Capital, the State, and Regional Development

Studies in Society and Space

Series editors **A J Scott and M Storper**

1 **Capital, the state, and regional development** M Dunford
2 **State policies, party politics, and regional change** R Hudson
3 **New industrial spaces** A J Scott

p **Pion Limited, 207 Brondesbury Park, London NW2 5JN**

Capital, the State, and Regional Development

M F Dunford

p Pion Limited, 207 Brondesbury Park, London NW2 5JN

© 1988 Pion Limited

All rights reserved. No part of this book may be reproduced in any form by photostat microfilm or any other means without written permission from the publishers.

ISBN 0 85086 123 3

Printed in Great Britain by Page Bros (Norwich) Limited

Preface

The main part of this book is devoted to several interconnected studies of Italian and French regional development. In these studies particular attention is paid to the establishment and development of industrial complexes. Most of the complexes concerned were centred on large-scale industry and the production of intermediate goods, and were located in less developed areas. But instead of simply describing the development of these nuclei of industrialisation, I have made an attempt to relate them to the overall processes of economic and social reproduction of which they were merely component parts.

More specifically, a short history of the regional problem in Italy and of the preindustrialisation phase of southern policy is followed by a macroeconomic analysis of the process of southern industrialisation in which investments in the oil, chemical, and steel sectors played a central role. Attention is also paid, however, to the development of a modern engineering sector in the Mezzogiorno in the late 1960s and early 1970s, and to the more general decentralisation of Italian industry in the 1970s. In this study the emphasis is on the overall transformation of the economy and society of the Italian South, and on the reasons why the structure of the Mezzogiorno was profoundly altered without significantly narrowing the gap between it and the rest of Italy. As in the case of many other underdeveloped areas, the South was transformed, and yet the inequality between it and the rest of the country was reproduced.

In order to focus in more detail on the processes of development of particular industrial poles, attention is then turned to the industrial complexes located at Dunkirk and Fos-sur-Mer, whose establishment and expansion were in part a consequence of trends similar to those operating in Italy. In both of the French examples the most important investments occurred in the steel sector, and the French state, via its industrial and regional planning policies, was one of the main social actors.

In the 1970s the construction of high-productivity plants on the coast was, however, to be linked with the rationalisation of older installations. In the final study the connections between the development of new capacity at Dunkirk and Fos-sur-Mer and the recent crisis in the old steel-producing regions in the Nord and Lorraine are accordingly outlined in some detail, and are considered in the context of the overall evolution of the French steel industry. The discussion is then widened further to include consideration of two other issues. One is the contrasts between the development of the steel industry in France and that in Italy and other European countries. The second is the impact of the new international division of labour that is emerging in this branch of production.

The primary emphasis in these case studies is on a number of interrelated empirical questions. Yet no study of uneven development or of any other topic can proceed without the use of concepts and theory. We are of course concerned with what are, ultimately, unique events. But even in explaining individual cases one is necessarily involved in the task of abstraction, and logical analysis as always plays an important role in aiding and clarifying our thinking about the real world. Indeed, in the absence of theory one would not know what questions to ask, what evidence to select, or in which ways different determinations might interact and be organised.

An argument of this kind does not imply a commitment to a priori modes of thinking. The theory used in the social sciences is itself derived by means of a process of abstraction from the real phenomena with which it is concerned. Moreover, the concepts and ideas arrived at in this way have the status of hypotheses which are in principle capable of being checked empirically and of being changed if and when they are shown to be inadequate: the concepts of social science are not, in other words, hypostates or ideal essences.

The use of theory does not necessarily result in reductionism. The process of abstraction leads to the identification of a sequence of increasingly abstract and general determinations. The resulting abstractions are one-sided facets of the reality being studied. In subsequently moving from abstract concepts to empirical reality a degree of *indeterminacy* will of necessity appear, simply because certain facets of the object being considered were ignored in the process of abstraction. As a result, concrete events cannot be inferred directly from abstractions.

In this book, for example, the basic concepts and categories are drawn from Marxism. The evolution of the economy cannot, however, be reduced to the class conflicts and value movements immediately associated with the process of accumulation of capital, just as the complex social relations of advanced capitalist societies cannot be reduced to the class antagonism between industrial capital and wage labour. The factors concerned are indeterminate and overdetermined or qualified by other factors. Yet the categories involved are, it will be argued, mental representations of important components of empirical reality and play a major role in explaining movements on the surface of society, just as intermediate-level concepts and the regularities which can be identified in the changing behaviour of human beings and in human history help to explain a large part of locally varying developments.

Because of this crucially important role of theory, the studies in this book are prefaced with a theoretical introduction. In that introduction most attention is paid to Marx's conceptions of capital and the state. The empirically oriented sections that follow were the product of a dialectical process in which a sequence of determinations from which that theory abstracts were integrated into the analysis, and in which concepts and interpretations were continuously revised and qualified. In the exposition the actual process of moving from the abstract to the concrete is not reconstituted in full. Nevertheless, the more abstract arguments developed in the early chapters are at work in the sections on Italian and French regional development, structuring the material and organising the analysis.

Consequently, whatever merits subsequent arguments might possess stem in large measure from the fruitfulness of the underlying theory as a source of hypotheses, research questions, and explanatory concepts.

Throughout the book the regional problem is viewed as a product of a spatial differentiation of social reproduction. In order to understand the character of a region it is therefore necessary to study (1) the changing role of the area's inhabitants in the changing national and international divisions of labour, and (2) the overall dynamics of the national and international economy.

What I shall argue is that the problems highlighted by the studies in this book are closely related to the underlying models of development of Italian and French society. National development, it will be suggested, was in each case closely related to what I shall call a regime of intensive accumulation and a system of monopolistic regulation which underpinned western growth after the Second World War. Internationally, the development paths of the two countries were related to the ways in which the Italian and French economies were inserted into the hierarchy of national economies headed by that of the United States of America. Accordingly, some of the major characteristics of processes of regional development and some of the specific ways in which inequality was reproduced were at least in part, it will be claimed, a product of the national variants of the model of intensive accumulation and the type of insertion in the US dominated world economy adopted in the two countries.

In the final chapter I shall develop this point. I shall argue that a more rational and equilibrated process of development presupposes, amongst other things, a new model of development, as well as new ways of determining the spatial distribution of economic activity. Underlying questions about models of development are, however, more deep-rooted questions. Of these, the most important concern the directions in which the social relations of production are to be changed.

In writing this book I have been helped by many people, but I alone am responsible for any errors and omissions. My debt to the work of other writers is acknowledged in the references in the text. Diane Perrons read and commented in detail on the whole manuscript, adding much to the clarity and quality of the argument. David Forgacs read the sections on Italy and directed me to ideas that have had an important impact on my interpretation of Italian development. In discussions with Fabio Arcangeli and Gioacchino Garofoli I learnt much about Italian research and about the structure and dynamics of Italian society. Peter Holmes read the sections on French industrial development, and through challenging some of my arguments helped me to express them more clearly and carefully, even if I did not respond adequately to the important points he made. Allen Scott's critical but encouraging remarks were of great help in the task of revision of earlier drafts of the manuscript. Successive versions of the manuscript were typed by Sue Adams, Pat Bennett, Fran Cook, Barbara Garrett, Alison Mudd, Wendy Turnquest, Yvette Stone, and Helen Warner, and half-worked-out ideas about illustrations were transformed with great skill into finished maps and diagrams by Susan Rowland. In addition, I would like to thank Irene Hames, whose careful copy editing helped identify many errors and inconsistencies, and all the staff at Pion who helped translate the manuscript into a finished book.

M Dunford
University of Sussex

To
Rose, Fred, and Anne Dunford

Contents

Part 1 Capital, the state, and the regional problem

1 Introduction: spatial inequality and social reproduction 1
1.1 Capitalism and spatial inequality 1
1.2 What is the regional problem? 4
1.3 Uneven spatial development 5
1.4 The evolution of the social and territorial division of labour 8

2 Capital and the space economy 11
2.1 Commodity production and the law of value 13
2.2 The circuit of industrial capital and the production of surplus value 14
2.3 The transformation of values into prices of production 17
2.4 The labour process and the production of surplus value 20
2.5 The development of the wage relation and of the process of labour 22
2.6 The accumulation of capital 28
2.7 Investment, technical change, and competition 29
2.8 The reproduction and regulation of the capitalist mode of production 32
2.9 The development of a regime of intensive accumulation: the national framework 34
2.10 Specialisation and the international division of labour: the principle of comparative costs 38
2.11 The theory of circular and cumulative causation 44

3 Capital and the state 48
3.1 Marx's conception of the state 48
3.2 The state and the anatomy of civil society 50
3.3 The state and the economy 52
3.4 The legal and institutional framework 53
3.5 Infrastructural investment and the general conditions of production 54
3.6 Externalities and state action 56
3.7 The general conditions of reproduction of the wage-earning class 56
3.8 Economic planning and the state 57
3.9 The state as entrepreneur 59
3.10 The restructuring of the state 60

Part 2 Regional policy and the development of the Italian Mezzogiorno

4 Introduction: the historical foundations of the southern question 61
4.1 Spatial inequality before and after Italian unification 61
4.2 19th century agrarian change 64
4.3 The southern agrarian bloc and national politics after unification 66
4.4 Italian development in the liberal era following unification 69
4.5 The formation of the '*blocco storico*' and the switch to protectionism 71
4.6 The South as a colony 73
4.7 Italian socialism and the southern question 75
4.8 The interwar years: fascism and global crisis 76
4.9 The Second World War and after 78

5	**The development of the Mezzogiorno in the preindustrialisation phase of southern policy**	80
5.1	The southern problem and the national economy in the years of reconstruction	80
5.2	The southern agrarian system in 1950	84
5.3	Early postwar development of the national economy and southern policy	91
5.4	Land reform	94
5.5	The policy of extraordinary intervention, 1950–1957	97
5.6	The process of agricultural change	98
5.7	Industry in the South in the 1950s	106
5.8	The industrial reserve army mechanism and the process of emigration	108
5.9	Social class and southern development	111
6	**The development and crisis of the Italian economy**	117
6.1	From economic recovery to 'economic miracle'	117
6.2	Unbalanced growth and crisis	123
6.3	The years of centre-left planning	125
6.4	The 'hot autumn' of 1969 and after	129
6.5	The oil crisis	137
6.6	The strategies of Italian capital	139
7	**A history of policies for southern industrialisation**	145
7.1	The policy for southern industrialisation from Law 634 of 1957, to 1965	147
7.2	Selectivity and the integration of southern policy with economic planning in Law 717 of 1965	150
7.3	Incentives policy and national programming in Law 853 of 1971	153
7.4	The reorganisation of southern policy in Law 183 of 1976	156
8	**Regional policy and the restructuring of capital: the expansion of industries producing energy and intermediate goods, and of a modern engineering sector in the Mezzogiorno**	162
8.1	The changing size, composition, and location of Cassa activity	162
8.2	Investment and the formation of capital in the Mezzogiorno: the role of regional policy	167
8.3	The dynamics of southern investment	169
8.4	Investments in energy and intermediate goods production	172
8.5	The development of the steel sector	173
8.6	The development of the oil and chemical sectors	185
8.7	Southern industry: cathedrals in the desert?	198
8.8	The diversification of state-sector investment: the case of Alfa Sud	200
8.9	Industrial restructuring and decentralisation: the case of FIAT	203

9	**Industrialisation and the reproduction of inequality**	208
9.1	Industrial development and the changing economy and society of the South	208
9.2	The evolution of output and employment in the South	213
9.3	Investment and employment in the South	218
9.4	The deteriorating trade balance of the Mezzogiorno	220
9.5	The changing geography of economic activity and population in the South	223
9.6	The spatial implications of the crisis of a regime of intensive accumulation	225

Part 3 Industrial complexes and the development of the French steel industry

10	**Capital accumulation, state intervention, and the development of industrial poles**	231
10.1	Industrial poles in French and Italian regional development	231
10.2	Monopolville: industrial and regional planning	233
10.3	Capital accumulation and the development of port and industrial zones	238
10.4	The role of state intervention in the establishment of maritime industrial development areas	240
10.5	The evolution of the French economy in the 1960s and early 1970s	241
10.6	The reorganisation of the state and of state intervention in the 1960s	242
10.7	The evolution of French regional planning	244
11	**The formation of a port and industrial zone at Fos-sur-Mer and the development of the Marseilles metropolitan area**	252
11.1	The origins and history of public intervention in the Fos maritime industrial zone	252
11.2	The structure and economic development of the Fos maritime industrial development zone	257
11.3	Employment and the Fos maritime industrial development area	274
11.4	Regional and urban planning in the Marseilles metropolitan region	282
11.5	Conclusion: industry and the urban environment	294
12	**The crisis and restructuring of the French steel industry**	296
12.1	The French steel industry at the end of the Second World War	296
12.2	The phase of reconstruction, 1945–1954	299
12.3	Open conflict between the steel industry and the metal-using industries, 1954–1960	305
12.4	Declining profitability and investment, stagnating output, and the Convention Générale État–Sidérurgie, 1961–1967	309
12.5	The Plan de Conversion de Wendel-SIDELOR	315
12.6	The steel crisis and the Plan Acier, 1975–1978	319
12.7	The Plan de Sauvetage de la Sidérurgie, 1978	323
12.8	The victory of the Left and the nationalisation of the steel industry	330
12.9	The 1984 Steel Plan	332

13	**Spatial implications of the steel crisis and steel production internationalisation**	337
13.1	Differential growth and the spatial redistribution of steel production	340
13.2	The origins of the French steel crisis	343
13.3	The steel crisis	346

Part 4 Conclusions and further remarks

14	**Conclusion: regional planning under capitalism**	349
14.1	Industrial development and the restructuring of capital	350
14.2	Industrial restructuring and political economy	351
14.3	The division of space	353
14.4	The theory of regulation	354
14.5	The development of Fordism	355
14.6	The crisis of Fordism	357
14.7	Beyond the crisis?	359

Glossary	365
References	369
Index	383

Part 1

Capital, the state, and the regional problem

Introduction: spatial inequality and social reproduction

1.1 Capitalism and spatial inequality
With the establishment and extended reproduction of capitalism significant material progress occurred. The process of economic and social development was, however, very uneven. Unevenness was in part sectoral: different areas of economic activity, the spheres of material and artistic production, and the social relations of production and legal relations, for example, all developed unevenly. But unevenness was also geographical. In each capitalist society, economic activity and the population it supported were polarised spatially: wealth and people were concentrated in a few districts occupying a relatively small part of the territory of the country concerned, and the rest was underdeveloped. As a result, geographical inequalities were widened, often quite sharply. Once capitalism had emerged the map of human activity underwent continual, rapid, and profound transformations. But just as economic development was accompanied by a reproduction of social inequality, the changing geography of capitalism was accompanied by a reproduction of spatial inequality.

In the preindustrial epoch there were of course significant gaps in the levels of material progress achieved by those living and working in different areas. Until the industrial revolution, however, differences in the value of gross marketed output per capita between the least developed and the richest country in the world were, according to Bairoch, of the order of only about 1.0 to 1.6. And in the case of microregions, but excluding a few small economies that played particularly important roles in international commerce, such as those of the Italian city republics of the late Middle Ages, the greatest gaps in average per capita income probably did not exceed a ratio of 1.0 to 3.0 (see Bairoch, 1981, page 14).

With the advent of industrial capitalism, however, disparities between rural areas and urban districts, between and within urban agglomerations in industrialising economies, and also between core and peripheral countries widened markedly.

In the first cycle of modern industrialisation the expansion of industry was concentrated in a few small regions. Many peripheral countries were deindustrialised, and virtually all of them were impoverished, relatively if not absolutely. By the 1830s the gap between developed and underdeveloped countries was much wider than in the early modern epoch, and until the 1860s the gap between the countries that were first to be industrialised and the rest of the world widened. In the second half of the 19th century the list of industrialised countries was enlarged. Within this group, inequality diminished as newly industrialising countries caught up with, and sometimes overtook, the early leaders. But disparities between the economies that had been industrialised and the nonindustrialised world increased very sharply at first, and continued to widen until the end of the

Second World War. After 1945, inequalities between these two broad groups of countries narrowed slightly. With the industrialisation of peripheral capitalist and some Third World countries, industrialisation was once again extended to new parts of the globe, and the number of centres of gravity was multiplied. Moreover, the ranking of national economies in the upper echelons of the hierarchy of nation states was modified, albeit slowly. Within the ranks of the industrialised countries, economies that had assumed a leading role at one stage in the history of industrialisation, such as the United Kingdom and, subsequently, the United States of America, did not succeed in retaining the dominant positions that had been achieved. Some economies, including the British and others which preceded it in the exercise of international hegemony, slipped down the hierarchy of nation states. At the same time, other economies rose, closing the gap and sometimes overtaking formerly more developed economies.

In the mid-1970s, however, in the industrialised economies average per capita income exceeded that of the nonindustrialised world by a factor of nearly 8.0, and the gap between the poorest and the richest country had reached nearly 1.0 to 30.0 (see Bairoch, 1981, pages 3–14).

The statistics used to measure and compare incomes internationally and interregionally must of course be used with extreme caution. What is measured is only the value of marketed output. Individual goods and services are given market valuations which frequently are not a good index of their value to society. The statistics collected for different regions and countries and at different moments in history are based on differing definitions, and vary considerably in reliability. Also, international comparisons involve the use of rates of exchange and are, consequently, distorted insofar as currencies are overvalued or undervalued.

However, reservations concerning the adequacy of existing measures of inequality cannot explain the differences the evidence reveals. At the level of the world system as a whole, significant inequalities did in fact emerge and were reproduced. Very few less developed economies actually succeeded in catching up with the most developed parts of the globe. The recent growth of newly industrialising countries heralds not the end of unequal development but, in most cases, only a differentiation within the less developed world (Lipietz, 1982c, pages 33–34). Within the ranks of the industrialised countries development was continually deepened or redirected, albeit with different degrees of success. As a result, virtually all of the economies that achieved high levels of development remained relatively prosperous.

What the historical record reveals is the coexistence of processes of differentiation of development alongside processes of equalisation (see Palloix, 1975, pages 163–165; Smith, 1984, pages 97–154). Initial differences are frequently amplified as a result of the interaction of virtuous circles of growth and vicious circles of decline. (In the process, many areas are actively underdeveloped while others are overdeveloped). Yet at the same time, differentials play an important part in generating strategies of adaptation in less developed areas. As a result of these adjustments an equalisation of the conditions of production and exchange occurs.

Over the long run the very fact of development and the possession of a competitive edge can itself act as a constraint on further transformations, allowing dominant economies to be overtaken by close rivals. Mechanisms of differentiation do not, in other words, always work in favour of the most highly developed economies, as is highlighted by the way the USA overtook Britain, and the recent emergence of Japan and the regions bordering on the Pacific Ocean: some one hundred years later than Marx and Engels anticipated, commercial hegemony may well be shifting from the Atlantic to the Pacific rim[1]. Only slowly and only in the cases of a few economies, however, have major changes in the hierarchy of nation states occurred. Internationally, only the dimensions and the map, and not the fact, of inequality have changed.

In his article, Bairoch (1981) does not discuss trends in intranational inequality. But similar arguments apply. Under capitalism, processes of regional development, as measured by the level and success of market- and profit-oriented activities around which social life is constructed, have been highly uneven. In almost all countries, substantial intraregional and interregional gaps in the value of marketed output per capita have emerged. Inequality at a regional level, defined in this way, exists in all developed capitalist economies and interacts with the map of international inequality to generate extremely wide gaps in the level of development attained in different regions in different countries (see figure 1.1).

Yet within each country the actual pattern of inequality has changed quite markedly. Some regional economies have been adapted in ways that have enabled them to act as major concentrations of activity over quite long periods and to remain relatively prosperous. On the other hand, many communities that were once active and thriving, often as the result of an extraordinarily rapid development of a narrow range of activities, have been converted, sometimes quite quickly, into devastated, derelict, and depressed areas. Other areas have been locked into a state of persistent relative poverty. What underlies the regional problem is, in other words, not simply unequal development with its roots in mechanisms of differentiation and equalisation. In almost every case it is a consequence of simultaneous and sequential overdevelopment and underdevelopment.

[1] "The centre of gravity of world commerce, Italy in the Middle Ages, England in modern times, is now the southern half of the North American peninsula .... Thanks to Californian gold and the tireless energy of the Yankees both coasts of the Pacific Ocean will soon be as populous, as open to trade, and as industrialised as the coast from Boston to New Orleans is now. And then the Pacific Ocean will have the same role as the Atlantic has now and the Mediterranean had in Antiquity and in the Middle Ages: that of the great water highway of world commerce, while the Atlantic will decline to the status of an inland sea" (Marx and Engels, cited in Davis, 1985, pages 61–62).

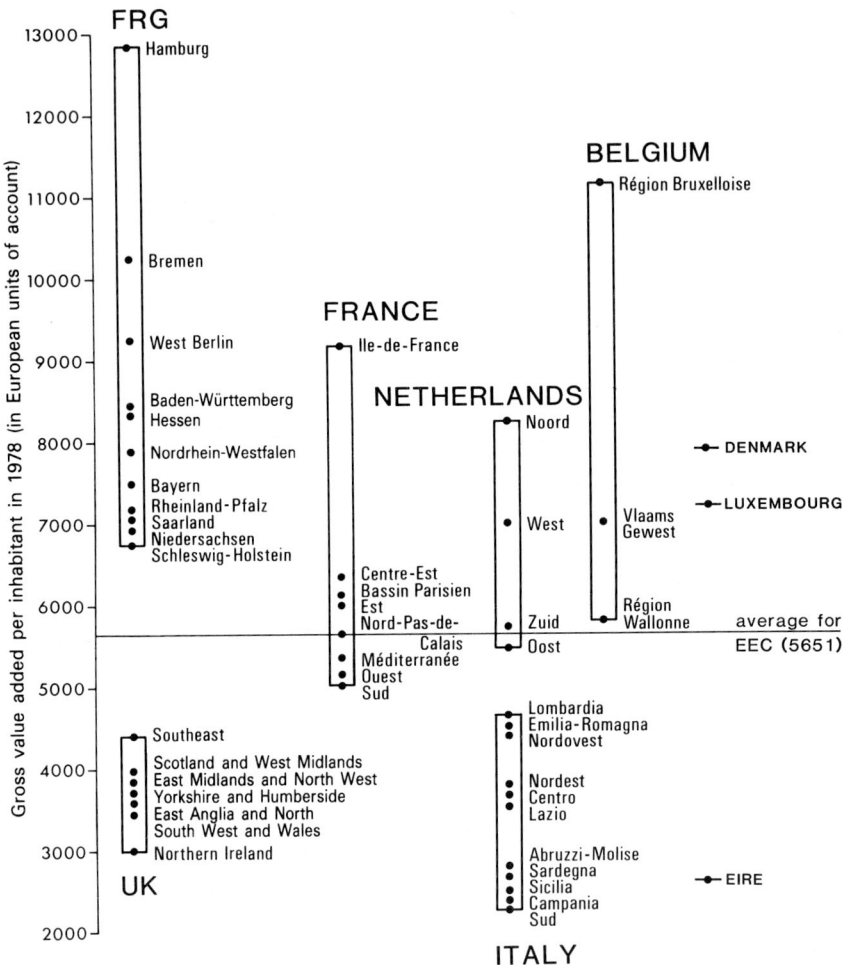

Figure 1.1. Interregional and international inequality in the EEC of nine in 1978. Source: elaborated from Eurostat (1979, pages 117–119).

1.2 What is the regional problem?

In speaking of regional problems it is of course usually to the existence of wide and persistent gaps in income per capita that one is referring. But underlying these inequalities are differences in (1) the rates of participation of the populations of different regions in income-yielding activity, and (2) the sectoral and occupational composition of economic life. Why is it a problem?

In part the problem is one of equity, involving questions of social need and equality. In capitalist societies resources, wealth, income, and influence are distributed very unequally. Thus a comparatively small number of people acquire an unjustifiably large share of social output and have a disproportionately large say as to what should be produced, whereas a substantial minority find themselves in a state of relative poverty. Superimposed on, and in part determined by, the distribution of wealth and influence in society is the geography of inequality. On the one hand, people suffer deprivation by virtue of the fact that they live in a particular part of a country. On the other, the capacity of a region's inhabitants to make decisions about the way in which their lives and work should be organised is frequently limited and externally controlled.

But the regional problem also involves questions of efficiency and of resource mobilisation. Almost invariably, uneven development is linked with the existence of important external costs and benefits not allowed for by market methods of resource allocation, and is associated with an underemployment and inefficient use of a country's resources (see also chapter 3).

Moreover the idea that there is a trade-off between equity and efficiency is in many ways a misleading one. A society can be egalitarian and efficient. In the terms of the theory of welfare economics one would be starting from a different initial allocation of resources, and society would simply end up at a different point on the production and utility possibility frontiers. On those frontiers both the organisation of production and the organisation of consumption are Pareto efficient (see, for example, Walsh, 1970, chapters 10-12; Lancaster, 1974, chapter 10).

The problems of equity and of efficiency of aggregate resource use are, it must be acknowledged, not problems for everyone: dominant interests are, for example, only concerned insofar as spatial problems place in jeopardy the stability of the social system or are seen as dysfunctional to individual interests. Whether or not the regional problem is a problem is, in that sense, a political question: a question of class politics as it is overdetermined by territorial interests.

1.3 Uneven spatial development

Very often studies of regional problems are confined to a listing and description of the varieties of local economy and society that exist. What I shall argue is that one of the most important factors underlying the diversity and variety of local landscapes, economies, and societies, and the seemingly different images with which they are associated, is uneven development. On this account, what appear at first sight to be problems that are unrelated can be seen at a deeper level as the product of an internal division and a spatial splitting up of social activity, with an assignment to the inhabitants of different areas of special roles in a wider and continuously changing interregional and international division of labour. What appears at first sight as a problem of a region that is poor is seen subsequently as a problem of a region of poor people and of social relations that result in a polarisation of wealth and poverty in society and in space (see Lipietz, 1977, page 26; Läpple and van Hoogstraten, 1980, pages 120-132). In short, what is happening in different areas is connected in a common history and with particular social relations, and if regional problems are to be solved, it is that history and those social relations that will have to be changed (Gramsci, 1978, pages 441-462; Williams, 1981).

At the root of the regional problem and of the process of uneven development lie (1) a continuously changing functional and spatial differentiation of the process of social reproduction, and (2) inequalities within and between functionally and spatially differentiated spheres of human activity (Läpple and van Hoogstraten, 1980, pages 117-132).

The process of social reproduction is an expression used to refer to the totality of processes involved in the production and reproduction of the means of human existence and of human life itself. It is composed of four interdependent moments: production, distribution, circulation, and consumption, where each of these moments is simultaneously material and ideal, and material and social (Dunford and Perrons, 1983, pages 352-357).

What is meant by material and ideal is that the course of the process of social reproduction is shaped by processes of material and ideal causality. The word ideal is used to refer to the impact of conscious goal-directed human activity. Of course the intended ends of human activity are often not accomplished, and unintended consequences frequently result, in part out of the interaction of different projects, and in part out of incomplete mastery and understanding of the material and social conditions in which activity occurs. The aims and projects of the individuals and groups of which a society is composed and the understandings actors have of their situations are nevertheless major factors in explaining its evolution. On the other hand, the process of reproduction is also shaped by the action and effect of (1) socially mediated natural conditions and (2) socially determined conditions on human activity. The effects of these conditions on human activity are subsumed under the concept of material causality.

I also suggested that the process of social reproduction is both material and social. What I meant was that the process as a whole results in the production and reproduction not only of the material basis of society and of its individual members, but also, and simultaneously, of the social relations and social classes of which the particular society is composed and of the ideas and meanings through the medium of which the processes of material and social reproduction and the experience of individual human beings are lived and understood. Almost any process of change is, in other words, simultaneously economic, social, political, cultural, and ideological, involving, perhaps, changes in the economy, in relations of class and gender, in styles of consumption and ways of life, in symbolic meanings, and in political and cultural attachments, amongst other things.

The word reproduction is, however, slightly misleading. The processes of reproduction and the demographic movements aimed at reproducing a society as a whole are at the same time new production. With the production of the means of subsistence and the reproduction of the human species, human needs are expanded, the division of labour is extended, social intercourse is increased, and the material and social environment is transformed (Marx and Engels, 1976, pages 32-45). As a result, the subjective and objective conditions on which a particular society is based are gradually modified and eventually suspended. Thus the ground is slowly prepared for the transition to a new type of society and new levels of material development.

In complex societies the process of social reproduction is split up into a large number of functionally differentiated activities, and the degree of cooperation and interdependence of the agents participating in production is increased. The way in which the activities involved in the process of social reproduction are split up into different and specialised branches, species, and subspecies of human labour, and in which individuals are made and channelled into particular vocations, is in fact one of the most important points that needs to be understood in explaining the spatial distribution of the entire body of social production. But what is split up must also be recombined. A study of the division and specialisation of labour must therefore be accompanied by an analysis of the mechanisms through which different functions are coordinated and individual work is made social.

All labour is situated in a particular location or locus standi. The extension and development of a functional differentiation of the process of social reproduction is consequently accompanied by the development of a territorial division of labour and of methods of territorial socialisation. On the one hand, the production of specific use-values or particular phases in the production of a single commodity, good, or service are confined to particular districts of a country, and, via mechanisms of coordination, a variety of aggregated spatial complexes of complicated intra- and inter-regionally interdependent functions of production, distribution, circulation, and consumption are established (Marx, 1976, pages 470-480; Läpple and van Hoogstraten, 1980, pages 117-132; Läpple, 1985, pages 55-59). On the other hand, the economic division of space that results is at the same time associated with a social division of space (see Lipietz, 1974, pages 21-39).

The structure of the space economy is thus determined in part by the processes of location and development of the differentiated activities, enterprises, and sectors of production of which the technical and social divisions of labour are composed. Individual activities are located, and are usually successful, only in areas where the natural, economic, social, and political conditions of production and reproduction are capable of satisfying the materially and socially determined requirements of the processes of labour involved. The location of particular functions and of particular enterprises thus depends upon the interaction of two elements. One is the characteristics of the activities involved and the general relations of interdependence within production. The second is the disposition of the conditions of production and reproduction, which themselves comprise (1) socially mediated natural conditions of production, such as raw material deposits and natural energy sources, and conditions of transport, such as deep-water harbours, and (2) socially and economically developed conditions of production and reproduction.

But, as with the technically differentiated work carried out within a single enterprise, the work of all of the increasingly specialised workers participating in the social division of labour must be recombined such that each type of work is established as a more or less interdependent part or branch of the collective production of society as a whole. In other words, what Marx (1976, pages 464, 468–469) called the collective worker must in its turn be formed as a result of a combining into a single mechanism of all of the specialised workers whose activities and products are mutually interdependent.

On account of the role of relationships of interdependence between differentiated activities, a single-plant or single-enterprise approach to the study of location and the structure of the space economy is insufficient: microeconomic approaches with their emphasis on the division of labour need to be integrated with macroeconomic analyses. The reason why lies in the fact that the spatial distribution of human activity also depends upon the possibility of systematically combining and coordinating the partial functions rendered independent by the division of labour, including functions of industrial production and of circulation, communication, and transport, individual and collective means of consumption, and the general conditions of production (Lojkine, 1976, pages 119–127; 1977, pages 123–159; Preteceille, 1976; Läpple and van Hoogstraten, 1980, pages 117–132).

The geography of any society, however, is not simply a product of the current development and location of that society's social production and population. It is also stamped by its history. On the one hand, the way in which geographical space is used and transformed in the course of the process of social reproduction is conditioned by the specific disposition of resources and people with which each successive cycle of human social activity is confronted and with whose modification or erasing it is associated. On the other hand, the geography of each country reveals elements of continuity whose roots lie in variations in the rate at which different objects are transformed and in the reproduction or partial modification, as a consequence, it must be emphasised, of a new logic of development, of historically given conditions. As a result, elements of inertia and continuity, and an effect of the past on the present, can always be observed (Dunford and Perrons, 1983, pages 352–357).

1.4 The evolution of the social and territorial division of labour
At one stage in human history, specific local economies and societies were relatively self-contained. The natural and social conditions of human

existence and the processes of development differed from those found in other areas, as did the modes of production and living and the products of different communities. But as and when these communities came into contact with one another, the differences between them called forth a mutual exchange of goods and services and a gradual conversion of an increasingly large number of products into commodities. The economies concerned were thus made into increasingly interdependent parts of a wider mechanism. With the generalisation of commodity production and, in particular, of capitalist commodity production, the inhabitants of each area were integrated much more fully into a national and international economy, and were assigned increasingly specialised and often new roles in wider and more developed divisions of labour. As a corollary of these developments, each region was integrated economically, politically, culturally, and ideologically into a nation state of which it was merely a constituent and subordinate part. (The word region originally meant kingdom. The idea of a region as a part of a larger entity is a relatively modern one.) Similarly, the development of a world market and the more recent internationalisation of capitalist production have acted as a stimulus to the development of supranational economic and political institutions, but without yet challenging the centrality of the system of nation states.

In *The German Ideology* Marx and Engels pointed out that division of labour mediated by commodity exchange itself developed initially by severing industrial and commercial labour from agricultural labour. As a result, an economically grounded separation of town and country into partial and interdependent structures of production and reproduction was established. With the further development of the division of labour, craft production was separated from commerce and a special class of merchants was formed. The subsequent extension of exchange beyond the immediate surroundings of the town led to a division of production between individual towns, with the inhabitants of each town specialising in different branches of industry. In areas with a relatively numerous and high density of population, and in which sufficient amounts of wealth had been concentrated, the next step was the rise of manufacturing. [It should be noted, however, that the density of population "is more or less relative. A relatively thinly populated country, with well-developed means of communication, has a denser population than a more numerously populated country with badly developed means of communication" (Marx, 1976, page 473).] With the rise of manufacturing the process of production was itself split up into a series of partial operations, and the territorial division of labour was given a new stimulus and a new level of complexity (Marx, 1973, pages 417-514; Marx, 1976, pages 472-473; Marx and Engels, 1976, pages 32-45, 64-74; see also Dunford and Perrons, 1983, part 2).

One of the consequences of the development of the forces of production was the disintegration and dissolution of feudal relations of production in the countryside and the separation of independent agricultural, industrial, and commercial workers from the means of production and consumption on which they depended. In other words, it led in a wide variety of ways to the formation of a class of free-wage labourers. At the same time, the means of production and consumption appeared in the form of alienable goods and services which could be bought and sold by those strata in whose hands money wealth had been concentrated. With the expansion of production on the basis of the class relations which accordingly developed, the regional organisation of social life and its processes of development and restructuring were gripped by the laws of capitalist commodity production and capitalist accumulation. At that point in history, industry and people were concentrated in urban agglomerations. In addition, farming was industrialised. The countryside was thus urbanised and the rural–urban dichotomy was dissolved: organisationally, space was transformed into a set of urban regions.

In subsequent chapters I shall consider one instance of integration of a region in which precapitalist relations of production predominated with a more developed capitalist society. But most attention will be paid to the development of industrial capitalism itself, and the impact of capitalist industrialisation on processes of spatial development.

A wide variety of models and theories have been advanced to explain the pattern of international and interregional specialisation and of geographical inequality to which I have referred. The list includes a number of ad hoc models, as well as pieces of analysis drawn from general economic, social, and political theory. In the next two chapters I shall attempt to develop the points made in the last section, and discuss in turn the national and international dimensions of inequality and the role of the state.

Capital and the space economy

Space is the context in which social reproduction occurs and by which it is conditioned. As a context it is a material reality providing resources which can be used to meet human needs and whose availability and disposition shape the activity aimed at meeting them. But it is also a social reality in the sense that the use of space is subject to a set of property rights which have a major impact on access to and use of the resources it offers. The development of a new industry in a region, for example, is dependent upon the availability of raw materials and infrastructural equipment, the acquisition of rights to use land, and so on. The activity which occurs in space in its turn modifies and transforms it. As a result, space is itself a product of the development of the activities of which the process of social reproduction is composed as well as, indirectly via the impact of space on activity and directly via inertia, of its own past.

What we must now go on to consider is the way in which human activity and the process of social reproduction can be conceptualised and understood.

The societies I shall be concerned with are modern capitalist societies. According to Marx, capitalism has two major characteristics. Capitalism is in the first place a system of commodity production in which goods and services are produced for sale on the market. In a commodity producing economy, decisions about what should be produced, how much, when, and where are made not in accordance with a social plan but privately and autonomously by individuals. As a result of these decisions a particular division of social labour is established. But the social validity of different activities and of decisions about resource allocation is only determined a posteriori when the products are sold on the market. If a buyer is found, the work involved is socially validated. But if someone who wants the good or service and who, usually, has the wherewithal to pay for it is not found, the product and the work involved in producing it are not recognised as socially useful.

It is also through the process of market validation that incomes are formed: as a result of the exchange of a commodity for a certain amount of the general equivalent or of money, the original owner is given a claim over an equivalent part of society's net output. The need of a producer to secure social validation of his or her own work, through the sale of the products of that work on the market for money, in order to establish a claim over the products of the work of others, is a monetary constraint (see Aglietta, 1979, pages 42–45).

What, however, differentiates capitalist commodity production from other commodity producing societies is the fact that work itself is structured by the wage relation. Under capitalism the population is polarised into two broad groups: a capitalist class in whose hands are concentrated the material and monetary wealth necessary to set the process of production in motion, and a wage-earning class separated from the means of production and consumption. In order to work and to secure a claim over a part of social production, members of the wage-earning class must consequently sell their capacity to work to capitalist employers.

In a modern capitalist society only one part of the process of social reproduction is structured by these relations. Many goods and services are not commodities. Included under this heading are things intended for the personal use of the producer, the products of domestic work, and collective goods and services supplied free of charge to the community. Also, some things that are bought and sold are not commodities. Natural resources and other gifts of nature which do not involve the intervention of human labour are not commodities, although where private property rights are established and enforced the owner can demand a rent of anyone wishing to use them. Activities concerned with selling and hiring out merely transfer rights of ownership over a product which is already in existence. As a result, many circulation services are not commodities. In addition, not all work is performed by a wage-earning class. In the market sector, petty commodity producers and owners who do not employ others are numerically significant, and in the nonmarket sector, domestic and voluntary work are not structured by the wage relation.

Thus, only a subset of the activities which contribute to the overall reproduction of society fall in the capitalist sector (see table 2.1). But it does not follow that other areas of work are unaffected by its development. On the contrary, very close interdependencies exist. The provision of collective goods and services is usually financed through taxation and government borrowing which depend upon and have important effects on the capitalist sector. The sphere of home life is shaped by what occurs outside: the rhythms and intensity of paid work and the incomes it yields, for example, are major determinants of domestic life.

In subsequent chapters I shall consider some of these interdependencies. My main concern, however, will be with events occurring in the capitalist sector of the societies we are going to study.

Table 2.1. A schematic partitioning of social reproduction.

	Commodity production	Noncommodity production
Wage relation	capitalist sector (private and public capital)	circulation sector state administration and collective services sector
Nonwage relation	self-employed and petty commodity sector	domestic and voluntary sector

2.1 Commodity production and the law of value

According to Marx, a commodity is something which has a use value and a value. A use value is something which is useful or has a utility, and as a result of its production society's material wealth is increased. The value of a commodity is a measure expressed in monetary form of the contribution made by one unit of the commodity concerned to the wealth of society.

The concept of value is connected with the concept of production. In political economy the act of producing is one of expending a certain amount of human labour on an ensemble of products in order to obtain a new set of products. As a use value any commodity is itself a result of the application of a specific amount of particular types of human labour, whereas at a societal level a particular vector of commodity outputs is associated with a particular distribution among various different activities of the total work performed.

In view of the central role played by production, the value of an individual commodity can be measured by the amount of socially necessary abstract labour required to produce it. A commodity's value is, in other words, made up of (1) the value transferred as a result of the using up of commodity inputs and the depreciation of plant and equipment, and (2) the value newly added by the producers. The values themselves are equal to the quantity of undifferentiated abstract labour needed in the average conditions of technique, skill, and intensity of work prevailing at the moment when the commodity is sold.

The average value added is a measure of a commodity's contribution to the wealth of society. It is itself measured by the average increase in incorporated labour, whereas the value of the net product expresses the aggregate expenditure of abstract social labour in a commodity producing economy. In the words of Duménil, "value is labour, and its measure is labour time" (Duménil, 1983, pages 429-434). Value is expressed, however, in the form of money. (The role of what Marx called the law of value was one of providing a conceptual understanding of reality and not a model of it: what was meant by law was a qualitative determination and not a regular quantitative relationship.)

Insofar as it can be exchanged against a particular quantity of another commodity or a particular amount of money, a commodity also has an exchange value or a money price. The determination of exchange values is explained by a law of exchange.

In much of *Capital* Marx assumes that exchange occurs at commodity values: the money price of each commodity is held to reflect labour time as it has been incorporated and to be equal, in fact, to its labour value multiplied by the reciprocal of the value of money or the monetary equivalent of an hour's work. (See Foley, 1982. In Foley's work the value of money is defined as aggregate direct abstract labour divided by aggregate value added.)

The process of exchange has two aspects. First, a commodity and the work involved in producing it are socially validated via exchange. Second, the exchange of a commodity for money gives the seller a claim over a part of society's net output equivalent in value to the value realised in exchange.

The amount of money for which a commodity exchanges and the fraction of society's direct work over which the sale of the commodity gives a claim may well be different from the fraction of aggregate direct social labour expended in producing it. In the first place some commodities will not find buyers, with the result that the producers will realise less value than they produced and will perhaps consider switching to new activities. Other factors such as monopoly, government intervention, and the exploitation of information differentials by middlepersons can result in price–value deviations. And where invested capital per worker differs over different sectors, and where rates of profit are equalised through competition, prices will deviate from values. (I shall come back to this point.)

As long as unsold commodities are not destroyed, the value created is conserved but is distributed in a different way from that in which it was produced. In other words, the labour value produced by the expenditure of abstract direct labour and given up in selling a commodity may differ from the money value added realised by the producers. In such cases a value transfer occurs, and exchange is unequal for individual and groups of producers. But the sum of the value gained and lost in exchange will be zero. Value is created in production, realised in exchange, and perhaps redistributed. Variations in prices associated with variations in the law of exchange thus result in changes in distribution but not in the quantity of value (see Foley, 1982, pages 40–42; Duménil, 1983, pages 429–434).

2.2 The circuit of industrial capital and the production of surplus value
Capitalism is, as has been mentioned, not simply a system of commodity production. Only after exchange has been generalised, such that not only all the products of labour but also the capacity of the producers to work are bought and sold as commodities, does capitalist commodity production develop. The development of capitalism presupposes, in other words, the establishment of new relations of production involving a concentration of monetary wealth and the means of production in the hands of one section of society, and the transformation of the rest of society into a wage-earning class composed of juridically free individuals who are nevertheless obliged by their lack of property to sell their capacity to work in order to survive. In these conditions, production itself falls under capitalist control and is organised in accordance with what is called the wage relation. The wage relation is in fact the most fundamental relation defining the capitalist mode of production. It is also the key to the production of surplus value or the economic form in which surplus labour is appropriated under capitalism.

In a capitalist society the production of use values occurs "only because and in so far as they form the material substratum of exchange-value".

But the capitalist producer of a commodity also wishes to produce a commodity whose value is greater than that of the elements purchased to produce it. It follows that "just as the commodity itself is a unity formed of use-value and value, so the process of production must be a unity, composed of the labour process and the process of creating value" or of valorisation (Marx, 1976, page 293).

According to Marx, the general formula for capital in the form in which it appears in the sphere of circulation is represented by the schema $M - C - M'$: a sum of money, M, is advanced to purchase commodity inputs, C, which are subsequently exchanged for a larger sum of money, M', where money is acting as capital as the sum originally advanced is increased in size or valorised (Marx, 1976, pages 252, 257).

In capitalist societies the process of production is itself under capitalist control and the fundamental form of capital in general is industrial capital. What distinguishes industrial capital is the fact that its circuit includes the direct capitalist process of production in which the value of the capital advanced is increased, or profit is made, by transforming and increasing the value of the commodity inputs. Industrial capital is advanced in five spheres of material production: the extractive industries, agriculture, manufacturing industry, energy production, and transport and storage.

In the circuit of industrial capital a sum of money, M, is advanced to purchase commodity inputs, C, comprising means of production, MP, and labour power, LP, bought respectively on the commodity and labour markets with the constant and variable parts of capital (see figure 2.1). At first it is assumed that all commodity inputs are sold and bought at their values. In the case of raw materials, semifinished goods, equipment, and plant the outlay is equal, in other words, to the abstract labour time socially necessary for their production multiplied by the monetary equivalent of an hour's work. The value of labour power must, however, be defined in a different way.

A wage earner sells his or her capacity to work to a capitalist employer in exchange for a money wage. The money wage is in effect a claim over a particular part of abstract social labour, and it can be converted into a quantity of abstract labour time by multiplying it by the value of money. The quantity that results can be interpreted as the value of labour power. The value of labour power is then equal to the amount of abstract social labour over which the money wage gives the wage-earning class a claim or the amount of labour time for which the worker receives on average an equivalent in the hourly money wage.

As long as prices are proportional to values, the value of labour power multiplied by the quantity of labour power sold is equal to the labour incorporated in the consumption goods on which wages are spent. If working-class consumption is regarded as equivalent to the reproduction of labour power as a commodity, the value of labour power can be said to be equal to the labour contained in the commodities used up in and necessary for, under the prevailing social and historical circumstances, its reproduction. In these conditions the definitions of the values of constant and variable capital coincide. But once prices deviate from values the similarity ceases to hold: money wages may well be determined but are not defined by the value of the commodities necessary for the reproduction of the wage-earning class (see Foley, 1982, pages 39-42).

In the next stage these commodity inputs leave the sphere of circulation and enter the sphere of production as elements of productive capital, P. In the capitalist process of production they are used to produce new commodities, C'. The value of these new commodities exceeds the value of the commodity inputs. In the process of production the value of the means of production used up is passed on to the new commodities. (The values of items of constant capital are measured, in fact, not by the values they inherit but are revalued according to the current conditions of production.) The increment in value is a consequence of the fact that the value added by labour in the capitalist process of labour is greater than the value of labour power. It stems, in other words, from the fact that the quantity of labour supplied in return for the money wage and the quantity of work performed exceed the number of hours for which the workers are paid.

At the end of the process of production the commodities, C', which have been produced enter the sphere of circulation and are offered for sale on the commodity market. On being sold they are converted into a sum of money M' ($M' = M + \Delta M$), and the value contained in them is realised. As a result, the capitalist class normally receives back the original sum of money plus an increment or an amount that has been added to the original outlay.

The argument can be restated algebraically. At the outset an amount of value, c, was advanced in the form of constant capital to purchase the means of production. In a sufficiently long period of time the entire value of the means of production would, under conditions of full realisation, be transferred to the products. In the same period the capitalist class will have advanced an amount of variable capital, v, in exchange for the labour power needed to transform the other material inputs into new commodities. In the process of production the value of the labour power employed is replaced by the value added to c by the wage-earning class. If the value added is denoted by the symbol l, the value of the initial commodity inputs is $c+v$, and the value of the final product is $c+l$. As a result, the value advanced has been increased by an amount s, equal to $(c+l)-(c+v) = l-v$. This increment in value, whose origin lies in the fact that the workers employed work for a longer period or at a higher level of intensity than is necessary to replace the money advanced in the form of variable capital, is called surplus value.

The circuit of industrial capital can be represented by a circular flow diagram, as in figure 2.1. The process whereby the value of industrial capital is augmented via the addition of surplus value is called the valorisation of capital, and the ratio of surplus value to the value of the variable capital advanced, s/v, is called the rate of surplus value.

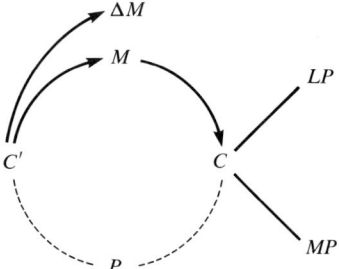

Figure 2.1. The circuit of industrial capital.

2.3 The transformation of values into prices of production

One reason why the formulation of Marx's theory of value that I have outlined is important is that it gives rise to a more satisfactory solution to the problem of transforming values into prices of production (see Foley, 1982; Lipietz, 1982a, pages 73-81; and Duménil, 1983; on whom the following account draws).

A commodity has a value that is proportional to the fraction of the overall labour of society that has been allocated to its production and which has been socially validated in exchange. In an assumed representative process of production the work performed adds value to the value which has been created by previous work and which has been incorporated in the means of production.

Suppose that a_j^i is the quantity of good i normally required to produce one unit of good j, where the branches of production identified are those that are separated by market relations and between which commodities are exchanged, and suppose that **A** is the corresponding matrix of input-output coefficients. Assume also that the methods of production do not alter, and that we are analysing the reproduction of an economic system: in other words, all production is realised, the means of production and consumption used up in the period of reproduction are replaced, and the surplus necessary for a regular process of accumulation is constantly replenished. In these conditions we have

$$\boldsymbol{u} = \boldsymbol{u}\mathbf{A} + \boldsymbol{l} = \boldsymbol{l}(\mathbf{I} - \mathbf{A})^{-1} \, , \tag{2.1}$$

where $\boldsymbol{l} = l_1, l_2, ..., l_n$ is the vector of quantities of abstract labour newly added to units of these goods in the period of reproduction, $\boldsymbol{u}$ is the vector of the values of the commodities, and where **A** is (1) nonnegative and indecomposable, and (2) nonsingular. **I** is the identity matrix.

Unlike in a simple commodity producing economy, in a system of capitalist commodity production, labour power assumes the form of a commodity. As a commodity it has a value, w, equal to the quantity of abstract labour, that the workers receive. The value received can be spent on the market according to the workers' needs and in order to reproduce their capacity to work from day to day. But labour power also has a use value: the capacity of producing abstract labour and of adding value to commodity inputs.

The value added by labour, V, is itself determined by the duration, λ, and the intensity, ε, of work. Suppose that $\boldsymbol{m}$ is the vector of quantities of labour power m_j that must be purchased in order to produce one unit of commodity j. If we know the duration, λ_i, and the intensity, ε_i, of work in sector i, the quantity of labour expended by the quantities of labour power $\boldsymbol{m}$ purchased to produce one unit is $\boldsymbol{l} = \boldsymbol{m}\mathbf{V}$, where $V_j^i = \lambda_i \varepsilon_i$, with $V_j^i = 0$ if $i \neq j$, and, by assumption, $\mathbf{V} = \mathbf{I}$ (Lipietz, 1982a, pages 84-85). (The argument can be extended to include the effects of arrangements concerning overtime working and the mobility of labour, which also have an impact on value added.)

The three parameters w, λ, and ε are the joint result of an historical process of class struggle and class conflict. Together they determine the rate of surplus value, or rate of exploitation, z, which is equal to the ratio of unpaid labour and the value of labour power, $(1-w)/w$, or of surplus value and the wage bill. By definition, $w(1+z) = 1$. It follows that the equation

$$\boldsymbol{u} = \boldsymbol{u}\mathbf{A} + w\boldsymbol{l} + zw\boldsymbol{l} = (1+z)w\boldsymbol{l}(\mathbf{I}-\mathbf{A})^{-1} \qquad (2.2)$$

is a modern vector representation of $c+v+s$. This formulation of the problem is due to Duménil, Foley, and Lipietz. What differentiates it is the fact that the value of labour power is interpreted as the share of the value added, $1/(1+z)$, which is actually paid to the working class, and whose money equivalent is spent at prices of production in order to satisfy socially determined needs. [Aglietta (1979) interprets a similar expression empirically as the real social wage cost or the wage cost per unit of value produced.]

Equation (2.2) yields

$$\boldsymbol{u} = (1+z)w \sum_{n=0}^{\infty} \boldsymbol{l}\mathbf{A}^n , \qquad (2.3)$$

where l_j is the quantity of abstract labour embodied directly in j, $\boldsymbol{l}\mathbf{A}_j$ is the quantity directly embodied in the means of production ($\mathbf{A}_j$ is the jth column of $\mathbf{A}$), $\boldsymbol{l}[\mathbf{A}^2]_j$ is the means of production of the means of production, and so on. $\sum \boldsymbol{l}\mathbf{A}^n$ is the aggregate quantity of abstract labour embodied in the commodities, and $w\sum \boldsymbol{l}\mathbf{A}^n$ is equal to the aggregate value received by the wage-earning class in the form of wages.

Since $\mathbf{V} = \mathbf{I}$, $\sum \boldsymbol{l}\mathbf{A}^n$ can also be interpreted as (1) the aggregate quantity of labour that has to be bought to produce one unit of each commodity, or

(2) the quantity of labour commanded by the wage paid to the workers employed: the quantity of abstract living labour set in motion, in other words, when the wage is advanced as an element of capital in the production of a unit of each commodity and its inputs.

The concept of labour commanded warrants some attention since it will be used later in this chapter. In commodity exchange the labour commanded by the wage is equal to v or its vector equivalent. But in a capitalist society what is exchanged is not only commodities but also capital or 'values in process'. As an element of capital the labour commanded by v is equal to $v+s$ or the totality of the value added. In volume 3 of *Capital* and in *Theories of Surplus-Value* Marx himself used the quantity of variable capital advanced by a capitalist employer as an index of the labour embodied or the value added by the workers consequently employed. On these occasions the quantity of variable capital v was, in other words, measured by the living labour it commanded and was used as an index of $v+s$ as "since the beginning of capitalist production the value of commodities is determined not by the labour they contain but by the living labour they command" (Marx, 1969, volume 2, page 397). Under capitalism the value of commodities is determined, in other words, by the value of labour power (Napoleoni, 1975, pages 39–43, 71–73; Lipietz, 1979, pages 302–303; 1982a, pages 76–78).

So far I have assumed that exchange is regulated by the value of products. Under capitalism that assumption is invalid. In an economy where commodities are exchanged as products of capital, or, more precisely, as products of workers employed by capital, exchange is regulated, according to Marx, by a system of transformed values or prices of production. Under this system the value added in the period of reproduction is redistributed over the commodities in such a way that the amount of profit received by each capitalist is proportional to the capital invested. If r is the general rate of profit,

$$\boldsymbol{p} = (1+r)(\boldsymbol{p}\mathbf{A}+w\boldsymbol{l}) = w\boldsymbol{l}\left(\frac{\mathbf{I}}{1+r}-\mathbf{A}\right)^{-1} \tag{2.4}$$

or

$$\boldsymbol{p} = (1+r)w\sum_{n=0}^{\infty}(1+r)^{n}\boldsymbol{l}\mathbf{A}^{n}, \tag{2.5}$$

where $\boldsymbol{p}$ is the vector denoting the prices of production. With the redistribution of value what results are the prices of production around which market prices oscillate. Instead of $w\sum\boldsymbol{l}\mathbf{A}^{n}$ we find, on the right-hand side of equation (2.5), the expression $w\sum(1+r)^{n}\boldsymbol{l}\mathbf{A}^{n}$: in a system of redistributed values the quantities of aggregate value received by the wage-earning class, and which can be exchanged against wage goods, are weighted, in other words, by $(1+r)^{n}$ (see Lipietz, 1982a, pages 76–78).

2.4 The labour process and the production of surplus value

The process of labour is a unity of the processes of production and valorisation and it is the site where surplus value is produced. The social logic on which it is based is indicated in figure 2.2.

With the help of this diagram the definition of the value of labour power and the determination of the rate of surplus value can be set out in a different way. In the diagram, T denotes the apparent duration of the working day in which the total mass of new value produced by society is created, T_n is the amount of abstract social labour time represented by the wage or what Marx called the value of labour power, and T_v is the uniform time in which new value is actually produced, where $T_n < T_v \leqslant T$. In this situation the value of labour power is equal to that fraction of abstract labour time supplied which actually has a counterpart in the wage or the wage share in value added. The difference between T_v and T_n is equal to the amount of surplus or unpaid labour time: the hours worked for which the wage-earning class receives no equivalent in the wage. And the rate of surplus value is represented by the ratio of surplus and paid labour time and can be written as $s/v = (T_v - T_n)/T_n$ (see Palloix, 1976, pages 49–51; Aglietta, 1979, pages 49–52).

If real wages are held constant, the rate of surplus value can be increased in two ways. One is by increasing absolute surplus value. In this case T_n is held constant and the amount of surplus labour time is increased by (1) extending the length of the working day, or (2) intensifying the labour process in order to reduce the amount of time during which the worker is 'idle'. With increases in the length or intensity of the working day, value added and the surplus value accruing to the employer are increased, as is output. The second way of increasing s/v is by increasing relative surplus value. In this situation T_v is held constant and T_n is reduced. If the real wage is held constant, a fall in T_n can only occur as a result of increases in the productivity of labour in the wage-goods sector or in sectors supplying it with means of production. No new value is produced. But with rising productivity output increases, and the unit values of wage goods fall, reducing the value of labour power and increasing the rate of surplus value. (Value is in fact the reciprocal of productivity.) A switch to new and cheaper sources of supply of commodities has similar effects.

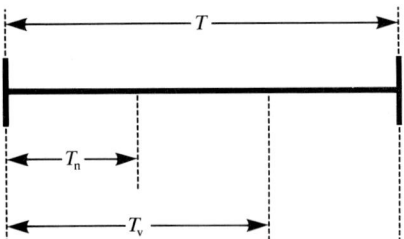

Figure 2.2. The division of the working day and the production of surplus value.

Increasing the rate of surplus value involves, in other words, increasing the difference between T_v and T_n. An increase in $(T_v - T_n)/T_n$ can be achieved, as was indicated in the last paragraph, in three analytically distinct ways. The first method involves operating on the difference between T and T_v, or on the 'porosity' of the process of production, and results in increases in the production of absolute surplus value. The gaps between T and T_v are of two kinds (see Aglietta, 1979, pages 113-114). On the one hand, delays are caused by insufficient coordination and control of operations. Included are the time lost in setting up production runs, in moving materials under transformation, and in shifting workers, the time involved in repairing and maintaining equipment, the time that passes between the execution of different operations, and 'idling' on the part of workers. On the other hand, the working day is interrupted and time is lost as a result of the inability of workers to sustain without interruption a certain pace of work and the need for periods of rest.

Increased cooperation, which occurs at first when a collective work rhythm is established by the workers themselves, but which is subsequently imposed by the continuous and uniform movement of the machine system and its speed of operation, enables capital to reduce this margin. The fragmentation of tasks and specialisation have, in the absence of strong working-class opposition, similar effects. With the extension of cooperation and the development of a more sophisticated division of labour each worker usually spends more time performing predefined tasks. The time lost in deciding how to execute a task is reduced, as is the time lost in changing from one activity to another or in setting up a job. In addition, the supervising and disciplining of factory workers offers another way of reducing the porosity of the working day.

The second method leaves the ratio of T_v to T unchanged but increases s/v by extending T. With the transition from extensive to intensive processes of accumulation strategies of this kind diminish in importance but are still reflected in the use of shift work and overtime working.

The third method involves increasing the difference between T_v and T_n by reducing T_n and increasing the production of relative surplus value. The most important way of reducing T_n is the introduction of new methods of production or principles of work organisation that enable productivity to be raised. The discovery of new and less expensive sources of supply of goods and services can, however, have the same effect. Alternatively the value of labour power employed in production can be lowered as a result of changes in the composition of the wage-earning class. One example is provided by developments in the sphere of production that enable skilled operations to be separated out and concentrated in the hands of a small group of highly qualified workers while the activities performed by the majority of the workers employed are routinised. Insofar as such a strategy of producing "the maximum deskilling of the maximum proportion of manual workers" and "the maximum skill in the smallest proportion of mental workers" is successful, the overall level of skill required is reduced, as is the value of labour power (Maignien cited in Palloix, 1976, page 48).

2.5 The development of the wage relation and of the process of labour
The development of the process of labour has been punctuated by several major transformations, as has the evolution of other facets of the wage relation, including the ways in which labour power is mobilised and the factors that determine the level and distribution of wages (see Boyer, 1979, page 9).

In the sphere of work a phase of manufacturing was superseded by mechanisation, whereas, at present, mechanisation is beginning to give way to automation or systemofacture. The examples I shall consider involve the second and third steps.

With mechanisation, production came to depend on the use of machine systems in which a series of tools and machines were driven by a mechanical source of energy via an appropriate transmission system (Aglietta, 1979, page 113). Some human knowledge and some of the qualitative characteristics of specific types of human labour were embodied in the new machine systems, and the tasks of workers were changed into ones of operating and controlling mechanical tools and machinery that were performing work that they themselves had once carried out. Very early instances of mechanisation can of course be identified. But only with the epoch of capitalist mechanisation did it assume real economic importance.

The principle of mechanisation was given a new impetus by the development of scientific management or Taylorism. Initially introduced in the engineering industries in the United States of America at the end of the 19th century, scientific management was developed with a view to, first, reducing the hold of craft workers over the organisation and tempo of production, and, second, increasing the amount of work each employee performed in a given period of time. What it involved was the development of general principles of work organisation aimed at accelerating "the completion of the mechanical cycle of movements on the job and [filling] the gaps in the working day" (Aglietta, 1979, pages 114-115). To this end, the activities of conception were separated from those of execution and placed in the hands of management, sharpening the division of mental and manual work. And through time-and-motion studies a sequence of simplified jobs made up of simple cycles of movement that could be performed by individual workers were identified. Output norms were set, payments were related to productivity, and surveillance and control were made more systematic. In the conditions that resulted, new methods of production and new specialised machine tools which could be operated by unskilled or, as the French say, 'specialised workers' were developed. The introduction of these new methods often involved costly investments in plant and machinery. To maximise its use and to reduce the risks of devalorisation, Taylorism accordingly culminated in the organisation of work teams: with a shortened working day the intensity of work was increased, gaps were reduced to a minimum, and shift working enabled the machinery to be operated almost continuously (see Aglietta, 1979, pages 115–116).

In the 1920s and onwards, Fordism, understood in its narrow sense as a principle of work organisation and of wage determination, was added. The word is used in this sense mainly to refer to the use of the semiautomatic assembly line (see, for example, Sabel, 1982, pages 32–34). Originally it was introduced in the vehicle manufacturing industry. In subsequent years, however, it was extended upstream into the production of standardised intermediate components and into other consumer-good and assembly industries. (What was involved was in fact a mechanisation of transfer. As a result, the developments concerned represented a qualitatively new stage in the transformation of industry.)

On the semiautomatic assembly line different segments of the process of production are integrated via a system of conveyors and handling devices that ensure movement of the material to be transformed past a sequence of positions where appropriate specialised machine tools are located. With its introduction, components were standardised, and a straightforward linear process of production was developed. "A condition of its success was a revolution in energy which generalised the industrial use of electricity and made possible the construction of high capacity motors" (Aglietta, 1979, page 118). But with it the partial Taylorised tasks of assembly line workers were simplified further and reduced in many cases to the repetition of a few elementary movements. At the same time, workers were fixed to jobs and positions that were rigidly determined by the configuration of the machine system, and the speed at which they worked was determined by the speed of movement of the line itself.

The development of Fordism was, however, subject to several external and internal limits (see Aglietta, 1979, pages 119–122; Coriat, 1983, pages 185–214; and also Coriat, 1984b). In the first place "the far-reaching transformations of the technical division of labour that the semi-automatic assembly line permits give an enormous boost to productive capacity and consequently demand social conditions consistent with the mass circulation of commodities on a rapidly increasing scale" (Aglietta, 1979, page 119). But with the increasing subdivision of jobs the costs in means of production associated with successive increases in the output norm tend to increase. According to Aglietta the reason why lies in the "great technical rigidity of the machine system" (Aglietta, 1979, page 119). With a need to find rapidly expanding markets and with rising fixed costs the valorisation of the capital advanced is increasingly problematic.

Internally at least three limits can be identified. One is the delays caused by inequalities in the cycles of movement of different workers. As a result, an amount of time "equal to the sum of those periods spent waiting by the workers with shorter cycles" is lost (Aglietta, 1979, page 120). A second concerns the effects of jobs that are intellectually undemanding, repetitive, and uniform in rhythm on the mental and physical health of individual workers. With the intensification of work, exhaustion increases, as does the likelihood of accidents. The proportion of defective products goes up, necessitating increased spending on quality control. In addition, irregular absenteeism tends to occur, requiring the employment of many more workers than are strictly necessary to operate plant and equipment. In the third place, the increasing collectivisation of work results in the abolition of any perceptible link between collective output and the effort of individual workers, prevents the identification of responsibility for defects, and tends to unify the workers in a struggle against their conditions of work. Indeed, in 1966–1974 a series of frequent and forceful revolts against the conditions of work in modern industrial plants occurred, often under the leadership of unskilled, immigrant, young, and women workers (see especially chapter 6, section 6.4). Involved were not only strikes and go-slows, but increased and irregular absenteeism, increased job turnover, and an increased proportion of poor-quality work. In addition, demands were made for equal rights for immigrant and female workers, an elimination of the lowest-graded jobs, automatic entry into skilled occupations, the establishment of regular promotion procedures for industrial workers, the incorporation of bonuses into the basic wage, and the elimination of piecework. "Taken together these demands constituted something close to a programme for the revision of workplace relations ... for which the working class actively fought and struggled" (Coriat, 1984a, pages 40–41). What followed was a crisis in the reproduction of the wage relation.

But with the advances in electronics and in information technology, automation is emerging as a new principle of capitalist control over production and is opening the way to a major new transformation of the process of labour.

The introduction of new instruments of measurement and control along with microprocessor technology enable information about the process of production to be collected, analysed, and stored as production is occurring. Information about a worker's deviation from prescribed standards with respect to rates of work, time out, and rate of material consumption can be monitored by supervisory staff in a central control room, and processes of production can be modified almost instantaneously. In assembly line industries the movement of materials can be altered according to the way work is proceeding, and the composition of output can be varied according to demand conditions. In process industries, processes of production can be monitored and, via feedback control mechanisms, almost instantaneously and continuously modified.

At the same time, machines are being developed that are capable of controlling their own operations and that are also polyvalent and capable of being quickly reprogrammed: many industrial robots can, for example, change tools and switch from one task to another very quickly. Along with the introduction of computerised models and a capacity to control large and complex systems, the flexibility of production is consequently increased, and in many areas of the economy methods of flexible specialisation are being adopted.

In addition, mechanisation is being given a new impetus since some complex, difficult, or dangerous tasks can be suppressed, and the number of workers required can frequently be reduced as one worker can supervise several machines, whereas the workers themselves can be moved around more easily.

After the generalisation of mechanical tools and the mechanisation of transfer, the control of machinery is, in other words, being mechanised. But with the help of information and microprocessor technology, not only production but also research and design and management and circulation are being transformed. Moreover, it is not simply individual or subsets of activities within the different spheres that are being automated. The spheres themselves are being integrated into complex self-adjusting systems, opening the way to what has been dubbed systemofacture (see figure 2.3 and Kaplinsky, 1984, pages 19-35).

At the same time, new methods of work organisation referred to as the recomposition of tasks, job redesign, job enrichment, and job rotation are being introduced. In some cases workers move between jobs. In some assembly line industries semiautonomous groups are formed and given a number of detailed and predefined tasks, including component control, the setting and supervision of machines, execution, and quality control. According to Aglietta, however, job rotation and job enrichment are simply the ultimate extension of the principles of Taylorism and Fordism: the tasks of setting machines are devolved only insofar as the specialised skills of the setter are no longer needed and the job has been deskilled, whereas all the other operations have individually been Taylorised. Yet by granting increased autonomy to the workers, productivity can be increased and quality improved. In conjunction with automation, job redesign is aimed in fact at increasing productivity and the intensity of work: wasted and unused time is eliminated, and control over each worker's performance is tightened. As a result, important increases in the speed and quality of production can be achieved. At the same time, efficiency in the use of tools and machines is increased, and energy consumption and the wastage of materials are reduced. What is more, the flexibility of production is increased: in particular, automation opens up the possibility of revolutionising small batch production.

Thus the transformations of the process of labour that are based on automation are resulting in a reduction in the amount of variable capital required to produce a given amount of value: in other words, absolute and relative surplus-value production are increased.

But surplus value "is only effectively realised if the equivalence relationships of exchange evolve in such a way as to counteract the tendency to the uneven development of Department 1 that follows from the rising organic composition of capital as the translation in the value field of the relative saving on labour-power". In the view of Aglietta, automation is likely to have two effects. On the one hand, "a far more advanced centralisation of production becomes compatible with a geographical decentralisation of operations". With the consequent increase in flexibility the capitalist class is presented with an opportunity of breaking up large working-class concentrations and creating an environment that minimises the convergence of struggles at the point of production. On the other, "a far-reaching modification of relationships between industries develops replacing electromechanical items of high value by electronic items of low value". As a result, "the development of electronics industries with simple and standardised

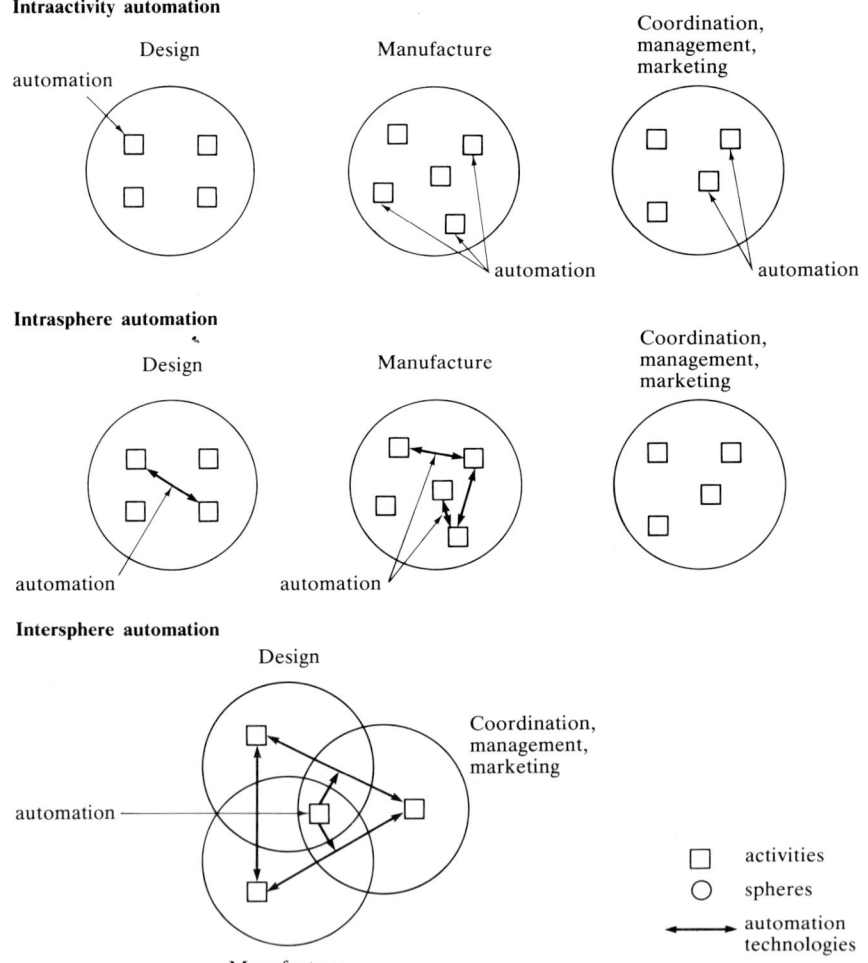

Figure 2.3. Three different kinds of automation. Source: Kaplinsky (1984, page 27).

production methods tends to lower the value of constant capital and consequently to counteract the rise in the organic composition of capital". Automation may, in other words, offer the possibility of transforming the relations of capitalist production in a way capable of safeguarding the reproduction of the wage relation (Aglietta, 1979, pages 125 - 127).

At present, however, what prevails is a state of crisis and uncertainty. Automation is proceeding, and the wage relation is being transformed, but only with a view to improving the profitability of capital in a situation devoid of prospects of steady growth.

In particular in the field of employment, not only are employers attempting to keep down wage costs, but increased flexibility is also being sought. Two main kinds of flexibility are involved. One is functional flexibility, which refers to the capacity of a firm to adjust the tasks performed by the workers it employs according to changes in demand, technology, or marketing policy. This kind of flexibility is achieved mainly through the recruitment of a group of polyvalent core workers. The second is numerical flexibility. Numerical flexibility refers to the ease and speed with which firms can adjust the number of workers employed to meet fluctuations in demand. (On this distinction and the arguments in the rest of this section see Atkinson, 1984, pages 11 - 19). In addition, of course, employers are seeking financial flexibility in the form of a capacity to alter the structure of pay according to the level of employment and the type of work each worker is doing and a limitation of fixed costs.

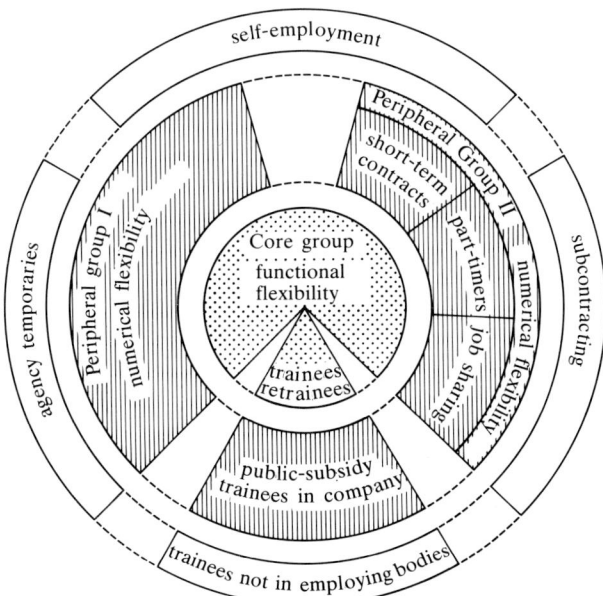

Figure 2.4. The flexible firm. Source: Atkinson (1984, page 16).

As a result of the strategy of seeking functional and numerical flexibility, the segmentation of the working population has been reinforced: functional flexibility has been closely associated with the employment of a group of core workers; numerical flexibility has been associated with variations in the numbers of peripheral workers (see figure 2.4). Included in the peripheral category are two groups of people. One is composed of the workers employed by subcontractors, specialised self-employed workers, and staff supplied by temporary-employment agencies. The second is made up of some of the firm's own employees. Included in this group are workers without career status who can be laid off or reemployed according to economic conditions, workers with temporary contracts of employment, part-time and casual staff, and people in groups with a high turnover whose numbers can easily be reduced by a policy of nonreplacement.

Whether and to what extent employers succeed in a dual-society strategy depends very much upon the goals, organisation, and strength of the working-class and trade union movements. In both the Italian and the French cases, transformations of the wage relation in this direction can nevertheless be observed.

2.6 The accumulation of capital

As the circuit of industrial capital is repeated, the production and realisation of surplus value is continually renewed. If the increment in value is consumed unproductively, a process of simple reproduction of commodities, of surplus value, and of the social relations of capitalist production occurs. But if the value of the capital advanced is increased through the transformation of part of ΔM into additional capital, the circuit grows in an outward spiral movement in a process of extended reproduction or accumulation of capital. The employment of surplus value as capital is what Marx meant when he referred to the accumulation of capital.

One frequent consequence of the accumulation of capital is that individual capitals grow in size. An increase in the size of individual capitals can occur in two ways. First, the amount of money capital advanced by an individual capitalist enterprise may increase, in which case a process of industrial concentration is said to be occurring. Second, formerly separate capitals may be merged, in which case growth occurs through industrial centralisation.

In *Capital*, Marx also pointed out that the extended reproduction or accumulation of capital on the basis of a stable ratio of constant and variable capital will come up against finite limits as more and more people are drawn into the production process, and as a relative shortage of labour develops. A process of extensive accumulation or capital widening is, however, to some extent self-correcting since, if the wage-earning class succeeds in these circumstances in pushing up the value of labour power, the rate of surplus value and the stimulus to invest will fall. Any subsequent decline in the amount of capital advanced will lead to a fall in the level of employment. Consequently, labour power will become relatively abundant once again, and the rate of surplus value can be restored to a higher level. "The mechanism of the accumulation process itself removes the very obstacle it temporarily creates" (Marx, 1976, pages 781-794). It does so through the reproduction of an industrial reserve army. With any slackening in the rate of accumulation, the size of the underemployed, unemployed, and marginalised strata of the reserve army of labour is increased. As a result, the share of wages in value added can be reduced, and the ability of capital to increase the production of absolute surplus value by lengthening the working day or increasing the intensity of work is also strengthened.

A more effective way of attempting to maintain the rate of surplus value and of sustaining the process of accumulation is by pursuing a strategy of intensive accumulation or capital deepening. In this case the proportion of constant to variable capital and the rate of relative surplus value are increased. Aggregate employment thus increases less rapidly than aggregate social capital, and shortages of labour power are less likely to occur.

Unregulated capital accumulation is, however, a contradictory process that is self-crippling.

2.7 Investment, technical change, and competition

In what ways do "the immanent laws of capitalist production manifest themselves in the external movement of individual capitals, assert themselves as the coercive laws of competition, and therefore enter into the consciousness of the individual capitalist as the motives which drive him [or her] forward"? After identifying this question concerning the microeconomic foundations of his theory at the end of his account of the concept of relative surplus value, Marx made some brief remarks about the role of competition in technical change (Marx, 1976, pages 433-438; and also Lipietz, 1979, chapter 9; 1980, pages 524-527).

Suppose a normal day's work of ten hours results in the transformation of means of production equal in value to that of ten hours of abstract labour into ten articles. As long as the articles are made in the average conditions of production the output of a day's work will represent twenty hours of abstract labour and each article two hours. Suppose also that the monetary equivalent of an hour of abstract labour is £1. The social value of the article, at which commodities are assumed to exchange, is equal to £2: £1 for the means of production used up, and £1 for the value newly added. If the value of labour power is represented by eight hours of work the daily wage must be £8. The rate of exploitation is $s/v = \frac{2}{8} = 0.25$. And the value of the commodity is $c + v + s =$ £1 + £0.8 + £0.2 = £2.

Suppose also that the capitalist concerned introduces a new method of production. The value of the constant capital required per article remains constant, but the apparent productivity of labour is doubled. As a result, twenty articles can be produced in a normal working day. "Even though the productivity of labour has been doubled, a day's labour creates, as before, a new value of [£10] and no more." But the value added is now spread over twice as many articles. "Only half an hour of labour-time, instead of a whole hour, is now added to the means of production while they are being transformed into each article." Thus, the new individual value of an article is $c + l$ = £1 + £0.5 = £1.50. "The real value of a commodity, however, is not its individual value but its social value." With the introduction of the new method of production the individual value of the commodity is less than its social value. "If, therefore, the capitalist who applies the new method sells his [or her] commodity at its social value of [£2], he [or she] sells it for [£0.50] above its individual value." Thus, an extra surplus value of £0.50 is realised. "On the other hand", continues Marx, "the working day [of ten hours] is now represented ... by [twenty] articles instead of [ten]". In order to sell the product of one day's work demand must double. "Other things being equal the capitalist's commodities can only command a more extensive market if their prices are reduced. [The capitalist concerned] will therefore sell them above their individual but below their social value at, say, [£1.80] each. By this means he [or she] still squeezes an extra surplus value of [£0.30] out of each." It follows, concludes Marx, that "there is a motive for each individual capitalist to cheapen his [or her] commodities by increasing the productivity of labour".

On this account the initial fall in price is a result not of the fall in value of the commodity, but of the need of an entrepreneur who is producing more commodities while advancing the same amount of capital to conquer a larger share of a market whose size in value terms is predetermined. For Marx, supply and demand are inextricably interwoven: the investment of capital in production determines the size and composition of distributed incomes, whereas the incomes so formed determine the size and composition of the output that can be realised. If the incomes distributed when capital is advanced remain consistent with an existing schema of extended reproduction, and a new method of production capable of increasing output is introduced, the increase in output comes up against unchanged conditions of demand. The employer who has raised productivity must therefore lower his or her offer price to conquer a larger part of an unchanged market (see Lipietz, 1980, pages 525-527).

Once the new method has been introduced the other producers whose sales have fallen must adapt to the new norms of production. The capitalist who has introduced the new method can invest the extra surplus value obtained to accumulate more rapidly than his or her competitors. As a result, the social value of the commodity concerned is reduced. But as soon as the new method of production has been generalised the difference between the individual value of the cheapened commodity and its social value disappears, as does the extra surplus value. Any fall in the price of a commodity alters the amount that the consumer can buy with his or her income. If the new method of production results directly or indirectly in a cheapening of wage goods, the general rate of surplus value is affected.

In my example the capitalist originally produced ten articles and sold them at £2 each, receiving £20. Since the value of the means of production was £10, five articles replaced the capital advanced. The value added was represented by the remaining five. Since the value of labour power was £8, four articles represented the value of labour power and one the surplus value, and $s/v = \frac{1}{4} = 0.25$.

After the change in methods of production, twenty articles were made, and, after the method's generalisation, were sold at £1.50 each, yielding £30. Of this sum, £20 or two thirds of the articles represented the value of the means of production used in one day's work. The value newly added was represented by the remaining £10 or 6.67 articles.

Suppose that the articles concerned were the means of consumption purchased by the working class. With the increase in productivity the time needed to manufacture the goods originally bought fell from eight hours to six hours and their value from £8 to £6. If the value of labour power is correspondingly reduced, surplus value increases from £2 to £4 and the rate of surplus value from $\frac{1}{4}$ to $\frac{4}{6} = 0.67$.

What impact do these developments have on the value rate of profit? The value rate of profit is defined as

$$r = \frac{s}{c+v} = \frac{s}{v+s}\left(\frac{c}{v+s} + \frac{1-s}{v+s}\right)^{-1}$$
$$= \frac{h}{k+1-h},$$

where $0 \leq h \leq 1$ and $0 \leq r \leq k^{-1}$: r is equal to 0 if s and, consequently, h are zero, and to k^{-1} if v is zero and h is 1. h is the share of profits in value added. k is the ratio of labour materialised in the means of production and the living labour employed. It is what Marx called the value composition or the organic composition of capital (see Lipietz, 1982b, pages 199-205).

In my example the initial value rate of profit calculated with unit values was $r_1 = 0.2/(1+0.8) = 0.11$. With the general introduction of the new method of production and in the absence of a fall in the value of labour power, the rate of profit would have fallen to $r_2 = 0.1/(1+0.4) = 0.07$. But if the commodities concerned were the only wage goods and the value of labour power was adjusted downwards, the rate of profit would have increased, reaching $r_3 = 0.2/(1+0.3) = 0.15$ (see figures 2.5a, 2.5b, and 2.5c, respectively, to emphasise the connection).

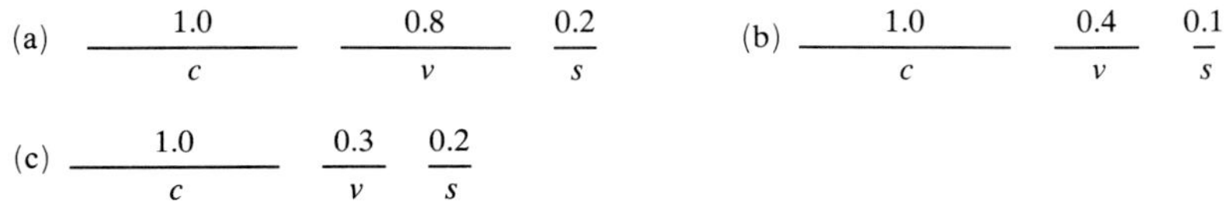

(a) $\frac{1.0}{c}$ $\frac{0.8}{v}$ $\frac{0.2}{s}$ (b) $\frac{1.0}{c}$ $\frac{0.4}{v}$ $\frac{0.1}{s}$

(c) $\frac{1.0}{c}$ $\frac{0.3}{v}$ $\frac{0.2}{s}$

Figure 2.5. Technical change and the value composition of the product.

As the organic composition of capital increases the maximum value rate of profit falls:

$$r = \frac{s}{c+v} < \frac{s+v}{c+v} < \frac{s+v}{c}.$$

Whether the organic composition does in fact go up depends on whether or not innovations are capital-using and labour-saving, as in my example, or labour-using and capital-saving. [On the controversy surrounding Marx's law of the tendency of the rate of profit to fall see Lipietz (1980, pages 514-527; 1982b, pages 199-207.]

2.8 The reproduction and regulation of the capitalist mode of production
From the point of view of an individual capitalist any activity is good as long as it yields a profit. But at the level of the economy as a whole all production is interdependent, as are the activities of distribution, exchange, and consumption. An expansion of one industry depends on the expansion of industries supplying necessary capital goods and intermediate inputs, as well as on an expansion of demand for its output. The availability of inputs is conditional upon supply decisions by other capitalists, whereas demand depends on other capitalists advancing money to purchase constant capital, and on the distribution of incomes in the forms of wages, rent, interest, and distributed profits to individuals who can then spend them on consumer goods and services.

The conditions necessary for equilibrium growth can of course be identified. Some of them are highlighted in Marx's reproduction schemas. In the reproduction schemas only two departments of production are identified: department 1, which is made up of the set of processes of production whose outputs are elements of constant capital, and department 2, in which means of consumption are produced for the wage-earners and capitalists of both departments.

In the simplest case of simple reproduction all surplus value or surplus revenue is consumed by the capitalist class. Simple reproduction is accordingly associated with a succession of identical cycles of production and a constant level of social wealth.

To simplify the analysis several assumptions are initially made (see, for example, Gouverneur, 1983, pages 103-105): (1) All activities are capitalist production activities. The existence of circulation and administration activities is disregarded. (2) The rate of surplus value and the composition of capital are the same in both departments. (3) In both departments all of the means of production have to be renewed at the beginning of each annual cycle of production. (4) The monetary expression of the working hour is £1. As a result, any symbol can be interpreted either as a value or as a price.

On these assumptions the equilibrium conditions are twofold. First, the supply of producer goods which is equal in value to the value of the output of department 1 must equal the value of the producer goods demanded by both departments. In other words,

$$c_1 + v_1 + s_1 = c_1 + c_2 . \qquad (2.6)$$

Second, the value of the aggregate supply of consumer goods produced in department 2 must be equal to the value of the goods consumed by the wage earners and capitalists of both departments. In other words,

$$c_2 + v_2 + s_2 = v_1 + s_1 + v_2 + s_2 . \qquad (2.7)$$

If equations (2.6) and (2.7) are simplified it follows that c_2 must equal $v_1 + s_1$. In other words, the demand of department 2 for producer goods must equal the demand of department 1 for consumer goods.

The analysis can be developed in several ways. First, the more complex case of extended reproduction can be considered. In this case, where one part of the surplus revenue is accumulated, output must be adequate to meet a replacement demand and an expansion demand corresponding to (1) the supplementary means of production exchanged against reinvested surplus revenue at the beginning of each new cycle, and (2) the supplementary means of consumption that will be exchanged against the additional wages paid in the new period. Second, changes in the norms of production that stem from investment and technical change and changes in the value and volume composition of demand can be included in the analysis.

Although the formal conditions of equilibrium growth can be identified, in the absence of systematic state intervention no planning mechanism exists that is capable of ensuring that they are satisfied. In a capitalist society an equilibrated development of the different types of activity of which the social division of labour is composed is not planned a priori or consciously organised. (Only in the case of the detailed division of labour within the enterprise does planning prevail.) The distribution of social labour among the various areas of economic activity is a result of the independent initiatives of thousands of capitalists, all of whom are advancing and readvancing money capital. As the values in process represented by this wealth move through their circuits an interlacing occurs. On the one hand, goods and services are exchanged with other capitalists and with the wage-earning class, affirming the validity of some activities. On the other, shortages and surpluses are identified. Adjustment depends on the market. If a product is in short supply its price will go up, attracting investment into that sector. And once output can be increased or new capacity comes on-stream, supply will increase, driving prices down again.

Yet if adaptation depends on a sequence of ex post adjustments (which can themselves, as is indicated in, say, cobweb cycle models, be destabilising), how do capitalist economies succeed in sometimes growing in a balanced way. At one level the acquired experience of a solution is itself one of the bases of a solution. On the basis of information gleaned from the monetary results of previous activity and acquired knowledge of market conditions, expectations about the results of renewed activity are formed. In conditions of relatively stable growth the cycle of production is likely to be renewed. Through the renewal of activity, capital and intermediate goods are bought, and incomes distributed to wage earners are spent, validating the activity of other capitalists and helping to confirm and reaffirm the original expectations. The conditions inherited from the past, and the expectations that these conditions will continue to prevail and that the norms of production and consumption will continue to evolve as they have in the past, are the foundations of a 'social mould' which can sometimes be described as a regime of accumulation (see Lipietz, 1984b, pages 5-6; and also Aglietta and Brender, 1984, pages 29-134).

A regime of accumulation is a systematic organisation of production, income distribution, exchange of the social product, and consumption. With the materialisation of a regime of accumulation the process of economic reproduction is characterised by a relative stability: changes in the amount of capital invested, its distribution between sectors and departments, and trends in productivity are coordinated with changes in the distribution of income and in the field of consumption.

Several schematic regimes of accumulation can be identified. In the 19th century a regime of extensive accumulation gave way to a regime involving a combination of extensive and intensive accumulation in which the investment of constant capital, including investments in iron and steel, railway construction, and shipbuilding, itself validated the growth of department 1. In the 1930s and after the Second World War in particular, it gave way in turn to a regime of intensive accumulation in which the conditions of existence of the wage-earning class were transformed through the articulation of mass production and mass consumption (see Aglietta, 1979, pages 66-72; Lipietz, 1984b, pages 6-7).

2.9 The development of a regime of intensive accumulation: the national framework

In subsequent chapters it will be argued that what underpinned Italian and French industrialisation after 1945 was in fact an unequal diffusion and a crisis of a regime of intensive accumulation and a system of monopolistic regulation.

With the extension and generalisation of Taylorism and Fordism and an emphasis on the production of goods capable of being produced in long runs and of yielding considerable scale economies, productivity increased rapidly. Yet the growth of capacity to produce goods and services and the emergence of new sectors producing vehicles and durable household equipment goods came up against limits of demand: in the 1930s consumption of these products was largely confined to relatively prosperous middle strata. As a result, a deep crisis occurred.

After the Second World War and after a phase of reconstruction a new wave of very fast growth occurred. On this occasion wages increased along with productivity. [In Italy the wage relation was generalised but wages were at first held down, the home market was dominated by middle strata who played an important part in the consensus-forming strategy of the Democrazia Cristiana (Christian Democrat Party, DC), and growth was export-led.] The share of household budgets devoted to food and necessary subsistence goods fell, and demand increased in line with the expansion of production capacity. Mass consumption emerged as a corollary of mass production, and the conditions of existence of large sections of the skilled and semiskilled wage-earning class were transformed. In 1959-1974, for example, the percentages of French workers owning consumer durables increased dramatically. In the case of cars it rose from 21.3% to 60%, televisions from 8.6% to 81%, refrigerators from 19.4% to 87%, and washing machines from 21.2% to 72.9%. The equivalent middle-class consumption ratios were all over 90% (Souyri cited in Davis, 1984, page 14; see also Souyri, 1983).

The transformation of the spheres of consumption and reproduction did not merely supply outlets for new types of consumer goods and enable a harmonisation of the development of the two departments of production. With the development of Fordism, workers suited to new kinds of work and capable of preserving and reproducing the skills and attitudes they required were needed. Accordingly, attempts were made to select and produce new types of worker with "new, more complex and rigid norms or habits of order, exactitude and precision", and indeed to transform the structure of society itself. Work was more wearying and exhausting, and demanded new levels of expenditure of muscular and, in particular, of nervous energy. Consequently, high wages were also paid to assist the process of restoring the strength and energy used up at work (see Gramsci, 1971b, pages 294-297, 298-306, 310-313).

The renewal of the opportunities for investment that resulted was eventually to be accompanied by a spectacular development of, first, industries linked with the transformation of the conditions of production (that is, production of plant, machinery and equipment), second, industries connected with the enlargement of the sphere of consumption (that is, production of housing and of cars and household equipment), and third, process industries connected with the supply of energy and intermediate goods.

Alongside the expanding output of capitalistically produced commodities and the growth of privatised mass consumption, a social security system and welfare state were developed. In the fields of education, health, and social security the state assumed a major role in the provision of a safety net and in the reproduction of individuals isolated from wider networks of support.

At the same time, the service sector expanded. Within the various groups of services, some declined, as in the case of private domestic services.

Some followed the overall trend. Many were transformed, as in distribution, with the development, at least in the French case, of self-service and large chain stores to serve an increasingly motorised and suburbanised society. Some grew explosively. The most rapidly expanding tertiary activities included services to firms, activities connected with financial circulation, and health and education. As productivity increased comparatively slowly, employment in these sectors increased particularly rapidly.

With the transformation of work and of the structure of the economy major occupational shifts occurred. In the French case the most rapidly expanding occupations were the ones that included scientific, technical, and other professional staff on the one hand, and middle and higher-level managers and administrators on the other. In 1954–1981 the '*professions libérales et cadres supérieurs*' increased from 2.9% to 8.6% of the active population, and the '*cadres moyens*' from 5.8% to 14.7% (see Thévenot, 1977, pages 4–5; 1985, page 551).

Underlying the development of services were a number of sets of factors. (Some of the more specific reasons will be considered in subsequent chapters.) Of particular importance was the establishment of a more developed division of mental and manual work and the growth of large organisations. As a result of these developments, white-collar employment increased within manufacturing itself, as well as in the tertiary sector, according to whether mental tasks and service work were performed internally, contracted out or bought in from specialised enterprises. A second major element was the development of the health, education, and social security systems. But also included were relations of complementarity, of differential productivity, and of differential profitability. In the Italian and French cases the last factor, which is itself connected with the fact that services are less subject to international cost competition than manufacturing, helps to explain the shift of investment from the manufacturing to the tertiary sector.

After the war, then, the crisis conditions of the 1930s did not recur. Instead, a wave of almost unprecedented growth occurred. What was it that differentiated the years after the Second World War from those that preceded it?

What had emerged were in fact new principles of regulation. The concept of regulation is used to denote a specific local and historical collection of institutional arrangements within which individual and collective behaviour unfolds, and a particular configuration of market adjustments through which privately made decisions are coordinated (see Boyer, 1978, pages 28–29; Boyer and Mistral, 1978, pages 2–5). Underlying it is a distinction between social action and institutional arrangements or the social conditions of human activity. Conflicts between classes and social groups, the strategies of enterprises and financial institutions which themselves are rooted in the fractioning of capital into interdependent private units, and the relation of these conflicts and strategies with various markets and the state are expressed, in each historical situation, in a collection of structural constraints which have emerged out of an historical process of class conflict, intercapitalist rivalry, and state action. Adjustments in each market accordingly depend on institutions or structures which possess a certain degree of autonomy, and cannot be reduced to a global mechanism such as that of supply and demand.

The stability of regulation presupposes a certain inertia of structures and institutional arrangements. But stability is only relative. The process of regulation itself engenders permanent movements which continually modify the character of social relations, the intensity of conflicts, and the relations of strength. Consequently, a type of regulation can only be identified as a result of a process of schematisation carried out for the purposes of theoretical analysis. Actual processes not only differ in a multiplicity of ways, but also are subject to a continuous dynamic caused by changes in the social and political relations underlying them. At certain critical moments in history the process of development brings into question previously formed constraints and opens up the subject of new forms of overall reproduction. Out of this real dialectic operating in each social formation, and out of the conflicts between classes and political groups, the strategies of organised social movements, and political processes unfolding within the state itself, specific types of regulation were developed.

After the Second World War the new social framework that emerged was one whose roots lay in, first, the defeat of an old style of conservatism and of fascism, and second, a more general adoption, albeit with more emphasis on private as opposed to collective activity, of some of the social reforms envisaged in the 'New Deal'. What it involved was a transition from competitive to monopolistic processes of regulation.

The main national institutional developments were fourfold.

(1) As a consequence, in part, of the struggles of the trade union and working-class movements the direct wage came to be determined via processes of collective bargaining, and wages were linked with productivity and the cost of living (see Boyer, 1978, pages 28 – 34).

(2) With the emergence of large oligopolistic firms and financial groups came the practice of administered pricing. As a result, the sensitivity of prices, of profits, and of investment to short-term market fluctuations was reduced. In addition, large financial savings could be amassed, and the intersectoral mobility of finance was increased.

(3) Credit money and a hierarchical banking system were developed. The rate of money creation was thus made endogenous. With these changes in the monetary system money wages could be freely negotiated, prices could be administered, and long-term investment plans could be implemented with less risk of losses through devalorisation.

(4) A social security system and welfare state were introduced, along with major reforms in the fields of urban and regional planning. With the adoption of Keynesian economic ideas and of other economic reforms

including, in some countries, elements of economic planning and state entrepreneurship, relations between enterprises and the state were modified.

So far attention has been confined to the reproduction of the capitalist sector of a national economy. However, the reproduction of society cannot, as has already been suggested, be reduced to the reproduction of this sector. Many activities within each national economy are not governed by capitalist relations of production: in the domestic sector, for example, relations of patriarchy usually prevail. Furthermore, each national economy exists within an international division of labour. Accordingly, together with a sheltered sector, an exposed sector dependent on internationally imposed conditions of production can be identified, and the analysis can be extended to cover the question of internationalisation (see Aglietta, 1982b, pages 7–10).

At an international level other institutional changes took place and shaped the environment in which the processes of national development occurred. Under the hegemony of the United States of America a new hierarchical international order was established. In the western world a US cultural model was imposed, US financial aid and technology were supplied to aid the recovery and secure the unity of the advanced capitalist nations, and internationally a new institutional framework was established with the decisions made at Bretton Woods and the setting up of GATT, the IMF, the OECD, and so on.

An analysis of the dynamics of the exposed sector is represented in the models of circular and cumulative causation. According to Aglietta, after the Second World War two interdependent virtuous circles were set in motion: first, a circle of high growth and high inflation of economies exporting durable consumer goods, and second a model of somewhat slower growth and less inflation of economies with technological superiority in capital goods sectors (see Aglietta, 1982b, pages 6–19). The Italian and the French economies were both instances of the first model.

2.10 Specialisation and the international division of labour: the principle of comparative costs

In capitalist societies values are formed at a national level. The conditions on which the wage relation depends are established and reproduced at the level of national economies whose structures and processes of regulation are characterised by important degrees of long-term autonomy. In this way, national contrasts in the development of the wage-earning class and in the process of wage determination are constantly renewed. Contrary to what is claimed in orthodox neoclassical economics, the functioning of market mechanisms does not lead to the establishment of an international equilibrium in which the prices of all goods, or even of all traded goods, and of the factors of production are equalised. Spatial differentiation cannot be dissolved (Aglietta, 1982a, pages 323–329).

As a consequence of the varying national histories of investment not only by national capitals but also by international firms, national systems of production differ, as do comparative costs. Suppose, as did Ricardo (1951, pages 128-149), that the costs of production in two countries are the ones set out in table 2.2. But let us interpret these costs as quantities of labour commanded by the wage weighted by a rate of profit which itself reflects the difficulty of producing wage goods in the country concerned [see equation (2.5)]. In this situation, multiplying them by the money wage yields the prices of production.

In the situation depicted in the tableau, Portuguese producers can produce both wine and cloth more cheaply than their English counterparts: the Portuguese have an absolute advantage in the production of both commodities. But in Portugal wine is comparatively cheap, since

$$\frac{m_{wp}}{m_{cp}} = \frac{80}{90} < \frac{m_{we}}{m_{ce}} = \frac{120}{100},$$

whereas in England cloth is comparatively cheap. Alternatively, one can say that Portuguese producers have a comparatively greater advantage over their English counterparts in the production of wine,

$$\frac{m_{wp}}{m_{we}} = \frac{80}{120} < \frac{m_{cp}}{m_{ce}} = \frac{90}{100},$$

whereas English producers have a comparatively smaller disadvantage in the production of cloth.

The value of commodities bought and sold on the international market is not formed in the same way as values on the national market. In Ricardo's own example, where the terms of trade were assumed to be 100:100, England ends up exchanging the produce of one hundred hours of work for that of eighty hours. In other words, an inequality of exchange occurs largely because, in Ricardo's view, of the international immobility of capital.

International values are formed in the process of interaction of relatively autonomous national economies, in which a correspondence is established between national price systems through the establishment of a rate of exchange which itself is a measure of the rate of exchange of wage labour between different national economies. At first, interaction is considered as comprising only (1) a process of international commodity exchange, and (2) the operation of an international monetary constraint in a context that is shaped, of course, by comparative costs and the dynamic of specialisation to which they give rise.

Table 2.2. The Ricardian Tableau for England and Portugal (in hours of work per yard of cloth or gallon of wine).

	England	Portugal
Cloth	100	90
Wine	120	80

International exchange can only be sustained if prices expressed in a common currency lie within certain limits and the international monetary constraint is respected. Suppose that d_w and d_c are the international prices of wine and cloth, and w_p and w_e the money wages in Portugal and England respectively, with all quantities being expressed in a common currency. International exchange will only occur if

$$\frac{m_{wp} w_p}{m_{cp} w_p} < \frac{d_w}{d_c} < \frac{m_{we} w_e}{m_{ce} w_e},$$

with

$$d_w = m_{wp} w_p \quad \text{and} \quad d_c = m_{ce} w_e.$$

In other words, it will only occur if the ratio of money wages expressed in a common currency satisfies the constraint

$$\frac{m_{ce}}{m_{cp}} = \frac{100}{90} < \frac{w_p}{w_e} < \frac{m_{we}}{m_{wp}} = \frac{120}{80}.$$

The inverses of total costs can be interpreted as indices of the productivity of labour employed to produce one unit of each type of commodity in the conditions of production prevailing in each country. It follows that each economy has a tendency to export those goods in whose production its productivity relative to that of its competitors is greater than the ratio of money wages expressed in a common currency. What must be emphasised, however, is that the process of formation of value does not imply that wages or wages per unit of output are equalised. All that is implied is that

$$\frac{m_{wp} w_p}{d_w} = \frac{m_{ce} w_e}{d_c}.$$

In other words, the wage costs per unit of value produced should be equal after specialisation.

For international exchange to occur a rate of exchange must be established. Suppose that the rate of exchange, e, is equal to one unit of the Portuguese currency per unit of the English currency. In other words, 1 escudo is equal to £1, or $e = 1$. Suppose also that the money wage in each country is £0.01. If the price of cloth in England is £1 the average price of cloth in Portugal expressed in units of the English currency is £(90/100), that is, £0.90. Similarly, the prices of wine are £1.20 and £0.80, respectively (see columns 1 and 2 in tables 2.3 and 2.4). In these circumstances the Portuguese economy has an advantage not only in the production of wine but also in the production of cloth. If trade were to occur the English economy would have a large trade deficit and the Portuguese economy a large surplus. What is required is a mechanism which will raise the international prices of all Portuguese products and lower the international prices of all English products until: (1) English producers can undersell the Portuguese in one of the two commodities, and England's comparative advantage has been translated into a competitive advantage; (2) resources have been transferred to the activities in which each country has a comparative advantage; and (3) the values of each country's exports and imports have been altered and the balance of payments of the two countries brought into equilibrium[2]. In the absence of these adjustments, protectionism and exchange controls would be the only way of avoiding an international economic war and a series of national economic crises.

According to Aglietta (1982a, pages 323-329), adjustment can occur in a number of ways. Wages in Portugal could rise, pushing up prices, while those in England fell, until $w_p = 1.11 w_e$, and the prices of cloth expressed in English currency were equal. As is indicated in the middle section of table 2.3, the desired result could be achieved by a 5.26% fall in English prices and an equivalent rise in Portuguese prices. In these circumstances England would be able to export cloth and to earn foreign currency with which it could pay for imports of wine. The prices set out in the middle section of table 2.3 are the lower limit at which the balance of payments of the two trading countries can be equilibrated. The upper limit occurs at the point at which the prices of wine expressed in the English currency are equal. At this point $w_p = 1.50 w_e$. One way in which this wage ratio could be

Table 2.3. International prices (in £) with fixed exchange rates and wage flexibility. (w_p and w_e are the money wages in Portugal and England, respectively, both expressed in a common currency.)

	$w_p = w_e$		$w_p = 1.11 w_e$		$w_p = 1.50 w_e$	
	England	Portugal	England	Portugal	England	Portugal
Cloth	1.00	0.90	0.95	0.95	0.80	1.08
Wine	1.20	0.80	1.14	0.84	0.96	0.96

Table 2.4. International prices (in £) with flexible exchange rates (e) and wage inflexibility. ($e = 1.11$ indicates 1 escudo equal to £1.11.)

	$e = 1.00$		$e = 1.11$		$e = 1.50$	
	England	Portugal	England	Portugal	England	Portugal
Cloth	1.00	0.90	1.00	1.00	1.00	1.35
Wine	1.20	0.80	1.20	0.89	1.20	1.20

[2] Whether gains from trade occur depends on assumptions of constant returns to scale in all processes of production and of full employment. In the presence of diminishing or increasing returns, costs would be affected by changes in the level of output, whereas the existence of unemployed resources would mean that the opportunity cost of producing the imported good domestically is zero, unless production can only occur if materials and capital goods are imported. In addition, inflexibility in factor markets must be ruled out along with the existence of costs of adjustment.

established is through a 20% fall in English wages and a corresponding increase in money wages in Portugal, as a result of which prices would be equal to those set out in the final two columns of table 2.3.

A second way in which adjustment could occur and the international flows of money corresponding to international commodity exchange could be equalised is through movements in the rate of exchange. Starting from the same initial position (that is, 1 escudo equal to £1), the rate of exchange would have to move in favour of the Portuguese until it reached the situation where 1 escudo was equal to £1.11 ($e = 1.11$) and the prices of cloth were equalised. But an upper limit to the depreciation of the pound also exists. In this case it is set by a rate of exchange of 1 escudo equal to £1.50 ($e = 1.50$), at which the prices of English and Portuguese wine would be equal (see table 2.4).

Movements in relative money wages or in the rate of exchange, caused by changes in the process of money income formation and the operation of an international monetary constraint, always occur, however, in conjunction with changes in specialisation. Each economy is normally capable of producing a range of commodities, and the constraint on the money wage ratio should be written

$$\frac{m_{ae}}{m_{ap}} < \frac{m_{be}}{m_{bp}} < ... < \frac{w_p}{w_e} < ... < \frac{m_{ce}}{m_{cp}} < \frac{m_{de}}{m_{dp}},$$

where a, b, and so on represent different traded goods. In other words, for a given money wage ratio and rate of exchange there exists an international division of social production with England exporting a quantity of each of the internationally traded goods to the left of w_p/w_e, which can be represented by a vector x_e, in exchange for imports from Portugal, whereas Portugal exports quantities of the other goods, represented by a vector x_p.

Suppose that England has a trade deficit, so that the international monetary constraint is not respected. In other words, $ep_p x_p > p_e x_e$, where p_p and p_e are vectors denoting the prices of production prevailing in Portugal and England respectively. In these conditions wages, or the exchange rate, or both, must fall in England and rise in Portugal. The wage ratio expressed in a common currency which links the two national price systems would accordingly be altered, moving to the right through the ranked array of comparative costs. As a result, the schema of specialisation should change, with commodities that were formerly exported by the Portuguese now being exported by the English.

The analysis must, however, be qualified in several ways. In the first place, any reduction in capacity and development of new spheres of activity must involve a scrapping of existing equipment, investment in new activities, and a redeployment of workers. Consequently, shifts in specialisation are neither smooth nor automatic. In addition, only if the English industrial system is highly diversified and integrated can exports be increased and imports diminished without very large variations in the wage ratio or in the exchange rate, and only if a country is capable of remodelling its industrial system and is not dependent on narrow market niches or crénaux can shifts in specialisation occur without serious dislocation.

Another difficulty concerns the effects and efficiency of monetary mechanisms. In the view of Ricardo, the mechanism through which adjustment would occur is the one posited in the classical quantity theory of money (see Shaikh, 1979; 1980a; 1980b). On this account, net transfers of gold, at first from England to Portugal, would be translated into movements in money price levels in the two nations. [One of the problems with this argument, as with neoclassical theory, is that it involves a treatment of a market economy independently of monetary factors: relative prices are deemed to be determined by real factors, and money is only introduced in order to determine the general price level. On the development and character of classical and neoclassical theory see Walsh and Gram (1980).] Whether or not monetary expansion and contraction have a direct effect on the price level has in any case been a subject of dispute in economics. According to Marx and Keynes, for example, changes in the supply of money have a direct effect only on the rate of interest: a fall in the supply of money results in an increase in the rate of interest, raising, incidentally, the costs of borrowing and impeding the new investment necessary for adjustment, and vice versa. In these and other circumstances adjustment may well fall on output instead of on prices (see, for example, Edwards, 1985, pages 123–137).

Under monopolistic regulation, wages and other costs are characterised by a certain inflexibility. In the face of, say, a fall in the rate of exchange, employers may choose not to adjust prices expressed in a foreign currency downwards. The competitiveness of the enterprise's output would thus remain the same, whereas its profit margins on export markets would increase (see Aglietta et al, 1980; 1981).

Adjustment is in reality, as we shall see in subsequent chapters, neither automatic nor self-equilibrating at full-employment levels of resource use. In this section my main aim was, however, not one of analysing in any detail the mechanisms of international adjustment. Instead a method of theoretical analysis was used simply in order to identify and describe the interaction of some of the major determinants or factors on which the evolution of the rate of exchange and of the international division of labour depend. The argument itself, which has been drawn from the work of Aglietta, is summarised in figure 2.6. Alternatively it can be stated algebraically by

$$e = \frac{p_e x_e}{p_p x_p} = \frac{w_e}{w_p} \frac{l_e[\mathbf{I}/(1+r_e) - \mathbf{A}_e]^{-1}}{l_p[\mathbf{I}/(1+r_p) - \mathbf{A}_p]^{-1}} \frac{x_e}{x_p}, \qquad (2.8)$$

and

$$\frac{ew_p}{w_e} = \frac{l_e[\mathbf{I}/(1+r_e) - \mathbf{A}_e]^{-1}}{l_p[\mathbf{I}/(1+r_p) - \mathbf{A}_p]^{-1}} \frac{x_e}{x_p}, \qquad (2.9)$$

where e is the rate of exchange at which each country's balance of payments would be in equilibrium and the international monetary constraint would be respected strictly, ew_p/w_e is the rate at which social labour is exchanged internationally, and the middle expression on the right-hand side of equation (2.8) and the first expression on the right-hand side of equation (2.9) is what I have called comparative costs. The historical process itself can, however, only be explained if the theory I have started to outline is elaborated in order to consider, amongst other things, intracommodity trade, and is supplemented by empirical analysis.

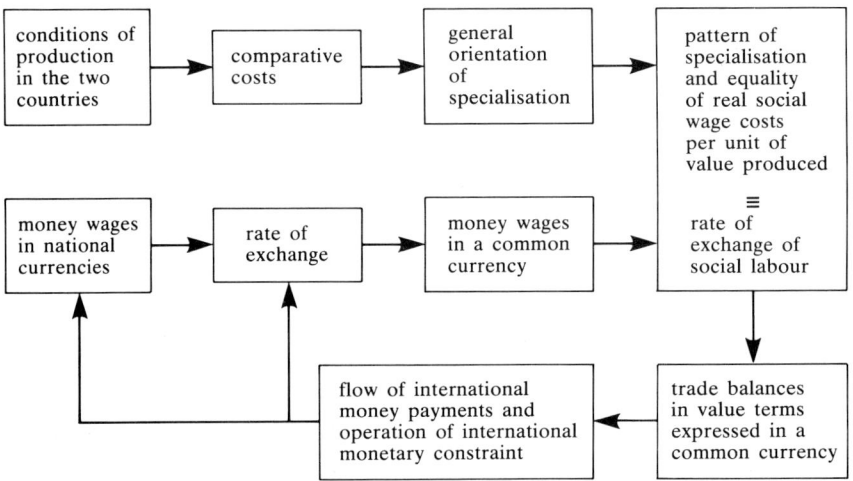

Figure 2.6. International specialisation and the international monetary constraint. Source: Aglietta (1982a, page 329).

2.11 The theory of circular and cumulative causation
The argument set out in the last section can be developed in a variety of ways. In particular it can be extended to include an account of the dynamic interaction of the schema of specialisation represented by the vectors x_e and x_p and the conditions A, l, and z or r, with which z is related, and of what Myrdal and Kaldor have called processes of circular and cumulative causation (see Myrdal, 1957, pages 11-22; Kaldor, 1970, pages 340-344; 1972, pages 1244-1245).

Models of circular and cumulative causation, along with an analysis of the underlying mechanisms of value formation, supply in fact one of the main explanations of uneven development. In them, inequality is seen as a product of the way in which growth itself creates the material and social conditions on which further growth depends: fast growth is self-reinforcing, as is slow growth.

According to the formulation of Kaldor, for example, natural resource endowments are only relevant in explaining the location of activities that are land based and raw material dependent (see Kaldor, 1970, pages 337–340). In the case of processing activities resource endowments and markets themselves are endogenous elements and not exogenous and naturally determined: as manufacturing activity expands in a particular locality the infrastructural and other conditions necessary for the success of new rounds of investment are supplied and constantly renewed. Thus, initial differences in the levels and rates of growth of activity are likely to be perpetuated in a cumulative spiral movement in which new investment, factor movements, markets, and trade interact dynamically with one another.

One of the key factors in Kaldor's explanation of the growth of a national or regional economy is the demand for the area's exports: in his view, increases in this particular component of demand play an especially important role in inducing new investment. The movement of exports in turn depends on the growth in demand for the products produced in the region and on the efficiency wage relative to that in other producing areas.

The efficiency wage is equal to the money wage divided by labour productivity. Within a country, differences in money wages are, it is argued, comparatively small as trade unions are organised nationally, and as there is a strong tendency for sympathetic movements in money wage rates to occur. Productivity growth, on the other hand, varies according to the rate of growth of output and employment. This dependence of productivity growth on output growth, which is summarised by Verdoorn's Law, is said to stem from several factors. In the first place, increases in an economy's resource endowment are largely endogenous, being determined by the rate at which technical progress is embodied in new equipment and, consequently, by the rate of output growth. In the presence of increasing returns, international and interregional trade can increase the original competitive advantage of one economy relative to another. Excess demand for labour in an area can cause international or interregional factor movements which can themselves generate increasing returns. (Similar mechanisms underly the relationship between productivity and employment growth that has been called Kaldor's Law.) As a consequence, therefore, of initial shifts in demand, which result in increases in regional output and factor movements, efficiency wages fall in the nations or regions that are prospering, stimulating further export demand, and so on.

As in the case of Myrdal's model, the existence of a variety of 'spread effects' is also recognised. Included are the diffusion of innovations, the stimulation of demand for complementary products from poor economies, diseconomies of congestion, spread effects associated with the mobility of workers which counteract the more frequently mentioned 'backwash effects', and, within a nation, built-in fiscal stabilisers.

The mechanisms highlighted in this model are concerned only with the movement of economic aggregates and with very broad sectors of activity identified in standard national and regional social accounts. Yet transactions within sectors and especially within the industrial sector or account are, as we shall see in subsequent sections, particularly important.

Information on interindustry transactions indicates the structure of production within an economy from the point of view of the dependence of any industry on other industries either as a supplier of inputs or as a purchaser of outputs. Suppose that every industry is given a production account and that the appropriation, accumulation, and external accounts of a region are consolidated. In these conditions the matrix for a closed regional economy assumes the form given in figure 2.7. In the column for each industry is recorded the value of its inputs divided between intermediate, or produced, inputs, represented by elements of the matrix $\mathbf{O}$, and the total value of factor, or nonproduced, inputs, represented by elements of the vector y (the vector y must include depreciation). In the row for each industry is recorded the value of its sales divided into sales of intermediate products to other industries, O, and sales to final users, f.

The input-output model is the main model associated with this display of accounts. It can be thought of as a means of calculating all the intermediate product flows required to support a given set of outputs of final goods. Once these outputs are known, the outputs and levels of income generated in the various industries can be calculated. The model is $\mathbf{O} = \mathbf{A}\hat{\mathbf{q}}$, where $\mathbf{A}$ is a matrix of coefficients such that $\mathbf{A}'i < i$, where i is a column vector the elements of which are units (ones), and where $\hat{\mathbf{q}}$ is a diagonal matrix whose diagonal elements are the elements of the vector q of outputs of industrial goods.

The solution of the model is obtained in the following way:

$$q = Oi + f, \qquad = Aq + f, \qquad = (I - A)^{-1}f. \qquad (2.10)$$

	Production account industries	All other accounts	Totals
Production accounts	O	f	q
All other accounts	y	0	y
Totals	q	y	

Figure 2.7. A regional accounts matrix.

The inverse $(I-A)^{-1}$, a sufficient condition for whose existence is that $A'i < i$, is known as the matrix multiplier.

Interregional linkages have important implications for the effects of an expansion of demand on a regional economy. Suppose that two regions have the following matrix multipliers:

$$\begin{bmatrix} 1.0 & 0.3 \\ 0.3 & 0.4 \end{bmatrix} \begin{bmatrix} 1.9 & 0.7 \\ 0.7 & 1.8 \end{bmatrix}.$$

Suppose also that the demand for the products of industry 1 in region 1 increases by £100 million. The multiplier attached to industry 1 in region 1 is equal to the sum of the column elements, or 1.3, so that output in region 1 expands by 1.3 × £100 million, or £130 million. Assume, however, that industry 1 in region 1 always buys 50% of its inputs from activity 1 in region 2. In these conditions the demand for the exports of region 2 increases by £50 million. As the multiplier for activity 1 in region 2 is 2.6, output in region 2 will expand by 2.6 × £50 million, or £130 million. Additional feedbacks are likely to occur from region 2 to region 1, and so a complete interregional input–output table would be more useful than tables for closed regions and import coefficients (see also Thirlwall, 1974, pages 5–10).

Several conclusions can be drawn from this argument. One is the fact that the impact of movements in demand on employment, output, and income depends in reality, as we shall subsequently see, on the character and extent of interregional linkages. A second is that the role of the export sector should not be overemphasised: the dynamics of a national or regional economy also depends on the level of import penetration. Consequently, a more useful distinction is the one between an exposed and a sheltered sector. Moreover, the size and development of the internal market is itself an important factor in explaining virtuous spirals of growth [see, for example, the way in which these arguments have been extended in Aglietta et al (1981) and Mistral (1982)].

In order to consider actual instances of disequilibrium growth, specific historical determinations must be introduced. Some of the underlying mechanisms are nevertheless highlighted by these models of circular and cumulative growth. But the identification of spread effects is not sufficient as an explanation of the sharp changes that have occurred in the hierarchy of national and regional economies: high levels of development sometimes give rise to inertia, especially where the extra running costs of long-established plants are less than the capital costs incurred in building new ones, or where the costs of new development are pushed up by the character and density of existing activity, although at moments of crisis the trajectory of development can change quite sharply. In parts 2 and 3 of this book these concepts will consequently be qualified in various ways. Attention will be turned first of all, however, to the role of the state in the economy.

3

Capital and the state

In the years after the Second World War the Italian and French states assumed increasingly important positions in national processes of economic and social reproduction (see, for example, the trends in French government spending depicted in figure 3.1). Included were major roles in the industrialisation of less developed areas. For this reason, the studies in subsequent chapters must be underpinned by a conception of the state and of its role in a capitalist society. In this chapter my aim is to outline some of the most general characteristics of that theory of the state.

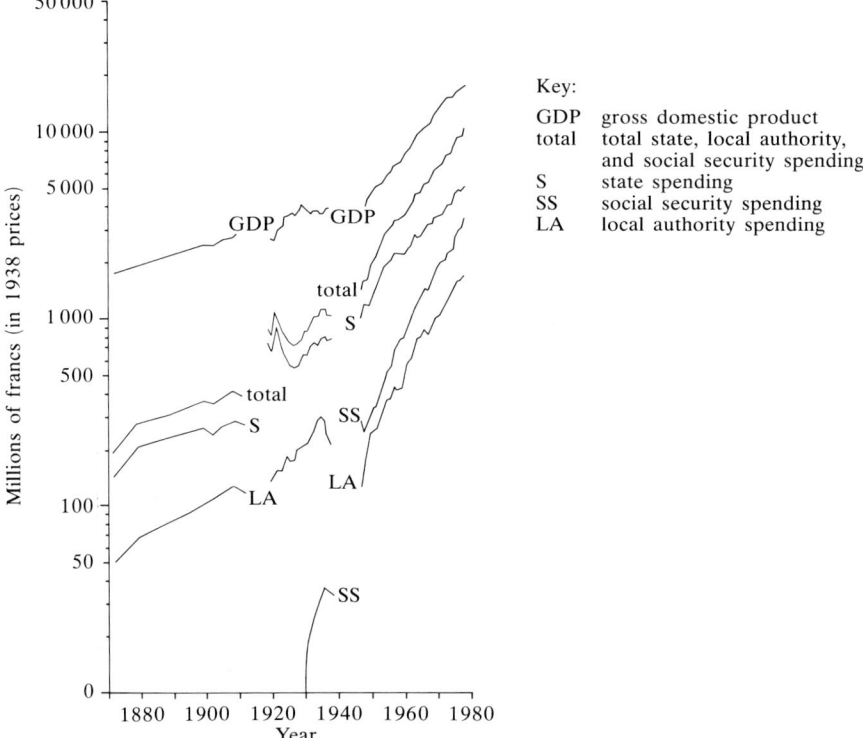

Figure 3.1. The evolution of French state spending and gross domestic product, 1872–1970. Source: Delorme and André (1983, page 34).

3.1 Marx's conception of the state

Very roughly, two types of theory of the state can be identified. First, there are a host of non-Marxist theories. In these the state is seen as being "charged with the representation of society as a whole, as standing above particular and necessarily partial interests, groups and classes, and as having the special function of ensuring that the competition between these interests, groups and classes remains orderly and that the national interest is not impaired" (Miliband, 1977, page 66). Second, there are a variety of Marxist theories of the state. What differentiates Marxist theories from others are two mutually dependent arguments. One is the view that in a class society the interests of different classes are fundamentally and irrevocably at odds with one another. The other is the related claim that the state itself is a form of class domination.

How is this conclusion reached? Some of the central arguments were set out in Marx's early writings, where two interconnected ideas were put forward. In the first place, the way in which the state is separated from society and appears as a separate sphere of public interests was explained. Second, the possibility of such a separation was challenged: according to Marx the real basis and content of the state remains the unequal class relations of the underlying social system.

The object analysed by Marx was the modern representative state, distinguished by three characteristic features: (1) parliamentary government with its source of sovereignty in the popular mass; (2) the division of spheres of action and of powers and rights into systems of general and particular interests; and (3) state-guaranteed equality before the law.

In the view of Marx the modern state was a product of modern civil society. In civil society, however, individuals are divided from and independent of one another: civil society is a sphere in which self-interest and competitive individualism hold sway and involves a kind of *bellum omnium contra omnes* (see Colletti, 1975, pages 28-37). In order, in these circumstances, to represent the common or general interest the state must be made independent of all interested parties and assume a separate existence. A common interest can only arise if the real divisions in society are abstracted from and denied value and significance in political life. Civil society is, accordingly, deemed as being composed of independent individuals, and the individuals concerned are considered politically and juridically equal. The liberty and equality of individual citizens can, however, only be established by abstracting from the class divisions in society. In this way, class divisions can be presented as mere social differences in private life which are of no consequence in political life. "The difference between the member of civil society and the member of political society", said Marx, "is the difference between the [tradesperson] and the citizen, between the wage-earner and the citizen, between the landowner and the citizen, between the living individual and the citizen" (Marx, 1975, pages 220-221).

The modern representative state rests, in other words, on a separation of state from society, of politics from economics, and of the sphere of public interests from the sphere of private interests. In the words of Poulantzas, "the people is itself erected as a principle of determination of the state not as agents of production distributed in social classes but as a collection of individual citizens" (Poulantzas, 1973, page 123). Since the resulting general interest of society as a whole is only arrived at by abstracting from reality, the real basis and content of political society must, however, be civil society with all its economic and social divisions (see Colletti, 1975, page 35). In other words, the class divisions and conflicts in civil society are not transcended.

Indeed, the political constitution of the modern representative state is, claimed Marx, the constitution and guarantee of private property. Yet the property rights and the formal equality and freedom of private individuals are the foundations on which the fragmentation of civil society and socio-economic inequality are based. In guaranteeing these rights the state itself plays an active role in perpetuating conflict and inequality. Individual citizens are granted the right to pursue their own interests independently of and sometimes against society itself. Accordingly, one of the state's goals is in actuality that of guaranteeing the reproduction of the class divisions and conflicts in civil society which it appears to be mediating. In short, the war of each against all is reproduced through the actions of the state.

The state should not therefore be seen as a neutral instrument whose activities can do good or ill according to who controls and uses it. Only through the transformation of the relations of production, the merging of the political and civil existences of civil society, and the development of qualitatively new types of political institution can, as has been reemphasised in recent analyses of the form of the state (see Jessop, 1982, chapter 3), radical change be effected.

3.2 The state and the anatomy of civil society
On this account the institutional organisation of the state and state activity are conditioned by the real movement of social classes and class conflicts in civil society. Class relations and relations of class strength develop within the framework of the actual historical process of social reproduction.

In a capitalist society, where significant, but not all, areas of social reproduction activity are structured by capitalist relations of production, class composition and conflicts depend largely on the dynamics of reproduction and accumulation of capital by which the actions of social subjects are structured. The underlying trajectory and mechanisms of society are themselves, however, the result of class conflicts unfolding in the reified context of the commodity, money, capital, and the state. In this sense, the development of society can be seen as a result of class struggles, whereas the composition, organisation, consciousness, and strength of social classes are shaped by the laws of accumulation.

State organisation and state action do not, however, arise directly from class struggles and the dynamics of the social system. Instead they are developed through specific political processes occurring in the institutional system of the state. The state anticipates or, more usually, reacts to events which occur in the actual course of the process of reproduction, which are expressed through class and other movements, and which are mediated through specific political channels and processes. What is more, the state itself can, as we shall see, be restructured.

These ideas have been expressed by, amongst others, Hirsch (1977). "The material reproduction of classes", he said, "is not identical with the reproduction of the institutional system of political domination which repressively and ideologically safeguards the material reproduction of classes .... What is required is a theory of the relations of classes and class fractions to political apparatuses and of the manner in which class movements and class struggles are transformed in the political system and determine its development."

This conception of the relation between the state and society has two advantages. First, the economic sphere is seen as embracing both material production and the production of social relations. Second, emphasis is given to concrete analyses of the political processes through which the interests of capital and of other social classes are established, requirements for state action are identified, specific projects and plans are formulated, and decisions and policies are implemented. In this way, analyses of party politics, of the changing composition of the ruling social bloc, of methods of representation of interests, of the structural selectivity of state action, of relations within the state, of administrative organisation and management, and of concrete measures and policies which are frequently ignored in Marxist writing on the state are given the attention they deserve. In addition, some of the problems associated with prevailing Marxist analyses of the state can be avoided (see Holloway and Picciotto, 1977, pages 81-85). Compared with theories in which state actions flow more or less directly from the requirements of capital, it has several advantages: the assumption that the state always acts rationally in the interests of capital is not made, the implication that only one course of action is open to the state is not present, the requirements of capital are not identified with the actual content of state action, social reproduction is not reduced to the dynamics of the capitalist sector, and the more general risks of economic reductionism and determinism are minimised.

A second broad approach rests on a concept of the relative autonomy of the state. In this group of theories the political level is often examined as an autonomous object of analysis and specific political concepts are developed. The simplifications of reductionism are avoided, and detailed accounts of the structure of the ruling class and of the trajectory of specific class conflicts are presented. But the connections between the state and the dynamics of the process of accumulation, the role of the state in reproducing the contradictions of capitalist development, and the connections between the political level and the anatomy of civil society are sometimes underexplored. Furthermore, the reasons why concrete class conflicts result in the reproduction of capitalism are not really explained.

3.3 The state and the economy

The specific state actions I shall consider must be explained concretely and historically. Nevertheless, several more general and abstract determinations identified in a lot of the theoretical writing on the state have much to contribute to an understanding of these developments.

In its aim of guaranteeing the reproduction of the relations of capitalist production and the accumulation of capital, the state plays two multifaceted roles. First, the state assumes a number of legal and economic functions on behalf of capital in general. As a result, it plays an important role in the process of economic reproduction, while at the same time organising bourgeois class interests and securing the cohesion of a ruling social bloc. Second, the state is a factor of social integration. Through means that are material and ideological, and that involve coercion on the one hand and the securing of consent on the other, the state attempts to ensure the cohesion of society. Opposition groups are disorganised, and class conflicts are channelled into forms that are consistent with the reproduction of capitalist domination. Where space for manoeuvre exists, important concessions are made, and the demands of some dominated, as well as of the dominant, strata are incorporated. Thus, through its role in guaranteeing material reproduction, through the repression and ideological domination and integration of dominated groups, and through a variety of concessions, the state seeks, in other words, the reproduction of bourgeois class domination and of class society.

One particularly useful way of analysing these two roles of the state, which transcends the division between the capital theoretical and class theoretical conceptions mentioned in the last section, has been developed in the work of Jessop (1983a, pages 89-109; see also Jessop, 1983b). In his account, state action is related both to accumulation strategies and to hegemonic projects and associated alliance strategies. An accumulation strategy is "a specific economic" growth model "complete with its various extra-economic preconditions and ... the general strategy appropriate to its realisation". A hegemonic project is a political, institutional, and moral strategy which is economically conditioned and relevant, but whose domain is civil society as a whole and not just the economic sphere (see the discussion of the process of social reproduction at the beginning of chapter 2). In it, the general interest is identified with a general institutional and policy framework and with a general programme of action which, on the one hand, advance the long-term interests of the hegemonic class or class fraction and, on the other, enable some of the goals of other allied or potentially allied interest groups to be attained. Through a programme that has a material as well as an ideological content the construction and reproduction of a wider social and electoral bloc is accordingly facilitated.

In practice, the ability of the state to act, in its economic capacity, as an ideal collective capitalist is circumscribed by its relations with individual capitals and by the existence of a variety of strategies of accumulation:

intercapitalist competition is itself reproduced in political forms in the state apparatus. In Italy after 1945, for example, increasing state intervention in the economy was accompanied by the development of close links between the political class and state industry. As a result, the state was ultimately incapable of acting rationally in the interests of capital in general. At the same time, industrial policy itself reflected not only the accumulation strategy of state industry, but also the hegemonic project of the Democrazia Cristiana. Any hegemonic project is of course grounded not simply in the capitalist sector of the economy, but also in civil society and the state. Consequently, some of the short-term interests of the hegemonic class must often be sacrificed so that concessions can be made to other social strata mobilised behind the project. In Italy, however, the very viability of state industry was, according to some, placed in jeopardy.

Some of the economic functions assumed by the state do nevertheless play a significant role in shaping the processes of national and regional economic development. In the next few sections I shall attempt to discuss the rationale of these activities. I shall argue that state action is in part a product of the contradictions and anarchy of capitalist reproduction. [Similar arguments have been developed by Scott (1980, chapter 8) and, in some cases, can also be found in the theory of economic welfare.] What we shall subsequently discover, however, is that many of the contradictions in response to which state action emerged are not transcended. As in the Italian case, the contradictions of capitalist development and the anarchy of the market are displaced but, ultimately, reproduced.

3.4 The legal and institutional framework
In a capitalist society many of the material and social preconditions of the processes of economic and social reproduction are established in the course of the reproduction of capital itself. Many of the use values which are to function as means of production in subsequent cycles of production and the social relations of production are, for example, reproduced as a result of the normal operation of the laws of capitalist development. In the simplest case, all that is required is that the legal and institutional conditions on which competition and the unimpeded circulation of commodities and money depends are guaranteed.

When capitalism was emerging the guarantee of freedom and equality and of rights over the ownership and transfer of private property played an active role in establishing and removing the restrictions on capitalist development. Similarly, in processes of economic integration, institutional and legal developments play an active role in eliminating discriminations (see Murray, 1971, page 88).

In more advanced capitalist societies legal measures are also used to place restrictions on some of the self-crippling aspects of capitalist accumulation. Included are actions against various restrictive practices, antimonopoly measures, and restrictions on trade unions.

The more active role does, however, persist. An important example is provided by rights of expropriation, compulsory purchase, and enforced development of land, as well as by the related activity of land banking. In this case the rights of private landowners are circumscribed for two reasons. One is that landownership is often highly fragmented and that individual owners of relatively small plots of land could block development simply by refusing to sell. The second is that an owner could prevent development by demanding the whole of the increment in value that follows the redevelopment of land. In the final analysis, however, the institution of private landed property has not yet been seriously challenged as state action has been "sporadic, discrete, and intermittent" (Topalov, cited in Scott, 1980, pages 155-156).

3.5 Infrastructural investment and the general conditions of production
With the extension of the division of labour every industry and every firm came to depend on independent branches of production. In *Grundrisse* Marx drew a distinction between the necessary conditions for a particular capital and its particular direct process of production, on the one hand, and the general conditions of production on the other. The general conditions are necessary use values not included in the direct process of production or used collectively. Included are the means of communication and transport, such as roads and canals, on which the ease of the circulation of commodities depends, and collective means of production, such as irrigation works, which augment the forces of production.

For an individual private capital to supply these use values, several conditions must be satisfied:
(1) Very large amounts of money capital must be obtained as the investments involved are usually large and costly.
(2) The investors must be prepared to commit money to projects in which capital turns over very slowly, and to accept the risks of having capital tied up in long-term ventures.
(3) The product must be sold either at a price at which the necessary and surplus labour are realised or in such a way that the investors receive a sufficiently large share of aggregate surplus value to get a normal rate of return on the capital invested.
The satisfaction of the last condition depends on several other factors. First, it must be possible, without incurring very high costs, to levy charges and to exclude third parties. In other words, the free-rider problem must not apply. Second, individual capitals must find it worthwhile to pay the price demanded.

The success of the project will also depend on the existence of a large volume of demand. Often, however, demand only arises after a facility has been constructed. The viability of many roads, for example, depends on the existence of a volume of traffic that will not be generated until after the roads have been built. For this reason, market mechanisms operating alone may well prove incapable of guaranteeing adequate levels of investment and supply.

Where investments in the general conditions of production are not capable of yielding an average rate of return on the capital advanced, adequate provision is likely to depend on state action. Suppose, for example, that after setting the constant capital consumed equal to zero the construction of a road costs twelve months work. If the value of labour power is equal to six months work a surplus value amounting to six months work is created. Suppose, however, that the road can only be sold for the monetary equivalent of six months work. No payment is made for the surplus labour performed. As a result, the surplus labour is not realised as surplus value, and the construction of the road is not a productive activity for capital. In this case, said Marx, responsibility for planning and financing road building is likely to be assumed by the state, which stands outside of the process of competitive valorisation of capital. Construction and maintenance work may well be undertaken by private capitals earning a normal rate of return on the capital invested. On completion, however, the product is exchanged not against the money capital of another capitalist, but against revenues raised by the state. The construction firms earn a normal rate of return on the capital advanced. But the work is financed not out of capital as capital, but out of state charges, taxes, and borrowing. Only with the fullest development of capitalism would these general conditions of production, thought Marx, be provided by capital (Marx, 1973, pages 524-533).

Similarly, where a natural or a natural spatial monopoly is involved, or where the provision of infrastructural equipment is associated with scale economies and with monopolistic production and supply conditions, state supply or state regulation may well occur.

What has been identified is the abstract possibility of state action to supply some of the general conditions of production. Questions as to what is a concrete object of state infrastructural provision, whose needs are met, why, what determines the timing of state action, and how charges are levied can only be examined concretely and historically.

In the societies I shall consider, state provision of communications and transport and other infrastructural equipment, of scientific and technical knowledge, and of other general conditions did play one other important general role: after the Second World War, state organisation of the general conditions of production was widely used as an element of strategies for growth at regional and national levels. In many less developed areas, for example, state infrastructural investment was very closely associated with the modernisation of farming and the implantation of new industrial activity, whereas at a national level, infrastructural projects assumed a very important role in supporting and sustaining the expansion of the capitalist sector.

3.6 Externalities and state action
In a capitalist society markets are not universal. As a result, many unpriced spillover effects exist. Included are a host of external diseconomies such as the destruction of some of the natural and social conditions of production caused by pollution, the degradation of the urban environment, and the reproduction of wide regional inequalities. In some cases the state acts with the intention of limiting external diseconomies, usually via changes in the economic and legal conditions of accumulation (see Scott, 1980, chapter 8).

Similarly, a variety of external economies exist. In such cases, where the economies concerned are advantageous to others but are overlooked in the ruling methods of economic calculation, output will be suboptimal in social terms unless state action occurs. In the absence of such intervention, what would prevail are significant gaps between social and private costs and benefits, and widespread inefficiency.

3.7 The general conditions of reproduction of the wage-earning class
The reproduction of the capacity to work of the wage-earning class is one of the preconditions of capitalist development. The act of buying and consuming commodities occurs, however, outside of the sphere of circulation of capital. Consequently, the adequacy of labour-power reproduction, as determined by the level of wages and the operation of noncommodified processes of reproduction, is not guaranteed. Furthermore, the needs of the working class cannot be reduced to a need to reproduce its capacity to work (see Preteceille, 1985, Preteceille and Terrail, 1985, chapter 2). Although the working class internalises at least in part the needs, as defined by capital, on which employment as specific kinds of wage earner depends, needs are also a product of each individual's autonomous search for self-fulfillment and development.

In capitalist societies the needs of the working class, as determined in these two ways, are not adequately met, and the way in which the working class itself spends the income it receives and manages its own consumption and reproduction may not meet with the complete approval of employers or of the political class. But on behalf of the collective interests of capital, and in the face of the demands of various social movements, some of the gaps in the individual, collective, and intergenerational reproduction of the working class and of the wage relation have been filled by the state. Included, for example, are state education and welfare policies (supplied as merit goods).

What usually happens is that the state assumes control over one part of the wages fund and uses the resources it obtains to finance the provision of collective goods (see Hirsch, 1978, pages 84–85). In this way income is redistributed within the working class. State action is, however, not simply a product of the incapacity of the wage-earning class to reproduce itself adequately. On the one hand, welfare provision is an element of strategies of integration and consensus. On the other, it is at least in part a result of the acquired economic and political strength of the working-class movement.

Indeed, other things being equal, the supply of collective goods and welfare benefits depends upon the share of value added falling to the wage-earning class increasing by an amount equal to the spending by the state on social consumption.

In this situation the value of labour power continues to be defined as the share of value added received by the wage-earning class. Only one part of it is, however, directly controlled by the working class. Insofar as the quantity and quality of the services supplied by the state correspond to the money deducted from the wages fund in the form of taxation, the value of labour power is unaltered. A reallocation of state spending in the direction of increased aid to capital would, however, represent a reapportionment of value added, and emerges consequently as a new stake in the struggle between capital and the working class.

3.8 Economic planning and the state

Under capitalism the process of economic reproduction is associated with sharp cyclical fluctuations and recurrent crises. Consequently, a range of instruments of state economic policy have been devised, most of which are situated in the sphere of circulation: demand management policies have been developed, the credit mechanism is manipulated, incomes policies have been used to shape the distribution of value added between capital and labour, and state spending has been used as an anticyclical measure and as an instrument of income distribution (see Fine and Harris, 1976a, page 99; 1976b, pages 170–173).

In order to plan the medium-term growth of capitalist economies, indicative planning methods have been adopted. Whether or not such methods are used depends of course on political factors. But underlying these developments are problems of coordination which market mechanisms have proved incapable of solving adequately.

Under capitalism, producers decide independently of one another what and how much to produce. Where supply depends upon investments with long gestation periods, very serious imbalances have a consequent tendency to occur. The reason why lies in two facts. First, the demand for a particular product will depend on the investment decisions of other capitalists, and these decisions are not known in advance by the producer concerned. Second, the availability of necessary inputs will depend on suppliers carrying out sufficient investment in capacity. In order to overcome the problems that result, some governments have tried to get capitalists to meet to discuss investment plans with a view to ensuring that investments are coordinated with one another and with state investments, and that problems of disproportionality do not occur. In this way, imbalances can sometimes be circumvented. However, the fundamental problem remains: methods of forecasting and planning are incapable of anticipating the evolution of the market, and the validity of social activity continues to be determined ex post facto.

State management and state planning are, however, not necessary characteristics of capitalist economic development, but reflect instead the hegemony or ascendancy of what van der Pijl has called a 'productive capital concept' (see van der Pijl, 1984, pages 1–20).

As Marx showed, capital exists in productive, commodity, and money forms. Associated with these different forms of capital are several important distinctions. First, the sphere of production, in which surplus value is produced and appropriated, is distinguished from the sphere of circulation, in which it is merely appropriated. Second, industrial, commercial, and banking capital are identified as analytically distinct types of capital (see figure 3.2). Different methods of appropriating shares of aggregate surplus-value correspond to these three types of capital. Industrial capitalists earn what Mandel called 'entrepreneurial and founder's profit' (Mandel, cited in van der Pijl, 1984, pages 277–279). The income of commercial capitalists is composed of commercial gains and interest payments derived from the use of money in commodity exchange, whereas the income of banking capital is made up of interest on money lent as capital. (In addition, a landed capital fraction receiving ground rent can be identified.)

Different strategic concepts correspond to these two spheres of activity. Very roughly, strategies of capacity utilisation tend to be supported by large industrial capital, whereas strategies of economic liberalism involving

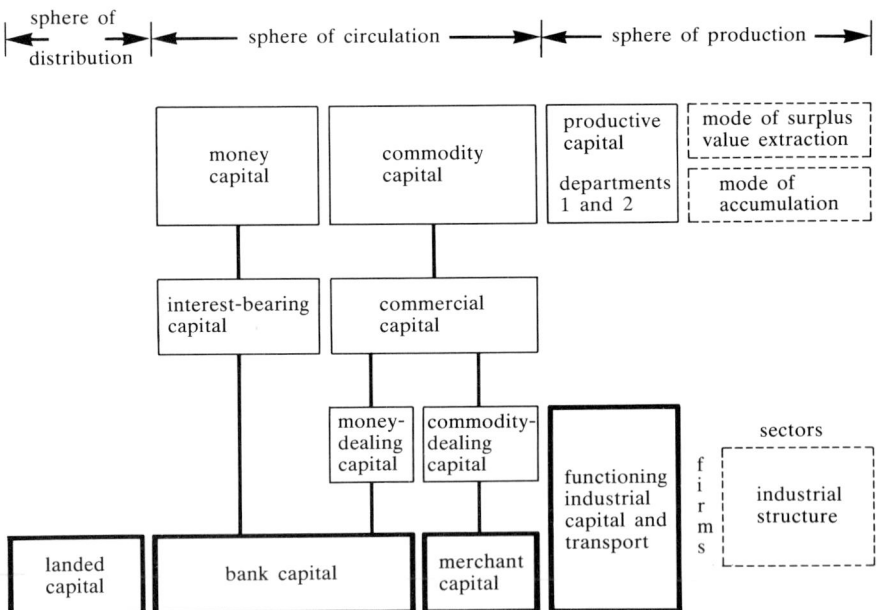

Figure 3.2. The functional forms and the major fractional elements of capital. Source: elaborated from van der Pijl (1984, page 6).

limited state social spending, self-regulating markets, and a sound currency tend to be favoured by those advancing money-dealing and interest-bearing capital. According to van der Pijl, the attractiveness of a particular strategic concept to groups other than the ones with whose ideology it most closely corresponds, and its relative strength, depend on the prevailing state of capitalist society (van der Pijl, 1984, pages 1-20).

In the course of the economic cycle the relative weight of these different fractions of aggregate capital and the perspectives of capitalists within each category tend to vary. Accordingly, the relative ascendancy of state economic management or of orthodox liberal and rentier perspectives may vary not secularly but cyclically.

3.9 The state as an entrepreneur

The separation of the state from society insulates state action from the requirements of competitive valorisation. But it also makes some of its actions blunt and unspecific. With the crisis of the 1930s, many capitalist states got increasingly involved in the restructuring of capital itself. A policy of restructuring capital through restrictions on credit and the supply of money is, however, unspecific in its effects. In the face of difficulties of accumulation and social reproduction some more specific types of intervention have consequently emerged. Aid is supplied perhaps selectively in the form of grants, loans at special rates of interest, and special tax advantages. The state may step in to plan the reorganisation of the conditions of valorisation of capital in specific sectors. And in some cases industries are nationalised.

Industries are nationalised for a variety of reasons, with political factors playing a particularly significant role. The specific causes and characteristics of Italian and French state entrepreneurship will be considered in parts 2 and 3. But some more general factors can also be identified:

(1) In sectors supplying necessary use values, where profits are inadequate owing to the limited extent of the market or the conditions of valorisation, nationalisation may occur.

(2) If an industry is monopolised by one producer and the monopolist fails to invest and reduce the costs of its output, the state may step in, especially where the group concerned survives by successfully charging monopoly prices. In such cases state action is likely to be dictated by a concern about the effects of the monopolistic situation on the rate of profit of other sections of capital.

(3) Industries are also nationalised because they are in crisis. States act to rescue firms from bankruptcy or to protect the financial sector from the losses that would occur if a bankrupt firm's debts had to be written off. State intervention may occur as a corollary of an injection of state funding aimed at improving the financial position of a firm. An industry in crisis may be nationalised so that the reorganisation of capital can be supervised directly.

Whatever the cause, nationalisation must, however, never be considered the final step, as an industry can always be reorganised and returned, at least in part, to the private sector.

Insofar as the nationalised industries aim at a rate of profit on the capital advanced that is approximately equal to the average, in order to cover the going rate of interest on loan capital, the state is advancing capital as capital and is itself acting as a capitalist. What the impact on the economy is depends on its specific pricing and investment policies.

3.10 The restructuring of the state

Changes in the role of the state in economic life are often accompanied by changes in the organisation of the political system itself. Included are, first, changes in the state apparatus aimed at adapting it to the changing relations between the state and dominant groups; second, changes in the organisation of the executive areas of government, and in the relation of these areas with those with party representation; and third, the development of ad hoc agencies and changes in the relation between the state and local societies. In determining the evolution of the processes of Italian and French regional and urban planning, administrative and political shifts of these types have played a major role.

The capitalist state is, it has been argued, a product of civil society, and state action is conditioned by the process of reproduction of capital. State intervention has, however, emerged in response to some of the contradictions of capitalist development as they have been expressed in specific situations. As a result, the social relations by which social life is structured have been changed and the operation of the mechanisms of capitalist development have been qualified and modified.

The fundamental contradictions of the process of reproduction of capital have, however, not been transcended. In spite of the major changes that have occurred in the development of Italian and French society, the contradictions of capitalist development, as we shall see in the chapters that follow, have been reproduced and have resurfaced in new forms.

Part 2

Regional policy and the development of the Italian Mezzogiorno

4
Introduction: the historical foundations of the southern question

In part 1 it was pointed out that spatial inequality widened with the rise of capitalism and was reproduced along with the reproduction of capitalism itself. With a view to explaining inequality, attention was subsequently turned to some of the mechanisms underlying the processes of economic reproduction and state action in capitalist societies. At various points empirical examples were introduced to illustrate the argument. But it was also emphasised that the use of the concepts introduced was invariably associated with a measure of *indeterminacy* which could only be overcome through an analysis of particular situations and of other determinations excluded from the more abstract system of concepts. My aim in part 2 is to develop an explanation of the interaction of capital and the state in the development of the Italian Mezzogiorno after 1945. Accordingly, much more attention will be paid to the particular characteristics of Italian economic development and of the Italian state. To set the scene, however, an account of the origins of the southern question is necessary.

4.1 Spatial inequality before and after Italian unification
The gap in Italy between the underdeveloped South, which occupies some 40% of the national territory, and the relatively prosperous North is often cited as one of the classical instances of geographical dualism within advanced capitalist countries. (The main territorial divisions of Italy are portrayed in figure 4.1. See also figure 4.2.)

The problem itself has roots which go back a long way into the history of the peninsula and the islands. At the very least, it can be traced to the division of Italy at the time of the fall of the Roman Empire, the foreign imposition of a feudal system in the South, and the subsequent development of autonomous city states in northern and central Italy (see Lill, 1984, pages 492-499; and also Aymard, 1982). However, the gap between the two main parts of the country was deepened quite markedly by the new processes of economic and political development that were initiated by their integration into the new Italian state.

The making of the new nation in the Risorgimento was accomplished through a series of annexations to Piedmont (Piemonte) of the preexisting and unequally developed Italian states and was completed in 1861. The regions that were brought together by the process of unification had experienced centuries of separate development, and were marked by extreme social and economic differences. Furthermore, unification occurred at a time when Europe already contained a number of more developed capitalist countries.

It is well known that the normal working of market mechanisms between and within capitalist societies, together with the processes of international and national economic integration, frequently increase existing geographical inequalities (Holland, 1976, pages 36-60). However, the evolution of an economy and of its constituent regions cannot simply be examined in the light of the operation of abstractly conceived economic forces. The integration of a country into the world economy and its adjustment to the prevailing international division of labour are not automatic processes. They depend at least in part on the class composition of the state and on the political and economic strategies it pursues, since these determinations mediate and, in their turn, condition the functioning of market mechanisms.

In the case of Italy, at the time of the Risorgimento, a variety of bourgeois elements were beginning to emerge in agriculture, industry, and commerce in the North. Capitalist farming was developing in the Po Valley, and some, albeit limited, capitalist industrial growth was under way. The woollen industry was developing at Biella in Piedmont, Schio in Veneto, and Prato in

Figure 4.1. The regions and main territorial divisions of Italy.

Tuscany (Toscana), the silk industry around Como and in Tuscany, and the cotton industry in the vicinity of Milan. Industries producing textile machinery, railway equipment, ships, and armaments, amongst other things, were also growing, along with related commercial activities and the social classes they supported (King, 1985, pages 30–32).

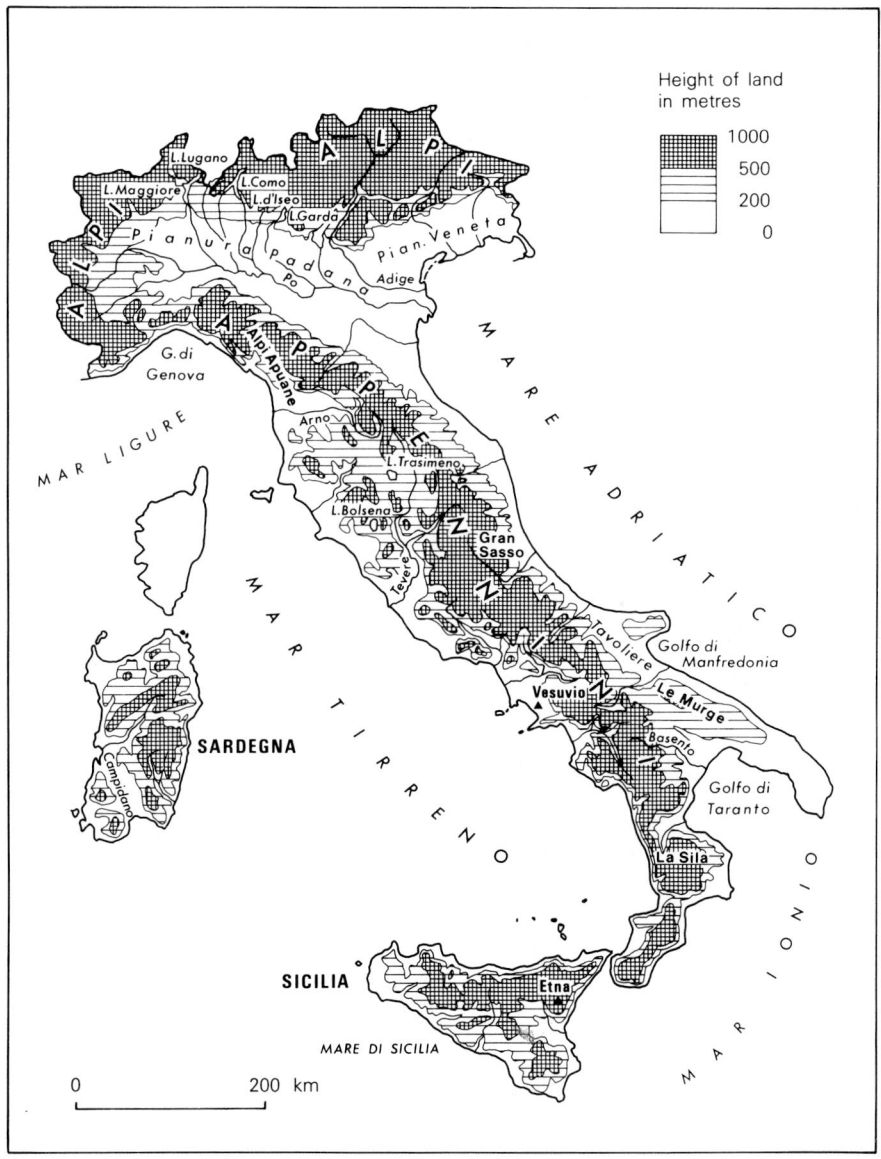

Figure 4.2. Italy: main relief.

Although constituting only a small part of the total population, the members of this rising class acted, along with various professional and bureaucratic strata, as the social base of the unification movement. The movement's essentially political aims of national independence and unity could be accomplished, however, by a limited bourgeois revolution, or what Gramsci (1971a, pages 106–114) called 'a passive revolution'. The lack of national independence in conjunction with foreign opposition also blocked a more radical programme, as did the weakness of the more democratic groups led by Mazzini, Garibaldi, and Pisacane. Instead, the leading role in the Risorgimento was played by the Piedmontese Moderate Party.

On account, however, of the relative weakness of the newly dominant Piedmontese and northern bourgeoisie, and because of the lack of mass peasant participation in the revolution, the northern bourgeoisie compromised with the landowning classes in the South and allowed them to retain their supremacy in that region. The result was the formation of a social bloc which was to have a profound influence on the subsequent course of southern and national economic development. On the one hand, the preservation of the economic and political position of the southern landed classes was to play an important role in blocking a solution to the agrarian question. On the other, the lack of substantial agrarian progress in the South and the integration of the region into the national economy were to make a significant contribution to the lack of industrial development in the Mezzogiorno, and to its continuing and deepening relative backwardness in the period up to the end of the Second World War.

4.2 19th century agrarian change

By the time of unification the land in the South had largely passed from the hands of the feudal nobility into those of a class of bourgeois landowners, and important changes in the organisation of agricultural production were under way.

In 1812, feudalism was formally abrogated, and in subsequent years the system of entails and primogeniture was abolished. In 1824, a law was passed enabling creditors to seize land in settlement of debts. With these steps the owners of land lost the rights attached to feudal property, including the administration of justice, local government, and taxation, which henceforth were to be among the rights and duties of the Bourbon state: the Kingdom of the Two Sicilies (1815–1859), with its centre in Naples. Until then, the common-use rights of the peasantry had been encroached upon as land was enclosed to establish exclusive pastoral and hunting zones for the barons, and as new farms were created. But with the replacement of feudal by modern private property the *usi civici* were abolished, and the compensation due to peasant communities was seldom received, giving rise to considerable hardship and numerous outbreaks of banditry in the southern countryside.

Most of the land that came onto the market, including portions of feudal and church land, royal demesnes, and communal land, was acquired by a variety of bourgeois elements present in the ancient feudal society of the South. In many cases the new owners tried to emulate the life-style of the aristocracy, and moved into the ranks of the nobility by purchasing titles and intermarrying. Thus, a new landed gentry emerged. Included in it were two groups. One was composed of new owners who succeeded in working their way up, in part replacing and in part merging with the old landowning aristocracy, as in the case of the rich upstart Don Calogero in Di Lampedusa's *The Leopard*. The second comprised those members of the feudal landowning class who managed to adapt to the changed conditions (see Blok, 1974, pages 36 – 57).

In 1860, the Italian state confiscated the landed property of the church and put it up for sale. Once again, the majority of the land sold was bought up by substantial owners, and the preexisting rights of the peasantry were abolished without compensation.

In the internal hill and mountain zones (see figure 4.2) the dissolution of the feudal system simply resulted in the replacement of the old landowners by new bourgeois owners. The system of farming underwent little if any change: the land under cultivation continued to be divided into small plots leased to peasants under precarious tenancy and sharecropping arrangements, and in the summer months cattle and sheep were still brought up from capitalist farms on low-lying land.

Nevertheless, until about 1880, as a result of the abolition of feudal rights and the resulting revolution in the legal forms of landholding, quite marked agricultural progress did occur. In some of the low-lying coastal and internal zones, in which the presence of malaria and the existence of clayey soils and an extremely arid climate had tended to restrict agricultural activities, new or noble landowners established some simple farms. As in the case of existing large farms, these estates were devoted to extensive wheat production and animal raising, and were worked by day labourers who supplemented their incomes through the cultivation of small owned and rented plots in the vicinity of the upland villages or towns in which they lived. At the same time, in some mainly coastal zones that were for the most part already used for more intensive types of farming, such as the cultivation of olives, vines, and citrus fruits, direct investment and management by landowners was associated with significant reorganisation and improvement of agricultural production.

These changes in the land tenure system and in the organisation of agricultural production were completed by about 1880. In subsequent years, bourgeois properties had a tendency to be subdivided. Increasingly, the owners of land took less and less interest in its cultivation. A large proportion of medium and small landowners were drawn towards the towns, and redirected their main interests towards the bureaucracy and the professions. In general, the owners of land were converted into urban-based rentiers, even if the farms owned were in areas in which production arrangements had been modified and the owners had been engaged in direct farming. At the same time, members of the urban petite bourgeoisie composed of doctors, lawyers, and public officials, along with *carabinieri*, acquired pieces of agricultural land.

With these changes in the character of landownership the land itself was increasingly leased to direct peasant cultivators under some form of agricultural contract, and the importance of day labourers declined. Consequently, southern agriculture came increasingly to be characterised by direct peasant cultivation of land owned by absentee landlords who received agricultural rents but played no active role in agricultural production and progress (Rossi-Doria, 1972b).

In view of the existence of this extremely backward type of agricultural organisation, the implementation, from 1880 onwards in particular, of policies which corresponded with the interests of the landowning class simply reinforced the underdevelopment of southern agriculture.

In the rest of Italy, however, more modern agricultural systems existed, and more progress was made. Under the *ancien regime* the prevalent type of tenure in most of northern and central Italy, except in mountainous areas, was the *mezzadria* or contractual sharecropping system. Under this system, each estate was divided into small holdings farmed by peasant families. These farming families used old-fashioned techniques and shared the expenses of production with the landowner. The produce was divided, usually equally, between the peasant family and the landlord. This system of production, and the highly dispersed pattern of settlement with which it was associated, persisted in much of central Italy. In parts of the more northern regions, on the other hand, capitalist farms employing wage labour were established, new farming methods were adopted, and new products were introduced (Lyttelton, 1979, pages 109-115).

4.3 The southern agrarian bloc and national politics after unification

The Mezzogiorno was drawn into the national movement by a crisis in southern society (Davis, 1979, pages 69-100). In the agricultural sector the old equilibrium of a set of societies organised around customary rights and paternalist relations between the peasantry and the nobility was destroyed by the integration of the South with the market in industrialising economies and the increasing commercialisation of farming. The old mechanisms of social integration were not, however, replaced by new ones. Instead the destruction of older social systems was accompanied by a general stagnation of processes of economic development and social change. What emerged were a number of economic and social systems characterised by a variety of types of capitalist underdevelopment, and what held them together was repression: "state repression, familial repression, and repression by cliques of clients and dependents, the so-called *clientelismo* of the South" (Arlacchi, 1983, page 16).

The problems encountered by the Bourbon regime in its strategy of developing a protected industrial sector contributed to its loss of the allegiance of the agricultural lobby. As a result, agricultural interests subsequently gave passive support to the process of Italian unification, but a sufficiently strong and well-organised modernising bureaucracy and a new political base within the state apparatus were not established (Davis, 1979, pages 88–100).

In the South, not only the peasantry, but also the 'intellectuals', lacked cohesion. The South was thus, in the words of Gramsci, a zone of "great social disintegration" (Gramsci, 1978, page 454). Southern society was also, in the view of Gramsci, a "great agrarian bloc". There were several reasons for this. First, the absence of an agricultural revolution in the South resulted in the reproduction of the class of large southern landlords or '*baroni*'. Second, the lack of dynamism in rural society placed limits on the extent of the market for industrial products, acted as a constraint on local accumulation and industrialisation, and prevented the emergence of a local industrial and commercial bourgeoisie of any significance.

In these conditions southern society was composed of a large class of agricultural workers and peasants who, argued Gramsci, were dominated economically and politically by an urban-based class of large landowners through the activities of a small 'intellectual' bourgeois stratum (see also Salvemini, 1973a). [The world '*intellettuale*' really means, in this context, someone who does cerebral as opposed to manual work. As is indicated with such clarity in Levi's (1982) *Christ Stopped at Eboli*, the qualitative meaning of the English word 'intellectual' is extremely misleading as a description of the middle strata in the traditional Mezzogiorno. Completely lacking in any kind of entrepreneurship or initiative these managers of land, doctors, and lawyers, in the words once used by Rossi-Doria, "were to social life what malaria was to physical life".]

In the predominantly agrarian South this intermediate stratum was made up of professional people and members of small and medium landowning families. As lawyers, doctors, and landowners, the members of this class played, along with the church, significant roles in the economic, social, and cultural life of each locality. But the political organisation of the new state also gave these same individuals the opportunity of playing a very important role in local political life.

After unification, the Piedmontese state adopted a centralised system of administration. At the same time, however, wide powers were delegated to local officials and to the *sindaco* or mayor of each community in particular. In this situation, the members of the local 'intellectual' bourgeoisie in each locality usually split into non-class-based political factions that competed for control of the local administration, for access to the resources that the local state could allocate, and for the local political and administrative posts that grew excessively, along with the associated networks of patronage.

As well as providing the political and ideological means for maintaining social control in the southern countryside, the agrarian bloc in the South acted as a counterweight to the northern industrial proletariat. In addition, it offered a political base for parliamentary representatives, who were able to play an important role in the construction of political alliances at a national level (see Bagnasco, 1977, pages 40-43; and Gramsci, 1978, pages 454-460). Furthermore, politics at a national level itself came to be characterised by related processes of *trasformismo*, with alliances being formed via a sharing out of, for example, contracts for public works.

As a consequence, a regional social bloc whose reproduction depended on the continuing underdevelopment of the South acquired an important role in national politics, and southern landowners were included in a national political alliance alongside the northern bourgeoisie. In turn, this national political bloc offered a way of maintaining social control in the South and in the country as a whole, while the state pursued a series of

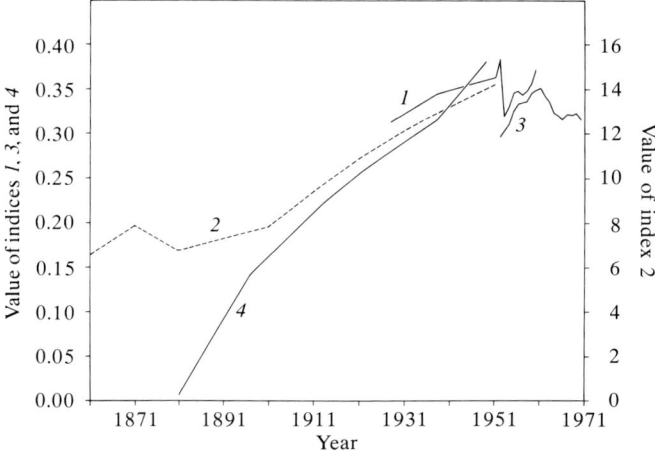

The index of regional inequality used is given by the equations

$$\frac{1}{\bar{b}}\left[\sum_{i=1}^{n}(b_i - \bar{b})\left(g_i \Big/ \sum_{i=1}^{n} g_i\right)\right]^{1/2}, \quad \text{for } i = 1, 2, ..., n,$$

where b_i is the value of the relevant indicator for region i, $\bar{b}$ is its mean value, g_i is the population of region i, and $g_i/\sum g_i$, $i = 1, ..., n$, denotes region i's share of the national population. On the graph, indices calculated with four different indicators are plotted:
1 Williamson's index based on estimates of net per capita output of the private sector in 1938 prices for nineteen regions.
2 Williamson's index based on estimates of the share of agriculture in total employment in nineteen regions.
3 Secchi's index obtained by computing three-year moving averages of an index calculated from estimates of net per capita income at 1963 market prices for the four main territorial divisions.
4 Secchi's index based on indirect long-run estimates of net per capita income at constant prices.

Figure 4.3. Regional inequality in Italy, 1861-1971. Sources: Williamson (1965, pages 26-28, 33-35, 57, 75) and Secchi (1974, pages 33-37, 42-54).

policies that played a vital part in encouraging and supporting industrial development in the North West. The class structure of the South and the composition of its dominant class thus had an important influence on the formulation of state policy, whereas the measures adopted by the state mediated and combined with the functioning of market mechanisms to reproduce and reinforce the economic and social imbalances that existed at the moment of unification (see figure 4.3).

The argument outlined in the last few paragraphs has been challenged by Romeo (1959). In his view, an agricultural revolution, in which the Italian peasantry made the sort of gains that their French counterparts won after 1789, would have slowed down national economic growth. Had such a revolution occurred, he argued, peasant consumption levels would have been higher, and the resources available for the infrastructural and industrial investments that enabled an Italy lacking in territory and natural resources to be "the only country in the Mediterranean area to create a great industrial complex and a highly developed urban civilisation" would have been reduced (1959, page 197).

The argument hinges on disagreements about the likely impact of the establishment of peasant property on the one hand, and the success of Italian industrial expansion on the other (Cammett, 1967, pages 213-222). What is clear is that the limited growth of productivity and output in southern agriculture, and the restricted development of an internal market for light industrial goods, provided little scope for the development of efficient southern industries and the emergence of a local entrepreneurial class. Instead, the southern market was dominated by low-productivity concerns that, as a consequence, were also unable to expand via sales on external markets and that were incapable of surviving when exposed to northern competition. Southern backwardness was accordingly perpetuated. Whether or not the lack of an agricultural revolution impeded the process of national economic growth thus depends on whether or not the resulting lack of dynamism in the South restricted national expansion more than southern underdevelopment contributed to it (Del Monte and Giannola, 1978, pages 68-73).

4.4 Italian development in the liberal era following unification
Until 1880, the Italian economy specialised in the production of agricultural commodities and imported industrial ones. Development was slow, and the gap between the North and the South did not increase much. Through increases in the production and export of cereals and Mediterranean products, agriculture in both areas successfully exploited the opportunities offered by rising prices and the policy of free trade pursued by the new state. The dismantling of tariffs between the various preexisting Italian states and the extension of the lower Piedmontese external tariffs to the South reduced the degree of protection enjoyed by southern industry, and contributed to the collapse of some major industries established around

Naples and Salerno under the Bourbon regime. On the whole, however, a very slow but relatively equalised process of industrial expansion occurred in the two parts of the country.

It is possible to identify several reasons for the slowness in Italian industrial development in the twenty years after unification. The extent of the domestic market for industrial products was held down by the penal levels of taxation necessitated by the government's desire to reduce the state's deficit and to balance the budget. Also, local manufacturing industries were often unable to compete with the foreign products allowed freely into the country under the state's liberal economic policies. Over one half of the government's own expenditure was used to meet military expenses and to pay interest on the national debt incurred largely by the Piedmontese in carrying through the unification process. A programme of public works and infrastructural projects was financed, as was a railway building programme. (Indeed, in 1860–1870 the length of the railway network was increased threefold, though in 1865 the first of two ultimately unsuccessful attempts to transfer the railway system in whole or in part to the private sector was made.) But these investments did not act as a major source of industrial growth. In the railway sector, for example, materials, machinery, and equipment were generally imported. Thus, instead of stimulating indigenous industrial development, state spending played a preindustrialisation role, helping to create the preconditions for subsequent as opposed to current industrial development.

The expansion that did occur, however, assumed very different forms in the two main parts of Italy. In the North, new investment and capital deepening occurred both in agriculture and in industry, laying relatively secure foundations for subsequent expansion. In the South, on the other hand, apart from the intensive development of the cultivation of Mediterranean tree crops that occurred for the most part in some coastal zones, very little technical progress took place in agriculture or in industry.

The lack of technical progress and of improvement in southern agriculture can be partly explained by the heavier incidence of taxation on farming in general and on southern farming in particular. But the main reasons lay in the structure of landownership and the organisation of agricultural production. In most cases, absentee landlords were able to obtain higher rents from extensive farming methods than from improved agricultural practices, and the incomes they received were used unproductively. At the same time, impoverished peasants lacked the security of tenure and the resources required to undertake the investments necessary for agricultural progress. In the areas dominated by large capitalist estates any increase in grain prices simply led to an extension of cultivation onto new land rather than new investments and more intensive farming on existing land. The cultivation of woodland and of marginal land in upland zones that had formerly been used as rough pasture aggravated the problems of erosion in the hills and of flooding in the plains.

4.5 The formation of the *'blocco storico'* and the switch to protectionism

In the years after the agricultural crisis of 1880 the two economies diverged, and the relative position of the South deteriorated sharply. From about 1878 the Italian state came to be organised by the historical bloc constituted by an alliance between the dominant northern industrial bourgeoisie and the subordinate southern landed bourgeoisie that was identified by Gramsci. In order to promote Italian industrialisation the state switched to a strategy of protectionism. At first the textile and engineering industries were defended. The customs barriers for industrial goods were increased substantially by the 1887 tariff, and protection was extended to some northern agricultural products. But in order to retain the support of the owners of large estates in the South, who derived most of their income from extensive cereal cultivation, the government also increased the duty on imported grain.

With the opening of the agrarian crisis, southern farming developed more slowly, only recovering towards the end of the Giolittian era in 1908, and declined in comparison with farming in the North. One of the reasons for this was that the implementation of the changes in state policy increased the obstacles to agricultural progress posed by the prevailing relations of agricultural production. The duty on imported grain increased grain prices and protected domestic producers from cheap corn imports from the USA. The policy of protection accordingly encouraged the cultivation of cereals for which the South was less well suited than the North, and which were produced extensively by some of the socially and technically most backward sections of southern agriculture. At the same time, the relative prices of grain and of industrial goods were pushed upwards. Consequently, the policies pursued by the state discriminated against the cultivators of Mediterranean products such as vines, olives, and citrus fruits. Furthermore, Italian protectionism was in violation of a commercial treaty with the French state. Not surprisingly, the French government took retaliatory action which seriously damaged Italian wine producers and provoked the wine crisis of 1888. In short, the measures adopted by the Italian state protected and impeded the reorganisation of some of the most backward parts of southern agriculture and placed the most dynamic parts in crisis (see Del Monte and Giannola, 1978, pages 49-53).

The redirection of state policy did, however, play an important role in launching and accelerating Italian industrial growth, and in opening the way for the development of large-scale industry. Industrial growth occurred in metal manufacturing with the development in particular of the Terni iron and steel mill to supply the naval sector, in engineering with state-supported investment in shipbuilding and railway engineering and the emergence of electrical engineering, in chemicals, in the textile sector, and in construction related activities (see King, 1985, pages 38-42). But modern industrial growth occurred mainly in the North. In the South, traditional artisan and family-based industries collapsed largely because of two factors.

One was the agrarian crisis and the related weakness of the local market. The second was the impact of northern competition to which southern industry was increasingly exposed as a result of the development of improved communications.

The subsequent upswing in industrial activity was, however, quickly followed by a recession that lasted until 1896. The volume of exports and the level of economic activity declined, and the speculative building boom that had given an impetus to the process of industrialisation collapsed. What followed was a series of banking scandals that resulted, amongst other things, in the dismissal of Giolitti as prime minister.

At the end of the 'great depression' the renewed expansion of the international economy was associated with a new phase of comparatively rapid development. Between 1896 and 1908, Italian industrial output grew at an average annual rate of 6.7%. Output increased in traditional industries, and especially in the textile sector, where a switch to electrical energy sources and significant mechanisation of spinning and weaving occurred. (On the eve of the First World War, textiles accounted for 20% of manufacturing output and 30% of employment.) Significant growth also occurred in more advanced and highly concentrated industries. Under state protection, iron and steel production was increased. The plant at Terni was expanded and modernised, new plants were constructed at Piombino in 1903 and Bagnoli in 1905, and in 1914, work started on the Ansaldo works at Cornigliano Ligure. Yet the Italian steel sector remained very small in comparison with the German, British, and French industries. Shipping and shipbuilding and the manufacturing of armaments were expanded, and a vehicle manufacturing industry was developed along with a whole range of related industries producing engines, tyres, electrical components, and so on. (In 1899, FIAT was, for example founded.) In addition, the rubber industry expanded, and important developments occurred in some parts of the chemical industry (see King, 1985, pages 42–47). Industrial growth was accompanied by marked increases in the production of electrical energy and, especially, of hydroelectricity.

In addition to the existence of industrial protection, the reasons underlying this "qualitative leap that put Italy in a class by herself among the nations of Southern Europe and the Mediterranean" (Webster, cited in King, 1985, pages 198–199) included state support for specific industries and specific constellations of industrial interests, on the one hand, and the activities of the new deposit and investment banks on the German model (the Banca Commerciale and the Credito Italiano), on the other.

Once again, however, industrial growth was concentrated on the industrial towns of Milan, Turin, and Genoa. In 1911, half of the firms with motor power were located in Lombardy (Lombardia), Piedmont, and Ligure (Liguria), which together covered 20.7% of the national land area and contained 27.4% of the national population. 64.1% of industrial employees worked in the North, compared with 14.9% in the Centre and 21.0% in the

South, and 38.7% (compared with 35.2% in 1901) worked in Lombardy, Piedmont, and Ligure (King, 1985, page 48).

With these developments in industry, the political weight of centralised industrial and financial groups enjoying close connections with the military establishment, the political class, and the state increased. At the same time, the model of industrialisation itself, along with the penetration of the domestic market by the more developed German economy in particular, were associated with a quest for outlets that was translated into a search for colonial space in the Balkans, East Africa, Libya, and Asia Minor, and with growing international rivalry (see King, 1985, pages 51-55).

In 1907, there was an economic downturn, owing mainly to the limited size of the internal market. At that point, considerable excess capacity appeared. As a result, in 1908-1914, industrial production grew much more slowly, at 2.4% per year.

4.6 The South as a colony
In 1881 and around the turn of the century, the problems caused by economic integration did lead to the introduction of some measures that involved the implementation of programmes of extraordinary public works in the South, and in 1904 the first measures designed to encourage southern industrialisation were introduced with the passing of the Special Law for Naples. The provisions of this law were subsequently extended to the rest of the southern mainland and islands. The aid given to the South was, however, limited in extent, and must be viewed in the context of government policies as a whole, that on balance discriminated against the South (Del Monte and Giannola, 1978, page 85).

Many classical southernist writers held that the underdevelopment of the South contributed in several ways to northern industrial expansion and to national economic growth, and that some of the most serious difficulties experienced in the South stemmed from government policies designed to encourage northern industrialisation. [The classical southernist tradition was made up of mainly conservative writers such as Villari, Franchetti, Sonnino, Fortunato, and Nitti (see Lill, 1984, pages 490-492). It must be distinguished from that which flowed from the more radical interpretations of the southern problem presented by Salvemini and Gramsci. A useful anthology of classical writings on the South is Caizzi, 1973.] The evidence for this view included reference to the damaging effects on the South of the protectionist policies pursued by the Italian state from 1878. But southernist writers also emphasised the role of movements of resources from the South to the North in perpetuating southern backwardness and promoting northern development. Their main argument was that there was a movement of capital from the South to the North caused not only by the greater profitability of investment in the North, but also by the operation of taxation, public spending, and selective credit policies. What was claimed was that taxes and net government borrowing in the South exceeded the sum of government transfers to southern residents and of government spending on goods and services produced in the region. Accordingly, the fiscal policies of the Italian state were seen as transferring resources to the North and as helping to promote northern industrialisation at the expense of the South.

It is obviously difficult to evaluate this claim. But Del Monte and Giannola have argued that many aspects of the Italian state's taxation and public expenditure policies harmed the southern economy, and certainly did not compensate for the existing inequalities between the two main parts of the country. In the two decades after unification, taxation was heavier in the South than in the North, and was more than proportional to the wealth and income of the region's inhabitants. At the same time, taxation policies mitigated against improvements in the structure of southern landholding. Taxes, and the sale of ecclesiastical property and of public offices mopped up local savings and deprived the southern agricultural sector of potential investment funds. On the expenditure side, the South probably received a share of state spending on public works that was proportional to its contribution to state revenue. Yet much of this expenditure was used unproductively to pay state employees, and the sums involved were quite inadequate compared with the needs of the region (see Del Monte and Giannola, 1978, pages 56-68, 101-102).

Although in the period preceding the First World War some of the capital requirements of northern industry were met by southern savings, the workers needed were largely drawn from within the region, as the transfer of workers from the agricultural sector, which was undergoing reorganisation, was sufficient to meet the needs of northern industry.

Until unification, emigration had been slight. In the 1860s, however, it increased, reaching 100 000 people per year by the end of the decade. After falling in the mid-1870s, it rose steadily, with an upward jump in the trend around the turn of the century, until the start of the First World war brought it to an end. At first, neighbouring areas in Europe and the Mediterranean Basin were the main destinations, but in the late 1880s these zones were supplanted by transoceanic destinations (see figure 4.4). In the years after 1881, emigration from the South started to increase rapidly, and in 1901-1911 it exceeded emigration from the central and northern regions. It was, however, largely directed abroad.

According to official statistics, in which the level of emigration was probably underestimated by at least 2 or 3 million, 14 million people left Italy in 1876-1914. About two thirds of Italian emigration was, however, temporary: of the emigrants going to Europe at least nine out of every ten returned, and emigration to the United States of America was increasingly temporary in character. In the twelve years preceding the war, between 300 000 and 400 000 emigrants returned to Italy each year, whereas, according to Foerster's estimates, 4.2 million people emigrated permanently. Of the emigrants, four fifths were men, and of these men most were in the early years of manhood. In the majority of cases the men who left were unskilled, came from peasant households, and were migrating temporarily in order to earn enough money to pay for a house and some land in their areas of origin (see Foerster, 1924, pages 4–43).

The loss of population imposed important costs on the South. Included were the resource costs of raising emigrants in the South and the output foregone as a result of their leaving the region. On the other hand, the remittances sent back to Italy by emigrants made an important contribution not only to southern incomes, but also to the country's balance of payments: calculations for the 1901–1913 period show that a commercial trade deficit of 10 230 million lire was more than offset by an invisible trade surplus of 12 291 million lire, of which over one half was composed of remittances from emigrants (Cafagna, cited in King, 1985, pages 43–44). Southern emigration, constituting a large proportion of national emigration, can thus be viewed as a second way in which southern underdevelopment contributed to national economic growth.

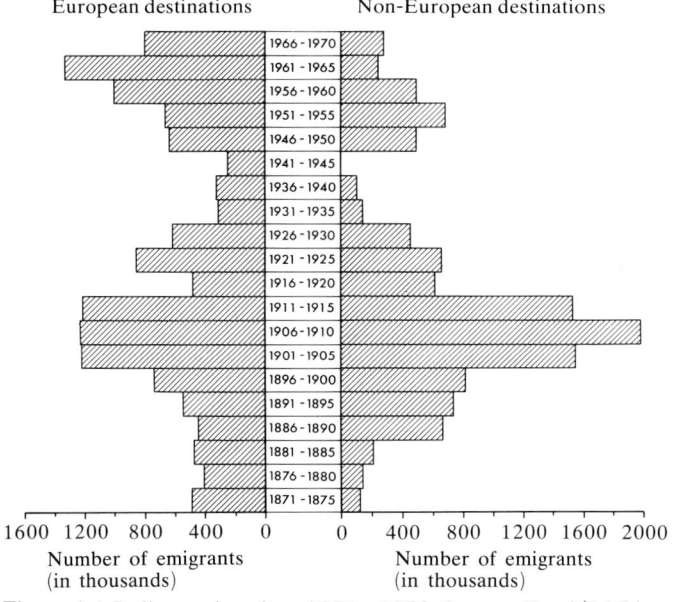

Figure 4.4. Italian emigration, 1871–1970. Source: Turri (1974, page 165).

4.7 Italian socialism and the southern question
The concentration of development in the North also had some important implications for the development of the Italian socialist movement. Between 1900 and 1910 especially, Giolitti, who was prime minister for most of this period, encouraged and pressed for political cooperation between the Italian bourgeoisie and social groups gravitating around the Italian Socialist Party (PSI) (Procacci, 1973, pages 368–388 and 407–412).

As a result of the compromises it made, northern socialism was held by some radical southernist writers, of whom the most notable was Salvemini, to have effectively renounced general political demands in favour of the sectional economic interests of workers in the North (see Salvemini, 1973b). The northern working class was, it was argued, incorporated and integrated with the prevailing model of development, and the gains it made occurred at the expense of the living standards of the peasant masses in the South. Increasingly, the northern working class appeared as a small and relatively privileged group with interests that were opposed to those of the southern peasantry, and the working-class movement lost its role as, in the words of Gramsci, a leader and guide of the dominated classes as a whole.

The tensions to which this situation gave rise in the PSI led to its division into various currents, and to the increasing detachment from the party of the radical southern middle class. The agrarian policy that it adopted in the critical period after the war also lost it much support in southern Italy (see Procacci, 1973, pages 368–388, 407–412).

In the 1920s, Gramsci was much concerned with this problem. He recognised that the strategy of the northern bourgeoisie involved the exploitation of this class division between the two main parts of Italy as a means of containing the class tensions that had taken shape with the industrialisation of the North. What he consequently sought to show was that the conditions prevailing in the two parts of the country were connected, and that the connection lay in the domination or hegemony of the industrial bourgeoisie over the system as a whole. It was Gramsci's belief that the demonstration of this connection established a basis on which an alliance could be constructed, under northern working-class leadership, between the southern peasantry and the northern working class. The foundations for this alliance lay, he argued, in the treatment of the southern question as a central problem of national development, and as a problem whose solution was a means for the transition to socialism (Bagnasco, 1977, pages 43–50; Gramsci, 1978, pages 441–462).

In the conditions prevailing in Italy at that moment in history, the formation of a social bloc composed of northern workers and southern peasants clearly afforded the only means of mobilising a majority of the population against the bourgeois state. But this conception of the social base and directions of an Italian socialist revolution was formulated in a period in which the fascists led by Mussolini had already come to power.

4.8 The interwar years: fascism and global crisis

The Italian economy grew more slowly in the period after the First World War than in the Giolittian period. With demobilisation unemployment soared, and in 1919 and 1920, industrial conflict increased dramatically. The conversion of the economy to peacetime production proved extremely difficult, and in 1921, in particular, many industrial concerns folded, including Ansaldo and Ilva (see Castronovo, 1980, pages 152–162).

In the improved international economic conditions that prevailed between 1921 and the great economic crisis of 1929, quite fast growth occurred. With economic recovery, the fascists who seized power in October 1922 succeeded in consolidating their position. In December 1927, a deflationary economic strategy was inaugurated, with the revaluation of the lire. Industrial concentration and centralisation accelerated. The authority of employers over the working class was increased, strikes were declared 'acts of war', existing working-class organisations were destroyed and replaced with fascist organisations, and in 1926-1936, wages were cut quite sharply. With the crash of 1929 the Italian economy was plunged into a deep economic crisis. In 1929-1932, industrial output fell by one third, and unemployment rose sharply. After 1933, however, industrial production recovered.

In earlier epochs, Italian growth had been restricted by shortages of indigenous capital, the weakness of the internal market, and recurrent problems with the balance of payments. It was these weaknesses, along with the impact of the great economic crisis of 1929, that lay behind the switch to protectionism, and that help to explain the development of policies aimed at making the country more autarchic and at generating resources that could be transferred to industrial production.

Various measures were adopted with a view to diverting resources towards industrial accumulation. The incomes of agrarian strata were, for example, increased. Income was transferred from the agricultural and other sectors to large industrial groups by means of taxation and credit policies, through the banking system, and by allowing the relative prices of industrial goods to move in favour of the products of monopolitistic groups (Corner, 1979, pages 254-265).

The fascist regime also acquired an entrepreneurial role as a result of rescue operations and the creation of the Istituto Mobiliare Italiano (IMI) in November 1931 and of the Istituto per la Ricostruzione Industriale (IRI) in January 1933. IMI was formed to provide medium-term and long-term credit to industry, and to shelter the deposit banks from the risks of industrial investment, whereas IRI was set up with a view to disengaging the banks permanently from industry.

In 1936, a major bank reform was passed, and IRI's second role of supplying new long-term industrial credit was given to IMI. In June 1937, IRI was, however, made into a permanent public body. On the eve of the Second World War it held more than 44% of Italian share capital. It accounted for 67% of national iron-ore mining, 77% of pig-iron production, 45% of steel production, 80% of shipbuilding, 22% of aircraft production, and one half of Italy's output of arms and ammunition. It played a major role in the field of maritime transport, and it controlled some electrical groups and the main telecommunications companies in northern Italy. As a result, the state came to assume a major role in the provision of both medium-term and long-term industrial credit, and an important one in the sphere of industrial production (see Castronovo, 1980, pages 196–204).

Special efforts were also made to encourage import-substituting industrial development. Included, for example, were investments in the oil and natural gas industries and in the hydrocarbons sector by the state-owned Azienda Generale Italiana Petroli (AGIP) and a subsidiary it established under the name of Azienda Nazionale Idrogenazione Combustibili (ANIC).

In addition, the fascist regime established corporations in which workers and capitalists were expected to cooperate to achieve common ends under state supervision. Through them, however, the main monopolistic groups such as FIAT in the vehicles sector, Montecatini in chemicals, and SNIA Viscosa in artificial textiles obtained direct access to the state planning system.

As well as preparing the ground for a policy of more active support for the expansion and modernisation of some key industries, these developments also involved at least the beginnings of a change in the composition of the ruling social bloc. Indeed, if, in the view of Castronovo, a dominant social bloc existed in the fascist epoch, it was based more on a fusing of large-scale industry and the state bureaucracy than on a coalition of industrial and agrarian capitalists (see the discussion in Pugliese, 1979, pages 72–74).

Once again, however, industrial expansion was largely concentrated in the North. The only important exceptions to this rule were some investments made by IRI in the Naples area in the mid-1930s, and the expansion of mining activities in Sicily (Sicilia) and Sardinia (Sardegna). Included in IRI's investments were some major developments in the iron and steel and engineering sectors, of which the most important was the modernisation of the Ilva steel plant at Bagnoli.

4.9 The Second World War and after
The long deterioration in the relative position of the South accelerated during the Second World War. In those years, resources were once again concentrated on war-related industries located mainly in the North, whereas the destruction caused by the war was most pronounced in the South, where the Allies first landed in 1943. The inequality continued to increase in the immediate postwar years, as the northern regions were favoured in the allocation of resources for reconstruction.

Nevertheless, the new processes of political and economic development that were set in motion in the late 1940s involved a major change in the model of southern development, as a result of which the Mezzogiorno was eventually to acquire a new and active role in the expansion of the national economy. Moreover, with these new developments went pronounced changes in the social and political complexion of the South, and in the composition of the ruling social bloc in the region and in the country as a whole. As a result, in fact, of the contradictions inherited from the

Risorgimento, the role of the southern landed bourgeoisie was in decline at least from the 1930s onwards. Yet it was only under the impact of the violent peasant struggles unleashed with the fall of fascism in 1943 that these contradictions finally resulted in its dispossession by the hegemonic element of the dominant class, and in the dislocation of the historical bloc identified by Gramsci. It was this act which initiated the new phase of southern and national development. After the destruction of the southern landed bourgeoisie, the dominant role in the South eventually passed to a high state bourgeoisie composed of strata controlling public and semipublic financial and industrial groups, on the one hand, and state bureaucracies administering public spending on the other. In the last section I indicated that a high state bourgeoisie had already started to assume a prominent role at a national level under the fascist regime. In the postwar period, however, it emerged as a major social actor in the South and as one of the main components of a new national social bloc (Pinnarò and Pugliese, 1979, pages 494–498).

5

The development of the Mezzogiorno in the preindustrialisation phase of southern policy

5.1 The southern problem and the national economy in the years of reconstruction

The outcome of the processes of national development outlined in chapter 4 provided the context from and in which a new model of economic and political development emerged after the Second World War. Two aspects of this context of development were particularly significant. One was the fact that the Italian economy was relatively backward compared with those of other capitalist countries in Europe. Second, Italy was characterised by very pronounced imbalances not only between the mainly agricultural southern regions and the rest of the country, but also between the more prosperous intermediate northeastern and central regions and the core northwestern regions that constituted the main centre of Italian manufacturing industry (table 5.1).

In the early 1950s, output and employment in Italy were still heavily dependent on the agricultural sector, and, compared with the situation in more advanced capitalist countries, industrial production made a relatively small contribution to Italy's gross national product (table 5.2). Moreover, it rested to a large extent on food processing and the manufacture of natural textile products, both of which were closely connected with the agricultural sector, rather than on modern manufacturing industries (table 5.3).

Table 5.1. Some indicators of regional differentiation in Italy in 1951: national accounts aggregates, employment, and population (percentage values given in parentheses). Sources: elaborated from ISTAT (1973, pages 7, 19–42; 1975, pages 3–6, 13–14).

	North-west	North-east	Centre	South	Italy
Gross income at current market prices (milliard lire)	4151.3 (38.6)	2125.0 (19.8)	2019.4 (18.8)	2452.3 (22.8)	10748.0 (100.0)
Total available resources at current market prices (milliard lire)	3716.0 (34.1)	2180.1 (20.0)	2092.4 (19.2)	2908.5 (26.7)	10897.0 (100.0)
Employment (thousands)	5342.9 (27.1)	4048.4 (20.6)	3810.6 (19.3)	6491.0 (33.0)	19692.9 (100.0)
Resident population (thousands)	11722.0 (24.7)	9399.0 (19.8)	8643.0 (18.2)	17654.0 (37.2)	47418.0 (100.0)
Gross per capita income (thousand lire)	354.1	226.1	233.6	138.9	226.7
Total per capita resources (thousand lire)	317.0	232.0	242.1	164.8	229.8

In the agricultural sector, output and employment were strongly concentrated in the largely agricultural South. But southern agriculture was particularly backward, owing to the small size and fragmentation of working units, the shortage of capital, and the system of tenure. It was also characterised by widespread underemployment: the South accounted in 1951 for 35.8% of national agricultural output but 42.6% of the total employment in agriculture (table 5.4). Agricultural output per person employed was equal to some 216 000 lire in the South compared with about 287 000 lire in the rest of Italy.

On the other hand, the country's industry and, in particular, its manufacturing industry were strongly localised in the Northwest. Regional inequalities in the level of labour productivity were even more pronounced in manufacturing industry than in the agricultural sector, with the South accounting, in 1951, for 12.4% of manufacturing output and 19.5% of manufacturing employment (table 5.4).

In the South, the manufacturing sector was in fact largely dominated by small-scale artisan and family-based enterprises operating in traditional industries, exploiting local agricultural resources, and serving local markets that were still protected from external competition by an underdeveloped transport network and the high cost of transporting commodities long distances. In the early 1950s, traditional consumption-good industries

Table 5.2. The sectoral distribution (%) of gross domestic product (at factor cost in current prices) and of employment in the main territorial divisions and in Italy in 1951. Sources: elaborated from ISTAT (1973, pages 7, 19–42; 1975, pages 15–18, 29–30).

	North-west	North-east	Centre	South	Italy
Gross domestic product					
Agriculture	14.4	28.7	19.4	34.0	22.9
Industry	49.8	31.9	32.2	23.7	36.7
manufacturing	43.1	23.4	23.9	14.8	28.8
construction	3.6	5.8	5.3	5.9	4.9
Services	30.5	30.5	35.0	29.5	31.1
Public administration	5.3	8.9	13.4	12.8	9.4
Total	100	100	100	100	100
Employment					
Agriculture	25.0	47.8	44.3	56.7	43.9
Industry	45.8	26.1	26.1	20.1	29.5
manufacturing	39.3	19.5	18.3	13.4	22.6
construction	5.3	5.7	6.3	5.5	5.6
Services	24.6	20.6	22.0	17.4	20.9
Public administration	4.6	5.5	7.6	5.8	5.8
Total	100	100	100	100	100

accounted for 64.7% of value added and 72.1% of employment in southern manufacturing compared with 44.1% and 55.1%, respectively, in Italy as a whole (41.2% and 51.0% in Italy excluding the Mezzogiorno) (table 5.3). The weight of the traditional sector in the regional economy was in turn reflected in the structure of employment in manufacturing industry: the South had 19.5% of Italian manufacturing employment (table 5.4), and yet it had 32.0% of independent manufacturing employment, and 28.1% of marginal or part-time employment, that is, of workers employed for up to thirty-two hours per week (ISTAT, 1973, pages 7 and 19–42).

Table 5.3. The sectoral distribution (%) of manufacturing output (at factor cost in current prices) and of employment in the main territorial divisions and in Italy in 1951. Sources: elaborated from ISTAT (1973, pages 43–66; 1975, pages 31–32).

	North-west	North-east	Centre	South	Italy
Output					
Food, drink, and tobacco	7.2	19.2	13.3	32.7	13.2
Textiles	19.3	14.6	11.1	4.4	15.4
Clothing and footwear	5.9	10.5	13.5	17.1	9.2
Leather and leather goods	1.3	0.5	1.3	1.2	1.2
Furniture and wood products	3.2	7.1	6.5	9.4	5.1
Metal manufacturing	8.1	4.6	7.7	2.9	6.9
Engineering	24.0	16.3	14.9	10.7	19.7
Transport equipment	6.9	5.1	2.9	3.6	5.6
Nonmetallic minerals	3.2	7.5	8.7	6.6	5.1
Chemicals and allied	10.5	7.7	9.9	7.9	9.6
Rubber	3.4	0.5	0.8	0.1	2.1
Paper	3.0	3.6	3.2	1.5	2.9
Printing, publishing, and other	3.9	2.9	6.2	1.9	3.9
Total	100	100	100	100	100
Employment					
Food, drink, and tobacco	5.4	12.5	10.4	20.7	10.4
Textiles	25.2	14.2	11.4	3.8	16.9
Clothing and footwear	10.3	18.5	20.0	30.0	17.1
Leather and leather goods	1.2	0.7	1.1	0.9	1.0
Furniture and wood products	5.8	11.4	10.2	16.7	9.6
Metal manufacturing	4.9	2.0	2.9	1.2	3.4
Engineering	23.8	19.8	18.1	14.8	20.4
Transport equipment	6.6	5.0	3.0	2.6	5.0
Nonmetallic minerals	3.7	6.3	8.5	4.7	5.1
Chemicals and allied	6.1	4.2	5.4	2.2	4.9
Rubber	1.6	0.3	0.4	0.1	0.9
Paper	1.7	1.8	2.1	0.6	1.6
Printing, publishing, and other	3.8	3.4	6.5	1.7	3.7
Total	100	100	100	100	100

Thus, the economic structure of the South was based on an agricultural sector in which productivity was low and on a small industrial sector dominated by traditional manufacturing industries. The region nevertheless contained 37.2% of the Italian population (table 5.1). Much of the Mezzogiorno was, however, mountainous (see figures 4.2 and 5.1), and consequently it was particularly densely populated. Yet the dense population of the South coexisted with high levels of unemployment and low levels of labour productivity amongst those who were employed. The interaction of these economic and demographic conditions meant that the incomes of those living in the South, and in its internal rural areas in particular, were very low.

In 1951, gross per capita income was only 61.3% of the national average (table 5.1). The distribution of income between the inhabitants of the region was extremely unequal, yet a very large proportion of the incomes earned by Southerners was nevertheless used for consumption. The per capita resources available in the region were augmented, however, by a large volume of net imports. In practice, a high proportion of the resources transferred to the South were used unproductively. But in volume, transfers were almost equal to the expenditure on investment in the region (Podbielski, 1978, pages 107 – 108).

Table 5.4. The territorial distribution (%) of gross domestic product (at factor cost in current prices) and of employment in each sector in 1951. Sources: elaborated from ISTAT (1973, pages 7, 19 – 42; 1975, pages 15 – 18, 29 – 30).

	North-west	North-east	Centre	South	Italy
Gross domestic product					
Agriculture	23.5	24.7	16.0	35.8	100
Industry	50.7	17.1	16.6	15.6	100
manufacturing	55.9	16.0	15.7	12.4	100
construction	27.2	23.1	20.5	29.2	100
Services	36.7	19.2	21.3	22.9	100
Public administration	21.3	18.7	27.0	33.0	100
Total	37.4	19.6	18.9	24.1	100
Employment					
Agriculture	15.5	22.4	19.5	42.6	100
Industry	42.2	18.2	17.2	22.5	100
manufacturing	47.2	17.7	15.6	19.5	100
construction	25.3	20.8	21.6	32.3	100
Services	31.9	20.3	20.4	27.4	100
Public administration	21.8	19.5	25.4	33.3	100
Total	27.1	20.6	19.4	33.0	100

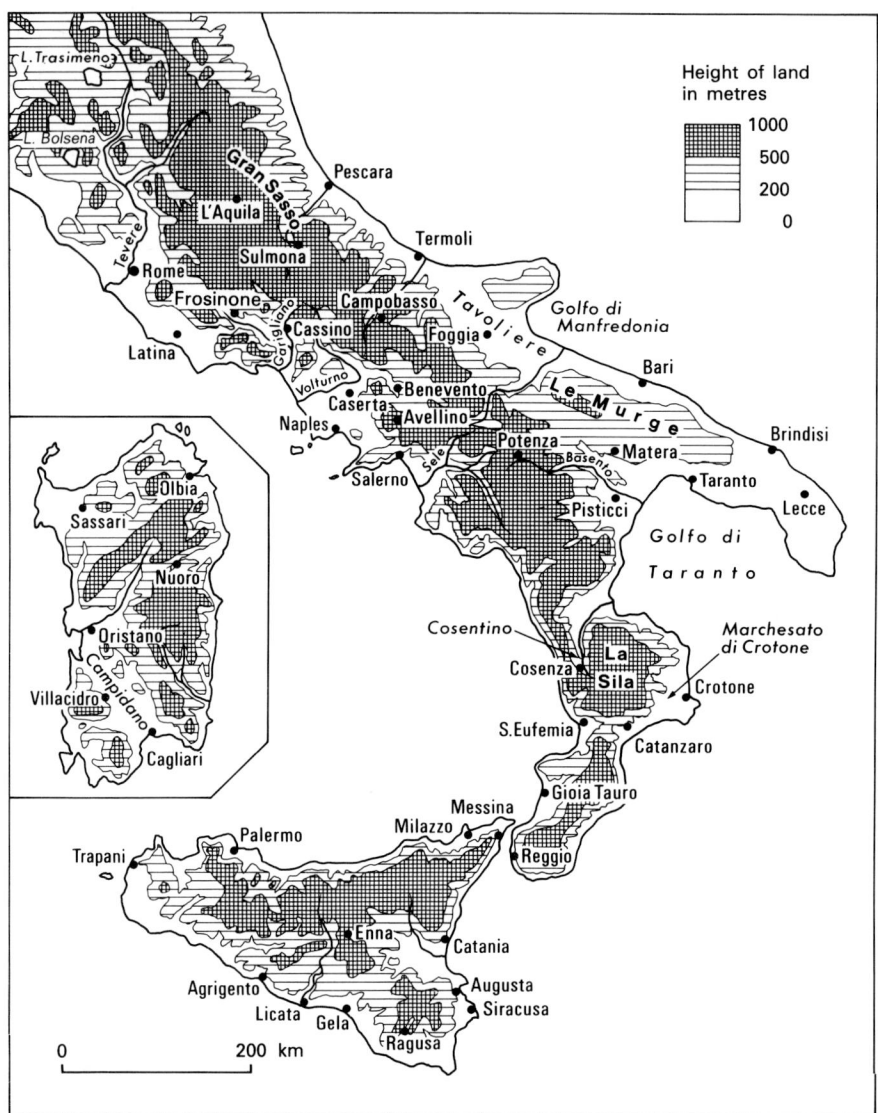

Figure 5.1. The Italian Mezzogiorno: main relief and settlements.

5.2 The southern agrarian system in 1950

After the Second World War what was first transformed was the agrarian economy of the Mezzogiorno. Accordingly, a more detailed account of the structure of southern agriculture must first be presented.

In 1950, three or four broad agricultural zones could, in the view of Rossi-Doria, be distinguished (see Rossi Doria, 1973, pages 167–192; Cosentino et al, 1979, pages 182–188; and also table 5.5).

Table 5.5. Agricultural zones and systems of tenure in southern Italy in 1950. In (a) values are expressed as a percentage of the South, and in (b) as a percentage of employment in each zone. Sources: Rossi-Doria (1948, page 57; 1950), cited in Tarrow (1967, pages 32, 34).

		Agricultural zone			
		capitalist latifundia	peasant latifundia	intensive ('*alberato*')	mixed ('*promiscua*')
(a)	Area	5	42	28	26
	Population	11	28	45	16
	Output	7	30	44	18
(b)	Peasant owner	23	36	37	58
	Tenant	24	21	22	18
	Sharetenant (*mezzadria*)	13	2	5	8
	Sharetenant (*colonia*)	10	22	20	9
	Sharecropper (*compartecipazione*)	4	6	4	2
	Hired help	27	14	12	5

5.2.1 The capitalist latifundia zone

The first of these areas was the capitalist *latifundia* zone. It was composed of dry farming areas in the *Mezzogiorno nudo* and dominated by extensively cultivated large capitalist estates. About 600 000 hectares of agricultural land situated mainly in the plains and valley bottoms, but stretching up on to the surrounding hills of the Mezzogiorno, were in this zone. Included originally were the Tuscan and Roman Maremma and the countryside surrounding Rome. These zones, however, lay outside the area that subsequently was officially defined as the Mezzogiorno. The other capitalist latifundia zones were all in the South: (1) the valleys of the Garigliano, Volturno, and Sele in the northwest of the region; (2) the Tavoliere in Apulia (Puglia), and the Metaponto in Basilicata; (3) some of the low valleys and plains of Calabria; (4) the plain of Catania and the Ionian plains of Sicily, and (5) the Campidano and the desolate coastal plains of Sardinia (see figures 4.1 and 5.1).

In the capitalist latifundia zone, between 60 and 80% of the agricultural land formed part of great capitalist estates, with some of the larger units occupying several thousand or more hectares of plain, along with pastoral and forest land stretching up into the hills and mountains. Moreover, the number of estates exceeded the number of proprietors. Accordingly, some families owned immense stretches of land. In the case of the most important proprietors of land in the Marchesato di Crotone in Calabria the amount of land held locally and elsewhere in Italy was such that in 1950: "Don Luigi Berlingieri possessed, as everybody knows, 22,500 hectares. Alfonso Barracco had only 17,000" (Repaci, cited in Arlacchi, 1983, page 127).

With the high degree of concentration of ownership went a system of agricultural production based on large and medium-sized units. At least one third of the land was still divided into large and medium-sized commercial farms operated directly by the owners with the help of agents and subagents (see Cosentino et al, 1979, pages 183–184). In some cases, large and medium-sized enterprises were rented out to tenant entrepreneurs. In Sicily, for example, *latifondo* enterprises were frequently let out on a *gabella* contract to *gabelloti*.

In these areas, which were continuously faced with the threat of drought on the one hand and malaria on the other, the farms were devoted to extensive cereal cultivation and animal raising. In order to be able to adjust quickly to fluctuations in the prices both of grain and of wool and cheese, investment in equipment, in improvements, and in fixed capital was minimised.

The activity of farming latifondo enterprises was centred on groups of farm buildings or *masserie* sprinkled around the countryside. In the 19th century the land was, as a rule, divided into three fields cultivated as follows: in the first year fallow, in the second wheat, and in the third pasture, except that in some cases a part of the fallow was put down to nitrogenous fodder crops capable of renewing the soil (see Blok, 1974, pages 42–84). What limited continuous and more intensive use of the land was, amongst other things, the labour intensity of growing fodder crops.

At least in some of the internal parts of Sicily the work involved in producing the cereal crop was effected primarily by dividing the fields marked for the cultivation of wheat into small strips and subleasing them on various short-term contracts to peasants, after the completion of the first ploughings in May. As a result, sharecroppers or sharetenants performed the tasks of ploughing, sowing, weeding, harvesting, transfer, and threshing. (An important implication of Blok's study is that the latifondo system should not be identified with the performance of wage labour.) Much of the other work was done by a wage-earning proletariat which included a large class of wretched *braccianti* employed on a casual or daily basis, or by some of the permanent employees of an estate. Among the latter were an overseer and armed guards who supervised agricultural work.

The pastoral areas were used by the frequently large flocks and herds of the owner or tenant and by the livestock owned by the shepherds and cattlemen they employed, or were subleased to other owners of livestock. In either case, grazing land was integrated into the cycle of movement of *transhumanza* in which flocks and herds moved from lowland farms where they spent the winter up on to the mountainous pastures in the summer months.

The workers on lowland farms usually lived not in the areas of plain, but in agro-towns in the surrounding hills of the peasant latifundia zone, and the extra labour employed in peak periods was supplied by people who often lived far away (see Blok, 1969; and 1974, pages 20–22). Throughout latifundia areas permanent settlement on the land was ruled out for a variety of reasons. Clearly malaria discouraged settlement in many low-lying areas. Insecurity and the widely dispersed character of the land worked by an individual peasant family encouraged urban living. The prevailing system of rotation implied short-term contracts and an absence of permanent settlement, as did the owners' or managers' aim of ensuring that production and the size of the working population could be adjusted quickly as market conditions changed.

The strategy of not allowing the peasants to invest, to have any security, or to have a permanent link with the land, enabled the rural population to be kept in a state of complete dependency and total availability. The landlords' aim of guaranteeing peasant dependency was secured not simply by preventing permanent settlement on the land. In the Crotonese, which Arlacchi studied, for example, the major way in which a large supply of obedient and cheap workers was secured was through both the reproduction of a permanent state of overpopulation and the autocracy of the great proprietors: not only did the great barons control the administrative and coercive organs of the state, but the groups of permanent armed employees used to supervise agricultural work were also used to keep the local population in order (see Arlacchi, 1983, pages 123–198).

In the capitalist latifundia zone productivity was comparatively high, but there was little stimulus to agricultural progress or intensive types of development. With adequate returns from directly managed land or with profits or rents maintained at high levels by competition for work and land amongst desperate peasants lacking alternative sources of income, landlords had little incentive to introduce more intensive systems of cultivation. At the same time, peasants who may have wished to invest were unable to save out of their inadequate incomes, had insufficient security, or were simply prevented from doing so.

By the end of the fascist decades, however, the capitalist latifundia had been pushed back by a number of factors. Included were the extension of intensive farming into adjacent coastal areas, the impact of land reclamation, the colonisation and settlement of reclaimed districts on the eve of the Second World War, and the way in which peasants who were being pushed down from the hills by the marginality of the conditions of existence in inland districts were managing to acquire small pieces of land or small holdings.

5.2.2 The peasant latifundia zone

The second of Rossi-Doria's areas was composed of the internal zones of extensive peasant farming devoted to cereal cultivation and wood pasture. It occupied an area of almost 5 million hectares, including much of the internal hill and mountain zones in the South. In the 19th century the majority of the land was owned by the large, medium, small, and very small bourgeois owners who had emerged with the dismantling of the feudal system in the South and the legal transformation of property rights that accompanied it. But by the end of the Second World War a large proportion of the patches or strips of land had fallen, as a consequence of a long and painful process of land acquisition, into peasant ownership.

In the 1940s, agricultural enterprises centred on masserie and employing wage earners were to be found. But usually the work was performed, as has been shown by Blok (1974) in his study of the western interior of Sicily, by subleasing small strips of land to extremely poor sharecroppers and sharetenants. In these cases, larger more compact pieces of land were subdivided into a multiplicity of small units. Moreover, the risks of bad harvests were largely borne by the peasant population, whereas the incomes of the owners, which flowed from the intense competition for land amongst largely landless peasants desperate for the opportunity of working and of earning the minimum necessary for survival, were maximised.

After the Second World War, a good 40% of the land was in fact held in the form of small rented tenancies, known as *affitti*, and of share tenancies on units on which no farmhouse or equipment was provided by the owner, which were known as *coloni*. Other types of arrangement also existed, and the contracts falling under these headings varied markedly: different percentages of the produce were taken by the owners, and the duration of the contracts varied, but generally were very short. As a result, the links between a peasant and the land he or she worked but did not own were very precarious.

Yet very large numbers of day labourers were also to be found, owing in part to the way in which production was organised and in part to the very high ratio of workers to land. In fact, day labourers were estimated as constituting almost 40% of those employed in farming in the peasant latifundia zones, and many peasants were forced by the inadequacy of their own holdings to seek supplementary work as day labourers or on contract.

A typical peasant combined, in varying proportions, a number of functions. On the one hand, a peasant would work for long hours on a number of tiny and widely dispersed plots that were in some cases owned and in other cases rented from the owners of the land or from medium or large tenants. On the other hand, a peasant would work as a wage earner, often in different and widely scattered latifondo or pastoral enterprises. The incomes received would accordingly be made up of what was produced on the land the peasant family owned, of the product of work on plots of land held precariously in the peasant's capacity as a share tenant paying a rent in cash or kind or as a sharecropper handing over a part of the product, and of the earnings from work as a wage earner.

In these areas the agricultural population crowded into large congested and insanitary rural towns perched on the hills and mountains. Immediately surrounding each town was a crown or *corona* of intensively farmed land where vegetables and fruit, vines, olives, and almonds were grown on miniscule plots which in the limit were capable of carrying only a few plants.

Stretching finally beyond the crown was a vast area of poor and badly eroded land devoted, according to the milieu, to cereal growing or grazing, with some woodland in the more mountainous parts.

Originally the corona was composed of the fiefs which feudal lords granted to those who settled in a village or town. On this land, long leases of small holdings were given to peasants and could be inherited. Such grants of land were made in order to attract and retain a permanent and resident group of workers who could be called upon to work on the large estates beyond the village or town. The leasing of microunits to peasant households thus complemented the operation of the large farms.

5.2.3 Intensive agricultural zones

The third broad area was composed of the traditional zones of intensive farming. With the widening of markets and the rising prices of grapes, citrus fruits, olives, and other Mediterranean products after the middle of the 19th century, intensive farming had devloped quite rapidly. Active in this process were merchants or industrialists, who had set up processing plants and had sought out suppliers, medium and small bourgeois elements, and, increasingly, peasants. In the interwar years, farmers in this sector suffered from a lack of access to foreign markets and inadequate commercial organisation. Yet by the 1940s, intensive farming occupied about 3 million hectares of agricultural land situated on parts of the coast and the sides of some of the plains, with larger areas on the Tyrrhenian coasts of Campania and Calabria, on the Adriatic coast of Apulia, and in the provinces of Catania and Siracusa in Sicily.

At one stage, bourgeois owners had predominated, and a good part of the work had been performed by wage earners residing in large towns on the edges of the intensive zones. But by the end of the Second World War, owner cultivators held nearly 60% of the land.

On the eve of the postwar epoch, 44% of the gross agricultural product of the Mezzogiorno was produced in these areas, and nearly one half of the southern population lived in them. Yet owing in the main to the fragmentation of landownership and of operating units, even the areas of intensive farming were, in the words of Rossi-Doria, "a world in crisis, a world incapable of resolving, in spite of the efforts made, the most elementary problems of civil life".

In subsequent years, agricultural activity was intensified in these areas. But the cultivated area was reduced, and some production was relocated, owing to the pressure on land from urbanisation and tourist development along the coast.

5.2.4 Mixed peasant farming zones

Also in the interior of the Mezzogiorno was to be found a fourth type of area, to which Rossi-Doria referred but did not consider in any detail. It was composed of a number of internal zones of mixed farming and mixed tree crop cultivation, and covered about 3 million hectares of land in hill areas.

It was concentrated in particular (1) in Abruzzi; (2) on the hills of Molise, in Sannio, and on the hills of Benevento, Avellino, and Salerno in Campania; (3) in the Conca Cosentina in Calabria, and (4) in the Sassarese, in Sardinia. Some 16% of the southern population lived in these zones. Almost 60% of the land was held by peasant owners, and 58% of those employed in

Table 5.6. The distribution of landed property in three different types of agrarian region, in Calabria, and in the Mezzogiorno in 1947. Sources: INEA (1947), cited in Arlacchi (1983, page 13).

Region	Units		Area	
	number	%	total (ha)	%
Very small units (0–2 ha)				
Cosentino	11 610	80.9	5 138	10.8
Crotonese	8 286	79.7	3 832	3.9
Plain of Gioia Tauro	22 328	87.1	9 312	19.0
Calabria	455 969	87.6	180 245	17.6
Mezzogiorno	3 948 189	85.4	1 869 253	19.3
Small units (2–10 ha)				
Cosentino	2 216	15.4	9 180	19.2
Crotonese	1 606	15.4	6 473	6.5
Plain of Gioia Tauro	2 587	10.1	10 562	21.5
Calabria	52 338	10.1	210 494	20.5
Mezzogiorno	551 655	11.9	2 199 457	22.7
Medium-sized units (10–100 ha)				
Cosentino	462	3.2	11 317	23.7
Crotonese	363	3.5	11 364	11.5
Plain of Gioia Tauro	694	2.7	17 746	36.2
Calabria	11 161	2.1	288 414	28.1
Mezzogiorno	112 239	2.4	2 888 468	29.8
Large property (100–1000 ha)				
Cosentino	64	0.5	15 939	33.4
Crotonese	130	1.3	44 085	44.7
Plain of Gioia Tauro	29	0.1	6 932	14.1
Calabria	1 218	0.2	289 329	28.2
Mezzogiorno	10 486	0.2	2 364 665	24.4
Very large property (>1000 ha)				
Cosentino	4	0.03	6 133	12.9
Crotonese	15	0.1	32 970	33.4
Plain of Gioia Tauro	2	0.01	4 520	9.2
Calabria	30	0.01	57 495	5.6
Mezzogiorno	204	0.01	360 359	3.7
Totals				
Cosentino	14 356	100	47 707	100
Crotonese	10 400	100	98 724	100
Plain of Gioia Tauro	25 640	100	49 072	100
Calabria	520 716	100	1 025 977	100
Mezzogiorno	4 622 773	100	9 682 202	100

agriculture belonged to the category of landowning peasants. The farms themselves were devoted to mixed farming, including cereal growing, the cultivation of tree crops, animal raising, and the production of fodder crops.

As an example one can consider the case of the Cosentino, where more than one half of the cultivated land was divided into units of less than 100 hectares. Moreover, that part of the area owned by bourgeois owners, who were very numerous and were drawn mainly from the urban professional classes, was most often let out on the basis of a peculiar sharecropping contract called a *colonia parziaria appoderata*. As a result, what developed was a society based on self-sufficient and self-regulating mixed peasant farming. It contrasted very sharply with the societies of the latifundia zone in the Crotonese and of the intensive export-oriented agricultural zone of the Plain of Gioia Tauro (see table 5.6, and Arlacchi, 1983, page 9).

5.3 Early postwar development of the national economy and southern policy

The development of the Italian economy after 1945 can be divided into several broad phases: a phase of economic reconstruction in the period 1945-1952 which gave way, successively, to one characterised by the establishment of the preconditions for export-led growth that lasted from 1952-1958, to the 'economic miracle' of 1958-1964, and to a phase characterised by recurrent crises and economic stagnation that opened in 1964. The redirection of southern policy and southern development must be considered in relation to these wider trends, with the first pre-industrialisation stage of regional policy being viewed as an element of the first and second of these phases of national development.

At the end of the Second World War, Italy faced deep economic problems, including a fall in industrial production, devastation of infrastructural and capital equipment, state deficits, and high inflation which was reducing the value of money wages and fixed incomes. In addition, of course, the fascist regime had fallen.

The phase of reconstruction can be divided into two main parts. The first one, which lasted from 1945 until 1948, was a period of political reconstruction coinciding with governments based on the collaboration of all the political forces which came out of the resistance movement. During this period the main priorities were connected not with the southern question but with the economic and political reconstruction of the country as a whole. Moreover, with the transformation of the Italian Communist Party (PCI) from a party of opposition to the system to a party of opposition within the system, what all the main political movements sought was a reconstruction of a market economy and of the social relations of capitalist production on the one hand, and the establishment of a bourgeois democratic state on the other (Salvati, 1972, page 4).

In 1947, with the increasing commitment of the United States of America to European recovery and the development of the Marshall Plan, together with the opening of the Cold War, the communists and socialists were expelled from the government. Shortly afterwards, the unified trade union confederation established in June 1944 was split by the defection, aided financially by the United States of America, of Catholic and Social Democratic elements. What resulted were three confederations between which there was intense ideological conflict and competition for working-class support that was itself often damaging to working-class interests: the Confederazione Generale Italiana del Lavoro (CGIL) associated with the PCI and the PSI; the Confederazione Italiana dei Sindacati Lavoratori (CISL) sponsored by the Christian Democratic Party (DC) and the Church; and the Unione Italiana del Lavoro (UIL) associated with many minor political currents, including in particular the Social Democratic Party (PSDI) (formed after the secession of the reformist wing of the PSI in January 1947) and the Republican Party (PRI). In 1948, the DC was confirmed in power in an election bitterly fought on the theme of the 'choice of civilisations' (see Lange and Vannicelli, 1982, pages 100 – 109).

The election initiated a new period which has been characterised as one of repressive development. It lasted until 1963. It was characterised by repression of the political and economic strength of the trade union movement and by working-class weakness (see Salvati, 1972, page 4). It also coincided with governments of the centre.

It was at this stage that the main lines for the subsequent development of the economy were laid down. On the one hand, it was decided to orientate the economy towards West European markets. Underlying this decision was the need to participate in international trade which was itself implied by two factors. One was the energy dependence of the Italian economy and the need to obtain essential raw materials. The second, which was more important, was the need to find outlets in a situation in which domestic demand was expected to be weak. On the other hand, the conservative coalition ruling the country opted for a classical liberal economic strategy involving tight credit, deflation, and high unemployment as well as openness to international competition. Undoubtedly this strategy helped create preconditions which explain in part the particular characteristics and tempo of Italian economic development in the years up to the end of the 'economic miracle'. But it also contributed to the accentuation of imbalances which were to play an important role in the subsequent crisis of Italy's economy and society.

By this stage in Italian history a new body of thought about the problems of the South called the '*nuovo meridionalismo*' had emerged. It was argued by those belonging to this new tradition that the development of the South depended upon a process of southern industrialisation, and that industrial development could be achieved not through the free play of market forces but only through systematic government intervention. What was envisaged was intervention occurring within the framework of the prevailing political and economic system with the aim of making it profitable for private capitals to invest in the South. In this way, it was argued, industrial development could be stimulated. In other words, it was believed that southern development could be promoted by government encouragement and assistance aimed at overcoming the initial disadvantages of locating private industry in the South. Furthermore, it was claimed by writers belonging to this tradition that the development of the South was necessary for and in the interests of the expansion of the national economy (Del Monte and Giannola, 1978, pages 121).

Some limited measures intended to encourage southern industrialisation were in fact introduced in 1947, 1948, and 1950. But the interventionist strategy proposed by the new southernist writers was not strictly compatible with the liberal economic policies adopted by the state. In any case, the main problem was still seen to be the reconstruction and development of northern industry, with a view to preparing it for international competition. Indeed southern industrialisation was actually opposed by northern industrialists who believed that it would result in a wasteful duplication of investments and would lead to the emergence of unwanted southern competition. Consequently, the first phase of southern policy was restricted to a preindustrialisation programme with resources directed towards agricultural development and a programme of public works.

The first phase of southern policy was initiated in 1950 with the passing of the land reform laws and the establishment of the Cassa per il Mezzogiorno. (The Cassa was originally established to undertake a programme of extraordinary public works which were to be coordinated with other interventions and were designed to promote land reclamation and improvement schemes and to provide economic and social infrastructure mainly in the South.) One of the reasons for introducing these two measures was the need to establish instruments and to formulate precise objectives for the use of international loans granted to Italy. The measures were largely designed, however, to defuse some of the social tensions stemming from the uneven development of the Italian economy and to contribute to the modernisation of southern agriculture. It was hoped that incomes in the South would be raised, providing an outlet for consumer goods produced by northern industries, and that the development of tourism, which was expected to play an important part in bringing the national balance of payments into equilibrium, would be encouraged.

At least in the short term, the measures introduced at this stage actually complemented some of the policies pursued at a national level. Indeed, southern policy helped lay the foundations for a process of national expansion that was to be concentrated in the northern regions and that was to lead to a marked increase in the degree of regional inequality (see figure 4.3).

From the early 1950s, the Italian economy expanded steadily through one economic cycle. In the next, it grew very rapidly on account of the growth of export and export-related industries located mainly in the industrial triangle in the Northwest.

The first cycle, which lasted from 1952 until 1958, was one of moderate growth in which the infrastructural foundations for export-led growth were laid and the modern industries that were to spearhead this process were strengthened. Industrial employment did not increase very rapidly, and the exodus from the countryside was comparatively slow at the national level, although some rural areas in the South experienced rapid depopulation. The main increases in employment occurred in construction and services. But these sectors frequently provided only precarious employment. As a result, an overall equilibrium of underemployment was preserved (see table 9.3).

The next cycle broadly corresponded with the 'economic miracle', and was characterised by rapid rates of growth of export and export-related industries and by marked increases in the international integration of the Italian economy. In this period, total employment started to fall, mainly because of the agricultural exodus. Industrial employment did not increase very rapidly, however, largely because of the rationalisation of traditional industries, particularly in the South (see table 9.3). The fall in total employment was accompanied by a fall in the size of the active population, and unemployment declined to reach its lowest postwar level in 1963.

These changes in labour market conditions prepared the ground for an increase in money wages which exceeded the rate of productivity growth. In conjunction with the effects of other structural imbalances associated with the process of export-led growth, the increase in the share of wages in value added contributed in turn to an earlier opening in Italy than in other advanced capitalist countries of a new phase of economic development, characterised by recurrent financial crises and protracted economic stagnation (Graziani, 1972, pages 13-15).

5.4 Land reform
During and after the Second World War, two major social movements developed in the Italian countryside. Just as had occurred after the First World War, returning veterans made a concerted attempt to break the hold of the latifondo system and to establish themselves as self-sufficient peasant proprietors. Motivated by deeply-rooted peasant aspirations for land, and confronted with the deterioration of living and working conditions in the South and the political crisis in the country, the peasant farmers and *braccianti* of latifondo zones came together in a militant movement for the occupation of uncultivated land. (The braccianti were landless agricultural labourers who were not fixed-wage earners but were hired by the day according to the work to be done.) At the same time, a movement of sharecroppers seeking an immediate improvement in the division of the product and in other clauses in sharecropping agreements emerged (Rossi-Doria, 1972a, pages 210-212).

The course pursued by the first of these movements led to a series of violent political struggles and occupations of uncultivated land in latifundia zones in the South. The conflicts themselves first broke out in 1943, when the political repression of fascism collapsed and the autocratic rule of the large southern landlords was undermined. But with continuing support from the Italian Communist Party the struggles of the southern peasantry were intensified after the 1948 elections (see Ginsborg, 1984).

At first the government responded by reforming land tenure contracts and by passing special decrees distributing some of the occupied land to participants in the land occupation movement. In the new Italian constitution of 1947 a transformation of large estates was stipulated. But only in 1950 and after some hesitation was a land reform introduced.

In the face of the communist-supported invasions of land, many estate owners guessed that an agrarian reform involving expropriation was very likely. Accordingly, virtually all *latifondisti* divided much of the property they owned among husbands and wives as well as born and unborn children and grandchildren, and sold shares to the more prosperous sections of peasant society. Only some of these transfers were countered by the provisions included in the land reform of 1950 that all transfers of land after 1 January 1948, when the new Italian constitution came into effect, would lack validity (see Blok, 1974, pages 76–78).

The land reform laws were designed in part to reduce social tensions in the countryside by forming a class of small peasant proprietors with an attachment to the land and an anticommunist ideology. Indeed, political considerations were major factors in determining the shape of the reform and its methods of implementation. In many areas, technical considerations and, in particular, the lack of skills and knowledge of agricultural principles amongst the braccianti, whose only experience was of tilling the soil and caring for cattle and sheep, led agricultural specialists to consider that cooperative enterprises would have had the best prospects of success. Yet priority was given to small peasant proprietorship, thought by the De Gasperi government to be conducive to the development of a conservative and Christian Democratic world view.

But the new laws also reflected a recognition of the growing incompatibility between the interests of the southern landed bourgeoisie and the exigencies of economic development. The measures pursued by the government were accordingly also designed to replace the large landed bourgeoisie in the South, although its members were generously compensated and were given the opportunity either of becoming capitalist farmers or of transferring their capital into urban construction and real-estate speculation (Pinnarò and Pugliese, 1979, page 497). It was intended in fact that the reform should facilitate the modernisation and intensification of agriculture in extensively cultivated zones located predominantly in the South. The land reform was thus mainly applied to areas of extensive farming in the capitalist and peasant latifundia zones. The reform itself was based on three laws passed in 1950: the Sila Law, the Stralcio Law, and the Sicilian Law. These laws resulted in the delimitation of nine special regions, in each of which an *Ente Riforma* was made responsible for the implementation of the reform (see figure 5.2). The tasks of the reform agencies included the expropriation of land, investment in rural housing and infrastructure, the creation of individually tenanted peasant farms, and the provision of technical, economic, and financial assistance to new peasant farmers.

The laws themselves were designed to protect capitalist farms and to cull most land from extensively cultivated estates. The criteria governing the

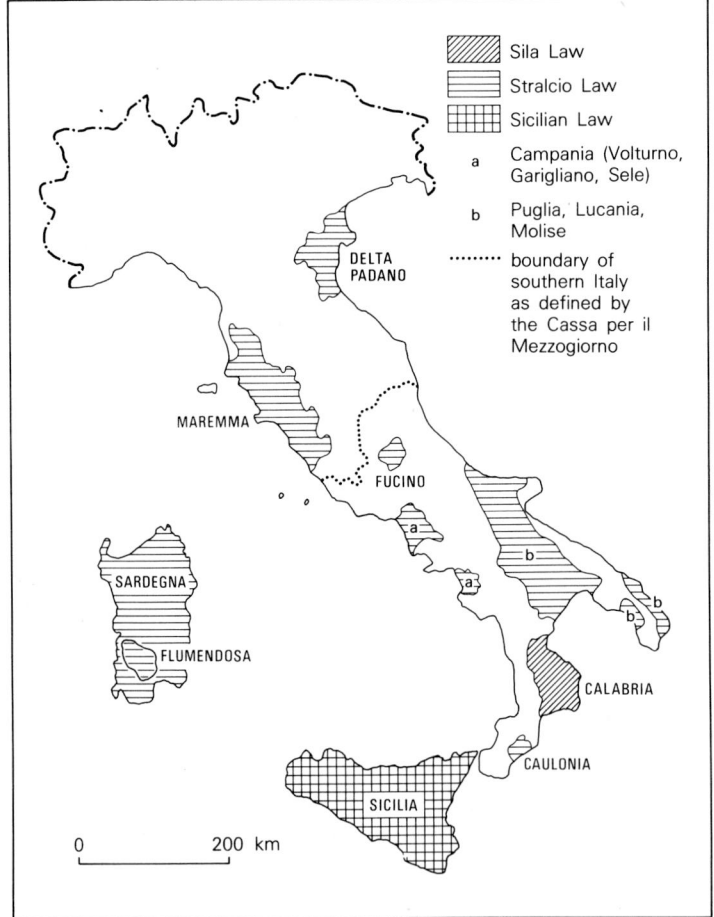

Figure 5.2. Areas in which the land reform was applied. Sources: elaborated from Clough (1965, page 409) and King (1973, page 48).

expropriation of land can be illustrated by the provisions of the Stralcio Law. In this case the amount of land to be expropriated was to be proportional to the total area owned, measured by its taxable income, and inversely proportional to the degree of intensity with which it was farmed, measured by the average assessed income per hectare. A provision for the residual third enabled landowners to retain part of the portion that could be expropriated, provided that they agreed to develop it in accordance with a plan prearranged with the reform agency. In addition, the law excluded some 'model farms' and certain livestock farms from expropriation. The landowners were paid compensation on the basis of the taxable value of the expropriated land in 1947 (King, 1973, page 47).

Compensation was quite generous; in Sicily, for example, under the provisions of the Sicilian Law, compensation to large landowners amounted in effect to an average of 40% of the market value of the expropriated land (Blok, 1974, page 78).

The reform resulted in the expropriation and acquisition of more than 750 000 hectares of land, of which more than 450 000 hectares were situated in the Mezzogiorno (see figure 5.2). The land in the South was taken from the very largest estates, and was used to create 32 000 '*poderi*' (small farms of 4-10 hectares, usually with a farmhouse on the holding), more than 33 000 '*quoti*' (small plots of 1-2 hectares designed to supplement incomes from other sources), and almost 17 000 agricultural lots, almost all located in Sicily and intended to supplement the incomes of landholding peasants (Cosentino et al, 1979, pages 208-209).

5.5 The policy of extraordinary intervention, 1950-1957

Also in 1950, Law 646 was passed. Under this law two bodies were created: a Committee of Ministers for the South (Comitato dei Ministri per il Mezzogiorno), and the Cassa per Opere Straordinarie di Pubblico Interesse nell' Italia Meridionale (usually abbreviated to Cassa per il Mezzogiorno). The Committee of Ministers was required to do two things. One was to prepare a programme of organic complexes of extraordinary projects, designed to promote economic and social development mainly in southern Italy. The second was to coordinate the activities of the extraordinary and ordinary public administrations. The Cassa, on the other hand, was required to frame the programmes, and to finance and implement the projects included in the plan adopted by the Committee of Ministers. But it was also enabled to entrust the execution of projects to appropriate entities.

The immediate intention of those who formulated the law was twofold. First, it was designed to provide, beyond the normal flow of public expenditure through the ordinary central and local administrations, a stable additional supply of funds for a programme of public works. Second, the preparation and execution of this programme were to be entrusted to new agencies that were more autonomous and more flexible than the ordinary public administration.

The Cassa was initially allocated 1000 milliard lire for a ten-year period, of which 77% was to be devoted to land reclamation and improvement, 11.5% to water supply and drainage, 9% to roads, and 2.5% to the development of tourism. The plan was subsequently extended to cover a twelve-year period, and the allocation of funds was duly increased to 1280 milliard lire, but almost 70% was still to be absorbed by agriculture (Podbielski, 1978, page 44).

The declared aim of the policy of extraordinary intervention was to create favourable conditions for the subsequent expansion of private-sector activities in the South. The investments made in the region were not, therefore, part of a development plan with specific targets and with appropriate instruments and adequate resources to attain these specified ends. The idea was instead that the Cassa's investment programme would (1) increase income and employment in the South, creating a market that could be supplied initially by northern industries, and (2) provide social overhead capital that would lay the basis for the subsequent expansion of private industrial activities in the South.

At first the infrastructural investments were mainly allocated to agricultural development and to projects connected with the land reform. Investments also occurred in the field of transport. The most striking involved the development of a motorway system linking the South with the North. [In Italy, however, roads were constructed and administered not by the extraordinary administration but, in the case of most non-southern motorways, by concessionary companies and, in the case of other roads, by the Azienda Nazionale Strade Statali (ANAS) and by provincial and communal organisations.]

5.6 The process of agricultural change

The activities of the reform agencies and related infrastructural programmes led to marked changes in the pattern of landholding and to striking changes in the products and productivity of agriculture in the reform districts. As a result, very pronounced changes occurred in the rural landscape (Franklin, 1961, pages 327–330).

One of the main effects of the reform was to increase the proportion of land held by a small peasant class and to reduce the proportion belonging to very large owners. These changes in the ownership of land did not stem only from the activity of land expropriation or acquisition and the assignment of land to peasant farmers. About 1 million hectares of land was bought with state help under provisions for the formation of small holdings. More importantly, a lot of land was transferred privately as a result of the impact of state action and the changing economic and political climate on the land market, and the increased willingness of landowners to sell.

The second major consequence of the land reform and associated interventions was the striking increase in output and in output per hectare in the southern reform districts located in the more fertile parts of the region, and especially in the irrigated areas of plain. Until the reform the productive potential of this land had been minimally exploited.

After stagnating in the early 1950s, the real agricultural output of the Mezzogiorno increased. In 1955–1959 it rose at 6% per year and in 1960–1967 at 5% per year compared with rates of 4% per year in the country as a whole. With growth went an increase in regional specialisation and in southern agricultural exports. In 1968–1973, on the other hand, output grew at only 1% per year in the South and in Italy (see also the data presented, according to a different periodisation, in table 5.7). Despite this growth in the South, the resulting levels of output per unit of land remained comparatively low. In 1973, each person working in farming in the South produced scarcely 70% of what was being produced in the rest of the country. The gap in levels of productivity was consequently virtually the same as the one that had prevailed in the early 1950s (see Del Monte and Giannola, 1978, pages 126–127; Cosentino et al, 1979, pages 180–182).

The impact of the reform and of other state policies was, however, very uneven geographically and economically. In conjunction with the functioning of market mechanisms they gave rise to a process of agricultural expansion that created a pronounced economic and geographical dualism within southern agriculture (Cosentino et al, 1979, pages 182–183; Mottura, 1980, pages 389–403; Mottura and Pugliese, 1980, pages 189–194). The process of expansion led to the development both of capitalist farms and of small peasant farms, with a limited presence of intermediate agricultural units combining features of both types of enterprise. In other words, what emerged was a structural dualism with two distinct sectors involving different forms of organisation of production, different levels of productivity, different perspectives on consolidation, and, finally, different roles in relation to the overall process of capitalist development (Mottura and Pugliese, 1980, page 171). Expansion also resulted in a related differentiation between the central areas of plain dominated by capitalist enterprises and the peripheral internal hill and mountain zones dominated by peasant farming.

The land reform contributed to this outcome partly by providing larger landowners with the stimulus and resources to establish economically sound farms. Medium and large capitalist farms were developed or established both on land that had not been expropriated and on the nonexpropriated parts of former estates. These enterprises were usually situated on more fertile soils in the lowland areas formerly dominated by large capitalist estates. The individuals setting them up had frequently amassed substantial investment funds in the form of compensation for expropriated land and from land sales on the open market. As a result, they were able to take advantage of the favourable conditions for agricultural expansion created by public intervention and by the work of the Cassa in particular, whose reclamation and irrigation schemes were concentrated in low-lying zones.

In these areas the investments carried out by the reform agencies and by the Cassa encouraged a marked intensification of agricultural activity and an expansion of production not only on capitalist farms but also on the peasant holdings created by the reform. The stimulus given to investment was, however, less pronounced in the case of peasant enterprises.

Of course, state agricultural spending was geared not only to the financing of large-scale reclamation and irrigation and other infrastructural schemes, but also to the sustenance of small landholdings and the small family farm. The peasant population was aided technically and financially. But what was created and sustained were peasant farms without a capacity for long-term survival and growth, and peasant farmers who were dependent on public funding controlled by clientelistic organisations. The farms were too small, were often situated on the poorest-quality land, and were not adequately supported by the development of new crops, equipment, marketing organisations, and associated food-processing industries.

In the short term, small family farms provided employment. But after 1958, as a result of the growing demand for industrial workers in the boom, and in 1964-1974, as a result of a more intense restructuring and rationalisation of the agricultural sector, the rural exodus accelerated. At the same time many small farms were abandoned, were turned into part-time farms whose peasant owners worked on a casual basis on larger farms or in forestry, construction, industry, or other types of activity, or were kept simply as a source of domestic consumption and as a means of obtaining different types of subsidy or aid.

According to official sources, in 1970 nearly 70% of peasant farms generated less than two hundred days of work per year, and consequently could not fully employ even one person, and nearly one third required less than fifty days of work per year. In lowland areas in the South only 50% of farms directly managed by a farmer or run on sharecropping lines actually had a full-time farmer, and more than 40% registered work on their own farms as a secondary occupation. In the hill and mountain zones about 60% of farms had a full-time farmer. But in contrast to the areas of plain, where jobs could be found on larger mainly capitalist farms, most of those who had a second or a first job off the farm worked in nonagricultural activities such as building and public works, and forestry and reafforestation, or were temporary emigrants. The number of family members working on the farms declined steadily. Indeed, amongst this group the problems of underemployment and dependence on off-farm work was even greater. In rural and specifically peasant farming households the proportion of family income from farming fell, whereas income from off-farm employment or, especially in the hill and mountain zones, from state relief payments assumed a more important role. Nevertheless, the peasant farming sector continued to be in many respects dominant. In 1970 it occupied about 60% of agricultural land in the South and accounted for more than 80%

of the work (Cosentino et al, 1979, pages 188-192; Mottura, 1980, pages 395-396).

In these predominantly peasant farming areas, which had formerly been part of the peasant latifundia and traditional mixed farming districts, agricultural production was not significantly improved nor was stable employment provided. The activities of the land reform agencies and intervention by the ordinary and extraordinary public administrations were more concerned with short-term income maintenance and other welfare considerations. In 1961, on the 73.2% of the agricultural and forest land of the South included in this type of area, only 53% of agricultural workers were employed, and only 45% of the region's net agricultural and forest output was produced (Pugliese, 1980, page 60).

After 1957 the actions of the Cassa were made more selective and differentiated, and the areas of high hills and mountains ceased to be ones in which major productive investments could occur. More importantly, with the law of renewal of the Cassa in 1965, it was decided that the Cassa's intervention should be confined to reclamation and irrigation of districts where the potential for capitalist agrarian development was greatest. At the same time, finance for land acquisition and improvement was to be allocated on the basis of the size of farm property. The result was that most of the territory of the South and almost all its poor districts were removed from the sphere of Cassa activity, and resources were channelled towards the capitalist sector. In these excluded areas the only actions in support of farming were henceforth to be those of the ordinary administration.

But with rapid industrial development and the increasing integration of Italy into the European and world economy, and with less social tension in the countryside, state intervention in farming was in general reorientated. Increasingly, the concern was with rationalising and improving the competitiveness of Italian agriculture.

Under the First Green Plan of 1961-1965, the resources available for agricultural development were increased. At that stage, state aid was still given for the formation and improvement of family farms. But state support, which was increasingly redirected to aid mechanisation, was only successful in the cases of areas of plain on the one hand, and of capitalist enterprises on the other, where costs fell and employment contracted. Under the Second Green Plan of 1966-1970, welfare considerations were less important, as were general programmes of public works. The authors of the plan explicitly developed the principles of (1) a selective distribution of aid to large and medium-sized enterprises, with a view to reducing their production costs through mechanisation, and (2) of a geographical concentration of aid on areas capable of rapid improvements in labour productivity.

National price-support policies and the agricultural policy of the European Economic Community (EEC) introduced from 1962 onwards generally operated in the same direction (see Mottura and Pugliese, 1980, pages 189-191). The agricultural policy envisaged in the Treaty of Rome of March 1957 was intended to modernise and increase the productivity of farming, to ensure an adequate standard of living for those who remained in farming, to stabilise agricultural markets, and to guarantee reasonably priced supplies to consumers. The financial instrument of the policy introduced after 1962 was the Agricultural Guidance and Guarantee Fund (FEOGA). It was divided into two sections: a guarantee section used to finance price-support policies, and a guidance section used to encourage the modernisation of agricultural structures. Priority, however, was given to the price-support policy. In the periods between 1965-1966 and 1968-1969 alone, spending in the guarantees section of the FEOGA grew tenfold from $240 million to $2600 million, whereas the expenses of the guidance section rose only from $80 million to $285 million (Pugliese, 1980, page 51).

The agricultural guarantee fund has been used, however, mainly to support the prices of continental products, such as cereals, milk and dairy products, and meat, and not of Mediterranean products. In 1962-1972, only 2.2% of the guarantee fund was allocated to fruit and vegetables, which are an important sector of southern agricultural production, and only 0.7% to wine (Podbielski, 1978, page 210). There are several reasons for the selectivity of support. One is that the EEC as a whole is dependent on imports of many of the products involved. A second lies in the existence of trading agreements with other Mediterranean countries under which industrial exports from EEC economies are matched by imports of agricultural products. But of most importance are reasons relating to the ways in which decisions are made in the EEC and the strength and method of representation of class interests.

At the same time, within any product category, policies of price support are most beneficial to large efficient farmers. As the unit costs of large capitalist farmers are much lower than those of middle-sized or poor peasants, and as size and levels of output of the two types of enterprise differ, capitalist farmers gain most, earning substantial excess profits. Often, excess profits are translated into high rents and capitalised in high values of land forcing up the costs of agricultural production. But insofar as high profits result also in high levels of investment, the costs of capitalist farmers are pushed down still further, and output is increased. By contrast, small peasant farmers are barely able to make ends meet. A system of price support only helps them by maintaining income levels and enabling them to survive for a while in farming. The reason why lies, amongst other things, in the fact that with the concentration of resources in the hands of rich farmers, productivity differentials are widened sharply, reducing the capacity of small farmers to compete.

What appears to have happened is that policies of price support have contributed in an indirect way to a controlled reduction in agricultural employment, and to the management of social consensus through the maintenance of barely adequate standards of living on farms and in areas not suitable for capitalist development. The problem is that policies of that kind are increasingly costly and result in particular in an overproduction of many of the supported products [see for example the discussion of the Mansholt Memorandum of 1968 in Mottura and Pugliese (1980, page 191) and Pugliese (1980, pages 50-64)]. The interests ranged against reforms involving the replacement of price support by direct payment to enterprises or limitations on payments to particular enterprises are, however, very powerful.

What I have just argued is that a sectoral and geographical dualism in southern farming was developed and deepened. In short, market mechanisms mediated by state and EEC intervention were more beneficial to the owners of large capitalist farms than to the peasant sector, which was marginalised. At the same time, more help was given to farming in coastal and low-lying internal zones than to that in internal hill and mountain zones. Overall, very little was done in particular to create the conditions necessary for the development of peasant farming in difficult areas.

Many small farms were finally abandoned, not only in the South but also in the rest of the country. In 1961-1971, the number of agricultural enterprises in Italy decreased by 686000, with the largest fall occurring amongst enterprises occupying less than 10 hectares of land. At the same time, the cultivated area was reduced by 1507500 hectares (Mottura and Pugliese, 1980, page 89). But the abandonment of land usually occurred in a chaotic and unplanned way. In the South, in particular, rigidities in the land market and technical problems which acted as an obstacle to the reorganisation of agricultural landholding and production did not give rise to effective action. Small and fragmented holdings were simply farmed more extensively, and peasant producers remained underemployed, sought supplementary jobs, emigrated temporarily, or relied on state transfers. Yet with a consequently underexploited agricultural potential, the Italian economy came to be burdened with an increasingly large balance of payments deficit in the agricultural sector. In 1958, it had a payments surplus of 35 European units of account (ECU). By 1981, it had a deficit of 4308 ECU (Mesplier, 1983, pages 80-81).

These changes in the structure of southern agriculture had important implications for the composition, location, and level of employment (see Cosentino et al, 1979, pages 197-207; and figure 5.3). The number of jobs in agriculture fell sharply, especially in the internal hill and mountain areas, but at a lower average annual rate than in the rest of the country (see tables 5.7 and 9.3). In 1951-1974, the number of independent workers, that is, peasants, sharecroppers, and sharetenants, fell by 1721500 or by 68.8%, whereas the number of dependent workers, that is, day labourers and other wage earners, fell by 326500 or by 27.8% (see figure 5.3). (One must always remember, however, that the second category included workers with very precarious jobs, and that wage earners could also work as peasant farmers on small owned plots.)

At first the number of dependent workers fell sharply as a result of the reorganisation of the latifondo system and the reform of landholding, on the one hand, and the recruitment of braccianti to work on public works and other building projects, on the other. By contrast, independent employment fell at only 0.7% per year.

After 1954, and especially in 1958–1964, agricultural employment fell more rapidly. What declined was employment in the peasant sector, particularly in the areas of extensive peasant farming and of traditional mixed farming. In the early 1960s, with a crisis of peasant farming deepening and also affecting the peasant sector in the areas of plain, independent employment fell even more quickly, averaging 12.8% per year in 1960–1963. It fell largely because, as industrial employment expanded in the more developed parts of Europe and northern Italy, peasants chose temporary emigration as the only way in which a peasant family could improve its position. At first it was hoped that enough could be earned in a few years to enlarge the family holding. These hopes were sadly ill-founded because earnings were not high enough to buy land and invest in improvements as land costs were pushed up, and because, in any case, the size of holding necessary for survival increased. So by the early 1960s, savings were used instead to buy or build housing or to set up service or artisan enterprises in the more rapidly growing towns of the region. In this way a stimulus was given to employment in the construction industry.

Yet at the same time, in 1957–1962, dependent employment increased (see figure 5.3). Indeed, at least in the areas of plain and nearby, some of the

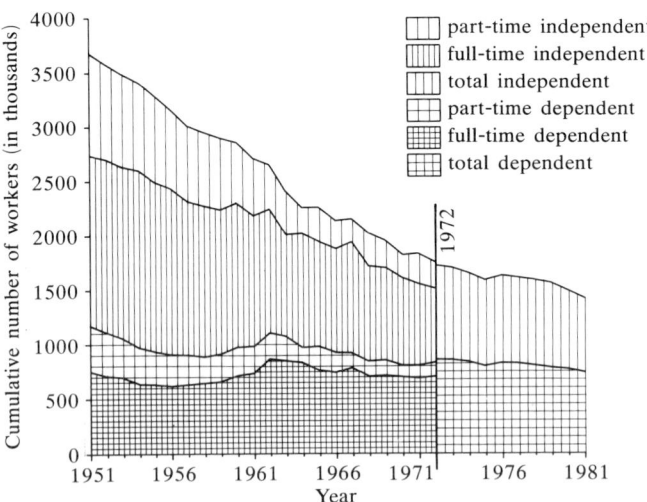

Figure 5.3. The changing class composition of southern agricultural employment, 1951–1981. Sources: elaborated from data in ISTAT (1973, pages 37–42; 1982, page 18).

new wage earners may well have been people who had formerly been classed as peasants but who now depended more on off-farm agricultural work. The reasons lay, respectively, in, first, the intensification of farming and the agrarian expansion whose roots lay in the investments in reclamation and irrigation and the improvements on capitalist farms, and second, the growing integration of capitalist and peasant farms.

After 1964, agricultural employment fell more slowly. The number of independent workers fell less rapidly owing to the greater difficulty in finding extraagricultural work and the growing weight of older men and women in peasant farming. Indeed, employment declined mainly as older agricultural workers dropped out of the active population without being replaced by younger farmers.

But after 1962, dependent employment also fell, and employment declined in the newly irrigated areas of plain and along the coast, as well as in the hills and mountains. At that stage, the development of capitalist farms was being redirected with an increased emphasis on mechanisation and capital deepening, supported by the state via subsidised prices, grants, and low-interest loans, instead of job-increasing investment and capital widening. Consequently, the demand for labour fell. Often the periods of demand for manual workers were shortened, with the result that the irregularity of the work offered increased. Moreover, much of the transformed work could be performed by unskilled workers. The demand for temporary labour was thus increased. The position of agricultural trade unions was consequently weakened, and in the face of inadequate incomes many agricultural labourers sought other jobs. (Where the unions did, however, have some success was in pressing for a guaranteed income in the form of welfare payments for farm workers or supplementary occupations.)

At the same time, wage work was taken on by members of peasant households. Of course the possibility of such a strategy was dependent on an ability to organise or reorganise work on their own holdings in such a way that the amount of work required was small when paid work on larger farms was on offer. Also, the fact that peasant households were able to support themselves, at least in part, played an important part in keeping down costs and ensuring the availability of temporary workers (see Pugliese, 1985, pages 131-138).

As a result, in short, of the interrelated processes of agricultural change, industrialisation, and migration, agricultural employment contracted and the class composition of rural areas was profoundly altered. What emerged was a reduced and spatially differentiated agricultural working population composed of individuals with extremely complex class locations and class interests: simultaneously and in different degrees, people working in farming were members of an agricultural working class, peasant or own-account farmers, and clients of the welfare state (see Pugliese, 1985, pages 123-137).

5.7 Industry in the South in the 1950s

The process of agricultural expansion and the policy of extraordinary intervention did contribute to an increase in output and income in the South. Between 1951 and 1958, output in the South rose at an average annual rate of 4.3% compared with 5.0% in Italy as a whole (table 5.7). But the expansion of local demand did not stimulate a strong process of local industrialisation.

In these years, southern industrial production did in fact grow at 7.5% per year compared with 7.6% nationally, and industrial employment increased at 3.8% per year compared with 2.9% in the country as a whole. But the underlying reasons included a major expansion in the South of the low-productivity construction industry, whose growth was stimulated by increased investment in infrastructural projects, by uncontrolled land and property speculation in urban areas, and by rapid urbanisation. Moreover, the growth of southern manufacturing industry was largely a result of the development of small firms in traditional industries that were closely connected with the local market and used extremely labour-intensive techniques. As a result, hardly any modernisation of the southern production system occurred at a time when the structure of northern manufacturing industry was being strengthened by a stronger concentration of resources on modern equipment-good industries and by improvements in labour productivity in traditional consumption-good sectors.

Table 5.7. Average annual percentage rates of growth of output and employment in Italy, 1951–1971. Sources: elaborated from ISTAT (1973, pages 7–12, 19–42; 1975, pages 15–18, 29–30).

	North-west	North-east	Centre	South	Italy
1951–1958					
Gross domestic product (at factor cost in 1963 prices)					
Agriculture	2.72	4.04	3.80	2.12	2.98
Industry	7.73	7.98	6.77	7.46	7.57
manufacturing[a]	(5.92)	(7.49)	(5.65)	(5.98)	(6.15)
construction[a]	(17.23)	(12.07)	(13.32)	(14.04)	(14.40)
Services	4.46	5.01	4.87	4.87	4.75
Public administration	2.23	2.58	3.52	2.94	2.89
Total	5.44	5.31	4.94	4.28	5.02
Employment					
Agriculture	−1.74	−4.06	−2.74	−3.09	−3.01
Industry	2.02	3.17	3.41	3.78	2.88
manufacturing	1.51	2.77	3.12	2.41	2.17
construction	5.56	4.61	4.89	7.25	5.80
Services	3.00	3.21	2.85	3.22	3.07
Public administration	1.17	0.99	3.24	1.80	1.89
Total	1.37	−0.03	0.80	−0.02	0.53

In fact, the widening of the southern market in the 1950s was probably more helpful to northern than to southern firms. The reason why was that many of the capital goods used in agriculture and many of the consumption goods purchased by the local population were supplied by firms based in the North. It has been shown, for example, that the multiplier effects of expenditures on infrastructural equipment were low owing to high

Table 5.7. (continued)

	North-west	North-east	Centre	South	Italy
1958–1964					
Gross domestic product (at factor cost in 1963 prices)					
Agriculture	0.31	3.88	0.76	2.19	1.99
Industry	8.32	8.98	6.63	7.03	7.96
manufacturing[a]	(11.26)	(12.36)	(10.85)	(11.48)	(11.42)
construction[a]	(14.19)	(15.97)	(9.49)	(11.09)	(12.88)
Services	5.83	5.49	6.19	6.37	5.97
Public administration	2.83	3.97	3.59	3.56	3.50
Total	6.30	6.16	5.13	5.05	5.74
Employment					
Agriculture	−6.66	−5.28	−7.34	−4.36	−5.50
Industry	2.12	2.99	1.51	1.60	2.06
manufacturing	1.69	3.09	1.19	−0.59	1.44
construction	4.11	3.30	2.83	5.10	4.07
Services	0.71	0.61	1.07	0.54	0.72
Public administration	2.76	4.12	3.18	3.37	3.34
Total	0.26	−0.18	−1.06	−1.01	−0.48
1964–1971					
Gross domestic product (at factor cost in 1963 prices)					
Agriculture	0.43	0.33	1.07	4.43	2.08
Industry	5.16	6.48	6.56	6.54	5.87
manufacturing[a]	(9.20)	(11.15)	(10.61)	(11.30)	(10.05)
construction[a]	(5.67)	(9.42)	(9.93)	(9.92)	(8.44)
Services	5.33	5.61	5.94	5.64	5.59
Public administration	3.67	2.41	2.21	3.03	2.82
Total	4.82	4.74	5.06	5.23	4.95
Employment					
Agriculture	−6.14	−5.30	−5.43	−2.89	−4.30
Industry	0.18	0.52	0.30	0.28	0.29
manufacturing	0.84	1.08	0.94	0.83	0.90
construction	−3.46	−1.40	−1.60	−0.43	−1.55
Services	0.80	1.42	1.88	1.10	1.23
Public administration	2.90	1.52	1.03	2.48	2.00
Total	−0.17	−0.46	−0.27	−0.40	−0.32

[a] In current prices.

leakages in the form of imports from the North and from abroad (Allen and MacLennan, 1970, page 50). Of course, increased demand for northern products was one of the objectives of the policy. But that goal was clearly in conflict with the other objective of laying the foundations for successful economic growth in the South.

Indeed, it has also been argued that, in the absence of measures designed to promote efficient local enterprises, the development in the 1950s of new transport facilities and the reduction in transport costs may, on balance, have been damaging to the southern economy. The subsequent integration of the two economies, the formation of a single national market, and the loss of natural protection in the South simply facilitated the penetration of southern markets by northern firms and undermined the chances of autonomous expansion in the Mezzogiorno. Many local firms did in fact collapse when they were eventually exposed to northern competition. Furthermore, the leading role in the process of industrial development that occurred in the South in the 1960s and early 1970s was played, not by local, but by externally controlled firms.

5.8 The industrial reserve army mechanism and the process of emigration

Within southern farming, then, a large group of underemployed workers were to be found. As a result, a potential supply of labour, or what Marx called a latent relative surplus population, existed in the southern countryside (see Holland, 1976, pages 36–47). In the 1950s and 1960s the development of capitalist farming and internal processes of restructuring were associated with a fall in the demand for labour, and repulsion effects that pushed workers out of farming. But the movement of workers into other sectors of the economy also depended, at least in part, on the extra-agricultural demand for labour and the capacity of those sectors to attract workers away from farming.

In the Mezzogiorno the development of marginal agricultural enterprises along with small-scale industry and commerce played a part in the regulation of the labour market. On the one hand, labour was released as and when it was needed. On the other hand, it was retained, and at least some excess labour was reabsorbed as and when demand in other sectors fell.

In addition, the rapid growth of employment in construction was accompanied by the enlargement of that special group of workers whose origin was agricultural, but whose occupation was in great part industrial, and which Marx called the 'light infantry of capital' or 'normal labour'. In the 1950s, major infrastructural and public-works projects and investments in the urban environment provided precarious jobs in a succession of projects and at a sequence of locations. Many of the workers who earned, in some cases, very high incomes from work on one or more projects, ultimately opted out of infrastructural employment and, perhaps after joining the pool of underemployed or unemployed urban workers, emigrated to find work in other regions. Work in construction thus often acted as a staging post or a medium through which workers passed on the way from jobs in the agricultural sector to jobs in the industrial and service sectors (see Holland, 1976, page 43).

After 1956 the flow of workers from these strata of the relative surplus population assumed considerable importance. In that year the rate of economic growth increased in Europe and in northern Italy. Adequate employment opportunities did not exist in the South, and so emigration from the Mezzogiorno increased and was redirected. The rate of foreign emigration increased, but transoceanic destinations declined in relative importance and European ones increased (see figure 4.4). International moves were less likely to entail the permanent emigration of whole families and much more likely to involve temporary movements of male manual workers. A large-scale and more permanent movement of southerners in working-age groups to the industrial zones of northern Italy was also set in motion (Mottura and Pugliese, 1972, pages 3-13).

During the twenty-five years between 1951 and 1975, 4420000 more persons emigrated from the South than moved into the region. The rate of net emigration increased from 0.96 persons per thousand inhabitants in 1952-1961 to 1.18 in 1962-1971, but declined markedly to 0.57 in 1972-1975, owing mainly to the reduction in the demand for labour in the receiving areas (Podbielski, 1978, pages 113-114. Slightly different data are given in table 5.8).

In the 1950s, as a result of the crisis of peasant farming and the absence of extraagricultural employment, emigration was most pronounced from the internal hill and mountain zones. In these areas residential populations fell sharply as their inhabitants migrated both to coastal zones in the South and to expanding industrial areas in the North and in the rest of Europe (table 5.8). In the 1960s, on the other hand, the main destination of emigrants changed from foreign countries to the central and northern parts of Italy. Two factors lay behind this change. One was increasing competition on European labour markets. The second was the acceleration in the early 1960s of northern industrial development. The fall in population continued in most of the internal zones. But rates of emigration from the areas of newly irrigated plain and the traditional areas of intensive farming showed sharp increases. One of the reasons for this lay in the rationalisation of capitalist agriculture. A second was connected with the large differences in income levels between agricultural and industrial occupations. In addition, the rapidly expanding urban areas, which had gained population through migration in the 1950s, experienced net losses of population through migration (table 5.8).

The supply of labour released by the reorganisation of southern agriculture, together with the availability of labour in the rest of the country, played a central role in facilitating the processes of European and of northern industrial development in the period up to 1963, mainly by raising the full-employment ceiling and restricting the growth of money wages.

At the same time, the increasing supply of agricultural products and increases in the productivity of labour in the agricultural sector helped to contain the costs of reproducing labour power. Consequently, wages increased more slowly than labour productivity, and the share of profits in national income increased, reinforcing the mechanism of accumulation.

The growing flow of remittances from emigrants helped to equilibrate the balance of payments and to increase incomes in the South. At the same time, of course, southern incomes were augmented by the expansion of agricultural production and the programme of investments in public works. As I have already pointed out, increases in per capita income in the South helped to widen the market for industrial goods. The new demand was, however, largely met by northern-based firms, and the lack of indigenous

Table 5.8. Net migration from the Mezzogiorno by elementary zones, 1951–1971 (numbers are given in thousands of persons). Source: G A Marselli, cited in Del Monte and Giannola (1978, page 166).

Elementary zone	Population in 1951		Natural increase		
	number	%	1951–1961	1961–1971	1951–1971
Appennine mountain	2807	16.1	367	228	595
Extensive agricultural	2275	13.0	305	232	537
Mixed hill	1696	9.7	212	160	372
Specialised arboricultural	2688	15.4	377	332	709
Cultivated hills in Abruzzi	397	2.3	33	25	58
Newly irrigated plain	820	4.7	148	144	292
Intensive agricultural	2204	12.6	352	373	725
Urban areas	4589	26.2	822	996	1818
Mezzogiorno	17476	100.0	2617	2490	5107
	Population in 1971		Net migration[a]		
	number	%	1951–1961	1961–1971	1951–1971
Appennine mountain	2286	12.4	−596	−519	−1115
Extensive agricultural	1967	10.7	−426	−418	−844
Mixed hill	1491	8.1	−321	−255	−576
Specialised arboricultural	2599	14.1	−410	−387	−797
Cultivated hills in Abruzzi	358	1.9	−73	−22	−95
Newly irrigated plain	956	5.2	−68	−88	−156
Intensive agricultural	2560	13.9	−174	−196	−370
Urban areas	6216	33.7	+18	−209	−191
Mezzogiorno	18435	100.0	−2052	−2097	−4149

[a] The net migration balance was estimated by adding the natural increase to the population present in 1951 and by subtracting the population present in 1961 or 1971.

industrial development and the selectivity of the process of emigration increased the dependence of the South on external resources.

Thus, as well as contributing to some important changes in the South, the regional policies introduced at the beginning of the period of repressive development were also important as measures of national planning. In that guise, it has been claimed by Bagnasco amongst others, policies for the South had two effects. First, the subordinated integration of the Mezzogiorno into the northern and national processes of accumulation was promoted. Second, the new functions that the southern economy and society were to assume in a new phase of externally oriented national development were planned (see Bagnasco, 1977, pages 52 – 53).

5.9 Social class and southern development
The policies for the South introduced in 1950 were in fact a compromise between the immediate need to improve conditions in the region and longer-term views about the prospects for national development (Graziani, 1976, pages 312 – 314). The reform agencies created many small farms whose existence alleviated unemployment for some sections of the rural population. But many of these enterprises had little prospect of long-term development. The somewhat indiscriminate provision of aqueducts and drainage systems, roads, schools, and electricity supplies by the Cassa helped to improve living conditions in the areas in which people were living at the time rather than in areas more suited to new forms of capitalist development. But these steps were not sufficient to keep people in the internal hill and mountain areas.

Yet by encouraging an increase in agricultural output in the capitalist sector and in some parts of the region, and by raising purchasing power in the South and enlarging the market for northern industrial products, the policies pursued by the Cassa and the land reform agencies also had effects which served dominant national interests. (Whether these effects were intended or not is another matter.) In addition, the creation of a network of marginal agricultural enterprises and the subsequent reductions in agricultural employment were connected with the management of an industrial reserve army mechanism that came to play an important role in the subsequent expansion of the national economy. In the words used by many Italian writers, the early policies for southern development thus had effects which at this stage were 'functional' economically to the development of the Italian economy as a whole.

The policies introduced in 1950 also had important social and political effects. Of particular importance was the fact that with the implementation of the land reform and the modernisation of southern farming the material and social conditions on which the southern landed bourgeoisie had depended were irreversibly changed, and the old ruling bloc composed of northern industrialists and southern landowners was finally dislocated.

From the 1880s onwards, the southern bourgeoisie, along with what Gramsci had called the 'intellectual' bourgeoisie composed of public officials and members of the liberal professions, had played an important part in securing social consent and maintaining social control in the South, and in reproducing social and political conditions within which national development could proceed. At the same time, it managed to construct a political base for itself in the South. The social groups dominant in the South thus acquired an important role in national politics. What followed was an ability to influence the formulation and choice of policies at a national level and to secure the implementation of measures that guaranteed the reproduction of these groups and of the power they exercised in the region and in the country.

The problem was that these measures resulted in the reproduction of backward agricultural systems because the landowners in the South received higher incomes from existing agrarian arrangements than they would have obtained had costly modernisation and improvement schemes been introduced. Commenting on the role of the southern landed bourgeoisie and on its opposition to the transformation of the latifundia system at the Convegno di Studi sui Problemi del Mezzogiorno at Bari in 1944, Rossi-Doria said:

> "The difficulty of the natural conditions certainly limits the advantages to be gained from transforming farming, but what reduces them to zero and blocks all change is the fact that, under the prevailing relations of production, landed property is in a position where it gets higher incomes than would be obtained with any other system of farming ... in contrast with so many elements of the landed bourgeoisie in Italy and in other countries the landed bourgeoisie of the Mezzogiorno does not play a progressive role in farming. It gives nothing to the land. And it appears to, and does, exploit the peasantry in a particularly harsh way. But one can say with justification that it is the force of circumstances, the weight of a system of social relations that keeps things that way. The reason why is that the situation of the southern bourgeoisie differs from that of the bourgeois elements whose virtues everyone extols. In the South self-interest in the shape of the prospect of increasing its own rents and profits does not act as a stimulus to progress as progress would almost always render its incomes smaller and more risky." (Rossi-Doria, cited in Pugliese, 1979, pages 68–69)

In the fascist era the role of the southern landed bourgeoisie began, according to recent research, to be reduced. And on the initiative of the capitalist bourgeoisie the dissolution of the ruling social bloc was set in motion. Of course, the fascist regime gave considerable support to agrarian interests insofar as oppression of subordinate rural strata was concerned, and the 'battle for wheat' represented in some ways a continuation of the protectionism accorded to southern cereal producers. In the 1930s, however, state policies aimed at channelling resources from the agricultural sector towards monopolistic industrial groups were introduced, and some important land reclamation and settlement schemes were carried through, extending peasant proprietorship.

Increased state intervention in the economy and modifications in the structure of Italy's political institutions were associated with a growing interpenetration of capital and the state, and the emergence, in the public and semipublic industrial and financial system and in the state itself, of an increasingly important state bourgeoisie. At the same time, as Castronovo (cited in Pinnarò and Pugliese, 1979, page 505) has argued, "the inflation of the staff of the state and para-state bureaucracy, the appointment of so many veterans to the administration, and so many small bureaucrats to the corporate agencies served to consolidate the influence of the small and middle bourgeoisie".

Yet it was only after the Second World War, when, with the passing of the land reform laws, the large landed bourgeoisie was dispossessed and ceased to form part of the governing class at a national level, that the ruling social bloc identified by Gramsci was finally dislocated. What eventually replaced it was, as I have already implied, a state bourgeoisie which had expanded not only under fascism but also after the war under Christian Democrat rule (see Pugliese, 1979, pages 71–75).

With the transformation of the southern economy, the social complexion of the Mezzogiorno was modified. Not only did the number of agricultural jobs fall, but, in the absence of adequate levels of employment and income in rural areas, rural depopulation and a rapid process of urbanisation occurred (see table 5.8).

In the cities there were not enough jobs in manufacturing. Instead, urban growth was fuelled by two factors. One was the growth of service employment and of jobs in commerce and the public administration in particular. The second was the expansion of the construction industry. The development of these two sectors was mutually reinforcing. On the one hand, the expansion of bureaucratic and other tertiary jobs stimulated the demand for housing and urban infrastructural investment. On the other, the physical expansion of a city and the increase in the size of its population created a demand for new tertiary activities and an increasing flow of public spending. Much of this tertiary employment was, it must be emphasised, of a low quality. The 'real function' of much government employment was "not so much to provide services or meet social needs as to give jobs". Indeed, as Becchi Collidà has remarked: "if one may properly speak of a lumpen proletariat in southern cities, it is not to be found by aggregating the thousands of semi-employed who are engaged in every possible way of seeking a means of sustenance. It is made up instead, of the thousands of recruits to the public employ who have no precise duties, are highly underutilised ... and receive a steady monthly salary" (Becchi Collidà, cited in Pinnarò and Pugliese, 1979, pages 512, 510; see also Becchi Collidà, 1979).

In the 1950s and early 1960s, owing to the interaction of these factors, many southern cities underwent processes of tumultuous growth. Accordingly, a class of urban entrepreneurs, linked with land and building speculation and with the construction industry which was clientelistically run by local notables, emerged. Along with the governing urban elites, these urban entrepreneurs acquired a dominant role in southern society and southern politics. Indeed, in these years these two groups not only assumed positions of power in the region, but also acted as a link between their localities and the central state. At the same time, moreover, a new tertiary bourgeoisie was consolidating its position as urban services grew in importance (see Pugliese, 1979, pages 77 – 80; and Allum, 1973a, pages 36 – 40; 1973b, pages 50 – 53, 296 – 324).

This phase of development was relatively short-lived. By the late 1960s, controls on speculation, the self-organisation of building workers, and a house building crisis were limiting the scope for profiting from urban construction. The result was that the strata depending on urban land rent ceased to play such an important role in the region.

More importantly, with the redirection of southern development several other changes in the class composition of the South were set in motion, laying the foundations for the construction of a new political bloc compatible with the modernisation and expansion of southern farming and a new form of integration of the Mezzogiorno with the national economy. In particular, the southern policy measures introduced in 1950 were associated with the creation of administrative and technical agencies to control the allocation of state funds, and whose capacity to undertake investments and to assist various social groups was used to co-opt political consensus around the ruling DC party. In 1954, Fanfani was elected Secretary General and succeeded De Gasperi. Under his leadership, a policy of systematically appointing Christian Democrat party members to all state and para-state posts was adopted and emerged, in fact, as a key element in the party's political strategy (see Allum, 1981, pages 318 – 319).

At the same time, social strata, such as peasants allocated land under the land reform and the beneficiaries of the Cassa's infrastructural investments, were reproduced. The material support given to these groups, along with the organisation of sections of civil society by DC controlled organisations such as the Federazione Nazionale dei Coltivatori Diretti (FNCD), played an important part in the mobilisation of social consent and social control in the South, and in the creation of an electoral base capable of ensuring the DC of the necessary support in the country.

In the mid-1960s, the policy of extraordinary intervention '*a pioggia*' gave way to one characterised by greater selectivity. But many of the actions of the ordinary administration fulfilled a similar function. On the one hand, frequently subsidised jobs increased rapidly in services and in the public administration. On the other, the flow to southern residents of invalidity and other pensions, of subsidies, and of other transfers increased. Some of the problems of unemployment and poverty were therefore eased, and a basis of consent was secured among petty bureaucrats and other state employees and among welfare recipients. What was wrong with this strategy was not that people were being paid, but that they were not being paid to do anything useful: irrationality and waste were justified by political expediency.

All of these processes of economic development and class recomposition were connected with the establishment of clientele structures within which relations of hierarchy, authority, and inequality prevailed, but which "succeeded in general in absorbing every incipient class alignment". These structures extended "from the politicians of the centre to local 'notables' and 'barons', administrators in the provinces, and peripheral state officials, to the main recipients of public money, big public works contractors, big building firms, 'subsidized' firms, right down through the *mafiosi* to the lowest levels of the masses, corrupted and deceived by the mirage of a 'post' " (Salvati, 1972, page 12). And in the coalition and structure of power that resulted, conservative elements originating in the older society of the South played an important part. What happened was in fact similar to what had happened under fascism, and had parallels with Tancredi's justification to his father of his participation in Garibaldi's Thousand in di Lampedusa's *The Leopard*: "if we want everything to remain the same, everything must be changed" (see Allum, 1981, pages 320 – 321).

In short, the expansion of the extraordinary and ordinary public administrations and of the resources they controlled were associated with a growth in the role of high-level bureaucratic and administrative groups who came to form one arm of an increasingly dominant state bourgeoisie. At the same time, the provision of jobs, the channelling of spending on public works, the distribution of agricultural and industrial credit and grants, and the spending by national insurance and pension funds were all characterised by clientelism which, along with the ideological appeal of anticommunism and of the Church, was one of the major planks on which Christian Democrat rule rested (see Allum, 1981, pages 315 – 317).

A second major element was added by the growth of the state holding companies and the modification, after 1957, of southern policy to promote a process of southern industrialisation under their leadership. What followed was "a southernisation of state industry, and a nationalisation of southern industry" (Pugliese, 1979, page 80). The financial and industrial arm of the state bourgeoisie linked with the state-run industries thus assumed an increasingly important role in the region.

With these processes of class restructuring went changes in the ruling bloc in the South (see Pinnarò and Pugliese, 1979, pages 497 – 498). The upper strata in the state bureaucracies controlling and administering public spending were able to consolidate local clientele structures. In turn, clientelism helped them to maintain social control in the Mezzogiorno and to command an electoral base that gave them considerable political weight in the region, and an ability to exercise a veto over processes of policy and decisionmaking at a national level. Also, the increasing role of the state sector in the national economy, and the part played by these groups in securing political stability and in the structure of power within the Christian Democrat party, gave the state industrial and financial bourgeoisie a major national role.

Thus, the old bloc composed of northern industrialists and large southern landowners came finally to be replaced by a new one based on an alliance, that was on occasions to be an uneasy one, between the industrial bourgeoisie and a state bourgeoisie (see Pugliese, 1979, pages 67–71, 80–90).

6

The development and crisis of the Italian economy

6.1 From economic recovery to 'economic miracle'

The modernisation and expansion of southern farming and the availability of a large industrial reserve army, which were related, as we have seen, to the effects of early southern policies, had important effects on subsequent Italian economic development, as did some of the changes in the structure of Italian industry which were connected with the policies for southern industrialisation introduced after 1957. But what were most fundamental in shaping the characteristics and tempo of Italian growth were some of the economic and political decisions made in the years of reconstruction and in the early 1950s.

At the outset there were at least two alternative development paths for the Italian economy. One favoured by the left was premised upon the use of internal demand and public spending as the primary stimuli to economic reconstruction and development, and entailed state intervention in key sectors (see Lange and Vannicelli, 1982, pages 100-109). Under this model, priority would have been given to investment instead of consumption goods, and more capital accumulation and growth would have occurred in the agrarian sector. Internally, the demand for consumer goods would have come more from working-class and less from middle strata, and investment in the provision of collective goods would have been greater. The social consequences of choosing this path would, in the words of Pizzorno (1981, page 110), have been "the expansion of a working class category in the industrial sector and a reduced exodus from the countryside directed towards the industrial rather than the tertiary sector".

But with the ousting of the PCI and PSI from the government, and the split in the trade union movement, the working class found itself without significant influence in the field of economic policy formation where it had tried to have an impact. Moreover, shop floor organisation, which had been developed covertly during the war and which had emerged afterwards to challenge managerial authority, had been weakened in part by the political role the union movement had played and the attempt to shape government policy (see Lange and Vannicelli, 1982, pages 100-109, 191-192). In subsequent years the employers succeeded in browbeating and bribing factory workers into docility:

> "At FIAT during the early 1950s at least 2,000 workers were fired for reasons having to do with political and trade-union activity; the reorganisation of work that accompanied the introduction of modern machines, many from the United States, provided ample possibilities for scattering groups of troublemakers and obstructing political friendships; and still other activists were exiled to undesirable departments, such as the *Officina Sussidiaria Ricambi*, nicknamed the *Stella Rossa* or Red Star. These punishments were combined with enticements to good behaviour such as a premium for regular

attendance .... An obvious sign that management had the whip hand in the 1950s and early 1960s was its power to lengthen and shorten the working day, declare lay-offs, and schedule vacations according to market conditions" (Sabel, 1982, pages 146-147).

Working-class weakness was one of the premises of the model of development that was actually chosen, and was a major factor in the success of the Italian economy in competing in export markets for those manufactured goods experiencing the most rapid rates of growth of demand. Indeed, the introduction in 1947 of a deflationary monetary and credit squeeze and of cuts in government spending by Einaudi in his capacity as DC Minister of Finance added to that weakness. The policy was aimed at controlling inflation and at increasing the competitiveness of Italian industry. But unemployment increased, and wages were forced downwards, disciplining workers and demonstrating the incapacity of the trade union movement to defend working-class interests.

Several other factors also kept down the costs of reproducing labour power. One was the existence of widespread marginal employment in backward sectors and backward areas together with high levels of unemployment. Almost 2 million persons, forming about 10% of the labour force, were officially unemployed in the early 1950s. In subsequent years, however, unemployment declined progressively to reach almost 500 000 persons, or 2.5% of the labour force, in the early 1960s. In spite of a high gross investment ratio and a relatively low incremental capital-output ratio, the supply of labour kept pace with the process of accumulation until the early 1960s. The elasticity of the supply of labour helped ensure that wages grew more slowly than labour productivity and that the share of profits in national income increased. The cost of labour per unit of industrial output was not as low as in some other European countries, but the availability of large pools of labour undoubtedly played an important role in Italian economic expansion in the wave of growth that lasted until 1963 (Ricossa, 1976, pages 297-299).

The last element contributing to the low reproduction costs of labour power was the extremely restricted development and satisfaction of working-class social needs. On the one hand, the level of provision of collective goods such as public housing, transport, and health and education services was extremely inadequate. On the other, the domestic market for consumption goods was restricted outside the ranks of the middle classes by low wages and a regressive tax system. Consequently, until the early 1960s, many parts of the home market continued to be supplied to a substantial extent by traditional consumption-good industries.

What I have argued so far is that the type of development chosen differed from the one favoured by the trade union and working-class movement in that it was dependent on low direct costs to industry. Owing in part to the consequent weakness of the home market it was oriented fundamentally to external rather than internal demand, with the demand for goods that were not exported coming mainly from middle strata. Included in this sector of society were two broad groups. One was composed of the owners of small agrarian and industrial enterprises. The second comprised the owners of small shops and of a wide range of professional or bureaucratic circulation and consumption related enterprises on the one hand, and the more highly paid white-collar workers on the other.

In Italy, middle strata were both numerous and influential, absolutely and also relatively. Compared with the situation in other capitalist economies in western Europe, the proportion of employers and own-account (self-employed) workers was in particular relatively high, whereas the proportion of wage earners was relatively small, as was the size of the new middle class (see, for example, the 1968 and 1971 data in table 6.1). After 1945, it was amongst this section of society and the peasantry, and also amongst Catholics, that the new political class sought the bases of a new consensus.

According to Pizzorno, Italian development came to be characterised by a predominantly individualistic organisation of consensus instead of one depending on an institutionalisation of collective demands. Inequality was allowed and was used as an incentive for people to seek the benefits the system was capable of distributing. In this type of organisation of consensus, middle strata, defined as that set of individuals who are in a position to prefer a project of individual improvement over that of a collective or sectoral improvement, played an important part. Accordingly, the bases of consensus were laid by enlarging the middle strata and by protecting its interests along with those of the peasantry.

Attempts were also made to establish a solidarity of interests between small employers and the marginal workers they employed by means of political protection and support aimed at enabling artisans and small businesses to survive, albeit precariously.

The strategy of reinforcing a petite bourgeoisie dependent on politically protected markets and of enhancing the security of marginal workers was complemented by another element that I have already discussed. Over the years, clientelistic criteria were developed and applied in the fields of public spending and the supply of state-controlled credit and in the execution of functions of licensing and interdiction on which an ability to carry on certain economic activities depended (see Pizzorno, 1981, pages 106–117).

Socially the economy's development path was consequently reflected in a retarded development of working-class categories in the industrial sector, a strong exodus from the countryside, and a strong development of the tertiary sector and of the middle strata connected with it (see Pizzorno, 1981, page 110).

The support accorded to these middle strata was, however, not total. In particular, the monetary and credit squeeze introduced in 1947 by Einaudi was aimed not only at controlling inflation but also at increasing the competitiveness of Italian industry. In subsequent years, small and medium-sized firms found it much more difficult to borrow, many small

Table 6.1. Occupation[a] and status in Italy, France, and the United Kingdom, 1968–1971 (expressed as a percentage). Source: elaborated from ILO; see also Burris (1980).

	France, 1/3/1968			Italy, 24/10/1971			United Kingdom, 25/4/1971		
	total	male	female	total	male	female	total	male	female
Employers and own-account (self-employed) workers	15.8	19.7	8.4	20.5	22.5	15.3	7.4	9.3	4.1
agriculture, forestry, and fishing	6.9	9.4	2.4	7.4	8.5	4.7	1.1	1.5	0.4
production and transport	3.1	4.4	0.6	5.4	6.6	2.3	2.4	3.6	0.3
tertiary	5.7	5.9	5.3	7.7	7.5	8.2	3.8	4.1	3.4
Family workers	7.0	2.7	15.2	4.6	2.7	9.7	0.0	0.0	0.0
Salaried employees and wage earners	75.1	75.8	73.7	70.0	70.5	68.6	87.5	85.4	91.2
agriculture, forestry, and fishing	3.1	4.4	0.9	6.9	6.4	8.2	1.8	2.4	0.7
production and transport	31.3	40.5	14.0	35.9	40.8	22.9	35.6	45.7	17.9
service	7.0	2.9	14.6	7.2	6.2	9.8	10.4	4.5	20.8
sales	3.8	3.0	5.1	2.4	2.3	2.7	6.9	5.2	9.8
clerical	11.6	6.7	20.6	10.5	9.5	13.3	17.4	10.7	28.8
administrative and managerial	1.8	2.4	0.6	0.3	0.4	0.1	3.6	5.2	0.8
professional, technical, and scientific	10.4	8.8	13.4	6.1	4.0	11.6	10.0	9.5	11.0
members of the armed forces	1.2	1.8	0.1	0.5	0.7	0.0	1.0	1.5	0.1
Individuals newly seeking work[b]	2.1	1.8	2.8	4.9	4.4	6.4	5.1	5.4	4.8
Total active population (in thousands)	20439	13316	7124	19807	14381	5427	25021	15884	9137

[a] The individual entries do not sum to the subtotals as some workers were not classified by occupation. Additional discrepancies are a result of rounding errors.
[b] Individuals seeking work for the first time are not classified by status.

firms in the productive sector were threatened with bankruptcy, and many uncompetitive enterprises were eliminated.

In fact the process of development of the economy and the successful participation of Italian industry in the expansion of international trade depended upon some major changes in the industrial structure of the country. Many of these changes were initiated in the years of reconstruction.

At the end of the Second World War the Italian industrial system was dominated by technologically backward traditional industries such as the food processing, natural textile, and wood processing sectors. It also included relatively advanced industries in the engineering, vehicle manufacturing, and chemical sectors (see table 5.3). Compared with the more developed west European economies, however, Italy's modern engineering and chemical industries were relatively small in size, whereas other industries that were subsequently to become important, like the iron and steel industry, were not only small but also were based to a large extent on traditional techniques of production.

In the postwar period the Italian economy continued to specialise in the export of some of the traditional industrial products of the textile, clothing, and shoe and leather goods sectors. Indeed it was the dynamism of these sectors that was subsequently to underlie the industrial success of some parts of the 'third Italy' (Bagnasco, 1977). On the other hand, the country's specialisation in food processing was lost owing to the relatively slow modernisation of Italian agriculture and the expansion of domestic demand.

More importantly, the structure of the economy was adjusted through a growing specialisation in the production of mass consumption goods, such as electrical household appliances and motor vehicles, for which world demand was expanding rapidly, and through a striking development of industries producing energy and intermediate goods such as chemicals and iron and steel that were necessary as inputs for the equipment-good sectors. Within these sectors, technology and principles of work organisation that had been developed earlier, in the United States of America in particular, were imported.

What was occurring was in fact the development of a model of intensive accumulation, which I have elsewhere called Taylorism and Fordism (see chapter 2, section 2.9). But in contrast to the models of development of the economies of core regions, domestic mass consumption did not at first develop as strongly alongside mass production. Instead, Italian growth was externally oriented, conforming quite closely to what Lipietz has more recently defined as peripheral Fordism. Through the articulation of its economy with that of more developed capitalist societies, Italian growth was, moreover, very fast, but associated with high rates of inflation (see Lipietz, 1985b; and also the discussion of international specialisation in chapter 2, section 2.10).

The development of firms that were comparatively advanced technologically and competitive on an international level, and the changes in the structure of Italian industry, can be attributed in part to the effects of international agreements and transfers of technology (see Graziani, 1976, pages 308-310).

After the inauguration of Einaudi's deflationary policy of economic recovery, major industries found themselves able to obtain funds and to undertake programmes of reconstruction and modernisation, but many marginal enterprises were bankrupted. In a similar way, the controlled liberalisation of foreign trade, the progressive opening of the Italian economy to foreign competition, and Italian participation in the process of European economic integration that culminated, in 1957, in the Treaty of Rome and the establishment of the EEC, help explain the survival and development of firms and sectors capable of competing on international or European markets.

The other major set of decisions shaping the direction of Italian development concerned the development of the state holding companies and state encouragement of large-scale investments in the production of intermediate goods and energy. In 1948, after some discussion as to whether its assets should be returned to the private sector, it was decided that IRI should survive. In 1953, the Ente Nazionale Idrocarburi (ENI) was set up to run several public and semipublic corporations in the hydrocarbons and natural gas sectors. Of these operations the most important was AGIP, which had been founded in 1926 to prospect for oil and to extract and refine it. In subsequent years, ENI's operations were extended into chemicals, nuclear fuels, and allied fields (see Allen and Stephenson, 1974, chapter 7). As a result of the relatively low costs of imported and national raw materials and of the programmes of investment these groups carried out, Italian firms were able to buy oil, steel, chemicals, and other intermediate products at highly competitive prices on the domestic market.

The expansion of these industries was given a major impetus by the provision of capital grants and loans for investment in these sectors in the Mezzogiorno from the early 1960s onwards. The new regional policies introduced after 1957 were, accordingly, used to promote a form of industrial development that was to play an important role in the process of national economic expansion.

As a result of the interaction of all of these factors, Italian economic development accelerated sharply and largely unexpectedly. In 1956-1961 the country's gross national product increased at 7.9% or more per year, giving rise in 1958-1964 to what came to be called the 'economic miracle'. At the time of the economic miracle, exports were the fastest growing component of aggregate demand. Next came fixed capital formation in the oligopolistic export and export-related sectors (Salvati, 1972, pages 7-12). In effect a process of export-led growth whose basis lay in an internationalisation of commodity capital led to extremely rapid economic development (see chapter 2, sections 2.10 and 2.11).

6.2 Unbalanced growth and crisis

In the short run the model of export-oriented development gave rise to very rapid economic growth. Yet at the same time it contained within itself elements that would subsequently bring it into crisis, in some cases by destroying its preconditions.

In particular, a number of economic and social disequilibria, including striking dualisms within the agricultural and industrial sectors of the economy, in its territorial organisation, and in the pattern of consumption, emerged or were reproduced (see Graziani, 1972, pages 31 – 53). Industrially, Italy was divided into a group of capital-intensive, high-productivity, high-wage export and export-related industries and a group of largely low-productivity, small-scale, low-wage industries producing for the domestic market. A pronounced dualism between advanced and backward regions which existed at the beginning of this period was reinforced by the concentration of the expanding export industries in the large and rapidly growing urban centres of the industrial triangle and also in nearby towns in the Po Valley and along the Milan – Venice axis. The speed and largely unplanned character of the process of urbanisation and the depopulation of rural districts created imbalances between town and country. In the sphere of consumption the model of export-led growth resulted in a dualism between individual and collective consumption. On the one hand, growth was accompanied by a restricted but nonetheless comparatively striking development of the national market for mass consumption goods. On the other, levels of provision of collective goods were limited.

A consequence of these disequilibria and imbalances was a rise in indirect costs to industry. In the industrial cities of the North, for example, the lack of investment in public transport systems and the inadequacy of collective equipment increased the pressure on land in the immediate vicinity of industrial zones and led to rapid increases in land prices, in housing costs, and eventually, in wages.

Most significantly, the intensity and form of the growth process was leading by the early 1960s to a level, composition, and distribution of demand for labour that reduced unemployment and created labour shortages, especially for 'skilled labour' in the most highly industrialised areas. Yet this tightening of labour markets occurred when there were still large amounts of underemployed and marginal labour in backward sectors and areas. Indeed, instead of recruiting migrants who had worked for a while in unskilled and unstable jobs in the North, some large firms made major efforts to recruit workers directly from the South.

The appearance of shortages of labour was also accompanied by a decline in the activity rate. The fall in the activity rate had begun in the late 1950s and continued throughout the 1960s. Amongst other things it indicated that considerable unemployment and underemployment had existed in the southern countryside. In an earlier era, in which the majority of people lived in the countryside, the wives of farmers were recorded as economically active because they helped with farm work. With the fall in agricultural employment and the absence of adequate alternative jobs, however, the inactive population was swollen.

In the past, backward sectors and areas had undoubtedly played an important role in regulating the labour market by releasing labour as and when it was required by more advanced sectors of the economy, and by reabsorbing some of the excess labour released by leading sectors when demand slackened. The shortage of labour of the early 1960s indicated that this mechanism was not sufficiently flexible or, at least, that it was not capable of providing adequate amounts of certain kinds of labour power.

In these conditions the movement towards something approaching full employment in existing industrial areas had the effect of strengthening the position of the working-class and trade union movements. In 1961-1963 a series of unofficial and official strikes occurred, with immigrant and northern workers in the industrial triangle playing a leading role. As a result, money wages increased sharply and grew more rapidly than the rate of productivity growth: "hourly wages went up by 15.3 per cent in 1962, 16.8 per cent in 1963, and 11.3 per cent in 1964, whereas the hourly productivity of industrial workers went up by an average of about 7 per cent in those years" (Vianello, cited in Sabel, 1982, pages 153-154).

The employers tried to counter the increase in money wages by raising prices. But the need to remain internationally competitive obliged them to bear part of the increase in costs themselves. As a result, profit margins were reduced, and the process of accumulation slowed down. The Italian economy had attained a state of 'precocious maturity', in the sense that it was experiencing many of the problems typical of industrial economies that had achieved a high level of resource utilisation, even though many of its own resources were subject to widespread underutilisation (Salvati, 1972, page 4).

The improvements in money wages, together with the reduction in the relative prices of many manufactured goods, stimulated private consumption. But rigidities in the supply of goods, which were connected with structural disequilibria in the economy, led to demand-pull inflation. The inefficient organisation of agriculture and retailing, and bottlenecks in traditional consumption-good industries caused prices to increase, giving a further impulse to wage increases. At the same time, land prices and housing costs continued to escalate due to the inefficiency of the building industry and the chaotic and largely unplanned character of the process of urbanisation. What these events indicated was that the strategy of keeping open spaces for individual profit-seeking and the absence of action to counter speculation, along with the inefficiency of the protected sector, involved, as was indicated more abstractly in chapters 2 and 3, widespread external diseconomies and high indirect costs. In the early 1960s, these high costs themselves helped disrupt the process of accumulation.

The economic miracle thus came to an end with an inflationary boom, and Italy's balance of payments position, which was aggravated by a strong outflow of long-term capital, deteriorated.

6.3 The years of centre-left planning

The crisis itself indicated that the mobilisation of resources for continued accumulation and a new wave of growth depended upon a rationalisation of the economic system and an elimination of the bottlenecks to growth (see Salvati, 1972, pages 21-29). A number of low-productivity sectors of production such as the agricultural sector, the building industry, commerce, and the public administration needed to be rationalised in order that labour could be released and the inflation to which they were contributing controlled. A reorganisation of the educational system so that it corresponded more closely with the needs of the economy was likely to be required, as was a use of territory in a way which would enable the labour available in less developed areas to be more fully utilised and the diseconomies associated with an excessive concentration of economic activity in large industrial cities and in the great cities of the Northwest in particular to be reduced. What was implied was a series of reforms aimed at reducing indirect costs by increasing efficiency and reducing the share of income received by rural and urban landowners, by commercial capitalists, by professional and bureaucratic groups, and by other middle strata.

The increasing political and economic strength of the labour movement was a second factor that helped to disrupt the old political equilibrium and the model of repressive development. But the formulation and implementation of a programme of reforms depended upon the establishment of a new reformist bloc, a political coalition capable of representing this bloc in parliament, and a new model of development.

A new coalition composed of large employers, of reform-oriented politicians, of scientific, technical, and managerial strata, and of some sections of the working class was indeed established. And in 1963 the government coalition was shifted to the left, when the DC dropped the PLI (the Italian Liberal Party) and brought in the PSI.

The centre-left government was formed in part as a means of dividing the labour movement and of integrating the non-communist part of it into a new political equilibrium. It was also seen as a means of regulating wages and of introducing a series of reforms aimed at improving living conditions and rationalising backward sectors of the economy.

The problem was that the reformist forces were unable to build a new social bloc and to achieve real political hegemony. The nationalisation of the electrical energy industry did eliminate one of the most powerful elements in the traditional industrial bloc, and a commission of inquiry into monopoly power was established. But, in general, the forces pushing for change were unable to get the main reforms through the political system or to implement those social and economic aspects of the National Plan that required interference with the pattern of export-led growth. Indeed, instead of helping to correct "the structural flaws of the Italian economy to which it had been originally addressed ... [the planning episode functioned as] another mechanism for the general expansion of government which went on in Italy in the 1960s ... and generally served to extend and deepen clientelistic and narrow interest-group linkages between the government parties ... [including the PSI] and a vast array of social strata, other than the organised working class" (Lange and Vannicelli, 1982, pages 120-121).

One of the reasons for this lay in the political strength of backward sectors which had in many cases been protected or created as part of the consensus strategy of successive DC governments. On the one hand, middle strata in the public and private sectors had acquired an ability to veto and obstruct reforms. On the other, the fact that certain fractions of the middle strata and marginal groups had shared interests was associated with the risk of a mobilisation of a fascist kind involving the petite bourgeoisie and marginal workers (see Pizzorno, 1981, pages 117-121). The crisis, moreover, was also a crisis for northern industry, as it would soon be for the industrial systems which had been developed in other advanced capitalist countries and whose basis also lay in the application and generalisation of the methods of scientific management and Fordism. In these circumstances it was clearly difficult to ensure that a rationalisation of backward sectors would coincide with increases in employment in modern equipment-good industries. Yet in the absence of new jobs in growing sectors, any social tensions provoked by a modernisation of the economy would have assumed increased severity.

Second, the alliance itself was weak. The major political parties represented a heterogeneous set of interests which could not easily be reconciled, and the unions were still comparatively weak. The CGIL and CISL refused to agree to a self-limitation of wage demands, let alone a legally sanctioned wages policy, and were diffident towards the planning experiment (see Lange and Vannicelli, 1982, pages 120-122).

In any case, once the centre-left government had been installed the monetary authorities responded to the problems of inflation and the country's balance of payments deficit in a traditional way, with the intention of creating the necessary conditions for a successful continuation of the postwar development model. A credit squeeze was introduced and a deflationary strategy adopted. The consequent depression in domestic demand was allowed to last for two years in the hope that the fall in activity and the rise in unemployment would hold down wages and encourage a restructuring of industry. In this way it was hoped that the ground would be prepared for a relaunching of investment and new gains in productivity (see Graziani, 1976, pages 325-326).

As a result of all of these factors the years of boom quickly gave way to a recession. The rate of growth of output fell and was followed downwards by the rate of growth of investment. The economic measures adopted by the state brought inflation under control and brought the balance of payments back into equilibrium. A reduction in total employment and an increase in unemployment occurred, and the rate of growth of money wages fell continuously (see figure 6.1).

Owing to the depression of the domestic market, exports once again played a leading role in Italian economic development, accelerating sharply in 1964 and constituting the main source of aggregate demand in the cycle between 1964 and 1971. But the recovery of the economy was much slower and less dynamic than expected. Moreover, the renewed expansion of income that did occur in the second half of the 1960s concealed some of the weaknesses of the Italian economy. One index of its malaise lay in the fact that total investment, which had fallen sharply in the period from 1964 to 1965, did not regain its 1963 level until 1969 (see Salvati, 1972, page 14), and manufacturing investment, which had grown at an average annual rate of 10.5% in the period from 1952 to 1962, increased at a rate of only 3.3% between 1962 and 1972. In addition, the rate of investment, that is, investment as a percentage of gross national product, fell markedly after 1962 (see also figure 8.1).

The trends in investment were a reflection of the particular ways in which Italian capital was restructured in the years immediately after 1964.

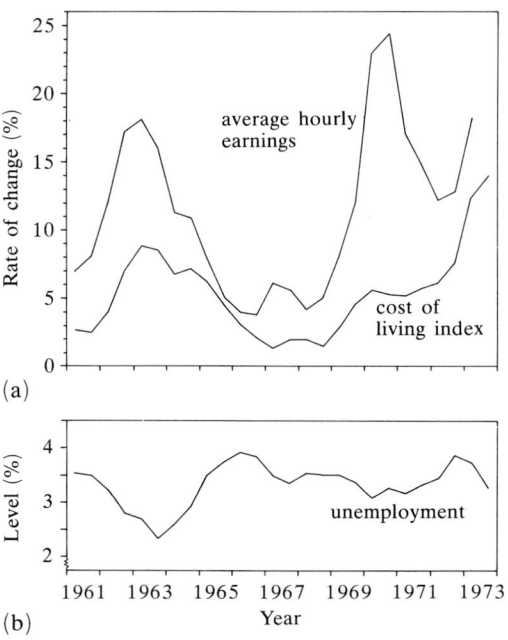

Figure 6.1. (a) Changes in earnings in manufacturing industry, and a union index of changes in the cost of living; and (b) the level of unemployment in Italy, 1961–1973. Source: Salvati (1975, page 91).

One consequence of the problems caused by the controlled recession and of the wish of many firms to conquer foreign markets was an intense and general concentration and centralisation of capital. Within large corporations like FIAT and Pirelli, production was internationalised. At the same time, the penetration of the Italian economy by foreign capital increased (Salvati, 1972, page 17).

The process of concentration was encouraged by state laws supporting mergers and the laws for the Mezzogiorno which allowed increasingly large projects to be supported, and it was reinforced by the reduction in internal financing and the increased dependence of industrial capitals on the credit system. "Between 1963 and 1973 the risk capital of firms was reduced by almost half: while in 1963 it represented 54.3 per cent of total financing, in 1973 it was down to 26.7 per cent. In the same period the rate of indebtedness of firms rose from 57.6 per cent of total financing to 69.1 per cent, and amongst external sources, short-term credit rose to 32.8 per cent" (Martinelli, 1980, page 78, referring to the results of a study by Alzona).

As a result of the privileged way in which resources were channelled to the state holding companies, which expanded in the South when the level of economic activity increased again, the state-controlled sector and the state bourgeoisie succeeded in strengthening their positions in Italian society: in 1963–1972 the share of the public sector increased from 19% to 24% of the total output of a sample of the largest one hundred and fifty firms, from 28% to 35% of invested capital, and from 20% to 24% of total employment (Martinelli, 1980, pages 77–78).

On the other hand, in sectors where Taylorist and, especially, Fordist principles of work organisation were used and where the intensity of labour was greater, employers sought to increase productivity not by undertaking new investment but by maximising the use of existing production capacity, by rationalising and reorganising tasks, and by intensifying the process of labour through increases in work speeds and related practices. This strategy involved reductions in personnel, and it was connected with the adoption of more selective recruitment policies aimed at increasing the relative importance of male workers in intermediate age groups.

In the 1960s output per person employed increased rapidly, although the rate of growth was lower than in the 1950s and declined during the course of the decade. But at the same time, inequalities in labour productivity fell markedly due to a comparative improvement in productivity levels in traditional industries. In the 'extensive' phase of accumulation in the 1950s, intersectoral and interregional inequalities in average hourly output had in fact increased. But in the 'intensive' phase of accumulation in the 1960s, both of these indices tended to decrease. These trends in intersectoral and interregional differences in labour productivity were accompanied by the opposite trends in wage differentials, which, after narrowing in the early 1960s, increased from 1962 until 1969 (Garofoli, 1976a, pages 101–120).

At the same time, a variety of rationalising interventions were being made by the state. As a result, the expulsion of labour from backward sectors and areas was accelerated, but without the creation of adequate alternative local employment. The Second Green Plan and the redirection of Cassa policies in the mid-1960s were examples of this type of intervention.

Despite the reduction in living labour employed and the increases in labour productivity achieved, the rate of profit did not regain the levels of the 1950s. The strategies employed by Italian capital were not able to raise productivity sufficiently to offset the effects of the overall increase in real wages, and the collapse in the rate of investment was leading to an increase in the age structure of the capital stock that would ultimately reduce the competitiveness of Italian industry.

6.4 The 'hot autumn' of 1969 and after

After the strikes of the early 1960s the unions and the industrial working class found themselves once again in a relatively weak position. On the shop floor, workers were unable to counter the attempt by employers to reorganise production and intensify work rhythms. In the national, industry-wide, wage bargaining round of 1965-1966, where minimum wages, working hours, and union rights were determined, the unions did not obtain very good results. And at a political level the unions did not have much effect on policy formation. At the same time, however, some important developments, whose origins lay in the mid-1950s, continued: in particular, attempts at rebuilding organisation at a factory level were made and more emphasis was placed on wages policy, the unions were moving away from the political parties with which they were aligned, and the strategies of the CGIL and CISL slowly converged (see Lange and Vannicelli, 1982, pages 113-124). In the North, however, the speedups and the rationalisation of work created dissatisfaction on the shop floor amongst often nonunionised southern assembly line workers who were being pushed to the limits of exhaustion, and also amongst northern craft workers. Similarly, the authoritarianism that characterised Italian industrial relations was a source of resentment amongst different sections of the factory proletariat. Consequently, the areas of common concern and the mutual trust that had been built up by different sections of the industrial working class during the industrial conflicts of the early 1960s were reinforced.

A number of other significant events also occurred in the development of the working-class movement. In January 1964, for example, shortly after the entry of the PSI into the government coalition a radical minority broke away to form the independent Partito Socialista di Unità Proletaria (PSIUP). In Turin, "the PSIUP won many craftsmen at FIAT to a plan for introducing factory councils composed of shop stewards or *delegati*. In 1969 these workers would play an important part in introducing the idea of *delegati* to the unskilled migrants" (Sabel, 1982, page 156).

As a result of these and other developments "the mass of factory workers, parts of the labour movement and the emergent intellectual elite were moving closer together and further away from the control of dominant institutions" (Sabel, 1982, page 157).

The recovery of the economy was slow and hesitant. After 1965 there were several years of renewed and relatively rapid export-led expansion. But in 1968-1969, increased raw material costs and increased costs of borrowing pushed up the rate of inflation. Owing in part to the segmentation of the Italian labour market, shortages of labour were experienced by employers in the modern sector. What followed was an explosion of social unrest and industrial conflict, whose high point coincided with the events of the '*autumno caldo*' of 1969.

The period of intense social and working-class mobilisation started in 1968 with the student demonstrations and mass rallies for pension reform. As in other countries, the growth of the student movement reflected dissatisfaction with the political, social, and cultural stagnation of western society and the subservience of national elites to foreign interests. But in contrast to other countries, students and left-wing intellectuals in Italy were much more eager to ally with the working class. As early as the mid-1960s, numerous contacts between students and factory workers had been established (Sabel, 1982, pages 156-157).

With shortages of labour being experienced by employers the working class grew more assertive, especially in the large northern industrial plants of which the FIAT works in Turin and other large metalworking establishments were exemplary. Subsequently, conflicts spread to other areas, sectors, and groups of workers where industrial action had been unusual: in and after 1968, white-collar workers and technicians went on strike in large numbers in companies. Included were SNAM Progetti (involved in oil prospecting and drilling and the design and construction of oil refineries and chemical plants, Italpianti (involved in the design and construction of steel mills, SIT Siemens (involved in the production of telephone and telecommunications equipment), Selenia in Rome (producing electronic equipment), and some of the installations of the National Committee for Nuclear Energy (CNEN). In the private service sector, conflicts occurred in the large retail and hotel sectors. In the state sector, public service employees and civil servants went on strike. (In this last case, however, what was often involved was an attempt to keep up with the gains made by industrial workers and to recover salary and status differentials.) Conflicts spread from large to small plants and from the more industrialised and urban areas of northern Italy to the Centre and the South (see Low-Beer, 1978, pages 38-42; Regalia et al, 1978, pages 104-111).

Overall the level of conflict increased from 7.26 hours lost per employee per year in 1959-1967 to 11.55 hours in 1968-1975, reaching a peak of 23.0 hours in 1969 (see figure 6.2 and Regini, 1980, page 52). In part the increase in strike activity in the late 1960s was connected with the negotiations for new wage agreements for the three years from 1970–1972. But there were also an unusually high intensity and proportion of plant conflicts.

In some of the early outbreaks of militant industrial action, older northern craft workers in metalworking, process and textile workers, and workers in plants where union organisation was weak figured prominently. But young semiskilled workers, who quickly learned of the central role they played in the organisation of production and of the capacity they had to disrupt it, were also involved. In the autumn of 1968, these mainly immigrant workers, along with students and rank and file militants, started to play an autonomous role in important conflicts, finally dominating the events of the 'autumno caldo'. At this stage, in particular, demands were made that went far beyond the reforms envisaged by the unions, and the rhythm and aims of the strikes were determined by grass-roots organisations. In addition, new forms of industrial conflict were invented and tried out. The unions had great difficulty in canalising the conflicts. In 1970, however, a new phase opened. By then the level of mobilisation had passed its crest. The unions took up many of the demands that had arisen spontaneously from the needs of different groups of workers and translated them into a strategy that secured the support of a majority of the working class. Union organisation and the system of industrial relations were transformed. But relations with employers and industrial conflicts were rationalised and subjected to union control and union-imposed restraint (see Regalia et al, 1978, pages 108–109).

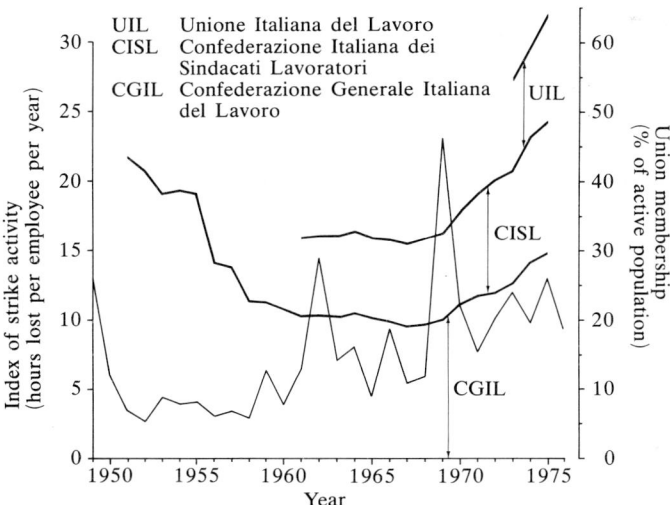

Figure 6.2. Union membership (heavy line) and industrial conflict (light line) in Italy, 1949–1976. (Union membership is plotted cumulatively.) Sources: elaborated from data in Crouch and Pizzorno (1978, pages 317–318) and Regini (1980, page 64).

The militancy and autonomy of immigrant workers was, by international standards unusual. As with other immigrants, the workers in the North were socialised neither into factory and modern urban life nor into unions. But in the rest of Europe immigrants were differentiated from the indigenous working class not only culturally but also by nationality and linguistically. In particular, many of them only held temporary visas, lacked the rights of citizenship enjoyed by nationals, and were more completely excluded from participation in political and trade union activity. In northern Italy, however, the immigrant workers occupying positions in the secondary labour market were from the South.

Innovative and radical tactics were a second important characteristic of the years 1968-1972. In particular, an emphasis was placed on the use of types of action capable of disorganising the cycle of production, of preventing production from restarting immediately after the end of strike activity, and of reducing production while continuing to work, so that the losses incurred by the company were maximised and the wages foregone by the workers minimised. Strikes were articulated over time ('spot strikes') and across space.

> "In 'rolling strikes' brief stoppages follow periods of work in sequences which differ from shop to shop, from line to line, even from worker to worker, in such a way that at the same time people are working while others are striking all over the factory. The result obviously upsets the production flow. The more rigid and integrated it is, the greater the impact. In chemical and steel factories this form of action sometimes seriously damaged plants or prevented them from functioning for many days after the end of a strike."

Another tactic was the go-slow.

> "To go slow on the assembly lines, the workers must every now and then let a piece pass without doing what is necessary to it. From 1970 to 1972 outstanding examples of this type of strike occurred in several big car, electrical appliance, and tyre firms. Sometimes when the 'missed out' job was hard to detect at the checkpoint or when, on the assembly line, each worker let a different piece pass, so that at the end not one completely assembled piece came out, these actions approached sabotage. However, no explicit cases of organised sabotage were ever recorded." (Regalia et al, 1978, pages 111-122)

The go-slow was one example of '*una lotta che pratica l'obiettivo*' or a struggle that puts its goal into practice. In this case the struggle's aim of enhancing working-class control over the pace and conditions of work or of reducing incentives were achieved without management agreement and were prefigured during the conflict itself (see Regalia et al, 1978, pages 114-191; Sabel, 1982, page 161).

In the third place, new and radical demands were made. Contractual demands went beyond the usual ones for improved wages. Equal wage increases for all workers were demanded with a view to reducing wage differentials, widening support, and increasing solidarity. Moreover, this demand was made not only by unskilled and semiskilled workers but sometimes also by skilled workers, whereas a less radical version of the implied egalitarianism was adopted by the unions. Skill hierarchies were also attacked, with demands for the elimination of many levels in the job hierarchy, collective upgrading, and guaranteed promotions. In addition, demands were made for job rotation, job enhancement, job enrichment, work groups, and production islands so that all workers learnt to perform maintenance and supervisory tasks. The workers pressed for a reduction in the length of the standard working week, restrictions on overtime and shift work, and the abolition of piece-rate systems. In addition, demands were made for more control over the organisation, pace, and conditions of work, and for the development of democratically controlled organisations representing working-class interests at the factory level (see, for example, Regalia et al, 1978, pages 122-132).

The events of the late 1960s did not just reflect dissatisfaction with Taylorist and Fordist principles of work organisation. Also condemned were other facets of modern urban life in the industrial cities of the North, existing institutions, and the centre-left government. In particular, discontent with rising unemployment, with lengthening journeys to work and inadequate transport services, with strained public services, with worsening housing conditions, and with urban congestion was growing. As a result, demands were made for improved public services and housing and for reduced distribution costs. Others were connected with the system of general economic planning and with the geographical location of investment, with demands for the location of more investment in the South being particularly prominent.

The existence of these demands alongside the contractual ones was important in several respects. It reflected the fact that for many southerners working in the north, an improvement in the working and living conditions of the whole of the working class was important. More significantly, it carried the conflict outside of the factories and acted as an important unifying element.

At first the employers were put on the defensive. In plants and sectors where the movement was strongest and the most militant action occurred the workers made major gains. What was more, as the unions gained control of the processes of conflict and bargaining, many of the gains made in the fields covered by collective bargaining and factory contracts were consolidated and generalised via the union's contractual policy and especially through the implementation of the Statuto dei Lavoratori or Workers' Charter passed in May 1970. After 1971, however, with the onset of a global economic crisis and the movement of the electorate, especially in the South, and of the government to the right, the employers' resistance hardened. At this stage, the position of the unions was changed to one of defending the positions already obtained, and in particular of protecting real wage and employment levels. The intensity of conflict was kept at a level accepted by management, establishing a new equilibrium in the field of industrial relations. Some significant concessions were made. But, judged by their success in achieving their main goal of defending wage gains and jobs, the unions were on the whole successful.

What then were the main results of the conflicts of 1968–1972? In the first place the unions were transformed and emerged as major actors in Italian society. Union membership increased, and union organisation was extended in small and medium-sized enterprises, in geographical areas in which the unions had previously been weak, and in sectors, such as public employment, in which the so-called autonomous unions were strongest (see figure 6.2). More representative and effective union organisations were established at factory level. The unions moved further away from the tutelage of the political parties, and the moves towards unity of action of the 1960s, especially among the metalworkers' federations, gave way with the Pact of Federation of July 1972 to the creation of "a federation of the confederations and of the confederally linked federations in a variety of sectors". The unions did, however, stop short of the full organic unity envisaged in November 1971, ensuring a continuing role for the different political currents in the union movement (Lange and Vannicelli, 1982, pages 125–135).

At the factory level, in the areas covered by collective bargaining and factory contracts, several important gains were made. The old *commissioni interne* gave way to the election of *delegati* by all, and not just unionised, workers in a shop, and to the creation of *consigli di fabbrica* or assemblies of shop stewards. At first the change occurred spontaneously in some large plants. Subsequently it was generalised via union action and the implementation of the Statuto. As a result, union activity was decentralised, with bargaining being conducted by the factory councils and the 'category' or industrial unions. Starting in 1971–1972, however, some recentralisation of union activity and collective bargaining occurred (see Regalia et al, 1978, pages 141–146, 148–149; and Regini, 1980, pages 53–55).

On the shop floor, job control was increased. The speed and organisation of work, the introduction of new technology, the mobility of workers, and layoffs were all turned into questions for continuous bargaining instead of ones where employers could exercise their own discretion. Job security increased. Indeed after 1971, and, especially 1974–1975, when inflation and economic crisis posed a threat not only to real wage levels but also to employment, the unions managed to maintain a de facto block on redundancies and, under the Cassa Integrazione Guadagni, obtained guarantees that workers in firms in crisis, who were 'temporarily' laid off either totally or in part, would be paid 93% of their net salary out of a state fund (see Regalia et al, 1978, pages 131–132, 135, 156). Thus, the incomes of workers who worked shorter hours or were laid off were guaranteed. Workers were, however, not the only beneficiaries. Any employer wishing to lay people off, not only found it easier to do so but also had the possibility of transferring the costs to the state.

With the introduction of plant bargaining and the new labour contracts in 1970, wages increased rapidly. In 1969-1970, as in 1963-1964, the monetary authorities responded to large increases in wages and widespread inflationary tendencies by introducing credit restrictions and a set of deflationary measures. But the measures were less strong than the ones taken in 1963-1964. The reason why lay in the fact that the PSI had suffered heavy losses in the 1968 elections. The party was pushed significantly to the left, and it agreed to continue its participation in the coalition only on certain conditions. On the one hand, it insisted that some of the reforms on which the centre-left coalition had originally been based be implemented rapidly. (The absence of significant structural reform was an important causal factor, alongside some of the more abstract ones identified in part 1, in the wage explosion and crisis of the late 1960s and early 1970s.) In practice, public spending expanded more quickly. However, significant reforms were not introduced, with the result that some of the inefficiencies contributing to the inflationary spiral were not removed. On the other hand, the PSI succeeded in ensuring that the new government was more accommodating to union demands.

Consequently, the demands for increased wages were not brought under control, and spread from national contracts into negotiations at firm level. In the years covered by the 1970-1972 national contract, average hourly earnings in manufacturing industry increased by some 20% per year (see figure 6.1), and in the first year of the new contracts, concluded with the start of a partial recovery at the end of 1972 and early in 1973, by 34.5%. In part the increases stemmed from the operation of the *scala mobile*, which was introduced in 1946 and under which wages are indexed on the cost of living. Nevertheless, and especially in the first period, very striking increases not just in money wages but also in real wages were secured (see Salvati, 1975, pages 89-95).

In the autumn of 1974 the unions pressed successfully for a reassessment of inflation adjustments. After a year in which the cost of living had increased by over 20%, the real value of working-class incomes was restored.

At the same time, employers were largely prevented by union strength from raising productivity and restoring profitability by reorganising work or laying off workers: in 1969-1973, employment held up, the number of hours worked per employee fell, and hourly productivity per employee increased only slowly (see Salvati, 1975, pages 79-89). In addition, almost all social welfare spending in Italy was financed through payroll taxes, which thus adds to wage costs, whereas increases in prices were constrained by the stability of the exchange rate and, in 1971-1972, by the stagnation of domestic demand.

Owing to the inability of the state to pursue a strong antiunion policy, and the capacity of the working class to prevent a fall in money wages, intensification of work rhythms, and reductions in personnel, the costs of labour per unit of output continued upwards, rising by 13.6% in 1970, 12.1% in 1971, 5.2% in 1972, and 12.2% in 1973 (see Salvati, 1972, pages 18–19; Salvati, 1975, pages 95–99). What followed was a shift in the distribution of income in favour of employees and dependent workers, and a strong profits squeeze.

Over a number of years, even in the face of a stagnation of the economy, in negotiations over contractual questions handled by the councils of factory delegates and the national federations, the unions were then very successful. As a result, the mechanisms of wage determination in particular were altered (see Salvati, 1979, pages 54–56), and the underpinnings of Italy's model of export-oriented development were destroyed.

But after 1970, attempts were made by the unions, or more specifically by the confederations, to go beyond work-place demands and to link them with broader social and economic policy goals. In this way the confederations were seeking a role as political protagonists pressing for reforms.

Several factors underlay these developments. In part the confederations were attempting to reaggregate the varying interests of different sections of the working class around certain unifying aims. At the same time, an attempt was being made to recentralise bargaining. But the unions were also wanting to represent the interests of a constituency beyond the one composed of employed and unionised workers. At least two reasons for this can be mentioned. One is the traditional politicisation of the trade union movement in Italy, and the concern of the CGIL in particular to act as a union representing the whole of the working class. A second is the fact that union strength depends on the breadth of union support. With underemployed, marginalised, and unemployed workers forming such a large and a possibly increasing fraction of the active population, the unions sought their support, but not without conflicts with the interests of existing union members being generated (see Regalia et al, 1978, pages 132–136).

In 1969–1971, general strikes articulated on a regional basis were used to support social demands including reforms of the housing, health, education, transport, pensions, and taxation systems, but with very disappointing results.

As early as 1971 and much more so after 1974–1975, questions of economic policy were given priority, with campaigns to defend employment levels and to develop the South. After the riots in Reggio di Calabria in 1971, for example, in which fascist groups were involved, a national demonstration calling for southern development was organised in the city, and demands were made that the investment plans of public and semipublic firms for the South be negotiated alongside the renewal of the national agreements. In 1973 and 1974, negotiations were started with the largest industrial groups with a view to getting them to carry out more new investment in the South.

More generally, calls were made for a new model of development. The unions pressed in fact for a set of measures to be carried out by the government and state institutions with a view to transforming quite radically Italy's strategy of development. Internal demand and public consumption were to be increased. The structural weaknesses of the economy were to be repaired and the conditions for full employment created, especially by dealing with the problems of the Mezzogiorno. The public sector was to be rationalised to get rid of waste and inefficiency, and the social services were to be reorganised and improved. In addition, a new fiscal policy capable of distributing the costs of government more equitably was demanded.

But politically the policy of reform and the aim of redirecting economic policy foundered on the inability of the confederations in particular to translate market strength into political action or into action by employers (see Regalia et al, 1978, pages 123-125, 132-136; Lange and Vannicelli, 1982, pages 128-131, 135-141).

6.5 The oil crisis

In 1972-1974, after some two years of stagnation, the Italian economy participated in the inflationary world boom that preceded the oil crisis. On this occasion, however, Italian growth was led not by exports but by the internal components of aggregate demand.

Several factors fuelled the recovery. First, there was a rapid and frequently speculative rebuilding of stocks. Second, an intense but brief wave of fixed investment in industry occurred: in the early 1970s the state holding companies and semipublic companies like Montedison, which were operating primarily in capital-intensive sectors, made large investments in the South with the help of the low-interest loans and grants available for southern development, and after 1971 many large private groups followed suit (see chapter 8, sections on steel, chemicals, vehicles). With the shift in the distribution of income in favour of wage earners and the generalisation of modern consumption norms, private consumption expanded. Finally, public spending underwent a process of sustained growth.

With the vigorous revival of domestic activity and the loss of competitiveness exports grew modestly, whereas imports expanded rapidly. At the same time, the terms of trade deteriorated, and a flight of capital was under way. What followed were increasing balance of payments difficulties. In February 1973 the lira was allowed to float and fell rapidly with respect to the currencies of Italy's main trading partners, thus enabling Italian capital to raise internal prices and profit margins. Overall profitability increased. But the unions responded with successful demands for increases in wages which, although smaller in real terms than the increases agreed under the 1970-1972 contracts, fuelled the process of inflation (Salvati, 1979, pages 53-61).

The increase in public spending which occurred prior to the elections of 1972 and in the recovery was, moreover, financed by increased borrowing rather than via an increased levy on those classes with greater fiscal capacity or who escaped government taxation. As a result, some of the foundations for a subsequent fiscal crisis of the state were laid, with the public-sector deficit rising to 10% of gross national product in 1976 according to the seriously inaccurate estimates of the Organisation for Economic Cooperation and Development (OECD) (Salvati, 1979, pages 53 - 61).

In 1975 the Italian economy participated in the deep world recession that followed the quadrupling of oil prices and the more general breakdown of the US dominated international economic order established after the Second World War. In the winter of 1975 - 1976 it made a rapid recovery. But the process of recovery was accompanied by a serious currency crisis that led to a sharp fall in the exchange rate of the lira and a new wave of inflation fuelled in part by the renewal of the main collective agreements in 1976, and especially by the revision of the system of indexation agreed in February 1975 (see OECD, 1977, pages 6 - 19; Salvati, 1979, pages 56 - 61).

At that point an important political shift was under way in Italy. In the national elections held one year early in 1972 the Right had made some gains, and in the years up to 1976 a series of weak and unstable governments were formed: a government of the centre was followed by a centre-left government, and by two minority governments depending upon support from the left. In the administrative elections of June 1975 the PCI made a great leap forward. A year later, in the general elections of June 1976, the PCI obtained 34.4% of the votes cast, compared with 27.1% in the preceding election and the 38.7% obtained on both occasions by the DC. The outcome was the formation of minority DC governments sustained in parliament by the parties of the Left, and the inclusion in effect of the PCI in the governing majority but not in the government (Salvati, 1979, pages 61 - 66).

What resulted was a relatively stable political situation which, along with an increased measure of self-restraint on the part of the trade union movement, provided the preconditions for a central bank strategy of economic stabilisation and austerity. Introduced in 1976 with a violent credit squeeze, the programme of austerity was sustained for two and a half years. Investment and economic activity stagnated, and unemployment, concentrated in the South and amongst women and young people seeking a first job, remained at a high level, with about 1.5 million people or 7% of the active population out of work. But there was a remarkable improvement in the balance of payments situation, with exports expanding once again from the end of 1976, partly as a result of cost advantages acquired through an expansion of subcontracting and putting out, and through the growth of the black economy. Inflationary pressures were, however, less easy to bring under control. In 1976 - 1978 prices and wages continued to increase quite rapidly. With only modest increases in labour productivity being achieved, unit labour costs in industry increased by about 12% (Salvati, 1979, pages 61-66).

Along with all other advanced capitalist economies, the Italian economy was, in other words, affected by violent oscillations in the level of activity and strong inflationary impulses. In Italy these movements were, however, more severe owing to the persistence of internal disequilibria: the gap between the North and the South, the underdevelopment of large parts of the agricultural sector, the uneven development of public and private consumption, the inflationary trends caused by speculation and inefficiency in the service sector and distribution, and the low level of efficiency in the public administration. Yet in the 1970s, effective reforms could not be introduced.

6.6 The strategies of Italian capital

After the autumno caldo, the working-class movement and the PCI emerged as major actors alongside the middle strata traditionally represented by the DC and the various fractions of Italian capital. What I have not considered is the way in which the industrial bourgeoisie reacted to the crisis and to the new political situation.

By that time, Italian industrialists were divided into at least two clear groups, represented by different organisations and standing in different relationships to the DC. On one side were the private business interests, represented by Confindustria. On the other was the state bourgeoisie, with its own Ministry of State Shareholdings since 1956 and represented since 1957 by Intersind.

After the Second World War the state sector had strong interests in declining sectors and continued to be used to salvage firms that on normal commercial criteria would have been closed. In the 1960s, rescued enterprises in the heavy engineering, shipbuilding, and textile sectors continued to record substantial net losses. But with the establishment of ENI under Mattei's aggressive leadership, the oil and gas industry, which was vital to industrial growth, was developed. IRI, meanwhile, carried out ambitious programmes of investment in the steel industry, in telecommunications, in motorway building, and in sea and air transport. In the 1960s, state-controlled enterprises were in general more modernist than the private sector in the fields of work organisation and industrial relations, and supported the centre-left strategy of planning and social reform. As a result, the state sector came to be seen by many observers as representing innovation, efficiency, and growth, as well as industrial democracy, while "still serving the ends of government economic policy and the interests of society as a whole" (Holland, 1972, page 1).

In the 1950s and 1960s the state holding companies expanded very rapidly. But the main investments were in sectors that required very large capital investments and involved levels of risk that were unlikely to have been accepted by the private sector. Furthermore, in the financing of investment, increases in the companies' endowment funds supplied by the government and access to the government-controlled funds for southern development played a significant role[3]. In these conditions a symbiotic relationship developed between the state holding companies and the state. At the level of specific strategies the state sector emerged as an instrument of party management of the economy, and, after the mid-1960s, managerial efficiency was subordinated not so much to social goals as to the interests represented by different factions of the DC and the party's strategy of regime building (see Martinelli, 1980, pages 75, 77-83; 1981, pages 89-93).

After 1970, not only did different sections of the industrial bourgeoisie adopt different strategies, but also some serious conflicts emerged within the dominant social bloc.

In sectors with a high capital intensity the state holding companies and semipublic groups such as Montedison both aimed at reducing the strength of the unions by making the role of the worker in production less important. For the managers in these firms in which growth required extremely large financial investments, access to special credit, including funds for southern industrialisation, and a close relationship with the state were necessary. Moreover, since new investment generated little additional employment, it was accepted that the problems of unemployment, exacerbated by the reduced opportunities for emigration, should be solved by increasing employment in urban services and by welfare spending.

Accordingly, in 1972 in the Senate hearings on the chemical industry, the president of Montedison, Cefis, traced an ambitious plan for the industry. It would, in his view, develop products with a high technological content and enter into other sectors such as building, health, food processing and agribusiness. Excess manpower in industry should be absorbed by the growth of the tertiary sector and of the public administration. And since sufficient extra employment would not be provided by these developments, an increase in welfare provision would be needed (see Graziani, 1976, pages 328-333; Martinelli, 1980, page 81).

As members of a party pursuing a policy of clientelism and welfarism, many elements and factions of the DC found this strategy congenial to the party's interests of consensus formation.

---

[3] The sources of finance were several: internally, amortisation funds, pension funds, retained profits, and sales of assets; and externally, state endowments or '*dotazioni*', issue of bonds without any equity element, long-term and medium-term bank loans, and short-term borrowing. (State endowments are capital grants. Endowment funds are not provided on a regular basis. Instead they must be applied for by the state holding company concerned with an argued case for the use to which they would be put. In return, the holding company is legally bound to give the Treasury 65% of net profits.) The subsidiary holding and operating companies were allowed to raise money by the sale of shares (see Posner and Woolf, 1967, chapter 5).

In sectors with a high labour intensity, including, in particular, the often export-oriented engineering and related sectors, in which private industrial groups were predominant, a different strategy was espoused. Industrialists were interested in restructuring operations aimed at containing labour costs and raising labour productivity, and a variety of measures intended to promote a more rapid modernisation of the industrial system and an increase in the international competitiveness of the national economy were advocated. At the same time, however, the firms in these sectors also depended on a widening of the domestic market and an expansion of exports as a means of achieving the scale economies and the high levels of capacity utilisation on which a reduction in production costs depended. Thus, after the autumno caldo a number of large private industrialists linked with firms like FIAT, Olivetti, and Pirelli started to stress the need for reforms aimed at improving living conditions and providing more efficient services, came out against indiscriminating policies of welfare of the kind practised in the South in particular, and proposed an alliance against strata occupying rentier positions in Italian society. Improved service provision was to be accomplished, however, not by new spending commitments, but by making more effective use of the resources already being allocated to public services and by eliminating inefficiencies and parasitic sectors that had developed merely to mop up unemployment. In this way, of course, it was hoped that indirect costs and the pressure for increased money wages in their own industries would be lowered.

At a political level the heads of the major private industrial groups criticised the role of the DC in managing the economy and its close relationships with the state sector. What they wanted was a government that mediated the interests of different elements of the dominant bloc and negotiated with the emergent political forces represented by the unions and the parties of the left.

Via Confindustria, over which these fractions of capital regained control in the early 1970s, several goals were sought. One was a role as a key political actor and a privileged but independent partner of government, with the quest for autonomy being translated on occasions into attempts to reach agreements directly with the unions and into a strategy of increasing the support given to smaller centre parties. A process of dialogue and negotiation with the unions was sought. In addition, a campaign in favour of the centrality of the firm and of private capital and against state interventionism and managerial inefficiency was conducted.

In the end it was the strategy favoured by private capital that prevailed. But the DC continued to play the major role in the political representation of business interests, and compromises had to be made with the state-controlled sector and with the DC's politics of patronage and welfarism (see Martinelli, 1980, pages 82–86).

At an economic level, however, major private industrialists supported a dual strategy vis-à-vis the working class. On the one hand, improved services and real wage increases were negotiated with factory workers in the primary sector. Indeed, after 1970, unionised industrial workers enjoyed considerable protection: real wages were protected by indexation, the mobility of labour within and between plants was rigidly controlled, firings were virtually out of the question, and workers laid off continued to get most of their normal earnings. On the other hand, many large employers sought to circumvent the increased strength of the union movement and to get union agreement to plans for work reorganisation. In the first place, hiring was frozen, and workers who left were not replaced: according to a study of the major industrial groups, accounting on average for one quarter of industrial employment, jobs in large private groups fell only slightly in the first half of the 1970s (see table 6.2). Second, specific operations or entire processes of production were subcontracted out and decentralised to small enterprises, semiartisan workshops, and outworkers to evade the job control and the high wages and other costs associated with work in central plants. In the third place, attempts were made to get agreements on rationalising and reorganising work.

The process of *decentramento produttivo* and the parallel development of an extralegal and invisible economy, providing in some cases second jobs for people regularly employed in the primary sector, are, as we shall see, components of a set of important sectoral and geographical developments in Italian industry.

After increasing at a rate of, on average, 7.5% per year in 1968–1973, investment in plant and machinery marked time, consistently exceeding depreciation only in medium-sized firms. After the mid-1970s, however, innovation and reorganisation of production and the renewal of production capacity were confined to a large extent to small and medium-sized

Table 6.2. Changes in employment (in thousands) in the major groups, 1971–1981. Source: Alzona, cited in OECD (1984, page 27).

	1971–1975	1976–1977	1978–1979	1980–1981
Total change				
All industry (excluding construction)	179.8	21.5	−26.2	−76.1
All major groups	160.3	−10.3	−24.3	−98.2
private	−13.0	−10.3	−7.1	−99.6
public	170.6	−0.3	−17.9	3.0
foreign	2.7	0.3	0.7	−1.6
Changes due to purchase or sale of firms				
All major groups	80.9	21.2	−13.3	−6.3
private	−9.2	14.8	−8.2	−22.6
public	90.1	5.6	−5.3	15.3
foreign	–	0.8	0.2	1.0

enterprises, whose numbers increased sharply: according to the census of industry and services the number of firms increased by 21% in the 1970s compared with 4% in the 1960s, whereas the average number of employees per firm fell from 77 in the early 1970s to 57 in the early 1980s.

The growth of these small and medium-sized firms was not, however, simply associated with low-technology production, with increased flexibility in the use of labour, and with the circumvention of tax and social security payments. In some cases a growing emphasis on robotics, computer-aided manufacturing, and precision engineering were involved, and frequently specialisation increased. Moreover, as a result of an increased emphasis on the final stages of production and on the manufacturing of high-quality goods, along with the depreciation of the lira, Italian firms were comparatively successful in exporting the products of traditional consumption-good sectors including food products, textiles, clothing, footwear, leather goods, and wood products where, however, competition from newly industrialising economies was and is strong. (Italy's international specialisation is indicated in figure 6.3.)

In the 1970s, large firms fared much less well, especially in the public sector. First, the state holding companies had already been weakened by the impact on decisionmaking of the competition between interest groups vying for access to state-guaranteed resources, on the one hand, and the DC's political management of the economy, on the other. Second, major investments had been carried out in sectors, such as oil, chemicals, and steel, which were badly hit by the crisis. In the third place, inefficient and failing private firms were rescued: in 1971–1975, employment in public-sector

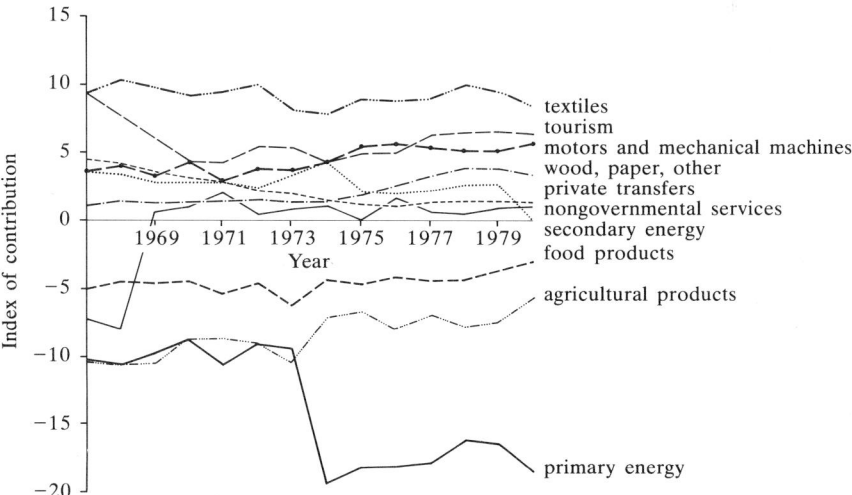

Figure 6.3. The contribution of different sectors to Italy's current balance of payments, 1968–1980. Source: CEPII (1983, pages 97, 120–126).

groups increased very substantially owing to the takeover of ailing units belonging to private firms and the government's employment support policy (see table 6.2). Finally, the methods of financing investment entailed a heavy dependence on external funds and high gearing. In growing rapidly, the state sector could not rely on self-financing or on increases in its endowment funds and the issuing of equity capital. Instead, long-term, medium-term, and, increasingly, short-term borrowing at fixed rates of interest were used as the means of financing investment. In general, a high degree of dependence on fixed-interest debt is advantageous for a company that is growing rapidly. But once profitability falls the already high proportion of profit that has to be distributed goes up, and once losses are incurred, indebtedness, high fixed costs, and difficulty in attracting funds place the companies concerned in much greater financial difficulty than less highly geared concerns (see Posner and Woolf, 1967, chapter 5; OECD, 1972, pages 71-81).

As a result of all these factors the state sector was to find itself in a state of deep crisis manifested in a series of political scandals, disastrous economic performances, and increasing indebtedness. In addition, investments in the South, whose development I shall go on to consider, were brought into question.

A history of policies for southern industrialisation

In the first half of the present century a variety of fiscal and customs concessions, which included the provisions contained in the Special Law for Naples, were granted to southern industry. In the first phase of southern policy, the industrial credit sections of the southern banks were strengthened, and, in 1953, three special credit institutes were reorganised or created to supply low-interest credit in the Mezzogiorno: Istituto per lo Sviluppo Economico dell'Italia Meridionale (ISVEIMER), which operated on the southern mainland, Istituto Regionale per il Finanziamento delle Industrie Piccole e Medie in Sicilia (IRFIS) in Sicily, and Credito Industriale per la Sardegna (CIS) in Sardinia.

These measures were, however, not especially important, and industry continued to be neglected. One reason why southern industrialisation was neglected lay in a certain scepticism about the possibility of national industrial development. More importantly, northern capital and the state were anxious to concentrate in the North the resources allocated to industrial development, and to avoid the development in the South, perhaps with state protection and subsidisation, of industries which might compete with existing or new industries in the North (Graziani, 1976, page 314).

In 1957 the policy of extraordinary intervention entered a new phase and was redirected to encourage industrial development in the Mezzogiorno. This modification in the direction of southern policy arose in part because inequalities between the North and the South of Italy had continued to increase during the preindustrialisation phase. In the 1950s in spite of the emigration of about 1.5 million people southern per capita income fell as a percentage of the national average. Moreover, the employment situation had not improved, since total employment had fallen and unemployment and underemployment continued to pose serious problems.

However, the change in southern policy also reflected some of the needs of Italian capitalism in a period of increasing European integration. In 1957 the EEC was formed. The successful exploitation of the opportunities offered by expanding international trade depended critically upon the structure and competitiveness of Italian industry. At that stage, competitiveness was dependent not only upon effective use of the advantages stemming from the low reproduction costs of labour power. It also depended upon the capacity of industries producing energy and intermediate goods to meet international competition and to provide necessary inputs for the expanding engineering industries. In other words, a strategy for national industrial development was almost certainly going to entail an expansion of investments, probably by the state holding companies in sectors producing energy, chemicals, steel, and so on.

The development of plans for an expansion of these sectors coincided with changes in southern policy. In the first place, large amounts of subsidised credit and grants for investment in the South were provided. Second, directives requiring the state holding companies to locate a specified proportion of their new and total investment in the Mezzogiorno were reaffirmed. And finally, a growth-centre strategy was established.

In the early 1960s, major investments by the state holding companies in industries producing energy and intermediate goods initiated the process of southern industrialisation, and much of the subsequent state-supported investment in the Mezzogiorno was associated with the expansion and restructuring of enterprises operating in these sectors.

The reformulation of southern policy occurred slowly. Change was slow, in part because investment decisions were guided by considerations of profitability and not by any assessment of the wider costs of concentrating development in the North. The South still tended to be viewed as a labour supply area, and the lack of spontaneous investment in the region, even with the availability of aid, was thought to justify the official view that the South suffered from a lack of entrepreneurship, an inefficient industrial system, and a general unsuitability for industrial development. The new political equilibrium between northern industrialists and a class of bureaucrats and speculators in the South could also only be preserved by postponing southern industrial development or by restricting it to isolated initiatives that did not interfere with the practices of local clientele structures (see chapter 5, section 5.9; and Graziani, 1976, pages 318–320). After 1957, policies for southern industrialisation were used almost continuously to support the development of large plants producing energy and intermediate goods in a small number of industrial zones, of which the most important are the Naples–Caserta zone and the Bari–Brindisi–Taranto triangle on the mainland, the Catania–Siracusa axis in Sicily, and the Ottana–Porto Torres zone in Sardinia.

But significant modifications were, nevertheless, made to the measures designed to secure industrial development. The changes reflected not only the impact and mode of functioning of existing measures, but also changes in the evolution of the national economy. In the 1960s, when it was realised that regional inequalities constituted a structural problem that was blocking the expansion of the national economy, and that the southern problem was a central problem of national development, new laws which sought to integrate southern policy with the national economic planning system were, for example, introduced. After the autumno caldo, when the increasing costs of reproduction of labour power were reducing the profitability of private investment, northern capitalists wishing to decentralise operations in comparatively labour-intensive branches of production sought changes in the system of regional aid. But before examining the spatial developments associated with successive sets of measures, the history of the policies themselves must be outlined.

7.1 The policy for southern industrialisation from Law 634 of 1957, to 1965
The policy of extraordinary intervention was formally modified by Law 634, which was passed in 1957 but which only came into effect from 1959 onwards. This law extended the duration of the activity of the Cassa per il Mezzogiorno until 1965, and increased its funds to 2040 milliard lire. It also brought the phase of preindustrialisation to an end, and ushered in a new phase in which industrial development was to be actively promoted. In all, three major innovations were introduced.

(1) A growth-centre policy based on the ideas of unbalanced growth and on a geographical interpretation of the concept of the growth pole or development centre was introduced. These centres were intended to be areas in which general infrastructural investment and industrial zones for new plants were to be concentrated. The aim was one of ensuring that complementary industries and services were developed alongside one another, and of establishing a diversified labour market, in the hope that external economies would reach a level that approached those existing in more advanced regions.

Subsequent legislation passed in 1959 and 1960 proposed that two categories of growth centre be identified. On the one hand, 'areas of industrial development' (ASI) were to be composed of a number of communes with a combined population of more than 200000 inhabitants and with several industrial estates. On the other, 'nuclei of industrialisation' (NI) were to be composed of one or two communes, usually with fewer than 75000 inhabitants, and with a single industrial estate.

The original law authorised the creation of growth consortia on the initiative of local bodies, although these consortia had to be approved by the Committee of Ministers for the Mezzogiorno. The consortia were to be responsible for drawing up a planning scheme for the area on the basis of criteria and directives laid down by the Committee of Ministers for the Mezzogiorno, and for carrying out and operating the works envisaged in the plan. The Cassa could make a grant to the consortia not exceeding one half of the expenditure incurred in the execution of the infrastructural work (Allen and MacLennan, 1970, pages 66-74).

In the end, local pressures, stemming from the widely felt desire to benefit or to profit from these provisions, led to a multiplication of consortia and of growth centres, with the result that by the early 1970s seventeen areas and twenty-nine nuclei covering a large proportion of the land area of the Mezzogiorno had been recognised (see figure 7.1).

(2) The state holding companies were required, by the law, to locate in the South by 1964-1965 not less than 60% of their aggregate investment in new industrial plant and not less than 40% of their total investment, and to act equally in all regions. (A similar provision had been included in Act 646 of 1950, but had been largely ignored.)

(3) Existing industrial incentives were widened and new tax concessions, capital grants, and loans at subsidised rates of interest were added.
(i) The fiscal incentives eventually involved partial or complete exemption from six forms of tax or duty for firms setting up, expanding, or modernising in the South. The incentive schemes also included some transport concessions (Allen and MacLennan, 1970, pages 54–55, 59–60).
(ii) The law introduced a system of capital grants. These grants were originally to be worth up to 20% of permissible expenditure for the establishment of small and medium-sized firms in communes with populations not exceeding 75 000 inhabitants and a shortage of industrial activities, and up to 10% of the expenditure incurred in purchasing fixed assets which had not been exempted from customs duties (Forte, 1979, pages 266–268).

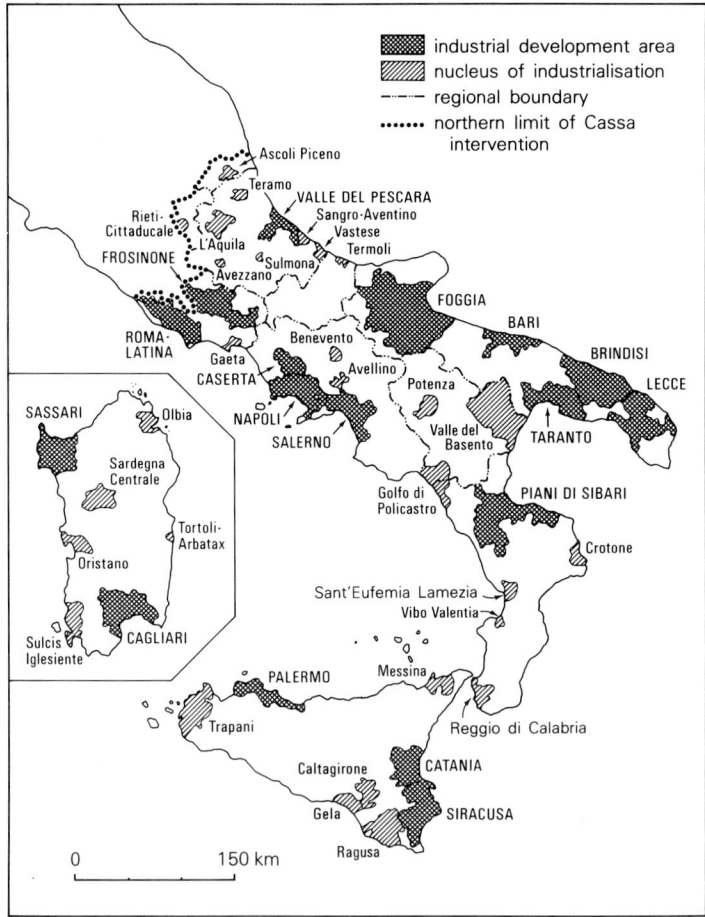

Figure 7.1. Areas of industrial development and nuclei of industrialisation in the early 1970s.

The criteria for awarding capital grants were subsequently defined more carefully and modified in various ways. The Cassa was eventually allowed to make grants worth up to 25% of the building costs of small and medium sized enterprises, with fixed assets not exceeding 6 milliard lire[4], locating or expanding in the South. The actual size of the building grant was to vary, with higher percentage grants for modern industries and large investments, for lower levels of investment per employee, and for location in growth centres. In addition, the Cassa could give grants worth up to 10% of the expenditure on machinery or equipment not exempted from customs duties, or up to 20% when it was purchased from southern suppliers (Allen and MacLennan, 1970, pages 55–57). The original aim of these subsidies was to encourage the development of a network of small and medium-sized firms able to provide a large amount of industrial employment in the South. But the need to release labour to promote northern industrial development and the need to attract modern industries led to successive modifications of this strategy. In subsequent years, financial assistance was progressively made available to larger enterprises through special provisions or through changes in the law which were introduced in 1959, in 1961, and in 1962. It was decided at first that financial assistance was to be made available only to enterprises with fixed assets not exceeding 6 milliard lire. But eligibility for grant aid was extended to the expansion of existing enterprises and to enterprises locating in centres with up to 200 000 inhabitants and in growth centres. Furthermore, in 1961 the limit of 6 milliard lire was made applicable not to the size of enterprise but to the size of each individual unit of production. As a result, aid was made available to enterprises of any size provided that the project was subdivided into several establishments. In 1962, Law 1462 made it possible for grants to be awarded for the first 6 milliard lire invested by firms of any size locating in growth centres. These modifications in the system of incentives, combined with the discretion exercised by the Cassa in the allocation of grants, opened up the possibility of grant aid being used to support major investments in southern growth centres by monopolistic northern groups and, more importantly, by the state holding companies whose new investments were increasingly to be located in the South.

(iii) Under the new law the Cassa was also entitled to advance medium-term credit at subsidised interest rates through the three special credit institutes which had been reorganised or created in 1953. At the same time, the right to advance low-interest loans in the Mezzogiorno was extended to medium-term credit institutes operating in the other regions of Italy. By the early

---

[4] After the British devaluation of September 1949 the exchange rate between the pound sterling and the Italian lira was approximately L1740 to £1. The basic unit employed in most Italian economic accounting is a milliard lire or one thousand million lire (L1 mld). It was equivalent to about £570 000. After the British devaluation of November 1967 it was equivalent to about £600 000.

1960s, loans were available at an interest rate of 4% for firms which were setting up, expanding, or being converted in the South with fixed investments in each unit of production or establishment not in excess of 6 milliard lire, whereas plants with fixed investments exceeding 6 milliard lire could secure loans at an interest rate of 5%. In addition, provision was made for special loans at interest rates of 3% for a period of fifteen years for investments of up to 1.5 milliard lire in new plant, and of up to 500 million lire for the expansion, modernisation, or conversion of existing plant. The loan could not exceed 70% of the cost of the project. A firm could receive a grant as well as a loan. But the grant and loan could not exceed 85% of the cost of the total investment (Allen and MacLennan, 1970, pages 58-59). The effects of these incentives on the attractiveness of southern locations was, however, partially offset by the extension of low-interest credit to small and medium-sized firms in the rest of Italy.

7.2 Selectivity and the integration of southern policy with economic planning in Law 717 of 1965

The next step in the development of southern policy occurred when the centre-left government passed Law 717 in 1965. This law extended the life of the Cassa up to 1980 and allocated it increased funds of 1640 milliard lire for the period 1965-1969 compared with 2216 milliard lire for the period 1950-1965. This sum was increased by 560 milliard lire in 1968 to cover the year 1970 and to help the Cassa through difficulties caused by the exhaustion of its funds for industrial development in 1968. The new law also resulted in the creation of a broad interministerial committee for the South, operating in the framework of the Interministerial Committee for Economic Planning (Comitato Interministeriale della Programmazione Economica or CIPE). This committee had the task of formulating pluriennial coordination plans, with a view to coordinating ordinary and extraordinary public activities in the South and providing the necessary link with the National Economic Plan. At the same time, an attempt was made to ensure that the work of the Cassa was additional to, rather than a substitute for, the activity of the ordinary administration, by introducing a requirement that at least 40% of all investment expenditure by the various ministries be located in the South.

The closer integration of southern policy with the national economic planning framework occurred largely because of a recognition of the connection between balanced regional development and the future progress of the national economy.

An equalisation of the level of development in different regions had in fact been one of the three main objectives of the Vanoni Plan for the period 1954-1964. But by the early 1960s the plan's regional objectives had not been met owing to the lack of expansion of extraagricultural employment. Indeed, the imbalances between backward and advanced regions had increased continuously, despite the fact that many of the growth targets on which fulfillment of the plan's regional objectives was thought to depend had been exceeded. One explanation for the nonachievement of regional targets was presented by Saraceno when he suggested that the plan had not anticipated certain stimuli to the process of national economic development which led northern management to seek to improve the competitive position of Italian industry and to increase capacity by expanding in the North rather than by locating major new ventures in the South. Included were the effect of foreign demand on the expansion of manufacturing industry, the effect of higher than anticipated rates of growth of income in the North on the growth of consumption-good industries, and the impact of EEC membership (see Holland, 1971, pages 71-90).

The first National Economic Plan, which was to cover the period from 1966-1970 also included quantitative objectives for southern development. Indeed, the location of 40% of new nonagricultural jobs in the South was one of the main objectives of the plan. The problem was that the plan itself, which was approved by the Council of Ministers (Consiglio dei Ministri) in January 1965, was not finally ratified by Parliament until March 1967, and if any attempt was made to meet its basic investment, employment, and regional targets, it failed completely. The plan's lack of success can be explained in part by the general economic conditions prevailing at that time. But it is also significant that the targets which were not achieved were the very ones whose fulfillment depended upon the establishment of adequate instruments and institutions to implement the plan, on the one hand, and upon active interference with and correction of the model of export-led growth, on the other. It is for this reason that the fate of the National Economic Plan is one of the more important examples of the general failings of the reformist programme of the centre-left government.

Around 1968 a system of planning agreements was introduced (known as the *contrattazione programmata*) in order to link industrial investment with the plan. This procedure involved negotiations between CIPE and large industrial firms, in part with the aim of comparing the southern investment intentions of the companies with the infrastructural provisions planned by the ordinary and extraordinary administrations. The object of the system was to check whether these investment decisions corresponded with the guidelines laid down by the plan, to encourage blocks of interdependent investments which were supported by industrial incentives and were located in well-equipped industrial zones in accordance with the needs of southern industrial development, and to secure a greater degree of correspondence between the investment plans of the major companies and of the public authorities. However, the initiative continued to rest with the companies, and the system itself simply afforded a framework within which large firms could exert pressure to secure from the state, financial assistance and infrastructural investments corresponding to their specific needs.

The new law itself was more concerned with rationalising interventions and provided for a much greater concentration of the activities of the Cassa than the preceding one. A larger part of the activities and expenditures of the Cassa were to be concentrated in areas capable of more rapid development. Included were designated irrigation districts and the agricultural areas connected with them, which covered about 3 million of some 11.5 million hectares of agricultural land in the South, areas of tourist development, and industrial development zones located mainly in the areas of plain situated near the coast. The achievement of some form of equal development within the South was to depend entirely on the activities of the ordinary public administration.

In the new law a marked shift in the composition of foreseen expenditure was proposed, with spending on industrial development increasing sharply. In addition, some important changes were made in the major provisions for southern industrialisation.

(1) The Cassa was given the right to take over some of the tasks connected with the executing of works and with the equipping of growth centres from the consortia, whereas the latter were required to promote and assist industrial ventures and to assume the tasks of managing and maintaining infrastructural works. The Cassa was also required to provide 85% of the finance for the provision of general infrastructural equipment and 40% for the provision of infrastructural equipment serving individual firms (Del Monte and Giannola, 1978, pages 290–291).

(2) The ruling that required the state holding companies to locate a specified proportion of their investment in the South was extended for five years.

(3) The funds allocated to industrial development were substantially increased. At the same time, the grants and loans were increased in value and were to be used in a more discriminatory way in favour of modern growth industries and growth centres, and in favour of projects meeting preestablished criteria.

(i) In principle, subsidised loans were granted for fixed investments up to a maximum of 12 milliard lire and could cover up to 70% of the cost of the investment. In the case of investments of more than that amount, the original ruling was that a loan on the additional investment could not exceed 50% of the sum granted in respect of the first 12 milliard lire. But in March 1968, fixed investments exceeding 12 milliard lire were made eligible for loans covering up to 40% of the whole investment but at interest rates that rose with the size of the investment on the condition that certain vague conditions were met. The actual proportion of admissible expenditure covered by the loans and the actual rate of interest depended on the location, industrial sector, and size of the investment. At that time, preference was given to (a) plants that were located in growth centres and in their industrial zones in particular; (b) modern growth industries such as the food processing, chemical, engineering, and capital goods sectors, and industries making considerable use of local resources; and (c) the larger sizes of investment within each of twelve industrial groups, where the sizes depended on what was considered to be an appropriate scale for plants in the relevant class (Allen and MacLennan, 1970, pages 85-88).

(ii) In addition, capital grants were made available for up to 20% of admissible investment expenditure in the case of fixed investments not exceeding 6 milliard lire. In the case of the part of an investment in excess of this amount but not exceeding 12 milliard lire, the maximum grant was 10%. In the case of investments exceeding 12 milliard lire, the grant on the amount exceeding this sum was originally limited to 50% of the grant conceded in respect of the first 12 milliard lire. This ruling was also amended in March 1968, such that enterprises with fixed investments in excess of 12 milliard lire could obtain grants equal to a maximum of 12% of their admissible expenditure, provided once again that certain vague conditions were fulfilled. The size of grant made to any enterprise could be increased by 50% for that part of the investment that involved expenditure on machinery produced in the South. The criteria for the actual award of grants were similar to those for loans, except that in this case the criterion of size gave preference to smaller instead of larger investment projects. It should also be noted that only new establishments with an investment in excess of 80 million lire could benefit fully from these incentives (Allen and MacLennan, 1970, pages 88-90).

(iii) The fiscal incentives applying to enterprises located in the South were extended up to 1980, and some changes and additions were made.

A growing body of criticism of the use of a system of capital incentives as part of a policy with the declared aim of providing industrial employment in the South, together with the impact of increasing unit labour costs on northern firms, led to the introduction in October 1968 of a system of labour subsidies. This ystem operated through reductions in social security payments for handicraft industries and industrial enterprises in the South, and was extended and made more generous in subsequent laws for southern development.

7.3 Incentives policy and national programming in Law 853 of 1971
The next law was passed in 1971. Law 853 was based on the view that the development of southern Italy should be the fundamental objective of the national economic plan, although in the end a specified national plan was not produced. The institutional framework for southern policy was, however, changed by suppressing the Interministerial Committee for Extraordinary Activities in the South (Comitato Interministeriale per gli Interventi Straordinari nel Mezzogiorno), and by transferring the planning and coordinating functions to CIPE, in order to integrate action for the South into the wider framework of national planning and national industrial policy.

At the same time, the southern regions created in the regional reform of 1970 were given a limited role in the formulation of policies for southern development. A consultative committee composed of the presidents of the southern regional governments was formed within the Ministry of the Budget and Economic Planning (Ministero del Bilancio e della Programmazione Economica), and the regions were given a role in the formulation of special projects (Allum, 1973a, pages 212-238). A few rather limited activities were delegated to the new regional governments, but the Cassa retained its functions of implementing southern policy and of financing and coordinating the activities of its associated organs. The Cassa was granted 7125 milliard lire for the period 1971-1975.

The Cassa was required to see to the complete implementation of programmes which had already been approved under the previous legislation. But the new law introduced some important changes in the way in which southern policy was to work in subsequent years. The most important innovation was the introduction of the new system of special projects. Under the heading of special projects were placed intersectoral and interregional projects involving (1) the construction of large-scale infrastructural works for general and for industrial purposes, (2) the use and protection of natural resources and of the environment, (3) the equipping of existing metropolitan areas or of new development areas, and (4) the promotion of economic activities in specific areas and specific productive sectors. The projects themselves could be formulated either by regional governments or by the Minister for Extraordinary Activities in the South (Ministro per gli Interventi Straordinari nel Mezzogiorno). Once formulated they were to be submitted to CIPE, whose task was to check that they corresponded with the national plan. The technical elaboration and implementation of these projects were to be undertaken by the Cassa or by related bodies.

In the new law an attempt was also made to increase the degree of state control over the investments made by large companies. The investment plans of some companies, including all of those with a share capital of not less than 5 milliard lire, and all investment projects involving the construction or expansion of industrial plants and costing more than 7 milliard lire had to be authorised by CIPE. The aim of this ruling was to ensure that these plans and projects were compatible with the directives for national economic planning and to limit new investment in areas suffering from congestion and from shortages of labour. It was intended that any company not submitting plans or projects, or ignoring rulings, should be penalised. But owing to the lack of effective sanctions, this attempt by the state to increase its ability to control the location of large private capitals proved to be quite ineffective.

State-controlled investments and expenditures were, however, directed more strongly to the South. The share of state holding company investment to be located in southern regions was increased from 60% to 80% for new construction, and to at least 60% for aggregate investment. The state holding companies were also required to submit annually a five-year investment plan for the southern regions.

At the same time, the system of industrial incentives was amended and aimed more specifically at the stimulation of small and medium-sized firms, and at giving CIPE more control over large investments. The new pattern is summarised in table 7.1. CIPE was required to determine the general directives for southern industrial policies. What was involved was the determination of directives that would encourage a less concentrated pattern of development in the South, and the choice of directives that concerned the way in which the loans and grants available to enterprises were to be graduated. But CIPE was also required to specify priority sectors for expanding and strengthening the national productive system and employment. All decisions concerning the eligibility for aid of investments by small and medium-sized firms and the grading of incentives were to depend upon the conformity of the project with the general directives outlined by CIPE. In the case of large enterprises, the grading of incentives and the provision of specific infrastructural equipment were to be negotiated

Table 7.1. The system of grants and loans for industrial development in the Mezzogiorno, 1971–1975. Sources: elaborated from OECD (1973, pages 50–53) and Belhadj et al (1975, page 27).

Size of enterprise	Class of enterprise	Loan as % of global investment[a]	% interest rate from September 1974[b]	Grant as % of fixed investment[c]
Small	investing in or reaching fixed assets up to 1.5 milliard lire	35	5.0	up to 35[d]
Medium	investing in or reaching fixed assets between 1.5 and 5 milliard lire	35–40	5.0	15–20
Large	investing in or reaching fixed assets of more than 5 milliard lire	30–50	7.5	7–12

[a] The global investment included investment in fixed assets, and inventories of raw materials and semifinished products. The maximum loan period was fifteen years for new initiatives and ten years for plant expansion, and so on, with a preamortisation period of three to five years.

[b] The market rate of interest at this time was about 13%.

[c] The grant could be increased by 10% for purchases of machinery and equipment manufactured in southern Italy.

[d] The maximum grant was increased to 45% for small enterprises locating in areas of intense depopulation, and could be increased by an additional contribution of up to 5% of fixed investment for small specific infrastructural works and labour training.

in the framework of the planning agreements system, and were to depend upon the general directives and also upon the directives of the national plan and any promotion and rationalisation programmes applying to the sector in question (Podbielski, 1978, pages 69-70; Forte, 1979, pages 356-372). One example of a regional and sectoral investment programme affected by the provisions of this law was the plan to reorganise the chemical industry (see chapter 8).

7.4 The reorganisation of southern policy in Law 183 of 1976

A new law regulating extraordinary intervention in the period 1976-1980 was passed in 1976. This law was based upon an agreement between all the major political parties. The members of the PCI abstained, to indicate the dissatisfaction of the party with the extension of the activity of the Cassa until 1980. But the decision not to vote against the law signified a marked change in this party's position after twenty-five years of opposition to the policy of extraordinary intervention. (Since 1950 the view of the PCI had been that the problems of the Mezzogiorno should be dealt with not by a separate agency but within a national economic planning framework.) What the decision to abstain amounted to was the adoption by the PCI of a more limited aim of changing the methods of management of the policy of extraordinary intervention rather than the policy itself.

However, the extension of the existing policy can also be explained by a convergence between several previously distinct positions. In the past, some of those who had defended the Cassa tended to see its activity as a means for setting the southern problem in the context of the programming, or planning, of national development. In the view of those holding this position it was the failure to develop a national planning system that had allowed the Cassa to manage a significant proportion of public expenditure, and to act as a largely autonomous agency and not simply as a technical instrument of planning. Of course what resulted was an increase in the importance of the Cassa as an instrument of social control and of political power in the South. Yet at the same time, the Cassa also came to be defended because of the inability of the southern regions and of the ordinary public administration to assume the planning functions it was performing.

The difficulty with the conclusion that the Cassa should survive was that the basic problem of overcoming the logic of additional intervention, however it was managed, was left untouched. What was needed was a radical change in the mechanisms of capitalist development which lay at the root of the deepening of the problem of the South, and that conditioned in terms of compatibility and efficiency any policy of intervention. In effect, the result of the decision by the PCI to abstain was that the demand for democratic planning receded into the background, largely because of the effects of the crisis, and the PCI found itself cooperating with a strategy whose aim was the recovery and rationalisation of the traditional model of development (Del Monte and Giannola, 1978, pages 294-301).

A history of policies for southern industrialisation 157

In Law 183 it was proposed that CIPE remain the main decisionmaking centre. CIPE was now required to approve, within the framework of the national planning system, a five-year plan prepared by the Minister for Extraordinary Activities in the Mezzogiorno (see figure 7.2). This plan was expected to set out the general and specific objectives for extraordinary intervention and to indicate its effects on employment, productivity, and income. In addition, two bodies were to be established to reinforce control

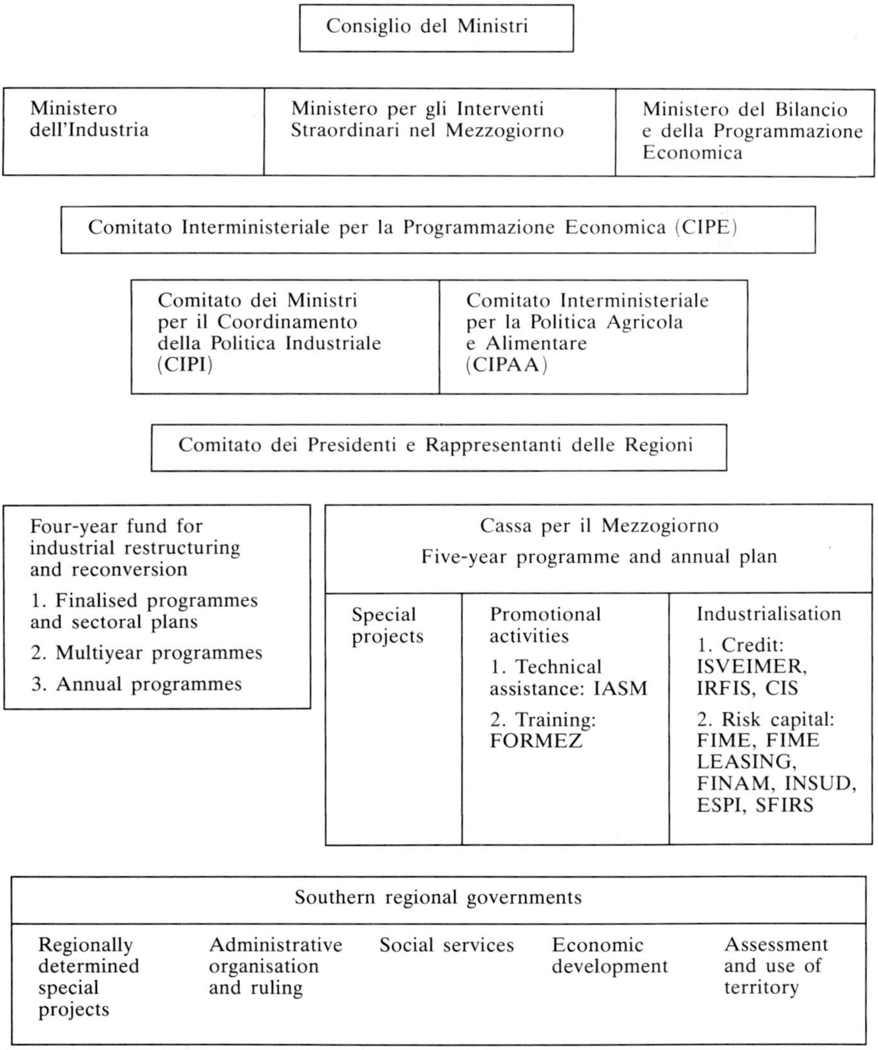

```
                    Consiglio del Ministri

Ministero          Ministero per gli Interventi     Ministero del Bilancio
dell'Industria     Straordinari nel Mezzogiorno     e della Programmazione
                                                    Economica

        Comitato Interministeriale per la Programmazione Economica (CIPE)

              Comitato dei Ministri          Comitato Interministeriale
              per il Coordinamento           per la Politica Agricola
              della Politica Industriale     e Alimentare
              (CIPI)                         (CIPAA)

              Comitato dei Presidenti e Rappresentanti delle Regioni
```

Four-year fund for industrial restructuring and reconversion	Cassa per il Mezzogiorno Five-year programme and annual plan		
1. Finalised programmes and sectoral plans	Special projects	Promotional activities	Industrialisation
2. Multiyear programmes		1. Technical assistance: IASM	1. Credit: ISVEIMER, IRFIS, CIS
3. Annual programmes		2. Training: FORMEZ	2. Risk capital: FIME, FIME LEASING, FINAM, INSUD, ESPI, SFIRS

Southern regional governments				
Regionally determined special projects	Administrative organisation and ruling	Social services	Economic development	Assessment and use of territory

Figure 7.2. The state and the regions in the institutionalisation of southern development policy: actors and roles in 1976.

over the formulation and implementation of southern policy: a permanent parliamentary commission to increase parliamentary control over the planning and implementation of extraordinary intervention in southern Italy, and a new committee of representatives of regional governments to secure regional participation in the definition and control of southern development policy.

The regions thus acquired some new functions. But the Cassa was still to implement state actions included in the plan approved by CIPE. It was also given the task of providing technical advice and assistance to the regional administrations, and, if requested by the southern regions, could carry out some regional activities using the region's own funds. A functional and organisational restructuring of the Cassa which would involve the inclusion of regional delegates on a new administrative council was in fact proposed. But in 1978, however, this proposal was suspended.

Special projects continued to be the main instrument of infrastructural policy, but the system of industrial incentives was revised once again.

(1) The law introduced reductions in social security charges that were to be added to the concessions made in 1968 and 1971. The new measure provided for payment by the state until 1986 of the full cost of social security contributions for additional labour hired by firms in certain sectors between July 1976 and December 1980, inclusive. Of the other major fiscal incentives, the most important included (i) a ten-year exemption from local corporate income tax on the profits of projects located in southern Italy, and of small and medium-sized firms located in central and northern Italy; (ii) an exemption from local corporate tax on up to 70% of profits earned in Italy and reinvested in industrial projects in the Mezzogiorno; and (iii) a 50% reduction for ten years in corporate income tax on the profits on southern investments.

(2) Capital grants were based on the size of fixed investment, that is, of the investment in buildings, machinery, and equipment. These grants could be equal to 40% of fixed assets for investments in new plants of up to 2 milliard lire or investments resulting in the expansion of existing plants up to 2 milliard lire, 30% on the share from 2 milliard to 7 milliard lire, 20% on the part from 7 milliard to 15 milliard lire, and 15% on the part exceeding 15 milliard lire. There were two reasons for these changes in the system of grading. One was to prevent a bunching of investments in the vicinity of the established size limits by reducing the percentage grant only for that part of the investment which exceeded the limits. The second was to reduce the risks of a less than optimal scale of operation (Podbielski, 1978, pages 203-204). These grants could be increased by 20% for investments in priority sectors for southern Italy, and by 20% for investments in particularly depressed areas. CIPE could temporarily or permanently exclude new enterprises in specific sectors or zones from grant provision, and was required to approve decisions on all grants to enterprises carrying

out or reaching investments in excess of 15 milliard lire. In addition, capital grants were extended to some offices of industrial enterprises, some research and design centres, and some commercial and service activities.

(3) The new law required the issue of provisions for the coordination and reorganisation of the entire national system of subsidised industrial credit, with the exception of that which was provided for reorganisation, reconstruction, and reconversion. It proposed the establishment of a national fund for subsidised industrial credit with a budget of 3200 milliard lire. 65% of this fund was to be allocated for southern investments. In the South, low-interest loans were to be advanced only for the construction of new plants involving fixed investments of less than 15 milliard lire or for expanding and modernising existing plants with less than 15 milliard lire of total investment. The loans were to be granted for 40% of the global investment at an interest rate equal to 30% of the market rate. In the depressed areas in central Italy, in the depressed zones in northern Italy, and in the rest of Italy, subsidised credit was only available to small companies. The maximum size of fixed-assets investment in new or existing enterprises, and the extent to which the interest rate was subsidised, were to be progressively less in each of these classes of area, and the loan was only available for ten years outside the Mezzogiorno compared with fifteen years for new plants in the South. Any loans plus grants for southern investment projects could not exceed 70% of the sum invested in fixed assets, except for investments in priority sectors or especially depressed areas. In calculating the size of investment projects, it was decided that henceforth industrial complexes consisting of more than one establishment should be considered as one unit when these establishments were located in one commune or were contiguous. This ruling was to apply even if the plants were owned by juridically distinct companies if the companies were part of a single group.

In cases where increases above the basic grant were expected, owing to investment in priority sectors or priority locations, the effective dividing line between an improvement and a worsening in the availability of capital grants and low-interest credit occurred around the investment level of 25 milliard lire. The largest improvements were for investments ranging from 1.5 to 5 milliard lire and from 5 to 15 milliard lire (Podbielski, 1978, page 203).

The financial provisions for this new stage in the development of southern policy were rather complicated. The Cassa, however, was allocated an additional 14 500 milliard lire and was allowed to raise a further 15 000 milliard lire. To this sum should be added the 2080 milliard lire allocated to the South from the national fund for subsidised credit. But, given the fact that some of these resources were not available for new programmes and that the real value of this sum was substantially reduced by rapid inflation, the resources available for new commitments deriving from the new programme were limited (see Podbielski, 1978, page 195-205; Forte, 1979, pages 405-419), and the share of medium-term and long-term

Table 7.2. The changing intensity of southern policy, 1951–1981. Source: Del Monte (1984, page 568).

Year	Index 1	2	G/V_m	3	4
1951	–	–	–	33.42	138.57
1952	–	–	–	34.46	144.74
1953	–	–	–	35.74	142.93
1954	–	–	–	34.96	143.05
1955	–	–	–	34.97	146.04
1956	–	–	–	36.61	149.98
1957	–	23.20	–	32.15	131.09
1958	–	26.05	–	32.84	136.78
1959	–	30.32	–	32.54	137.81
1960	–	42.72	–	33.26	144.13
1961	0.61	29.45	0.07	32.65	142.73
1962	0.90	33.32	0.09	33.36	148.80
1963	1.31	41.72	0.10	35.30	147.59
1964	2.06	39.43	0.13	33.98	146.94
1965	2.37	40.79	0.29	34.07	140.69
1966	1.30	33.36	0.26	33.89	142.63
1967	2.65	28.15	0.52	33.61	140.67
1968	2.24	21.45	0.43	32.07	141.15
1969	2.27	25.48	0.53	32.30	139.82
1970	3.04	37.72	0.59	35.69	151.12
1971	4.36	44.88	0.21	37.15	151.51
1972	5.46	52.88	0.46	38.59	155.53
1973	2.87	39.19	0.46	35.95	149.51
1974	3.31	42.00	0.44	36.37	148.06
1975	3.92	41.12	0.68	36.17	145.23
1976	2.49	25.80	0.62	36.39	158.74
1977	1.84	22.27	0.54	33.63	146.13
1978	1.50	20.93	0.55	33.45	145.03
1979	1.42	20.88	0.62	32.59	141.27
1980	1.06	25.94	0.47	25.33	147.24
1981	0.99	24.76	0.45	24.40	142.83

The indices used are:
1. an index of the intensity of regional policy: $(G + L_m)/V_m$;
2. an index of the intensity of regional industrial policy as compared with national industrial policy: $(I_m^s + L_m + G)/(I^s + L + G)$;
3. an index of the intensity of regional policy: $(I_m^s + L_m + G + C_m + I_m^g)/(I^s + L + G + C + I^g)$;
4. an index of the intensity of regional policy: $(C_m + I_m^s + I_m^g)/(C + I^s + I^g)/V$;

where
- G are venture capital grants,
- L is credit granted at a national level,
- L_m is credit for industrialisation of the South (Mezzogiorno),
- I^s are investments in Italy of state-controlled enterprises,
- I_m^s are investments of state-controlled enterprises in the South,
- V is value added in manufacturing industry at a national level,
- V_m is value added in manufacturing industry in the South,
- C is public consumption at a national level,
- C_m is public consumption in the South,
- I^g are investments in public works at a national level,
- I_m^g are investments in public works in the South.

lending accounted for by the subsidised lending by the special credit institutions declined.

In 1977 a new five-year plan for southern development was passed, as was an important law on the coordination of industrial policy (see Forte, 1979, pages 426-439). My account of southern industrialisation and of the functioning of southern industrial policies will, however, be concerned mainly with developments in the period up to about 1974. Consequently, only the effects of the first three laws (Laws 634, 717, and 853) will be considered in any detail. But in examining the way the laws worked I shall also highlight some of the problems, including the less than optimal scale of some investments and the splitting up of large projects, reflected in the changes in southern industrial policy introduced with the passing of Law 183 in 1976.

What, in conclusion, can one say about the intensity of southern policy? Several useful indicators have recently been presented by Del Monte (see table 7.2, and Del Monte, 1984, pages 563-569; see also Del Monte, 1986, pages 142-143). What his indicators suggest is the following conclusion. Until 1972 or, on the indicator G/V_m, 1975, the strength of measures in support of industrial development in the Mezzogiorno increased. Afterwards, however, it fell as the emphasis in overall Italian industrial policy changed to one of aiding the restructuring and reconversion of sectors and companies in crisis and increasing the competitiveness of Italian exports (see table 7.3, and Del Monte, 1986, pages 129-133).

Table 7.3 The percentage distribution of industrial assistance by type, 1961-1980. Source: Bank of Italy, cited in Del Monte, (1986, page 130).

Type of assistance	1961-1968	1969-1973	1974-1980
Regional development			
preferential loans	17.5	26.0	10.7
investment grants	3.4	4.1	7.6
Export competitiveness	23.6	27.2	40.4
Aid to small and medium-sized firms	35.3	27.5	13.9
Sectoral restructuring and reconversion	20.2	15.2	27.4
Total	100.0	100.0	100.0

In the next chapter, the question to which I shall first turn concerns the impact of southern industrial policy, and of its strengthening, on the development of the Italian South in the years preceding the oil crisis.

8

Regional policy and the restructuring of capital: the expansion of industries producing energy and intermediate goods, and of a modern engineering sector in the Mezzogiorno

8.1 The changing size, composition, and location of Cassa activity

In the period 1950-1975 the overall scale of Cassa activity expanded. But until 1971-1975, expenditure by the Cassa remained well below 1% of gross national product. In a southern context, of course, Cassa spending was more important. In the first four quinquennia it constituted between 3.5 and 3.9% of southern gross domestic product, and in 1971-1975 it increased to 4.5% (Podbielski, 1978, pages 75-76).

The switch to an industrialisation programme was associated with a marked change in the composition of Cassa commitments and expenditures. Until the introduction of the special projects in the early 1970s, commitments connected with infrastructural programmes declined in relative importance, whereas those linked with incentive schemes increased. Instead of giving priority to direct investment, emphasis was increasingly placed, in other words, on the supply of money and credit and on financial intermediation. At the same time, of course, the sectoral composition of Cassa activity was redirected. After 1960, commitments connected with the promotion of industrial development increased rapidly. Within a few years industrial interventions were consequently made into the major category of Cassa activity (table 8.1).

In most years the spending by the Cassa was not additional to social spending by the ordinary administration but was, as the PCI had feared when the Cassa was set up, a substitute for it. Consequently, the original intention of making available additional funds for the South over and above those provided by the normal administration was not realised (Del Monte and Giannola, 1978, pages 301-305).

Over the years, the Cassa's share of investment in public works in the South increased. It rose from 15.5% in 1951-1957 to 31.2% in 1958-1965 and, after falling to 21.5% in 1966-1971, increased to 56.6% in 1972-1974. Correspondingly, of course, the contribution of the ordinary administration declined. More importantly, the proportion of the ordinary administration's overall expenditure on public works allocated to the South tended to fall, even though at a national level total real expenditure increased. Of the aggregate spending by the ordinary administration: in 1951-1957, 41.9% was allocated to the Mezzogiorno; in 1958-1965, 30.9%; in 1966-1971, 37.3%; and in 1972-1974, 26.7%. Quite clearly, the provisions included in the laws for the Mezzogiorno requiring the ordinary administration to allocate 40% of its expenditure to the South were of limited effectiveness. Moreover, the Cassa devoted a much higher proportion of its expenditure on public works to infrastructural equipment of an economic kind than did the ordinary administration. Other things being equal, the process of substitution thus occurred at the expense of the already inadequate levels of provision of collective goods and social facilities in the South.

In the case of the incentives policy, spending was highly concentrated sectorally, by size of enterprise, and by geographical location. In the years

Table 8.1. The percentage composition of Cassa commitments, 1951–1975. Source: Podbielski (1978, pages 82, 78).

Sector of intervention	1951–1955	1956–1960	1961–1965	1966–1970	1971–1975	Total
General infrastructures	32.3	20.0	22.7	21.7	17.9	19.8
water supply and drainage	10.8	12.0	12.1	10.9	9.3	10.1
roads	12.1	5.8	6.6	7.3	6.2	6.7
railways	9.4	2.2	1.3	–	–	0.7
ports and airports	–	–	1.3	2.2	1.6	1.5
hospitals	–	–	1.4	1.3	0.8	0.8
Agriculture	57.1	49.7	23.7	15.4	10.2	17.0
infrastructures	51.6	39.1	17.0	11.8	7.3	13.1
incentives	5.5	10.6	6.7	3.6	2.9	3.9
Industry	–	1.3	17.1	41.1	41.3	34.8
infrastructures in industrial areas and nuclei	–	–	2.3	2.9	7.3	5.3
capital grants	–	0.5	5.4	10.3	11.5	9.6
contributions to workers' housing	–	–	–	–	1.1	0.6
subsidised interest	–	0.8	9.4	27.9	21.4	19.3
Tourism	1.9	1.9	1.9	1.6	1.4	1.6
infrastructures and archaeological works	1.9	1.9	1.9	1.4	1.2	1.4
incentives	–	–	–	0.2	0.2	0.2
Special projects	–	–	–	–	14.5	8.9
infrastructures	–	–	–	–	14.5	8.9
credits	–	–	–	–	–	–
Other interventions [a]	8.7	27.1	34.6	20.2	14.7	17.9
Total	100	100	100	100	100	100
Total (milliard lire)	736.3	941.3	1281.3	2882.9	9351.3	15193.1

[a] These commitments include those in the sectors designated as handicrafts and fishing, technical progress and cultural development, areas of particular depression, earthquake areas in Sicily, Cassa credit operations and participations, and credit interventions based on foreign funds.

up to 1975, 40.5% and 19.5% of the fixed capital formation financed by the special and other medium-term industrial credit institutes operating in the Mezzogiorno were allocated to investments in the chemical and metal manufacturing sectors respectively (see table 8.2). In both sectors the total financing and the value of the low-interest loans provided were roughly proportional to the fixed-assets investment expected. Accordingly, about 41.3% of the subsidised loans conceded up to 1975 was given to the chemical industry, and some 21.9% to the metal manufacturing sector. Furthermore, of the 1442 milliard lire distributed in the form of grants, the same two sectors were allocated 20.7% and 16.4% respectively (Cassa per il Mezzogiorno, 1976, pages 44, 51, 63).

The size distribution of investments supported by the system of industrial incentives can be explained in part by the large size of plant required to achieve economies of scale in the production of intermediate goods. In the period up to 1960, 0.3% of the projects financed involved fixed investments in excess of 5 milliard lire and received 19.3% of the funds for industrial development. In the period up to 1970, the corresponding figures were 1.6% and 46.8% respectively (table 8.3). Some of the changes in the size

Table 8.2. The percentage sectoral distribution of expected fixed industrial investment financed by the special institutes and by other institutes able to provide medium-term industrial credit in the Mezzogiorno, 1951–1975. Sources: elaborated from Cassa per il Mezzogiorno (1976, page 50; 1978, page 51).

Sector	Up to 1960	1961– 1965	1966– 1970	1971– 1975	Total
Extractive industries	0.9	1.0	1.2	0.3	0.6
Food, drink, and tobacco	17.8	6.4	5.1	3.7	4.8
Textiles	4.8	3.1	1.8	1.7	2.0
Clothing, leather, leather goods, and footwear	1.9	1.2	0.7	0.5	0.7
Furniture and wood products	2.7	1.5	1.2	0.8	1.0
Metal manufacture	3.4	29.1	20.1	18.0	19.5
Engineering	11.5	8.1	18.0	13.4	13.5
Nonmetallic minerals	12.9	8.8	5.8	3.7	5.1
Chemicals and allied industries	31.2	28.5	33.4	46.1	40.5
Rubber and rubber products	0.5	1.1	1.2	1.1	1.1
Cellulose and synthetic and artificial fibres	0.2	1.6	2.3	6.8	4.9
Paper, printing, and publishing	5.4	4.2	2.5	1.2	2.0
Other manufacturing industries	1.4	1.2	0.9	1.2	1.1
Electricity, gas, and water	1.9	2.5	3.8	0.7	1.6
Transport and communications	2.6	0.7	1.3	0.6	0.8
Other industries and services	0.8	1.2	0.8	0.4	0.6
Total	100	100	100	100	100
Total (milliard lire)	642.4	2731.7	3892.8	11977.6	19244.5

distribution of investments can be attributed to inflation. But clearly, up to 1975, aid for southern industrialisation was increasingly concentrated on a small number of large plants.

Assisted industrial development in the Mezzogiorno was also geographically concentrated. In part, the unevenness of development can be explained by the unequal distribution of infrastructural equipment. But the role of the incentives policy in financing large capital-intensive plants was also important.

By 1975, 81.4% of the fixed capital formation financed by the special and other medium-term industrial credit institutes operating in the South had occurred in four regions: 26.5% in Sardinia, 21.6% in Apulia, 17.6% in Sicily, and 15.7% in Campania (Cassa per il Mezzogiorno, 1978, page 49). Sardinia and Apulia both received more of this investment than would have been expected on the basis of the distribution of the southern population, with Sardinia's proportion substantially exceeding its share of the South's inhabitants.

Investment was also strongly concentrated in the growth centres. By the early 1970s, 88.8% of the fixed capital formation funded by these credit institutes had taken place in the seventeen areas and twenty-nine nuclei that had been designated by then, even though these zones contained fewer than one half of those living in the South (table 8.4). The frequently criticised

Table 8.3. The financing of and expected fixed investment (in percentages) in industrial plants funded by the special and by other medium-term industrial credit institutes in the Mezzogiorno, by size of investment in fixed assets up to 1975. Source: elaborated from Cassa per il Mezzogiorno (1976, pages 42–47; 1978, pages 44–45).

Size of investment in fixed assets (million lire)	Up to 1960 expd inv	fin	1961–1965 expd inv	fin	1966–1970 expd inv	fin	1971–1975 expd inv	fin	Total expd inv	fin
≤100	15.9	19.9	4.4	6.7	1.7	4.3	0.4	1.4	1.7	3.3
100–200	9.6	9.7	4.4	6.0	2.6	2.6	1.1	1.0	2.2	2.3
200–500	14.4	15.0	7.0	9.4	5.0	5.3	3.0	2.6	4.3	4.5
500–1500	15.4	15.6	8.7	12.3	8.3	11.2	7.9	7.5	8.3	9.1
1500–5000	22.4	20.5	16.8	26.9	15.7	20.5	7.0	8.8	10.7	13.9
5000–20000	18.6	15.9	19.2	24.0	21.3	23.8	14.5	17.4	16.7	19.5
>20000	3.7	3.4	39.5	14.9	45.3	32.3	66.1	61.3	56.1	47.4
Total	100	100	100	100	100	100	100	100	100	100
Total (milliard lire)	642.4	350.6	2731.7	1242.6	3892.8	2088.7	11977.6	6321.2	19244.5	10003.1

Note: The figures for expected investment from 1960 onwards are based on more recent estimates than the others in the table.

expd inv, expected investment; fin, financing.

Table 8.4. The percentage expected fixed industrial investment financed by the special and by other medium-term industrial credit institutes in the Mezzogiorno, by sector and by areas of industrial development (ASI) and nuclei of industrialisation (NI). Source: elaborated from Cassa per il Mezzogiorno (1972, pages 92–93).

ASI and NI[a]	Food, drink, and tobacco	Textiles	Metal manu-facture	Engi-neering	Non-metallic minerals	Chemicals	Cellulose, synthetic and artifi-cial fibres	Paper	Other sectors[b]	All sectors
ASI Napoli	10.5	13.4	24.4	44.3	5.6	3.0	4.6	7.4	11.5	13.9
ASI Taranto	2.3	–	55.7	1.6	5.8	1.3	–	0.3	0.8	11.2
ASI Sassari	2.3	0.6	0.2	0.3	1.8	7.0	6.1	0.6	3.0	7.1
ASI Cagliari	4.1	5.3	0.9	0.7	6.6	14.9	2.1	0.4	2.5	6.8
ASI Siracusa	0.8	–	0.1	0.8	2.4	14.7	–	0.8	4.9	6.2
ASI Roma-Latina	8.8	6.0	1.6	6.1	3.7	2.0	–	2.5	7.9	3.7
ASI Frosinone	2.7	14.9	0.2	11.3	2.3	1.5	2.4	17.3	3.6	3.6
NI Sulcis Iglesiente	0.1	–	8.7	0.3	0.1	4.5	–	–	1.9	3.4
ASI Brindisi	1.1	0.1	0.1	0.6	0.4	8.6	–	–	0.4	3.3
NI Sardegna Centrale	0.3	0.2	–	–	0.1	2.1	61.3	–	–	3.0
NI Gela	–	0.2	–	0.1	0.2	7.8	–	–	0.2	2.9
ASI Palermo	2.9	2.0	0.3	5.2	2.9	1.7	0.3	0.4	9.1	2.8
ASI Bari	3.4	1.5	2.2	6.6	2.0	0.5	0.1	0.8	5.1	2.4
ASI Caserta	2.6	1.1	0.2	4.6	7.9	1.2	0.2	0.1	3.4	2.2
ASI Salerno	8.6	8.2	0.7	2.0	3.6	0.1	2.8	1.8	2.9	2.0
All ASI and NI	78.2	68.6	98.2	94.7	77.2	92.4	93.1	68.8	77.4	88.8
Location outside ASI and NI	21.8	31.4	1.8	5.3	22.8	7.6	6.9	31.2	22.6	11.2
Total	100	100	100	100	100	100	100	100	100	100
Total (milliard lire)	563.2	224.5	1429.8	992.0	603.7	2904.2	287.0	217.9	845.5	8067.7

[a] ASI, Area di Sviluppo Industriale; NI, Nucleo di Industrializzazione.
[b] Sectors with fixed investments up to 2.5% of the general total.

proliferation of areas and nuclei of industrialisation did not prevent a strong concentration of industrial activity on a few centres. By 1971, 45.2% of the fixed investment supported by the industrial credit institutes operating in the South had occurred in five out of forty-six areas and nuclei: Naples, Taranto, Sassari, Cagliari, and Siracusa.

This concentration of investment in a comparatively small number of growth centres was particularly pronounced in the metal manufacturing industry, and was fairly strong in the engineering and chemical sectors (table 8.4). As a result, some centres were highly specialised. In 1971, 98% of the investment in Gela, 92.6% in Brindisi, about 85% in Sassari, Siracusa, and Messina, and 77.7% in Cagliari were in chemical and related industries, and 87.9% of the investment in Taranto aided by these credit institutes was in metal manufacturing (Cassa per il Mezzogiorno, 1972, pages 90-91).

8.2 Investment and the formation of capital in the Mezzogiorno: the role of regional policy

The expenditures incurred by the Cassa made an important contribution to southern capital formation. In 1951-1975, investments made or induced by the Cassa accounted for 30.3% of total fixed capital formation in the South, and for as much as 56.8% of total industrial investment, which increased quite substantially in the same period (Podbielski, 1978, pages 88-91).

As estimates of the effect of Cassa activity these official calculations are, however, misleading. On the one hand, the inclusion of the induced effects of Cassa activities alongside the money it actually spent rests on the assumption that investments supported by the Cassa would not have taken place without its support, and that the other parts of the southern economy would have developed in the same way had the Cassa not existed. On the other hand, they imply that public policies were the major if not the sole cause of the pattern of southern development.

The introduction of policies for southern industrialisation did indeed coincide with an acceleration of industrial investment in the Mezzogiorno. The system of grants and loans reduced annual capital costs and provided the greatest encouragement to relatively capital-intensive industries which actually dominated the process of southern industrialisation. Indeed, in the period 1965-1976, subsidised lending by the special credit institutions, net of repayments made on outstanding loans, was nearly equal to 18% of Italian gross fixed investment (see Capuggi, 1981, pages 76-78). Moreover, public and semipublic companies, which were required to locate a certain proportion of their new and overall investment in the South, played a major role in the process of industrial development.

But in explaining the correlation between these sets of events, the leading role does not have to be attributed to regional policy. The development and location of economic activity depend on many factors. The availability of state aid is only one of them, and its effects can vary widely. At one extreme, where firms are engaging in 'rent-seeking' strategies, state policy has no significant effect other than to transfer additional resources to firms that successfully seek state support for projects whose justification is largely independent of state policy. At the other, state action may have a major impact on the decisions of firms. What I shall argue is that the system of incentives did have important and often contradictory effects on the composition, size, and location of investments in the Mezzogiorno, but it was not the sole, or even the most important, factor. Southern industrialisation depended also on the capacity and willingness of the capitals concerned to invest in the region. More importantly, it was profoundly shaped by the strategies for expansion, at a national level, of some major Italian companies that had chosen a programme of investments largely on the basis of commercial criteria and that had, in some cases, already chosen the South as a preferred base for their expansion.

The system of incentives, however, was and is not an independent variable. In fact the direction of causality can also be reversed. At the same time as some of the investments that were to be located in the South were being planned, the groups involved pressed the state for a system of incentives that corresponded with their own needs, that reduced the annual capital costs of projects located in the Mezzogiorno, and that were consistent with trends in location that existed, in some cases, independently of the availability of grants and loans for southern development (see Graziani, 1978, pages 365-366; 1979, pages 47-49). The way in which successive laws for southern development were formulated and implemented depended at least in part on the interests and needs of companies locating in the South and elsewhere in Italy as well as on a variety of politically mediated national economic and political goals. (At the same time, of course, the development of policy was also shaped by the perceived inadequacies of existing measures and the potentialities of new ones as instruments of southern policy.) Instead of being interpreted as independent factors, the process of policy formation and the system of grants and loans should accordingly be seen as endogenous elements determined by particular configurations of class interests and class strengths and particular processes of political mediation.

In other words, regional policy must be seen as being conditioned as well as conditioning. Its effectiveness should consequently be seen as depending in part on its degree of correspondence and compatibility with prevailing micro- and macroeconomic conditions. Included under this heading are, on the one hand, the economic strategies of groups which were prepared to expand in the South or could only expand by locating in the South, and, on the other, the model of national development.

Viewed in this way, the weight given to regional policy is reduced. Undoubtedly it had a major impact on the trajectory of development. But as a result of the effects on the location of industry and on the evolution of policy of (1) the strategies of those groups which chose the South as a base for the restructuring and expansion of the capital they controlled, and (2) the model of economic and political development chosen by the Italian state, the leading roles in southern development must be attributed to these two factors.

8.3 The dynamics of southern investment
The proportion of gross national capital formation located in the South increased from 22.3% in 1951 to 24.2% in 1961 and to 32.3% in 1971, and the southern share of gross national fixed capital formation in industry increased from 15.0% in 1951 to 18.4% in 1961 and to 37.9% in 1971 (see ISTAT, 1975, pages 3-6; and table 8.5).

The growth of investment was accompanied by a major increase in the role of the state holding companies in the Mezzogiorno. In 1961-1971, the proportion of total state-holding-company investment located in the South increased from 37.4% to 56.1%, and the share of the state sector in total southern investment increased from 12.4% to 22.6%. In the case of industrial investment, slightly higher proportions were located in the South, and the state-holding-company share of southern industrial investment increased from 36.3% to 46.8% (see also table 8.5).

The industrial investments carried out by the state sector were, however, strongly concentrated in the energy, hydrocarbons, petrochemical, and steel sectors. For this reason, the growth in investment was not matched by corresponding increases in employment. In the same period, the proportion of total employment in the state holding companies located in the South increased from 19.6% to 25.2%, and their share in total southern employment increased from 1.0% to 2.0%. In 1961, 22.1% of state-holding-company industrial employment was located in the South, compared with 27.3% in 1971. The corresponding shares of southern industrial employment were, however, only 4.5% and 8.8% respectively (Podbielski, 1978, pages 159-160).

Investment in the Mezzogiorno occurred in two waves (see figure 8.1, and also table 8.5). The first one occurred in the period 1959-1963 and coincided with the introduction of policies for southern industrialisation. The southern investment process itself was dominated by a wave of investment in industry and, in particular, by some major investments by the state holding companies in the steel and hydrocarbons sectors. But with the onset of a recession in 1963, and with the completion of the major projects undertaken by the state sector, southern industrial investment fell sharply.

A second wave of investment in the Mezzogiorno occurred in the years 1969-1974. The upturn in investment was more pronounced and was dominated to a much greater extent than the previous one by investment in industry. It also differed from the previous one in that it did not coincide with an expansion of industrial investment at a national level. In the conditions prevailing in Italy in the late 1960s and after the autumno caldo, investment in the Mezzogiorno was carried out by (1) the state holding

Table 8.5. Investment and manufacturing output in the Mezzogiorno as a percentage share of the Italian totals, 1951–1981. Sources: ISTAT (1975, volume 4, tome 1, tables 15 and 40, tome 2, tables 12 and 21; 1983, volume 11, tome 1, tables 3 and 9) and Del Monte (1984, page 565).

Year[a]	Gross fixed investment		Gross fixed industrial investment		Manufacturing investment of state holding companies[b]	Manufacturing value added at factor cost	
1951	22.3		15.0			12.4	
1952	23.9		14.3			12.6	
1953	26.0		17.1			12.5	
1954	24.9		14.2			12.8	
1955	26.2		19.1			12.5	
1956	25.0		17.0			12.6	
1957	23.8		14.6		23.2	12.6	
1958	24.2		15.1		26.0	12.3	
1959	23.4		15.9		30.3	12.1	
1960	24.2		17.6		42.7	11.7	
1961	24.2		18.4		40.0	11.4	
1962	25.3		22.1		43.1	11.3	
1963	26.9		26.2		51.7	11.7	
1964	28.0		30.2		52.5	12.3	
1965	27.8		27.7		53.3	13.0	
1966	27.4		23.6		47.3	13.2	
1967	28.2		24.1		42.1	13.4	
1968	27.6		24.3		38.0	13.1	
1969	28.2		27.0		45.6	13.2	
1970	29.3	31.0	30.4	26.3	53.6	13.0	13.6
1971	32.3	33.1	37.9	33.9	60.8		13.7
1972	33.3	33.3	43.4	36.7	65.0		13.3
1973	32.0	31.6	43.2	32.4	57.7		13.5
1974		31.2		31.2	46.4		14.1
1975		31.9		31.1	44.5		14.1
1976		31.8		29.2	35.8		14.0
1977		30.6		25.7	34.7		13.8
1978		29.7		22.1	34.2		14.1
1979		30.0		20.1	38.7		14.6
1980		28.8		20.5	48.3		14.6
1981		29.1		21.3	46.8		15.0

[a] In 1974 a new national accounting system was adopted. As a result, the national accounting data for the years up to 1974 recorded in the left-hand columns cannot be compared directly with the new series recorded in the right-hand columns. A comparison of the overlapping 1970–1973 data indicates the effect of the new accountancy system on the aggregates.

[b] The data collected by the Ministry of State Shareholdings differ from the data collected by ISTAT. Once again, absolute values should not be compared. The data can, however, be used as indicators of trends.

companies which were seeking to strengthen and diversify their activities in the South and in the country as a whole, and (2) large private groups. Investment by private-sector groups was concentrated in the chemical industry, where a competitive process of expansion was under way, and in engineering, where some lines of production were being restructured and decentralised.

In 1974 the second wave of capital formation in the South came to an end. It was followed by several years in which the process of accumulation, especially in industry, slowed down markedly (see Del Monte and Giannola, 1978, pages 178–187; Giannola, 1982). The slackening of investment coincided with a standstill in investment in the South by the state sector. In the recession of the 1970s, state holding companies were involved in a series of rescue operations and takeovers of unprofitable and loss-making enterprises in the Centre and the North. In addition, most of the state-sector companies started to make significant losses. As a result, the resources available for new ventures or for investment in the South were smaller than would otherwise have been the case, and the state holding companies failed

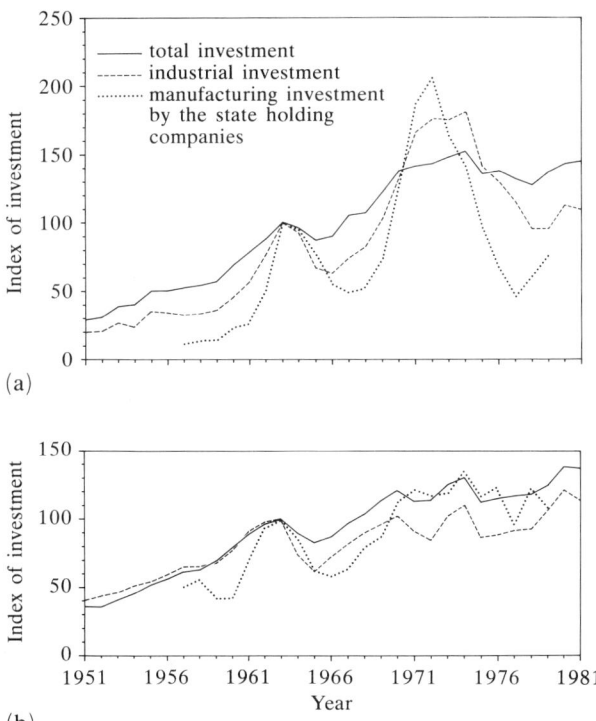

Figure 8.1. Investment in (a) the Mezzogiorno and (b) the rest of Italy, 1951–1981. (Index numbers, 1963 = 100.) Sources: elaborated from data in ISTAT (various years) and Giannola (1982, page 71).

to meet the requirements included in the 1971 legislation that they locate 80% of their new and 60% of their total investment in the Mezzogiorno (Podbielski, 1978, pages 160-162). Many of the investments in the South were left uncompleted or were placed in difficulty. Included, of course, were shipbuilding and ship repairing concerns. But with the rise in energy costs, the comparatively slow growth of the national economy, and the breakdown of the model of development, chemical, artificial fibre, and metal manufacturing firms were also affected.

At the same time, new investment by large private corporations dropped off, and consequently, large investments in modern industry by large extraregional groups or firms virtually came to an end. What growth in establishments and employment did occur was largely a result of the setting up and expansion of small and medium-sized firms, mainly in traditional sectors. Of the new plants some were owned by small and medium northern firms, but most were under southern entrepreneurship. The contribution of small firms to employment was, however, limited (on these developments see Arcangeli and Vitiello, 1982, pages 99-131; Giannola, 1982; Martinelli, 1985, pages 65-71).

8.4 Investments in energy and intermediate goods production

One of the most striking characteristics of the southern industrialisation process was the way in which it was based on the development of industries producing energy and intermediate goods. Included in the late 1950s and early 1960s were large investments in electrical generating plant and the nuclear power station at Latina. But more striking were some major oil and petrochemical projects and the Taranto steelworks, which absorbed such a high proportion of the aid for southern development.

In the first wave of southern industrialisation, large petrochemical investments were made in eastern Sicily, and petrochemical and steel developments were carried out in the Bari-Brindisi-Taranto-Ferrandina region. In the second wave, new chemical and related developments occurred, and the Taranto steelworks was expanded. By 1974, 54% of the crude oil refined in Italy was processed in the South, and 92% of Italian aromatic hydrocarbons, 80% of methanol, 86% of propylene, and 84% of ethylene were produced in the Mezzogiorno. In addition, more than 35% of Italian steel output was produced in southern plants (Belhadj et al, 1975, pages 17-18).

Underlying the expansion of these industries were a number of sectoral, national, and geographical factors, with a critical role being played by those sectoral developments which shaped the characteristics of the investments which were located in the South and the strategies of the groups that carried them out.

8.5 The development of the steel sector

In Italy the steel industry was largely dependent on imported raw materials, and up to the beginning of the Second World War was predominantly based on the melting of scrap iron. After the First World War, output rose rapidly from an annual production of 1.3 million tonnes in 1917 to 2.3 million tonnes in 1929. In 1932, however, it amounted to only 1.1 million tonnes.

In 1933, IRI was formed, and in 1937 its steel interests were regrouped under the sectoral holding company Finsider. Under the leadership of Sinigaglia, the ground was duly prepared for an ambitious programme of modernisation and expansion of the state sector based on integrated shore-based production. The rationale of the concept was simple:

> "a shore-based location would enable iron ore, coking coal and the other main inputs for steel making to be secured in bulk by sea from the lowest cost world producers and delivered to the plant itself with no additional transport costs and the minimum of handling costs. The full production cycle from ore through pig iron to rolled steel products also would be undertaken with minimum handling and no transport costs through continuous production on one site. Finally the finished products themselves could either be transported to local markets by rail or road, or re-shipped by sea to international markets or other national ports for inland distribution. At all stages of production economies would be secured both from large-scale production and from minimisation of transport and handling costs" (Wormald, 1972, pages 94–96).

To these elements should be added the extra increments in productivity offered by the possibility of combining the increased continuity of the cycle of production with the mechanisation of production and transfer discussed in chapter 2. In Italy, moreover, the case for the application of this formula was given added justification by the country's almost total lack of high-grade iron ore and coking coal.

With the formation of a large steel group in the public sector, the large capital outlays implied by such a strategy could be found. In 1936 a plan to build an integrated plant at Cornigliano in Genoa, where IRI already had a scrap-based plant, was pushed through, and in 1946 a plan for the modernisation of the steel industry was drawn up under Sinigaglia. By 1948 an integrated plant had been reconstituted at Cornigliano, after the dismantling of the original one by the retreating Germans, and was in production. In addition, integrated production had been introduced by Finsider at Piombino, and at Bagnoli near Naples (see figure 8.2).

At the same time, IRI proposed a rationalisation and expansion of these three plants. Under this scheme came plans for plant specialisation: at Cornigliano, hot-rolled flat products, of which coil, hoop and strips, plate, and sheets are examples, along with coated products were to be produced; at Piombino, merchant bars, wire rod, sections, and rails; and at Bagnoli, concrete-reinforcing bars, wire rod, beams, and hoop and strips. At Novi Ligure, cold-rolled coil and sheets were to be manufactured.

The investments involved were extremely ambitious. Indeed only after Sinigaglia had secured a long-term contract with FIAT could work proceed on a new plant at Cornigliano. In 1953, however, when the European Coal and Steel Community (ECSC) was opened, it came on-stream.

In 1951–1961, Italian steel production increased by 170% from 3 million tonnes per year to more than 8 million tonnes. A fundamental role was played by the state sector. In 1953–1960 the output of the state sector increased by 310% compared with 135% in the country as a whole, and by 1960 the state sector provided nearly 85% of Italian pig iron, nearly 54% of steel, and 50 to 60% of rolled products. In addition, the costs in the state sector were reduced, and offer prices were stabilised (see Castronovo, 1980, pages 289–291; and table 8.6).

Figure 8.2. The location of the Italian steel industry in 1981. Source: EEC Commission (1982, page 95).

Without doubt the expansion of the state steel sector played an important part in meeting the growing demand for steel and in preventing a growing dependence on imports. The development of plants of increasing size and of increasingly specialised processes raised productivity and lowered costs to the benefit of user industries, including the rapidly growing engineering and transport equipment sectors. Moreover, the introduction of integrated methods played an important part in stabilising prices in the face of the notoriously irregular oscillations in the availability and price of scrap metal. As a result, the once highly protected Italian steel industry was able to stand up to foreign competition, and Italy was able to join the ECSC. By guaranteeing supplies of good-quality steel at internationally competitive prices to user industries, the modernisation and expansion of the state steel sector amounted in fact to a programme not only of import substitution but also of growth promotion (see Wormald, 1972, pages 94-97).

In November 1958 a plan prepared by a committee headed by Saraceno envisaged for 1962 an annual steel consumption of 9.1 million tonnes compared with 6.4 million tonnes in 1958. To meet internal needs an increase in national production from 6.3 to 8.7 million tonnes per year was judged necessary. Also, integrated production was favoured as the method of production. At that stage, almost two thirds of Italian steel production came from

Table 8.6. Iron and steel production in Italy, 1960-1974 (in thousands of tonnes). Source: elaborated from IRI (various years).

	1960	1961	1962	1963	1964	1965	1966	1967
Pig iron								
Finsider	2277	2654	3205	3404	3167	5160	5942	6859
Other producers	406	402	351	336	331	330	317	435
National total	2683	3056	3556	3740	3498	5490	6259	7294
Steel								
Finsider	4430	5004	5391	5452	5020	7420	8164	9265
Other producers	3799	4121	4366	4705	4773	5261	5475	6625
National total	8229	9125	9757	10157	9793	12681	13639	15890
	1968	1969	1970	1971	1972	1973	1974	
Pig iron								
Finsider[a]	7377	7284	7828	8209	9180	9808	11436	
Other producers	449	497	504	327	235	225	250	
Natonal total	7826	7781	8332	8536	9415	10033	11686	
Steel								
Finsider[a]	10042	9443	9685	9631[b]	10951	11622	13561	
Other producers	6922	6985	7592	7821[b]	8864	9373	10242	
National total	16964	16428	17277	17452	19815	20995	23803	

[a] Including from 1969 the output of the Acciaierie di Piombino jointly owned with FIAT.

[b] In 1971 Breda Siderurgica was transferred to Cogne and its steel output was reallocated from Finsider to other producers.

small and medium-sized miniplants in which scrap metal was used. In each of these plants, located mainly in the Po Valley, electric arc methods were used to produce some 150 000 to 300 000 tonnes of steel per year. The problem with electric arc methods was that they did not benefit from scale economies and were subject in periods of rising demand to rising prices of scrap metal. Moreover, the ECSC was planning a revision of the scrap price equalisation system, and had set as a target for the end of 1965 a cutting of scrap consumption by one half. Also, imports of scrap from outside of the ECSC were to be restricted (Castronovo, 1980, pages 291–292). All of these factors contributed to the advocacy of a switch to integrated production.

In line with the Saraceno report, Manuelli, as president of Finsider, pressed for a new integrated shore-based plant, originally proposed in 1956 but put off owing to the 1957–1958 recession. In spite of the fact that it was not the original site preferred by Finsider's technical planning staff, senior personnel in IRI along with the southern lobby, sections of the state technocracy, and some powerful elements of the political class argued the case for a southern location at Taranto.

Why was a location in a primarily unindustrialised region chosen? The answer to that particular question is a difficult one. Clearly a number of social and political considerations were involved. In some respects, however, the location was an economically rational one.

In the Mezzogiorno, many coastal sites were and are well positioned for access to sources of raw materials and Mediterranean markets. The site at Taranto is comparatively well situated in relation to supplies of coking coal from the USSR, Poland, the Federal Republic of Germany, and Australia, and of ore from Mauritania, the USA, the USSR, and Australia. Some inputs were available locally. And much of the output of tubes was exported (Belhadj et al, 1975, page 47).

Integrated steel plants also require large areas of nonseismic land and uncongested ports with deep-water access. In addition, the processes involved pose problems of pollution. Consequently, new installations need to be located away from the more congested existing centres of industry and population. Suitable conditions could be found in the South as well as, of course, in other parts of Italy.

With respect to labour supply the site at Taranto offered some advantages. Through investing in an area without a tradition of work in the steel industry, new methods of production and of work organisation could be introduced more easily than in established industrial areas, especially where union organisation and working-class job control were strong. Moreover, as the city itself had an industrial history the firm could hope to draw on a pool of workers with experience of industrial work and, in some cases, skills that would be relevant to work in a modern steel complex.

In developing integrated steel complexes very large amounts of capital are required. The availability of increased resources for southern development, the increased priority attached to investments in industry, and the prospect of obtaining subsidised loans and grants by locating in the Mezzogiorno were consequently major attractions, especially for companies such as Finsider that were envisaging major programmes of expansion and were heavily dependent on fixed-interest borrowing. What was more, a gradual revision of the system of incentives in the light of the investment strategies of the groups that were planning to locate in the South was secured (see chapter 7, section 7.1). With these modifications large-scale capital-intensive projects could be subsidised yet more heavily and the planned restructuring and expansion of large and mainly semipublic companies could be aided.

The economic and social problems of the region were of course also relevant. In contrast to many parts of the South, the province of Taranto had an industrial past. At the end of the First World War a state-run arsenal, a privately owned shipyard, and related engineering firms provided jobs for 11500, 16000, and 2000 people respectively. But by 1957, employment in the arsenal had fallen to 3260 workers and in the shipyard to some 4000 workers. Also, since the end of the Second World War the number of small engineering concerns had fallen by more than one half, from thirteen to six. With the collapse of the old industrial base of the town, other activities serving local markets were weakened, and what jobs were to be found were increasingly concentrated in the service and construction sectors. Thus, unemployment was high, standing at about 22% of the active population, emigration was substantial but less than the immigration of people leaving the surrounding countryside, and average per capita income was extremely low (see Chapman, 1983, pages 173-188).

In short, the social and political problems existing in the area, along with infrastructural investment and the availability of subsidised loans and grants for plant, machinery, and equipment were important, but not the only locational factors explaining why a new steel project was to be implanted at Taranto in the Mezzogiorno.

From the outset the project was opposed by Italy's private steel producers, with Falck and Frumento, as, respectively, head and research director of the Falck steel company, playing a prominent role. Almost immediately, FIAT in conjunction with Innocenti proposed as an alternative a privately dominated but mainly publicly financed integrated plant of their own at Vado Ligure. At that stage the private sector, which included vehicle manufacturing firms that produced steel for their own use, was not only anxious to prevent the expansion of the state sector but also to secure a state-funded restructuring of largely protection-dependent private steel making.

In 1957-1958 the demand for steel fell. (Steel demand was subject to quite sharp ups and downs.) With this short-lived recession the strategy of the private opponents of the project changed to one of contesting the demand forecasts included in the Saraceno report, and of questioning the need for new capacity. But by 1958, FIAT was seeking new medium-term supply contracts with the state-sector plant at Cornigliano, thus weakening the position of the electricity supply firms which dominated Confindustria, of the private firms specialising in steel production, and of other sections of the private sector opposed to the scheme more out of a general disagreement with the growth of the state sector and a concern with the impact of large public investments on the distribution of credit.

In spite of private opposition and a disagreement between IRI and Finsider, it was nevertheless decided in June 1959 to go ahead with the project. To finance it, internally generated funds were supplemented by an addition of 80 milliard lire to IRI's endowment fund, which was then transferred through the sectoral holding company to the operating company undertaking the investment. A capital grant of 5.3 milliard lire and a loan of 55 milliard lire at a 5% interest rate were provided by the Cassa, and a loan from the European Investment Bank and Finsider bonds made up the rest of the funding (see table 8.7, and Wormald, 1972, pages 100–102). (In view of the scale of the project and the fact that no return might be expected for four or five years, equity funding was not sought.)

Table 8.7. The financial aid granted or requested for the development of the Taranto complex. Source: IRI (1970, page 33); see also Wormald (1972, pages 100–102).

	Capital grants		Low-interest loans		Value of the aid (% fxd inv)[a]
	milliard lire	% fxd inv	milliard lire	% fxd inv	
Stage I (up to 3 million tonnes) Fixed investment L401 mld	5.3	1.3	55.0	13.7	3.1
Stage II (3–4.5 million tonnes) Fixed investment of L200 mld	24.0	12.0	100.0	50.0	19.5
Stage III[b] (4.5–5.8 million tonnes) Fixed investment of L265 mld, plus working capital of L15 mld	31.8	12.0	196.0	70.0	28.4
Total	61.1	7.0	351.0	39.8	14.6

[a] The value of the aid was calculated on the assumption that market finance could not have been secured at a rate of less than 7.5% for stages I and II, and 8.5% for stage III. On subsidised loans the rates of interest were 5% in the case of stage 1 and 4% in the cases of stages II and III.

[b] In stage III, grants were calculated as a percentage of the costs of the fixed investment, comprising the overall costs of buildings, site connections, equipment, and machinery, whereas soft loans were calculated as a percentage of the total investment costs, comprising the fixed investment costs and the cost of inventories for one cycle of production.

% fxd inv, percentage of fixed investment.

In the second half of 1961 a welded steel tube plant with a maximum annual capacity of 350 000 tonnes came on-stream, and in 1964 the running in of the new complex with an annual steel making capacity of 3 million tonnes was completed. As a result, a potential shortfall in national steel production was reduced, thus improving the balance of trade of the Italian economy. Furthermore, the new plant was characterised by high levels of efficiency in the use of materials, and automation in steel making and mechanised rolling methods enabled strikingly low manning levels to be realised. Indeed, with the development of the new integrated shore-based complex at Taranto, the Italian public steel sector established itself as the European group most closely following the strategy adopted in Japan.

In April 1961, Italsider was formed by merging the Cornigliano and Ilva companies. In the early 1960s the capacity of the Italsider coastal plants at Cornigliano and Bagnoli was expanded and modernised, as was that of the Piombino steelworks, and the capacity of the cold-rolling mills at Novi Ligure was raised to 650 000 tonnes per year. Within the state steel sector, steel production was henceforth to be concentrated on large ore-based plants, whereas more specialised and high-quality products were to be produced in smaller concerns by Dalmine, Terni, Terninoss, and Breda Siderurgica. At the same time, increased emphasis was placed on oxygen steel making methods and especially on the Linz–Donawitz process. By the mid-1960s, as much as 80% of the group's steel output was being produced in integrated mills. Almost 40% was being produced by the Linz–Donawitz process at Taranto and Bagnoli, and nearly one half was being produced in the South (see IRI, 1966, pages 101–108).

In 1966 a supplementary expansion programme was announced in order to meet a projected shortage of capacity. Amongst other things, the capacity of the Taranto works was to be increased from 2.4 to 3.6 million tonnes of pig iron per year and from 3 to 4.5 million tonnes of steel per year. A new cold-rolling mill with an initial annual capacity of about 500 000 tonnes was to be added, in part to attract user industries to the South. (At that stage the Alfa Sud project was under consideration.) In addition, a plant capable of producing 90 000 tonnes per year of medium-diameter welded pipes was to be built by Dalmine. At Bagnoli a new Linz–Donawitz steel plant was to be added, and a continuous casting facility was to be installed. In January 1967 the plan was approved by CIPE, and the aid for the investment at Taranto granted by the Cassa was significantly larger than that allocated to the first stage of the project (see table 8.7). In 1970 the new southern capacity was almost completed.

Yet in April of that year a new steel expansion plan elaborated by a technical advisory committee was submitted to the government. At the end of November it was approved by CIPE. In the view of the technical experts involved, annual Italian steel consumption was likely to stand at 25.5 million tonnes in 1975 and at 30.4 million tonnes in 1980, with the possibility of these levels being attained two years earlier. (A significant expansion of demand was also expected by other European steel producers including, as we shall see in part 3, the French.) Accordingly, it was proposed that Italsider's capacity be increased from 10 or 11 million tonnes per year to more than 24 million tonnes by the end of the decade. What followed was a plan to expand the capacity of the Taranto plant from 4.5 to 11.5 million tonnes of steel per year, and a proposal to build a fifth integrated shore-based plant in the Mezzogiorno.

The '*raddoppiamento*' of Taranto was itself a source of some controversy, since the existing plant was already of the size at which scale economies were maximised. But as a working class with relevant skills and traditions already existed, along with some of the necessary infrastructural conditions, the decision to proceed went ahead. What happened, however, was not an enlargement of the existing works but the construction of a second one imaginatively called Taranto 2 (see table 8.8).

As a result of these major steel-making investments in the early 1980s, employment in the steel plant alone stood at some 20 000 people, with an additional 8000 workers employed by subcontractors to operate and maintain the plant (see table 8.8). Additional industrial development carried with it, however, many environmental, social, and cultural costs in a city whose population had grown from some 140 000 inhabitants in the 1950s to some 250 000 in the 1980s, with an increase of more than 60 000 occurring in ten years (see Viola, 1985).

The second decision concerned the fifth integrated steel centre. In March 1970, CIPE announced that of the sites considered in Sicily, Sardinia, and Calabria it preferred Gioia Tauro. According to CIPE, it had the advantage of being a noninsular location, adequate railway and motorway connections, and ample fresh water and electricity supplies. In January 1971 the choice of Gioia Tauro was confirmed. (The site was, however, in a seismic zone with a rich agricultural potential.)

At first a cold-rolling mill with an annual capacity of 1 million tonnes was to be built. Initially it was to be supplied with intermediate products from Taranto, but by the second half of 1978 it was to be completed with an integrated steel mill of its own with a capacity of 4.5 million tonnes per year.

Table 8.8. The development of the Taranto steelworks. Source: Nuova Italsider (1985, pages 2 – 3).

Year	Investment (milliard lire)	Annual steel capacity (million tonnes)	Employment
1964	400	3.0	4 000
1970	200	4.5	10 000
1975	1 326	11.5 [a]	20 000

[a] Coils, 8 million tonnes; plates, 2 million tonnes.

The cost of the project was estimated at 1290 milliard lire, excluding infrastructural investments. On completion the new plant was expected to provide about 7500 jobs in an area of high unemployment and underemployment and very limited industrialisation, and in a region where marginalisation and poverty had recently been translated into rioting in which fascist elements had played a prominent part. At the end of the 1970s, when these new investments had been completed, some 75% of IRI's and 60% of Italian steel production was expected to come from the enlarged Taranto plant, the improved Bagnoli plant, and the new Gioia Tauro complex.

By January 1972, however, a new plan had been submitted. According to IRI, changing technological and economic conditions, including the development of methods of direct reduction and the emergence of steel producers in the newly industrialising countries, underlay the change of plan. In February of that year the revised plan was approved by the Ministry of the Budget and Economic Planning.

The new project was to be carried out in two stages. In the first stage a cold-rolling mill of 1 million tonnes per year capacity was to be constructed. In the second an electric steelworks producing 500 000 tonnes per year of steel and a rolling mill producing 3.5 million tonnes of hot-rolled coils per year were to be added. The initial investment was reduced to 662 milliard lire, with infrastructural costs estimated at an extra 98 milliard lire. At the same time, IRI was demanding compensation for the very high costs of development at Gioia Tauro and was insistent that it would not proceed until the site was ready and the port at least partially useable.

In April 1974 the planning and construction of the infrastructural equipment were made the object of a special project in order to speed up the development of the port and industrial zone (see the discussion of special projects in chapter 7, section 7.3). CIPE also decided that the incentives to be conceded should equal the maximum allowed under Law 853 and not the larger amount requested by Finsider (see table 8.9). In the view of the company the poor bearing of the land, high seismic risks, and the problems of environmental protection made Gioia Tauro a high-cost site, and, for these reasons, the aid granted by the state was held not to be adequate. Accordingly, the company continued to press for additional aid in the form of either an increase in IRI's endowment fund or additional regional aid.

As the years passed, problems were encountered in equipping the port and industrial zone, and costs increased. After the oil crisis the demand for steel fell, whereas the new capacity at Taranto had come on-stream. Owing to the poor prospects for a plant producing cold-rolled products and the difficulty of importing intermediate goods, a new plan was submitted in the spring of 1975. The size of the cold-rolling mill was reduced to 650 000 tonnes per year, and the size of the electric steelworks was increased to 1.25 million tonnes per year with a prereduction unit of 400 000 tonnes per year.

Also included was a 1 million tonne per year hot-rolled sheet mill and a 0.6 million tonne per year zinc plating mill. The cost of the plant was estimated at 1145 milliard lire. In the first phase 4300 jobs were expected, rising on completion to 7500.

In 1975-1976 the port works were started. But by 1976 the steel crisis was seen as structural and not conjunctural. Added to which, IRI was faced with a cash flow crisis. After another change of plan the project was slowly and quietly dropped, more through default than as a consequence of a specific decision.

Undoubtedly, changing conditions in the international steel market played an important part in the saga of the fifth integrated works. But so too did the increasing financial problems of the state steel industry.

In the 1960s and early 1970s the investment plans of IRI were extremely ambitious: in the South, for example, the development of the ultramodern Taranto works and the extension of Piombino were accompanied by the Alfa Sud project, the extension of the Cementir cement works at Taranto and the construction of a new one at Maddaloni, northeast of Naples, as well as investments in transport and telecommunications (see table 8.10). But as with other rapidly growing public-sector groups, IRI's self-financing capacity and additions to its endowment fund fell far short of its investments

Table 8.9. The expected costs of and the cost per job at the V Centro Siderurgico at Gioia Tauro. Source: Ministero per il Mezzogiorno (1974, page 113).

	Investment costs [a,b] (milliard lire)	Cost per job (millions of lire)	
		7500 jobs	5500 jobs
Spending by IRI			
fixed investments	582.0	77.6	105.8
working capital	80.0	10.7	14.5
total	662.1	88.3	120.4
State spending			
capital grants	70.0		
interest relief	190.0		
infrastructural works	190.0		
other	110.0		
total	560.0	74.7	101.8
Grand total	1182.1	157.6	214.9

[a] The grant of 12% and interest relief implied by a loan equal to 70% of the investment provided at a rate of interest of 4% are as requested by IRI. The aid is in fact equal to the maximum help that could be given under Law 717. Under Law 853 of 6 October 1971 a maximum of 50% of the investment could be covered by subsidised credit and the rates of interest were raised from 4 to 6%, and subsequently to 7.5%.

[b] The costs of antiseismic works estimated as costing 40.0 milliard lire are included twice: once under fixed investments, and once under other state spending. In the grand total they are counted only once.

in plant and equipment. In financing its growth it had to rely instead on external borrowing, at the cost of growing indebtedness and a disproportionately small ratio of own funds to group fixed assets (see table 8.11).

Table 8.10. The IRI group's investments by sector, 1960-1974 (in milliard lire). Source: elaborated from IRI (various years).

Sector	1960	1961	1962	1963	1964	1965	1966	1967
Manufacturing[a]	80.7	130.6	180.1	352.7	367.9	280.4	225.9	165.4
steel	49.5	85.1	119.9	295.6	310.7	240.1	183.5	117.8
engineering	14.6	29.2	41.4	35.1	27.9	20.5	24.9	25.0
shipbuilding and repair	10.7	8.4	8.2	8.5	9.8	4.7	3.9	10.4
Services[b]	217.9	255.4	310.7	209.4	230.6	283.6	280.4	348.4
Grand total[c]	298.6	386.0	490.8	562.1	604.9	569.3	512.2	518.9

	1968	1969	1970	1971	1972	1973	1974
Manufacturing[a]	190.7	246.3	413.6	699.5	804.8	783.5	697.8
steel	107.4	129.0	223.2	414.5	530.0	563.5	445.1
engineering	43.2	73.3	140.3	202.5	167.9	103.3	88.3
shipbuilding and repair	16.8	10.3	8.0	7.6	11.0	15.8	35.2
Services[b]	390.2	320.2	320.7	414.4	537.3	770.6	906.4
Grand total[c]	585.6	655.3	871.7	1261.1	1535.6	1818.8	1852.0

[a] Manufacturing total includes cement, electronics, food processing, and other sectors not included in the table.
[b] The service sector includes telecommunications, shipping, airlines, and radio and television amongst others.
[c] Manufacturing plus services plus infrastructure and construction.

Table 8.11. Net own, government, and market contributions to the coverage of the IRI group's capital requirements, 1968-1974 (in milliard lire). Source: elaborated from IRI (various years).

	1968	1969	1970	1971	1972	1973	1974
Self-financing	233.7	295.9	267.1	304.8	361.7	704.6	803.5
State contributions to endowment fund	81.0	77.9	79.9	225.0	245.1	220.0	225.0
Equity	16.5	25.6	10.0	26.5	29.2	23.8	3.4
Medium- and long-term debt	260.2	175.4	257.0	585.9	927.9	1278.3	410.8
Short-term borrowing and other transactions	−66.8	17.6	434.5	313.4	118.6	−56.5	1062.3
Total financing	524.6	592.4	1048.5	1455.6	1682.5	2170.2	2505.0

As early as its 1968 Annual Report, emphasis was being placed on the problems that resulted. Arguments concerning the need to compensate the group for the extra costs associated with the external diseconomies of locating in the South as well as with politically determined constraints on rationalisation were frequently expressed, and were used throughout the late 1960s and early 1970s in support of requests for increases in endowment funds, refunding of the Cassa, and changes in the system of grants and low-interest loans for southern development, on which increasing reliance was placed (see, for example, IRI, 1969, pages 17-21). Added to all this, in 1969-1972 the group's integrated steel plants were hit by a wave of industrial conflicts and increased absenteeism. "In the last four years the Finsider group has suffered an overall loss of 15.6 million working hours and about 5 million tonnes of steel compared with annual operational plans" (IRI, 1973, pages 16-18). At the same time the costs of labour increased, as did the costs of raw materials, of transport, and of loans. In 1970-1972, large operating losses were recorded (see table 8.12).

In the case of IRI as a whole the problems of indebtedness and of a weak financial base were exacerbated by the losses incurred not only in steel but also in Alfa Sud, in shipbuilding, and in other sectors. In addition, delays occurred in the provision of endowment funds, and the economic strategy of its constituent companies was increasingly influenced by questions of job protection, by the interests of the political class, and by the growing political manoeuvring of senior personnel (see Castronovo, 1980, pages 313-319).

The investments of the state holding companies in the steel industry had played a major role in creating conditions necessary for national growth that would not have been provided by the private sector. Until the crisis the tendency to bring the capacity of plants to levels which, at least in the short term, appeared to exceed demand was associated with large increases in productivity, and played a major role in transforming the Italian economy into a major steel producer capable of supplying user industries with high-quality steel under long-term contracts and at internationally competitive prices. And with the exception of the Bagnoli works, which was in need of restructuring, the coastal plants owned by the group were technologically sound. On many indicators the position of the state holding sector in the

Table 8.12. The operating profits and losses of the IRI group's manufacturing companies, 1968-1974 (in milliard lire). Source: elaborated from IRI (various years).

	1968	1969	1970	1971	1972	1973	1974
Total	−1.2	−14.2	−40.4	−89.0	−68.1	−25.6	−73.0
of which:							
iron and steel	12.0	14.6	−9.7	−42.4	−35.3	14.2	33.0
engineering	−10.3	−15.5	−15.7	−18.5	−17.7	−37.1	−98.0
shipbuilding and repair	−2.9	−10.7	−14.5	−17.3	−13.2	−6.0	−8.8

Regional policy and the restructuring of capital 185

Italian economy was strengthened. But the impact of the crisis and the method of financing development ultimately transformed what many had seen as a model of capitalist success into a recipe for economic disaster.

8.6 The development of the oil and chemical sectors
Investments in the oil and chemical industries, which were quantitatively even more important than those in steel, were carried out in many parts of the Mezzogiorno (see figures 8.3 and 8.4 and King, 1985, pages 217-220).

With the rise of Middle Eastern oil production, major oil refineries were developed near centres of consumption and also at sites that were well situated in relation to Mediterranean oil tanker routes. Oil refining was

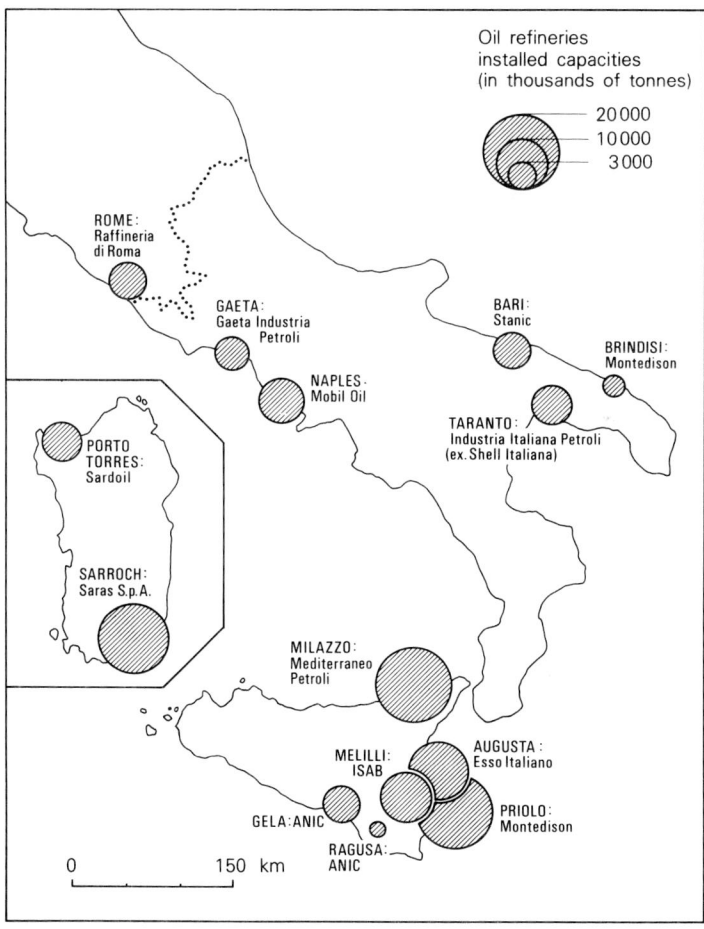

Figure 8.3. The location of major oil refineries in the Mezzogiorno in the early 1970s. Source: Mariani, reproduced in King (1985, page 216).

accordingly developed not only on the southern mainland but also in Sardinia and, in particular, in Sicily. Consequently, in 1960–1977, Sicily's share of national capacity increased from 14 to 33% (King, 1985, pages 214–215).

In 1957 work started on Montecatini's integrated petrochemical plant near Melilli and in 1959 on its ethylene cracker at Brindisi. In 1962 the construction of the Rumianca Sud complex at Assemini near Cagliari in Sardinia was under way. In the early 1950s oil was discovered at Ragusa and at Gela in Sicily. At both places ANIC developed major petrochemical projects, with the organic chemical complex that came on-stream at Gela in

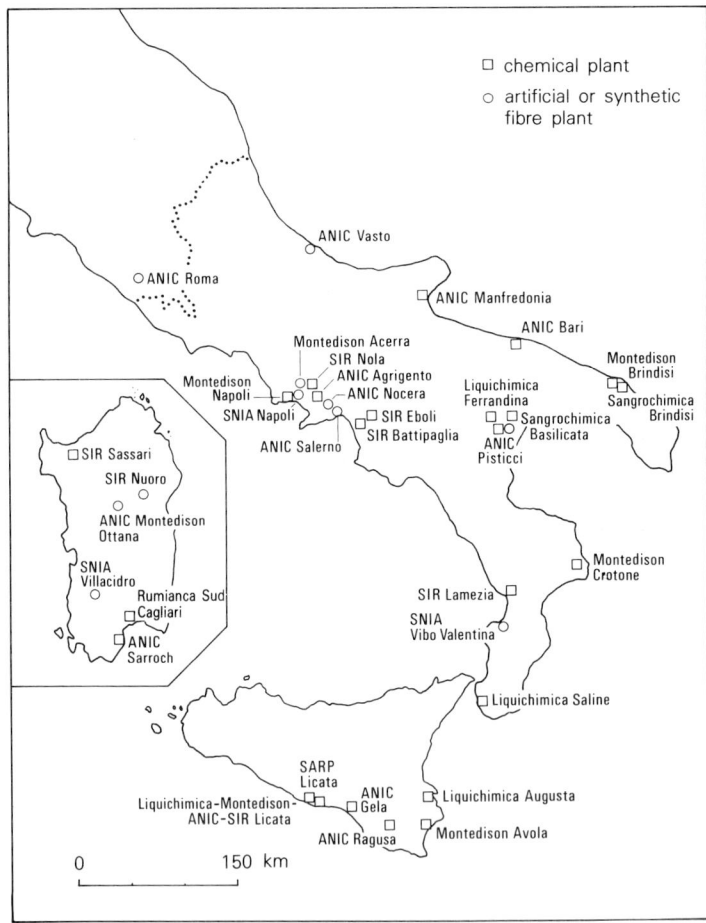

Figure 8.4. The location of existing and projected chemical and artificial or synthetic fibre plants in the Mezzogiorno in 1978. Source: Ministero dell'Industria, reproduced in Chapman (1983, page 407).

1962 involving an investment of some 1000 milliard lire. Subsequently, methane was found in the province of Enna in Sicily, at Ferrandina and Grotole in Basilicata, and at Gagliano in Sicily. With the discoveries in Basilicata it was decided that, although most of the gas should be piped to Bari, about one third should be used locally. In 1964, alongside AGIP's gas extraction operations, an ANIC acrylic plant consequently came on-stream, and in 1965 a caustic soda and PVC plant, owned at first by Pozzi and subsequently Liquichimica, was operational.

In the late 1960s and early 1970s a second wave of chemical investment occurred in the South. New petrochemical plants were developed by ANIC at Manfredonia, Saras Chimica at Sarroch in Sardinia, and Liquichimica at Augusta in Sicily. Additions were made to existing state-owned complexes at Gela and Pisticci, and a new acrylic and polyester plant was developed jointly by ANIC and Montedison at Ottana in central Sardinia.

At the same time some major new private investments were made. At Porto Torres near Sassari in Sardinia the Società Italiana Resine (SIR) petrochemical complex, which dated from the early 1960s, was enlarged via the continuing construction and extension of a set of functionally interdependent but legally independent units (see table 8.13). In the synthetic textile sector SNIA Viscosa invested in an acrylic plant at Villacidro in Sardinia, a new polyester plant was constructed in Naples, and a new polyamide line was developed at Castellaccio south of Rome (see King, 1985, page 154), and SIRON started work on an acrylic plant at Sarcidano in central Sardinia. In addition, in 1975 work started at Acerra, northeast of Naples, on the new polyester plant owned by Montedison's artificial and synthetic textile company, Montefibre.

What resulted were several major concentrations of employment and activity in the petrochemical and synthetic textile sectors but not in downstream activities. In these foci in Naples, Brindisi, the Basento Valley, southeastern Sicily, Cagliari, and Sassari, chemical development provided significant numbers of well-paid jobs, at least until the chemical crisis of the 1970s (see table 9.1). Yet these gains occurred at a cost that included environmental damage and increased costs of living. As Hytten and Marchioni indicated in the conclusion of their study of Gela (1970; cited in King, 1985, page 218),

"The presence of industry ... has accelerated the process of socio-economic marginalisation of the peasant class. ... If state industry wants to be an instrument of social development of the South ... it must do more for those who are excluded from the industrialisation itself".

Why, however, did these developments which transformed the South into a major focus of Italian oil and chemical production occur? The answer depends on the reply to two sets of questions. On the one hand, one has to explain why decisions to carry out certain investments were made. On the other, one has to explain why southern sites were chosen.

After the Second World War, coal was supplanted by oil as the primary source of energy in spite of the opposition in Italy of private electricity generating interests. Within the chemical sector a switch occurred from inorganic to organic chemicals and, within the organic group, from coal-based chemicals to ones based on oil and gas. Consequently, the integration of the oil and chemical sectors increased, and the major oil companies intervened on a massive scale in the chemical industry. In Italy the main chemical groups invested the major part of their capital in petrochemical plants. In subsequent years the oil-based and gas-based chemical sectors expanded very rapidly, at first under private-sector control.

In 1953 the government decided, in the face of bitter opposition, to set up ENI to exploit the recently discovered natural gas deposits in the Po Valley. After its establishment the new state-controlled group expanded at an astonishing speed. Moreover, in order to reap the benefits of increased backward and forward integration it entered new fields, moving upstream from the exploitation of methane and petroleum deposits into engineering, and downstream into the petrochemical and synthetic textile industries. Success in getting access to concessions to prospect for and extract oil and gas, and an ambitious programme of investment, enabled ENI to develop a national oil industry capable of competing with the 'seven sisters' and of reducing the weight of multinational corporations in the Italian economy. At the same time, investments in the chemical sector, located increasingly in the South, enabled it to make inroads into the formerly dominant position occupied by leading private-sector groups, of which the most important was Montecatini.

The decision that a state-controlled industry should get involved in the development of cheap energy and chemical products, which itself was part of a strategy of modernising the Italian economy in a context of increasing international economic integration, was in fact one of the major reasons underlying the early industrialisation of the South. Investments in the sectors involved were important in providing essential inputs for other parts of the national economy, but were usually large and risky and unlikely to be carried out by private-sector groups. Yet at the same time the possibility of investing in these sectors provided state firms with scope for expansion which they were anxious to grasp and which competing private-sector companies were anxious to close off.

In 1962 the electricity supply industry was nationalised, leaving the private electricity companies with a huge amount of capital to invest. As early as 1950, Edison, which was the largest of the companies involved, was sufficiently worried about the threat of nationalisation to turn towards the chemical industry, and after 1962 most of the indemnity funds it received were invested in chemical and petrochemical projects, preparing the ground for the subsequent merger with Montecatini. The private sector of the Italian chemical industry was thus strengthened, and its capacity to resist the attempt by ENI to break into the field was significantly increased (see Posner and Woolf, 1967, pages 40-42).

In the 1960s the Italian chemical industry was dominated by four oligopolistic companies: on one side was ANIC, which was state owned, and on the other were Montedison (which was larger than the rest put together), SIR, and Liquichimica, which were privately controlled. In the last years of the decade, however, the growth of Montedison started to lag. It also started to run short of cash and plunged deeply into debt, so that in 1970-1972 major losses were recorded. Most of the other major groups needed to modernise plant and equipment and were in difficult financial positions. Also, each of them was anxious to improve its market position vis-à-vis that of its rivals and to increase its control of Italian chemical production.

What followed was a competitive process of acquisition, restructuring, and expansion, subsequently referred to as a 'chemical war', in which each of the main chemical groups carried out major programmes of investment.

Many of these investments were located in the South, and several factors explain why southern locations were chosen. The South offered large and uncongested coastal sites that were well positioned for access by sea or via a network of oil and gas pipelines to sources of raw materials and Mediterranean markets. With vertically integrated cycles of production characterised by extremely limited linkages with the external surroundings, oil and chemical complexes needed few contacts with the local economy and society. As long as some general and specific infrastructural equipment was provided, and as long as a small number of ancillary service functions were set up, enterprises operating in these sectors could be implanted comparatively easily in the relatively underdeveloped industrial environments of newly industrialising regions. Consequently, a strategy of producing energy and intermediate goods was likely to be selected by companies seeking to expand in nonindustrial areas. Also, in view of the fact that the extra costs of transport involved were very low, companies operating in these sectors were unlikely to be disadvantaged by the choice of locations in areas such as the Mezzogiorno. An abundant supply of workers existed, and, although workers with industrial experience and the skills required for more demanding jobs were often lacking, managers and more skilled workers could be brought in from older industrial regions.

Most importantly, investments in the production of intermediate goods and energy also required very large amounts of capital. Throughout the 1960s the availability of increased resources for southern development, the increased priority attached to investments in industry, and the prospect of obtaining subsidised loans and grants by locating in the Mezzogiorno were consequently major attractions, especially for companies that were envisaging major programmes of expansion and were dependent on fixed-interest borrowing. The system of incentives itself was revised, in part in the light of the investment strategies of the groups involved. As a result of these changes, large-scale capital-intensive projects could be subsidised, and the restructuring and growth of large and often semipublic companies in sectors with a high capital to output ratio could be given substantial state aid. Once the system of aid had been determined, investments were tailored especially by SIR to maximise the level of financial support (see table 8.13, and chapter 7, sections 7.1 – 7.3).

The central role played in the development of the chemical industry by the provision of regional aid was highlighted by the evidence on the case of Sardinia presented by the president of CIS to a 1972 parliamentary enquiry into the chemical industry and the Montedison crisis.

Between 1951 and 15 October 1972, decisions on the financing of industrial development made by the Sardinian credit institute were expected to involve an advancing of 805 milliard lire, and agreements were reached on operations costing 515 milliard lire. Owing to the island's strategic location in relation to major oil routes, along with the development of new and improved infrastructural equipment and the availability of grants and low-interest loans, sites in Sardinia were attractive to companies interested in establishing new oil refining, petrochemical, and synthetic textile complexes. Thus 326 milliard lire, or 63% of the total on which agreements had been reached, were used to finance investments in the chemical sector. These funds were provided in respect of projects which were expected to entail investments of 690 milliard lire.

Of the funds allocated to the chemical sector, 69.0% was allocated to primary chemicals, 30.4% to synthetic textiles, and 0.6% to fine chemicals and parachemicals. 54.3% of the financing for primary chemicals was granted to the group of companies belonging to SIR and operating at Porto Torres, 32.0% to the Rumianca complex at Assemini near Cagliari, 9.7% to ANIC's plants at Sarroch, and 4.0% to its Ottana plant. In the case of synthetic textiles, 5.8% of the financing was conceded to the company owned by SIR at Porto Torres, 73.1% to Siron at Ottana, 10.5% to SNIA Viscosa for the development of its plant at Villacidro, and 10.6% to other projects. As a result of these decisions, 33.0% of the financing was allocated to the province of Cagliari, 39% to Sassari, and 28.0% to Nuoro (Bologna, 1973b, page 76).

The strategy of developing industries producing energy and intermediate goods in the Mezzogiorno was confirmed in the Chemical Plan which had been approved by CIPE earlier in the summer of 1971. After the crisis of the late 1960s and early 1970s a reconstruction of the forces and relations of production was under way. In part this reconstruction was to be accomplished by means of industrial programmes aimed at restoring profitability through the privileged development of high-productivity sectors rather than by means of general plans. In the view of Bologna, the Chemical Plan represented the choice of the chemical industry as a major sector for special support and as a propulsive sector in a new phase of capitalist expansion. In 1972 the "Programma di promozione dell'industria chimica" of the Ministero del Bilancio e della Programmazione was published.

Included in this report, that turned out to be the only official planning document produced in connection with the Chemical Plan, were proposals for the development of the primary sector (Bologna, 1973a, page 40-47).

The starting point was an analysis of the development of the Italian chemical industry. It was indicated that the chemical industry's growth rate had been higher than the average for Italian manufacturing industry. In the period 1965-1970, however, the Italian chemical industry had lost ground in comparison with the longer-established industries in other European countries. In the view of the authors of the report, its deteriorating position could be observed above all in a serious slowing down in the growth of exports. The relative backwardness of the Italian industry was attributed to its concentration on the construction of large plants producing primary chemicals and to the lack of emphasis upon the production of fine chemicals and parachemicals. This type of industrial structure and the need to import chemical products with a higher unit value than those exported were held to be largely responsible for the deteriorating balance of trade in chemical products. In short, the structure of the Italian chemical industry was thought to be inadequate for competitiveness on the international market.

The arguments outlined above led to a second series of observations in which it was pointed out that the plants producing primary chemicals were now inadequate in size and location. In each case, Italian companies had pursued policies of upstream integration. But the complexes constructed when the industry was being expanded and consolidated in the late 1950s and early 1960s were now too small to reap the economies of scale necessary for international competitiveness, and were geographically dispersed in integrated poles rather than concentrated in integrated areas of chemical development.

In the early 1970s the requirement was, it was argued, twofold. On the one hand, production structures should be based on one or, at most, two steam cracking plants capable of producing 500 000 tonnes of ethylene per year and linked via pipeline with the plants using ethylene. On the other hand, a system of integrated areas of chemical development containing oil refineries producing various oil fractions, plants producing primary organic chemicals such as olefins and aromatics, and plants using these products to produce intermediate and derivative chemicals needed to be established. In the report it was pointed out that steam cracking plants should be constructed by consortia, so that the companies involved could pursue a strategy of moving downstream and could concentrate more easily on the more profitable activities of manufacturing fine chemicals and finished products. In this way the tendency towards vertical integration and the associated duplication of facilities could be broken, and the companies could become more specialised.

These two sets of observations, along with the assumptions that the gross product of manufacturing industry would grow between 1971 and 1980 at an average annual rate of 7.5 to 8% whereas that of the chemical sector would increase at 11%, formed the basis on which the proposals contained in the report were elaborated.

The authors on the Chemical Plan envisaged the construction of a series of plants. In the period 1971–1980 the development of these plants was expected to involve investments costing 4500 milliard lire in 1970 prices. About 1200 milliard lire was estimated as the amount that would be required in the three years between 1971 and 1973 to carry out investments on which decisions had already been made by the companies. To this sum should be added some 2500 milliard lire for the development of efficient industries producing fine chemicals and parachemicals. In general, secondary industries of this kind required less fixed capital formation, but were only likely to be successful if large expenditures on research and development and marketing were incurred.

The employment estimates were subject to considerable uncertainties. At the time, forecasts suggested that the investments connected with the programme for promoting the development of the primary chemical sector might create about 80 000 to 85 000 new jobs, increasing employment from 170 000 persons in 1968 to 250 000 in 1980. In the cases of the fine chemical and parachemical sectors the prospects for expansion were expected to create an additional 100 000 jobs, with employment expanding from 110 000 jobs in 1968 to 210 000 in 1980.

Within the overall framework for the development of the industry, specific proposals for the development of the primary chemical sector were put forward. In the expectation of an annual demand for ethylene of 2.285 million tonnes in 1975 and 4.420 million tonnes in 1980 compared with an annual capacity of 1.050 million tonnes in 1970, four areas in which development might occur were identified: the Po Valley, Apulia, Sardinia, and Sicily.

In the case of the Po Valley a process of restructuring had been set in motion in the late 1960s with the construction of a new steam cracking plant at Porto Marghera, the completion of existing plant, the rationalisation of a number of establishments, including the closing of plants at Mantua, and at Ferrara, near Bologna, and the installation of a network of pipelines linking centres of production. At the same time, changes in the work process and in the size, structure, and composition of the labour force were implemented. In the report, however, it was argued that insufficient refining capacity, inadequate port installations, and proximity to congested and densely populated areas made it a matter of reconstructing the chemical industry to improve its competitiveness, rather than of undertaking further development.

In Apulia, where Montedison ought, in the view of the authors of the report, to increase the capacity of its plant at Brindisi to 400 000 tonnes per year if it were to operate efficiently, a process of expansion was expected to be a problem in that the Montedison plant was isolated from the plants at Manfredonia and at Ferrandina and Pisticci in Basilicata, and that these plants were not using ethylene as a basic material. In 1968, only 30% of Montedison's sales were to other plants in the South, and in 1974 only 15% of its production was destined for plants in Apulia (Belhadj et al, 1975, page 43).

In Sardinia, SIR was planning the construction of two large steam cracking plants which were expected to have an annual capacity of 570 000 tonnes of ethylene. But in the report it was suggested that these investments would only be economical if investments in plants in intermediate zones using the derivative products were increased correspondingly.

Only Sicily was left. In the report it was argued that this region was the most suited for new chemical development, both because of the possibility of linking the Montedison plant at Priolo with the ANIC plant at Ragusa, and because of the island's very large refining capacity which, in 1973, amounted to 56 million tonnes per year. "Sicily", it was concluded, "appears therefore to be the area which most adequately suits the directions of development we have advocated and the constraints on their achievement" (cited in Bologna, 1973a, page 46).

What is interesting about the Chemical Plan is that it included the proposal that the model of southern industrialisation which had been proceeding for more than a decade should continue, except that the new investments aimed at improving the competitiveness of the primary chemical sector should be more concentrated and should go into areas in which chemical complexes had already been developed. The decision to concentrate development in Sicily was made on economic grounds, and many of the new investments were aimed at increasing the technological content of existing installations and raising the capital to output ratio. In those conditions, any expansion of capacity was unlikely to generate many new jobs.

With the wave of chemical growth of 1970-1974, investment grew more rapidly than in other advanced European countries. The quickening of the accumulation process made up in part for the relatively slow growth of investment in the Italian industry in 1964-1968, and it helped to overcome the twin problems of a lack of optimal scale and of an excessive geographical dispersion of plants producing primary chemicals like ethylene and ammonia.

But the trade balance in chemicals continued to deteriorate, and the terms of trade did not cease to be unfavourable. Italy's share in world chemical production continued to decline from its peak in 1960. The Italian industry's loss of competitiveness on export markets, particularly in advanced countries, was not stemmed. In 1968-1975 the levels of profitability of the major Italian chemical companies declined, and eventually indebtedness increased, and substantial losses were recorded.

The lack of profitability was in part a product of the Italian industry's concentration on the production of widely used primary chemicals with a low technological content, and an unbalanced development of the primary and secondary sectors. Of particular importance in explaining this weakness, which was, of course, highlighted in the report on the chemical industry, were two factors. One was the rivalry and the anarchic and uncoordinated competition between the main groups. The second was the strategies of integration that resulted from the absence of planning at an industry level (see Pennachi, 1977, pages 31–38).

In the cases of companies such as Montedison and SIR, what emerged was a combination of high degrees of vertical integration with high degrees of horizontal integration, called 'diagonal integration'. The strategy of upstream integration and the policy of organising production so as to use fully the products of earlier processing instead of in the light of market factors necessitated high levels of investment on the part of each company and resulted in a lack of specialisation. Indeed, in the absence of collaboration what ensued was a duplication of plants frequently constructed on a scale which was less than that which would have minimised average unit costs of production, a geographical dispersion of establishments, excess capacity in some branches of chemical production, and a dissipation of research and development spending.

International comparisons also indicated that the Italian chemical industry was organisationally backward, inefficient in the use of capital, slow in innovating and in adjusting to changing prices and rates of exchange, and less internationalised.

Of course in a sector in which rapid technical progress was occurring and in which plants quickly became outdated, the timing of investments was also important. The system of grants and low-interest loans also seems to have contributed to the choice of plants of less than optimal scale, and must have encouraged the general emphasis on high-capital-intensity investments and the preoccupation with technological rather than organisational improvements.

The main reasons for the pattern of development of the Italian chemical industry and its problems in the 1970s were, however, threefold. One was the anarchic and uncoordinated competitive conflict between the main groups. The second was the industry's intermediate position between the chemical industries of industrialised countries with strong economies, specialising in more sophisticated chemical products, and the industries of East European and oil producing countries with new capacity for the production of primary chemicals and certain advantages in costs in an epoch of rising energy and raw material prices. The third was the crisis that hit the economies of the West in the 1970s.

One example of the problems caused by the rivalries between the main groups is provided by the events that followed the decision made in the late 1960s by ANIC to increase its involvement in the rapidly expanding synthetic textile sector by constructing an acrylic and polyester plant at Ottana in central Sardinia (see Trevisan, 1979). Montedison joined with ANIC, providing 50% of the capital and undertaking to cover the costs of producing 50% of the plant's output and to sell through its own distribution network the output whose costs it met. But SIR also decided to take advantage of the generous state aid available for investments in central Sardinia, and started to construct a plant that was identical near the ANIC-Montedison complex.

Production at ANIC-Montedison commenced. But costs were high: an extreme example of the problems that occurred concerns the question of labour supply (see King, 1977, pages 97-98). Some two thirds of the new factory workers were shepherds or came from agricultural or pastoral families. Moreover, a policy of encouraging the shepherd workers to remain in the villages where they were living and to commute to work was adopted. But early plans for an improved road network were largely unimplemented, with the result that journeys to work were often long and arduous. The new workers also had difficulty in adapting to the regime of industrial work, and, consequently, in the early years absenteeism was very high, on occasions reaching 25% of a shift.

More importantly, after 1974 the demand for polyester and acrylic fell (see figure 8.5). Unable to sell its share of the output, Montedison's

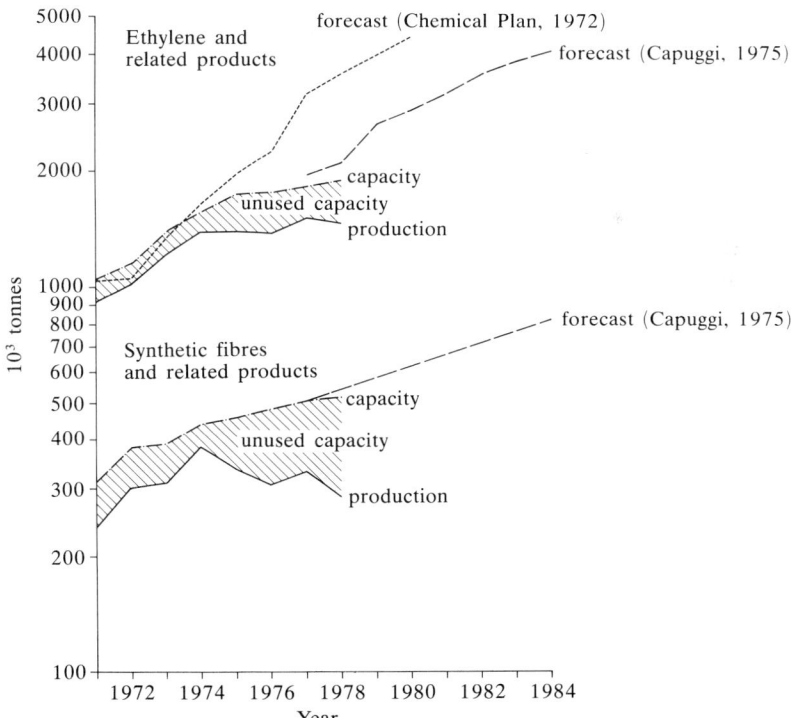

Figure 8.5. Italian ethylene and synthetic textile capacity and output in the 1970s. Sources: Ministero del Bilancio e della Programmazione Economica (1972) and ENI (1976), reproduced in Chapman (1983, pages 385, 387).

Table 8.13. SIR group and other chemical and related investments in the Porto Torres industrial zone in 1978. Source: IASM (1979, pages 23–33).

Company	Main products	Area covered (m^2)	Area of site (m^2)	Employment[a] (thousands)	Investment (millions of lire)	Start of activity	State[b]
SIFA	acetone and phenol	80000	80000	93	6300	1962	O
ALCHISARDA	styrol and cumene	70000	70000	265	12000	1963	O
Idrogenazioni	furfuryl alcohol and 'cicloesanolo'	20000	20000	40	2100	1963	O
SIR	paraffin waxes refining	80000	80000	200	12000	1964	O
STIRAL	polyethylene AP	60000	60000	152	12000	1965	O
ETB	polyethylene BP	50000	50000	115	12000	1966	O
SARDOX	sulphuric acid, ammonia, and urea	90000	90000	204	12000	1966	O
SIRAM	caprolactam and ammonium sulphate	50000	50000	210	6000	1966	O
SARDOIL	diesel fuel and petrol refining	200000	200000	115	12000	1966	O
SIRBEN	xlitols	50000	50000	135	12000	1966	O
SARDAR	butadiene	50000	50000	53	11800	1966	O
FIBRASIR	polyester fibres	20000	80000	254	6000	1968	O
SICO	copolymers and ethylene	10000	20000	50	6000	1969	O
SIRTENE	polyethylene	20000	30000	65	6000	1969	O
SIRCRIL	polyacrylic fibres	40000	40000	152	6000	1968	O
OXISIR	'oliocorostano'	20000	30000	40	6000	1969	O
SIRCLOR	'cloro elettrolitico'	40000	40000	40	6000	1969	O
TITANSIR	titanium dioxide	30000	30000	60	5000	196	O
SARDESA	soda ash and alkylbenzene 'benzolo'	30000	30000	78	6000	1967	O
SIO	heavy residual oils	30000	30000	70	6000	1969	O
SIR	ethylene	30000	30000	70	5000	1969	O
VICLOSAR	vinyl chloride	40000	40000	40	6000	1969	O
POLISARDA	polyvinyl chloride powders	30000	30000	164	6000	1969	O
SIRFIN	polyvinyl chloride	40000	40000	80	6000	1968	O
SIP	polyethylene glycol 'etereftalato'	30000	30000	72	6000	1970	O

Regional policy and the restructuring of capital 197

Table 8.13 (continued)

Company	Main products	Area covered (m²)	Area of site (m²)	Employment[a] (thousands)	Investment (millions of lire)	Start of activity	State[b]
SIRFOS	triple superphosphates	30000	30000	120	5000	1970	O
PARASIR	paramylum	40000	40000	55	6000	1970	O
ELSAR	nitrile elastomers	42395	42395	80	6000	1973	O
Esso Standard	oil storage	15000	15000	20	150	1959	O
AGIP	oil storage	33000	33000	28	250	1964	O
VINILSARDA	vinyl acetate	40000	40000	(90)	6000		C
GLICOSAR	ethylene oxide	10000	10000	(60)	6000		C
SIRION	ammonium sulphate and hydroxylamine	10000	10000	85	6000	1976	O
SIRAL			28000				C
SIRTIL	titanium sulphate	27543	27543				C
SIREF	polyethylene AD		35000	85	6000	1976	O
SARDA Polimeri	polyallomers		200000	90	6000	1976	O
SARDA Plastificanti			36267		6000		C
SIRFIL							C
SIRGUD							C
SARDA Maleica			20554				C
BUTAL			12893				C
SIREX			28000				C
PETROCOCHE			62980				C
SULFOSARDA			36120				C
SARDA Aromatici			78491				C

[a] Expected employment given in parentheses.
[b] O, operational; C, under construction.

synthetic textile company reneged on the agreement it had made. Since ANIC was not in a position to carry the whole of the financial burden on its own, it announced that it would have to close the plant. Yet in the face of the state of uncertainty about the plant's future and the fate of its workers, a few kilometres away SIR continued to construct a duplicate plant, capable on completion of producing 180 000 tonnes per year of the very fibre that lay unsold in the warehouses of ANIC-Montedison.

With the 1970s crisis of the chemical and synthetic textile sectors many investments were left incompleted. Most striking was the case of SIR, which had financed its very rapid expansion via recourse to credit and, especially, to the aid available for southern development. In the 1960s and early 1970s, for example, it developed at Porto Torres a fifteen square kilometre complex centred on an oil refinery capable of processing 5.3 million tonnes of crude oil per year, a reforming plant, and one of the largest steam cracking units in Europe. But in order to maximise the grants and subsidised credit received by the group the complex was developed by setting up some thirty separate companies (see table 8.13). Each of the companies established and progressively enlarged small units in which special groups of interrelated products were manufactured for exchange with other companies on the site and within the group. But as the amount of aid conceded depended on the size of investment, and as each of the units was comparatively small, very high levels of support were obtained.

After the early 1970s the completion of outstanding projects was increasingly delayed. Attempts were made by SIR to wrest incentives for southern development from the government to shore up the group's financial position, but in the mid-1970s, prior to the collapse of the group he controlled, Rovelli and some of his associates were accused of fraud against the Italian state and of tampering with balance sheets. In particular, it was alleged that 1858 milliard lire, which equalled 70% of the group's investment, was demanded of agencies supplying aid for southern development, that some 90% of the funding demanded was granted, and that financial aid was received by SIR for chemical plants which were never completed. It was of course as a result of these and other developments that some major changes occurred in the Italian government's policies for southern development, whereas the chemical crisis itself opened the way to the stepping in of the state to salvage SIR and also to rescue the other chemical companies that found themselves on the verge of bankruptcy. (On some of the more recent developments see King, 1985, pages 153-156, 223-227.)

8.7 Southern industry: cathedrals in the desert?

In my discussion of the development of the steel and the oil and chemical industries in the South, what I have emphasised is the way in which decisions on the size and composition of investments were made primarily by the groups themselves. Of course political connections were important, political mediation was always involved, and political considerations shaped the evolution of the sectors concerned and the location of many projects. Where uncertainty about a course of action existed, as at Taranto, ministerial opinion was likely to be a decisive factor. But what mattered most were questions of commercial viability, profitability, and capital growth in a context shaped not only by the availability of aid but also by other technological, organisational, market, and spatial factors.

The programme of southern industrialisation that resulted has, however, been widely criticised as a strategy for regional development. The large-scale, capital-intensive, and externally controlled projects implanted in the Mezzogiorno were normally not integrated with the local economy, but had strong links instead with plants located outside of the region. Only a limited contribution was consequently made to local output and employment either directly or indirectly, through the stimulation of ancillary industries. At the same time, local networks of small and medium-sized firms were sometimes damaged by competition from the new arrivals, and the polarisation of development in the South was increased. Thus, many of the developments in the Mezzogiorno were characterised as 'cathedrals in the desert'.

According to the critics, the ends and the means were inconsistent with one another. In the name of a policy aimed at solving social problems, a system of incentives to capital investment was introduced which resulted in "a kind of selection in reverse whereby the kind of enterprises whose creation was stimulated are also those which can contribute least to the creation of a vital and self-sustaining industrial system" and in which the jobs generated are smallest in relation to the capital advanced (Graziani cited in Podbielski, 1978, pages 176-177). In addition, the aid to industry in the South was double-edged. With the subsidisation of capital investment, other things being equal, the value losses incurred by a firm in writing off plant and equipment were reduced, and the devalorisation of capital accelerated. Thus the commitment of an enterprise to a region was correspondingly reduced.

Some people have claimed that many of the arguments of the critics of southern policy are spurious. In the view of Novacco, for example, it is

> "as if one had preferred a desert without cathedrals or as if investments were determined in accordance with our desires or with social requirements rather than linked to market prospects ... and [as if one were] losing sight of the role which large plants, even though they are costly, also have to play in an economic system whose efficiency cannot be measured or guided only in terms of industrial employment" (Novacco, cited in Podbielski, 1978, pages 180-181).

In the eyes of the policymakers and of those concerned with the implementation of regional development policy, its shaping and mode of operation could themselves be justified in several ways. The decisions about what should be placed in the South lay, it could be argued, not with regional development agencies but with the people in control of industry, and only those investments with some prospects of success in a market environment could reasonably be supported. In any case, some of the investments made in the South have provided relatively stable employment.

In these answers the reality depicted by the notion of cathedrals in the desert is not really being contested. Instead, the existence of other options is being denied. What are being highlighted, in other words, are political questions concerning the feasibility of different instruments and the choice of an underlying model of development.

Indeed, in the early 1970s, southern policy was subjected to considerable criticism by the heads of a number of Italian companies and some leading politicians on the grounds that it was unwise to commit such large amounts of money to a strengthening of the chemical and other industries with a high capital to output ratio. A number of reasons underlay this criticism, with the rivalries and conflicts within the dominant bloc being especially significant. In particular, employers in the privately dominated equipment-goods sectors, whose companies' profitability had fallen with the intensification of industrial conflict in 1969 - 1972, were pressing for reforms and a reallocation of resources, with a view to reducing costs in northern industrial areas and helping the groups they controlled to restructure and use territory in a new way (see Garofoli, 1976b, pages 177 - 178).

8.8 The diversification of state-sector investment: the case of Alfa Sud

At first much of the investment in the Mezzogiorno by state holding companies was in energy production and in chemical and metal manufacturing, with the groups themselves sometimes acting as instruments of national economic policy as well as working out strategies of self-expansion. But from the middle of the 1960s onwards, increasing resources were committed to investment in engineering and electronics, and new investments in these sectors were starting to be located in the South.

Increasing investment by state holding companies in equipment-good industries in the South was associated with the adoption by several of these companies of policies of sectoral diversification and of a strategy of progressively transferring their manufacturing base to the Mezzogiorno. A number of state-sector companies were, in other words, interested in diversifying into sectors that were expanding nationally and internationally and that could be commercially successful in the South, mainly in order to strengthen the economic and financial position of the firms concerned. As a consequence, however, the state sector was coming into competition with capitalists in the private sector, whose activities had previously been in many respects complemented. But by choosing to invest in the South, the state holding companies could expect to secure sufficient support from the southern lobby and from state personnel concerned about the growing problems of employment in the Mezzogiorno to overcome private opposition.

The most striking example of this type of development was the Alfa Sud plant located at Pomigliano d'Arco near Naples (see Amin, 1983, pages 6-26). The Alfa Sud project was originally put forward in the autumn of 1966 by the president of the state-owned Alfa Romeo group, and was subsequently approved by IRI and CIPE.

Underlying the project were Alfa Romeo's demand forecasts which, in 1967, predicted that the demand for volume cars would double in the next fifteen years, as long as the prices of raw materials and energy remained low. In the light of these forecasts it was decided to add to the group's range of products by starting to produce middle-priced, medium-capacity (1000-1500 cc) vehicles. The proposed project met with the not unexpected opposition of FIAT: in the view of Agnelli the project was clientelistic, and would create excess capacity in the sector. Significant support for the project came from Christian Democrat politicians and their clienteles. The charge of clientelism was, however, denied by Alfa Romeo. In any case, what really concerned FIAT was not simply the possibility of excess capacity, but the appearance of a new competitor.

As a result of the decision to locate at Pomigliano d'Arco in the South, however, not only did the group gain access to the aid for southern development and help IRI to comply with restrictions on the location of state holding company investment, but also the political backing necessary to overcome FIAT's opposition could be mobilised. At the same time, Alfa Romeo hoped to circumvent some of the problems it was facing in Milan: on the eve of the industrial conflicts of the late 1960s, living costs in northern cities were rising, labour markets were tightening, and working-class job control was increasing. At that stage, not only were wages lower in the South, but unemployment was high and trade union organisation was absent.

The choice of Pomigliano d'Arco itself, where another Alfa Romeo plant and an Aeritalia plant were already located, was determined by two other considerations. One was the need to start production as quickly as possible. In the car industry a new model had a life expectancy of about eight years. If the costs of an investment were to be recouped, early launching of a new model was consequently essential. In the second place, Alfa Romeo was anxious to minimise construction costs. The advantage possessed by Pomigliano d'Arco was the availability of a disused airfield owned by IRI. Furthermore, an adequate network of roads and railways already existed, and the site could be reached comparatively easily from many parts of the Neapolitan agglomeration where Alfa Romeo planned to recruit many of its new employees.

On completion, a large number of jobs were created. Most of the managerial, technical, and administrative staff were, however, recruited in the North, whereas many of the local people who got jobs were drawn not from the inactive, unemployed, or young people joining the job market, but from other firms. The plant remained dependent on Alfa Romeo's headquarters in Milan. The effect on the development of local supply industries was smaller than expected, and most pronounced in the case of the cleaning and maintenance of equipment, services, food provision, and similar activities.

In the first decade of its operation the project was, however, not very successful. Output was consistently less than capacity, and fluctuated in an erratic way owing to high levels of absenteeism on the one hand, and shop floor conflicts and the impact they can have in a plant with a rigid cycle of production on the other. According to the firm, the lack of profitability lay in the "non-industrial mentality of the workers and the inexperience of the internal union in mediating between the shopfloor and management". At first a policy of carefully selecting workers by means of criteria aimed at identifying an individual's suitability and willingness to comply with the norms of modern industrial work had been employed. But with the passing of the Statuto dei Lavoratori in May 1970 the recruitment area was extended, increasing the average length of journeys to work, and control over recruitment passed to local employment offices. As a result, Alfa Romeo did not get the type of workers it wanted (see Amin, 1983, pages 10-14).

The underlying problem was, however, more deeply rooted. The plant itself was based on the Taylorist and Fordist principles of work organisation applied in Alfa Romeo's Milan plant. Moreover, the entire cycle of production from manufacturing of parts to final assembly was concentrated in one works. After the industrial conflicts of 1969-1971 a plant of that kind could not really be expected to yield high levels of productivity, no matter where it was located.

In spite of the fact that Taylorism and Fordism as principles of work organisation were in crisis, Alfa Romeo sought a reestablishment of the old conditions of growth. In a context of recession, attempts were made to weaken working-class job control, reestablish managerial authority, increase mobility, and intensify work. The aim was one of raising productivity by means of the resources already at the firm's disposal and without investing in new plant and new methods of production.

The strategy adopted by Alfa Romeo was not sufficiently successful, and so by the end of the 1970s and early 1980s a change of policy was under way. On the one hand, semiautonomous work groups were being introduced as part of an internal restructuring of the plant. On the other, a joint venture with Nissan was planned. Under this agreement a new assembly plant was to be built in the Naples area, and engines for the new plant were to be supplied by Alfa Sud, ensuring that its engine shop would operate at full capacity. In short, after a long delay there were some signs that the new principles of work organisation and the automation of production with which other car producers had been experimenting were going to be introduced into Alfa Romeo's southern plants.

8.9 Industrial restructuring and decentralisation: the case of FIAT

At the end of the 1960s and in the early 1970s the high intensity of industrial conflict and a crisis of profitability in plants in the heavily industrialised and urbanised Northwest gave way to a major restructuring and decentralisation of Italian industry. In these conditions, investments in the production of equipment and related goods were located in the South by some of the large private oligopolies. Included were Olivetti, Pirelli, and, perhaps most strikingly, FIAT.

Until the early 1970s, most of FIAT's activity in vehicle manufacturing and ancillary areas such as steel and chemical production were concentrated in the Turin metropolitan area. From 50430 employees in 1950, the FIAT group had grown to 150621 employees in 1970, of whom some 60000 were employed in the Mirafiori car works. Until 1973, more than 83% of the group's Italian employees worked in Turin. In 1961-1971, employment in FIAT increased from 25 to 33.3% of the province's industrial employment. Without counting the people employed by subsidiaries and subcontractors, in 1973 one out of every three industrial employees in Turin worked for FIAT (Freyssenet, 1979b, pages 261-263).

In the car sector the divison of labour within the firm was associated with a differentiation of head office functions, a research centre, a machine-tool and tooling unit, and engineering and assembly plants. But the different establishments were all located within an area with a radius of about twenty kilometres. As a result, the scale economies associated with mechanised assembly line methods could be exploited to the full.

With output expanding rapidly, large numbers of unskilled workers were drawn into the city. In the Turin region in 1966-1970 the company recruited 90100 new employees. The commune of Turin itself had a net migration gain from the South of 83727 persons. At the end of 1973, 48% of FIAT's employees and 68.1% of its nonprofessional workers were people who had been born in the South compared with 35.1% and 20.9%, respectively, who had been born in Piedmont (Freyssenet, 1979b, pages 261-265).

In spite of the inadequacy of the city's housing stock, transport systems, and social equipment the firm avoided paying any of the social costs of congestion. Wages were held down, and productivity increased in part through the use of authoritarian methods of plant management.

In the 1970s the company's strategy was changed. First, the internationalisation of production was accelerated via direct investment and production under licence in the Mediterranean, Eastern Europe, and Latin America, amongst other places. As a result, in 1973-1979, production in Italy fell from 72.5 to 57.7% of FIAT's car production (see Amin, 1982, page 51). Second, production within Italy was restructured and decentralised, with the development of new plants in the Mezzogiorno (see table 8.14 and figure 8.6). The change of strategy was prompted by several factors. In the late 1960s, market conditions were such that new investments were initiated to meet the demand for small and medium-capacity cars. In the end, however, the growth of demand was not sustained. With the onset of the recession an increasing proportion of sales were of replacement instead of new vehicles, giving way internationally to increased competition and an acceleration of the processes of concentration and centralisation of capital.

A second factor was the crisis of Taylorism and Fordism as principles of work organisation. On the one hand, the existence of what Aglietta has called 'balance delay time' was placing an increasingly sharp technical constraint on productivity growth, and increases in productivity were increasingly costly in terms of additional investment (see Aglietta, 1979, pages 116-122). On the other, the militancy of the working class had increased. The factory despotism employed by FIAT management was no longer adequate as a means of controlling the work situation. Instead, the factory proletariat was using its newfound capacity to disrupt the cycle of production to secure greater job control and improved conditions of work and pay: wages were pushed upwards, job classifications were amended, new limits were placed on overtime working and the length of the working week, health and safety conditions were improved, and the company's capacity to direct workers and to lay them off was reduced. Also in the face of high levels of absenteeism, manning levels had to be kept high, thus adding further to the costs of production (see chapter 6, section 6.4). Outside of the plant, serious problems of urban congestion caused by several decades of net in-migration were at last having a major impact on the costs of large employers.

In these conditions new investments were made in the Mezzogiorno. Several factors account for the choice of southern locations. In the first

Table 8.14. Trends in employment in FIAT's Italian car plants, 1948-1977. Source: Freyssenet (1979b, pages 250-251).

	Date of establishment	1948	1960	1971	1974	1977
In Turin and its province						
Lingotto	1923	5090	5100	7629	7500	9300
Volvera Ricambi	1925	1028	2500	1689	1600	1850
Mirafiori	1939	16535	31000	60000	49000	37400
Rivalta	1967			15710	15000	14450
Villar Perosa	1969			185	350	400
Torino Stampe	1975					1170
In the rest of Italy						
Florence	1942	513	na	1092	1800	1775
Vado Ligure	1970			762	1400	1350
Termini Imerese	1970			820	950	2250
Bari	1970			na	2800	na
Cassino	1972				5000	6500
Sulmona	1972				1000	950
Termoli	1973				2900	2030

place, investments in the South and especially in depressed rural areas were supported by government aid. In most cases the new plants were located in rural areas near small provincial towns: in areas that had been depopulated some of the additional housing and social infrastructural equipment needed already existed. What also attracted the firm was the social and cultural composition of the working population in the areas chosen. In the light of FIAT's experience in 1969-1972, an attempt was made to recruit male workers with an average age of at least thirty, who were politically conservative, and who had diverse occupational backgrounds, including small-scale farmers or agricultural, commercial, and service-sector workers.

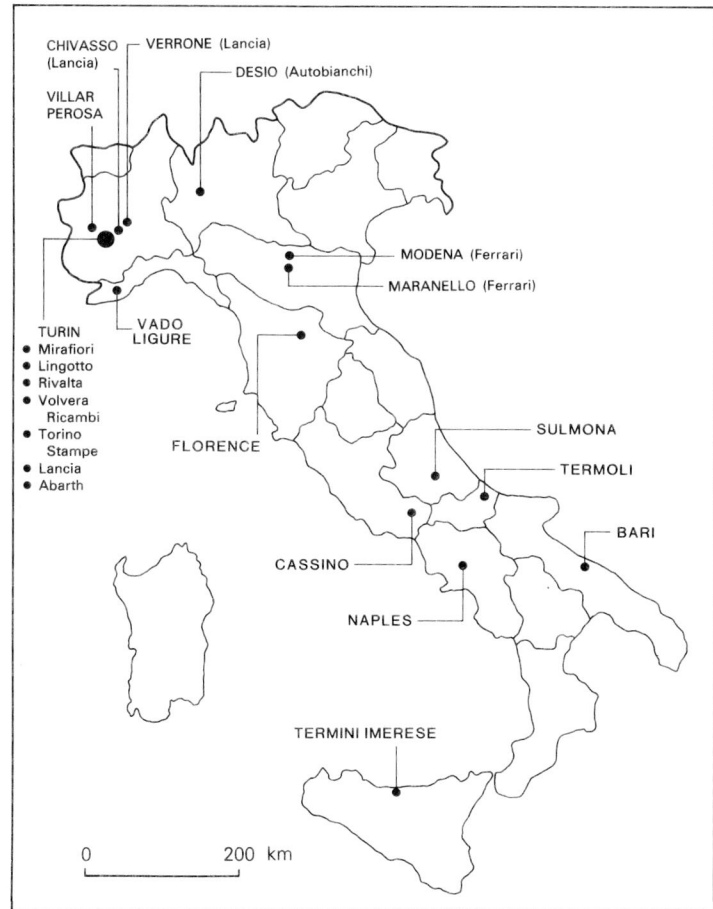

Figure 8.6. The distribution of the FIAT group's (FIAT, Autobianchi, Lancia, Ferrari, and Abarth) Italian car plants in the mid-1970s. Source: elaborated from Freyssenet (1979b, page 270).

In many cases the people concerned had a second job, but the increased absenteeism this implied was considered to be less important than the expected impact a diversity of interests would have on the collective identity of the new factory work force. What the company wanted was to avoid the militancy of a young urban industrial working class. In the end, of course, industrial conflict did occur. But a new type of manual worker moulded to the firm's new requirements was nevertheless created (see Amin, 1982, pages 76–80).

In contrast to what happened in the case of the earlier development of the Alfa Sud complex, the southern FIAT plants were not replicas of the integrated works developed in the Northwest. In the words of Agnelli, who was the president of FIAT:

"The labour conflicts in the factories have taught FIAT's management an elementary truth: large plants like Mirafiori can no longer be governed and therefore the FIAT system must be reformed. What was decided was to create factories in the South, but in a certain way ... one does not create a Mirafiori in the South, but several small plants. What these plants have in common is that they are independent of one another" (Agnelli cited in Amin, 1983, page 74).

After 1969–1972, traditional methods of restoring profitability had been largely closed off. In the case of FIAT, authoritarian and rigidly hierarchical managerial relations were retained. But a strategy of subdividing the production cycle, of reducing the degree of vertical integration, and of duplicating and decentralising different operations was adopted. In the new and in existing plants new principles of work organisation were introduced, and some areas of work that were dirty, dangerous, and conflict ridden were automated (see the discussion of automation and systemofacture in chapter 2, section 2.5).

In the first of these three developments the cycle of production was split up into different operations, including the manufacturing of particular mechanical parts, such as engines and gearboxes, and assembly work. Some of the operations isolated were sold off or subcontracted. Many of the others were made the object of work in independently-run small and medium-sized plants. And with the aid of a computerised administrative system, strategies of multiple sourcing and of decentralisation of production were adopted. An engine and gearbox plant was accordingly constructed at Termoli, and a similar plant was built in Poland. The Termoli plant was used to supply an assembly plant at Cassino with which it was connected by an EEC financed road. But its output could also be used to supply other assembly plants.

In establishing small and medium-sized decentralised plants the aim of the group's management was threefold. First, it hoped to break down the working-class solidarity built up in the large plants in Piedmont. Second, in large integrated plants the level of output of one shop was dependent on the output of other related cycles of production. With the fragmentation and decentralisation of production, FIAT's management hoped to prevent the spillover effects that occurred in integrated plants, and to acquire an increased capacity to vary the output of different stages of production according to conditions of demand. Third, the new strategy was seen as a way of guaranteeing the continuity of output. A number of other changes were also made with a view to reducing the impact of industrial conflicts and mechanical breakdowns on the continuity of production. At Cassino, for example, four independently-run lines were introduced to assemble one model.

The second main development was the introduction of production islands and semiautonomous groups. In areas of assembly work characterised by high levels of conflict the Taylorist and Fordist principle of asking one person to carry out one task was dropped. Instead, work groups were introduced. Within each group, jobs, whose skill content remained low, could be rotated. As a result, workers were given more control over the volume of output, though line speeds were still determined by management. Quality control was improved. In addition, each group was paid a collective bonus according to the volume of output. An individual worker was thus made responsible not so much to supervisory staff as to his or her colleagues. After the conflicts of the late 1960s and early 1970s a strategy of responsible autonomy was, in other words, being experimented with (see Friedman, 1977, pages 77-79).

In the third and last place some functions were automated. Included were panel pressing, spot welding, riveting, and paint spraying. In the case of spot welding, some skilled manual workers were replaced by robots and by a smaller number of skilled engineering and polyvalent maintenance staff. In other cases, dangerous and unpleasant work or processes where conflicts were common were involved.

At Mirafiori some even more striking developments occurred: in 1978 an automated magnetic machine transfer system was introduced, and in 1980 an automated engine assembly unit was opened. In each case new automated methods of moving parts to assembly stations where islands of workers were employed opened up the possibility of eliminating the assembly line. Not only did many jobs disappear and transfer time fall; the composition of output could also be altered as demand changed. If malfunctions or industrial conflicts occurred, the route along which parts were moving and the intensity of work at different stations could be altered with the help of a central computer. Moreover, the social composition of the work force was changed (see Amin, 1983, pages 66-72; Rollier, 1986).

In the early 1980s, productivity increased sharply, managerial authority was reestablished, and FIAT's profits recovered.

Industrialisation and the reproduction of inequality

9.1 Industrial development and the changing economy and society of the South
In the period up to 1975 the Mezzogiorno was integrated as an essentially open economy into the national economy, and the South was industrialised. As a result, the structure of the economy and society of the region was transformed. Interregional inequalities in output, employment, and income were, however, not substantially narrowed, and new types of inequality were produced. Indeed some of the most striking consequences of the modernisation of southern agriculture and of the implantation of modern industries in the region were the accompanying deterioration in labour market conditions and in the trade balance of the Mezzogiorno, and the way in which social tensions were translated from the South's rural areas to its towns and cities.

What must first of all be emphasised in outlining the consequences of twenty-five years of southern development are the profound changes in the economy and society of the Mezzogiorno. The most striking change was the development of modern industries in the region: in 1957–1975 a sequence of large industrial investments were made in the South (see table 9.1). The result of this was that the structure of the southern industrial system was fundamentally altered. A modern working class was formed. An indigenous industrial bourgeoisie, however, did not emerge. The reason why lies in the fact that the process of southern industrial investment was dominated by large monopolistic companies with headquarters outside of the region, and especially by externally controlled semipublic groups.

The leading role of public enterprises in the industrial development of the Mezzogiorno is indicated in table 9.2. In it are recorded the sales, fixed assets, and employment accounted for in 1973 by three hundred and fourteen companies, distinguished by the location of their establishments and the financial group to which they belonged. In the Centre–North, enterprises in the public group accounted for 10 to 14% of the various totals, whereas in the South, on the other hand, the corresponding range was 32 to 44%.

The domination of the southern economy by public groups was particularly striking in the South's major manufacturing industries. In metal manufacturing, public enterprises accounted for more than 90% of the southern totals; in chemicals, petrochemicals, and pharmaceuticals, public groups accounted for about 35% of production and assets and 20% of employment; and in mechanical and electrical engineering, public enterprises accounted for about 25% of the southern totals.

Industrialisation was, in other words, externally controlled and largely dominated by the public sector. Investments by the local bourgeoisie were primarily in the service sector or in urban land and property speculation: most of the energy of local entrepreneurs was devoted not to manufacturing

Table 9.1. Industrial establishments in the southern provinces employing 1000 or more people at the end of 1978 or in 1981[a]. Sources: Saraceno (1980); Guglielmetti and Padovani (1981a; 1981b).

Company	Type of group[b]	Sector	Year[c]	Commune	Region	Employment 1978	Employment 1980
Italcantieri	public	shipbuilding and repairing	1783	Castellammare di Stabia	Campania	2440	2339
Cantieri Navali Riuniti	public	shipbuilding and repairing	1850	Palermo	Sicily	3610	3538
Italsider	public	iron and steel	1910	Naples	Campania	7800	7681
Acciaierie Pugliesi	local private	iron and steel	1923	Giovinazzo	Apulia	1200	981
SNIA Viscosa	mixed	synthetic and artificial fibres	1923	Naples	Campania	1500	1424
Montedison	mixed	primary chemicals: phosphatic fertilisers	1928	Crotone	Calabria	1000	957
FMI Mecfond	public	mechanical engineering	1930	Naples	Campania	1270	1250
IAM (SACA)	public	aerospace equipment	1934	Brindisi	Apulia	1000	980
Mobil Oil	foreign private	oil refining	1937	Naples	Campania	1050	880
Italtrafo	public	electrical engineering	1938	Naples	Campania	1190	1222
Alfa Romeo	public	motor vehicles, parts, and accessories	1939	Pomigliano d'Arco	Campania	2990	3042
Aeritalia	public	aerospace equipment	1952	Bacoli	Campania	4490	4561
Selenia	public	electronics and telecommunications	1952	Naples	Campania	2150	2181
SEBN	public	shipbuilding and repairing	1954	Pozzuoli	Campania	1350	1304
Olivetti ICO	national private	electronics and telecommunications	1955	Melilli	Campania	2000	1641
Montedison	mixed	primary chemicals: petrochemicals	1957	Salerno	Sicily	6500	6313
Marzotto Sud (Issimo)	national private	textiles and clothing	1958	Brindisi	Campania	1490	1170
Montedison	mixed	primary chemicals: petrochemicals	1959	Marcianise	Apulia	4400	4637
GTE	foreign private	electronics and telecommunications	1960	Sulmona	Campania	1650	1627
ACE	foreign private	electronics and telecommunications	1960	Maddaloni	Abruzzo	1500	700
Face Standard	foreign private	electronics and telecommunications	1961	Taranto	Campania	1200	1193
Italsider	public	iron and steel	1961	Bari	Apulia	20780	21251
Officine Calabrese	local private	motor vehicles, parts, and accessories	1961	Catania	Apulia		1004
SGS-Ates	public	electronics and telecommunications	1961	Caserta	Sicily	2100	2097
3M Minnesota Italia	foreign private	secondary chemicals	1961	Sta Maria Capua Vetere	Campania		1118
SIT Siemens (Italtel)	public	electronics and telecommunications	1962		Campania	4670	4662

Table 9.1 (continued)

Company	Type of group[b]	Sector	Year[c]	Commune	Region	Employment 1978	Employment 1980
ANIC	public	primary chemicals: petrochemicals	1962	Gela	Sicily	4250	2983
Adriatica Confezioni	public	textiles and clothing	1962	Chieti	Abruzzo	1600	1406
Brema-Firestone	foreign private	rubber tyres and rubber products	1962	Bari	Apulia	1350	1251
Pneumatici Pirelli	national private	rubber tyres and rubber products	1962	Villafranca Tirrena	Sicily	1450	1375
Rumianca Sud	mixed	primary chemicals: petrochemicals	1962	Assemini	Sardinia	1100	1335
ANIC	public	synthetic and artificial fibres	1963	Pisticci	Basilicata	3000	2860
Filati Industriali	mixed	textiles and clothing	1963	Villacidro	Sardinia	1200	596
SIR Alchisarda	mixed	primary chemicals: petrochemicals	1963	Porto Torres	Sardinia	3250	769
Società Italiana Vetro	public	glass and glassware	1963	San Salvo	Abruzzo	2900	2860
Ideal Standard	foreign private	nonmetallic minerals: ceramic bathroom accessories	1964	Salerno	Campania		1285
IRE	foreign private	electrical engineering	1964	Naples	Campania	1950	931
SIT Siemens (Italtel)	public	electronics and telecommunications	1964	L'Aquila	Abruzzo	4940	4906
Texas Instruments	foreign private	electronics and telecommunications	1965	Aversa	Campania	2200	1185
Intesa	public	textiles and clothing	1965	Gagliano Castelf. (Enna)	Sicily		1113
Belleli Sud	national private	mechanical engineering	1966	Taranto	Apulia		1118
ICROT	public	iron and steel	1966	Taranto	Apulia	2000	1987
SNIA Viscosa	public	synthetic and artificial fibres	1966	Villacidro	Sardinia	1400	1300
Harry's Moda	private national	textiles and clothing	1967	Lecce	Apulia		1305
Alfa Sud	public	motor vehicles, parts, and accessories	1968	Pomigliano d'Arco	Campania	15330	15161
Monti Tescon (M. d'Abruzzo)	public	textiles and clothing	1968	Monte Silvano	Abruzzo	1500	1317
Alluminio Italia-Alsar	public	metal manufacturing: aluminium	1969	Portoscuso	Sardinia	1300	1508
FIAT	national private	motor vehicles, parts, and accessories	1969	Modugno (Bari)	Apulia	2700	2700
FIAT-Allis	national private	mechanical engineering: earth moving equipment	1970	Lecce	Apulia	2000	3790
FIAT	national private	motor vehicles, parts, and accessories	1970	Termini Imerese	Sicily	2200	3204
Olivetti	national private	mechanical engineering	1970	Marcianise	Campania	1100	1192

Table 9.1 (continued)

Company	Type of group[b]	Sector	Year[c]	Commune	Region	Employment 1978	Employment 1980
FIAT	national private	motor vehicles, parts, and accessories	1971	Sulmona	Abruzzo	1000	1021
SIT Siemens (Italtel)	public	electronics and telecommunications	1972	Palermo	Sicily	2170	1666
Indesit Sud	national private	electrical household goods	1973	Aversa	Campania		5114
FIAT	national private	motor vehicles, parts, and accessories	1973	Termoli	Molise	2900	3025
Fibra del Tirso	mixed	synthetic and artificial fibres	1974	Ottana	Sardinia	2300	1977
Magneti Marelli	national private	electrical engineering	1974	San Salvo	Abruzzo	2400	2383
Sofim	national private	motor vehicles, parts, and accessories	1974	Foggia	Apulia	1000	812
Also	foreign private	food, drink, and tobacco: ice cream	1975	Caivano	Campania		1030
Montefibre	mixed	synthetic and artificial fibres	1975	Acerra	Campania	1800	922
FIAT	national private	motor vehicles, parts, and accessories	1978	Flumeri	Campania		1177

[a] Data on the southern provinces of Lazio and Marche are excluded.

[b] The groups to which these companies belong, and by which they are controlled, are differentiated into: private groups originating in the South, in the North, and abroad; public groups; and mixed groups (groups which started out as private ones, which entered into crisis, and in which the state took a large holding).

[c] The year in which construction began.

industry but to an exploitation of the opportunities offered by the urban growth that it helped fuel.

The second main component of change in the southern industrial system was the decline in the absolute and relative importance of traditional industries. In these sectors, locally-owned firms producing for the local market with outdated methods of production had predominated. Consequently, the decline of firms in these sectors was paralleled by the decline in the relative importance of the small independent industrial bourgeoisie in the Mezzogiorno.

In 1976–1980 the situation changed somewhat. The chemical and steel sectors were in crisis, and major investments by large extraregional groups virtually came to an end. But a more dynamic role was played by smaller northern firms, and especially by small southern firms operating mainly in traditional sectors.

At the end of 1980, of 10 889 manufacturing establishments owned by firms with ten or more full-time employees in the Mezzogiorno, 84.8% were owned by southern entrepreneurs. Yet only 39.6% of jobs were, however, in southern-owned firms. Southern firms were small (see figure 9.1), and 72% of southern establishments and 68.5% of employment were in traditional sectors. Three fifths of southern manufacturing employment was in establishments wholly owned by or controlled by extraregional groups. In general, the plants of nonsouthern capital were large (see figure 9.1), and were involved in modern sectors. Indeed, amongst these externally controlled establishments were most of the southern plants in modern

Table 9.2. The sales, fixed assets, and employment of the main Italian companies, by location of establishment and by ownership structure, in 1973 (percentage values). Source: Graziani (1979, page 44).

	Sales	Fixed assets	Employment
Mezzogiorno [a]			
Public enterprises	37.67	43.87	32.09
Montedison	18.91	16.39	31.33
FIAT	9.01	14.18	7.98
Independent enterprises	34.41	25.56	28.60
Total	100.00	100.00	100.00
Centre-North			
Public enterprises	10.22	13.53	13.46
Montedison	6.07	7.78	8.64
FIAT	2.61	3.52	4.32
Independent enterprises	81.10	75.27	73.58
Total	100.00	100.00	100.00

sectors and almost all of those in electronics, transport equipment, steel, and chemicals (Martinelli, 1985, pages 57-65, 72-73).

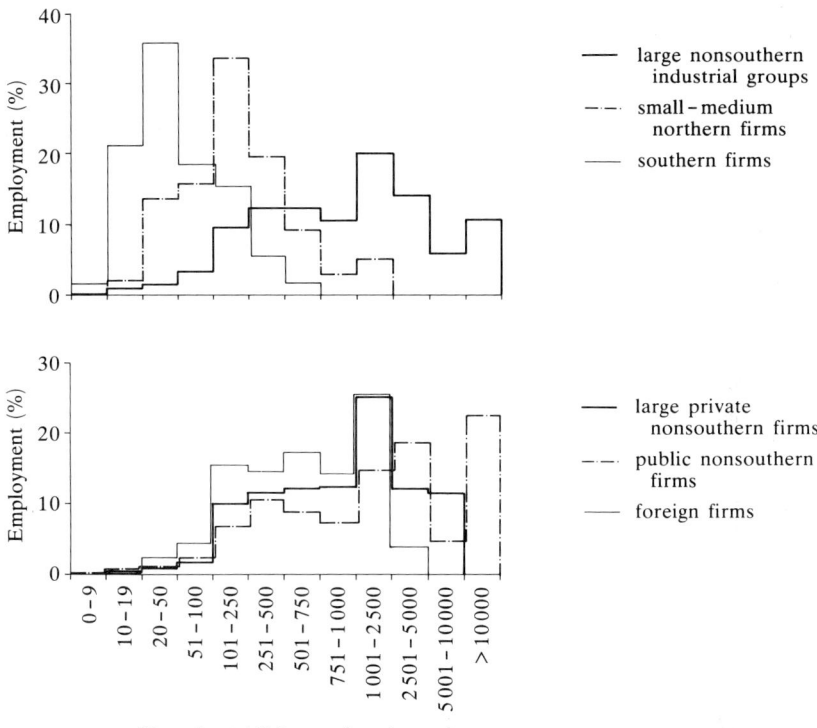

Figure 9.1. The distribution of manufacturing employment in plants owned by firms with ten or more employees in the Mezzogiorno, by size of establishment and main ownership group, in 1980. Source: elaborated from data in Martinelli (1985, page 60).

9.2 The evolution of output and employment in the South
In 1951-1961 the share of the South in gross domestic product at factor cost declined from 24.1 to 23.6%. It then increased slightly, to reach 24.5% in 1971 and 25.0% in 1975 (Podbielski, 1978, pages 105-106). The fact that there was such a limited equalisation of regional output levels, despite the fast expansion of southern investment, can be explained by the fact that the incremental capital to output ratio was higher in the South than in the rest of the country. The difference was particularly marked in the case of southern industry.

In its turn the magnitude of the capital to output ratio can be explained in part by the sectoral composition and low regional multiplier effects of southern investment. On the one hand, traditional industries stagnated.

On the other, the chemical and metal manufacturing sectors, which required extremely large investments per unit of output, especially in the branches producing primary products, expanded. In the rest of Italy the firms operating in traditional industries were more competitive and maintained output growth more successfully than those in the South, and the modern engineering industries that led the process of national economic expansion had a larger weight in the industrial system. After 1960, incremental capital to output ratios were lower in the sectors that were strongly represented in the North than in those sectors and branches on which the southern industrial system was based. In addition, it was northern firms that secured increases in output and labour productivity through rationalisation without investment in the 1960s. The effects of the composition of southern investments on output growth were reinforced by the fact that southern industrialisation was based on the implantation of externally controlled plants, which established few links with the local economy and whose multiplier effects were felt in the advanced regions rather than in the vicinity of the plants themselves (see Podbielski, 1978; pages 110-111, and 142-143).

The southern accumulation process also had important effects on the evolution of employment and on the movement of unemployment and activity rates. As in the case of changes in output, there was a general tendency for labour market conditions to worsen in the South in comparison with those in the rest of the country (see Podbielski, 1978, pages 111-115). Official unemployment statistics, which, like official employment data, are notoriously unreliable and understate the relevant magnitudes, recorded substantial reductions in the level and rate of unemployment both in the South and in the Centre-North. But these improvements were much more pronounced in the more prosperous parts of the country. In the South the rate of unemployment declined from 9.2% in 1951 to 3.9% in 1961, but rose to reach 4.5% in 1971 and 5.1% in 1975, whereas in the rest of Italy it fell from 8.7% in 1951 to 3.0% in 1961, 2.5% in 1971, and 2.4% in 1975.

Since the end of the 1950s the Italian economy has been characterised by particularly low and declining activity rates. But not only is Italy's activity rate amongst the lowest in Europe: in 1951-1975 it declined even when the economy was going through a process of rapid growth. In other European countries the activity rate was stable or decreased only slightly.

Up to 1975 the size of the population in working age groups increased slightly. But in the country as a whole there were low and declining activity rates for women in all age groups, and sharply declining rates for men in the age groups 14-25 years and 55 years and over. Activity rates were nevertheless much lower in the Mezzogiorno than in the rest of the country, and they fell equally steeply in both areas. According to official statistics, they declined from 41.1% in the South and 48.9% in the Centre-North in 1951 to 33.0% and 38.9%, respectively, in 1971, and to 32.5% and 38.7%, respectively, in 1975.

This progressive fall in Italian activity rates started a widespread discussion about the way in which labour markets operated and about the characteristics of the accumulation process in the country as a whole. In the literature on the topic at least four different interpretations of this phenomenon can be distinguished, based, respectively, upon the following explanatory elements. One set of interpretations stressed the role of changes in the supply of labour caused by changes in the preferences of workers. A second focused on changes in the demand for labour due to the fall in the level of investment and attempts to increase labour productivity through selective recruitment strategies. A third stressed the impact of the expulsion of less skilled workers from factory employment and the segmentation of the labour market caused by the success of trade unions in narrowing wage differentials. The last sought to link fluctuations in employment and unemployment not with changes in the operation of labour markets, but with changes in the process of accumulation and in the strategies of capital. In particular, emphasis was placed on the objective need for capital to reproduce an industrial reserve army (see Graziani, 1977, pages 8-11).

These debates contributed much to an understanding of Italian labour market phenomena. Some of the reasons for falling activity rates were not properly identified, however, until awareness of the extent of marginal employment and of the black economy increased: in 1975 a sample survey conducted by a research institute added about 3 million jobs to those recorded by ISTAT, and in 1977 a revised survey method added about 1 million people to the employed population, and 2 million to the labour force (Bruno, 1979, page 133).

In Italy, total employment, as measured by official employment statistics, increased in the 1950s but declined from the early 1960s until the early 1970s. In the Centre-North an increase in the 1950s just outweighed a decrease in the 1960s. In the South, on the other hand, overall employment fell continuously from the beginning of the 1950s.

The decline in southern employment occurred because the outflow of labour from agriculture was not matched by a sufficient growth of extraagricultural employment. The decrease in agricultural employment exceeded the expectations of the planners, but the main problems stemmed from the less than expected and very limited growth of manufacturing employment (see tables 5.7 and 9.3). In the South, employment increased rapidly in the construction industry, in the public administration, and in the service sector. But this growth was largely a product of (1) an increase in precarious and low-productivity employment in the construction industry and in backward service activities, and (2) new jobs in already overexpanded and inefficient state bureaucracies. As we shall see, the expansion of more or less precarious forms of employment in the building industry and in services and of unproductive state employment, as well as the existence of mass emigration, can be attributed in part to the lack of alternative

Table 9.3. Employment[a] change in the Mezzogiorno and in Italy, 1951–1972 (in thousands). Source: elaborated from ISTAT (1973, pages 7–18, 37–42, 61–66).

	Mezzogiorno					Italy				
	1951–1958	1958–1964	1964–1969	1969–1972	1951–1972	1951–1958	1958–1964	1964–1969	1969–1972	1951–1972
Agriculture	−725.6	−693.4	−293.7	−208.3	−1921.0	−1666.0	−2007.0	−944.0	−668.0	−5285.0
Industry	386.7	169.6	6.9	4.3	567.5	1273.9	919.1	52.0	−31.0	2214.0
manufacturing	157.3	−36.0	16.7	33.6	171.6	723.7	465.2	157.1	136.0	1482.0
construction	226.4	203.3	−11.3	−28.5	389.9	536.4	444.5	−119.1	−160.5	701.3
Services	279.8	46.2	109.9	16.8	452.7	970.6	222.7	295.7	272.0	1761.0
Public administration	50.3	94.4	77.1	33.0	254.8	159.5	282.2	180.4	90.0	712.1
Total	−8.8	−383.2	−99.8	−154.2	−646.0	738.0	−583.0	−415.9	−337.0	−597.9
Consumption-good industries[b]	113.5	−73.5	−17.0	−33.6	−10.6	352.2	83.0	−22.9	−76.2	170.1
permanent	−13.6	39.7	1.4	−19.0	8.5	−10.4	290.5	32.8	−32.3	280.6
dependent	12.1	56.8	19.3	−3.4	84.8	30.9	313.4	70.8	8.2	423.3
independent	−25.7	−17.1	−17.9	−15.6	−76.3	−41.3	−22.9	−38.0	−40.5	−142.7
marginal	127.1	−113.2	−18.4	−14.6	−19.1	362.6	−373.5	−55.7	−43.9	−110.5
dependent	75.4	−71.9	−7.0	−9.6	−13.1	204.8	−205.4	−17.0	−32.5	−50.1
independent	51.7	−41.3	−11.4	−5.0	−6.0	157.8	−168.1	−38.7	−11.4	−60.4
Equipment-good industries[c]	16.9	3.3	5.9	43.8	69.9	208.9	346.0	140.9	128.6	824.4
permanent	16.0	14.0	20.6	43.6	94.0	186.7	370.9	200.4	126.0	884.0
dependent	15.3	14.6	19.5	41.1	90.5	159.6	357.8	187.2	126.6	831.2
independent	0.7	−0.6	0.9	2.5	3.5	27.1	13.1	13.2	−0.6	52.8
marginal	0.9	−10.7	−14.5	0.2	−24.1	22.2	−24.9	−59.5	2.6	−59.6
dependent	−1.2	−0.3	−12.1	0.0	−13.6	6.7	15.6	−50.6	2.0	−26.3
independent	2.1	−10.4	−2.4	0.2	−10.5	15.5	−40.5	−8.9	0.6	−33.3

Table 9.3 (continued)

	Mezzogiorno					Italy				
	1951–1958	1958–1964	1964–1969	1969–1972	1951–1972	1951–1958	1958–1964	1964–1969	1969–1972	1951–1972
Intermediate-good industries[d]	26.9	34.2	27.8	23.4	112.3	162.6	202.2	39.1	83.6	487.5
permanent	23.4	36.3	29.1	23.6	112.4	158.0	207.2	42.9	83.8	491.9
dependent	24.5	37.2	29.2	23.1	114.0	150.9	204.0	44.2	83.8	482.9
independent	−1.1	−0.9	−0.1	0.5	−1.6	7.1	3.2	−1.3	0.0	9.0
marginal	3.5	−2.1	−1.3	−0.2	−0.1	4.6	−5.0	−3.8	−0.2	−4.4
dependent	3.5	−2.1	−1.3	−0.2	−0.1	4.6	−5.0	−3.8	−0.2	−4.4
independent	0.0	0.0	0.0	0.0	0.0	0.0	0.0	0.0	0.0	0.0

[a] Permanent and marginal employment broadly correspond to full-time and part-time employment, whereas dependent and independent employment broadly correspond to employees and self-employed persons. Owing to effects of rounding errors, column and row subtotals and totals cannot always be derived from table entries.

[b] Traditional and current consumption-good industries: food, drink, and tobacco; textiles; clothing and footwear; leather and leather goods; furniture and wood products; printing and publishing; and other manufacturing industries.

[c] Equipment-good industries: engineering; and transport equipment.

[d] Intermediate-good industries: metal manufacturing; nonmetallic minerals; chemicals and allied industries; rubber; and paper.

industrial jobs and to the overall model of southern and national industrial development (Del Monte and Giannola, 1978, pages 188–197).

9.3 Investment and employment in the South

One of the most striking characteristics of the southern development process was the coexistence of a sharp increase in industrial investment with an extremely limited expansion of employment in industry, excluding construction. Whereas in 1951–1973 the share of the South in national industrial investment increased from 15.0 to 43.2%, over the same period its share of industrial employment decreased from 19.6 to 17.7%. As has been pointed out by Graziani, the process that many have described as one of industrialisation without development could perhaps be more adequately described as one of development without employment (Graziani, 1978, pages 366–371; 1979, pages 49–65).

One reason for the modest contribution of investment to the growth of manufacturing employment lay in the concentration of southern investment in increasingly large projects in sectors and branches with high and rapidly increasing capital intensities. Until the late 1960s, modern engineering industries with medium capital intensities were located overwhelmingly in the Centre–North. The investments undertaken in the South accordingly led to an increase in output and employment that was low compared with the outcome that would have ensued from a more diversified set of investments (table 9.4).

The most important factor explaining the limited growth of industrial employment in the Mezzogiorno was, however, the decline of independent and dependent employment in traditional consumption-good sectors (see table 9.3). In these industries, artisan and family-based types of organisation, and archaic methods of production predominated. In comparison with small and medium-sized firms operating in these branches in other parts of Italy, southern concerns were on the whole more labour intensive and less competitive.

In the early 1950s, small firms had increased in number and size in the South. The reason for this was that southern firms still enjoyed a relatively high degree of protection from outside competition, owing to the existence of high transport costs and the small size of the local market. Towards the end of the decade, however, the integration of the region with the rest of the national economy and the trend towards a single national market were accelerated, in part as a result of the impact of the policy of extraordinary intervention. In addition, the flow of resources to the South was expanding, southern incomes were increasing, and the mode of consumption of the region's inhabitants was changing. Consequently, the protection enjoyed by southern firms was reduced. The interests of northern firms in penetrating southern markets increased, and markets in the Mezzogiorno could be supplied without locating in the region.

In the 1950s, small and medium-sized firms in the Centre–North had in fact been restructured to increase their competitiveness on export markets. The gap in competitiveness had consequently been widened, and so in the 1960s and early 1970s, northern enterprises were able to outcompete southern firms and quickly captured a large share of sales in the South.

Increased competition on the product market thus gave way to a sharp increase in import penetration. With the implantation of modern industry in the region, competition increased on the labour market as well. As a result of these two factors many marginal firms in the Mezzogiorno collapsed.

Table 9.4. Average investment per person employed, by sector and size of investment (in million lire in current prices)[a]. Source: elaborated from Cassa per il Mezzogiorno (1973, pages 55–56).

	Up to 1960	1961–1964	1965–1968	1969–1972
Sector				
Extractive industries	3.0	3.6	15.2	18.1
Food and drink	3.0	6.4	7.9	7.1
Tobacco	0.9	4.3	3.9	2.6
Textiles	1.9	6.1	8.4	7.7
Clothing	0.9	1.6	2.2	3.6
Footwear, leather, and leather goods	1.6	2.4	3.9	2.2
Furniture and wood products	1.6	3.6	6.4	6.8
Metal manufacture	3.3	55.5	30.6	54.2
Engineering	2.4	4.0	8.2	6.8
Nonmetallic minerals	2.8	6.4	8.9	12.4
Chemicals and allied industries	10.3	26.4	62.5	44.3
Rubber products	6.1	12.3	12.8	11.1
Cellulose and synthetic fibres	3.0	12.2	12.7	30.4
Paper and paper products	3.7	17.7	25.8	5.3
Printing and publishing	1.6	3.7	9.6	4.6
Plastic products	5.4	5.4	6.2	8.4
Photographic, phonographic, and cinematographic products, and other manufactures	1.5	5.6	8.3	5.0
Electricity, gas, and water	9.1	69.8	144.3	30.0
Transport and communications	5.1	9.1	30.3	35.9
Other industries and services	1.4	3.1	6.8	12.9
Total	3.3	10.2	16.2	18.6
Size of investment				
<1500 million lire	2.2	4.4	6.1	5.3
1500–5000 million lire	6.8	10.4	21.9	10.5
>5000 million lire	17.9	57.9	39.1	43.6
Total	3.3	10.2	16.2	18.6

[a] These estimates are based on expected fixed investments and expected levels of employment in projects financed by special and by other medium-term credit institutes.

9.4 The deteriorating trade balance of the Mezzogiorno

Over the period as a whole the gross per capita income of southern residents increased slightly as a proportion of the national average. At first it fell, dropping from 61.3% of the national average in 1951 to 60.3% in 1961. Subsequently, however, it increased to reach 65.6% in 1971 and 68.9% in 1975. This overall improvement is often attributed to two factors. One is increases in the comparative level of labour productivity in southern industry. The other is the emigration of some 4.4 million people between 1951 and 1975. (What would have happened had these people not emigrated is, however, not usually considered, nor can it easily be determined.)

In the case of total per capital resources a more pronounced increase occurred. Southern resources increased from 71.7% of the national average in 1951 to 73.3% in 1961, 85.1% in 1971, and 84.2% in 1975. The difference between income and resources was, however, the product of a rapid growth of net imports into the region. The latter increased from 15.7% of total internal resources in 1951 to 18.2% in 1971 and 18.5% in 1975. (A set of similar figures for the period up to 1973, when the methods of national income accounting were revised, are set out in table 9.5.)

A continuous and increasing imbalance in the external accounts of the Mezzogiorno was in fact a second striking characteristic of the southern development process (the first was the absence of significant industrial employment growth). In 1951-1973 the level and growth of the South's external deficit was mainly a product of the size and growth of net imports of goods and services into the region. An outflow of profits on externally financed investments was, however, a second contributory factor (see table 9.5).

The deteriorating trade balance of the South was largely financed by an expanding volume of net transfers into the region. The latter were composed in part of remittances from emigrants. Incomes distributed to southern residents by the public administration in the form of subsidies, pensions, and grants were particularly important (see figure 9.2). (Incomes received in this way helped fuel consumption of imported goods, but were also saved and used to finance a variety of small-scale investments. To a large extent, however, these incomes served to create and to preserve precarious forms of employment and a variety of unproductive activities.) In addition, a decreasing but nevertheless significant net inflow of capital occurred.

Graziani has pointed out that the mechanism lying behind this phenomenon and behind the development process as a whole was a pattern of infrastructural and industrial investment that increased aggregate demand without promoting a balanced expansion of the productive system. The flow of industrial investment and of public expenditure into the Mezzogiorno increased income and demand in the region. Industries producing energy and intermediate goods were established. But industries producing items of industrial equipment or modern consumption goods did not develop on a significant scale in the South itself.

The expansion of demand for goods and services that could not be imported led in fact to a rapid development of local production. The construction industry and commercial and distributional services connected both with the maintenance of plant and equipment and with consumption activities expanded rapidly. These industries were almost entirely under southern entrepreneurship. But the firms concerned tended to provide only relatively precarious employment for comparatively unskilled and low-paid workers.

Table 9.5. The balance of payments of the Mezzogiorno in relation to gross income, 1951–1973. Source: ISTAT (1975, volume 2, pages 6, 12).

Year	Net exports (%)	Net exports of goods and services (%)	Net income from abroad (%)	Net current transfers from abroad (%)	Current balance (%)	Gross income (%)	Gross income (milliard lire at current prices)
1951	−18.6	−15.8	−2.8	8.6	−10.0	100.0	2452.3
1952	−24.0	−21.4	−2.6	10.1	−13.9	100.0	2614.2
1953	−19.5	−16.9	−2.6	10.3	−9.2	100.0	3018.6
1954	−20.2	−17.5	−2.7	10.8	−9.4	100.0	3142.9
1955	−23.4	−20.7	−2.7	11.5	−12.0	100.0	3397.0
1956	−20.6	−18.2	−2.4	11.5	−9.1	100.0	3772.9
1957	−17.8	−15.6	−2.2	10.8	−6.9	100.0	4076.7
1958	−18.6	−16.4	−2.1	12.9	−5.7	100.0	4296.4
1959	−18.9	−16.9	−2.0	13.6	−5.3	100.0	4478.0
1960	−24.4	−22.2	−2.2	13.7	−10.6	100.0	4742.9
1961	−21.2	−19.3	−1.9	13.7	−7.5	100.0	5378.2
1962	−24.9	−23.3	−1.6	15.4	−9.5	100.0	5951.9
1963	−25.5	−23.9	−1.6	16.7	−8.8	100.0	7047.7
1964	−25.0	−23.4	−1.6	14.9	−10.1	100.0	7634.6
1965	−17.6	−16.2	−1.3	17.0	−0.6	100.0	8536.2
1966	−18.7	−17.4	−1.3	17.3	−1.4	100.0	9139.5
1967	−18.9	−17.3	−1.6	16.6	−2.3	100.0	10151.8
1968	−18.6	−17.1	−1.5	17.9	−0.7	100.0	10786.9
1969	−19.4	−18.0	−1.4	19.0	−0.3	100.0	11910.4
1970	−23.5	−21.9	−1.6	19.0	−4.5	100.0	13061.4
1971	−22.2	−20.8	−1.4	20.0	−2.2	100.0	14481.8
1972	−24.4	−22.9	−1.5	18.7	−5.7	100.0	15647.5
1973	−26.1	−24.0	−2.1	18.5	−7.7	100.0	18628.7

The trade balance is equal to net exports of goods and services plus net income from abroad, and the current balance in the balance of payments is equal to the difference between net exports and net current transfers to the rest of the world. The current balance is assumed to be equal to net investment abroad, that is the net increase in the value of external assets acquired by southern residents less the net increase in the value of assets in the South acquired by nonresidents. Total available resources are equal to gross income plus net imports.

In the manufacturing sector, on the other hand, the increase in demand led in most cases to an increase in imports rather than to an expansion of local production. The growth in imports was most pronounced in the case of producer goods: department 1 industries (see chapter 2, section 2.8) were not well represented in the southern industrial system, and so most items of capital equipment had to be imported. But in consumption-good sectors the results were similar. In the 1960s and early 1970s the pattern of consumption switched away from traditional consumption goods and towards the modern products of northern-based industries. Moreover, as a result of the loss of protection and of the increases in local wages and production costs that followed the implantation of modern enterprises in the South, southern concerns operating in traditional sectors declined in relation to their northern counterparts.

Woman to get pension at 33

From George Armstrong in Rome

MRS ROSANNE de Luca, who has worked in the administrative office of Genoa University for 14 years, is to retire on a pension of £335 a month. Mrs De Luca, married with two children, will be 33 this year.

It is not certain that she is the youngest pensioner in Italy. Her early retirement was made possible by a law of about 10 years ago, aimed at creating more job openings for school leavers. If she wants to Mrs De Luca can take on a new job, without losing her pension, and in another 15 years will be entitled to draw two pensions.

The news of her retirement comes at the time when the Fanfani Government is fighting in Parliament to have its new, heavy tax measures approved by Parliament. On Wednesday a section of the tax bill was passed by only one vote. Mr Fanfani says that the Treasury urgently needs billions more lire to plug a deficit.

One way to reduce public spending would be to examine the cases of the 400,000 Italians under 50 who are drawing old age pensions, which normally do not begin until 62 or 65. But that would take years and the taxes now sought could bring in immediate cash.

Another category of pensioners is those who have qualified as "handicapped" and who account for one tenth of the population, excluding the blind and the deaf mute. In southern Italy, the "invalids" reach even higher percentages.

In Isernia, 22 per cent of the inhabitants are drawing "handicapped" pensions and in Benevento it is 21.5 per cent. At 5.5 million, Italy has more than double the number of pensioned invalids than France or Germany.

To qualify, one must have a doctor's certificate which says that the pensioner's ability to earn his income — which is sometimes interpreted to mean "maintain his former life style" — has been reduced by more than one third. Because of the large number of people entitled to pensions, the State-run pension funds are now without funds.

Figure 9.2. State transfers and the fiscal crisis of the state. Source: Armstrong (1983).

The mechanism which lay behind the problems of inadequate local employment and declining activity rates led also therefore to the deteriorating trading position of the southern economy. The problems of employment were alleviated by emigration, when jobs could be found elsewhere, and by the expanding levels of employment in services and the public administration. At the same time, the continuing flow of public funds to the South played a major part in financing the progressive expansion of net imports into the region. The availability of resources in the South was increased to levels that considerably exceeded what would have been provided by local production on its own. As a result, these transfers from the rest of the country to the Mezzogiorno, together with the flow of externally financed investments, emerged as major characteristics of the southern economy.

The channelling of resources to the South helped to maintain aggregate demand and to mop up local unemployment. Inequalities between the South and the rest of the country were diminished and social consensus in the South was by and large maintained. The size of the southern market was increased. But in many cases the resources involved were used in ways that had very little to do with the satisfaction of human needs or indeed with augmenting the capacity of the southern economy: money was spent, and jobs were created unproductively, inefficiently, and wastefully. One of the main priorities seems instead to have been one of augmenting the power and influence of the clientelistic bureaucracies controlling the allocation of the jobs and incomes deriving from transfers of this kind.

The inhabitants of the Mezzogiorno were thus locked into a position of economic and political dependency. The growing external debt of the Mezzogiorno did not represent a sum of resources that had to be repaid, and so it did not produce the same consequences as a balance of payments deficit for a national economy. But the transfers involved, along with limited tax receipts, played an important role in the growing fiscal crisis of the state at local and national levels. The resources available for the satisfaction of human needs and for investments by private-sector employers, whose profits were not directly dependent on state financing, were also reduced, giving rise to the strong opposition to the model of southern development of, respectively, the political Left and some sections of northern capital.

9.5 The changing geography of economic activity and population in the South

To these changes in the structure and relative position of the South compared with the rest of Italy should be added the fact that development within the South was extremely unequal. In 1963–1974 the rates of growth of income per capita varied significantly among the different regions of the South, with the fastest increases occurring in Abruzzi, Basilicata, and Sardinia, and the least rapid in Campania and Apulia. In 1975, there were wide inequalities between the poorest regions, which at that time were

Calabria, Molise, and Basilicata, and the richest, which were Sardinia and Abruzzi. In addition, there were marked inequalities between the internal hill and mountain zones and the coastal areas of the Mezzogiorno.

Some of the most pronounced changes in the internal structure of the Mezzogiorno were, however, those connected with the rapid and chaotic process of urbanisation. In 1951, some 4.6 million people, or 26% of the population, lived in eight 'metropolitan areas': the cities other than Pescara with 100 000 or more inhabitants. In 1976, 37% lived in thirteen cities with more than 100 000 each. (The city of Salerno is included in the Neapolitan agglomeration.) In the same period, the population of the large cities of the South increased by 2.7 million people. Of this increase, 0.7 million was a product of the addition of five cities to the list of large urban areas, 0.3 million was a result of the addition of some new communes to the metropolitan areas of 1951, and 1.7 million was a consequence of an increase in the population within the 1951 limits. Accordingly, the increase in the South's urban population was a result more of an increase in the density of population in the metropolitan areas of 1951 than an extension of the urbanised area (see Cafiero and Busca, 1970, pages 18–32; Cafiero, 1979, pages 859–861; and table 9.6).

The process of urbanisation was of a very different type from the one which occurred in the North. In most cases it took place without a

Table 9.6. Changes in the resident population in urban areas and in the rest of the Mezzogiorno, 1951–1976. Source: Cafiero (1979, page 861).

Urban area	Resident population (thousands)		Change in population (thousands)	Average annual rate of change (%)
	1951	1976		
Pescara	127.30	234.10	106.80	2.47
Naples	2 780.80	3 847.30	1 066.50	1.31
Foggia	97.50	153.30	55.80	1.83
Bari	325.00	469.00	144.00	1.48
Taranto	168.90	243.80	74.90	1.48
Cosenza	57.00	102.40	45.40	2.37
Reggio Calabria	153.90	192.80	38.90	0.91
Palermo	541.40	739.60	198.20	1.26
Catania	413.90	588.00	174.10	1.41
Messina	228.70	274.50	45.80	0.73
Siracusa	86.70	138.00	51.30	1.88
Sassari	70.10	116.00	45.90	2.04
Cagliari	145.50	254.20	108.70	2.26
All urban areas	5 196.70	7 353.00	2 156.30	1.40
Rest of the Mezzogiorno	12 488.70	12 487.80	−0.90	<−0.01
Mezzogiorno	17 685.40	19 840.80	2 155.40	0.46

corresponding growth of industrial employment. Consequently, it was associated with the emergence of a vast urban subproletariat, employed in marginal and precarious activities or in public and semipublic jobs. In places in which an adequate number of jobs of this kind were not available the people belonging to this layer had no option but to seek temporary work or join the ranks of the unemployed and inactive population.

With the growth of cities lacking an adequate economic base, the problems of unemployment and underemployment and of low income were concentrated in urban areas. The towns and cities of the South, especially the largest agglomerations of Naples and Palermo, thus came to replace the countryside as the regional foci of social tension and social conflict.

9.6 The spatial implications of the crisis of a regime of intensive accumulation

The changing structure of the economy and society of the South is only one aspect of recent changes in Italian spatial organisation. At the end of the Second World War the major regional contrast was between the backward, mainly agricultural, southern regions and the rest of the country. Until 1964 this contrast was largely preserved, owing to the concentration of economic expansion in the industrial triangle in the Northwest, in the Po Valley, and along the Milan–Venice axis. After the early 1960s, however, this structure was modified, not only by the development from the late 1950s onwards of large-scale industry in the Mezzogiorno, but also by the relative decline of the economy of the industrial triangle and by the steady growth of small and medium-sized enterprises in the northeastern and central regions.

One index of these recent changes in the economic structure of the Italian regions is provided by estimates of regional output growth (table 5.7). In 1951–1958 and in 1958–1964, output increased rapidly in the Northwest and the Northeast, and at less than the national average rate in the Centre and the South. In the period 1964–1971, however, output growth fell below the national average in the Northeast and the Northwest, and exceeded it in the South and the Centre. The trends in industrial output are even more striking. Industrial production grew at rates exceeding the national average in the Northeast and the Northwest in 1958–1964, and in the South, the Northeast, and the Centre in 1964–1971. This slowing down in the growth of the Northwest and the development of industry in the Northeast and the Centre can also be traced by examining various other statistical indicators, including those relating to investment and employment.

What these trends highlight was the existence of a broad differentiation within the more advanced part of the country. In the Northwest, large-scale industries were predominant, much of the population lived in large metropolitan areas, and growth was slowing down. In the Northeast and the Centre, on the other hand, small-scale industries and small and medium-sized settlements were more important and significant growth was occurring.

As a result of the identification of these and other economic and social contrasts, Bagnasco has distinguished not just a developed North and an underdeveloped South but 'three Italies' (Bagnasco, 1977, pages 13-14).

The relative decline of the economy of the dominant northwestern regions, and the decentralisation of production and employment in more labour-intensive activities to the northeastern and central regions and the Mezzogiorno can be explained in part by the problems of congestion in established industrial centres. The changing geography of Italian development can, however, only be fully understood in the light of the crisis of the model of intensive growth and the changing trajectory of the Italian economy.

Until the late 1960s, growth involved amongst other things an application of the methods of scientific management and Fordism to the process of labour in modern equipment-good industries, as well as in other sectors of the economy. With these developments, productivity increased rapidly. At the same time, external and internal demand grew more or less in line with output, enabling the economy of the Northwest in particular to expand comparatively rapidly (see chapter 2, section 2.9). Owing, however, to the structural imbalances of the Italian economy and the dynamics of class conflict in the industrial triangle, the Italian variant of this regime of accumulation was placed in crisis comparatively early.

The context of the relative decline of the economy of the Northwest is, in other words, a crisis of a model of development. In an immediate sense, however, its decline is a product of the problems of specific branches of production. Of course, even in sectors in difficulty some firms can grow. In the Northwest, however, what are in difficulty are not just certain industries. Within industry what usually exists is a relatively small number of major enterprises involved in large-scale production, and a large group of small satellite enterprises. The satellite enterprises are linked to large firms by relations of (1) market dependence, (2) financial dependence caused by the shortages of capital experienced by many small firms, and (3) technological dependence stemming from the use by small firms of technologies developed and passed on by larger ones (Graziani, 1977, pages 18-20). What is in crisis is also this kind of industrial structure, which itself is characteristic of Fordism.

Under Fordism, substantial scale economies were realised, but only at the expense of large capital outlays on plant and equipment that was characterised by a high degree of rigidity. Should delays and bottlenecks interfere with the regularity of output or demand, and sales fall, high fixed costs would have a very damaging effect on profitability. As a result, only with regularly increasing sales and an ironing out of economic cycles did this regime of accumulation take off. Nevertheless, several important adaptations to the problem of reconciling the scale and rigidity of investments with oscillations in demand did occur.

In the first place, investments in large-scale production installations tended to occur in order to meet only the regular component of demand. Oscillations in demand were accommodated in part via sharp changes in the level of activity of smaller companies with lower fixed costs and higher levels of labour intensity.

Central companies did of course adapt. In economic downturns, marginal workers were laid off and output was reduced. The change in output was, however, less marked than the change in demand, not simply as a result of the greater impact of recessions on smaller enterprises, but also as a result of a building up of stocks. With a subsequent increase in demand, stocks were run down, enabling sales to increase more rapidly than output. Stock adjustments, in other words, allowed companies to reduce the effect of demand variations on production levels. At the same time, of course, stocks offered a buffer against holdups in the supply of inputs and against the wastage and costs associated with inadequate quality control in supplier companies. Although expensive to hold, the costs of lower levels of capacity utilisation caused by delays and shortages of necessary materials and equipment were greater.

With the crisis of Fordism, however, oscillations in demand increased sharply in size and predictability. As a result, the costs of stock holding increased and the advantages of large-scale production declined. What proved relatively more successful was what Piore and Sabel have called 'flexible specialisation' (see Piore and Sabel, 1984, pages 19–48). (What it offered, however, was a way of adapting to technological and market uncertainty and to economic instability rather than a new engine of growth.)

In the Northeast and the Centre, where industrial growth is more vibrant, there are a small number of large and long-established industrial complexes, including the steel complex developed at Piombino to exploit the ore from Elba, and the chemical complexes at Porto Marghera near Venice and at Cervignano between Venice and Trieste. These complexes are, however, not connected with the rest of the economies of these two regions, and in the sectors that are expanding a new kind of industrial structure composed of a network of small and medium-sized firms is predominant. In the Northeast, these firms are in traditional and modern sectors, whereas in the Centre they are predominantly in traditional industries in which Italy faces competition from less developed countries.

The expansion of manufacturing industry in the northeastern and central regions occurred as a result of processes of restructuring and productive decentralisation. In Italy, productive decentralisation is the name given to a tendency, that can also be observed in the more advanced regions of the country, for activities or phases of work that formerly took place in large factories to be transferred to small and medium-sized firms, or to be put out to domestic workers, and for small and medium-sized firms to grow more rapidly than large ones.

A significant part of the labour employed in this way forms part of the black economy. As a result, some of the work involved is not revealed in the official statistics collected from firms. The workers employed are not remunerated in accordance with collective agreements, and the individuals who employ others do not pay the necessary insurance and social security contributions. The identification of a second labour market, composed of some of those workers who were originally thought to be unemployed and inactive but who were employed instead in precarious activities for low wages and in poor working conditions, helps explain the somewhat anomalous movement of activity rates in Italy to which I have already referred.

There are a variety of forms that this process can assume and a variety of ways in which it is connected with the national process of accumulation. In many cases productive decentralisation was a strategy adopted by capital to increase the rate of exploitation after the success of the organised labour movement in increasing wages, improving working conditions, and enhancing job control and job security in the late 1960s and early 1970s.

The growth of small firms counters the strength of the labour movement by contributing to the division of the working class into three layers: (1) unionised factory workers whose numbers are reduced by the strategy of productive decentralisation, (2) the less organised or unorganised workers employed in small enterprises or working at home, and (3) the more secure but internally divided workers employed in the public and semipublic sectors. To the effect of these divisions should be added the advantage for capital of an increase in numerical flexibility in the field of employment (see the discussion of flexibility in chapter 2, section 2.5). Small firms tend to have a capacity to hire and fire labour and vary working hours without trade union problems, and home workers are not guaranteed regular employment. In addition, the rate of exploitation can be increased. First, the direct and indirect wage can be depressed. Small firms are able to pay low wages. Frequently, insurance and social security contributions are not paid, especially when employing workers with another job and a main employer who pays their contributions. Also, extensive use is made of underpaid female labour. Second, working conditions are more likely to be unhealthy and dangerous, and the expansion of small firms is often associated with an intensification of work speeds, longer hours, and payment by the job (see Graziani, 1977, pages 16–18).

Where these considerations are dominant the development of small and medium-sized firms is often a product of a defensive reaction by capital to the current crisis and to the intensification of international competition associated with the emergence of a new international division of labour. In Italy, for example, an ability to increase the rate of exploitation through the extension of archaic types of organisation of production is particularly important in maintaining the international competitiveness of many of the largely independent small and medium-sized firms in traditional industries that still account for an important share of the country's exports (see figure 6.3).

As well as countering the strength of the trade union movement and the job control built up by existing groups of workers, subcontracting and the decentralisation of economic activity offered a way of increasing the flexibility of production in the face of the increasingly frequent fluctuations in demand and the uncertainty characteristic of the present financial crisis of capitalism (see Sabel, 1982, pages 209-219, 220-227).

In the area that is centred on Emilia-Romagna and that stretches northwards into Veneto and southwards into Toscana and in part into Marche, however, many small and medium-sized firms do not simply depend on low wages, bad working conditions, and job insecurity, or even on flexibility in the use of workers. In the Centre and Northeast, many small firms are successful on national and international markets owing to remarkable processes of specialisation and integration of different stages in the production of a commodity. Through interfirm specialisation, industries in particular localities achieved significant scale economies (see Garofoli, 1981, pages 395-403; 1985, pages 61-62). In contrast to the satellite development of the Northwest, individual enterprises have a variety of suppliers and outlets and, as a result, more autonomy. Many firms have specialised in the production of medium- and high-quality products with a high design content. Sophisticated management systems and complex articulations of manufacturing and marketing have been developed, and many small and medium-sized firms use modern technologies.

The fact that the new processes of labour based upon automation and the recomposition of tasks are being developed has led many commentators on the process of productive decentralisation to link the emergence of this new type of industrial structure with a new model of capitalist development and a transition to a postindustrial society. Whether small firms will finally survive the shakeout that usually follows a period of innovation and change is open to question, as is the extent to which small firms can retain some independence vis-à-vis the merchant capitalists organising decentralised industrial systems. What is clear is that automation makes it possible for a more advanced centralisation of capital to be compatible with a geographical decentralisation of manufacturing and assembly operations (see Aglietta, 1979, page 127). With the decentralisation of production and employment onto a network of small and medium-sized establishments a diffused pattern of industrial and urban development will occur, with small and medium-sized enterprises achieving scale economies where necessary through their concentration in small but specialised areas, and the establishment of this new type of industrial and spatial structure helps to overcome the problems of congestion and of rapidly increasing infrastructural costs confronted in existing industrial centres (see Garofoli, 1985, pages 52-62; see also 1978, pages 51-64).

The questions as to whether or not there is a capitalist solution to the present crisis and capital can establish a new regime of intensive accumulation depends, however, not only on transformations in the sphere of work. The use of new methods of production capable of restoring profitability must be accompanied by changes in the macroeconomic environment of capitalist development. Included under that heading are new forms of socialisation of the mode of consumption, and a major expansion of the demand for new consumption goods or a sharp reduction in the length of the working week. In the Italian case the processes of adjustment are made more difficult. Sections of the economy and territory are underdeveloped. The Italian economy has a strong specialisation in some of the very industries that are being decentralised to newly industrialising countries. In addition the path of change is obstructed by many of the structural imbalances that still characterise the Italian economy.

Part 3

Industrial complexes and the development of the French steel industry

Capital accumulation, state intervention, and the development of industrial poles

10.1 Industrial poles in French and Italian regional development
In the 1960s and 1970s there were several major trends apparent in the reorganisation of the space economies of advanced capitalist societies. First, there was a tendency towards a tertiarisation and deindustrialisation of metropolitan regions. Second, manufacturing employment was decentralised to less industrialised and often to predominantly rural areas. In the third place, major shore-based industrial complexes centred around firms producing energy and intermediate goods were developed, and existing plants in older industrial areas were rationalised.

The aim of this study is to focus more closely on the third of these three trends. In this chapter and the next, what I plan to do is examine in some detail the evolution of a couple of industrial poles that were promoted by the French state in the 1960s and 1970s. In chapter 12 the development of the industry around which these poles were structured will be considered. Very little attention will be paid to the other types of development.

In chapter 8, I outlined the way in which major industrial complexes were developed on coastal sites in the Mezzogiorno. At least until the middle of the 1970s, when a crisis emerged in the chemical sector in particular, the development of firms producing energy and intermediate goods in areas and nuclei of industrialisation was supported and encouraged by the state as (1) an element of a strategy of national economic development and of expansion of specific capitals, and (2) a component of a policy for the development of backward areas in the south of Italy.

It has already been shown that investments in these sectors played an important role in transforming the economic and social structure of underdeveloped areas in the Mezzogiorno, and on the whole gave the South a new and active role in the national and international economy. But what was essentially a process of dependent industrialisation made only a limited contribution to the solution of problems of unemployment and underemployment in the South. Moreover, the process of industrialisation was an unbalanced and, in some cases, a wasteful one, and itself played a significant role in the creation of new contradictions. As a result, the wave of investment in the energy and intermediate-goods sectors in the Mezzogiorno had effects that did not correspond closely with the declared objectives of policies for regional development which were used to support it.

The gap between the aims of regional policies and what was achieved should not be surprising, since the criteria used in deciding whether or not a particular project should be encouraged and supported were not aimed primarily at altering the operation of market mechanisms in order to achieve a more equitable distribution of employment and a self-sustained process of development in the South. The measures adopted were such that the state could do little more than alter the geographical distribution of costs, on the one hand, and encourage and modify the initiatives of capitals in the private and public sectors on the other. In fact any policy for southern industrialisation had to be broadly consistent with a model of national capitalist development whose sectoral and geographical dynamic was extremely unbalanced. What was given priority was, in short, a development path chosen because of its correspondence with the strategy of accumulation of dominant economic interests and the hegemonic project primarily of the Democrazia Cristiana.

The aim of the state was mainly one of modifying and redirecting the process of spatial development. State action in its turn had three broad goals. One was to support the growth of specific capitals. The second was to correct, insofar as it could, the tendency of market mechanisms to result in developments that were harmful to dominant interests or socially irrational, and to coordinate public and private action. At the same time, however, state action was also organised with a view to keeping in check social tensions and maintaining consensus.

In many cases the grants and loans for southern development accordingly functioned as general investment incentives, subsidising the growth of firms that were playing an important role in a strategy of externally oriented national development, that in quite a few instances might well have been attracted to the South by other considerations, and whose investments were far from ideal as components of a programme for regional development. In the case of the second goal, however, the capacity of the state to act rationally in the interests of capital in general was limited. In the Italian chemical industry, for example, state financing of waves of investments by competing sections of capital enjoying different degrees of state support resulted in a wasteful duplication of capacity. Intercapitalist rivalry was reproduced, in other words, within the state itself (see chapter 3, section 3.3). In short, the priority that was and that could have been attached to a rational use of the nation's resources, equality, and a balanced process of territorial development was not very great. Instead, southern policy tended to function as an instrument both of national strategies of accumulation and of regional and national strategies of hegemony and consensus.

The use of grants and loans to encourage the implantation and expansion of enterprises in capital-intensive branches of production in industrial complexes in the Mezzogiorno was, however, only one example of a more general tendency for regional policy to be integrated with, subordinated to, and even to become an instrument of national economic planning. The formation of large-scale industrial development zones as centres for industries producing energy and intermediate goods, and the construction of related port facilities was also a striking feature of state strategies for the reshaping of the geography of France.

In the 1960s and early 1970s some large capitals and the French state planned and developed major maritime industrial poles at Le Havre and on the Lower Seine, at Dunkirk in the Nord, and at Fos-sur-Mer near Marseilles. At the end of the 1970s the construction of two new but smaller complexes occupying sites of about 500 hectares each on the Atlantic coast was announced: one was to be established at St Nazaire on the Loire estuary and one at Verdun near Bordeaux.

The complex centred on Le Havre is based on oil and petrochemical industries. Amongst other installations, however, are plants owned by companies in the metal manufacturing and mechanical engineering sectors. The complexes at Dunkirk and, in particular, at Fos-sur-Mer also include oil and petrochemical industries. What characterises them, however, is the existence of large integrated iron and steel works whose construction, in conjunction with the rationalisation of older steel plants in traditional steel-producing regions, made these zones into two of the most important centres of French steel production.

The aim of this study is to examine some of the connections between the development of these zones and the crisis in long-established steel-producing regions, on the one hand, and state regional and industrial policies and the restructuring of the French steel industry, on the other. I shall begin with a brief account of the structure and development of the complex at Dunkirk.

10.2 Monopolville: industrial and regional planning

The maritime industrial development area at Dunkirk on the Northwest European industrial plain is an extension of a port which was already the third most important in France, and of an existing industrial zone on which an integrated iron and steel plant was built between 1959 and 1962. The implantation of the steelworks was accompanied by an initial extension of the port and its facilities. As a result of the decision to centre a major industrial platform on it, however, a new deep-water port was constructed between 1972 and 1976, and a new industrial zone was developed to the west of the existing one.

The new maritime industrial development zone was planned to occupy about 7680 hectares, of which some 60% was scheduled for industrial development. Yet by the end of 1976 only about 1500 hectares of the land originally intended for development in the western extension of the existing industrial zone had been allocated. Of this amount, some 1200 hectares was being used for industrial purposes. An additional 900 hectares had been prepared but had not been developed. The development of the industrial zone was expected to be accompanied by the expansion of existing industries and the implantation of new ones. In practice there was less expansion and less diversification of the zone's industrial base than was originally expected. One result is that the complex is frequently described as being monoindustrial.

The centrepiece of the zone is the steelworks owned by the Union Sidérurgique du Nord de la France (USINOR). Its annual steel-making capacity reached 1.8 million tonnes in 1964, 4 million tonnes in 1972, and 8 million tonnes in 1975. The plant itself is used for the production of sheet metal products. In the early 1980s it was composed of two coking units, four blast furnaces, two steel-making units, and a hot rolling mill, all of which are located on a 450 hectare coastal site. To the installations of Dunkirk should be added the Mardyck cold rolling mill on a 250 hectare inland site. In 1977 the steelworks employed nearly 13 000 people compared with 500 when the original plant was opened in 1962.

These two establishments were connected upstream with energy and gas production. At Dunkirk, electrical energy was provided by a thermal power station. In the early 1980s a nuclear power station was added. Oxygen as well as acetylene and other gases were produced in an Air Liquide plant. Downstream, the steel industry was linked with other metal manufacturing industries, and with heavy engineering and shipbuilding and ship repairing firms. Included were an enterprise at Leffrinckoucke owned by Creusot-Loire, and others at Dunkirk owned by Vallourec, La Compagnie Universelle d'Acétylène et d'Électrométallurgie, La Compagnie Française d'Entreprises Métalliques, Constructions Métalliques de Provence, and France-Dunkerque.

These industries played a particularly important role in the provision of local employment. Out of 35 885 manufacturing jobs in the Dunkirk agglomeration in 1975, the iron and steel industry and the primary processing of metals accounted for 17 305, and shipbuilding and ship repairing accounted for 8905 (Green, 1979a, page 64).

The decisions to proceed with the construction of a new deep-water port surrounded by a large industrial zone and to build a new power station at Gravelines near Dunkirk were strongly influenced by the declared intention of Péchiney and Kaiser to establish a plant producing alumina. The intention of the two groups was to use the alumina produced at Dunkirk to supply the aluminium smelters they owned at Flessingues in Holland and in the Federal Republic of Germany. Soon afterwards the alumina project was dropped. At least three explanations were given for the withdrawal of Péchiney and Kaiser. One emphasised the impact of opposition from the environmentalist lobby to plans for the disposal of the red mud created in the process of alumina production. A second attributed it to high electricity costs at Dunkirk. A third suggested that it stemmed from the adoption by the companies involved of a new locational strategy entailing the location of primary processing at sites near the point of extraction of bauxite (Green, 1979a, pages 85–86).

In the oil and petrochemical sectors a number of investments occurred. On the basis of, amongst other things, expectations about the development of the alumina plant, an existing oil refinery was extended, and a new one was constructed. In December 1978 a steam cracking plant with an initial ethylene capacity of 225 000 tonnes per year came on-stream. Of this, 150 000 tonnes was to be used to produce 150 000 tonnes of low-density polyethylene, and the rest was to be piped to Belgium to be processed. As a result, there was at that stage little scope for the attraction of downstream chemical activities and for the diversification of the local chemical industry, especially as there was no intention of linking the region with the network of ethylene pipelines in northwest Europe (Green, 1979a, pages 45-47). Other local chemical firms included a company producing boric acid, and two companies producing plastics. Of the latter, one was owned by the Lesieur-Cotelle group, and manufactured plastic bottles for the edible oils it produced at Dunkirk.

A Lafarge Fondu International plant producing aluminous cement completes the list of major investments on the new industrial zone. Its output was composed of 150 000 tonnes per year of semifinished products for export to the United States of America for further processing, and 100 000 tonnes per year of finished products. As it was fully automated, only sixty people were employed in the aluminous cement works. The other industries attracted to the zone included those involved in constructing the industrial installations and port facilities, and miscellaneous activities like warehousing (Green, 1979a, page 40).

In the years after the establishment of the steelworks a number of local bodies had pressed for the extension of the port and industrial zone at Dunkirk. The decision to proceed with the construction of a maritime industrial development area of international dimensions was actually taken, however, only when a decision was made to include the project in a national strategy spelt out in the Fifth and Sixth Plans.

At that point, international economic integration was increasing, as was the internationalisation of capital. In that situation the main aim of the country's planning strategy was one of strengthening the national economy, and the Dunkirk maritime industrial development area was seen as contributing to that goal. The inclusion of the Dunkirk complex in schemes for national economic modernisation stemmed from two factors. One was its potential role in increasing the attractiveness and competitiveness of the main French ports. The second was the role of the steelworks at Dunkirk in plans for reorganising and modernising the French steel industry.

The Dunkirk project was, however, also promoted on regional grounds. In the 1960s the growing imbalances between Paris and the provinces and the problems caused by declining agricultural and industrial employment and by marked emigration from the Nord-Pas-de-Calais region led to the formulation of a regional plan for the metropolitan area based on Lille (see figure 10.1).

The region's main job losses were occurring in the three major industries established by regionally-based capitals in the 19th century. One was the textile industry, which was most heavily concentrated in Lille, Roubaix, and Tourcoing, but which also provided an important share of local employment in many other centres including Calais on the coastal plain, Fourmies, and Avesnes. In this sector, employment was declining because of the rationalisation of the industry, the restructuring of the leading companies, and the introduction of automated installations in the face of increasing foreign competition and the loss of protected colonial markets. The coal industry was in financial difficulties. One of the reasons why, argued the nationalised industry employers and unions, lay in the effects of government price controls. In the 1960s these financial problems, along with the increased use of alternative sources of energy, were leading the industry to shed labour. The third industry was metal manufacturing. In this sector, employment was stable at a regional level but was declining in towns like Denain and Valenciennes in the Sambre Valley owing to the reorganisation and relocation of production.

In the mid-1960s a number of vehicle manufacturing plants were located in the Sambre Valley and in the Mining Basin, partly to use some of the labour released by the decline of the region's traditional industries. The new jobs provided by the car industry were, however, not sufficient in number to replace those lost in the old, regionally-based, industries. Indeed, at the end of the 1960s, employment projections were indicating that between 40 000 and 50 000 new jobs would have to be provided by 1975, of which some 35 000 would have to be concentrated in the Mining Basin, if high levels of unemployment and emigration were to be avoided. (In the event, unemployment did increase significantly, as did emigration.)

It was in this context that the proposal written into the Sixth Plan for the establishment of an internationally competitive industrial complex at

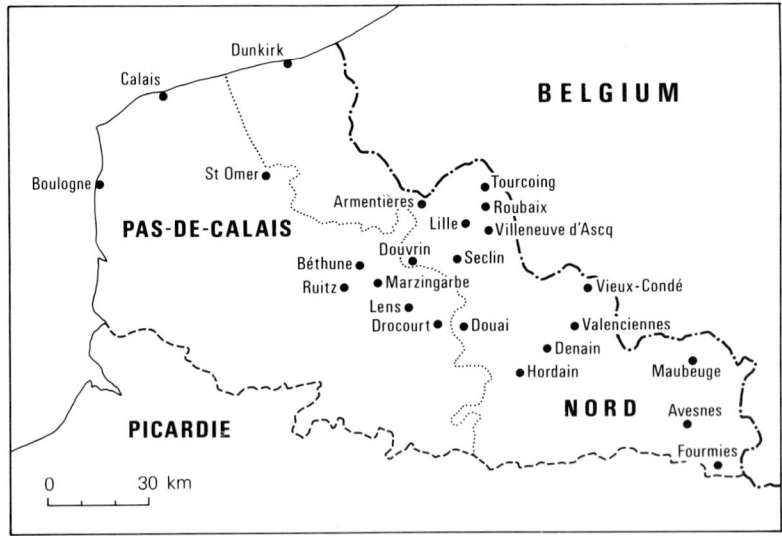

Figure 10.1. The Nord region: areas referred to in the text.

Dunkirk was included in a regional plan formulated by the central and regional authorities. The declared goal of the plan was the conversion of the metropolitan region centred on Lille into a pole of industrial development of international dimensions.

More specifically, three aims were set out in the regional plan. One was to promote the development of a maritime industrial development zone specialising in the production of energy and basic intermediate goods at Dunkirk on the coastal plain. The second was to encourage the implantation of ancillary processing industries in the hinterland of the port in accordance with the growth-centre idea. A new counterbalancing metropolis based on the Lille-Roubaix-Tourcoing agglomeration was planned as a centre for research, management, and teaching activities. In addition, a new town was to be developed near the *métropole d'équilibre* as a centre for science-based industries.

The main instrument for achieving these objectives was to be the development and improvement of infrastructural equipment. The strategy set out by the authors of the plan was one of developing port facilities and of preparing industrial sites at Dunkirk. In the rest of the region activities were to be attracted by the presence of intermediate-goods industries on the coastal plain. In addition, new communications networks were planned in the expectation that they would play a particularly important role in attracting new activities to the region. Included were a Channel Tunnel and associated international and interregional road, rail, and canal systems, and an improved regional communications network linking the main urban centres.

Subsequent development was, however, strongly concentrated around Dunkirk, and the regional economy was not adequately diversified. This concentration of development resulted in the creation of large disparities between the expanding and contracting parts of the region. One of the most striking was the coexistence of labour shortages and a lack of skilled labour around Dunkirk with an excess supply of labour around Calais and Boulogne on the coastal plain and in the internal industrial areas. These labour market disequilibria were marginally reduced by the development of the communications network and by a widening of the labour market area of the new complex to include Calais and the edge of the Mining Basin. But with rising unemployment, and especially after the announcement of the 1979 steel plan proposing the shedding of many jobs in areas in which there was virtually no alternative employment, the generally marked and persistent imbalances gave rise to serious conflicts over the location of industry within the region.

Unlike the complex at Dunkirk, the one at Fos-sur-Mer involved the development of a wholly new port and industrial zone on a green field site, and was situated in a region that was in general underindustrialised but that already contained a dominant set of modern industries in the shape of the oil and petrochemical concerns located around the Étang de Berre. As in the case of the project at Dunkirk, however, national and regional arguments were used to justify development.

The Marseilles metropolitan area had been largely bypassed by the industrial revolution. Instead its development was based on the commercial role of Marseilles as a port and transshipment point linking France with its overseas empire. By the 1960s this traditional role was declining in importance, and many of the traditional industries linked with the port, such as the food processing and the shipbuilding and ship repairing sectors, were stagnating. With these changes came pressures for a restructuring of the regional economy.

In the late 1960s the expansion and development of the region's oil and chemical industries required the establishment of new port facilities in addition to those already existing at Lavéra west of Marseilles. At the same time the modernisation of the French steel industry was thought to entail as a matter of urgency the development of a second integrated shore-based plant, for which the site at Fos was one of the alternatives that was being considered.

As we shall see, it was these factors that ultimately led to the promotion of a new industrial zone at Fos. In the first place, however, we shall consider the connections between the development of major coastal industrial complexes and the mechanisms of capital accumulation and state action outlined in chapters 2 and 3.

10.3 Capital accumulation and the development of port and industrial zones

In an abstract sense the development of maritime industrial development zones indicates the way in which the evolution of the economy and the establishment of new conditions of production and exchange were resulting in a revaluation of some of the natural and social qualities of coastal sites. The attractiveness of coastal sites with access to natural deep-water channels and with large amounts of undeveloped flat land was increased by two factors in particular. One was the strategy, in industries producing energy and intermediate goods, of constructing large integrated plants to obtain economies of large-scale production. The second was increased use of imported supplies of energy and raw materials and the interrelated development of methods of large-scale maritime transport. Indeed the port of Dunkirk not only afforded the desired geographical conditions but also occupied a strategic position at the entrance to the North Sea. The site at Fos offered similar but less congested conditions at a strategic intersection of trade routes on the tideless Mediterranean.

An explanation of the increased importance of these geographical conditions and of these developments in economic life lies, however, in the modalities of reproduction of capital in the manufacturing industries concerned and in sea transport (Castells and Godard, 1974, pages 51-55).

In process industries like the steel and petrochemical industries there was a marked concentration and centralisation of capital at national and even at international levels. In the case of the steel industry the processes of concentration and centralisation stemmed in part from the need in the 1960s and 1970s to reorganise the industrial system through a massive devalorisation of capital, and in both branches the problems of financing accumulation in sectors involving large investments in fixed capital were significant.

The concentration and centralisation of capital were accompanied by some technical and social changes in the organisation of production and by an increasing emphasis upon the development of large integrated or interconnected plants frequently located on a single coastal site. In these sectors, at least until the mid-1970s, not only were new units of production characterised by an increasing scale of production. In addition, a tendency existed for an increasing integration within one complex of interdependencies between separate units of production. As a result, human intervention was considerably reduced, and handling and transport costs were lowered.

A minimisation of human intervention was important for two reasons. One was its role in reducing the indirect costs of production and increasing the speed of turnover of circulating capital. The second was the way it contributed to ensuring continuous and uninterrupted production: at that stage the continuity of production was coming to play an ever more important role in determining the ability of capitals in these sectors to realise the increasing amounts of value immobilised in increasingly capital-intensive plants.

At the same time the process of production was being internationalised. Increasingly, alternative or higher quality sources of energy and raw materials were being imported, with dependent countries emerging as some of the major sources of supply. In the advanced countries new plants tended accordingly to be located at points at which fuels and raw materials could be imported and from which metal, oil, and chemical products could be reexported. Consequently, the relationship of a site to existing and potential transport networks along which commodities of this kind could be moved played an important role in determining the location of a plant. Included, of course, were not only sea transport, but also road, rail, and pipeline networks.

As the years passed, however, some new trends in the international division of labour were set in motion. On the one hand, much of the new capacity for refining oil and for producing primary chemicals and steel was located in less developed and newly industrialising countries. On the other, the economies of the more developed countries were moving downstream. (I shall return to this point later when discussing the steel crisis in chapters 12 and 13.)

Increases in the internationalisation of capital and in international economic integration were closely associated with (1) some revolutionary changes in the means of communication and transport, (2) the coordinated development of different transport modes, and (3) the planning and the development of transshipment points with improved cargo and passenger handling facilities. In the case of sea transport these processes stemmed in part from the unremitting attempts by capitals engaged in maritime transport and in port activities to reduce the time and costs of circulation and to increase the speed of turnover of the capital they were advancing as well as of the items which they handled. Indeed, only through reducing costs vis-à-vis their rivals could a carrier or port succeed in the competitive struggle to attract cargoes and supply hinterlands.

In the 1960s and 1970s the pursuit of competitiveness was associated with a growing use of extremely large and specialised vessels whose time at sea had to be maximised to secure a normal rate of return on the large amounts of capital locked up in them. In the case of sea ports, success in the struggle to attract traffic accordingly came to depend in part upon their ability to receive and cope with large and specialised vessels, and to ensure rapid access and turnaround for them so that the amount of time they spent in the port was minimised. The development of ports able to cope with large vessels was emerging as an important stake for the shipbuilding and ship repairing industries.

Changes in the methods of transporting goods by sea depended upon the development of sea ports on metropolitan coasts with deep access channels. Specialised handling facilities and large amounts of space were also needed for modern cargo handling techniques. At the same time, however, the success of the ports themslves depended on the implementation of major programmes of investment in installations and handling methods, and the introduction of new methods of cargo handling enabled port authorities to employ a new and less skilled dock labour force. As a result, charges could be lowered and competitiveness increased further.

10.4 The role of state intervention in the establishment of maritime industrial development areas

The second major agency involved in the establishment of maritime industrial development zones was the state. The state played a central role in preparing and reproducing the material and social conditions necessary for national economic expansion and in strengthening national capitals and the national economy. In planning and developing internationally competitive industrial poles, several types of state intervention designed to secure these general objectives were fused.

In the first place, strategies devised by capital and the state in the framework of systems of national economic and sectoral planning for strengthening specific branches of production, modernising the national port system, and increasing the competitiveness of the national economy were involved. The establishment of maritime industrial development zones was also encouraged through the completion of infrastructural investments receiving less than the normal market rate of return and the provision by the state of grants and low-interest loans to companies locating in them.

In the French case the state played a particularly important role in these areas. Improvements and extensions to port facilities and improvements to road, rail, and canal networks were carried out and managed. Industrial and commercial sites were developed and equipped, and let or sold to private users. In addition, the provision of housing and services for the workers assembled to build and operate the zones' infrastructural equipment and industrial installations was coordinated and supported. As infrastructural equipment was heavily subsidised, however, investment grants were not generally provided: the help the French state gave with the financing of investment was usually confined to low-interest loans.

Also involved in the development of shore-based industrial complexes was state regional planning policy. In the French case most of the new industrial zones were located in depressed or less developed areas, were planned by regional planning agencies, and were supported by regional development funds. Moreover, the development of industrial poles was associated with industrial rationalisation schemes whose social consequences were managed by the state in part by means of its regional policies.

10.5 The evolution of the French economy in the 1960s and early 1970s

The general determinations outlined in the last section were as always mediated and modified by more specific factors and translated into new port and industrial complexes through more specific processes of accumulation and state intervention. Some of the most important of these specific factors were the economic and political processes connected with (1) the opening of the French economy to international competition in the late 1960s, and (2) the approaching recession of the 1970s.

A movement away from traditional protectionist policies had begun with the formation of the EEC in the late 1950s. At that time the French government introduced liberal economic policies in an attempt to solve the balance of payments problems which emerged in the early years of European economic integration. According to Boyer and Mistral these measures contributed to a stagnation in real wages and a reduction in the share of wages in national income. The resources released by this change in the distribution of income were diverted towards accumulation, with the result that the French economy was characterised by a high rate of investment and rapid growth until new problems of competitiveness began to appear in the late 1960s (Boyer and Mistral, 1978, pages 2-29).

To prepare the economy for competition on the world market, proposals for the creation in each sector of a small number of enterprises of international dimensions were included as a priority objective in the Fifth Plan (1966-1970). After 1968, attempts to adjust the structure of the French economy in the light of the growing internationalisation of capital and increasing international economic integration were associated with a redirection of the accumulation process and an emphasis by the state upon the twin themes of industrialisation and selective public intervention.

In the early years of the plan period a rapid process of concentration and centralisation of capital did occur, and financial resources were redirected towards large-scale industry. After 1968 the rhythm of accumulation increased with an acceleration in the rate of growth of investment in industries producing equipment and intermediate goods. Partly as a result of increases in wages after the events of May 1968, industrial investment was generally aimed at increases in labour productivity rather than in output, but it nevertheless resulted in a rapid expansion of dependent employment in the equipment-goods industries. With demand expanding and productivity increasing, accumulation continued without coming up against any serious obstacles until 1973. (On the development of the French economy see also Lipietz, 1984a, pages 15 – 64.)

10.6 The reorganisation of the state and of state intervention in the 1960s
The increasing relative importance of those sections of French industry which were most concentrated and which were leading the internationalisation of French capital was associated with changes in the structure and composition of the dominant social and political bloc. In 1958, when this process was beginning, the Fifth Republic was established. Soon afterwards, the state apparatus was reorganised and state policies were redirected with a view to accelerating monopolistic accumulation as much as possible without disrupting the overall balance of class forces.

In this phase of political development, which lasted until the early 1970s, the structure of the state apparatus was changed (see figure 10.2). Mainly via the ministerial cabinets, the upper echelons of the civil service were fused with the executive, and steps aimed at increasing their independence and reinforcing their power were taken. At the same time, bodies which bypassed traditional channels of communication and gave large industrial groups immediate access to the upper levels of the state apparatus were created, with the result that the representation of the bourgeoisie and of the new hegemonic class in particular passed to the summit of the state. The roles of the executive and of the central administration were redefined, as were their relationships to parliament and to the political parties. Within the central state apparatus a new division of labour and new management techniques were adopted with a view to, first, centralising information, conception, and control, and, second, improving the rationality of administrative action. At national and local levels a whole set of special-purpose centrally appointed administrative bodies were established. The agencies concerned were organised along horizontal lines, acted outside traditional, vertical, and segmented hierarchies, and were used so as to integrate and co-opt those willing to collaborate with the administration. In addition, new regional institutions were set up, mainly with the aim of bypassing traditional administrations in the periphery and their clienteles (Sallois and Cretin, 1976, pages 234 – 253).

As we shall see, these attempts at increasing the influence of the central administration and making its actions more effective, along with the state's policies of modernisation, generated major institutional and political conflicts. Included were conflicts with the vertically organised traditional administration in the periphery, with local authorities, with locally elected representatives and local notables closely linked with the prefectorial system, with local interests threatened by modernisation, and even with parliamentary deputies who were more attentive to local demands than was the central state. Indeed the opposition that came from local notables, small and medium proprietors and businessmen frightened by the administration's policies for economic and social modernisation and economic expansion, and regionalist movements concerned about the relationship between the state and local societies, was an important factor in the defeat of early attempts by the state to transform the administration of the regions and in the defeat of de Gaulle himself (see Dulong, 1976; 1978; Birnbaum, 1980, page 102 – 108)

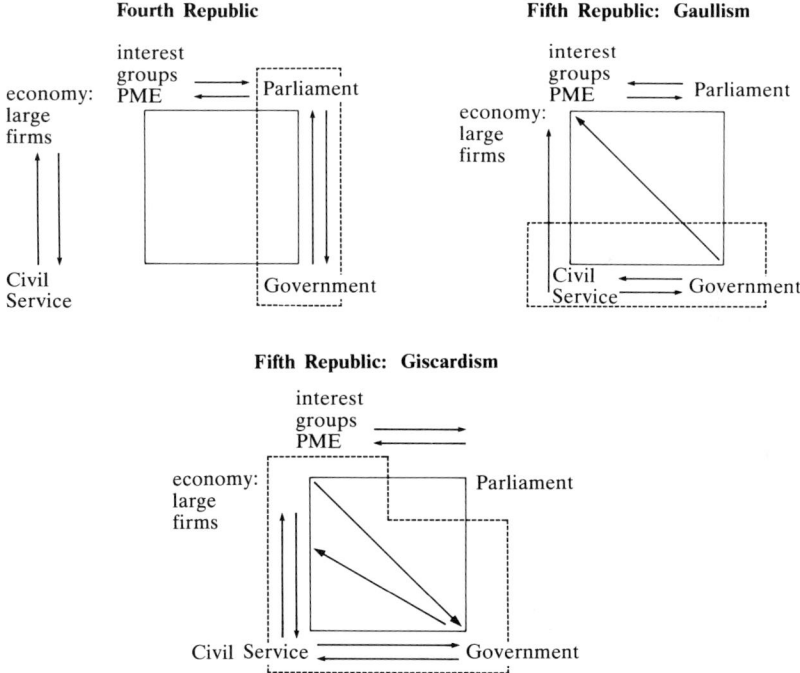

Figure 10.2. The changing structure of the French state apparatus under the Fourth and Fifth Republics. PME stands for Petites et Moyennes Entreprises. The boxes represent the main elements of French society and the main elements of the state apparatus; the arrows indicate the most strongly developed political networks and relationships; and the broken lines indicate which elements were incorporated into the key decisionmaking structures. Source: Birnbaum (1980, page 95).

What underpinned these contradictions, faced not only by de Gaulle but also by Pompidou who succeeded him, was the ultimate impossibility of reconciling two goals. One was that of technical and economic modernisation. The second was the goal of defending the interests of declining social strata and of upholding the traditional political and cultural values on which the hegemonic project of Gaullism largely rested. Nevertheless, in this period that ended in the early 1970s, changes in the state apparatus and in the composition of the ruling social bloc did occur and were translated into changes in the party system and in state intervention in the economy. In particular, with these changes a programme of industrial restructuring was elaborated in which (1) increased weight was given to profitability as the criterion of rationality in the allocation of resources, and (2) development was more closely oriented to the international market.

Insofar as state action was concerned, the modernisation drive wanted by many large industrial groups was tempered by political considerations. The programme written into the Sixth Plan (1971-1975) differed, for example, from the one preferred by many large industrialists. The reason for this was that the government was worried that with fast industrialisation there might be problems of maintaining social cohesion. If the industrialisation process were very rapid, it was argued, the interests of the small and even the medium bourgeoisie would be damaged. The rate of rural depopulation and the rate of decline of small-scale industry and commerce would accelerate sharply. The rate of employment change among dependent workers would increase substantially. Moreover, a marked change in the composition of public spending in favour of industrial development would be necessary. In order to avoid undue conflict and social unrest the state therefore chose spending programmes that implied a slower process of accumulation than was desired by the most powerful elements of French industrial capital.

The new political conjuncture outlined in this section was also important in another respect. In the early 1960s, regional planning was redirected and integrated with policies for increasing the international competitiveness of the French economy. An explanation of these changes lies not only in changes in the economic sphere, but also in the changing structure and role of the French state (Castells, 1976, pages 192-195; see also Bleitrach and Chenu, 1975; Castells, 1975; 1978; Biarez, 1982).

10.7 The evolution of French regional planning
The origins of French regional development and regional planning policy lie in the problems posed by the historic centralisation of economic, political, and cultural life in Paris. After the Second World War, processes of economic and social modernisation accentuated the country's territorial disequilibria. As a result, economic activity continued to be concentrated in the capital. The economic and social structures of traditional France were broken up. Much of rural and provincial France was depopulated, and old industries in the provinces declined.

After an early emphasis, in the field of regional planning, upon the problems associated with the gap between Paris and what Gravier called the 'French desert', several other themes were added. One was the need to correct the imbalance between the east and the west of the country. A second was the goal of preventing regional inequalities from acting as a serious constraint on the rate of national economic growth. In addition, the problem of reconverting declining industrial regions was given greater emphasis.

In its early stages, regional planning was a central government initiative implemented by a department formed in 1945 in the Ministère de la Reconstruction et de l'Urbanisme (Construction Ministry). The main aim was one of controlling the reconstruction and development of urban areas and encouraging the decentralisation of industry from the Paris region.

In 1954-1955, perspectives on regional planning began to be widened from ones of town planning and industrial decentralisation to encompass a much more comprehensive view of decentralised economic development. At the same time the administration of regional planning started to undergo change to accommodate the new perspective. In particular, the Commisariat du Plan began to move into the regional planning area alongside the Construction Ministry and proceeded to encourage the preparation of regional action programmes for each of the twenty-two programming regions set up in June 1955. With the change in perspective, went increased emphasis on the collection of data and a steady development of theory and techniques for regional planning (Boudeville, 1966, pages 155-157).

In the early 1960s, new national policies for regional development were introduced, and the institutional and administrative framework for regional planning was transformed. The division of regional planning activity between the Construction Ministry and the Commissariat du Plan was settled in favour of the national planning system, and in 1963 the Délégation à l'Aménagement du Territoire et à l'Action Régionale (DATAR) was set up as a central regional planning agency on the model of the Commissariat du Plan itself. The intention was that DATAR should be a small and flexible body headed by a minister but attached to the Prime Minister's office. It was given the tasks of coordinating and initiating regional development activities and implementing the regional priorities of the central administration. At the same time, it was hoped that it would succeed in getting round the bottlenecks created by the existence of tradition-bound, autonomous, and functionally specific ministries. The new agency was given specific powers and control over specific financial resources. DATAR was not, however, intended to act on its own. Instead, it was expected to work in conjunction with the existing structures of bureaucratic competence and power. Its activities were meant to supplement and stimulate those of the various national ministries, and its success was to depend to a large extent upon its ability to influence the objectives and practices of the ministries themselves.

Over the preceding twenty years or so the distribution of the French population had been modified, and the role of the local notables who had traditionally managed communal and departmental institutions had declined. The technocracy was particularly concerned to accelerate this process and to increase its ability to bypass old regional elites and existing local administrations. One instrument it chose to achieve this goal was the construction of a regional tier of the administration. The establishment of new institutions would contribute, it was hoped, to a reconstruction of the system of local political power and increase the political weight of modernising groups.

Although this political and economic goal was a central factor in the central administration's attempt to rationalise and centralise local administrative action, technical arguments, including in particular the need to improve the horizontal coordination of state action at a regional level, were also advanced.

In 1964, several decrees were passed which resulted in the creation in each of twenty-one regions of a regional administrative conference headed by a centrally appointed regional prefect and his or her mission. Each regional prefect was given certain rights of consultation and information on broad questions of national planning as they related to the region he or she headed. In addition, the prefects were given powers to carry out specific regional planning duties, of which the most important was that of elaborating and reporting on the execution of the regional tranche of the national economic plan. (The regional tranche of the plan was essentially a capital budget for a five-year programme of intraregional public investments.)

A second result of these decrees was the establishment in each of the regions of a Commission de Développement Économique Régional (CODER). The intention was twofold. On the one hand the new commissions were planned to replace the Regional Expansion Committees which had emerged autonomously in some of the regions in the 1950s. On the other it was hoped that they would be dominated by representatives of 'progressive' forces and not by traditional dignitaries. The CODERs were to be composed of local politicians, nominees of the Prime Minister, and representatives of local corporate interests, with the first two groups providing 25% of the membership each and the third the rest. The regional prefects were legally required to consult the CODERs on the regional aspects of the national plan.

The regional reform was accompanied by the introduction of a new set of national procedures for regional and urban planning and new institutions were created to apply them. One example was the decision taken in 1966 to set up the Organismes d'Études d'Aménagement des Aires Métropolitaines (OREAM). The OREAMs were to be established in order to prepare long-term structure plans for metropolitan areas and were to be appointed and financed through DATAR and by the central government.

With these steps the role of the central state was strengthened, and the old relations between local societies, local authorities, and the upper echelons of the state apparatus were disrupted (see figure 10.2). However, the new bodies did not succeed in legitimising the new forms of social and political control. Indeed, in the referendum submitted to the population by de Gaulle on the 27 April 1969 the regional reform, together with some proposals for the reform of the Senate, were defeated along with de Gaulle himself. In July 1972 a new law establishing regional councils was passed. But it involved a marked retreat by the state from its earlier position (Sallois and Cretin, 1976, pages 249-251).

These organisational changes were closely associated with an increasing integration of regional planning with the medium-term plans for national economic expansion, and with the introduction of more selective forms of intervention. Steps to integrate national and regional planning had occurred progressively from 1958. The most important changes came, however, with the inclusion in the Fourth Plan (1962-1965) of a new procedure for regionalising the plan's public investment programmes. This procedure represented a move towards specifying the type and amount of infrastructure to be allocated to each region in order to achieve its planned development while paying attention to the objectives of the national plan and the constraints on their attainment.

The new procedure also stemmed, however, from the complementarity of some of the activities involved in national and regional planning and from the role played by infrastructural policies in strategies for growth. In particular, through the planning of differentiated and selective forms of infrastructural provision, infrastructural policies have two effects. On the one hand, surplus value is redistributed between capitals. On the other, privileged conditions of accumulation are provided for selected capitals (see chapter 3, sections 3.3 and 3.5; and Hirsch, 1978, pages 90-97).

In the Fifth Plan (1966-1970) the integration of national and regional planning was carried much further. The most important objective of the Fifth Plan was to change the form and structure of many French industries to make them competitive on EEC markets. A corollary of this aim was an increase in the rate of productive investment. An implication of the priority attached to these objectives was, it was argued, that regional policy "must, in a highly competitive situation, give every opportunity to the 'strong' regions whose economic potential can benefit the whole economy. In the 'weak' regions, on the other hand, it must seek to promote development which will become self-sustaining so that these regions can play a part in the schemes for modernisation and expansion" (Commisariat Général du Plan, cited in Allen and MacLennan, 1970, page 178). In the Fifth Plan, regional policy was accordingly integrated more closely with and used as an instrument of, first, a strategy of industrialisation aimed at preparing the French economy for increasing competition on EEC markets, and, second, a national economic policy aimed at achieving rapid economic growth. A similar decision was embodied in the Sixth Plan (1971-1975).

In the early 1960s, significant changes also occurred in the strategy for regional development. Of these changes one set were closely correlated with the integration of national and regional planning. In 1964, state aids for industrial development were reorganised with the country being divided into five zones (see figure 10.3). These zones were ranked according to the priority attached to government aid to industry. At one end of the spectrum were the cities of the underdeveloped western part of the country in which subsidies for industrial development were to be high and almost automatic. In these centres, grants were to be of the order of 20% of total investment for the establishment of a new factory and 10% for the extension of an existing one, compared with 10% and 5%, respectively, in the rest of this zone. The second zone was composed of the so-called conversion areas with

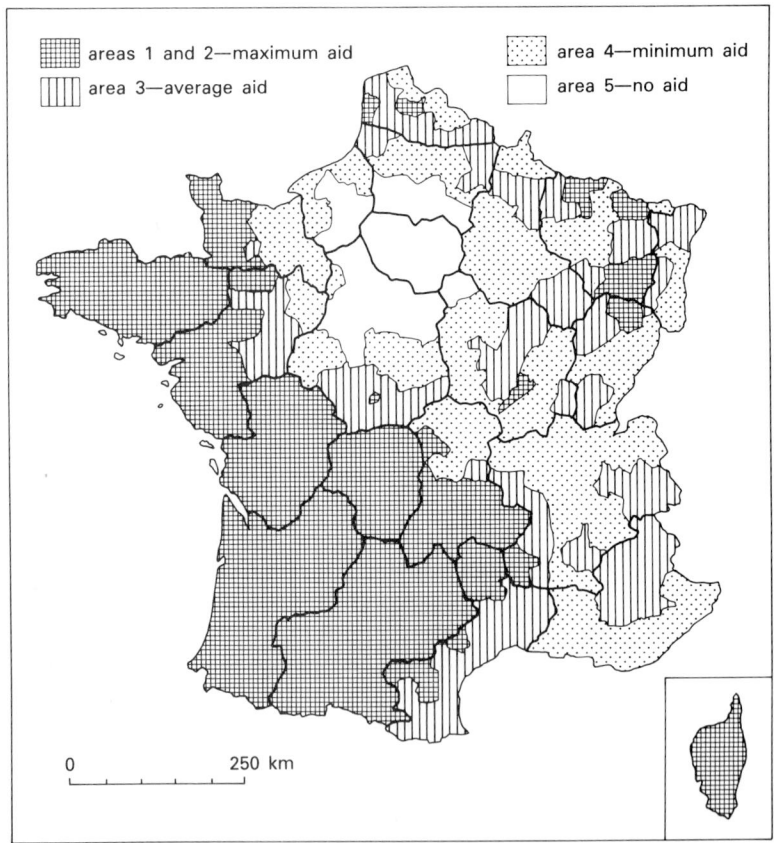

Figure 10.3. Areas in which firms were eligible for regional development aid in 1965. Source: DATAR (1965).

a high proportion of jobs in declining industries and a lack of alternative employment. The third zone was made up of slow-growing towns in the more affluent parts of France, in which industry was to be eligible for certain fiscal concessions. In the fourth zone, covering the more prosperous parts of the country but excluding the Paris region, eligibility for reduced taxation was to depend upon the individual merits of the project. No special advantages were to be granted to industries locating in the fifth zone centred on the Paris agglomeration (Boudeville, 1966, pages 158-161).

The reorganisation of regional aid was accompanied by the introduction of a second set of more selective regional policies involving the concentration of development in a small number of preselected areas which were to be planned in such a way as to yield the maximum in economies of scale and external economies. Under this heading fell some of the most striking regional planning policies introduced by the French state between 1962 and 1965.

One of the most important was the policy of establishing eight métropoles d'équilibre as a means of reducing congestion in Paris and of promoting development in the provinces (see figure 10.4). This policy was initially formulated by the Commission Nationale de l'Aménagement du Territoire (CNAT) during the course of preparatory work for the Fifth Plan. The intention was twofold. First, investment was to be concentrated selectively on eight provincial metropolises in order to equip them with modern transport and communications facilities, high-quality infrastructural equipment, improved services, and outstanding cultural and intellectual institutions. Second, the development of high-level tertiary and decisionmaking functions and of significant regional elites was to be encouraged. What was intended was to assist the development of metropolitan centres which would be sufficiently large and well-equipped to be capable (1) of acting as economic and demographic counterweights to the Paris agglomeration, (2) of growing sufficiently rapidly and diffusing sufficient growth to their hinterlands to enable the provinces to participate in a process of national economic expansion, and (3) of reequilibrating the national urban system.

In line with the more general application in French planning of the principle of a selective concentration of public investment to enhance the competitiveness of the national economy, the state also sought to organise the development of major metropolitan areas like Paris and Lyon in such a way as to enable them to assume and maintain the roles of major growth centres in the European economy. In addition, it was decided to support the establishment of internationally competitive industrial complexes combining high-quality infrastructural equipment with large-scale industry on the Lower Seine, at Dunkirk, and at Fos-sur-Mer.

These two sets of general priorities were associated with two rather different and to some extent contradictory models of spatial development. On the one hand, a model of development aimed at controlling the growth of Paris and correcting the imbalances between an underdeveloped and slow-growing homogeneous region in the west of the country and a more prosperous one in the east was implied. On the other, a model of economic polarisation around selected urban foci was proposed.

In practice, the state's global strategy and its close connection with large-scale industry meant that public investments were not distributed in accordance with the objectives of French regional policy. In the 1960s and early 1970s considerable emphasis was placed instead upon the promotion of the Paris agglomeration as an important international metropolis and as a centre for the head offices and research departments of large national and international firms and for specialised commercial and financial activities. In addition, DATAR came to play a major role in implementing the *grandes options* of French industrial policy and took a growing interest in the provision of urban infrastructural equipment around coastal industrial complexes whose role as regional development initiatives was questionable.

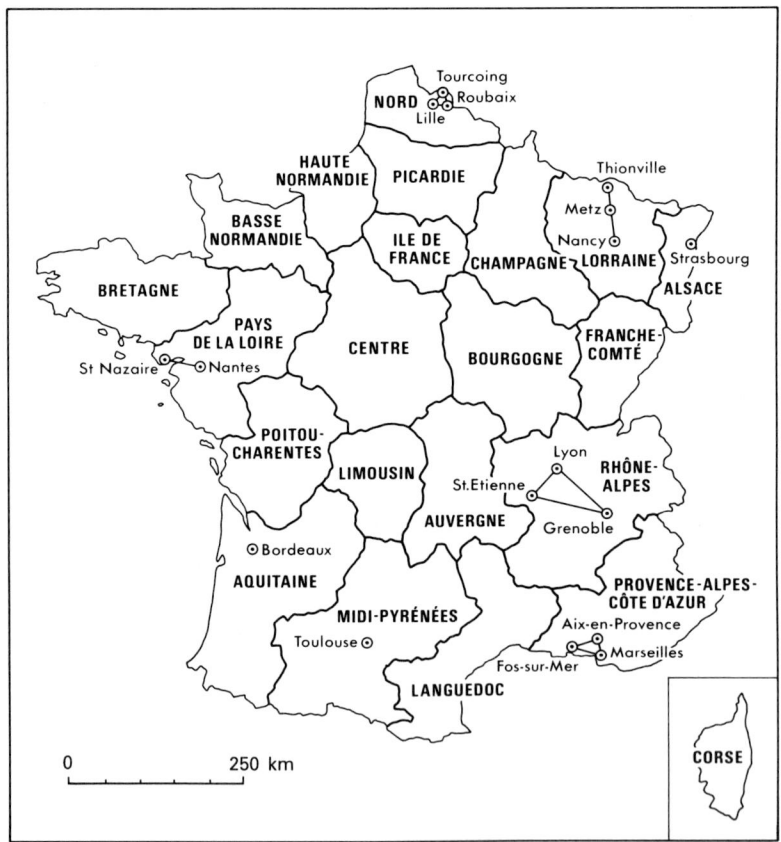

Figure 10.4. The métropoles d'équilibre and the French programming regions.

The priority given by the state to projects of this kind is only indicative of a gap between the state's actions and its regional policy objectives. Stronger evidence of such a gap is provided by some estimates produced by Prud'homme (1974) of the distribution of public expenditure in the late 1960s. For the period of the Fifth Plan an index of per capita central government expenditure on public investment projects indicates that two of the most favoured regions were the Paris region and Haute Normandie. As the richest regions in the country, these areas were not supposed to receive special help.

11

The formation of a port and industrial zone at Fos-sur-Mer and the development of the Marseilles metropolitan area

The creation of the port and industrial zone (Zone Industrialo-portuaire or ZIP) at Fos-sur-Mer was, in the words of President Pompidou, "the great national regional planning operation of the Sixth Plan" (cited in Bleitrach and Chenu, 1975, page 375). What was to result was a complex capable of rivalling Rotterdam as the Europort of the South (see Paillard, 1981, pages 36-37).

The complex itself includes a new port linked with the old established port of Marseilles but adapted to the new conditions of maritime transport. Amongst other types of vessel, the new installations are capable of receiving large specialised ships carrying crude petroleum and refined petroleum products, liquefied natural and petroleum gas, solid fuels, ores, and containers. In addition, the zone contains a very large industrial complex based on energy production and petrochemical industries, together with iron and steel and metal manufacturing.

The development of the area was originally contemplated in the early 1950s, when it was considered as a possible location for an integrated shore-based iron and steel plant. The site was initially developed, however, as an oil storage area and, from 1965, as a petroleum port able to receive large oil tankers. The installation of oil handling facilities occurred for two reasons. On the one hand, the port at Lavéra was becoming too small to cope with the growing volume of oil imports and the increasing size of tankers. On the other, any deepening of the access channels to Lavéra posed serious difficulties. These developments and the subsequent implantation of other private companies, as well as the construction of facilities for receiving large ore carriers and container ships which could not be received at Marseilles, depended, however, upon a process of land assembly and a programme of public investments in infrastructural equipment.

11.1 The origins and history of public intervention in the Fos maritime industrial zone

The development of the port and industrial zone at Fos-sur-Mer was initiated in 1962 when the Chambre de Commerce et d'Industrie de Marseille (CCIM) started to purchase land in the area. In all, 955 hectares were acquired. In 1963 a mixed development company known as the Syndicat Mixte d'Aménagement et d'Équipement de la Région du Golfe de Fos was formed by the area's local authorities and some local business interests. One of its actions was to buy the land acquired by CCIM, along with an additional 536 hectares. In subsequent years, however, land purchase was increasingly undertaken by the central state. The state acquired some 4000 hectares through the Fonds National d'Aménagement

Foncier d'Urbanisme. Some land was obtained through the expropriations that followed the declaration of several Déclarations d'Utilité Publique. Further, a Zone d'Aménagement Différé was established, giving the state the right to preempt land sales on 1450 hectares north of the road and rail loop (see figure 11.1). In 1969 the land assembled by the state as well as the usable land, amounting to 1100 hectares, acquired by the mixed development company was allocated to the Port Autonome de Marseille (PAM). PAM was, however, largely independent of the mixed development company and of the interests it represented. In all, some 6500 hectares of land was acquired over a period of eight years for PAM at an approximate cost of 55 million francs (Cultiaux, 1975, pages 35-36).

In order to ensure the coordination of the project at a national level, in January 1964 DATAR entrusted the preparation of an overall plan for the development of the area to an interministerial working party, the Groupe Central d'Aménagement du Golfe de Fos. In addition, loans were obtained, and preliminary studies were commissioned from private consultants. In November 1965 the resulting plan was approved and was given the status of a national regional planning directive by the Conseil Interministériel pour l'Aménagement du Territoire (CIAT). The first stage of the port and maritime works had, however, already been approved in December 1964. In March 1965, work on an oil terminal had begun, and in July 1965 work started on the access channel and the first dock. In December 1965 the second stage of the works was approved.

In April 1966, PAM was formed as a result of the passing, in 1965, of the law on autonomous maritime ports. As a result of this law, which was applied to the six main ports in France, central government control over the overall planning and financing of major port and industrial zones was increased, whereas development and management were decentralised to local port authorities. The autonomous ports were to be public agencies with a civil management and financial autonomy placed under the public works ministry. The head of the port authority was to be nominated by the government, and its board was to include twenty-four other members, of whom one half were to be appointed by the state. The government appointees were to include state representatives and the representatives of port users. The remaining twelve members were to be representatives of the local Chamber of Commerce, local authorities, and port employees.

The new law also included important provisions for state financing of port and industrial zones. It required the state to (1) reimburse the port authorities for expenditures incurred in purchasing private land, (2) meet 80% of the costs of dredging channels and constructing breakwaters and docks, and 80% of the costs of quays and other basic facilities, and (3) pay for the maintenance of channels, sea walls, and so on. The superstructures of the port and equipment on industrial zones were to be provided by the port authorities. The activities of the port authorities not covered by central government funding were to be financed in two ways. One was out of port dues and taxes. The second was out of rents and revenues from the leasing or sale of prepared sites and quays.

In the 1960s and 1970s the actions of the port authorities were governed by commercial criteria. But state subsidisation of their activities meant that port and industrial installations were financed by capitals receiving a very low rate of return. Consequently, the users of these port and industrial zones were in effect subsidised and received privileged treatment from the state. This tendency was reinforced by the provision of other items of infrastructure and of other services at rates that did not correspond to their real costs. In this category were to be found railway and other transport equipment, telecommunications systems, and electrical energy. All of the installations concerned were provided as a result of investments by public agencies, sometimes with the help of loans from the port authority, and the goods and services they supplied were frequently sold at prices that were particularly favourable to private industrial users (Castells and Godard, 1974, pages 67-68).

With the formation of PAM and the transfer to it of responsibility for the development of the port and industrial zone, the task of plan preparation was vested in a body which was separate from the local authorities and members of the local bourgeoisie that had formed the mixed development company. Once established, PAM proceeded to prepare the *Plan-Masse* for the development of an area of 7290 hectares. In it, 5520 hectares were scheduled for industrial and commercial development. Early in 1967 the plan was approved by the government, and PAM was placed in charge of the development of the maritime industrial development zone.

At this stage PAM received financial help from the state. Additional funds were borrowed from financial institutions. With this money PAM proceeded with (1) the construction of the channels, sea walls, docks, and quays and of an oil terminal, (2) the consolidation and preparation of the land area, and (3) the development of infrastructural and transport facilities including protective works, a drainage and water supply system, and a road network. In addition, steps were taken to accelerate and increase the quality of nationalised-industry investments in a railway network, telecommunications equipment, and an electricity supply system. The infrastructures linking the port and industrial zone with the national road and motorway network were provided by the state. PAM also prepared sites for service industries and other enterprises connected with the major industries expected to locate in the new industrial zone. The expenditure incurred from the moment when feasibility and technical studies were approved by the government in May 1962 until the end of the Fifth Plan amounted to some 0.5 milliard francs[5] (see table 11.1).

In the period of the Sixth Plan, public investment was required not only to continue the development of the port and industrial zone. Items of social

---

[5] A milliard francs is one thousand million francs.

infrastructure had also to be provided and the urbanisation process in the wider region, in which there were already serious delays in the provision of communications facilities and housing, had to be planned. A special programme for Fos was accordingly included in the Sixth Plan. It was divided into three major projects:

(1) The first project was concerned with development of the port and industrial zone and of the waterways in accordance with expectations about the use of the port.

(2) The second was the finalised programme for urbanisation around the Étang de Berre. This programme was established and implemented according to the specific arrangements for new town development. The urbanisation process was, however, different from the one characteristic of new towns. On the one hand it was a response to industrial development. On the other it was to involve the expansion of existing towns and to be discontinuous in accordance with the structure plan for the Marseilles metropolitan area.

(3) The third project was concerned with the main infrastructural facilities. It included proposals for a major reorganisation of the road network and the development of links between Fos and Marseilles, Arles, and Salon (see figure 11.5).

Table 11.1. Expenditure (in millions of francs) between 1962 and 1970 on the preparation of the port and industrial complex at Fos-sur-Mer[a]. Source: Cultiaux (1975, page 38).

Operations	PAM	State	Total	Comments
Land acquisition (about 6500 hectares)	55		55	About 51 million francs of the expenditure incurred by PAM was reimbursed by the state as from 1970
Works relating to the oil port and trade in hydrocarbons				
infrastructural works	30	90	120	
superstructural works	50		50	
Works relating to the ore and container quays				
infrastructural works	10	20	30	
superstructural works	25		25	
Development of ZIP				
general works	30	100	130	
superstructural works	90		90	
Total	290	210	500	

[a] During the same period, payments of up to some 350 million francs were made.

The planned expenditure on these special projects is set out in table 11.2. To this sum should be added the increases in the costs of these projects that occurred in subsequent years, a variety of expenditures on the protection of the environment and on the provision of equipment and services which were not included in the special programme itself, and the costs of a number of other public investments of which the most important were in the urban fabric of the region. After including estimates of the costs of these items the level of expected expenditure on public facilities amounted to something in excess of about 2.5 milliard francs. The amount of private-sector investment devoted to the creation or extension of factories in the region of Fos and the Étang de Berre was equal to about 12 milliard francs (Cultiaux, 1975, pages 42-48). Of the 12 milliard francs invested in the region between 1971 and 1975, almost 10 milliards were invested in the zone at Fos between 1971 and 1973.

The programme of public investment in the provision of port and industrial infrastructures, and of canal, road, and railway networks and airport facilities continued into the period after the Sixth Plan. In 1976 the construction of a third deep-water dock and of a commercial quay was planned. Work started in 1978, and the new quay was due to come into service in 1980. At the same time, existing port facilities continued to be improved and extended.

Table 11.2. Expenditure (in millions of francs) planned under the special programme for Fos-sur-Mer and its region in the Sixth Plan, 1971-1975. Source: Cultiaux (1975, pages 43-44).

Main projects	State	Others	Total
ZIP and waterways			
land acquisition	50.00	15.00	65.00
works relating to the port and port facilities	252.00	194.75	446.75
development of ZIP		155.00	155.00
waterways	34.85	6.95	41.80
total	336.85	371.70[a]	708.55
New urbanisation	369.20	315.60[b]	684.80
Major infrastructural facilities[c]	411.30	–	411.30
Total	1117.35	687.30	1804.65

[a] Mainly PAM.

[b] Mainly the local communities and developers.

[c] Excluding telecommunications (75 million francs) and SNCF (Société Nationale des Chemins de Fer) (25 million francs).

11.2 The structure and economic development of the Fos maritime industrial development zone

The traffic, excluding bunkering, of PAM increased from 46 million tonnes in 1964 to 100.5 million tonnes in 1973, but declined slightly from 1974 to reach 93.6 million tonnes in 1978. That handled by Fos was almost zero in 1964 but reached 28 million tonnes in 1968, 61 million tonnes in 1973, and 73.2 million tonnes in 1978. These changes in the traffic handled by the port were primarily due to changes in the hydrocarbons trade. In PAM as a whole the traffic in crude oil and petroleum products increased from 35.5 million tonnes in 1964 to 82.3 million tonnes in 1973, but declined from 1974 to reach 73.5 million tonnes in 1978. The growth in the hydrocarbons trade was accompanied by a considerable increase in bulk cargoes to which the imports of coal and iron ore for the SOLMER steelworks made a major contribution (see Cultiaux, 1975, pages 55-57; PAM, 1980, page 3).

The structure of the Fos maritime industrial development zone is illustrated in figure 11.1 and is summarised in table 11.3. The industrial complex was launched in 1962 when petroleum storage facilities and an operations centre for the south European oil pipeline linking Lavéra with Karlsruhe in West Germany were established on a 208 hectare site at La Fenouillère, northwest of Fos-sur-Mer, by the Société du Pipeline Sud-Européen (SPLSE).

With the development of the oil port at Fos, new investments were made. The oil storage complex at La Fenouillère was linked with the new oil port, the capacity of the storage equipment was increased, the capacity of the existing pipeline was tripled, and new pipelines linking Fos with Oberhoffen-sur-Moder and with Lyon were constructed. In all, more than 1.5 milliard francs were spent. The oil port at Fos was also connected with an oil refinery established in the industrial zone by Esso in 1965, and with an oil terminal opened in 1969 by Shell, British Petroleum (BP), and the Compagnie Française de Raffinage (CFR). Shell, BP, and CFR use this terminal to supply their own long-established refineries at Berre, Lavéra, and La Mède and, with the development of the oil port at Fos, decided to expand the capacity of these older refineries (see table 11.4). In addition a storage area for refined oil products imported by sea was constructed on a 27 hectare site by the GIE Dépôts Pétroliers de Fos.

In 1970 the energy base of the zone was extended as a result of the decision by Gaz de France (GDF) to locate a methane terminal at Fos. With this development, Algerian natural gas from Hassi R'Mel was liquified at Skikda in Algeria, transported to Fos, and transformed at this plant. The refrigerants released by this process are supplied to an Air Liquide plant established on an adjacent site to produce oxygen and nitrogen. In turn, Air Liquide supplies Gaz de France both with heat to reheat and vaporise the liquified natural gas, and with nitrogen gas to inject into the methane. At the same time, oxygen and nitrogen are supplied by Air Liquide to the oil and petrochemical, and metallurgical industries in the area. Interdependencies of this kind were and are of course important locational factors.

PAM also attempted to launch a joint venture with local petrochemical companies to import and store liquefied petroleum gas (LPG) at Fos. With the cost of naphtha increasing, LPG seemed to offer an alternative feedstock for the petrochemical industry. LPG was already being imported through Lavéra. What PAM was proposing was that its capacity to handle this traffic be enlarged mainly by developing a new and relatively isolated oil berth at Fos for what are hazardous tanker operations. Some temporary steps to

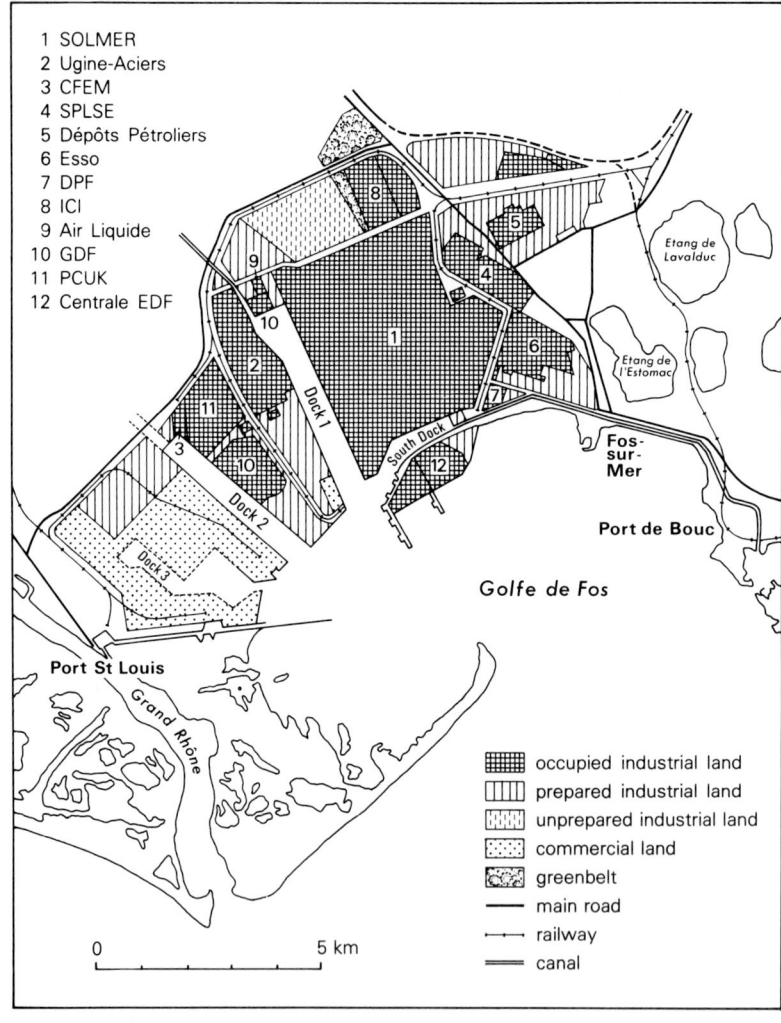

Figure 11.1. The structure of the Fos maritime industrial development zone.

Table 11.3. The early large investments in the Fos Maritime industrial development area. Source: elaborated from Robert (1974, page 64) and Cultiaux (1975, pages 68–77).

Company	Production	Activity and productive capacity in tonnes	Commencement of operation	Size of site (hectares)
Société Lorraine et Méridionale de Laminage Continu (SOLMER)	integrated iron and steel works producing flat steel products	stage 1: steel plant $> 3\,500 \times 10^3$ year^{-1} rolling mill $4\,500 \times 10^3$ year^{-1} stage 2: steel plant $7\,000 \times 10^3$ year^{-1}	1st quarter 1974 4th quarter 1973	1560
Ugine-Aciers (Péchiney–Ugine Kuhlmann)	production of special steels	stage 1: special steels 200×10^3 year^{-1} stage 2: stainless steel 400×10^3 year^{-1}	4th quarter 1973 3rd quarter 1975	275
Compagnie Française d'Entreprises Métalliques (CFEM)	production of heavy metal structural elements	metallic structures 25×10^3 year^{-1}	3rd quarter 1972	12
Esso	oil refining	refining of crude oil 3000×10^3 year^{-1} 8000×10^3 year^{-1}	2nd quarter 1965 3rd quarter 1973	275
Imperial Chemical Industries (ICI)	production of high-pressure low-density polyethylene	high-pressure low-density polyethylene 60×10^3 year^{-1} 70×10^3 year^{-1}	3rd quarter 1972 4th quarter 1973	132
Société des Produits Chimiques Ugine Kuhlmann	production of chlorine	chlorine 80×10^3 year^{-1}	4th quarter 1975	183
Air Liquide	liquefaction and distillation of air to produce oxygen and nitrogen	oxygen gas 800 day^{-1} liquid oxygen 120 day^{-1} liquid nitrogen 120 day^{-1} 90% pure nitrogen gas 900 day^{-1} pure nitrogen gas 340 day^{-1}	3rd quarter 1972	7.8
Gaz de France	reception, storage, regasification and distribution of liquefied natural gas from Skikda in Algeria	methane $3\,500$ m^3 year^{-1} treated	4th quarter 1972	15.5

[a] The wide hot strip mill was also able to roll stainless steel produced by Ugine-Aciers.

handle LPG were taken. But although Shell-Chimie and Naphtachimie both expressed an interest in the project, they were reluctant to participate in it in the absence of a third partner (Green, 1979c, page 3).

The importation of crude petroleum and the development of refining capacity were associated with the development of the region as an important focus for the petrochemical industry. In the two main centres at Berre, where Shell-Chimie is located, and at Lavéra, where Naphtachimie, Rhône-Progil, and Oxochimie constitute a large complex, are plants which produce the full range of basic organic products.

By about 1974, local production of ethylene amounted to some 40% of national production. Of particular importance in expanding local capacity was the development by Naphtachimie in 1970–1972 of a steam cracking plant with a capacity of 400 000 tonnes per annum, together with a unit producing ethylene oxide in the vicinity of Lavéra. In 1975 the capacity of the steam cracker was increased to 500 000 tonnes per annum (Cultiaux, 1975, page 59).

In 1970, Imperial Chemical Industries (ICI) decided to establish a plant producing low-density polyethylene by the high-pressure process at Fos. One of the reasons for this was the possibility of piping ethylene from the Naphtachimie plant at Lavéra. ICI was also attracted by the availability and the characteristics of the site. However, the main reason for the choice of Fos lay in the fact that it provided a manufacturing and distribution base in southern Europe for a commercial strategy oriented towards markets in the Mediterranean and in the Middle East.

Table 11.4. The growth of the refining capacity of oil refineries in the region of Fos and the Étang de Berre and in France, 1965–1980. Source: Cultiaux (1975, page 59) and UCSIP (1980, page 57).

Company and region	Location	Date of establishment	Refining capacity on 1st January (millions of tonnes)				
			1965	1970	1973	1978	1980
Shell Française	Berre	1931	6.00	7.00	10.24	13.50	13.50
Société Française BP	Lavéra	1933	4.40	4.40	13.50	11.50	8.50
Compagnie Française de Raffinage	La Mède	1934	6.40	10.24	10.24	10.50	9.80
Esso SAF	Fos-sur-Mer	1965		3.00	3.00	8.00	8.00
Total (Fos and the Étang de Berre)			16.80	24.64	36.97	43.50	39.80
Méditerranée– Rhône			20.53	32.37	48.20	58.30	54.57
France			61.93	105.24	144.05	171.24	166.84

The petrochemical base of the zone was widened by the completion in 1976 of Produits Chimiques Ugine Kuhlmann's (PCUK) fully-automated chlorine and soda plant. (This group was formed in 1972 as a result of a merger between Péchiney and Ugine Kuhlmann.)

In August 1977, Shell-Chimie and PCUK announced a joint investment programme costing 3.5 milliard francs. The centrepiece of this plan was the construction by Shell-Chimie of a new ethylene cracker with a capacity of 350 000 tonnes per year. When it came on-stream at the end of 1980, the number of steam crackers in the region was to reach four and the total ethylene capacity 1.05 million tonnes per year. At the same time, Shell-Chimie was constructing a polyvinylchloride plant, and one of its subsidiaries was expanding its output of high-pressure polyethylene from a plant on the Berre site. PCUK was increasing the capacity of its chlorine plant from 80 000 to 150 000 tonnes per year. In addition, a new mono-vinylchloride plant was under construction on PCUK's site at Fos by a new jointly owned subsidiary of Shell-Chimie and PCUK called Vinyl-Fos. 60% of the funds for it were to be provided by Shell-Chimie, and the rest by PCUK (Green, 1979b, page 48; 1979c, page 5).

The infrastructural and industrial investments at Fos accordingly created some of the conditions for the development of an important Mediterranean centre of integrated energy and primary chemical production. Yet very little development of downstream activities occurred. In the early 1980s, polyethylene and synthetic rubber were produced locally, but few final products apart from insecticides and animal proteins were produced in the region (see Green, 1979b, page 31). The local chemical industry has some important competitive advantages deriving from the qualities of the zone's infrastructural and production facilities, the low costs of importing raw materials, and the scale of production. But in the absence of new downstream industries, what happens to the zone is clearly going to depend very heavily upon the extent to which these advantages prove sufficient to counteract the tendency for the production of primary petrochemical products to be decentralised to newly industrialising countries and especially to areas where energy is cheap.

The main element in the new industrial zone was, however, an integrated shore-based iron and steel plant established by the Société Lorraine et Méridionale de Laminage Continu (SOLMER). With the development of this plant to produce flat steel products from imported ore and coal, the industrial base of the zone was widened to include an industry centred on the processing of a second major raw material.

The idea of developing an iron and steel plant at Fos had been put forward as early as 1954. The origins of the SOLMER project lie, however, in a report prepared in 1963 and 1964 by a working party composed of representatives of the steel companies participating in the Société Lorraine de Laminage Continu (SOLLAC), in which Fos was identified along with Le Havre as a possible location for a second shore-based integrated iron and steel works. At first, however, the majority of the industrialists involved preferred the site on the English Channel (see Paillard, 1981, pages 71-74).

In the technical and economic conditions prevailing at that time, large integrated plants in which some stages in the production process were beginning to be automated had the highest levels of labour productivity. In comparison with other types of new plant they also had the lowest costs of production (see chapter 8, section 8.5).

At the same time, mining in countries with high-grade ore and high-quality coking coal deposits was being mechanised, and large-tonnage ore carriers and other specialised means of large-scale maritime transport were being developed. As a result, the costs of transport were falling, and the competitiveness of imported raw materials was increasing. In the 1960s, steel companies in metropolitan economies accordingly started to switch to imported supplies of iron ore and coking coal. With the construction of large-scale integrated plants on the coast adjacent to deep-water channels the advantages of a switch to new sources of raw materials could be maximised, as could the economies associated with the exploitation of improved means of maritime transport not only to import raw materials but also to export steel products.

In spite of these advantages, however, it was not until December 1969 that the decision to build a second coastal plant and to locate it at Fos was announced.

The decision to proceed was closely connected with processes of financial centralisation and industrial restructuring orchestrated by the state and aimed at countering the decline in the rate of profit in the steel sector, at relaunching investment, and at rationalising and modernising the productive system. In the case of the Lorraine-based groups who held a controlling interest in SOLLAC, some of the most relevant of the state-initiated processes commenced in the late 1960s. In 1968 the groups holding shares in SOLLAC merged. The group that resulted was called Wendel-SIDELOR. At the beginning of 1973, however, further reorganisation occurred, when Wendel-SIDELOR and SACILOR were merged. The new group also assumed the name Société des Aciéries et Laminoirs de Lorraine (SACILOR) (see figure 11.2).

At the time when the Sixth Plan was being prepared the position of the groups concerned seemed to be improving. In a climate of optimism about the future of the industry the first stage of the SOLMER works was written into the plan as a priority objective. Along with proposals for doubling the capacity of the existing shore-based complex at Dunkirk from 4 to 8 million tonnes of steel per year and constructing the Mardyck cold rolling mill, the decision to build the new plant was a central component of a strategy for improving still further the industry's competitiveness, and expanding French steel-making capacity from 28.8 million tonnes per year in 1972 to 36.1 in 1975, in line with President Pompidou's policy of industrialising the country.

Fos-sur-Mer and the development of Marseilles 263

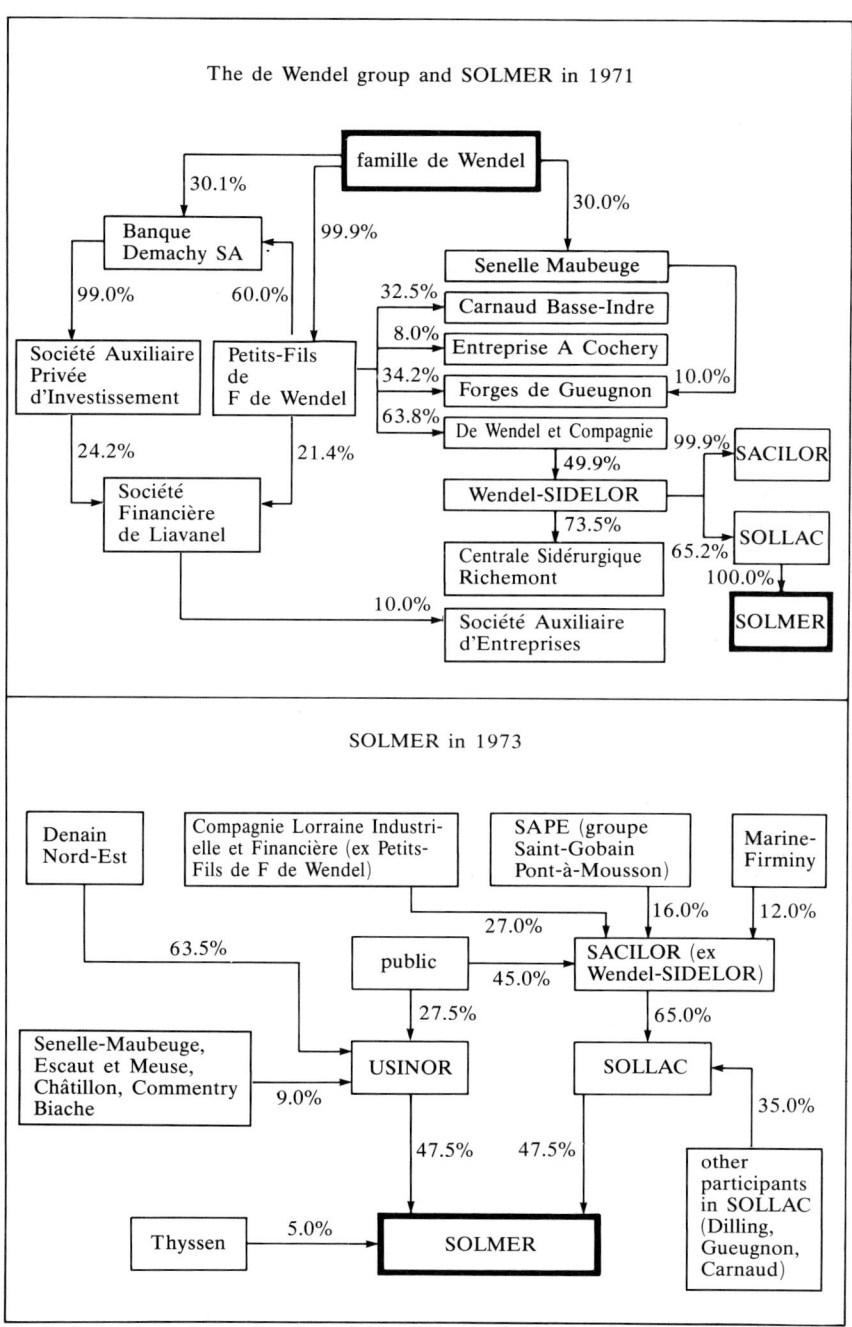

Figure 11.2. The structure of SOLMER in 1971 and 1973. Source: Paillard (1981, pages 73, 135).

The government approved the project as soon as it was announced in December 1969. In November 1970 the decision was confirmed, and SOLMER was formed as a subsidiary of SOLLAC. Construction of the installations included in the first stage of the project commenced in October 1971 and was completed between October 1973 and June 1975.

By the end of this phase the works was equipped with (1) steel-making facilities capable of producing up to 3.5 million tonnes of steel per annum, (2) a slabbing mill and continuous casting facilities for the direct production of semifinished products, and (3) a continuous wide hot rolling mill and finishing facilities for the production initially of up to 4.5 million tonnes per year of steel sheet or strip. In a second stage, commencing in 1976, a heavy sheet metal workshop was to be added, the capacity of the iron- and steel-making units was to be doubled, and a cold rolling mill was to be installed. At that stage it was expected that SOLMER's total installed capacity would eventually reach 20 million tonnes of steel per year. With the reappearance of excess capacity and the crisis in the steel industry in the second half of the 1970s, however, all of these expansion plans were postponed. (Compare the French case with that of the Italian industry discussed in chapter 8, section 8.5.)

The decision to locate at Fos rather than at Le Havre, or even at a site on the Atlantic coast, is frequently attributed to government pressure on a company which would have preferred one of the other locations. Of course location at Le Havre would have reinforced the disequilibrium between the north and east of France and the rest of the country. However, elements within Wendel-SIDELOR also opted for Fos. One of the main reasons was that a site on the Mediterranean was thought at that time to afford the most advantageous position from which the company could pursue a new economic and commercial strategy aimed at restoring profitability (see Robert, 1974, page 65). The fact that the government provided low-interest loans on very favourable terms obviously enabled it to exercise some influence over the locational decision, and locations for which such assistance was not available were likely to be ruled out.

Of some 6.1 milliard francs originally thought to be necessary to implement the first stage of the project, 1.85 milliard francs were lent by the state on extremely favourable terms from the Fonds de Développement Économique et Social (FDES). Another 1.8 milliard francs or so were borrowed from banks and financial institutions. Consequently, only some 0.8 milliard francs had to come from SOLMER's profits and only about 1.7 milliard francs from the companies investing capital in it. Of the 4.1 milliard francs estimated as required to construct the second stage of the project, however, 3.1 milliards were to be found out of the profits obtained from the operation of the installations built in the first phase. In the event, the conditions on which this plan for financing the project depended were not realised. In 1971, Wendel-SIDELOR found itself in financial difficulties. As a result, a conversion plan was prepared with a view to rationalising and modernising the company's installations in Lorraine and raising its profitability to the average level being achieved by other large steel companies in Europe. By the beginning of 1972, SOLLAC had only managed to put up 0.4 milliard francs of the capital required to develop the Fos complex. (The main reason for this lay in Wendel-SIDELOR's lack of profitability.) Moreover, in each of the next four years, Wendel-SIDELOR had to spend a formerly unanticipated annual sum of 0.4 milliard francs on a conversion plan.

In the Autumn of 1972, as a result of its inability to meet its share of the projected expenditure out of its internal resources and of increases in the costs of constructing the complex, Wendel-SIDELOR was forced to seek further help from the state and to look for new partners to help finance the Fos project. Subsequent negotiations with USINOR and with Italian, Spanish, and German companies eventually resulted in the inclusion in SOLMER of USINOR alongside SOLLAC. At the same time, the state stepped in to modify the original financial arrangements. In a new plan announced in February 1973 the estimated cost of the first stage of the project was increased from 6.1 milliard to 7.7 milliard francs. (Similar data to the ones discussed in the text are set out in table 11.5.) Some 2.3 milliard francs were to be obtained from the issue of shares and from the provision of capital by the companies participating in SOLMER. Included were an additional 0.8 milliard francs FDES loan provided at a low rate of interest to the participants in SOLMER, and a 0.45 milliard franc loan made by a nationalised bank to a new finance company controlled jointly by SOLLAC and USINOR. With these loans the contributions to be financed out of Wendel-SIDELOR's and USINOR's internal resources were accordingly

Table 11.5. The original plan and the plan of February 1973 (prior to the entry of Thyssen) for financing stage 1 of SOLMER. Source: elaborated from Paillard (1981, page 135).

	Finance (milliard francs)			Finance (milliard francs)	
	1st plan	2nd plan		1st plan	2nd plan
Shareholders' contributions			*Internally generated funds*		
de Wendel[a]	1.70	0.50	Profits[b]	0.80	0.80
USINOR		0.30	*Loans*		
Other		0.20	FDES	1.85	1.85
State banks		0.50	Banks, etc[c]	1.80	1.80
FDES		0.80	Other		1.00
Total	1.70	2.30	Total	3.65	4.65

[a] de Wendel and other partners in SOLLAC.
[b] SOLMER's gross operating profits.
[c] Banks, financial institutions, GIS, GI-FOS.

reduced to about 1.0 milliard francs. USINOR advanced 0.4 milliard francs to match the sum that had already been put up by Wendel-SIDELOR.

At the end of March 1973, August Thyssen Hütte AG joined SOLMER. The German group took 5% of the capital with the possibility of increasing its shareholding to 25% at a later stage. The two main French producers were to divide the rest of the capital equally between themselves. In January 1978, however, the German company decided not to take up its option and withdrew from SOLMER.

The remaining sum of about 5.4 milliard francs was to be covered in several ways. 0.8 milliard francs was to come out of depreciation allowances and retained profits generated in SOLMER's first two years of operation, and some 3.6 milliard francs were to be borrowed. Both of these items were as envisaged in the earlier plan. What was new were additional long-term loans worth 1.0 milliard francs.

In effect the companies participating in SOLMER were only expected to provide about 1.0 milliard francs from their internal resources. Some 0.8 milliard francs were to be financed out of SOLMER's operating profits. The state was to provide 2.65 milliard francs in the form of FDES loans, and about 3.25 milliard francs were to be borrowed from a variety of banks, financial institutions, and specialised agencies lending money in the steel sector (Cultiaux, 1975, pages 68 – 70; Freyssenet, 1979a, pages 125 – 134).

Quite clearly, state financial aid played an important role in promoting the project. In all probability, however, it was not tied to the choice of Fos. On the other hand, state infrastructure provision, to the extent that it preceded and was independent of the actual locational decision, was probably more constraining from a geographical point of view. Insofar as its distribution was a determining factor, government decisions played a significant part not only in the investment decision but also in determining the choice of Fos as a location for the new steelworks. But to what extent were the government's decisions as to where infrastructural equipment was to be developed independent of the locational preferences of the company and to what extent were they harmonised with them?

The company's selection of Fos as a site for a new plant was undoubtedly one aspect of a new and more offensive commercial strategy oriented towards the conquest of markets on the French Mediterranean coast, in countries bordering on the Mediterranean, and in the Middle East. In the late 1960s, markets in these areas were thought to offer more growth potential than some of the larger north and northwest European markets because of two factors. One was the expected development of metal-using activities in Mediterranean France and in some countries bordering or accessible from the Mediterranean. The second was the existence of less competition from other European steel producers. (Other sections of French capital were adopting similar strategies.) Moreover, at the level of national planning, the choice of Fos coincided with the strategic aims of the French state of (1) making the Marseilles metropolitan region into a major industrial and commercial pole in the Mediterranean Basin capable of challenging similar poles in Italy and Spain, and (2) preserving French economic domination of the Mediterranean Basin in conditions in which the international division of labour was changing.

The success or otherwise of the company's strategy would depend, however, not only upon the diversification and development in the predicted direction of the regional and national economies concerned. Also important was the competitiveness of the steel produced at the new plant. To a large extent the competitiveness of the project was guaranteed, it was thought, by several factors. First, the most modern and technically sophisticated production techniques available were to be adopted. Second, the processes involved in making iron and in making and rolling steel were to be automated and integrated. In the third place, the scale of production was to be optimised. All of these factors were expected to give rise to high levels of labour productivity and a high level of efficiency in the use of working capital. Once the plant had been run in, and as long as it were operated sufficiently near its capacity to approach full efficiency, operating costs could reasonably be expected to be very low.

The development of new works does, however, involve high additional capital costs. Although operating costs are lower, newer works burdened with heavy development expenditures are in the short term often characterised by higher total costs of production than older works. What is more, the full loading of new plants is often associated with the incurring of losses as a result of the retiring of older capacity which has not been fully depreciated. In the longer term, however, the construction of new installations plays a particularly important role not only in expanding capacity but also in determining a company's competitive strength. One reason is that once a plant has been constructed the capital costs of a project are sunk costs. Ex post, though not ex ante, sunk costs are not relevant. In that situation, cost comparisons should accordingly be based on differences in operating (and, in a rational world, social) costs.

Economic viability, however, is not the same thing as financial viability. When prices are high, older steelworks may be able to survive for many years, and, in recessions, companies with outdated installations are sometimes in a financially stronger position than those with high overhead costs. In the steel industry, companies undertaking major investment programmes are in many cases unable to rely on internal sources of funding and as a consequence find themselves heavily in debt. When demand slackens and prices fall, companies with a high level of indebtedness must sell to meet their prior charges burden, are unwilling to participate in cartel arrangements and to restrict output, and are prepared to produce and sell steel as long as prices exceed their operating costs. One result of this type of behaviour is that the size of any fall in prices is increased. In these conditions, companies that have invested in modern facilities may well succeed in seizing markets from their competitors, but only at the expense of incurring significant financial costs. Furthermore, very strong pressure is placed on rival firms to participate in an unbridled race to increase their own productivity levels.

In these conditions, of course, the state will sometimes step in, overruling market rationality in the name of some kind of technical rationality (see chapter 3, section 3.6). On the one hand, an attempt may be made to prevent prices from falling too far. On the other, capacity cuts are likely to be planned at the level of the industry as a whole in order to ensure that closings are based on economic cost considerations and to socialise the costs of devalorisation.

In the case of SOLMER the works was in structure and design highly efficient. With the recession in the steel industry in the second half of the 1970s, however, the active commercial role planned for SOLMER was undermined, and the second stage of the project was postponed. As a result, the role of the works in the development of the industry and the region was to differ from the one which had originally been envisaged.

The competitiveness of the plant was not solely dependent on the internal organisation of production. As with other installations occupying sites at Fos, the competitiveness of the steelworks was expected to be enhanced by several characteristics of the location. In the case of SOLMER the relevant characteristics included relatively low construction costs and the availability of local raw materials. In addition, the structure of the local economy and of the local and regional labour markets added to the area's attractiveness.

One advantage of the site at Fos was that it afforded a large expanse of uncongested and undeveloped flat land adjacent to natural deep-water channels. The value of the land for industrial development had already been substantially enhanced by state infrastructural investments. Included were new port facilities, a communications network linking the zone with the rest of the national territory, and public utilities such as power stations, telecommunications equipment, aqueducts, and drainage networks. Consequently, the site was a particularly attractive one for companies that used imported raw materials and exported or moved their products by sea. In addition, PAM had a policy of allowing companies locating at Fos to buy or lease extremely large sites with ample room for subsequent expansion at very low prices or rents. The original site included 5520 hectares of industrial land. Of 2935 hectares allocated to industrial users by PAM by the beginning of 1974, 1560 hectares had been sold to SOLMER, although only about 400 hectares were being used in the first stage of the project. Ugine-Aciers had bought 275 hectares but was using only 15 hectares. ICI was using only 12 out of 130 hectares. The allocation of such a large proportion of the land available for industrial development to a few companies placed severe limits on the possibility of other enterprises locating in the zone and quickly led PAM to seek to extend the maritime industrial development area to the Northwest.

A second advantage of the site for the firms lay in the fact that the area was relatively unpopulated. The absence of densely settled areas in the immediate vicinity of the zone enabled the companies locating at Fos to make relatively low initial investments in antipollution devices and to set up plants involving dangerous processes. The lack of strict pollution controls in the early years of development of the complex reduced the costs to the capitals involved of investing in the port and industrial zone. What resulted, however, were levels of pollution that had particularly damaging consequences for the local landscape, local ecological systems, and the quality of life of the region's inhabitants (see Paillard, 1981, chapter 7).

A network of nationally-, regionally- and locally-based subcontracting firms capable of meeting the needs of large-scale capital-intensive enterprises producing energy and intermediate goods existed and was developed in the locality. In addition, a differentiated and abundant supply of labour needed to construct the complex and to carry out less skilled jobs in new industrial establishments was to be found. According to many observers the availability of workers played an important role in the development of industry at Fos. At that stage in the steel industry's development the production cycle in large integrated plants was characterised by increasing continuity and automation. With these developments significant changes were occurring in the technical division of labour and in the skill composition of the labour force. When major changes of this kind occur, companies often seek to recruit labour at a national level or from areas where the industry concerned is absent to obtain workers without a long tradition of working in it. This type of consideration reinforced the attractiveness of the site at Fos.

The development of the SOLMER works was accompanied, however, by a major scheme for rationalising Wendel-SIDELOR's operations. Under this plan about 10 650 jobs were to be lost in Lorraine. In accordance with the terms of a social agreement between the employers and the steel unions, substantial numbers of workers had to be offered transfers to Fos. As a result, some of the problems that might otherwise have been posed by the inadequacy of local industrial training schemes and by the lack of an adequate local supply of skilled labour could be overcome, but fewer new workers could be recruited.

More than 6000 of those employed by SACILOR-SOLLAC applied for transfers to SOLMER. At the end of 1973 some 2200 of the 3400 persons employed by SOLMER had come from Lorraine. 2400 workers were eventually transferred, including 500 workers from a steelworks at Micheville near Longwy which was to be closed. Of these workers, 69.6% were engineers, technicians, supervisors, and office workers. At the beginning of 1975, transferred workers accounted for 90.1% of SOLMER's engineers, 71.8% of the supervisory staff, 50.2% of its technicians, 43% of its office workers, 58.9% of its 'special' workers, 32.3% of its tradesmen, and 12.9% of its unskilled workers (Freyssenet, 1979a, page 46). By the end of 1975, only some 2600 of about 6500 persons employed by SOLMER had come from the local départements of Gard, Vaucluse, and Bouches-du-Rhône. The workers originating in these three départements filled 29.8% of the skilled and 58.3% of the unskilled jobs in the new steelworks (Fabre, 1976, page 6). Many of the other unskilled jobs were filled by immigrant workers.

The actual proportion of skilled jobs provided by SOLMER itself was increased by the company's recruitment policy. In 1977, some 6700 persons were directly employed by SOLMER. It has, however, been estimated that, at any one moment, another 2000 people would, on average, be working on the site. Of the latter, a much higher proportion were thought to be manual workers than in the case of SOLMER's own labour force (see Broda et al, 1978, page 444). The reason for this is that in operating as well as in constructing the new steelworks, SOLMER adopted a strategy of subcontracting certain kinds of work to other firms and of relying to a considerable extent upon the use of temporary labour recruited either directly or, more usually, indirectly via subcontractors from temporary employment agencies. In fact, in integrated and automated process industries there is at present a general tendency for capital to attempt to limit direct employment to management and production activities. Activities occurring upstream and downstream of the immediate production process are often subcontracted, as are tasks relating to the provision of the conditions within which production takes place, and some of the work involved in maintaining, repairing, and modifying machinery and industrial installations (see the discussion of employment flexibility in chapter 2, section 2.5.).

In the case of SOLMER, some research and development activities are subcontracted to national and even to multinational firms. More significantly, some of the maintenance, construction, and repair work, which is particularly important in modern process industries, is also subcontracted. In some cases this work is delegated to national firms employing polyvalent skilled workers, and temporary workers are recruited as and when they are needed from national-level temporary employment agencies. Otherwise, the work concerned is subcontracted to local firms, which are often small or medium in size and family-owned, which are almost always structurally linked to local temporary employment agencies, and which employ large amounts of skilled labour on a temporary basis.

Services such as the transport of personnel, catering, cleaning, and security, as well as some office jobs, are often carried out by workers who are not permanently employed by the company. Industrial cleaning, the handling of raw materials, by-products, and finished products, and the recovery and recycling of scrap metal are also subcontracted, as is distribution. Some of the more unpleasant manual and industrial cleaning jobs are carried out by unskilled workers and labourers employed by national companies which came to the area from Lorraine and the Nord in the wake of the steel industry, and which are linked with national financial groups with interests in the steel sector. These firms make widespread use of immigrant workers and of other sections of the marginalised proletariat. With the temporary employment agencies with which they are connected, these companies play an important role in regulating part of the local secondary labour market.

Other industrial cleaning jobs and some of the semiskilled tasks connected with handling raw materials and products and the provision of transport services, as well as jobs like office cleaning, tend to be subcontracted to locally-owned family firms employing workers who are, on average, more skilled and better paid than those employed by national firms of the type included in the last group. As with their national counterparts, these local firms also make very extensive use of temporary workers supplied by temporary employment agencies to which the subcontracting firms themselves tend to be structurally related. Accordingly, the activities of these firms are situated at the point at which the delegation of relatively unskilled work by a leading company intersects with a local labour market on which male and female immigrant workers, young people, and women seeking employment are particularly numerous. As a result, an important role in structuring the conditions of demand and supply of local labour is also played by these local family-owned firms.

In short, tasks which need to be done promptly but irregularly are assigned as far as possible to outside agencies. Some work is delegated to temporary workers or to firms that use temporary labour as part of a conscious policy of limiting the recruitment of permanent workers. Also certain dirty, difficult, and often dangerous jobs are allocated to workers not directly employed by the company. As a result, the jobs retained by SOLMER for the workers it employs directly are generally more skilled, more secure, better paid, and involve a shorter working week (Broda and La Bruyère, 1979, pages 34-41).

During the 1970s, subcontracting increased in importance. Between June 1974 and September 1975 two leading steel companies, which were located on the Fos maritime industrial development zone and which were employing about 7500 people directly, employed a permanent equivalent of 141 temporary workers. In the cases of the firms to which SOLMER and Ugine-Aciers subcontracted work, a permanent equivalent of 622 temporary workers were employed. Between September 1975 and September 1977 the corresponding figures were 199 and 1183 respectively.

In the first of these two periods, the leading companies used temporary workers mainly to work in offices as typists, secretaries, punch-card operators, and so on, whereas, in the second period, unskilled manual workers constituted the most important type of temporary labour used. Of the temporary labour hired by subcontractors a good three quarters were, in both periods, skilled manual workers, although a group of about twelve of the subcontractors hired about 70% of the unskilled manual labour employed on a temporary basis. In the second period, work was given in all to two hundred and eight subcontractors in the region of Fos and the Étang de Berre. One hundred and twenty-two of the latter employed temporary labour, and fifty-six, which were particularly closely linked with the main steel companies, used about 70% of the total temporary labour employed. More than 90% of the latter was recruited from thirty-four temporary employment agencies in the region, with the rest being obtained from agencies in other centres such as Marseilles, Aix, and Arles (see Broda, 1976; Broda and La Bruyère, 1979).

The reasons why SOLMER decided to adopt a strategy for managing the labour force which resulted in the paradoxical coexistence of advanced technologies and archaic forms of superexploitation lay in two main factors. One was the development of new and specialised roles in the technical division of labour. The second was the conscious adoption of a new capitalist strategy for increasing the rate of profit. In particular, the company was intent on segmenting the fractions of capital and the workers not playing a direct role in the process of production, and on reducing its investment in certain kinds of equipment and certain types of labour power. The extent to which employers succeed with a strategy of this kind obviously varies historically and geographically. In the case of the state-controlled Italian steel industry the unions have, for example, been relatively successful in protecting the workers employed by subcontractors (see Rhodes, 1985, pages 209-216).

As with the policy of recruiting labour from different parts of the country and from different countries, SOLMER's strategy contributed to a segmentation and to differentiated forms of management of the collective worker. The differences in the composition of the labour force that resulted were, moreover, reinforced by related differences in the processes of reproduction and in the ways of life of different sections of the population. The traditions of struggle and the existing forms of organisation of the local labour movement were broken down, and trade union militancy would, it was hoped, be limited. At the same time, the flexibility with which labour could be used within the sphere of production would, it was intended, be increased, whereas costs would be reduced, and the continuity of production and the realisation of the large amounts of value immobilised in the works would be more easily achieved (Broda et al, 1978, pages 435-445).

Many of the subcontractors and temporary employment agencies were established or moved to the area with the implantation of the steel industry in the early 1970s. As has, however, been suggested, the existence in the locality of a group of local firms to whom maintenance work could be subcontracted, and of a differentiated supply of labour capable of being used both in the construction phase and in the operating phase in accordance with SOLMER's strategy for managing the labour force, did play an important role in attracting the steel industry to the area.

Shortly after the plant came on-stream the demand for steel fell, and in 1974 a protracted steel crisis opened. The commercial strategy on which the development of the complex had been based was in ruins. The second stage of the project was postponed. And until February 1977, production did not exceed 50% of the plant's capacity: only in two short periods of three and a half and two and a half months, respectively, were the two blast furnaces operated together. Output was equal to 1.655 million tonnes of steel in 1975 and 1.825 million tonnes in 1976.

In the new plant the productivity of labour was high, standing at about four hours thirty minutes per tonne of steel. Shortly before the announcement, at the beginning of 1977, of a new plan for restructuring the steel industry (known as the *Plan Acier*) a new strategy of producing coils as cheaply as possible was adopted. In accordance with this strategy, both blast furnaces started simultaneous operation (see figure 11.3). In that year, output increased to 2.784 million tonnes compared with a capacity of 3.5 million tonnes per annum (Broda et al, 1978, pages 426-428).

The implantation of an integrated iron and steelworks widened the industrial base of the Fos maritime industrial development zone not only by adding a new basic industry, but also by stimulating a small number of related investments. The establishment of the SOLMER works was a major factor in the decision by Ugine Kuhlmann, or Péchiney-Ugine Kuhlmann as it was to become in 1972, to locate a plant producing special steels at Fos. The reason why was that some of the steel ingots produced by Ugine-Aciers were able to be and were rolled on the continuous wide hot rolling mill included in SOLMER's investment programme. In the first stage of the project a steel-making unit capable of producing 200000 tonnes per year of special-alloy steel, rolling mills, and finishing mills were constructed. In the second stage, a second steel-making unit with an initial annual capacity of 400000 tonnes of stainless steel was to be built. In 1984, however, it was decided that the plant should be closed (see chapter 12, section 12.9).

The other major investment occurred when the Compagnie Française d'Entreprises Métalliques (CFEM) decided to locate its fifth main plant at Fos. This decision was made mainly because of CFEM's role in constructing

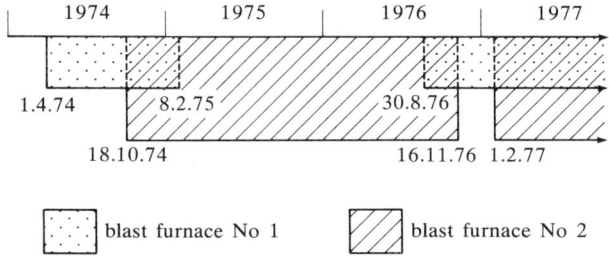

Figure 11.3. The operation of the SOLMER steelwork's blast furnace capacity. Source: Broda et al (1978, page 426).

infrastructural equipment and industrial installations included in the port and industrial complex. The plant itself came into service in October 1972. In it is produced heavy metal equipment such as boilers, bridges, offshore platforms, and oil rigs.

Two other metalworking plants exist. One is Ferifos, occupying a 14 hectare site, where rolling stock is maintained and repaired. The second is the Otto Lazard plant, occupying a 3 hectare site, where scrap iron is recovered and treated. Some service activities and subcontracting firms are also located in the zone on a 48 hectare site at Le Ventillon, a 64 hectare site at La Feuillane, and a 7 hectare site at La Petite Feuillane. Others are found in nearby industrial zones.

11.3 Employment and the Fos maritime industrial development area

The establishment of the new port and industrial zone was not only intended to be part of a programme of national economic expansion. It was also presented as one of the central components of a programme of planned regional development aimed at solving some of the problems of employment in the Aire Métropolitaine Marseillaise (AMM). [AMM is an area stretching from Marseilles to Aix, Arles, and Port St Louis. It includes fifty-nine of the one hundred and nineteen communes and 85% of the population in the Bouches du Rhône département (see figure 11.6).]

In the 1960s the region of Provence-Alpes-Côte d'Azur, the département of Bouches du Rhône, and the Marseilles metropolitan area all suffered from low and falling activity rates, especially for women, and from rising rates of unemployment. In planning documents written in connection with the preparation of a structure plan for AMM, both of these sets of labour market conditions were attributed to discrepancies between rapid rates of population growth and high rates of net immigration on the one hand, and slow rates of employment growth on the other. In addition, industrial jobs were lacking, and a comparatively high proportion of employment was in the tertiary sector (see table 11.6). One reason for this was that the region had been largely bypassed by the industrial revolution and had come to depend to a large extent upon the commercial role of the port of Marseilles.

The old port of Marseilles and almost all local industries were in turn largely dependent on the traditional and protected colonial trade with the countries of the Union Française and the Zone Franc. In 1954, Vietnam gained independence. With the war in Algeria, exchanges with North Africa were intensified. In the 1960s, however, the process of decolonisation was accelerated. As a result, most of the traditional functions of the port were undermined, and many of the traditional port-related industries which had developed around Marseilles were declining. Moreover, many of these declining activities had a high labour intensity. At the same time, some of the small number of industries which had been set up in the region to exploit local raw materials such as salt, lignite, limestone, and bauxite were also in decline.

Table 11.6. The growth of employment in AMM and in France by sector, 1962–1968, with projections for 1985 (figures are in thousands, with percentages in parentheses). Source: Cultiaux (1975, page 26).

Sector	1962 AMM		1962 France		1968 AMM		1968 France		1985 AMM[a]		1985 France[b]	
Energy and transport	64.872	(15.5)	1357.700	(7.2)	64.780	(13.7)	1542.320	(7.7)	100.000	(11.4)	1799.500	(7.8)
energy	12.867	(3.1)	361.400	(1.9)	12.779	(2.7)	380.920	(1.9)	15.000	(1.7)	294.500	(1.3)
transport and telecommunications	52.005	(12.4)	996.300	(5.3)	52.001	(11.0)	1161.400	(5.8)	85.300	(9.7)	1505.000	(6.5)
Industry and agriculture	112.059	(26.7)	8921.900	(47.0)	113.236	(24.0)	8179.760	(40.9)	245.000	(28.0)	8573.900	(37.0)
agriculture	14.572	(3.5)	3759.000	(19.8)	14.551	(3.1)	3006.820	(15.0)	8.000	(0.9)	2370.000	(10.2)
food processing industries	24.578	(5.9)	640.100	(3.4)	22.342	(4.7)	654.900	(3.3)	27.000	(3.1)	625.000	(2.7)
metal-manufacturing and chemical industries	48.116	(11.5)	2577.800	(13.6)	52.600	(11.1)	2663.200	(13.3)	150.000	(17.1)	3386.300	(14.6)
other industries	24.793	(5.9)	1945.000	(10.2)	23.743	(5.0)	1854.840	(9.3)	60.000	(6.9)	2192.600	(9.5)
Commerce	54.364	(13.0)	1878.000	(9.9)	64.678	(13.7)	2223.060	(11.1)	105.000	(12.0)	2636.500	(11.4)
Building and public works	52.253	(12.4)	1841.300	(9.7)	59.545	(12.6)	2207.240	(11.0)	105.000	(12.0)	2039.000	(8.8)
Services	136.205	(32.4)	4965.200	(26.2)	170.081	(36.0)	5849.860	(29.3)	320.000	(36.6)	8137.100	(35.0)
services other than the administration	74.064	(17.6)	2842.200	(15.0)	92.852	(19.7)	3363.820	(16.8)	180.000	(20.6)	4759.800	(20.4)
administration	62.141	(14.8)	2123.000	(11.2)	77.229	(16.4)	2486.040	(12.4)	140.000	(16.0)	3377.300	(14.6)
Total employment	419.753	(100.0)	18964.100	(100.0)	472.320	(100.0)	20002.240	(100.0)	875.000	(100.0)	23186.000	(100.0)
Total population	1140.780		46500.000		1351.710		49778.540		2300.000		59760.000	
Activity rate (%)	36.8		40.8		34.9		40.2		38.0		38.8	

[a] The 1985 figures for AMM are taken from the Livre Blanc de l'AMM.
[b] The 1985 figures for France are taken from the Ducros-Fraisse report.

Some large-scale and modern industrial installations had been developed. At Gardanne a large aluminium plant processed imported bauxite, and in the west of the region around the Étang de Berre, new enterprises in the rapidly growing oil, petrochemical, and aircraft manufacturing sectors had been established. The plants concerned were, however, externally controlled and, for the most part, capital intensive. As a result, relatively little employment was provided.

Starting out from these problems the authors of the structure plan projected and set as targets an increase in the active population of AMM of more than 400 000 people between 1968 and 1985 and of more than 800 000 people by the year 2000. (The structure plan was approved in December 1969.) During the period 1962-1968, 11 000 new jobs had been created each year. In the plan a marked increase in the rate of job creation was envisaged: 17 000 jobs per annum were to be created during the Sixth Plan, 24 000 per annum during the Seventh Plan, and 33 000 per annum during the Eighth Plan. This increase in employment was to be accompanied by an increase in the population of AMM from 1.4 million people in 1968, to 2.3 million in 1985, and 3.2 million in the year 2000. As a result, the area's activity rate was expected to increase from 34.9% in 1968, to 38% in 1985, and to 40% in 2000.

In addition, significant changes in the structure of employment were envisaged, with the tertiary sector declining in relative importance and a substantial increase occurring in the number of industrial jobs. By 1985 the development of the port and industrial zone at Fos was expected to (1) generate 30 000 new jobs in port activities, in energy production, and in the petrochemical and metal manufacturing sectors, (2) attract 50 000 new jobs in upstream and downstream activities, and (3) induce 80 000 new jobs in the building industry, public works, public services, and private services. The remaining 240 000 new jobs expected by 1985 were to be generated by complementary activities. Of the latter, some of the most important were to be stimulated by the development of Marseilles as a high-level service centre which, with the development of the maritime industrial development zone at Fos, was intended to elevate the region to the status of a growth pole of European dimensions.

At the moment when the Sixth Plan was being formulated the official view was that 12 000 new jobs would be created at Fos by 1975 and that an additional 18 000 new jobs would be generated by the multiplier effects of the zone's activities. However, these forecasts and the longer-term projections included in the original structure plan proved to be exceptionally ambitious. Soon afterwards the projections were reduced dramatically: instead of 160 000 new jobs by 1985, only 80 000 were, it was said, going to be generated by the development of the port and industrial zone. The estimate of 30 000 jobs by 1985 for the complex itself was, however, retained. In subsequent years the employment estimates were reduced still further. In 1975, for example, the figure for the expected number of jobs in the zone's primary industries in 1985 was revised downwards by the Mission Interministérielle pour l'Aménagement de la Région de Fos–Étang de Berre (MIAFEB) to between 15000 and 20000 jobs.

The reasons for these revisions were twofold. First, employment was hit by the crisis of the 1970s. Second, it was increasingly felt that there was likely to be less diversification of the regional economy than had originally been anticipated. Owing in particular to the quality of the communications network linking the area with the rest of the national territory and the absence of significant external economies, only a small proportion of the new industrial jobs generated by the project needed, it was realised, to be located near to Fos (see Kinsey, 1978, pages 247–250). Increasingly, the expectation was that the only activities that were going to be attracted to the region in the near future were those which would generate only small amounts of direct and indirect local employment in relation to the capital advanced.

Not only did the development of the Fos maritime industial development zone not have the effects on the level of employment envisaged by the early structure planning documents and by the authors of the Sixth Plan, it also created severe disequilibria on the local labour market.

The simultaneous and rapid development of the principal industrial installations led to an extremely and unexpectedly rapid increase and an equally rapid and unplanned fall in employment in the temporary tasks associated with construction (figure 11.4). Almost all of the large plants were built in the early 1970s within a few years of decisions by each of the companies concerned to locate at Fos. In particular, the SOLMER works was, considering its size, developed very quickly indeed. The reason for this lay, of course, in the wish to maximise the profitability of the project. After these few years, however, the level of construction activity on the site and in the surrounding region was very much lower.

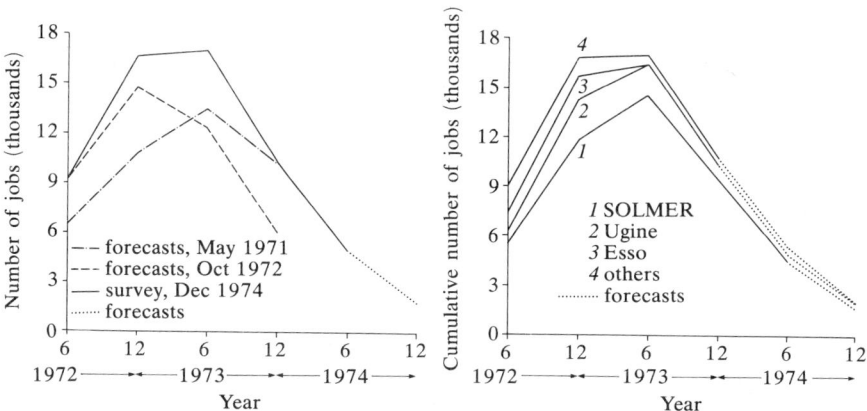

Figure 11.4. The evolution of employment in construction on the Fos maritime industrial development zone. Source: Cultiaux (1975, page 61).

Very fast construction could, however, only be accomplished by making widespread use of an unorganised and mobile labour force composed of workers who were willing to work for long hours in poor and often dangerous working conditions. Construction workers also had to be prepared to endure long journeys to work and to put up with bad living conditions. Several factors were at the root of these problems. One was the speed with which the zone was developed and the anarchy of the site's development. (On the chaos that accompanied the construction of the complex see Paillard, 1981, chapter 3.) Advance planning was woefully inadequate, as was the coordination of the different activities involved in the site's development. The local road network was quite incapable of coping with the construction traffic and the journeys of the areas's new residents. In addition, major delays occurred in the supply of housing and services, with the most serious problems occurring with the large influx of construction workers. In 1983, for example, nearly 18 000 workers were employed on the site, yet only 6 000 temporary lodgings were provided. As a result, immense strain was placed on the area's existing social fabric.

Not surprisingly, a high proportion of this labour force was composed of immigrant and temporary workers. Evidence on the origin of the construction workers is limited. But when the number of workers employed in construction on the site reached its peak of about 17 000 early in 1973, between 10 000 and 12 000 of them were believed to be immigrants.

The completion of the bulk of the construction work was accompanied by a sharp increase in unemployment in the area. One reason for this was that the number of jobs in construction activities exceeded by a substantial amount the number of permanent and temporary workers required to operate the port and industrial installations.

In December 1973, 5 233 people were permanently employed in the main establishments, and smaller firms located in the port and industrial zone employed another 500 or so people (table 11.7). Between December 1970 and June 1973, 7 236 additional permanent jobs, of which 2 330 were industrial jobs, were created in the commune of Fos and in the six neighbouring communes. Quite a high proportion of the increase in employment in this slightly wider area was concentrated in the communes of Fos and Martigues. But a much lower proportion than was expected occurred in the manufacturing sector. By the end of 1975 the number of permanent jobs stood at 8 834 compared with the peak figure of about 17 000 in construction and the target of 12 000 permanent jobs included in the Sixth Plan.

A second reason explaining the rise in unemployment was that some of the permanent jobs created by the incoming firms were of a type that did not match the industrial traditions or the employment needs of the region. Furthermore, the inadequate development of industrial training programmes meant that the local population was not given much opportunity of adapting to the needs of the new enterprises. Instead, many of the jobs created by the new companies were given to workers from outside of the region. Of the 4739 workers employed by SOLMER at the end of March 1974, only 40% came from the three local départements. Nearly 40% had been transferred from Lorraine, and the rest came from other parts of France and from abroad. In fact SOLMER consciously sought to recruit labour at a national level by setting up recruitment centres in Lyon and Paris as well as in Fos, Marseilles, and Montpellier (Cultiaux, 1975, page 64).

Table 11.7. The growth of permanent employment (in thousands) by company on the Fos maritime industrial development zone, 1970-1982. Sources: first six columns Cultiaux (1975, page 61) and rest of data PAM (1983).

	Dec 1970	Dec 1971	Dec 1972	Dec 1973	Dec 1974	Dec 1975	Oct 1975
SOLMER	–	300	980	3432	6082	6582	6582
Ugine-Aciers	–	2	62	722	1020	1128	1128
Esso	196	225	294	298	298	301	301
ICI	–	20	170	186	198	198	198
CFEM	–	1	138	232	308	246	246
Ferifos							139
DPF							39
AL							57
GDF							50
PCUK							105
SPLSE							119
PAM							358
Others[a]	187	216	363	363	363	379	762
Total	383	764	2007	5233	8269	8834	9322
	Sept 1976	Autumn 1977	Dec 1978	Dec 1979	Dec 1980	Dec 1981	Dec 1982
SOLMER	6565	6898	7114	6948		6153	6187
Ugine-Aciers	1146	1222	1169	1112		1141	1167
Esso	317	335	346	373		374	370
ICI	194	189	185	154		149	163
CFEM	230	215	145	138		229	261
Ferifos	133	118	114	112		117	122
DPF	40	41	43	42		44	45
AL	58	58	59	58		59	53
GDF	53	54	54	62		67	79
PCUK	108	117	144	216		554	557
SPLSE	120	124	125	126		123	125
PAM	392	409	422	425		521	528
Others	796	804	817	825		931	952
Total	9356	9780	9920	9766	9535	9531	9657

[a] PAM, SPLSE, GDF, AL, DPF, and other employers.

The workers arriving from other parts of the country tended to occupy a particularly high proportion of the more skilled positions, while locally-recruited workers tended to get the less skilled jobs. In fact the recruitment of workers from other regions was frequently explained by reference to the existence of local shortages of skilled labour. Any lack of the requisite skills on the part of the local population must, however, itself be explained. In the case of Fos several particularly important factors can be identified. One was the recruitment strategies of the firms themselves. The second was the region's different industrial traditions. A third was the lack of success and limited extent of industrial training and retraining programmes. As the port and industrial zone were developed a number of public and private agencies with the tasks of recruiting and training labour were of course set up. The incoming companies were likewise engaged in this kind of activity. However, priority was given to construction work. In addition, some attempts were made to modify the local educational system and to set up training centres with a view to providing potential workers with new skills and to inculcating the psychological attitudes thought to be appropriate and necessary for modern industrial work. These steps were, however, out of phase with the launching of new industrial activities in the area (see Robert, 1974, page 72; Cultiaux, 1975, pages 64-66).

As a result then of the investments in the port and industrial zone and induced investments in neighbouring communes, employment and the size of the active population increased, but by less than was anticipated. Not only were the direct employment effects of the firms setting up at Fos much lower than the expectations of the zone's planners as depicted in successive sets of employment forecasts. The indirect effects were also much smaller than expected, and indirect job creation occurred much more slowly than expected. One reason for this was that some local firms went to the wall (see also chapter 9, section 9.1). The second was simply that the magnitude and speed of multiplier effects were overestimated.

The balance between industrial and service employment in the region was not significantly altered. Nor is the development of the zone now expected to overcome the problems of local unemployment and underemployment. In particular the industrial growth that did occur had no significant impact on the problems of female employment experienced in the region. At the end of March 1973, only 16% of all jobs, excluding those in building and public works, in the seven communes around the Golfe de Fos were for women, compared with 32% nationally. Yet the industry attracted to the area created jobs primarily for men.

In addition, the new industries did not significantly increase the quality of the jobs available for the region's inhabitants. In the early stages about one half of the jobs created in new factories in the region of Fos and the Étang de Berre were for unskilled workers and labourers (Cultiaux, 1975, page 64). Even though this proportion may have fallen over the years, it has had particularly important repercussions on the development of the region.

In particular, it meant that the effective demand for housing and services was relatively weak. At the same time, growing pressures on the existing stock of housing led to a rapid increase in housing prices and to strong wage inflation.

The policy of establishing a maritime industrial development area at Fos was, it seems, relatively successful in encouraging the development of internationally competitive enterprises in sectors producing energy and intermediate goods. In the early 1980s most of the plants were considered efficient and modern. In 1981, for example, the SOLMER steelworks along with the coastal complex at Dunkirk needed only three hours of work per tonne of steel produced. As a result, it had a level of productivity that was amongst the highest in Europe and comparable with that of Japanese plants. With the exception of Ugine-Aciers, the industrial establishments on the zone, though not all of the workers they employed, were, consequently, able to ride out the crises in their sectors.

The pursuit of profitability and the satisfaction of human needs are, however, contradictory goals. In particular, the aim of maximising growth did not prove capable of reconciliation with the objective of planned regional development. On the cost side, the development of the port and industrial zone was expensive both in terms of the amount of expenditure involved and in terms of the dislocation caused in the region and in other parts of the country. On the benefit side, some jobs were provided. The jobs created were, however, few in relation to the capital advanced.

The aim espoused by growth-centre theorists of creating a broad-based and integrated industrial structure in the region by encouraging the implantation of propulsive industries was thus not achieved. Instead, the region was endowed with a series of cathedrals in the desert: isolated and large-scale industrial installations whose local multiplier effects are extremely limited because of their incorporation into national and international organisation and marketing structures. To a large extent the development of the complex reinforced the role of the Marseilles metropolitan region as an importer of raw materials and an exporter of semifinished goods to other parts of the country, and as an area dependent on incoming firms for technical knowledge and on in-migrating workers to fill skilled jobs. Consequently, the aim of contributing to a rapid process of economic growth was not achieved. In 1982, only 22 000 jobs were, it was argued, a result of the Fos operation, instead of the original forecast of 77 000 to 197 000, and the area's population stood at fewer than 60 000 people instead of the predicted 210 000 to 540 000 (see Planque, 1983, page 5).

One explanatory factor was, of course, the onset of the crisis. A second was the fact that the multiplier and polarising effects of the development were seriously overestimated. With the internationalisation of production and with the transformation of the spheres of communications and transport, economies of agglomeration were weakened, and integrated industrial complexes were much less likely to develop. In the 1970s, in particular, the spatial dynamics of capitalist industrialisation was, in other words, undergoing a profound change that the planners had not anticipated. Moreover, any realistic assessment of the impact of other similar complexes, including the one at Taranto in Italy, should have generated some scepticism about the validity of the concepts of spatial polarisation on which the planners had drawn.

In 1984, the closing of one of the main establishments on the zone was announced. Added to existing employment difficulties, the decision to close Ugine-Acier's ultramodern plant was instrumental in the designation of an area that was a growth pole of the late 1960s and early 1970s as a zone that was, in the mid-1980s, in crisis.

11.4 Regional and urban planning in the Marseilles metropolitan region

So far, the creation of a maritime industrial development area at Fos has been interpreted as an expression of a correspondence between the material and social conditions prevailing at Fos and the changing needs of large enterprises in sectors producing energy and intermediate goods and of capitals engaged in maritime transport.

On one side of this equation lay the strategies of capital in these branches of production and circulation and the aims and actions of the other agents participating in the development of the port and industrial zone. In the last section, these strategies were shown to be a part of processes of accumulation unfolding in and shaped by an economic and political context in which the economic and spatial organisation of the activities involved were undergoing change in order to enable them to expand and remain competitive and profitable on international markets. In spite of the fact that it was largely determined by capitalist interests, state action also, however, played an important part in regulating the reproduction of capital and influencing processes of economic development. As a result, emphasis was also placed on the ways in which the strategies pursued by capital were shaped by processes of state intervention.

On the other side of the equation were the changing material and social conditions in which these processes unfolded, by which they were conditioned, and which they modified (see also chapter 1, section 1.3). In earlier sections these conditions were themselves interpreted as products of the previous evolution of the local economic and political system. But of particular importance was the recent modification of these conditions as a result of (1) the infrastructural policies pursued by the port authorities and the state, and (2) steps taken by the state and by the firms investing in the area to assemble workers to construct and operate the port and industrial installations.

Of course none of these processes were simply technical. In each case their real content was one of class struggles and conflicts. Included were the struggles involving the steel companies, whose aims were largely determined by a need to increase the rate of profit, and steelworkers seeking to preserve their jobs. In addition, conflicts occurred between the central administration, whose aim was the construction of the new complex, and significant numbers of the inhabitants of AMM, who were opposed to the new model of regional development and to its imposition from above by capital and the state.

As has also been indicated, the planning and development of the port and industrial zone at Fos were also presented as part of a policy of planned regional development. What I now want to do is to approach this side of the problem from a slightly different perspective: instead of asking whether the project might or might not meet regional development goals, I shall consider the ways in which regional planning was or was not essential for the success of the project.

The process of economic expansion initiated at Fos was bound to have repercussions extending beyond the industrial zone. Consequently, the implantation of new enterprises had to be coordinated with the overall restructuring and development of the regional economy. The success of the new maritime industrial development area depended, however, not simply upon the success of measures connected with the organisation of production and of the market for labour at Fos and in the rest of the region. It also depended upon the implementation of measures connected with the development of the spheres of consumption and social reproduction, and with the organisation of a system of political and ideological domination around the new port and industrial zone (see Bleitrach and Chenu, 1977).

The segmentation of workers in the sphere of production into a group of relatively stable and permanent workers on the one hand and a group of insecure and marginalised workers on the other was carried over into the sphere of social reproduction. A network of dwellings and services had to be provided in a coordinated way to meet the needs of the people attracted to the area. In addition, the social tensions generated by the resulting changes in the structure of the region and by the contradictions between the optimal conditions of expansion of the new enterprises and the optimal conditions of life of the region's inhabitants had to be managed. The project had, in other words, to be situated in a broader programme for the development of the region. Support given to the process of industrialisation had to be accompanied by other forms of state action aimed at managing the development process and the contradictions it engendered. Included under this heading was the setting up of institutional structures adequate to these new tasks.

Accordingly, with the development of the region in the direction planned by capital and the state, the institutional framework of state action was itself restructured (see chapter 3, section 3.10).

In February 1966, in line with the policy of developing Marseilles as one of the métropoles d'équilibre, the Organisation d'Études d'Aménagement de l'Aire Métropolitaine Marseillaise (Marseilles OREAM) was set up. Its role was the preparation of a long-term structure plan for a region containing fifty-nine of the one hundred and nineteen communes in the left-wing-dominated département of the Bouches du Rhône.

An OREAM was an interministrial study group which was largely financed by DATAR and was closely dependent upon the central administration. It had the task of preparing, in conjunction with the elected representatives included on its coordinating committee, a draft plan and a *schéma d'aménagement* specifying the general pattern and the main stages in the development of a metropolitan area until the year 2000. Once approved, the schéma d'aménagement was to form the basis on which decisions about a number of public investment projects were to be made and the framework within which more detailed land-use plans were to be prepared.

In the case of the Marseilles region, the Livre Blanc de l'Aire Métropolitaine Marseillaise was approved by the government in January 1969, and the Schéma d'Aménagement de l'Aire Métropolitaine Marseillaise was approved by CIAT in December 1969. The outline strategy of the schéma d'aménagement was based on the assumption of an increase in the population of AMM of about 2 million people in a period of about thirty years. More specifically, the area's population was expected to expand from 1.35 million inhabitants in 1968 to 2.3 million in 1985 and 3.2 million in the year 2000. In addition, employment was to increase by some 400 000 jobs by 1985 and by about 800 000 jobs by the year 2000, with some 160 000 of the first 400 000 new jobs being created directly or indirectly as a result of the development of the port and industrial complex at Fos.

The outline strategy's main proposals were for a new use of space that involved two main processes. One was the development of Marseilles as a centre of managerial and high-level tertiary activities in accordance with the strategy for promoting métropoles d'équilibre and the development of industrial activities to the west of the Étang de Berre. The second was a dense and discontinuous process of urbanisation that involved the expansion of existing towns rather than the creation of new ones, namely, the expansion of Marseilles, Aix, and Arles, and of towns in the areas southeast and west of the Étang de Berre.

The urban areas of Marseilles and Aix were to be developed as tertiary centres predominantly but with nearby industrial zones. In the case of Marseilles, the central area was to be renewed and the use of land changed to make way for high-level tertiary activities, managerial and administrative functions connected with the industrial zone at Fos, and luxury housing. In addition, secondary commercial centres were to be developed, and industrial and some service activities were to be decentralised under the impact of rising rents and the restructuring of the urban area. In the end the development of Marseilles did not really complement that of Fos, and the city was not very successful in attracting high-level tertiary activities. Nevertheless, the process of urban renewal envisaged by the plan created many opportunities for members of the local bourgeoisie to engage in land speculation and property development. Port activities were displaced towards the west, and the city was deindustrialised as existing enterprises collapsed or moved out. The zone around Vitrolles to the southeast of the Étang de Berre was to be a centre for industrial activities decentralised from Marseilles, whereas Vitrolles itself was to be given new tertiary functions.

Because of the development of economic activity at Fos and of related activities to the north of the port and industrial zone, the area around the Golfe de Fos and on the west bank of the Étang de Berre was expected to experience rapid demographic growth, with its population increasing fivefold from some 100 000 inhabitants in the late 1960s to 550 000 inhabitants by the end of the century. It was pointed out that this increase in the area's population would lead to a major increase in the demand for housing and for various items of collective consumption. In the plan it was proposed that this demand should be met by expanding existing urban centres. Much of the increase in population was to be accommodated in the two principal centres of Martigues–St Mitre-les-Remparts in the south and of Miramas–St Chamas in the north, in the intermediate centre of Istres, and in the external centre of Salon. Some growth was also to occur around Port St Louis.

In other words, population growth was to occur around Marseilles, Aix, and in the zones east and west of the Étang de Berre. In addition, the area around Arles in the northwest of the region was scheduled for some development.

Correlated with this plan for the distribution of population and economic activity was a set of transport investment proposals. In the outline strategy the various elements of the urban system were to be linked together with a much improved transport network, and links between AMM and the rest of the national territory were to be improved. In particular, the intraregional road system was to be developed. Two motorways were to lead into the north of Marseilles, one was to be built to the east, and one was to cross the urban agglomeration. A boundary road was to be constructed around the Fos maritime industrial development area, and fast roads or motorways were to link Fos with Arles, with Marseilles, and with the Paris–Marseilles motorway at Salon (figure 11.5).

In short, the schéma d'aménagement set out, in the light of the establishment of a port and industrial complex at Fos and of a métropole d'équilibre at Marseilles, a broad sketch of the long-term restructuring and development of AMM. It outlined proposals for the provision of transport and communication facilities, and it included plans for the development and equipping of industrial sites and urban areas around the new industrial complex. It was thus not surprising when the government's approval of the schéma d'aménagement was given the status of a national regional planning directive.

Since about one half of the expected increase in population was to occur in the region of Fos and the Étang de Berre, more detailed structure plans had to be prepared for this area. The task of preparing a Schéma Directeur de l'Aménagement et de l'Urbanisme for the zones east and west of the

Étang de Berre was given to a study group set up in October 1969 called the Mission d'Études et d'Aménagement des Rives de l'Étang de Berre (MAEB).

What MAEB proposed was that in the west, development should be concentrated in two broad areas within easy commuting distance of Fos. One was composed of Port de Bouc, St Mitre-les-Remparts, and the parts of the commune of Martigues to the north of the Caronte Channel. The combined population of these three districts was planned to increase from 43 300 inhabitants in 1968 to 80 000 in 1976 and to 150 000 in 1985. The second zone included Istres and Miramas. In these communes the population was planned to increase from 23 900 people in 1968 to 42 000 in 1976 and to 104 000 in 1985. In the east, population was expected to increase from 42 000 inhabitants in 1968 to 80 000 in 1976 and to 165 000 in 1985. The growth was to be concentrated in Vitrolles and in the northwest of the commune of Les Pennes Mirabeau (figure 11.5). These proposals were approved by an interministerial committee in February 1971 (Cultiaux, 1975, pages 25-33).

At about the same time, a special programme for Fos and the Étang de Berre was included in the Sixth Plan: quite clearly, considerable importance was attached by the state to the development of the maritime industrial development area, and regional planning activities were seen as having a significant part to play in coordinating processes of industrialisation and

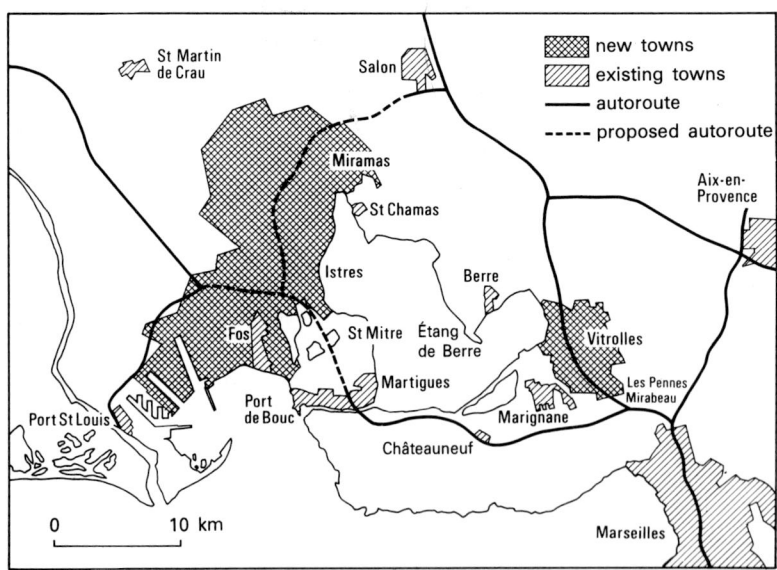

Figure 11.5. New town and infrastructural investment in the département of the Bouches du Rhône.

urbanisation at a regional level. Included in this programme were three projects involving (1) the development of the port and industrial zone, (2) the construction of a road system, and (3) an urbanisation programme for the region of Fos and the Étang de Berre. The third project was based on the one formulated by CIAT. 27 500 new dwellings were to be constructed, of which 21 500 were to be built in the western zone. Services were to be provided. And sites for industrial and service activities linked with the leading industries at Fos were to be developed. In addition, plans were to be prepared and land was to be assembled for subsequent urbanisation. Some 85% of central government expenditure on this programme was included as a subprogramme in the Sixth Plan's finalised programme for new town development. Consequently, the project was to benefit from the prioritisation and individualisation of finalised programmes in the annual state budget. Furthermore, it was to be controlled largely by the Groupe Central des Villes Nouvelles (GCVN).

Up to this point the only role of the local authorities had been one of being consulted on the main options of the development plan. Once these plans had been prepared, however, the state had to secure the cooperation of the local authorities. The reason for this was that implementation could only proceed with their help because of the role of local authorities in financing and carrying out urban development activities. The central administration also wanted the local authorities to be regrouped and consolidated, in part so that their activities could be coordinated. Several other considerations also had an impact on the actual course of action chosen by the central administration. On the one hand, some of the companies were hesitant to proceed with the construction of new industrial installations at Fos until plans for the provision of housing and services were being implemented. On the other, the central state was anxious to reduce the capacity of local communist municipalities to influence the pattern and speed of the process of urbanisation.

In these conditions the state decided to bypass as far as it could the existing local authorities and the traditional administrative agencies in the region, and opted for a centrally directed form of new town development. In October 1971, CIAT decided to include fourteen communes in the Étang de Berre region in an Établissement Public d'Aménagement (EPA), and in December 1971, on the recommendation of GCVN, but against the advice of the Conseil Général of the département of the Bouches du Rhône and of the coordinating committee of the Marseilles OREAM, it proposed that the Boscher Law be applied.

The Boscher Law, which had been passed in July 1970, was designed to overcome some of the technical and political problems of new town development. What it proposed was (1) that new towns be separated from existing communes to exempt existing urban areas from the expenditure incurred in meeting the needs of the incoming population, and (2) that the financial resources of areas of revenue generating industrial and commercial development be fused with those of areas of residential development requiring large amounts of expenditure on housing and services.

In areas of new urbanisation designated by the state, a new authority, whose finances were to be detached from those of the commune or communes from which it had been formed, was to be set up. If the communes involved wished to participate in the planning and development of the new urban area, the new authority could assume the form of (1) a Syndicat Communautaire d'Aménagement (SCA), administered by a committee whose members were to be elected by the existing councils of the participating communes, or (2) a Communauté Urbaine. Otherwise it was to assume the form of a separate Ensemble Urbain. In each case the regrouping of communes was to be accompanied by many special advantages, including the provision of capital grants, fiscal exemptions, increased subsidies, special credit facilities, and accelerated approval of public works projects.

Control over the process of urbanisation and the task of implementing broad plans for the development of the area were, however, to be carried out by a technical planning unit. This unit could be either a Société d'Économie Mixte, which would be dominated largely by the participating communes, or an Établissement Public d'Aménagement (EPA). An EPA would have on its administrative council at least equal municipal and state representation, but would be largely controlled by the central administration. Apart from government representation on its administrative council, its director, the composition of its council, its powers, the method of appointment and powers of its president, and its objectives were to be determined by the Conseil d'État. Such a technical agency would generally be responsible for the preparation of planning studies, land acquisition, and activities connected with site development and infrastructure provision.

In the case of the area around the Étang de Berre the state did not try to include all of the communes affected by the process of urbanisation that was stimulated by the development of the port and industrial zone at Fos in a single body. Instead, it proposed the establishment of one SCA composed of two communes to the east of the Étang de Berre, and two SCAs to the west. Of the ones in the west, one was to be composed of the towns of Fos, Istres, and Miramas, which all had right-wing majorities, whereas the other was to be formed by three of the communes with communist majorities, namely, Martigues, Port de Bouc, and St Mitre-les-Remparts. The remaining communist-held communes of Port St Louis and St Chamas were to be excluded (see figure 11.6).

The criteria used in selecting the participating communes and in drawing the boundaries were designed in part to ensure that the new institutions covered the main areas of new urbanisation and combined areas of revenue generating activities, such as Fos and Martigues, with those zoned mainly for housing and services. The areas were also drawn up, however, so as to ensure that the new institutions would not be dominated by the opposition.

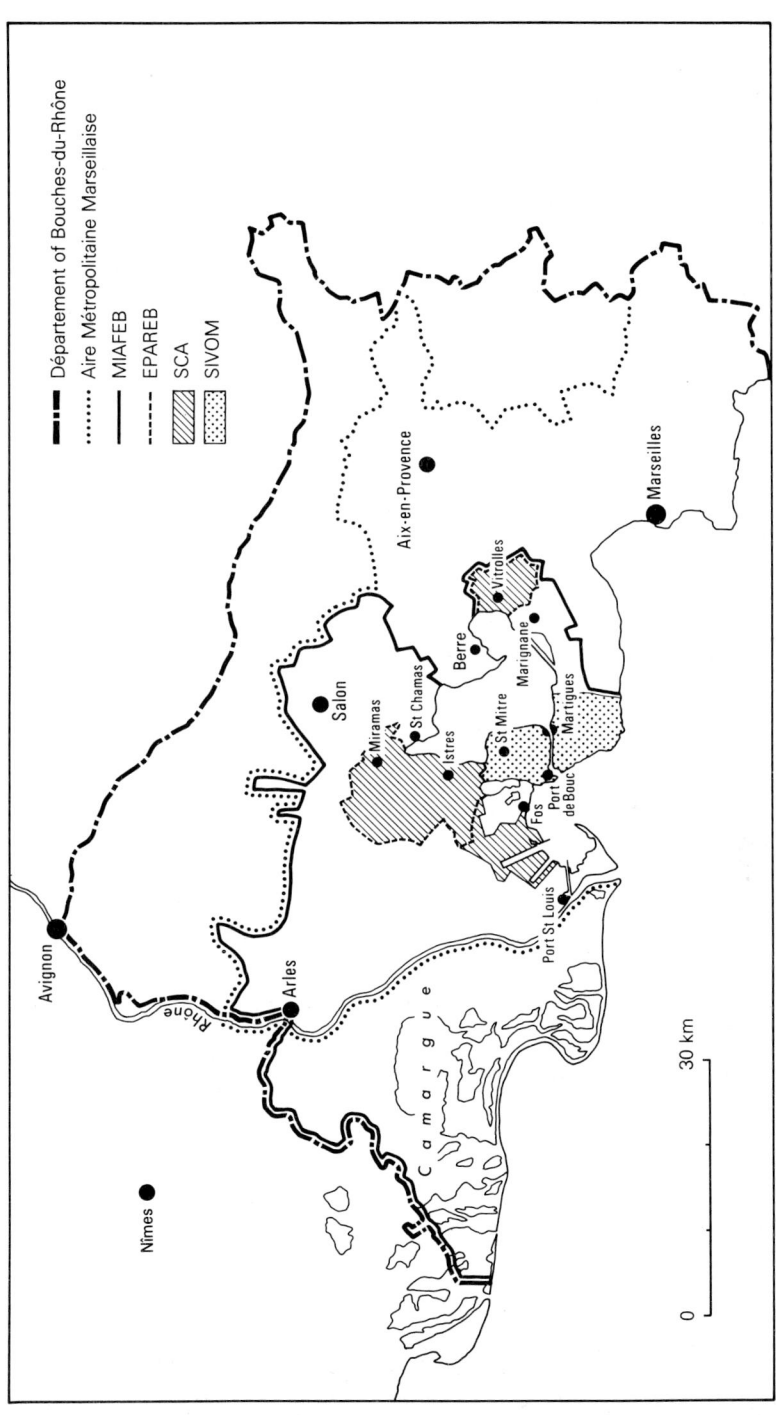

Figure 11.6. The political geography of the département of the Bouches du Rhône.

In addition, the state attempted to set up an EPA rather than a locally responsive Société d'Économie Mixte as the technical unit. The intention of the state was that this agency should carry out planning activities not just in the areas included in the SCAs but in fourteen communes in the area around the Étang de Berre.

This attempt by the central state to set up new and more centralised administrative bodies and to implement a process of urbanisation whose characteristics it had itself largely determined stimulated very widespread and almost unanimous opposition from local authorities in the region and resulted in a confrontation between local politicians and the central government which lasted right the way through 1972. The establishment of ad hoc bodies also interfered with the traditional responsibilities of the field services of the administration, and so the government's proposals were also opposed from these quarters. The ensuing battle has been documented by Vieille (1977, pages 386-406). (On these events see also Paillard, 1981, chapters 4-6.)

The struggle that resulted is in fact of more general significance. After the early 1960s the French state made frequent attempts to bypass local bodies, to set up new institutions providing a new and more direct link between local societies and the summit of the state, and to impose new forms of class domination and direction compatible with a new phase and specific form of capitalist development. As a result, many conflicts were generated at the periphery of French society.

In the case of AMM, general opposition from the local municipalities was led by the Mayor of Marseilles and was directed against the application of the Boscher Law. (The city of Marseilles was in fact a socialist fiefdom headed by Gaston Deferre.) The application of this law was said to be unacceptable. On the one hand, it involved the establishment of organisations which reduced and interfered with traditional communal rights. On the other, it was seen as an instrument that was being used to reshape the region politically by subdividing it in an artificial way, by discriminating between different local authorities, and by vesting authority in centrally controlled bodies rather than in intercommunal organisations covering the whole of the area affected by the development of the Fos maritime industrial development zone. The Boscher Law was also thought to be technically inapplicable. First, it was argued that the provisions of the law were unsuited to developments that involved the rapid expansion of an existing urban system with established services in which, as a result of pressure from local representatives, new urban growth was not to assume the form of independent satellite units. Second, the urbanisation process differed from the one characteristic of most new towns in that the rate of population growth depended directly on the rate of growth of local industrial employment.

The central government's initial reaction to this opposition was twofold. On the one hand, it first sought to exploit some of the differences between the communes. To this end most emphasis was placed on the cleavages between (1) the powerful metropolis of Marseilles and the other satellite local authorities to its north and west, and (2) left-wing and right-wing communes. On the other hand, the central administration attempted to use its control over funds for urban development to secure compliance with its preferred plan.

Nevertheless, some of the local authorities held out and remained adamant about their unwillingness to cooperate with the state on the terms it had spelled out. In the region itself, mounting criticism of the privileged treatment of the steel industry, of the appalling living conditions of many of the temporary construction workers, and of the potential environmental effects of the project was successfully directed against the central administration. In addition, serious delays were occurring in the provision of housing and of other types of social infrastructure. As a result, the state was eventually forced to retreat from its original position. But by making a series of separate agreements, in which it made significant concessions, with about one half of the communes involved, the central administration succeeded not only in securing the cooperation of at least some of the local authorities but also in keeping the general initiative. The main agreements were the following.

(1) In December 1972 the communes of Fos, Istres, and Miramas formed an SCA. Contrary to the original proposal, the government agreed that this SCA should include the whole of the communes of Istres and Miramas so that these communes would benefit from the special financial advantages available for new town development even for projects occurring in older neighbourhoods.

The government also had to compromise with the Mayor of Fos. One of his main demands was that the commune be developed to a greater extent than was envisaged in structure plans prepared for the area by the OREAM and the MAEB. Because of its proximity to the industrial zone and because of the position of the commune in relation to the airport at Istres only a relatively small increase in the town's residential population had been proposed. This decision conflicted with the interests of those sections of the population with something to gain from new development at Fos. The Mayor's second main demand, which was related to the first, was that controls over pollution and over the deterioration of the environment be increased. The government made concessions in relation to both of these demands. In addition, it granted the town certain special rights with respect to the collection of taxes. The participation of the commune of Fos in the SCA was thus secured.

Soon afterwards the state had to step in again to settle disagreements between Fos and the other two communes over the structure of control of the SCA. On this occasion the compromise organised by the state was once again relatively favourable to Fos.

(2) The communist municipalities of Martigues, St Mitre-les-Remparts, and Port de Bouc refused to join an SCA or to be associated with the proposed EPA. All they would accept was the establishment of a multipurpose, intercommunal district benefitting from the full financial advantages available under the Boscher Law. By holding out and blocking projects for which they had not received adequate financial support from the state, the government was eventually forced to allow them to form a Syndicat Intercommunal à Vocation Multiple (SIVOM) as a means of coordinating development and of providing services at an intercommunal level. The SIVOM was set up in July 1973 and was given special financial support by the state. This support was broadly in line with what the municipalities had been demanding.

(3) On the east of the Étang de Berre the commune of Vitrolles won acceptance of its demand to manage its own urbanisation and was given a status equivalent to that of an SCA.

In the case of the remaining communes, which were to be less affected by the urbanisation process connected with the development of the port and industrial zone, and which were not included in the group of communes whose urbanisation was to be aided by the funds allotted to the finalised new town development programme incorporated in the Sixth Plan, assistance was to be given in relation to specific projects from funds deducted annually from the Fonds d'Intervention pour l'Aménagement du Territoire (FIAT).

In March 1973 the state also managed to set up the Établissement Public d'Aménagement des Rives de l'Étang de Berre (EPAREB). However, its area of operation was reduced from the area that had originally been proposed, to include only the three communes participating in the SCA and the commune of Vitrolles. In addition, its management council was to include a majority of local elected representatives, and its activities were to be restricted to land-use operations. In particular, the granting of construction contracts was to remain in the hands of the communes.

What the state lost on this count was, however, largely regained through the creation in the same month of the Mission Interministérielle pour l'Aménagement de la Région de Fos–Étang de Berre (MIAFEB). MIAFEB was a new, locally-based interministerial planning mission set up to succeed the MAEB. Twenty-four communes were included within its boundaries. In this broad region MIAFEB was given extremely wide powers to enable it to study and plan the development process, to coordinate, finance, and implement the plans it prepared, and to carry out associated programmes of public works. More specifically, it had two sets of functions. On the one hand, it was given the role of coordinating interventions by the different state services connected with the analysis and implementation of regional planning policies, equipment provision, and the public financing of development. On the other, it assumed the functions of the traditional departmental administration in the field of public works: the elaboration of planning documents such as Schémas Directeurs de l'Aménagement et de l'Urbanisme (SDAUs) and Plans d'Occupation du Sol (POSs), land assembly, control over the allocation of construction permits, development of the main drainage system, and the building of roads and motorways (Cultiaux, 1975, pages 25-33). On these issues MIAFEB was only required to consult elected officials and was directly answerable to the Prefect.

On the initiative of the Mayor of Marseilles, fourteen of the local communes had formed a Syndicat Mixte as a means of coordinating their actions themselves rather than having them coordinated by a body escaping their control. With the setting up of MIAFEB and the establishment in 1975 of the Mission Interministérielle de l'Aménagement des Bouches du Rhône (MIDAM), however, a major imbalance was created between the central administration and the local authorities at the spatial level at which the urban effects of the development of the port and industrial zone had to be coordinated, because no equivalent locally-based representative body existed.

In short, the strong desire of the communes in AMM to preserve their autonomy was exploited, as were some of the material and ideological differences between them. In addition, some concessions were made to the communes most closely connected with the development of the port and industrial zone. As a result, the opposition to the state's original plans for the reorganisation of local government in the region of Fos and the Étang de Berre and to its industrial and regional policies was segmented. The central state gained a substantial degree of control over the urbanisation process. And, albeit with some delay, the main urban planning and equipment decisions included in the Sixth Plan were implemented.

In section 11.1 we saw how the state played a central role in the development at Fos-sur-Mer of a maritime industrial development zone of international dimensions. It organised and financed the assembly of land and the provision of infrastructural equipment, and state-controlled resources were used to aid the concentration and centralisation of capital and industrial restructuring in energy and intermediate-goods production in which some of the enterprises which were to be located at Fos were involved. In this section I have tried to show how centrally-directed forms of regional planning were used as a means of doing two things. One was to alter the structure of the local administration and of local political power. The other was to organise and finance the restructuring of the regional economy and the construction of an urban environment on which the success of a port and industrial zone of national importance depended. Once again, capitalist interests were at stake: in promoting a process of urban development, a variety of opportunities for profitable investment were created for builders and developers and for the large financial groups lying behind them, as well as for those who had acquired development land in the region.

11.5 Conclusion: industry and the urban environment

The early history of the Fos maritime industrial development area ended with the ensuing expansion of the region's population and with the process of urbanisation. In the case of the state, activities connected with the assembly of land continued. Not only was the state anxious to build up land banks in order to facilitate subsequent urban or industrial development. It was also seeking to overcome some of the problems caused by land speculation and by the fragmentation of landownership. But some of the most striking aspects of this story were those surrounding the delays and shortcomings in the provision of housing and services.

Not only with the beginning of the work connected with the construction of the main industrial installations and the sudden expansion of a floating population of workers was housing and service provision inadequate. The provision of housing and of transport, educational, health, social, recreational, and cultural facilities for permanent workers was also subject to delays and shortages in the early years, and was characterised by the mediocrity of much of what was produced.

In the early 1970s, serious housing shortages led to a sharp increase in rents and housing costs, fuelled speculation, and resulted in a large amount of long-distance commuting. Added to this, the early arrival of permanent workers and their allocation to housing ahead of families on housing waiting lists was a source of tension.

The construction programme envisaged by the Sixth Plan was initiated in 1971–1972. In the period 1971–1973, 12 000 new dwellings were started in the seven communes adjacent to the port and industrial zone, but only 7136 were completed, compared with an expected number of 10 600 and an estimated need for 12 500. Of these dwellings, some 55% were Habitations à Loyer Modéré (HLMs).

Very extensive use was made of the Zone d'Aménagement Concerté (ZAC) procedure in house building, since it allowed development to occur on unequipped sites as long as the developers were prepared to put in the necessary amenities. Two consequences followed: (1) rents and selling prices increased rapidly; (2) densities were high, the amounts of open and parking space provided were small, and the quality of much of the collective equipment was poor. Moreover, the unsuitability of high-density housing for workers doing shift work, together with the dependence on public financing as a means of meeting the quantitative housing targets, led to a relative overproduction of local authority rented housing and excess demand for free-standing private dwellings. The distribution of housing thus reinforced social segregation and long-distance commuting.

By the mid-1970s, however, quantitative shortages in the provision of housing were proving to be less serious than they might have been, because of an increase in the recruitment of local workers, lower than expected increases in employment, a stifling of effective demand by increases in housing costs, and the building of new housing in more distant communes.

In its turn, the urban history to which allusion has been made in the last few paragraphs created some of the preconditions for and gave way to a new history. It is the history of the organisation of work in the new industrial installations and in other parts of the regional economy, of the changing patterns of consumption and social reproduction of different sections of the local population, of changes in the systems of political and ideological domination in the region, and of the repercussions of these changes in the region's economic and political structure on the lives and political traditions of its old and new inhabitants. But instead of pursuing this path, which has been explored by Bleitrach and Chenu (1979) and Paillard (1981, chapter 10), we shall switch our attention to the restructuring of the industry on whose implantation the development of the port and industrial zone was largely based.

12

The crisis and restructuring of the French steel industry

The development of the port and industrial zones at Fos-sur-Mer and at Dunkirk was closely bound up with the restructuring of the French steel industry. Not only were new steel mills developed at these sites. With the addition of new capacity on the coast, older plants in the traditional steel-producing areas of the Nord and Lorraine were run down. In this chapter my aim is to focus on this wider context and to outline the development and crisis of this sector of the French economy. [Much of the argument draws on the work of Freyssenet and Imbert (1975a; 1975b) and of Freyssenet (1979a; 1983); additional material has been drawn mainly from official publications. The underlying theoretical concepts have already been introduced in part 1.]

12.1 The French steel industry at the end of the Second World War

At the time of the liberation the French steel industry was made up of about thirty family-based companies and their subsidiaries, and of one hundred and seventy-seven plants, of which sixty-six were integrated. These plants had an annual capacity of some 11 to 12 million tonnes of steel.

The industry was largely based on the exploitation of the deposits of iron ore with a low ore and a high phosphorus content which were to be found in Lorraine, as were the industries in Belgium, Luxembourg, and the Saar. Much of the coking coal and coke used by the French industry was imported from the Ruhr. Not surprisingly, therefore, the main centre of the industry was in Lorraine. (The main centres of steel production are shown in figure 12.1. A more detailed map of Lorraine is provided in figure 12.2.)

The region of Lorraine had been a centre of iron production for more than three hundred years. Its growth as a steel-producing region dates, however, from the discovery in 1878 by Gilchrist and Thomas of a method of making steel from ores with a high phosphorus content. In 1938, works in the region accounted for the production of 78% of the country's pig iron and for 67% of national steel production. Not until the early 1960s did the region begin to lose its dominant position.

At the end of the war this region could be subdivided into several zones. One around Nancy in the South included the Neuves-Maisons, Pompey, and Pont-à-Mousson plants. In the North there was a second steel-producing zone which could itself be divided into several parts:
(1) In the Pays Haut, in the North, the Longwy Basin and the valley of the Chiers contained five integrated plants: Mont-St-Martin, Senelle-Maubeuge, Saulnes, La Chiers, and La Providence à Rehon. Nearby Villerupt had three plants: Aubrives-Villerupt, Micheville, and Audun le Tiche.
(2) The Moselle valley contained the plants of Thionville, Rombas, Hagondange, and Uckange, and the tributary valleys of the Fensch and the

Orne included the Knutange and Hayange steelworks and the Joeuf, Moyeuvre, Homécourt, and Auboué works, respectively.
(3) In addition, there were some rerolling works to the northwest in the Ardennes.
Of these, the Saulnes works, with the exception of its modern wire rod mill which was attached to USINOR's Longwy plant, was closed in the mid-1960s. The Auboué works was closed in 1966. And in 1968, in accordance with a plan for the rationalisation of the iron foundry industry, the Aubrives-Villerupt plant was closed by Pont-à-Mousson SA. In 1970 it was demolished. In 1973 the Moyeuvre works was closed and subsequently demolished. (Most of the works which still existed at the end of the 1960s are indicated in figure 12.2.)

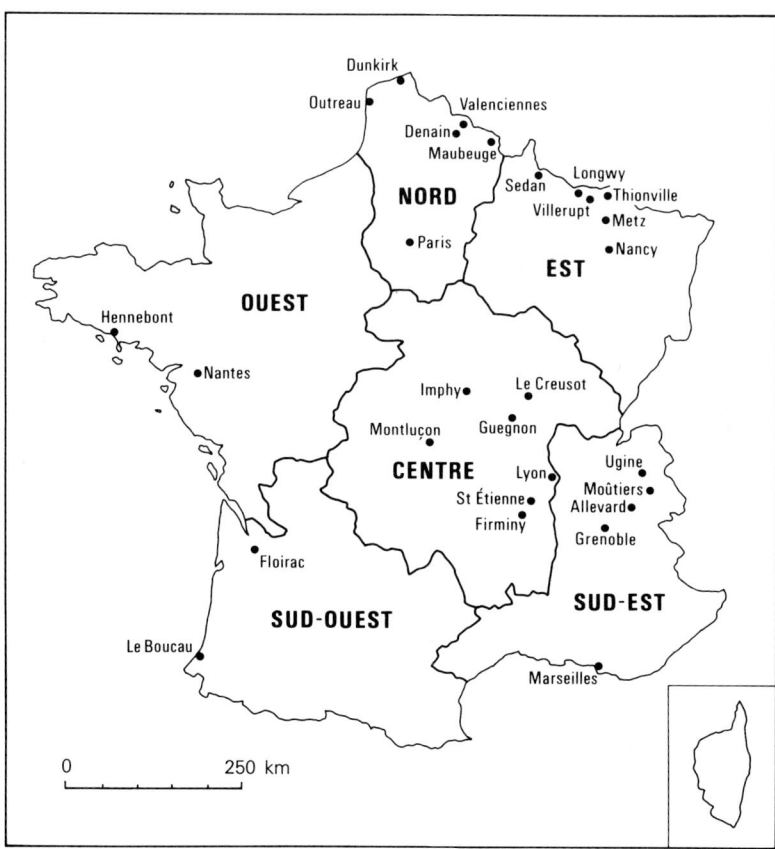

Figure 12.1. The distribution of the French steel industry after the Second World War.

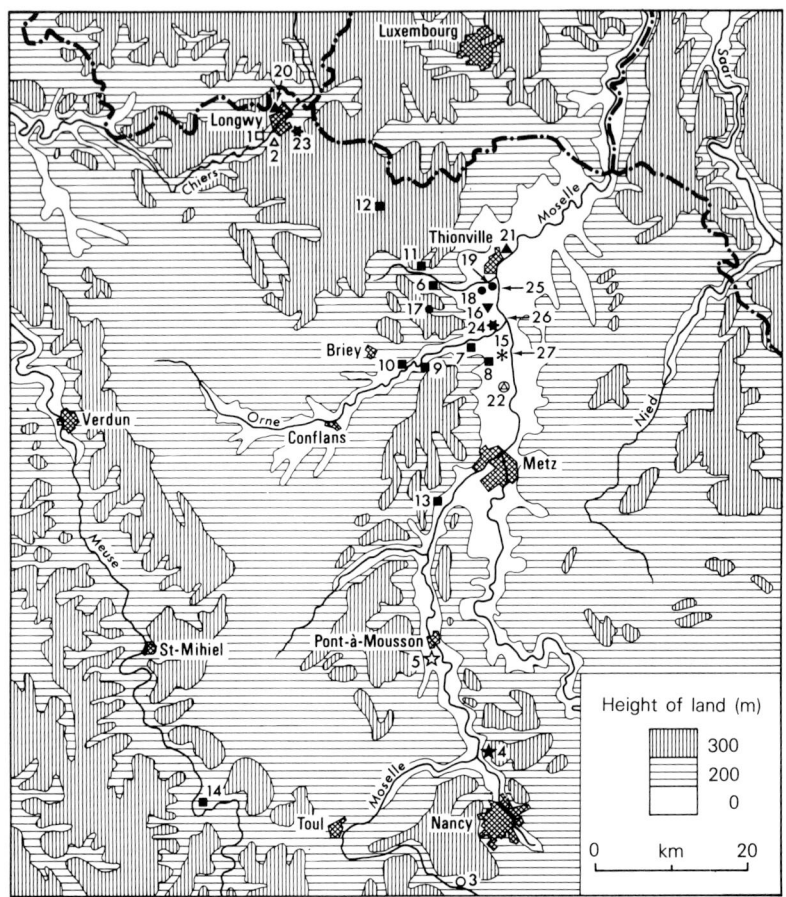

□ Hauts-Fourneaux
  de la Chiers
  1 Longwy-Bas
△ Cockerill-Ougrée-Providence
  2 Rehon
○ Aciéries et Tréfileries
  de Neuves-Maisons Châtillon
  3 Neuves-Maisons
★ Aciéries de Pompey
  4 Pompey
☆ Pont-à-Mousson SA
  5 Pont-à-Mousson

■ SACILOR
  6 Hayange
  7 Gandrange-Rombas
  8 Hagondange
  9 Joeuf
  10 Homécourt
  11 Knutange
  12 Micheville
  13 Ars-sur-Moselle
  14 Sorcy
✲ SAFE
  15 Hagondange
▼ Hauts-Fourneaux
  de Saulnes et Uckange
  16 Uckange

● SOLLAC
  17 Sérémange
  18 Florange
  19 Ébange
▲ USINOR
  20 Longwy
  21 Thionville
⊛ IRSID
  22 Maizières-les-Metz
✸ 23 Centrale Électrique
    d'Herserange
✸ 24 Centrale Électrique
    de Richemont
  25 Port d'Illange
  26 Port de Richemont
  27 Port d'Hagondange

Figure 12.2. The distribution of the steel industry in Lorraine in the early 1970s. Source: Centre d'Information des Industries Lorraines (1974c, pages 40–41).

The second main steel-making region was the Nord, where plants based on local supplies of coal accounted in 1938 for 19% of national steel output. In this region, integrated plants were to be found at Denain, at Valenciennes-Trith-St Léger, and at Louvroil-Maubeuge. In addition, a significant number of small and medium-sized processing plants were located in the valleys of the Sambre and Escaut.

Other steelworks were located in the Centre–Midi. These plants, which were to be found in the centre of this area near Le Creusot, in the upper reaches of the Loire near St Etienne, and in the Alps to the northeast of Grenoble, were originally developed to exploit local supplies of coal and iron ore. In subsequent years, however, works in the Centre–Midi were equipped with electric furnaces and converted for the production of special steels from scrap metal.

The fourth and last group was made up of a set of coastal plants that used imported ore and coal or exploited small local deposits of the necessary raw materials. Included were the Le Boucau works on the Basque coast, the Floirac works in the département of Gironde, the Basse Indre works at Nantes, the Hennebont works in Brittany, the Mondeville works at Caen, the Paris-Outreau works at Boulogne, and the Les Dunes steelworks at Dunkirk. All of these steelworks had been constructed before 1914, except for those in the Nord, which had been reconstructed in 1918 (Freyssenet, 1979a, pages 16–18).

12.2 The phase of reconstruction, 1945–1954

By the end of the Second World War, mechanisation was beginning to occur more widely in the steel industry. With mechanisation and with improved methods of preparing ores for smelting, the size of blast furnaces and the efficiency of blast furnace operations were increasing. (The steel production cycle is outlined in figure 12.3.) Of more importance, however, was the development of methods of continuous rolling. With this advance, the transfer of steel in the rolling process was mechanised.

The adoption of continuous rolling techniques was connected with important changes in the division of labour and in the composition of the labour force employed in the steel sector. In the first place, workers with traditional craft skills were no longer needed (some of the workers with traditional craft skills could, however, be employed to carry out activities like quality control). Second, some tasks formerly undertaken by unskilled labourers were mechanised. With the introduction of these new Taylorist methods of production, knowledge and skill were concentrated in the hands of a small group of engineers and technicians involved in the design of machinery and in the organisation, analysis, and supervision of the production process. New skilled maintenance jobs were created for electricians and mechanics. In the case of production workers, however, the situation changed in a different direction. The workers concerned were of course reskilled in the sense that they had to be capable of adapting to new forms of factory discipline. All that they were required to do, however, was execute simple operations determined by the group of engineers and technicians or imposed by the design of the machine system. In the sphere of production, the old combination of *ouvriers de métier* or *ouvriers professionnels* and *manoeuvres* was, in other words, losing ground to a rising group of *ouvriers spécialisés* (ouvriers spécialisés are unskilled workers whose task is to operate a specialised machine).

The French steel industry was much less mechanised than those in the United States of America and in some other European countries. According to the estimates of the 1946 Commission de Modernisation de la Sidérurgie, the optimum capacity of a steel-making plant stood at 1 million tonnes per annum. Allowing for certain special types of production, twenty-four plants rather than one hundred and seventy-seven were accordingly thought to be

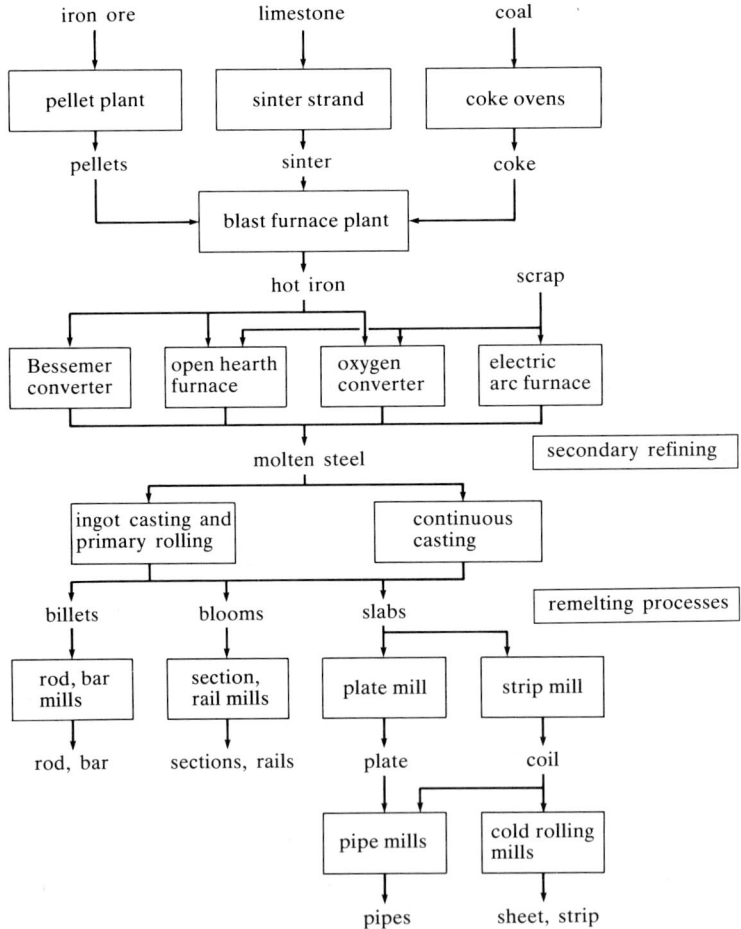

Figure 12.3. The steel production cycle.

sufficient to produce the 12 million tonnes of steel per year that the industry was capable of producing. What resulted was a comparatively low level of labour productivity, and the selling prices of steel tended to be high. The problem of productivity was, however, compounded by another problem.

In the French steel industry there was a strong emphasis upon the production of shaped products with specific uses in relatively unmechanised industries. As a result, the production of wire rod and of flat products was underemphasised. It was this second group of products that could be continuously rolled. Moreover, the products concerned were the ones needed by the metal-using industries which were based on mass production techniques and on the use of unskilled workers. In the 1950s it was of course these industries which were to grow rapidly, and these products for which the growth in demand was to be most pronounced. After the war, no serious employment problems would have been caused by a modernisation of the steel industry, because of the general shortage of labour in the country. A switch towards the production of good quality wire rod and sheet steel was, however, held back. The reason for this was the desire of the steel companies, particularly those based in Lorraine, to continue specialising in and exporting semifinished and long products. The companies concerned were much less interested in meeting the needs of a new national market for flat products about whose growth they were sceptical (see Freyssenet, 1979a, pages 23–26).

The structure of the industry was a second obstacle. Any reorganisation of production and output of this kind would have immediately required a series of major mergers. Only via mergers could the industrial system have been rationalised such that the best of the existing installations were used and the others closed. Mergers were also a precondition for the generation of the large amounts of capital needed for investment in modern mechanised units of production.

A concentration and centralisation of capital and a restructuring of the industry could not easily occur. On the one hand, the industry was dominated by a large number of companies of approximately equal size. On the other, the steel owners were reluctant to merge and were generally unwilling to coordinate and rationalise their steel-making activities. (For a self-portrait of one of the *maîtres de forges*, Henri de Wendel, see Padioleau, 1981, pages 10–12.) In addition, the industry was able to acquire the investment capital it wanted through the activities of its powerful trade association, the Chambre Syndicale de la Sidérurgie (CSSF), which had inherited the role of the old Comité des Forges of studying and defending the economic, industrial, and commercial interests of the French iron masters. Through a subsidiary organisation of CSSF called the Groupement de l'Industrie Sidérurgique (GIS), state-guaranteed debentures were issued. Investment capital was thus raised without recourse to mergers or the forging of alliances with sources of financial capital, and the industry was insulated from the criteria that the banking system and other financial institutions would have applied (see Padioleau, 1981, pages 15-23; Rhodes, 1985, pages 203-204). Nor would the state intervene to achieve these ends. The section of the Premier Plan de Modernisation et d'Équipement (1947-1952) that dealt with the steel industry was essentially a compromise between the wishes of the steel companies, pressures from the main metal-using industries, and the state's own goals (Freyssenet, 1979a, pages 29-31). All that really happened was that the Commisariat du Plan amended the suggestions of the steel modernisation commission by proposing the construction of two wide hot rolling mills and of several cold rolling mills to increase the amount and competitiveness of sheet steel production. In addition, economies in the use of living labour were to be achieved by means of the electrification of existing rolling mills.

At that time the most modern wide hot rolling mills, which were being constructed in the USA, had an initial capacity of 1.8 million tonnes per year. Individually, of course, none of the French companies produced steel on a sufficient scale to warrant the development of modern rolling facilities. In these conditions what emerged was an unsatisfactory compromise: mainly because the investments involved would be broadly commensurate with the resources and steel-making capacities of two groupings of French companies, the French industry opted for two mills with an initial capacity of 0.7 million tonnes per annum each. Both of the new projects were financed by the state out of the Fonds de Modernisation et d'Équipement and were aided by Marshall Plan funds. In April 1947 the Société des Forges et des Aciéries du Nord et de l'Est and the Société des Hauts-Fourneaux, Forges, et Aciéries de Denain et Anzin decided to order a wide hot sheet rolling mill from the USA, and in 1948 these two Nord-based companies merged to form the Union Sidérurgique du Nord de la France (USINOR) (see table 12.1, and on the subsequent development of the complex see table 12.2). The new rolling mill was installed at Denain, where iron and steel making was to be progressively expanded and modernised and came into service in 1950, as did the cold rolling mill corresponding to it, which was located at Montataire in the Oise Valley.

Once the social and political situation had been stabilised at the end of 1948, four companies based in Lorraine and three companies controlled from Lorraine formed the Société Lorraine de Laminage Continu (SOLLAC). SOLLAC was created as a cooperative venture to construct and operate the second wide hot rolling mill envisaged in the First Plan. The new works was also equipped with steel-making capacity and with two cold rolling mills. It came on-stream at the end of 1953. SOLLAC was supplied with pig iron or steel by the companies participating in the cooperative: material was supplied by each of the companies involved in proportion to its interest in the venture, and an equivalent share of the sheet steel produced by SOLLAC was bought back at cost price.

In the early 1950s the launching of the European Coal and Steel Community (ECSC) stimulated several mergers. In 1950, SIDELOR was

Table 12.1. The centralisation of capital in the French iron and steel industry, 1945–1976. (Vertical bars indicate year organisation was set up.) Source: elaborated from Freyssenet and Imbert, 1975a, pages 135–136).

Société des Forges et Aciéries de la Marine et d'Homécourt	→ 1950 SIDELOR
Société des Aciéries de Micheville	→ 1950 SIDELOR
Société des Fonderies de Pont-à-Mousson	→ 1951 De Wendel et Compagnie
Société Lorraine des Aciéries de Rombas	→ 1950 SIDELOR
Les Petits Fils de François de Wendel	→ 1951 De Wendel et Compagnie
De Wendel SA	→ 1951 De Wendel et Compagnie → 1968 Wendel-SIDELOR → 1973 SACILOR
Société Métallurgique de Knutange	→ 1963 Société Mosellane de Sidérurgie → 1968 Wendel-SIDELOR
Union des Consommateurs de Produits Métallurgiques et Industriels	→ 1964 SACILOR → 1968 Wendel-SIDELOR
	1948 SOLLAC
	1971 Société des Profilés et Tubes de l'Etat
	1973 SOLMER
Société des Hauts-Fourneaux, Forges et Aciéries de Denain et Anzin	→ 1948 USINOR → 1966 USINOR-Lorraine
Société des Forges et des Aciéries du Nord et de l'Est	→ 1948 USINOR
Société des Aciéries de Longwy	→ 1953 Lorraine-Escaut → 1966 USINOR-Lorraine
Société Métallurgique de Senelle Maubeuge	→ 1953 Lorraine-Escaut
Société d'Escaut et Meuse	→ 1953 Lorraine-Escaut
Société des Hauts-Fourneaux de Saulnes	→ 1960 Société des Hauts-Fourneaux et Forges de Saulnes et Gorcy → 1966 Société des Hauts-Fourneaux Réunis
Société Métallurgique de Gorcy	→ 1960 Société des Hauts-Fourneaux et Forges de Saulnes et Gorcy
Société des Forges et Aciéries du Nord et de la Lorraine	→ 1966 Société des Hauts-Fourneaux Réunis
Société des Hauts-Fourneaux de la Chiers	→ 1977 Compagnie Industrielle Chiers-Châtillon
Société des Forges de Châtillon, Commentry Biache	→ 1977 Compagnie Industrielle Chiers-Châtillon
Société des Aciéries et Tréfileries de Neuves-Maisons Châtillon	→ 1977 Compagnie Industrielle Chiers-Châtillon

Table 12.2. The development of some of the major French steel plants, 1950–1981. Sources: Centre d'Information des Industries Lorraines (1974c, pages 39–71), Freyssenet and Imbert (1975a, page 224), and Dahmani (1983, page 141).

	Complex				
	Denain	SOLLAC (Lorraine)	Dunkirk		Fos-sur-Mer
Owner of complex	USINOR	SACILOR	USINOR		SOLMER
Stage number			1	2	1 2 3
Date of entry into service	1950	1953	1962–63	1973–77	1973–74 1985
Blast furnaces		pig iron supplied by a cooperative of participants	3: 4Mt	4: 8Mt	2: 3Mt 3: 6Mt
Steelworks					
Bessemer converter	3/50t	4/55t converted into 4(LWS oxygen converters)/65t (1975)			
open hearth furnace	3/100–150t	4/180–200t			
oxygen converters	4(LD)/62t	1(Kaldo)/140t (1960) replaced by 2(LWS)/240t (1978)	3(LD)/160t	3(LD)/160t 3(LD)/200t	2/280t 3/280t
Annual steel-making capacity	2.5Mt	3Mt (in 1975)	4Mt	8Mt	3.5Mt 7Mt ≥10Mt
Continuous casting				4Mt	2Mt
Rolling mills					
slabbing mill	1: 1.5Mt 1: 1Mt	1: 3Mt	1: 3.5Mt	4Mt	1: 3.5Mt 5Mt
wide hot rolling mill	1: 2.5Mt (1965)	1: 3Mt	1: 2–3Mt	1: 4–5Mt	1: 3.5Mt 1: 6Mt
heavy plate mill			1: 1Mt	1: 1.5Mt	1: 1Mt

t is capacity in tonnes; Mt is annual capacity in million tonnes; 3: 4Mt is 3 units with an aggregate capacity of 4 million tonnes per year; 3/50t is 3 units with a capacity of 50 tonnes each; LWS is Loire–Wendel–Sprunck converter; LD is Linz–Donawitz converter.

formed from four Lorraine-based companies. In 1951 the two companies owned by the de Wendel company were combined to form a single company. And in 1953, five companies with interests in the production of tubes and heavy plate formed Lorraine-Escaut. Only the last of these mergers, along with the one resulting in the formation of USINOR, laid the basis for a geographical consolidation of production and a fusing and modernisation of existing installations. The remaining fifteen or so companies sought to remain independent by specialising (see table 12.1).

The targets for steel production included in the First Plan were broadly achieved, but goals connected with the overall levels of labour productivity and the restructuring of the industry were not. Furthermore, the works aimed at preparing for an increase in capacity from 12.5 million tonnes per year in 1952 to 15 million tonnes in 1955 were not started. Investment accordingly fell short of the level projected in the plan, and much of it was used to patch up old installations which remained in use owing to the relatively high level of demand for steel (Freyssenet, 1979a, pages 32–36).

In the Second Plan (1954–1957), new targets were set as a result of the negotiations within and among the Planning Commission's sectoral commissions and working groups, the Ministry of Industry, CSSF, and the steel companies themselves. On this occasion, only a small increase in capacity to 14.3 million tonnes per annum was envisaged.

Instead of the expected 33% increase, domestic demand went up by 47%. In the ECSC, demand increased by 43%. Although some efforts were made to increase the production of wire rod, the demand for flat products was underestimated and the demand for heavy sections overestimated. There was, in general, a lack of planned investment in new facilities and new processes and in the balanced expansion of the various phases of iron and steel making, and too much emphasis was placed upon the modification of existing installations.

As in the case of the years up to 1954, these characteristics of the industry's development can be attributed to two factors. One was the limited resources available to each of the companies individually. The second was the widespread adoption of a policy of minimising short-term capital expenditure by carrying out piecemeal improvements to existing facilities (Freyssenet, 1979a, pages 36–39).

12.3 Open conflict between the steel industry and the metal-using industries, 1954–1960

The phase of reconstruction was followed by a wave of almost uninterrupted expansion. However, the French steel industry did not gain from it to the same extent as did the steel industries in other advanced capitalist countries, and did not respond in a way that would have enabled it to cope with the more competitive market conditions which characterised the years after 1961.

Output increased from 10.6 million tonnes in 1954 to 17.3 million tonnes in 1960. This increase of 63% was slightly less than the average of 66% for countries belonging to the ECSC, and was much less than the increases recorded in Japan, Italy, the Netherlands, and the FRG (see the 1950–1960 data in table 13.2). More importantly, output growth was much less than the increase of 100% in domestic demand. Exports rose sharply in 1955, but were subsequently held at between 3.5 million and 4 million tonnes per year. As a result of the lack of investment in new capacity, the French industry found itself unable to meet the needs of its traditional clients. More significantly, it was also unable to meet the needs of the country's metal-using industries. Steel users in France had to rely increasingly on expensive imported steel: in 1954–1960, steel imports increased from 1 million to 2.9 million tonnes.

A shortage of domestic capacity and the high price of imported steel led to open conflict between the steel industry and the main metal-using industries. Obviously, the interests of French capital as a whole lay in exporting manufactured goods with a high value added rather than steel. But on account of the structure of the French industrial system, this economy-wide aim did not coincide with the short-term interests of the individual capitals involved. At that time, no iron and steel company was sufficiently strong to absorb or control a large group of metal-using industries, as in the case of Krupp in the FRG, and there was no large engineering company or motor vehicle manufacturer capable of developing an important iron and steel manufacturing division as FIAT had done in Italy.

The employers in the iron and steel industry advocated an increase in domestic steel prices as a means of reducing the relative attractiveness of exporting. The government, however, was determined to resist demands for more rapid increases in the prices of manufactured goods containing steel and refused the steel employers' request. In order to counterbalance some of the effects of its actions on the steel industry itself the government also introduced some measures aimed at limiting cost increases and at facilitating investment in the steel industry. Nevertheless, when the steel companies sought to explain the difficulties that they subsequently experienced, considerable emphasis was placed upon the effects of the low prices of the period 1954–1960, which in the view of the companies, were caused by direct and indirect state action (see Freyssenet, 1979a, pages 59–63).

Of more importance in limiting the profitability of steel production in France, however, were three other factors. In the first place, capacity was inadequate. Second, there was too much rolling capacity for products for which demand was growing slowly and too little for flat products, wire rod, concrete-reinforcing bars, and other products which were more in demand and whose prices were increasing more rapidly. In the third place, the cost price of pig iron was high owing to a lack of investment in the preliminary processing of ores and a lack of efficiency in the use of coke.

By the mid-1950s, important changes necessitating new investment were beginning to occur in the steel industry. One was the growing use of oxygen steel-making processes (see figure 12.4). With these methods a wide range of good quality steels could be produced in less time and with three times less direct labour than the open hearth process. (In the steel industry productivity is normally measured in this way, indicating the relevance of the value concepts introduced in chapter 2.) At the same time, reductions in the cost of maritime transport and the mechanisation of mining were beginning to make it profitable to exploit deposits of high-grade ores in Mauritania, Brazil, Liberia, Australia, Sweden, and Canada. The impact of these developments on expected costs along with the opportunities for establishing mechanised production outside traditional steel-producing regions were beginning to make it optimal to develop new coastal complexes using high-grade imported ores. In the wake of the Japanese, Italian, Dutch, and German industries a group of French companies headed by USINOR accordingly decided to construct a small plant at Dunkirk. The initial scale of this project was subsequently increased. In 1959, however, the minority associates pulled out, leaving USINOR to finance the project on its own and to carry the risks associated with a high level of indebtedness.

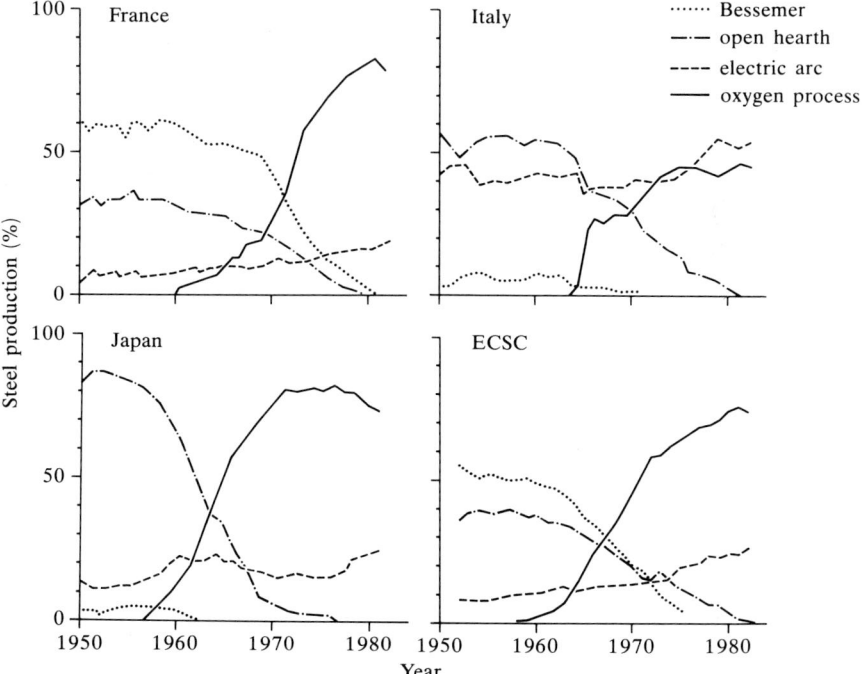

Figure 12.4. Crude steel production, by process, in France, Italy, the ECSC, and Japan, 1952–1982. Sources: elaborated from EEC Commission: Eurostat (1983, page 21) and Poznanski (1983, page 312; 1985, pages 15–16).

In the wave of expansion that preceded 1960 the response of most of the steel companies was simply one of maximising the use of existing capacity and of those installations that had recently come on-stream. Even at the time of the preparation of the Third Plan (1958 – 1961) the majority of the steel owners were still not sufficiently confident that expansion would continue at the same rate to be prepared to invest in new capacity. In any case, the resources necessary to build new plants on their own were lacking. With rising steel prices, however, the pressure on the steel companies to merge declined. In these conditions the strategy that predominated was one of maximising short-term profits so that each of the companies would subsequently be able to develop new mechanised installations of their own. The strategy of maximising the use of existing installations and the lack of mechanisation and of productivity growth had two important results. On the one hand, it led to the recruitment of relatively large numbers of workers of a traditional kind, whose skills were often specific to the steel industry. On the other, it was associated with a concentration of these workers in monoindustrial areas.

Between 1954 and 1960, employment in the French steel industry increased by some 20 000 jobs, with most of the new jobs being concentrated in the East in general and in the northern steel-producing basin in Lorraine in particular. The population of this basin increased by 3.06% per year between 1954 and 1962, compared with 1% nationally, and many new immigrant workers, mostly from Italy and Algeria, were drawn into the region. At a national level the proportion of immigrant workers in the steel industry increased from 26% to 30% (Freyssenet and Imbert, 1975a, page 255). Via policies of land acquisition and other methods of controlling processes of local development, steel firms also sought to ensure the existence of situations of monopsony in the markets for labour in the areas where they were operating: as in the past, the steel companies were anxious to prevent the entry of other industries likely to compete with them for local labour.

As a result of all of these factors the steel firms were themselves laying some of the foundations of subsequent regional crises.

Only when the Interim Plan (July 1960 – December 1961) and the Fourth Plan (1962 – 1965) were being prepared did the steel companies and the state agree not only to make up for delays that had occurred in meeting the objectives of the Third Plan, but also to make a major effort to increase capacity and to modernise the industry. Capacity was planned to increase to 20 million tonnes per year in 1962 and 24.5 million tonnes per year in 1965. In 1959, construction of the new works at Dunkirk commenced. De Wendel announced its intention of constructing a new integrated plant with an eventual capacity of 4 million tonnes per annum in the Orne Valley. In addition, studies connected with the development by SOLLAC of a second coastal plant were to be undertaken.

The financing of the implied programme of investments in existing as well as in new works depended to a large extent, however, upon continuing expansion. This expansion did not occur. As a result, the hopes of the Gaullist regime of reconciling the interests of the steel companies with those of the metal-using industries and of avoiding a social and regional crisis by means of a combination of output growth, productivity growth, and stable levels of employment were dashed.

12.4 Declining profitability and investment, stagnating output, and the Convention Générale État-Sidérurgie, 1961-1967

In 1961 and 1962, world steel production stagnated, and until 1970 it increased much more slowly than in the period 1954-1960. In the ECSC there was a recovery in 1964, but stagnation quickly set in again and lasted until 1968. Competition increased sharply both on the international market, as heavily indebted Japanese producers sought to sell at almost any price, and in ECSC countries. As a result, prices fell.

The intensification of international competition caught the French steel industry ill-prepared. The industries of many rival countries were more concentrated and had secured the advantages of large-scale production, whereas the situation rents associated with the availability of low-cost iron ore, which had constituted the basis of the competitiveness of the French industry, were no longer as advantageous as they had been in the past. The turnover and gross profits of each of the French companies, with the exception of USINOR, stagnated. (USINOR was able to compete successfully by virtue of the entry into service of the Dunkirk plant in 1962.) Consequently, most French producers were unable to generate the resources required to carry out their planned investment programmes. In contrast to the steel industries in Belgium, Luxemburg, and the FRG, which were facing similar problems, the French companies resisted the option of merging to form companies with more resources for investment and greater borrowing capacities, of rationalising, and of developing new installations. Instead, planned investments were put off, and the companies hoped for a recovery in the demand for steel.

In 1964, de Wendel and SIDELOR did finally decide to participate in a cooperative venture to construct an oxygen steel-making unit at Gandrange. But with the renewed stagnation of demand after the recovery in 1964, the general strategy adopted in 1961 was reinforced. As a result, French capacity increased more slowly than that of many other European countries, imports increased, and the country's traditional trade surplus in steel declined.

The situation was exacerbated by the fact that at this stage in the industry's development the operation of the law of value was beginning to impose new norms of production requiring even larger amounts of capital (see chapter 2, section 2.7; and Freyssenet, 1979a, pages 96-100). Some processes, including the preparation of ores and the rolling process, were beginning to be automated, and steps were being taken with a view to automating the whole of the steel-making process.

Automation helps overcome the limits to productivity growth imposed by the speed with which human operatives can carry out instructions and by their ability to control the rate at which they work. With automatic production control the regulation of production is concentrated in the hands of a single, computer-controlled and self-correcting central control system. The analysis and interpretation of centralised information, research into methods of improving the system, and tricky changes in it are carried out by a restricted group of engineers, technicians, and highly skilled maintenance workers. The operatives simply have to observe a set of dials. The amount of capital for which each worker is responsible will have increased, as will, in some respects, the responsibility associated with his or her job. Overall, however, operatives tend to lose the limited degree of initiative left to them by mechanisation. At the same time, some of the maintenance staff are deskilled, and in some cases maintenance workers simply acquire a specialisation in one part of the process. The automatic and centralised detection of faults grows in importance. In addition, increasing emphasis is placed upon the replacement of faulty units with standardised parts, with a view to minimising the amount of time during which costly installations are out of action. Insofar as these developments occur at the expense of repair work, the old skills of maintenance staff are devalued.

Processes of continuous casting were also being introduced, and methods of direct reduction capable of at least partially supplanting the blast furnace as a source of iron for steel making were being developed (see figure 12.5).

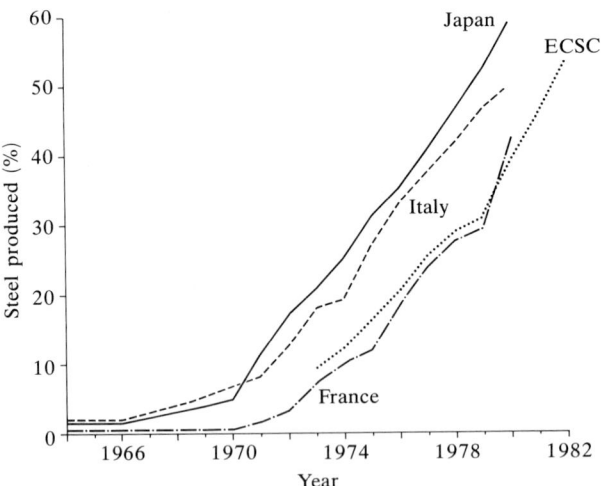

Figure 12.5 Steel produced by the continuous casting process in France, Italy, the ECSC, and Japan 1952-1982. Sources: elaborated from EEC Commission: Eurostat (1983, page 20) and Poznanski (1983, page 370).

In both cases the aim was to short-circuit long, tricky, or expensive stages in the production of steel.

One other development with important implications for the scale and characteristics of investment in the steel industry can be identified. In the 1960s, ministeelworks, of the kind established around Brescia in Italy and in the FRG, were proving very successful. As a result, the advantages of methods of production involving the transformation of ore compared with scrap-based methods were perhaps less clear-cut than at the turn of the decade, whereas after 1974 or so, ministeelworks were to acquire a competitive edge (see Dahmani, 1983, pages 150–153).

At the same time, a regional crisis was emerging in Lorraine. In the early 1960s, employment was declining in agriculture, in the textile and clothing industries, and in coal and iron mining, and employment in the steel industry was stagnating. Some 53 000 jobs were estimated as being required by 1970 if net emigration from the region was to be avoided. Yet the prospects for jobs in new sectors were low: about 85% of the steel produced in the region and a high proportion of other local resources were exported for further processing, local services and commerce were weakly developed, and there was no real regional metropolis.

The first blows were struck with the closing of several works in the iron foundry industry in the middle and late 1960s and with the rundown of the iron mines (see figures 12.6 and 12.7; and Freyssenet, 1979a, pages 70, 73–75, 92–96). Between 1952 and 1960 the output of the iron mines in Lorraine increased from 38.4 to 62 million tonnes. In the same period, exports to Luxembourg, Belgium, and the Saar rose. However, after 1957 some of the industry's more distant clients started to meet part of their growing needs by importing higher grade ores from Third World countries and from Sweden. This loss of markets was one of the reasons for the mechanisation of mining. As a result of this mechanisation, productivity increased and employment in iron mining declined from 26 553 workers in 1952 to 23 594 workers in 1960 (see figure 12.7). The output of the iron mines peaked at 62.1 million tonnes in 1962. Afterwards it declined owing to the fall in demand from steel producers in the Nord, Belgium, and the Saar, and the absence of a compensating increase in demand from producers in Luxembourg and Lorraine. The availability of local ore was no longer a guarantee of the competitiveness of locally produced steel, and the decision to construct installations for enriching ore had occurred too late.

This fall in demand had the biggest impact upon mines producing ore for the open market. The owners of these mines responded in several ways. The number of shafts was reduced. Only the more easily worked and higher quality seams were exploited. More modern and powerful equipment was used. In addition, the number of workers employed was reduced. Opposition from the miners and spectacular acts like the seventy-nine-day occupation of the Sancy mine at Trieux only secured certain rights to reemployment and compensation. Between 1960 and 1967, employment in the iron mines in Lorraine fell from 23 594 to 13 058 persons.

This conflict was followed by a clash between the workers and the employers in the steel industry.

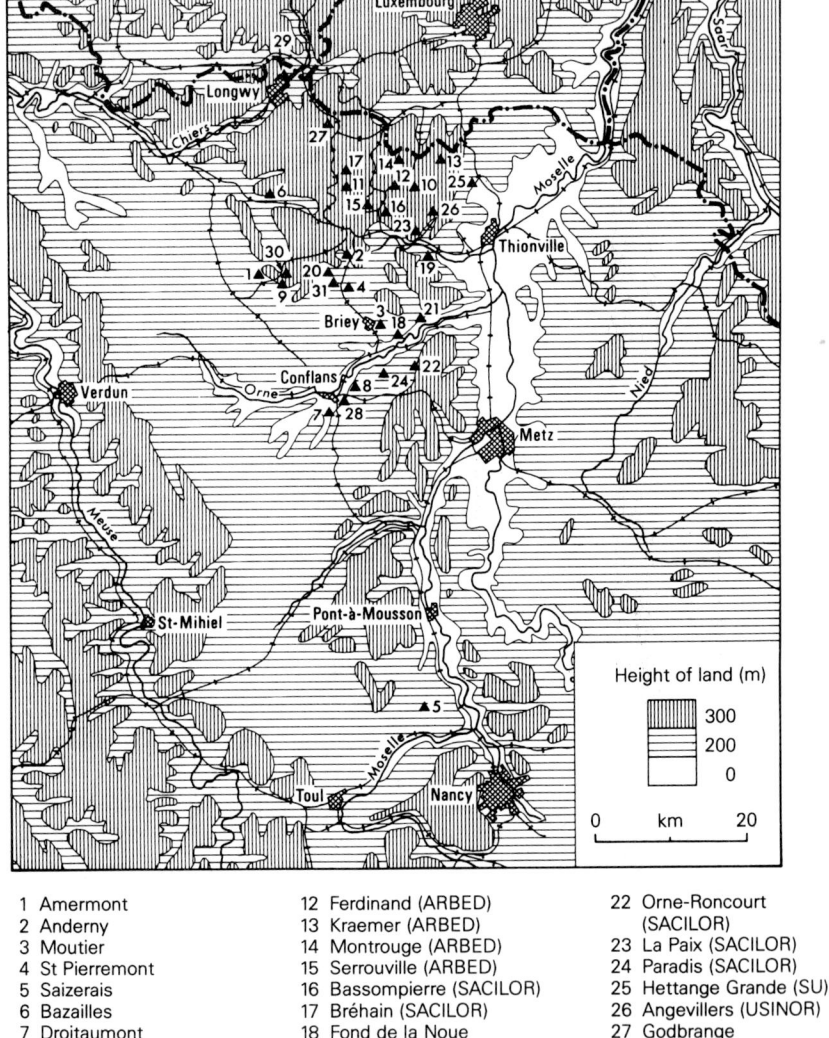

1 Amermont	12 Ferdinand (ARBED)	22 Orne-Roncourt
2 Anderny	13 Kraemer (ARBED)	(SACILOR)
3 Moutier	14 Montrouge (ARBED)	23 La Paix (SACILOR)
4 St Pierremont	15 Serrouville (ARBED)	24 Paradis (SACILOR)
5 Saizerais	16 Bassompierre (SACILOR)	25 Hettange Grande (SU)
6 Bazailles	17 Bréhain (SACILOR)	26 Angevillers (USINOR)
7 Droitaumont	18 Fond de la Noue	27 Godbrange
8 Giraumont	(SACILOR)	28 Jarny (USINOR)
9 Joudreville	19 Hayange (SACILOR)	29 Longwy (USINOR)
10 Ronchonvillers-Adélaide	20 Mairy (SACILOR)	30 Piennes (USINOR)
11 Errouville (ARBED)	21 Moyeuvre (SACILOR)	31 Tucquegnieux (USINOR)

Figure 12.6. The distribution of the iron mining industry in Lorraine in the early 1970s. Source: Centre d'Information des Industries Lorraines (1974a, pages 12–13).

In the Fifth Plan (1966-1970) there were proposals for (1) an increase in steel-making capacity to 26 million tonnes by 1970, (2) increases in productivity, (3) improvements in the quality of the steels produced, (4) the completion of preparatory studies in connection with the development of a new coastal works, and (5) research into automation, continuous processes, and new steels. The associated investment programme was estimated as costing 7.5 milliard francs over five years, to which should be added 4.5 milliard francs for loan repayments. CSSF publicly announced that the steel companies were not in a position to finance the investments involved in fulfilling the objectives of the Fifth Plan. The reasons for this lay in two related factors. One was the industry's lack of profitability. The second was a shortage of investment funds. Underlying these problems, it was repeatedly argued, was one major cause: government price controls that had cost the industry some 3 milliard to 5 milliard francs. Thus responsibility for the industry's difficulties lay not with the companies but with the state.

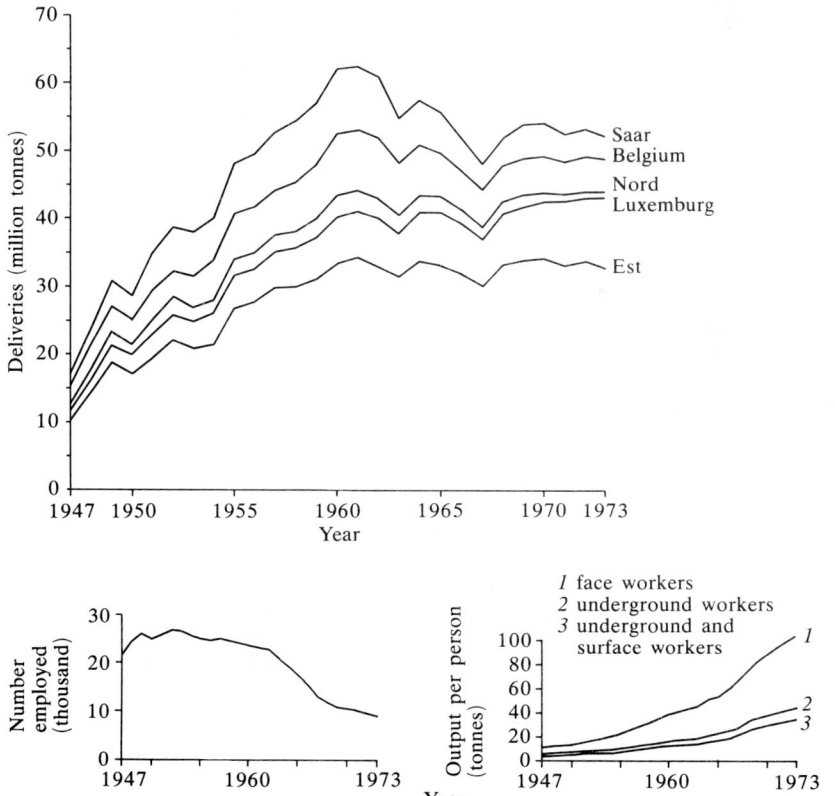

Figure 12.7. Deliveries by market area, employment, and productivity in the iron mining industry in Lorraine. Source: Centre d'Information des Industries Lorraines (1974b, pages 21-22).

In 1966 an agreement with the government was signed called the Convention Générale État-Sidérurgie, whose application depended upon its being followed by agreements between the state and each of the companies. In it the government agreed to CSSF's demands for reductions in the costs of transport and of coal and coke. In addition, it promised to help with the financing of an investment programme estimated as costing 10 milliard francs by lending 2.7 milliard francs from FDES at an extremely low rate of interest and by easing other loans. In return, the companies agreed to regroup on a geographical basis, forming one set of companies in the Nord and one in Lorraine, with special steels being produced in the Centre-Midi. The activities of the new groups of companies were to be coordinated and rationalised. The aim of the agreement was to raise productivity by 5% per year on average. An increase of this magnitude was expected to lead to a loss of 15 000 jobs, of which some 7000 to 10 000 were expected to occur as a result of natural wastage and limitations on recruitment. The companies were also required to participate in schemes for reemploying workers who lost their jobs, and in a policy of industrial diversification in steel-producing areas. In addition, they had to come to an agreement with the unions over the job losses.

The workers in Lorraine tried to oppose what was essentially a process of capitalist rationalisation. However, the unions did not succeed in identifying an alternative to those of accepting capitalist modernisation and the deskilling and job losses associated with it, or of defending the status quo and risking the eventual bankruptcy and disappearance of the enterprises concerned. Consequently, the strikes of 1967 did little more than secure some improvements in the Convention Sociale de la Sidérurgie de l'Est. What was important, however, was the fact that with this agreement the principle of no redundancy without reemployment was first introduced into the private sector (Freyssenet, 1979a, pages 105-112).

With the Convention Générale État-Sidérurgie a number of important changes in the French steel industry were initiated. One of the most important occurred in 1966 when USINOR's holding company absorbed Lorraine-Escaut and its holding company. What resulted was a new production company called USINOR-Lorraine, and the new holding company assumed the name of Denain-Nord-Est-Longwy (DNEL). The decisions taken by USINOR for the *Plan Professionnel* were to concentrate its effort on two plants producing flat products, namely Dunkirk and Denain, and to make the newly acquired works at Longwy the main centre for the production of those long products for which demand was thought to be increasing. The pipe-making plants formerly owned by Lorraine-Escaut were regrouped into a company called Vallourec.

The other important change occurred when SIDELOR merged with the Société Mosellane de Sidérurgie to form SIDELOR-Mosellane, in accordance with promises given in making agreements with the state in February 1967, and the new group merged with de Wendel to form

Wendel-SIDELOR. A new agreement with the state was signed in December 1968, and the Plan Professionnel began to be applied in 1969. The competitiveness of Wendel-SIDELOR, however, was not increased adequately. On the one hand, mistakes were made by SACILOR, which had been established in 1964 as a cooperative by de Wendel and SIDELOR, in equipping the new Gandrange plant. (The plant at Gandrange was to be the centrepiece of a plan for rationalising the production of long products.) In addition, the group's plants remained integrated and independent of one another and were not made sufficiently specialised (Freyssenet, 1979a, pages 112-115).

One of the consequences of what happened in the years between 1960 and 1967 was that the French steel industry lost ground in comparison with its competitors. Output increased by 13.7% compared with 23.4% in the ECSC as a whole, 93.1% in Italy, 75.5% in the Netherlands, and 35.2% in Belgium (see table 13.2). More importantly, its efficiency and the level of investment were comparatively low. A second consequence was that from 1964 the French steel companies started to place strong limitations on recruitment. As a result, the number of workers employed fell from 130 800 in 1964 to 114 100 in 1967. A further 5 500 jobs were to be lost in 1968.

12.5 The Plan de Conversion de Wendel-SIDELOR

The expectations on which the Plan Professionnel rested were proved wrong. In the period 1968-1970 the demand for steel and steel prices increased sharply. The French steel companies were anxious to operate existing installations at as near full capacity as possible. Consequently, employment increased, and in 1970 the number of steel workers regained its 1966 level. However, the French industry lacked the capacity necessary to meet the additional demand for flat products. Imports therefore increased, and this growth in imports was reinforced by the lack of competitiveness of plants producing concrete-reinforcing and other merchant bars. The country's trade balance in steel moved into deficit for the first time. By the time the Sixth Plan (1971-1975) was being prepared, however, productivity had increased, mainly because of the high level of capacity utilisation, and profitability had been restored.

Included in the Sixth Plan were proposals for an increase in steel-making capacity from 25.8 million to 35.6 million tonnes per year. (Its main goal, it will be recalled, was to accelerate French industrial development.) Of this output, 55% was to be produced by means of oxygen steel-making processes (see figure 12.4). In addition, new rolling mills for the production of flat products and special steels were to be constructed. With a view to increasing productivity, old installations were to be taken out of service, and employment was to be reduced by about 13 000 jobs. The capacity of the Dunkirk works was to be increased from 3 million to 8 million tonnes per year, a cold rolling mill was to be constructed at Mardyck near Dunkirk, and a new coastal complex was to be built at Fos. Self-financing out of depreciation allowances and retained profits, new capital, and the sale of shares were expected to cover 54% of expenditures on new developments. The state was expected to be involved only in the financing of the Fos project, providing 29.5% of the funds required (see chapter 11, section 11.1).

Two aspects of this strategy were to be most significant in the long-term. One was the fact that the demand forecasts on which the decisions were founded were to prove much too high. The steel companies were thus to be left with substantial excess capacity. The second was the decision to proceed with the Fos project. Not only did the decision to construct rest on an illusion of expansion, the plant itself lacked an industrial hinterland. It was, of course, intended to supply Mediterranean markets. But with the subsequent world crisis, international steel prices fell much more sharply than national ones, posing severe difficulties for SOLMER. Also, the absence of a radical reorganisation of SACILOR's plants in Lorraine on the model of the restructuring of the industry in the German Ruhr was to place Lorraine's steel-producing future in jeopardy.

In the short run, however, the conditions on which productivity growth and the proposals for financing the investments included in the plan depended were not realised. By the time the construction of the complex at Fos began, Wendel-SIDELOR was no longer in a position to meet its share of the projected expenditure. Its inability to finance the project led both to a search for new partners for Wendel-SIDELOR, which ended with the inclusion of USINOR and August Thyssen Hütte AG in SOLMER, and to the preparation of the Plan de Conversion de Wendel-SIDELOR with a view to restoring the company's profit margins.

The central planks of the Plan de Conversion or the *Plan Dherse* of 1971 were the decisions not to develop a large new works in Lorraine and simply to rationalise Wendel-SIDELOR's existing industrial system. The plan had three main aims. One was to economise on investments, particularly by maximising the use of scrap metal in the steel-making process. The second was to reduce the number of installations in service. Only the most modern units were to be kept, and these installations were to work continuously. In the third place, all of SOLLAC's installations for the production of flat products were to be retained. The production of merchant bars and concrete-reinforcing bars was in part to be abandoned: in the field of long products the group was to specialise in the production of rails and heavy sections, with their greater profitability and more assured future. More specifically, the following proposals were made. Twenty out of thirty-one blast furnaces were to be retained, with some being enlarged and modernised and a new one being constructed at Joeuf. Four steel-making units were to be kept (SOLLAC, Gandrange, Rombas, and Hagondange) and three were to be closed (Micheville, Hayange, and Homécourt). SOLLAC's wide hot strip mill and cold rolling mills were to be retained, as were the universal plate mill at Homécourt and the three wire rod mills at Joeuf, Rombas, and Knutange. Two mills for rolling heavy sections at Rombas, one at Hayange, and one at Hagondange were to be retained, whereas the one at

Micheville in the Pays Haut was to close. In all, another 10 650 jobs were to be lost.

The Plan de Conversion de Wendel-SIDELOR was accompanied by a change in the structure of the group. Wendel-SIDELOR absorbed its subsidiary, SACILOR, and its two parent companies, de Wendel SA, excluding the establishments included in the Société des Profilés et Tubes de l'Est, and SIDELOR-Mosellane. At the beginning of 1973 the name of the group was changed to Société des Aciéries et Laminoirs de Lorraine (SACILOR). The outcome was the formation of a group specialising in the production of long products. Flat products were the specialism of SOLLAC and SOLMER, and steel plate and sheet were produced by the Société des Forges et Aciéries de Dilling in the Saar (see Freyssenet and Imbert, 1975b, pages 52–59; Freyssenet, 1979a, pages 129–132).

The failure of the strikes in May 1971 at Knutange and in the Fensch Valley made the workers sceptical about the possibilities of undertaking successful action against the plan. Only the support organised by the Parti Communiste Français (PCF) for the communist municipality of Villerupt had any real success: the mill for rolling rails at Micheville and 650 jobs were saved by the decision to set up a new company and to supply the works with semifinished steel from the nearby Rodange-Athus plant across the border in Luxembourg.

The number of people employed by SACILOR-SOLLAC fell by 11 069 from 60 452 to 49 383 between 1971 and 1975. The decline in employment would have been even greater had there not been a boom in the steel industry in the period 1973–1974. In addition, the saving of the rail rolling mill at Micheville preserved 650 jobs, and the extension of the life of the blast furnaces at Knutange saved 150. The greater than expected reduction in the length of the working week had a similar effect. On the other hand, the decision not to construct the third blast furnace planned for the plant at Joeuf meant that some new jobs expected in the conversion plan were not created (Freyssenet, 1979a, pages 145–146). Because of the deterioration in the general employment situation the number of voluntary departures fell by one half. Some 2000 workers went into early retirement, 2400 of 6000 applicants were transferred to Fos, and more than 7000 were transferred to other plants in the region (see chapter 11, section 11.3). Some of these workers had already been moved in the late 1960s, and some were former miners recruited by the steel industry in the period 1964–1970. After one year, 30% of them had not regained the real wage obtained before the move, 10% had been demoted, with 80% staying on the same grade and 10% being promoted, 25% had changed over to shift work, and 65% were faced with marked increases in the length of their journeys to work (Freyssenet, 1979a, page 46).

The loss of jobs in SACILOR-SOLLAC and the accompanying fall in the number of temporary workers employed directly and indirectly by the companies involved, along with the stagnation of employment in plants belonging to other companies, had important effects on the region and its inhabitants, although the exact effects varied between groups of the population and localities. In five years only about 2200 new government-aided jobs were created in the steel-producing basin. As a result, there was a marked net loss of jobs.

The reorganisation of the industry and the implementation of the Plan Dherse and of the earlier Plan Professionnel had several other important effects. Workers were moved from the works at Joeuf and Homécourt in the Orne Valley, Knutange and Hayange in the Fensch Valley, and Micheville in the Pays Haut to works in the Moselle Valley. There was also a marked ageing of the labour force in Lorraine's steel industry, with the proportion of forty to sixty year olds increasing from 28.8% in 1961 to 45.8% in 1975.

Between 1968 and 1975 every commune except Gandrange, Rombas, and Thionville lost population, especially as young people seeking employment moved away. In the early part of this period the rate of depopulation was, however, kept in check, especially in the Pays Haut, as the number of people crossing daily to work in the steel industry in Luxembourg and in new engineering industries in the Saar increased. The actual number of people crossing the border daily from the départements of Moselle and Meurthe et Moselle increased from some 2000 in 1960 to 7900 in 1968 and 22 500 in 1974. With the deepening of the crisis in 1974, however, this safety valve was removed (Freyssenet, 1979a, pages 146–155).

In 1974, USINOR and de Wendel disputed the control of Marine Firminy, which held 50% of the shares in a holding company which controlled Creusot-Loire. In the end, the de Wendel family in the shape of the Compagnie Lorraine Industrielle et Financière (CLIF) came out on top and found themselves at the head of an empire extending from the mining of iron ore to heavy engineering (Freyssenet and Imbert, 1975a, pages 59–62; Freyssenet, 1979a, pages 159–161).

The significance of this struggle was that by the early 1970s, radical changes were starting to occur once again in the conditions on which competitiveness depended. The highly concentrated Japanese industry had acquired a marked competitive advantage, partly because of the cheapness and flexibility of the contract labour system used in Japan. In addition, new steel industries, often financed with international credit money, were being developed in less advanced countries. In the FRG, the steel employers were already coming to the conclusion that, as German workers could not be employed on the same terms as the Japanese, even with automated plant, steel could not be produced as cheaply. Consequently, German firms were attempting to move downstream into construction engineering and into the export of equipment and of technical and engineering knowledge. The French companies were starting to draw the same conclusions as their German counterparts. The struggle for control of Marine Firminy was one index of an anxiety to get a foothold in the production of special steels and in the manufacture, assembly, and installation of equipment and of structural metal products.

12.6 The steel crisis and the Plan Acier, 1975-1978

In the mid-1970s the movement to a new stage in the development of the division of labour and in the geographical distribution of economic activity was associated with the disruption of the growth process in the advanced capitalist world. Very quickly the boom which had occurred in the steel industry in the years 1969-1974 gave way to a sharp fall in the demand for steel. Steel prices fell, excess capacity reappeared, and in developed market economies a protracted steel crisis opened.

In developed countries the rate of growth in the demand for steel was declining for several reasons. Some steel-using industries economised on steel or were decentralised. The rate of growth in the demand for consumption goods slackened. And steel stockholders and steel users ran down the stocks accumulated for precautionary or speculative reasons in the preceding boom. At the same time, automation was occurring. New steel industries were being established in newly industrialising countries, and existing ones were expanding in the centrally planned economies. By 1974 the development of efficient producers in these zones and in Japan was having an important effect upon international price formation and upon the competitiveness of long-established steel industries in advanced capitalist countries in the West. What was consequently emerging was a new international division of labour.

With the increase in oil prices this process was pushed further. On the one hand, the imported-energy-dependent Japanese sought to increase their competitiveness and their sales of equipment to oil producing countries, whereas the Germans reacted by accelerating the internationalisation of their consumption-good industries and by moving downstream and increasing the competitiveness and international importance of industries producing means of production. On the other hand, newly industrialising countries used some of the additional resources acquired as a result of increases in the prices of raw materials as well as international loans to create or expand their own steel industries. At that very moment, however, a large amount of new capacity was coming on-stream, and many of the steel companies involved were heavily indebted and obliged by this fact to sell as much steel as they could, as long as the prices they received covered their running costs.

In 1975, output fell by 19.5% in the ECSC of nine, 19.6% in the USA, 12.7% in Japan, and 8.3% in the world as a whole. Only in 1978 did world production regain its 1974 level. The reason why it reached new heights lay, however, in the expansion of steel production in the centrally planned economies and in newly industrialising countries, and not in renewed growth in developed market economies (see table 13.1).

The fall in demand and in output was accompanied by a sharp fall in prices at a time when the costs of raw materials and of transport were continuing to increase. What was most significant were the events on the international market. The amounts of steel sold on the international market were in fact relatively small in relation to world production. But with the contraction of domestic markets and rising costs, competition on the world market intensified, verging on economic warfare. In one year, export prices fell by some 40 to 50%. As a result losses were made by many steel companies, with the size of the loss varying with the extent of the company's indebtedness. French firms and the French industry were particularly heavily in debt (table 12.3). In the years 1975-1977, SACILOR-SOLLAC lost 4.745 milliard francs and USINOR 4.526 milliard francs (Freyssenet, 1979a, pages 165-167; see also table 12.3).

In 1975 the employers in France, Belgium, and Luxembourg began to put strong pressure on the EEC Commission to use the powers contained in the ECSC treaty to fix minimum prices, to institute production quotas for the industries of member countries, and to limit imports into the EEC. The arguments in favour of protectionism and of an agreement between the companies to limit their own output were opposed by the German and Italian companies and their governments among others. In the German case this opposition stemmed in part from the fact that the financial position of the leading steel companies was satisfactory because of their low indebtedness, the size of their reserves, and their diversification into other sectors. In addition, dominant groups in the FRG were concerned about the effect of an increase in steel prices on the costs and competitiveness of manufactured goods containing steel, and about the impact of retaliation on EEC economies which were particularly dependent upon exporting.

With the ending of the recovery in 1976, however, an anticrisis plan called the Simmonet Plan was adopted. The adoption of this plan was followed in 1977 by the adoption of the Davignon Plan as a framework within which the steel industry could be restructured at a European level (Freyssenet, 1979a, pages 174-179).

In France, in 1975, a sectoral study group for the steel industry was working on the Seventh Plan (1976-1980). Its report indicated that neither the steel companies nor the government expected the crisis to persist.

Table 12.3 The development of the French steel industry, 1973-1977. Source: Curry (1978).

	1973	1974	1975	1976	1977
Output (million tonnes)	25.3	27.0	21.5	23.2	22.1
Turnover (milliard francs)	24.3	35.5	28.5	32.6	34.2
Cash flow (milliard francs)	2.5	5.2	−2.6	−2.5	−4.1
Net profits (milliard francs)	0.9	2.3	−3.7	−4.0	−6.1
Medium- and long-term debt (milliard francs)	20.5	23.7	28.3	33.9	38.0
Employment (thousands)	151.5	157.6	155.5	153.7	142.7
Output per person (tonnes per person)	171.8	175.0	137.3	150.0	149.0

Indeed, at the end of the plan period, steel output was expected to stand at 32 million to 35 million tonnes. (In reality it was to equal 23 million tonnes.) Similarly, in the preamble to the Seventh Plan report adopted in July 1976 the crisis was spoken of in the past tense, and output was expected to grow at 5.5 to 6% per year instead of only 3% (Stoffaes, 1984, page 300). In short, the demand for steel was expected to increase again in the near future. The main companies and the government were consequently able to agree on a conjunctural strategy of riding out the crisis through recourse to short-time working. Needless to say, the costs of this strategy were to be met largely by the government and the workers. The other option of redundancies was, however, ruled out, and thus employment in the steel industry, which had risen from 146 000 workers in 1970 to 158 000 in 1974, only fell to 153 700 in 1976. (The number of temporary workers fell much more sharply. Nevertheless, the fact that employment was higher in 1976 than in 1970 was to add to the severity of subsequent events.) In addition, some new investment was planned, and the government lent the companies 1.547 milliard francs from FDES.

Only with the ending of the recovery which began in 1976 was it concluded that the crisis was going to persist. This realisation led to the preparation of the Plan Acier. However, the content of the plan was revealed only slowly over a period extending from December 1976 to late in 1977 for fear of its political repercussions in the months leading up to the municipal elections of March 1977.

The aim of this new plan was to make the steel industry competitive in the long term while maintaining capacity at its existing level of 33.3 million tonnes per annum. Some of the older installations which were duplicated by newer ones were to be closed. More modern installations like the SOLMER works, which had not been operating at anywhere near its capacity, were to be fully loaded. In addition, the capacity and competitiveness of modern installations were to be increased through new investments. The resulting plan was expected to lead to the loss of 16 100 jobs between April 1977 and April 1979, of which some 13 400 were to be lost in Lorraine.

The actual plan was composed of several volets. A financial volet included provisions for state funding of a programme of investments in works in return for which the companies were expected to make certain financial, industrial, and social commitments. In the industrial volet one of the clearest new decisions was that the SOLMER works should operate at full capacity. A second was USINOR's decision to drop plans for modernising the Thionville works and to close everything except the electric arc furnaces and the foundry and forging shop. Operating the remaining installations was expected to require only 800 of the 4200 workers employed at Thionville. This decision was presented as a condition for the survival of USINOR's works at Longwy. In addition, the Société des Forges de Châtillon, Commentry Biache, the Société des Hauts-Fourneaux de La Chiers, and the Société des Aciéries et Tréfileries de Neuves-Maisons

Châtillon merged to form the Compagnie Industrielle Chiers-Châtillon (CICC) (see table 12.1). With this merger the basis was laid for a rationalisation programme involving the rundown of the La Chiers plant near Longwy. On this occasion the decision to reduce employment was not accompanied by guarantees that the workers concerned would be redeployed. What followed was a series of demonstrations and protest actions against the plan and in particular against its employment implications. These struggles were, however, largely ineffective. More importantly the unions agreed to take part in discussions about the social volet of the plan, and Force Ouvrière accepted the employers' proposals for minimising the number of redundancies, enabling the plan to go ahead.

The regional volet of the Plan Acier was composed of a series of measures that were intended to provide alternative jobs in Lorraine. Of these measures, which were announced in the course of 1977, the most important were the agreements with leading motor vehicle manufacturers to create, by 1984, 8000 government-aided jobs in or near the steel-producing basin.

As far as the financial and industrial restructuring of the holding companies with steel interests was concerned other options did of course exist. In particular, the metal-using companies owned by each holding company (CLIF, DNEL, and CICC) could have been placed under the control of each group's steel company. Had a policy of this kind been adopted, several advantages would have followed. On the one hand, the integration of the steel industry with downstream activities would have been closer. On the other, the resources available for the reorganisation of steel production would have been augmented. However, the holding companies were opposed to strategies of this kind. One reason was that the ability of shareholders to switch resources between activities according to their relative profitabilities would have been reduced. The second was the fear that, if steel and steel-using sectors were more closely integrated and if the Union de la Gauche were to win the March 1978 elections, the extent of any nationalisations that were to occur might increase. In this situation what tended to happen was that several largely independent groups were formed. Of these groups one would be composed of those companies which were directly involved in primary metal processing. Accordingly, activities whose future was uncertain, and which the holding companies were in all probability prepared to see nationalised, were grouped together. The companies whose activities were more profitable and which the holding company concerned was anxious not to lose were conversely placed in a different group. An integration of metal manufacturing and metal-using activities was therefore sacrificed on grounds of narrow financial expediency (Freyssenet, 1979a, pages 196–200).

12.7 The Plan de Sauvetage de la Sidérurgie, 1978

The assumption on which the Plan Acier was based quickly proved to be unfounded. In 1977, output fell to 22.1 million tonnes, and only about 60% of capacity was in use. In 1978, output recovered slightly but only reached 22.8 million tonnes, and prices did not rise as expected. On the other hand, the reductions in employment envisaged by the plan were more than achieved. In the three companies that had signed the social agreement with Force Ouvrière, employment fell by more than 20 000 jobs (Malézieux, 1980, pages 187-188).

In 1977 the steel companies were making yet larger losses (see table 12.3), and thus borrowing had to continue as the only means of covering these deficits and meeting the companies' prior charges burden. At the end of the year the companies owed 38.1 milliard francs. This sum amounted to 111% of their turnover. Interest payments alone were equal to 11.7% of their turnover (Malézieux, 1980, page 186). In the autumn, with the steel companies on the verge of bankruptcy, work started on the formulation of a new plan. After the elections in March 1978, in which the Right gained a victory, the contents of the plan started to be made public. On the 20 September 1978 it was announced.

What this plan represented was a major change in the structure and development of the French steel industry. With its approval, the government stepped in to save the industry but without nationalising it, and the state's strategy was altered from one of conjunctural support to one of aiding structural reorganisation. Unprofitable installations were to be closed, but no new capacity was to be added. As far as the industry's organisation was concerned the options of forming more powerful multinational groups, of placing the steel industry under the control of metal-using industries, and of nationalising the industry were rejected. In the Plan de Sauvetage de la Sidérurgie the formula adopted involved state acquisition of majority control of SACILOR-SOLLAC and also of USINOR-Châtillon-Neuves-Maisons (UCNM) which itself was formed as a result of a merger between USINOR and the Société Sidérurgique Châtillon-Neuves-Maisons. (The second of these groups had been established in September 1977, when, as part of a reorganisation of CICC, works producing ordinary steels and rolled products at Neuves-Maisons, Longwy, Anzin, and Blagny, and a plant producing special steels at Isbergues had been grouped together.) (See table 12.1; and Freyssenet, 1979a, page 200.)

With these steps CSSF lost its role in the allocation of state aid and in the financing of investment, and the centres of decision-making were more clearly defined. Moreover, some transnational restructuring was set in motion: USINOR with the industries in Belgium and Luxembourg, and SACILOR with the Saar and Luxembourg. However, no serious efforts were made to coordinate the activities of the two main French groups (Stoffaes, 1984, page 308).

The aim of the financial plan was threefold. The cost of servicing the outstanding debt of the steel industry was to be reduced substantially; the repayment of loans was to be deferred for as long as possible; and the main steel companies' own funds were to be reconstructed to forestall the need to borrow again in the near future. Special arrangements were made to reduce the cost of (1) loans of 9 milliard francs from FDES, (2) bank loans of 9 milliard francs, and (3) loans amounting to 13.5 milliard francs from GIS, the Crédit National, and some other sources. An amortisation fund was set up by the state, the Crédit National, and the Caisse des Dépôts et des Consignations to protect and repay small investors. Most significantly, 2 milliard francs of debt to the state and to some other public investors were converted into shares in the capital of two finance companies controlling, directly or indirectly through holding companies, the steel companies themselves.

The resulting structure of USINOR after its absorption of Châtillon-Neuves-Maisons, and of SACILOR-SOLLAC is indicated in figure 12.8. (Vallourec, controlled by DNEL, and the Aciéries de Dilling, controlled by Marine-Wendel, both of which were making profits, had to be included in the new groups. Companies involved in construction engineering and in the production of special steels were, however, not included.)

As a result of these steps, the annual financial costs of the steel companies involved were reduced to 1.2 milliard francs per year or to some 5% of their turnover, and some of their debt was practically written off. Some restrictions were placed on the activities of existing shareholders, but provisions were made to enable the old majority shareholders to reassume control by settling their debts once the companies concerned had been placed back on an even keel (Freyssenet, 1979a, pages 205-209, 218-220).

Alongside these financial and organisational changes new technical plans were prepared. In essence, production was to be concentrated upon the most efficient installations, with a view to operating them at or near full capacity, whereas installations and works whose profitability was judged to be insufficient were to be taken out of service and closed.

In the case of SACILOR-SOLLAC the response was the following. In its least competitive installations at Hayange, Hagondange, and Rombas, four eight-hour shifts were replaced by three or two eight-hour shifts. The works owned by SOLLAC, the Gandrange plant, the continuous rod mills at Joeuf and Rombas, and the joist and rail mill at Hayange were to be updated in order to increase productivity, sometimes with the institution of a regime of discontinuous working. These measures were expected to lead to the loss of 8500 out of 35800 jobs, and to 2500 redundancies. As far as closures were concerned, only the coking unit and blast furnaces at Hagondange were targeted. The absence of significant closures helped to minimise the social tensions generated by SACILOR-SOLLAC's proposals. The proposals themselves, however, seemed unlikely to be adequate to the task of establishing a coherent and competitive set of installations in the company's long products division, even after a subsequent round of closures, and new investments were likely to be required to safeguard the flat products division (Freyssenet, 1979a, pages 109-112).

The steps proposed by USINOR were much more radical (see figures 12.9 and 12.10). One of the most striking was the decision to increase the production of pig iron and steel at Dunkirk and to end steel making at Denain. The rolling mills at Denain were to be supplied for the time being with slabs shipped from Dunkirk along the Dunkirk-Valenciennes canal. Cold rolling was to continue at Montataire, Mardyck, and Biache. A small plant at Blagny in the Ardennes was to be closed. The ultramodern and highly specialised factory at Isbergues was to form, on its own, a separate operational division of the company. Steel plate was to be produced by using the recently automated mill at Longwy and a mill at Dunkirk whose capacity was to be doubled. These changes in the flat products division were expected to lead to the loss of 5400 jobs by the end of 1980.

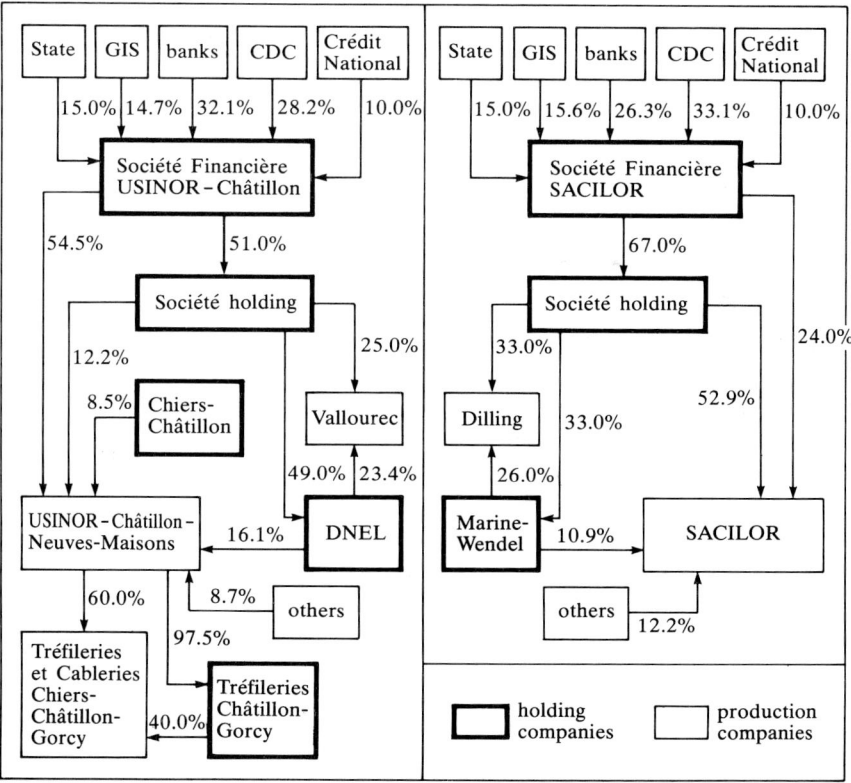

Figure 12.8. The structure of USINOR and SACILOR in 1978. Source: Marger (1979, page 10).

326 Chapter 12

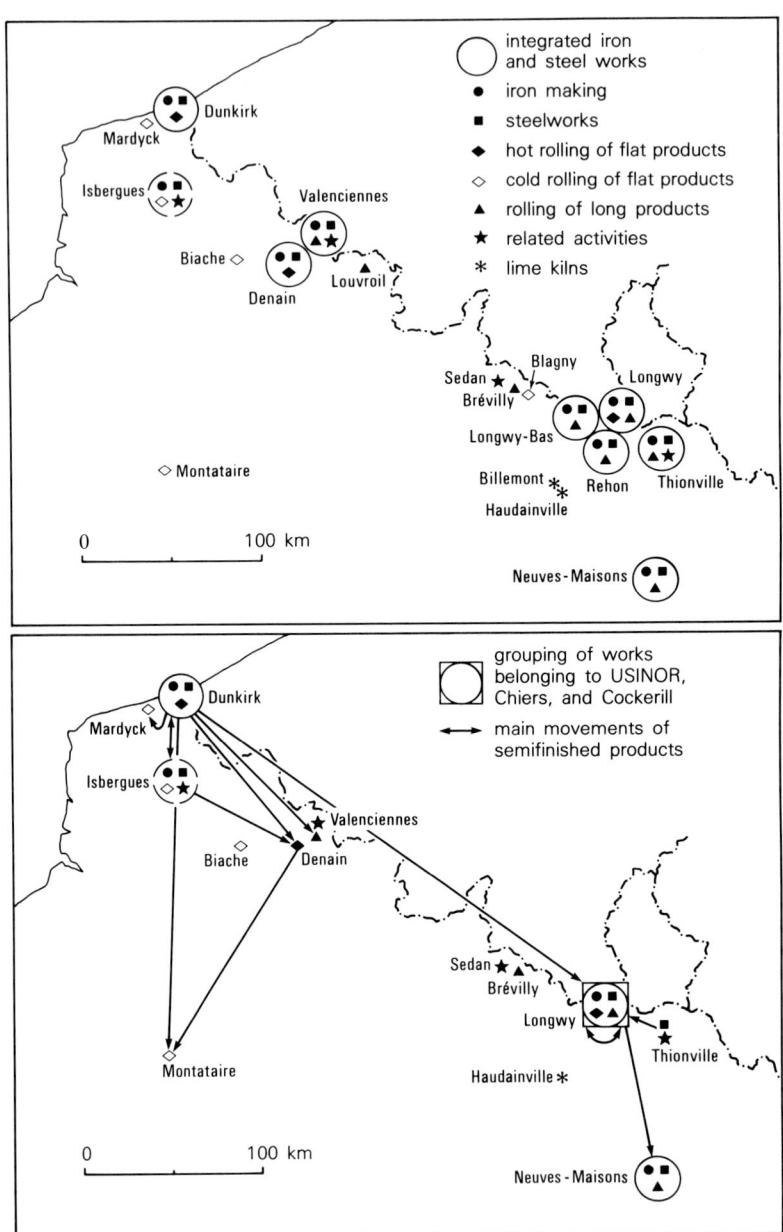

Figure 12.9. The restructuring of USINOR: reorganising production.
Source: Malézieux (1980, page 191).

The crisis and restructuring of the French steel industry 327

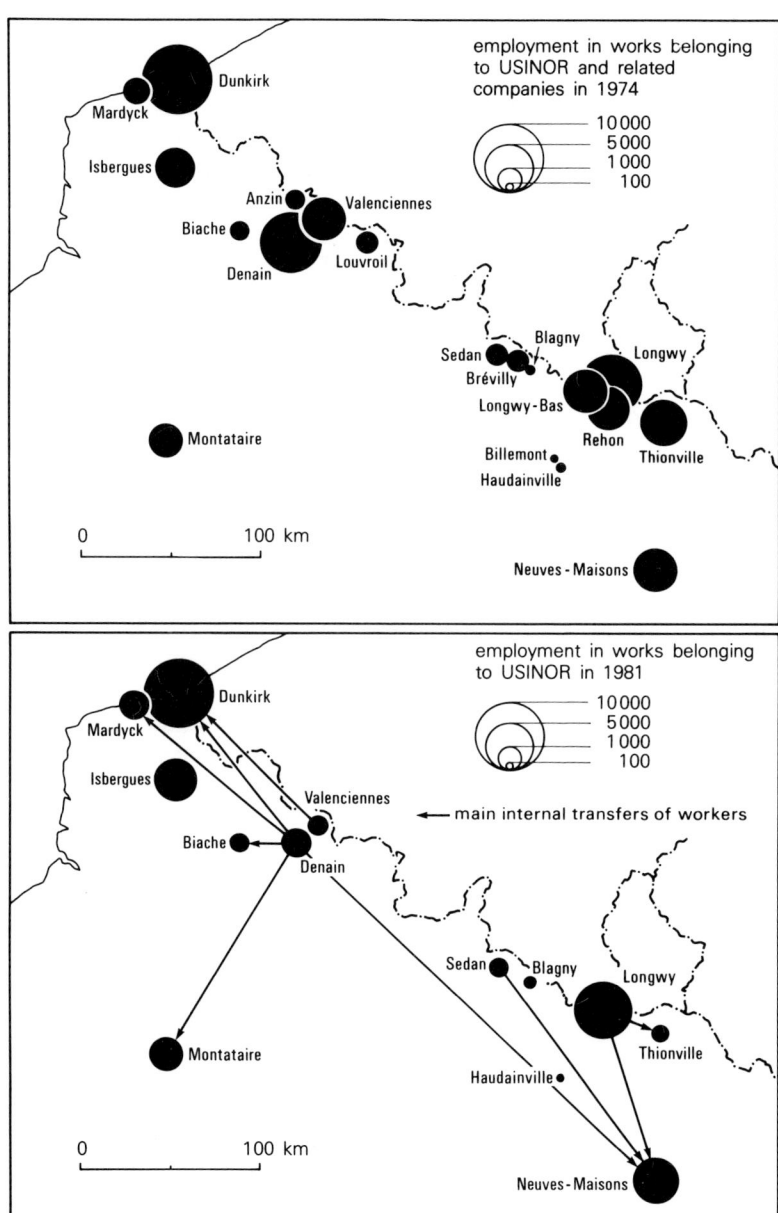

Figure 12.10. The restructuring of USINOR: employment change.
Source: Malézieux (1980, page 193).

In the area of long products USINOR had already decided to concentrate on the production of wire rod and large and medium-sized joists, manufacturing bars, and concrete-reinforcing bars in miniworks owned for the most part by subsidiaries. The continuous wire rod mill at Anzin was to be closed along with the rest of the works. A decision had already been taken to close the mill at the La Chiers plant. This decision left the mills at Longwy and at Neuves-Maisons. The joist mills at Longwy and Valenciennes-Trith-St Léger were to be retained, with the one at Valenciennes being supplied with blooms by the Dunkirk works. Most significantly, the decision to equip the works at Longwy with an oxygen steel-making unit was reversed. Instead the works was to be supplied, it was decided, with steel from Neuves-Maisons, where oxygen steel-making equipment was already being installed, and from the plant at Rehon which was owned at that time by Cockerill, whose base was in Belgium. In the period up to the end of 1980, with this reorganisation of the company's long products division, some 7000 jobs were expected to be lost. But since hardly any new investment was contemplated, the proposals were seen as doing little to increase the chances of long-term survival of the steel industry in Lorraine (Freyssenet, 1979a, pages 212–216).

In all, the Plan de Sauvetage de la Sidérurgie implied a loss of 21 750 jobs between the end of April 1979 and the end of 1980, of which some three quarters were to be lost in 1979. Of this total, some 14 000 jobs were to be lost in the steel-producing basin in Lorraine, with Longwy in particular being badly affected. In the Nord, the town of Denain was to lose a disproportionate number of jobs. The new jobs in vehicle manufacturing promised for Lorraine were far from being created, and the number to be generated at Thionville by Renault had been reduced from 1100 to 300. In Longwy only 850 jobs had been created since 1970, even though employment in the steel industry had fallen by 5075 jobs. This loss of jobs had been accompanied by a sharp fall in employment in subcontracting and in public and private service activities. The magnitude of these job losses, the exhaustion of many of the possibilities of early retirement, the concentration of many of the job losses in the towns of Longwy and Denain, and their presentation without any form of compensation for the communities and individuals involved led to violent working-class opposition. Some factories were occupied, roads and railway lines were blocked, police stations and the offices of employers' organisations were attacked, a free radio station was set up at Longwy, *ville morte* [6] operations were carried out, and wide-ranging demonstrations were organised throughout the first half of 1979 (see Noirel, with Azzaoui, 1980; Noirel, 1981).

---

[6] A 'ville morte' is a ghost town. All activity is brought to an end and the town is closed off from the outside world in order to highlight the likely impact of the collapse of its economic base.

In the face of this opposition, some measures aimed at, first, limiting the social effects of the plan, and, second, disorganising the opposition were introduced. But the main financial and economic decisions were retained without being altered in any fundamental way.

In July 1979 a social agreement was signed by all the interested parties except the Confédération Générale du Travail (CGT) and the Longwy branch of the Confédération Française Démocratique du Travail (CFDT). The age of retirement in the steel industry in the Nord and Lorraine was reduced to fifty-five years and to fifty years for some workers. Schemes for transferring workers to other plants or other industries were set up. An extra grant of 50 000 francs was offered to workers prepared to give up their jobs. If, however, the workers concerned were immigrants and were prepared to return home, another 10 000 francs was added. With the development of the French steel industry significant numbers of immigrant workers had been recruited. In 1975 in the Eastern region, for example, nearly 38%, and in the country, nearly 26% of the industry's workers were immigrants (see table 12.4). As part of a strategy of managing the crisis a disproportionate share of the job losses were to fall on this group. The aim of these measures was to avoid compulsory redundancies and to overcome opposition to the plans of the government and the steel companies. In addition, reconversion companies offered temporary maintenance and engineering jobs to some workers whose jobs were disappearing (Malézieux, 1980, pages 192-194).

Table 12.4. Foreign workers in the French steel industry and by nationality in the eastern region steel industry (in percentages of the workers employed). Source: elaborated from Freyssenet and Imbert (1975a, pages 255-256).

	France	Convention sociale Est							
		all	Italian	Belgian	Spanish	Portuguese	Polish	Algerian	Moroccan and Tunisian
1948	29.90								
1954	26.00								
1960	29.60								
1966	26.80	36.60							
1967	26.00	35.59	16.05	2.93	3.10	1.50	1.68	8.05	0.74
1968	25.80	35.00	15.39	2.83	2.89	1.46	1.48	8.90	0.71
1969	26.70	35.82	14.83	2.44	3.39	1.68	1.30	9.73	1.06
1970	27.30	36.56	14.34	2.21	3.02	1.98	1.11	9.97	2.63
1971	26.40	35.67	14.14	2.18	2.60	2.09	1.10	9.80	2.59
1972	25.60	35.35	14.10	2.01	2.52	2.34	1.02	9.98	2.19
1973	25.90	37.12	13.83	1.85	2.26	2.47	0.97	11.47	2.58
1974	26.00	38.44	13.34	1.68	2.36	2.49	0.88	12.41	3.57
1975	25.50	37.69	13.12	1.63	2.37	2.57	0.78	12.03	3.61

The Fonds Spécial d'Adaptation Industrielle (FSAI) was set up by the government to attract new industry to the regions concerned. In addition, the car industry was, it was announced, going to provide yet more new jobs. Some 7800 jobs were to be created, of which 5100 were to be located in the Nord and in the Ardennes. 925 new jobs were to be provided in Lorraine, including 191 in the steel-producing basin in the north of the region (Freyssenet, 1979a, page 218). These measures were, however, unlikely to do much to revitalise the economies of the area around Denain and Valenciennes or of the steel-producing areas in Lorraine. The financial and social volets of the plan nevertheless cost the state something in the region of 30 milliard francs in 1980 prices (Stoffaes, 1984, page 304).

12.8 The victory of the Left and the nationalisation of the steel industry

In 1974–1981, employment in the steel industry in Lorraine fell from 80 618 to 41 767. Of these workers, only 6% were less than twenty-five years old and 8% were over fifty years old. In the same period, jobs in the iron mines declined from 8854 to 3781. Of the 11 700 jobs in the car industry promised in 1977 and 1979, only 4000 had been created. At the end of 1980, nearly 35 000 people were unemployed in the steel-producing zone, and about 16 000 people crossed daily to work in the Saar and in Luxembourg (see table 12.5; and Freyssenet, 1983, pages 79–80). 1981 was a census year. When the results were announced, one of the most striking features was the extent of the fall in population in Lorraine and in the northeast of the country (see Laborie et al, 1985, pages 13–51, 79–109).

On the 10 May 1981 the Left swept to victory in the national elections. Many factors explain this historic change. The disastrous economic and regional consequences of the development of the French economy after the monetarist turn of the Barre government was one of them (see Lipietz, 1984a, pages 58–61; and also Ross and Jenson, 1981, pages 72–92).

Table 12.5. Output and employment in the French steel industry, 1974–1981. Sources: CSSF(a) (various years) and CSSF(b) (1980; 1982).

	Output (thousands of tonnes)			Employment		
	1974	1978	1981	1974	1978	1981
Est	14 251	9 800	8 064	80 618	62 851	41 767
Nord	9 026	7 611	7 969	40 910	35 229	26 725
Centre	1 086	800	na	14 748	12 928	10 463
Sud-Ouest	173	132	na	1 390	1 169	1 138
Sud-Est	1 494	3 708	na	12 687	12 668	10 986
Ouest	993	790	na	7 276	6 478	6 112
Total	27 023	22 841	21 258	157 629	131 323	97 191

na, data not available.

At the end of 1980, however, the European steel industry had entered a new phase of crisis. Underlying it were several sets of factors. Some, including the cyclical downturn that followed the second increase in oil prices and the adoption of strict monetarist strategies in Britain and the USA, were conjunctural. Others were structural (see chapter 13, section 13.3). On this occasion no major European steel producer avoided losses. In the French case, SACILOR lost about 1.9 milliard francs in 1980 and nearly 3 milliard in each of 1981 and 1982 on an annual turnover of some 17 milliard francs. The situation of USINOR was not much better. On a larger turnover of some 24 milliard francs it lost about 4 milliard per year in 1981 and 1982. Substantial losses were also recorded, however, by the British Steel Corporation, the Belgian industry, and Italsider as well as by ARBED, Thyssen, Estel, Krupp, and Klöckner (Stoffaes, 1984, page 290). At the EEC level, however, the Davignon Plan was already in place. What it provided was a crisis cartel that could set minimum price levels and quotas and that could protect the European industry against dumping while long-term restructuring was carried out.

At the end of 1981, USINOR and SACILOR were nationalised along with many other parts of the industrial and financial system in the framework of the laws extending the public sector. Moreover, the nationalisation of Péchiney – Ugine Kuhlmann (PUK) allowed Ugine-Aciers to be linked with SACILOR. New managing directors were appointed, and trade union representatives were given seats on management councils. While new decision-making structures were established, the plans for the industry's development proposed when the Left was in opposition were quickly forgotten. Instead, measures that amounted to a continuation of the ones adopted in 1978 were presented as necessities imposed by the economic crisis and the French steel industry's lack of adjustment to new technological and market conditions. With the new government's election almost all French steel-production activity was transferred to the two groups, and ways of coordinating USINOR's and SACILOR's activities were considered. The rationalisation and modernisation of existing capacity continued. Increased emphasis was placed, however, on downstream integration into the production of special steels and engineering with a view to increasing the value added by the steel groups and reconquering the home market, and more resources were to be devoted to research.

In August 1982 a new steel plan was announced. The plan had several aims. One was to meet the current losses of the two steel companies. The second was to assist a strategy of modernisation and restructuring aimed at a return to profitability. Measures to cope with the plan's social consequences were also proposed.

Instead of an annual capacity of 34 million tonnes, advocated ahead of the elections by the PCF, or of 31 million tonnes, suggested by the Parti Socialiste (PS), annual capacity was to fall to 24 million tonnes by 1986.

[The target was derived from the Judet Report (Judet, 1982).] After 1984, new closings were envisaged, especially at Longwy, Vireux-Molhain, Joeuf, Villerupt, and Pompey. In addition, a programme of modernising investments was proposed. In 1981-1986, USINOR was to spend 9 milliard francs and SACILOR 8.5 milliard. Included were renewal of the Dunkirk works, the rolling mills at Montataire, Ugine-Acier's plants for special steels in Savoy, the Les Dunes works in the Nord, and the works at Hagondange in Lorraine, and a complete reconstruction of SOLLAC's and the Gandrange rolling mills.

Owing to the reduction of the length of the working week the number of jobs to be lost as a result of these closures and of modernising investments was more limited than would otherwise have been the case. Nevertheless, 11 000 to 12 000 jobs were to go, with one half of the losses occurring in Lorraine. As a counterpart to these job losses, early retirement and retraining schemes costing some 2 milliard francs per year were envisaged. In addition, changes occurred in the field of regional planning. In particular, more emphasis was placed on reindustrialisation and the reconstruction of the industrial fabric of the steel-producing regions through the development of small metal-using industries.

To finance new steel company investments and cover steel industry losses, state financial aid was given to USINOR and SACILOR. In addition, some 3.2 milliard francs were set aside for investments by steel group subsidiaries and for reconversion operations. Overall, in 1982-1986 the French government proposed to spend a sum (in 1982 prices) of 10 milliard francs per year on the steel industry. [The steel plans of 1966-1981 had altogether cost some 60 milliard francs (Stoffaes, 1984, pages 309-310).]

12.9 The 1984 Steel Plan

According to the European Commission, the European steel industry had an excess capacity of some 50 million tonnes per year. On these estimates, in 1986 French output was expected to stand at some 17 million to 21 million tonnes. As a result, in 1983 the Commission proposed that capacity be reduced by some 30 million tonnes and that no national steel industry get state support after 1986. With this reduction, capacity utilisation would, it was argued, stand at about 70%, leaving sufficient leeway to meet any unanticipated increase in demand. Under this proposal the Italian industry was thus to reduce annual capacity by 5.8 million tonnes, the British by 4.5 million tonnes, the German by 7 million tonnes, and the French by 5.3 million tonnes (Stoffaes, 1984, pages 310-311).

In March 1983 a second important development occurred: after a short expansionary experiment the French government changed course. What it adopted was a deflationary programme that in turn added to the reduction in the demand for steel. In 1983, output stood in fact at only 17.5 million tonnes compared with an annual capacity of some 23 million tonnes. In the same year USINOR and SACILOR made losses of nearly 10 milliard francs (in 1984 similar losses were recorded). USINOR had already reduced employment by 2000 jobs and SACILOR by 4200. But with another 5000 to be lost (under the 1982 plan), additional reductions amounting to 4000 jobs were announced by the two groups. The announcement of new financial losses occurred, however, at the moment when the government was embarking on its austerity programme and was intent on limiting its 1984 spending on the nationalised industries to 12.85 milliard francs. In the event, USINOR and SACILOR were given less money in 1984 than in 1983. The reason why less money was given was that the state wished to give more priority to the development of the electronics and car industries: in the view of the government, supporting the steel industry would have required most of the resources it had allocated and would have jeopardised its plans for other sectors on whose success depended that of the French economy (Stoffaes, 1984, page 311).

In the face of these state spending targets some outstanding investment decisions were made and some of the earlier strategic industrial decisions were reconsidered. To cut losses some loss-making plants producing products for which excess capacity existed were designated for closure. At the same time, to reduce spending, investment plans were cut back and modified.

At the end of March 1984 a revised plan was announced. The ECSC's requirement that the main French steel companies return to profitability was put off by one year to 1987. The country's projected steel-making capacity was reduced slightly to some 23 million tonnes. What was most significant, however, were a set of investment and disinvestment decisions mainly affecting the production of long steel products (the main decisions are set out in table 12.6). With them, job losses were to go up very sharply. In 1982-1986, 11000 to 12000 were to be lost. In 1984-1987, 20000 to 25000 were to go.

Underlying these decisions were several factors. In the first place a decision was made to place more emphasis on the production of simple steel products from scrap metal by means of electric arc methods. At that stage there were five miniworks in the country with an average annual capacity of some 200000 tonnes each, and a sixth works with a capacity of 500000 tonnes per year was planned. In Spain, on the other hand, there were sixteen, in Japan fifty, in the USA sixty-one, and in Italy eighty-one (see Dahmani, 1983, pages 150-153). Internationally, many miniworks were developed in the 1970s. Indeed in the framework of the Seventh Plan about ten new French minimills were tabled with the ECSC. Had these projects gone ahead, some 3.5 million tonnes of capacity would have been added by the end of 1980. On account of the situation of crisis, however, the ECSC blocked the French plans. In the past, miniworks had been used to produce relatively low-quality products from scrap and lacked scale economies. With the crisis, however, increased production capacity, improved rolling methods, and continuous casting allowed more sophisticated products to be manufactured and costs to be reduced. Also, methods of production and output could be adjusted much more quickly in the light of changing conjunctural conditions, overhead and energy costs were lower, and construction periods were shorter. As a result, electric arc methods were gaining ground. In Brescia, for example, the costs of producing concrete-reinforcing bars, wire rod, and small girders were up to 30% less than those of French ore-based producers. Not only were the French exporting some 3 million tonnes of scrap per year. Owing to the increasing competitiveness of miniworks, the home market was being lost to imported products from Italy and elsewhere. Consequently, the government decided on the construction of electric steelworks for the production of long products at Neuves-Maisons and Longwy.

Second, the decision to close a wire rod mill was required of the French government by the ECSC. Of the four mills in the country the state considered the one at Neuves-Maisons and the one at Rombas, finally

Table 12.6. The socialist government's main decisions for the steel industry, 29 March 1984[a].

Plant	Decision
Lorraine	
SACILOR Serémange	construction of a cold rolling mill producing flat products confirmed
USINOR Longwy	retention of the blast furnace supplying the wire rod mill; switch to electric steel making for the steel girder mill
USINOR Neuves-Maisons	switch to electric steel making for the wire rod mill
SACILOR Gandrange-Rombas	closing of the wire rod mill and decision not to build a universal rolling mill
SACILOR Hayange	retention and modernisation of the rail rolling mill
Outside of Lorraine	
USINOR Valenciennes	modernisation of the steel girder mill
USINOR Dunkirk	heavy (33 mm or more) sheet and plate mill project approved
SACILOR Fos	closing of Ugine-Aciers
SACILOR Caen	blast furnace to be retained and reconsidered in 1986

[a] These decisions were in addition to those made in the 1982 Steel Plan which involved the closure in whole or part of installations at Vireux-Molhain in the Ardennes (USINOR), at Denain in the Nord (USINOR), at Joeuf in Lorraine (SACILOR), at Villerupt in Lorraine (SACILOR), and at Pompey in Lorraine (SACILOR).

choosing to close the second. What caused most controversy was the related decision not to go ahead with the construction of a universal rolling mill at Gandrange. The project itself had been proposed by SACILOR. At that stage, SACILOR was producing shaped products at Hayange, Villerupt, Rombas, and Hagondange. What the group wanted was to concentrate production at Gandrange. The project was, however, expected to cost at least 1.5 milliard francs.

Instead of approving the project, the government, which was split on the question, decided to spend 0.6 milliard to 0.7 milliard francs on a modernisation of existing installations, of which one at Valenciennes was owned by USINOR and the other at Hayange was owned by SACILOR. In effect the government chose a path favoured by USINOR and the workers at Valenciennes instead of the one for which SACILOR had been pressing. Amongst other considerations two were important. On the one hand, it was argued that the construction of the universal rolling mill would have made it difficult for SACILOR to get out of the red by 1987 (at that stage the EEC was insisting that state subsidisation of steel industry losses should cease after 1976). On the other, the Gandrange plant used the comparatively expensive local ore. With this decision, however, the 2.2 million tonnes per year steel-making units at Gandrange and the jobs of 6700 people in Lorraine were placed in jeopardy (see Le Boucher, 1984a; 1984b). In addition to these developments, USINOR and SACILOR were required to coordinate investments, marketing, and research, and in order to rationalise activities and operate in the long products and special steels sectors, common subsidiaries were formed.

Job loss was to occur without redundancies. Instead, early retirement was proposed along with some 10 000 *congés de conversion*. Under this scheme some 10 000 workers were to be retrained on full pay. In addition, financial incentives were offered to encourage job creation in conversion poles so that at the end of the conversion holidays there would be new jobs for the workers concerned. Via these measures and via government pressure on nationalised firms, some 4000 jobs were promised, mainly in the electronics industry. Nevertheless, the socialist and communist government was acting against the interests of some of its own political supporters, and sufficient new jobs could not be guaranteed. In spite of the definition of comparatively generous accompanying social measures the new industrial plan accordingly stimulated another wave of violent working-class opposition in Lorraine and Marseilles.

The plan, however, was not a simple extension of the strategy of earlier right-wing governments. In several ways the measures of 1984 also represented a turning point in steel industry policy. The strategy of closing only inefficient plants and of successively modernising others was ended, and decisions were made about the destiny not just of individual plants but of whole regional industrial systems. In particular, Lorraine's industry seemed destined to be reduced to SOLLAC's flat products plant and some works producing long products not from ore but from scrap. Increased weight was also placed upon restructuring at the European level with USINOR working with Cockerill-Sambre, and SACILOR with ARBED. In addition, as a result of the weakening of SACILOR, a merger of the two main French groups was made more likely. Should these developments occur, European steel production will come to be concentrated in the hands of a few transnational groups and a few transnational regions.

Spatial implications of the steel crisis and steel production internalisation

After the Second World War, steel output increased rapidly but irregularly in the advanced capitalist countries and also internationally. Accompanying this process of expansion were marked increases in the amount of capital used per person employed and in the productivity of labour. In many countries with long-established steel industries the growth in productivity exceeded output growth, with the result that employment in this sector tended to decline. Moreover, the job loss that did result was frequently concentrated in largely monoindustrial regions and occurred at times when little alternative employment was available.

These processes were accompanied and reinforced by a strong movement towards a new distribution of steel production at international, national, and intranational levels (tables 13.1, 13.2, and 13.3). At a world level the market shares of developed market economies fell, especially in the 1970s, whereas those of newly industrialising countries and of centrally planned economies increased. In 1974-1978, for example, the share of ECSC producers in

Table 13.1. World crude steel production, 1960-1981 (in millions of tonnes, with percentages given in parentheses). Sources: elaborated from CSSF(a) (various years) and United Nations Economic Commission for Europe (various years).

	ECSC[a]	DME[b]	CPE[c]	LDC[d]	World
1960	98 (28.4)	231 (67.0)	105 (30.5)	9 (2.5)	345
1965	114 (24.9)	306 (67.0)	135 (29.6)	16 (3.5)	457
1970	138 (23.2)	395 (66.4)	178 (29.9)	22 (3.7)	596
1971	128 (22.0)	370 (63.7)	188 (32.4)	23 (3.9)	582
1972	139 (22.0)	405 (64.2)	199 (31.5)	27 (4.3)	631
1973	150 (21.5)	459 (65.8)	210 (30.1)	29 (4.1)	697
1974	155 (22.0)	461 (65.0)	216 (30.5)	31 (4.4)	708
1975	126 (19.4)	388 (60.1)	225 (34.8)	33 (5.1)	646
1976	134 (19.8)	413 (61.1)	225 (33.3)	38 (5.6)	676
1977	126 (18.7)	397 (58.9)	235 (34.9)	42 (6.3)	674
1978	133 (18.5)	417 (58.2)	251 (35.1)	48 (6.7)	716
1979	140 (18.8)	439 (58.8)	253 (33.9)	55 (7.3)	746
1980	128 (17.9)	404 (56.3)	253 (35.3)	60 (8.4)	717
1981	125 (17.7)	397 (56.1)	250 (35.3)	61 (8.6)	708

[a] The output of the ECSC is also included in the DME data. The output of Denmark, Eire, and the UK, which joined in 1973, is included from 1960 onwards.
[b] The developed market economies (DME) are Western Europe (excluding Yugoslavia), North America, South Africa, Japan, Australia, and other Oceania.
[c] The centrally planned economies (CPE) include the USSR and Eastern Europe, China, and DPR Korea.
[d] The less developed countries (LDC) are Latin America, Africa (except South Africa), the Middle East, and Asia (except Japan, China, and DPR Korea).

Table 13.2. Crude steel production in the ECSC, 1950–1981 (in millions of tonnes, with percentages given in parentheses; includes output of Denmark, Eire, and the UK). Sources: CSSF(a) (various years) and EEC Commission: Eurostat(a) (various years).

	Belgium	Denmark	Eire	FRG	France	Greece	Italy	Luxemburg	Netherlands	UK	ECSC[a]
1950	3.778 (7.80)	0.123 (0.25)	–	14.018 (28.95)	8.652 (17.87)	–	2.362 (4.88)	2.451 (5.06)	0.490 (1.01)	16.554 (34.18)	48.429
1960	7.180 (7.34)	0.318 (0.33)	0.030 (0.03)	34.100 (34.85)	17.281 (17.66)	–	8.229 (8.41)	4.084 (4.17)	1.941 (1.98)	24.683 (25.23)	97.846
1965	9.162 (8.04)	0.412 (0.36)	0.050 (0.04)	36.821 (32.33)	19.604 (17.21)	–	12.681 (11.13)	4.585 (4.03)	3.138 (2.76)	27.438 (24.09)	113.891
1970	12.607 (9.13)	0.473 (0.34)	0.080 (0.06)	45.140 (32.62)	23.773 (17.22)	–	17.277 (12.51)	5.462 (3.96)	5.030 (3.64)	28.315 (20.51)	138.058
1971	12.446 (9.71)	0.471 (0.37)	0.081 (0.06)	40.313 (31.47)	22.859 (17.84)	–	17.452 (13.62)	5.241 (4.09)	5.083 (3.97)	24.174 (18.87)	128.120
1972	14.532 (10.45)	0.505 (0.36)	0.077 (0.06)	43.705 (31.43)	24.054 (17.30)	–	19.815 (14.25)	5.485 (3.93)	5.585 (4.02)	25.321 (18.21)	139.052
1973	15.523 (10.34)	0.445 (0.30)	0.110 (0.07)	49.521 (33.0)	25.264 (16.84)	–	20.995 (13.99)	5.925 (3.95)	5.631 (3.75)	26.649 (17.76)	150.063
1974	16.225 (10.42)	0.535 (0.34)	0.112 (0.07)	53.232 (34.20)	27.023 (17.36)	–	23.803 (15.29)	6.447 (4.14)	5.835 (3.75)	22.426 (14.41)	155.638
1975	11.583 (9.22)	0.559 (0.44)	0.082 (0.07)	40.415 (32.16)	21.530 (17.13)	–	21.836 (17.38)	4.624 (3.68)	4.823 (3.84)	20.198 (16.07)	125.650
1976	12.145 (9.06)	0.722 (0.54)	0.058 (0.04)	42.415 (31.64)	23.221 (17.32)	–	23.447 (17.49)	4.566 (3.41)	5.189 (3.87)	22.274 (16.62)	134.037
1977	11.256 (8.93)	0.685 (0.54)	0.058 (0.05)	38.985 (30.92)	22.094 (17.52)	–	23.334 (18.50)	4.329 (3.43)	4.927 (3.91)	20.411 (16.19)	126.079
1978	12.601 (9.50)	0.863 (0.65)	0.066 (0.05)	41.253 (31.11)	22.841 (17.23)	–	24.283 (18.31)	4.790 (3.61)	5.590 (4.22)	20.300 (15.32)	132.598
1979	13.443 (9.59)	0.804 (0.57)	0.072 (0.05)	46.040 (32.84)	23.360 (16.66)	–	24.250 (17.30)	4.950 (3.53)	5.801 (4.14)	21.464 (15.31)	140.184
1980	12.321 (9.64)	0.734 (0.57)	0.028 (0.02)	43.838 (34.31)	23.176 (18.14)	–	26.501 (20.74)	4.619 (3.62)	5.272 (4.13)	11.277 (8.83)	127.766
1981	12.283 (9.61)	0.612 (0.48)	0.033 (0.03)	41.610 (32.57)	21.258 (16.64)	0.909 (0.71)	24.778 (19.39)	3.790 (2.96)	5.472 (4.28)	15.321 (11.99)	125.113

[a] The output of Denmark, Eire, and the UK, which joined in 1973, is included from 1950 onwards.

world production fell from 22% to 18.7%. In the ECSC itself the countries most affected were Luxembourg, the FRG, and Belgium. Italy was least affected. The output of the French industry fell by just over the average for ECSC countries, whereas within the country, production was transferred from Lorraine and from the internal parts of the Nord to new coastal works at Dunkirk and Fos-sur-Mer.

With the world recession of the 1970s and 1980s the steel industries of the advanced capitalist countries in particular were confronted with a deep structural crisis. In the first place, demand declined, competition increased, prices fell, and major losses were recorded. Second, with the rise of the steel industries of Japan, the Soviet-dominated COMECON (Council for

Table 13.3. Crude steel production in France 1950–1981 (in millions of tonnes, with percentages given in parentheses). Sources: CSSF(a) (various years) and CSSF(b)(1981, page 20; 1982, page 19).

	Est	Nord	Centre	Sud-Ouest	Sud-Est	Ouest	France
1950	6.119 (70.72)	1.703 (19.68)	0.464 (5.36)	0.063 (0.73)	0.099 (1.14)	0.204 (2.36)	8.652
1960	11.339 (65.62)	3.970 (22.97)	0.831 (4.81)	0.117 (0.67)	0.307 (1.78)	0.717 (4.15)	17.281
1965	12.309 (62.79)	5.245 (26.75)	0.851 (4.34)	0.060 (0.31)	0.377 (1.92)	0.762 (3.89)	19.604
1970	13.989 (58.84)	7.146 (30.05)	1.128 (4.74)	0.106 (0.45)	0.590 (2.48)	0.814 (3.42)	23.773
1971	13.527 (59.17)	6.781 (29.66)	1.020 (4.46)	0.128 (0.56)	0.481 (2.10)	0.922 (4.03)	22.859
1972	13.873 (57.67)	7.561 (31.43)	0.987 (4.10)	0.119 (0.49)	0.562 (2.34)	0.952 (3.96)	24.054
1973	14.003 (55.42)	8.494 (33.62)	1.039 (4.11)	0.143 (0.57)	0.572 (2.26)	1.013 (4.01)	25.264
1974	14.251 (52.74)	9.026 (33.40)	1.086 (4.02)	0.173 (0.64)	1.494 (5.53)	0.993 (3.67)	27.023
1975	10.235 (47.54)	7.072 (32.85)	0.956 (4.44)	0.160 (0.74)	2.228 (10.35)	0.879 (4.08)	21.530
1976	10.932 (47.08)	7.932 (34.16)	0.896 (3.86)	0.138 (0.59)	2.517 (10.84)	0.806 (3.47)	23.221
1977	9.841 (44.42)	7.185 (32.52)	0.784 (3.55)	0.127 (0.57)	3.483 (15.76)	0.701 (3.17)	22.094
1978	9.800 (42.91)	7.611 (33.32)	0.800 (3.50)	0.132 (0.58)	3.708 (16.23)	0.790 (3.46)	22.841
1979	10.234 (43.81)	8.092 (34.64)	0.752 (3.22)	0.147 (0.63)	3.249 (13.91)	0.886 (3.79)	23.360
1980	9.423 (40.66)	8.328 (35.93)	na	na	na	na	23.176
1981	8.064 (37.9)	7.969 (37.5)	na	na	na	na	21.258

na, data not available.

Mutual Economic Assistance), and the newly industrialising countries, the international distribution of steel production was, as I have just indicated, changing. Third, revolutionary changes in technology and in the process of production were under way.

As a result of the consequent restructuring of the industry, steel industry employment declined sharply in most ECSC and advanced capitalist countries. Between the end of 1974 and the spring of 1978, employment fell by 25.9% or 5998 jobs in Luxemburg, by 22.5% or 14338 jobs in Belgium, by 12.5% or 19636 jobs in France, and by 10.9% or 24218 jobs in the FRG. Between the end of December 1974 and December 1978, UK employment declined by 16.0% or by 31500 jobs. Only in Italy did employment in the steel industry not fall (Freyssenet, 1979a, pages 171–172). With these and more recent job losses, unemployment in old steel-producing regions rose sharply.

13.1 Differential growth and the spatial redistribution of steel production

The steel crisis itself played an important role in accelerating changes in the distribution of steel production. Companies whose installations had not been fully automated were forced to modernise them as quickly as possible if resources were available for investment, to close outdated installations, and to use fully the most modern ones. By contrast, companies with wholly modern facilities sought to operate them as near capacity as possible. With any subsequent increase in demand the market shares of the companies whose plants were fully automated and had been operating at less than full capacity would increase (see the discussion of technical change in chapter 2, section 2.7, and the data on technical change in the steel industry in figures 12.4 and 12.5).

In an industry such as steel, in which capital costs form such a substantial proportion of total costs, a redistribution of production according to differential productivity is, however, not automatic. (On the structure of costs in the French industry see table 13.4.) Companies that have recently carried out large-scale investments are likely to be heavily indebted, whereas companies with less efficient installations whose capital costs have

Table 13.4. The changing structure of annual costs in the French steel industry, 1960–1978 (in percentages). Source: CSSF, cited in Dahmani (1983).

	1960	1969	1978
Raw materials	25.4	21.7	19.7
Energy	22.0	18.1	19.1
Labour	24.1	29.6	30.5
Other expenses [a]	28.5	30.6	30.7
Total	100.0	100.0	100.0

[a] Mainly the financial charges associated with the financing of investments.

at least in part been met may conversely find themselves in a comparatively strong financial position. In situations where excess capacity exists, market mechanisms cannot ensure therefore that schemes of rationalisation are governed by efficiency criteria. Within a country, what is normally also required is either the formation of larger financial units able to assess as a whole the balance of gains and losses associated with different rationalisation schemes, or state intervention aimed at devalorising some capital that has not been fully depreciated.

In the case of the ECSC it was market and planning mechanisms of these kinds that lay behind recent changes in the location of steel production. In the 1970s and early 1980s, one of the most striking changes was the relative growth of the Italian steel industry: in 1974-1978, its share of output increased from 15.3% to 18.3%. In the 1970s the nationalised sector of the Italian industry made losses because of its low level of capacity utilisation and its high degree of indebtedness (see table 13.5), but the Italian industry had some of the most modern installations and one of the highest overall levels of labour productivity in the ECSC (table 13.6). By contrast, the share of the French industry remained more or less constant. Until the adoption of a policy of a strong currency by the Barre government, the franc had fallen in international value, and the industry's labour costs were comparatively low. (International value formation was discussed theoretically in chapter 2, section 2.10.) Adjustments of a monetary kind do not, however, constitute an adequate basis for long-term competitiveness. What is critical is the structure of the industry itself.

In the last chapter, I showed how at the end of the 1970s the companies and the government in France responded to the crisis by closing outdated installations and fully loading the most modern ones. In other words, competitiveness was sought at the expense of a fall in capacity. If, however, the demand for steel were to increase, French steel users would have to import steel from low-cost foreign suppliers. The economy's dependence on imports would thus, other things being equal, increase, and the share of the French industry in ECSC steel output would fall. Underlying these possibilities were two factors. On the one hand, in the absence of new investment the industry was inefficient. Although the French industry had ultramodern plants at Fos and Dunkirk, it also had one of the lowest average levels of labour productivity. In 1978 it employed 137 000 workers to produce 22.8 million tonnes of steel compared with the employment of 96 000 workers to produce 24.4 million tonnes in Italy. It also had an extremely high level of indebteness. On the other hand, a strategy of seeking competitiveness through capacity cuts alone leaves an industry without the capability of short-run increases in output.

The strategy adopted corresponded closely with the liberal and pro-European views of the French Government, and with the liberal recommendations of the EEC Commission. In particular, it was consistent with an increase in European economic integration and with the view

Table 13.5. Steel capacity utilisation (including independent steel foundries) in the ECSC, 1960–1982 (in percentages). Source: EEC Commission: Eurostat(b) (various years).

	Belgium	Denmark[a]	Eire[a]	FRG	France	Italy	Luxemburg	Netherlands	UK[a]	ECSC
1960	88.9			94.5	96.7	94.3	99.6	93.5		87.5
1961	84.8			90.7	94.7	93.0	97.7	90.2		83.3
1962	87.9			85.6	88.1	91.4	93.7	82.2		87.5
1963	85.1			79.5	84.0	92.5	90.3	79.7		90.0
1964	88.6			91.2	91.6	83.7	94.2	84.4		84.2
1965	87.5			80.9	86.5	84.6	93.5	88.8		78.6
1966	80.2			74.2	83.4	78.0	84.7	93.5		80.1
1967	78.4			76.9	82.6	82.9	79.2	97.3		85.7
1968	83.5			86.0	84.1	86.6	85.0	96.3		89.0
1969	89.6			89.6	91.0	81.4	93.3	96.3		86.2
1970	85.0			84.8	91.0	81.3	90.7	95.0		76.5
1971	79.5			69.7	84.0	77.1	85.6	90.8		81.5
1972	90.8			76.7	87.0	78.4	88.2	94.3		86.3
1973	92.1	80.9	92.8	84.2	90.0	74.9	91.3	92.0	92.5	86.9
1974	91.2	94.7	81.5	88.1	88.5	82.5	96.0	95.7	80.3	66.1
1975	60.9	81.5	60.4	64.3	64.0	66.6	61.5	76.1	74.2	68.0
1976	66.0	59.0	64.0	64.0	70.0	70.0	56.0	67.0	76.0	63.0
1977	59.0	58.0	52.0	58.0	66.0	68.0	53.0	60.0	71.0	66.0
1978	63.0	73.0	76.0	60.0	71.0	68.0	63.0	67.0	73.0	69.0
1979	68.0	68.0	80.0	67.0	73.0	65.0	68.0	69.0	75.0	63.0
1980	63.0	66.0	na	66.0	71.0	67.0	72.0	62.0	40.0	63.0
1981	69.0	68.0	na	61.0	71.0	60.0	58.0	64.0	61.0	63.0
1982	58.0	65.0	na	55.0	63.0	58.0	55.0	51.0	55.0	57.0

na, data not available.
[a] Denmark, Eire, and the UK joined the ECSC in 1973.

that countries in the EEC should specialise in the production of those commodities in which their economies had a comparative advantage. The problem with this type of adjustment is that in the absence of increased economic integration the external constraint is tightened. As long as the economies of the EEC act as largely independent economies and as long as austerity is internationalised through monetarism, European-level rationalisation schemes can, other things being equal, damage the prospects of growth in countries in which import dependence is significantly increased.

Table 13.6. Labour productivity in the steel industry in the ECSC, 1970–1981 (in hours worked by manual workers per tonne of crude steel). Sources: EEC Commission: Eurostat(a) (1977, pages 5, 72) and Eurostat(b) (various years).

	Belgium	Denmark	Eire	FRG	France
1970	7.88			7.63	9.29
1971	7.63			7.68	9.20
1972	6.60			6.76	8.38
1973	6.09			6.22	7.87
1974	6.01			5.86	7.40
1975	6.78	6.02		6.58	8.41
1976	6.40	4.83		6.33	7.60
1977	6.19	4.76		6.46	7.17
1978	5.20	3.71		5.89	6.35
1979	4.90	3.98		5.42	5.71
1980	4.99	4.22		5.41	5.19
1981	4.65	4.58		5.31	4.93
	Italy	Luxemburg	Netherlands	UK	ECSC
1970	6.55	6.79	4.82		
1971	6.54	6.85	4.72		
1972	5.94	6.36	4.33		
1973	5.70	5.87	4.29	10.46	7.05
1974	5.38	5.47			
1975	5.44	6.63	6.13	12.63	7.65
1976	5.48	6.35	5.88	10.89	7.14
1977	5.42	6.09	5.77	11.88	7.20
1978	5.18	4.84	5.14	10.93	6.46
1979	5.15	4.48	4.84	9.95	5.96
1980	4.88	4.42	4.99	17.70	6.20
1981	4.92	4.56	4.39	7.70	5.30

13.2 The origins of the French steel crisis

From the early 1960s onwards the development of the French steel industry involved massive dislocation and an enormous waste of human resources, of resources invested in steel plants, and of economic and social infrastructural equipment. At one level, the reasons lay in the inability of French capital either to modernise the steel industry or to manage processes of adjustment.

At a deeper level, however, that inability was itself rooted in the specific structure of the French steel industry and in the underlying contradictions of the growth process in capitalist economies.

In the last chapter emphasis was placed upon three elements in particular. One was the strategy of patching up existing installations and the lack of mechanisation and automation in the French industry (see figures 12.4 and 12.5). In the 1950s, insufficient modernisation played a central role in the reconstruction of a large traditional working class and the concentration of this working-class population in largely monoindustrial regions. In the 1960s and 1970s the French industry accordingly lost competitiveness, and in the early 1970s, increases in output were met through new increases in employment. As a result of this undercapitalised process of growth, the subsequent employment crisis was to be intensified. The second element was the domination of the industry by small family-based firms and the slowness and shortcomings in the processes of concentration and centralisation of capital. Owing to the unwillingness of the capitals concerned to cooperate with one another and to coordinate their activities, a modern, rationally organised and technically efficient steel industry did not emerge. In the third place, the steel industry was not adequately articulated with metal-using industries. Consequently, a strong 'filière acier' was not developed (see Freyssenet, 1979a, pages 232-234; and figure 13.1).

In the 1960s and 1970s the French state made several attempts to overcome some of these social contradictions, but with little success. In those years the main aim of French planning was to encourage the expansion of large firms with a view to promoting the growth of exports and adjusting the structure of the French economy to changes in the structure of the

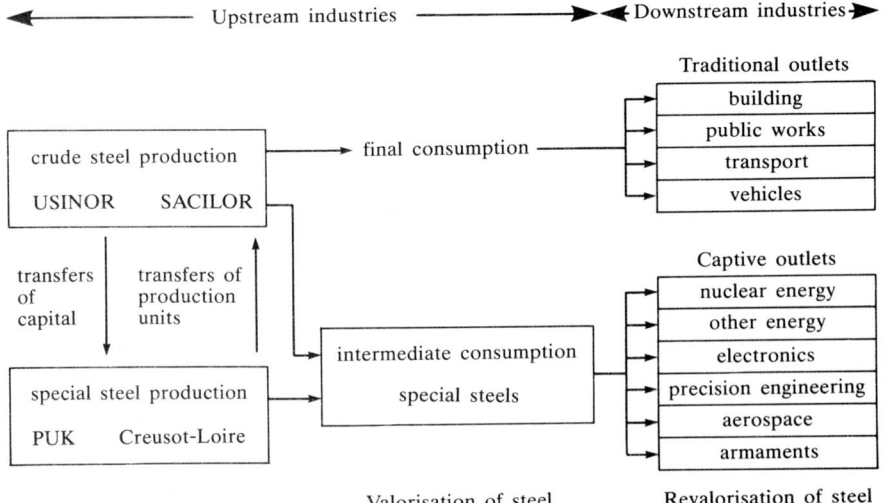

Figure 13.1. The filière sidérurgique. Source: Dahmani (1983, page 137).

international market. Accordingly, regional planning was integrated with and subordinated to a strategy of industrialisation conceived with this aim in mind. One result of this decision was that very little was done to reconvert declining industrial regions, and the establishment of internationally competitive industrial poles at Dunkirk and Fos-sur-Mer was only achieved at enormous expense. At the level of the industry, two large national firms came to account for almost all national production. Investments were more closely coordinated, and employment fell. But a 'filière acier' was not reconstructed. Although specific crises were managed, the contradictions, whose roots lie in the very structure of the relations of capitalist production, remain.

The decisions made by French capital and the state were in fact broadly in line with the forms of international redistribution of economic activity and with the types of hierarchisation of developed capitalist economies that were a consequence of largely unmediated market mechanisms after the mid-1960s. In particular, the French economy became heavily dependent for investment goods upon more developed capitalist economies. Other development options did, however, exist. One alternative to this type of model was a self-centred form of economic development aimed at recapturing the domestic market in the field of investment goods, at reducing the dependence of the economy on other countries for the techniques of production on which its competitiveness depends, and at securing a pattern of development capable of guaranteeing a fuller utilisation of the country's resources (see Mistral, 1979, pages 17-18).

Views of this kind had some impact upon the arguments put forward by the main unions in France. In the late 1970s the CGT and the CFDT tried not simply to oppose the government's and the steel companies' plans for reorganising the industry (see in particular the discussion of 'proposition force' trade unionism in Ross, 1982, pages 164-169; 1984, pages 57-62). An attempt was also made to develop alternative plans capable of coping with the crisis and of modernising the industry in ways which corresponded more closely with the interests of the workers and which could increase working-class control over the industry's subsequent development. Both unions were, in particular, critical of the demand forecasts used to justify reductions in capacity. These forecasts were based on the assumption that the branches of economic activity likely to develop in France in the medium term would require less steel than those which had led the country's expansion process in the past. Underlying this assumption, however, were, it was argued, a series of decisions that amounted to abandoning certain activities in which profitability was low but which played an important role in meeting human needs. Amongst other things, it implied agreement with new trends in the international distribution of industry and in international inequality. In particular, capitalist firms were expected to continue locating less skilled assembly work in less developed and newly industrialising countries, whereas the production of items of industrial equipment and research and development work would continue to be located in the capitalist metropolises. With this pattern of development much of any increase in the demand for steel and in steel production would, it was argued, occur in less developed countries. In addition, the decision that certain key industrial sectors, like those producing machine tools and investment goods, would continue to be weakly represented in the French industrial system was effectively confirmed.

The unions sought to oppose these forecasts and the assumptions on which they were based by arguing for an expansion of the building and public works programme to meet the needs for housing and for items of economic and social infrastructure. In addition, they demanded an industrial policy aimed at establishing a coherent industrial system which could be planned at a national level, and at linking the steel industry with metal-using and investment-goods industries. If this type of strategy were adopted, the unions argued, the demand for steel would be greater than the government was expecting, and the country's steel-making capacity would not need to be reduced.

The CGT and the CFDT were both opposed to the decision to pull out of the production of certain types of steel products and to the associated increase in the degree of European economic integration and in the dependence of the country on imported steel. The unions accepted, however, that a plan for modernising and restructuring the industry and for increasing productivity would result in the employment of no more and perhaps fewer workers. Consequently, demands for reductions in the working week and for a diversification of the economies of steel-producing regions into related industrial activities also played a central role in their plans. In addition, modernisation was expected to entail some changes in the skill content of work in the industry. Attempts were accordingly made to specify modernisation programmes offering workers increased initiative and control in changing working situations.

Many of these ideas were to be taken up in the first year after the victory of the Left in the 1981 elections. What happened under that economic strategy is discussed by Lipietz (1984a, pages 113-241). In the steel industry the original goal of reversing the industry's contraction was, as we have seen, revised. With the economy locked into a recession, demand was low, and with large losses continuing, the danger was that the steel industry would absorb a very large proportion of aggregate investment. Yet the consequent decisions to cut capacity and to reconsider quite radically the industry's trajectory could only occur at the expense of substantial unemployment.

13.3 The steel crisis
What underlay the choice of strategies were of course not simply the goals of the actors, but also a series of conjunctural and structural constraints that themselves were a product of the functioning of market mechanisms.

(No steel industry was abandoned to the market as a result of, amongst other things, balance of payments and strategic considerations, the threat to the liquidity of the financial system posed by the bankruptcy of heavily indebted steel groups, and the social and political implications of the collapse of large steel producers. Instead, the state stepped in to nationalise or finance steel groups and to protect the industry against Japanese, COMECON, and newly industrialising country competition, or to establish crisis cartels. Nonetheless, an underlying market logic prevailed.) Within the steel industry, conjunctural and structural cycles tend to be amplified owing to the stocking and destocking of downstream industries and the dependence of the steel sector on the equipment-goods and construction sectors whose cycles are more pronounced than consumer-goods industries. Second, with high fixed costs, competition tends, in situations of excess capacity, to result in sharp price falls.

In the 1970s and 1980s a series of structural factors were also very important (see Stoffaes, 1984, pages 288-293). Within advanced countries, it was often argued, the age of steel had ended in the sense that the elasticity of steel consumption with respect to increases in aggregate output had fallen from more than two at the turn of the century to something approaching zero. The composition of final output was changing, economies were being made in steel use, and steel substitutes had emerged, whereas amongst the users of the industry's products, new high-quality steels were required. Internationally, newly industrialising countries, where the demand for steel was high, had installed modern domestic capacity, and on the world market, prices were determined in part by Japan's very low costs and in part by strategies of 'dumping' steel at less than its cost of production. Major changes in products and processes were also under way. New quality alloy steels were of increased importance, and new sources of raw materials were being exploited. In addition, competitiveness was increasingly dependent on the transformations in production associated with energy saving and conservation, continuous casting, direct reduction, continuous process technologies, and computer-controlled production, management, and distribution systems, and in the face of sharp oscillations in demand the speed with which the output and production technology of miniworks could be adjusted gave them significant advantages compared to large integrated plants. In these conditions, old established ore-based plants are left facing an immense gulf in productivity, while new ones need to operate at high levels of capacity utilisation.

The central problems are, however, not ones of technology. At the root of the crisis lie the dynamics of accumulation in a capitalist society, the problematic role of the market in coordinating economic activity, and the difficulty of ensuring that resources are fully used while enabling adaptation and adjustment to occur.

Part 4

Conclusions and further remarks

Conclusion: regional planning under capitalism

In the late 1950s and 1960s most of the economies of the West were growing comparatively rapidly. The process of development was, however, extremely uneven. In the Italian Mezzogiorno, an agrarian reform along with a large-scale infrastructural investment programme had not prevented a growing divergence between the South and the rest of the country, and in the Marseilles metropolitan region, decolonisation added problems of adjustment to an area already lacking industrial employment. One policy response was the development of new industrial poles.

Underlying the adoption of this type of strategy were, amongst other things, the ideas of several writers on regional planning theory concerned with the concept of polarised development and growth pole theory (see Weaver, 1984, pages 82-86). The idea of growth poles was initially introduced by Perroux. According to Perroux, leading industrial sectors could act as strategic growth poles within interindustrial space: with any expansion of activity in these sectors, growth would be extended throughout the economy via a network of interindustry transactions or input-output relations. This economic conception of growth poles was developed into a notion applicable to geographical space by Boudeville, whereas other writers, including in particular Hirschman, used the concept of growth centres to connect "theories of unequal development and the idea of inducing growth through integration of the space economy".

In *The Strategy of Economic Development*, Hirschman (1958) argued that there was a tendency for development to be polarised around certain initial growth points. After a while, however, the never-ending search for resources and markets would ensure that 'trickle-down' or 'spread' effects would predominate. According to Hirschman,

> "... we may take it for granted that economic progress does not appear everywhere at the same time and that once it has appeared powerful forces make for a spatial concentration of economic growth around the initial starting points. Why substantial gains may be reaped from overcoming the 'friction of space' through agglomeration has been analysed in detail in the economic theory of location. In addition to the locational advantages offered by existing settlements others come from nearness to a growing centre where an 'industrial atmosphere' has come into being with its special receptivity to innovations and enterprise ... .
>
> ... there can be little doubt that an economy, to lift itself to higher income levels, must and will first develop within itself one or several centres of economic strength. This need for the emergence of 'growing points' or 'growth poles' in the course of the development process means that international and inter-regional inequality of growth is an inevitable concomitant and condition of growth itself" (Hirschman, cited in Weaver, 1984, page 83).

In order to overcome disparities in welfare between different regions the process of polarised development was itself to be extended into depressed areas or into areas without a major history of industrialisation, through the establishment of growth centres connecting such areas to the economic growth impulses generated within a wider economic system. Although what would result would be an unbalanced process of growth within underdeveloped areas, the development that ensued would in turn, it was argued, produce tensions and stimuli that would result eventually in growth at subsequent points. A second consideration was also important. Underdeveloped areas lacked much of the infrastructural equipment characteristic of modern industrial areas. If infrastructural investments were concentrated in particular growth centres, however, modern industrial environments could be developed.

With the implementation of growth pole strategies, processes of peripheral industrialisation did indeed occur. Most investments were, however, in plants characterised by a high capital intensity and an integrated cycle of production. Sectorally, investments in intermediate goods predominated. And as far as ownership was concerned, most of the new plants were new establishments owned by large extraregional groups. Accordingly, the numbers of jobs generated were small in relation to the capital advanced. Also, the fact that most of the industrial establishments were integrated and acted as a part of international or interregional cycles of production implied a lack of strong linkages with local industry. Consequently, local multiplier effects were very limited. Moreover, investment occurred in sectors in which demand fell during the 1970s and international competition was intense. In short, the developmental consequences originally anticipated did not occur.

In the view of growth centre theorists, development is inherently unequal, but growth centre strategies were seen as a way of reducing overall inequality. In the absence of the anticipated developmental results that expectation was not fulfilled. The gaps between less developed and developed areas considered as a whole were generally reproduced, and development at these new points was in practice connected with a reduction in the level of economic activity in other areas. A striking case was provided by the example of the old French steel-producing regions.

The impact of processes of peripheral industrialisation must, however, not be underemphasised. In many areas, new well-paid jobs were created, a modern industrial working class was established, and output and incomes were increased.

14.1 Industrial development and the restructuring of capital
The adoption of new regional planning measures with a view to promoting industrial development in less developed areas did have important effects on the processes of industrial development studied in earlier chapters. The processes of policy formation and implementation were, however, not independent of developments occurring in industry itself. In fact the character and timing of developments in regional policy were shaped politically by industrial interests, and the effectiveness of the policies that were

introduced depended in large measure on the extent to which they were consistent with the investment strategies of the groups concerned.

In earlier chapters I have shown that investments in the oil, chemical, and steel industries in the Italian Mezzogiorno were a product of the economic strategies of expansion and restructuring of the state and nonstate groups involved. Similarly, a serious interest in the development of the port and industrial zone at Fos-sur-Mer was a product of the identification of the zone as a potential site at which the groups connected with SOLLAC could set up an integrated shore-based steelworks with a view to preparing to meet an anticipated increase in the demand for steel and strengthening the competitiveness of the French industry. In the vehicle manufacturing industry the development of the Alfa Sud plant was linked with Alfa Romeo's strategy of diversifying into a sector where it would be competing directly with private-sector car producers, whereas the establishment by FIAT of a number of car plants in the Mezzogiorno was shown to be a result of the adoption of a new management strategy after the 'hot autumn'.

Just as the choice of location cannot be considered independently of the economic and managerial strategies of the groups concerned, the subsequent development of new investments in less developed areas cannot be understood without analysing nonlocational factors. In the 1970s, for example, many industrial projects were left incomplete, some comparatively new establishments were closed, and many workers were laid off, with important effects on the income levels and the consumption and reproduction strategies of the households affected. To understand these events what is required is an analysis of the evolution of the global economic crisis and of the mechanisms underpinning the appearance of excess capacity and the strategies of capitalist rationalisation and working-class recomposition with which it was related.

14.2 Industrial restructuring and political economy

Underlying these changes in the structure and location of industrial and of other types of economic activity were the investment and disinvestment decisions of large corporations, the economic and industrial policy decisions of the political classes at national, regional, and local levels, and the actions of trade unionists and other social actors. At a more abstract level the developments concerned can be viewed as a product of the interaction of the actions of a variety of individual and collective actors with intentions and goals, with resources and instruments, and with knowledge of the situations they confront and the means of attaining different goals. Accordingly, questions concerning the content and character of the resources at society's disposition, the ownership of resources, the conditions governing access to them and the way they can be used along with an analysis of the elements which shape and condition the goals and intentions of the various social subjects need consideration.

The individual actions involved were in every case a complex product of specific and general factors. In many cases, for example, individual actions were a product of the application of general criteria to particular situations: the principles of scientific management are, to consider one case, abstract principles that were applied in many different industrial contexts. In that situation the exact effects were composed of several elements: effects that were a product of the particular situation, and effects that were a result of the general method.

The developments in particular industries and particular localities were, however, not simply a product of an adding up of individual events. Individual events interact with one another and shape each other's trajectory. What happened as the result of the construction of a new steel mill depended on the evolution of demand, on investments in industries and spheres in which steel was used, on investments by other firms in the same sector, and on politically mediated processes of competition which condition and select individual decisions and actions. In other words, the process of development depended not only on the actions of different actors, but also on expectations about the context of action which condition decisions ex ante and on the effects of the conditions themselves which determine the results of decisions ex post.

Any explanation of the interaction of goal-determined actions and of the effects on actions of the material and social conditions in which that interaction occurs depends on the use of concepts and theory. In the studies in earlier chapters the concepts that I used were drawn from Marxist political economy. To explain the dynamics of agrarian and industrial change I drew on concepts of valorisation and accumulation of capital, analysed the transformation of the sphere of work, and discussed inter-capitalist competition and the schemas of economic reproduction. The actions of the state and political processes were explained with the help of Marxist analyses of the role of the state in capitalist society, along with the more specifically political concepts of Gramsci.

Accordingly, the processes of chemical development in the Italian Mezzogiorno were explained by reference, amongst other things, to the competitive processes of expansion of private and state chemical groups, and underlying the external movement of individual capitals and the laws of competition were "the immanent laws of capitalist production" which accordingly "enter into the consciousness of the individual capitalist as the motives which drive him [or her] forward" (Marx, 1976, page 433). Out of that argument emerges not only an understanding of processes of regional change, but also elements of a critique of capitalist development. With the crisis, for example, problems of excess capacity emerged, and much capacity had ultimately to be scrapped. In a context of monopolistic regulation the costs of devalorisation were in part passed on via a type of capital cost inflation (see De Vroey, 1984, pages 384-396) and in part socialised through the placing of workers in Cassa Integrazione and through the nonremuneration of infrastructural investments. The anarchy and waste that resulted were themselves shown to be a result of the 'chemical war' and, at a more abstract level, of the inadequacy of the market as a means of coordinating economic activities and the weaknesses and limitations of state industrial and regional planning.

Throughout the studies in earlier chapters it was repeatedly indicated, however, that empirical reality cannot be derived immediately from abstract concepts. Theoretical analysis of the interaction of general determinations can only occur as a result of a process of abstraction in which certain facets of the reality under consideration are set on one side. As a result, theoretical arguments are indeterminate. Insofar as the abstractions are good ones some of the central aspects of the particular situation under study will be grasped. Nevertheless, the actual complexity of empirical reality can only be reproduced through a process in which what has been excluded is added back in. In a similar vein it was argued that attention must be paid to the institutional framework of capitalist development, and the dynamics of accumulation itself was treated not simply analytically, but also historically, with the help of concepts of regimes of accumulation, capitalist regulation, and hegemony.

14.3 The division of space

Spatially the world was divided into a set of economic regions each of which had relations with the exterior. Abstracting from the division of town and country, the urban hierarchy and the internal organisation of urban regions a variety of types of area were identified, including areas such as Sardinia, Sicily and the Neapolitan metropolitan region in Italy, the Mezzogiorno and the Italian industrial triangle, the Italian and French national territories, and larger areas such as the European Community.

The regions identified were in each case characterised by a set of social and economic relations resulting from the region's history. At any moment in history the inhabitants of the region, and in particular dominant social groups, are faced with choices concerning the way in which the region's resources and characteristics are to be exploited, and the manner in which the area's economy is to be integrated into the wider system of regions. What results is a particular dynamic of development and a specific set of interregional relations. Yet, although the population of each region has in principle the possibility of choosing, resisting, or altering a development path, interregional relations formed in the past and the relation of internally-based groups with the exterior weigh on its trajectory. As a result, centre–periphery relations of the kind I have discussed are a cause, as well as a result, of the socioeconomic character of underdeveloped areas. The question as to which is more important is one whose answer depends on circumstances. At a national level, however, the internal character and internal class and political composition of the region are, as Lipietz has argued, in the last instance probably most important.

Indeed in the studies of processes of reproduction in earlier chapters, attention was given mainly to the national level. The reason for this is two-fold. On the one hand, nation states were the level at which political, legal, and monetary authority were concentrated, at which a capacity to use nonmarket methods of income redistribution were focused, and at which social contradictions and class conflicts were and are in the main regulated. On the other hand, the nation state's we have considered were distinct monetary spaces amongst which economic transactions were regulated by comparative costs and within which relations with the exterior were associated with a monetary constraint. Insofar as incomes exchanged against the products of other countries must have an almost immediate counterpart in export earnings of an equivalent value, internal national resources have a special part to play in the regulation of social conflicts. Accordingly, compromises among social groups, even if organised at a regional level, depended largely on the use of resources provided at a national level, as in the case of the resources supplied to alleviate the effects of industrial restructuring in the French steel-producing regions and the funds supplied by the Italian government for the development of the Mezzogiorno (see Lipietz, 1985a, pages 11-15).

14.4 The theory of regulation

The starting point of the theory of capitalist regulation is the view that in a society or national economy in which capitalist social relations are predominant, social reproduction is fundamentally problematic. In periods of crisis, economic reproduction is subject to extremely serious disruption. Yet historically, periods of crisis have alternated with phases of growth and development. (In the 20th century the phases of growth have been few and far between.) It was to explain these phases of development that the concepts of a regime of accumulation and of regulation were introduced. (The question as to whether or not one can meaningfully speak of regimes of accumulation at a regional level was not considered.)

A regime of accumulation is said to be present if there exists a relatively equilibrated development of the different departments of production and sectors of economic activity. Underlying it is accordingly a situation in which transformations in the spheres of production and consumption are characterised by a certain regularity such that the decisions of individual and collective actors, made in accordance with the results of past activity, which themselves are materialised in the economic landscape, and expectations of a reproduction of those conditions, are validated.

In passing it should be noticed that in characterising processes of development attention was also paid to the connections between the capitalist sector and areas of economic activity not structured by capitalist social relations, including household reproduction units and family farming on the one hand, and between the region concerned and other communities on the other. Social relations of, for example, patriarchy and ethnicity, which also shape the processes of production and reproduction, were, however, not considered explicitly.

Underlying the coherence of the strategies and the expectations of different social subjects and the overall coordination of economic activity is also a mode of regulation. A mode of regulation is a collection of institutional arrangements and rules of behaviour. Included under this heading in a capitalist society are at least three sets of arrangements: (1) mechanisms connected with the regulation of the wage relation, including the determination of the length and intensity of the working day, the reproduction of skills, conditions of employment, and direct and indirect wages; (2) monetary mechanisms; and (3) modes of competition within the capitalist sector and between it and other noncapitalist spheres. A mode of regulation is itself a product of political processes occurring within the state and of processes of class conflict unfolding within civil society, and its institutionalisation is closely associated, as Lipietz has suggested, with the hegemony of a particular social bloc: "a regime of accumulation is the basis of the material existence of a hegemonic bloc which itself is the guarantor of a mode of regulation that in its turn pilots the reproduction of the regime of accumulation" (Lipietz, 1985a, page 11).

14.5 The development of Fordism

In earlier chapters most attention was paid to one particular regime of accumulation. Underlying it were developments in the organisation of work combining elements of Taylorism and Fordism as well as innovations in continuous process technologies. With high-volume production these high fixed-cost technologies resulted in a rapid growth in the productivity of labour. Although the amount of fixed capital per head rose sharply, substantial reductions were achieved in the unit value of commodities. At first, investments in these new methods of production and in new sectors producing vehicles and household equipment came up against limits of demand: in the 1930s, consumption of these products was largely confined to relatively prosperous middle strata. As a result, a deep crisis of under-consumption occurred.

After the Second World War and after a phase of reconstruction a new wave of very fast growth occurred. On this occasion wages and incomes increased in line with productivity. With rising real incomes and changes in the mode of consumption in favour of the products of new industries, demand increased and reinforced the expansion of production capacity, and investments in new capacity fuelled the demand for capital equipment. Mass consumption thus emerged as a corollary of mass production, and the conditions of existence of large sections of the skilled and unskilled working class as well as of middle strata were transformed.

The transformation of the spheres of consumption and reproduction that resulted did not merely supply outlets for new types of consumer goods and enable a harmonisation of the development of the two main departments of production. Workers suited to the new kinds of production and capable of preserving and reproducing the skills and attitudes they required were needed. As Gramsci pointed out many years ago, the development of Fordism was associated with (1) attempts to transform the structure of society and to select and develop new types of worker with "new, more complex and rigid norms or habits of exactitude, order, and precision", and (2) high wages, which were necessary to restore the strength and energy worn down by forms of work that were more wearying and exhausting, and that demanded new levels of expenditure of muscular and, in particular, nervous energy (see Gramsci, 1971b, pages 294-297, 298-306, 310-313).

The renewal of the opportunities for investment that resulted prepared the ground for a spectacular development of the consumer-goods and construction industries, and the growth of these sectors stimulated the demand for investment goods and for energy and intermediate goods such as steel and plastics. As a result, a space was created for the expansion of those industries on which Italian and French development was based, at the same time as other related developments occurred in the agrarian and in older established industrial sectors, in services, and in the sphere of domestic life.

What differentiated the years after the Second World War from those that preceded it were new principles of regulation of economic and social life. Out of the conflicts among classes and political groups, the actions of organised social movements, and political processes unfolding within the state itself were developed a set of institutional arrangements within which individual and collective action was to occur. In the West the new social framework was one whose roots lay in the defeat of an old style of conservativism and of fascism and in the adoption of some of the social and institutional reforms foreshadowed in the 'New Deal'.

Of these developments the most important included the consolidation of new monetary arrangements on the one hand, and the development of methods of collective bargaining and the linking of wages with productivity and the cost of living, along with the emergence of the welfare state, on the other. The exact situation did, however, differ from one country and one industry to another. In Italy, for example, the wage relation was extended to wider areas of economic activity, but in comparison with other countries wages were at first held down, and the home market was dominated by middle strata who played a major role in the hegemonic bloc constructed around the Christian Democrat Party.

At the same time, the process of expansion had an international dimension. A new hierarchy of national economies was established under the hegemony of the United States of America: US technology was exported, as was a US cultural model, and a set of important international institutions were established, including the Marshall Fund, the Organisation for European Economic Cooperation, the General Agreement on Tariffs

Conclusions and further remarks 357

and Trade, and the International Monetary Fund. Indeed it was within this framework that Italy's ruling social coalition adopted an export-oriented growth strategy, and the existence of relations of complementarity between virtuous circles of growth played an important part in the dynamism of Italian development in the years up to 1964, as did the same relations in the rapid growth of the French economy in the 1960s and early 1970s (see Aglietta, 1982b, pages 6-19, 26-35). But just as some aspects of pre-1970 Italian and French regional industrial development can be illuminated through an analysis of the mechanisms of growth underlying the postwar boom, so can the developments of the 1970s and early 1980s be explained in part through an analysis of the crisis of that model of development.

14.6 The crisis of Fordism

Towards the end of the 1960s, Fordism was losing momentum. Increases in productivity were increasingly difficult to attain in the sense that any increment in value added per person required increasingly large amounts of capital investment. Moreover, working-class and trade union movements were succeeding in increasing the share of wages in value added. As a result, the rate of profit started to fall, increasing the difficulty of financing accumulation.

In subsequent years, moreover, new investment was, at a societal level, increasingly job-replacing: with aggregate productivity increasing, the work necessary to produce the means of production used up in producing a commodity and the new work required to transform inputs into output was falling. All new investment creates jobs, but insofar as demand is unchanged the output of new high-productivity plants will outcompete that of older less efficient plants where the intensity of work is greater. As a result, older plants will be closed, aggregate employment will fall, and unemployment will increase, placing increasing strains on the welfare state and increasing the costs of financing it.

Initially employers responded by transferring parts of the production cycle to low-cost areas, frequently outside of the already industrialised countries (see Fröbel et al, 1980, chapter 2; Lipietz, 1984b, pages 30-33). Accordingly, the internationalisation of capital was accelerated. With that development, however, wages in particular were seen as a determinant of competitiveness and not as an element of final demand. Outlets were to be found, in other words, in areas where the companies concerned were not contributing to the formation of money incomes on which a capacity to buy goods and services depends. As a result, the mechanisms of regulation linking internal demand and supply were compromised.

At the same time the share of banking capital in aggregate surplus value increased, as did rentier incomes. With the delinking of the dollar from gold, international liquidity increased dramatically allowing the use of the savings centralised by US banks to finance industrial development in the periphery (see van der Pijl, 1984, pages xvii-xviii).

Until towards the end of the 1970s in the countries we have studied, essentially Keynesian policies were employed, preventing a sharp fall in aggregate demand. With the switch to monetarism, however, a policy of austerity was introduced, which via its effects on international demand was quickly internationalised.

Austerity in one country reduced world demand. Imports into the country concerned were diminished at the expense of producers in other countries, and any consequent reduction in costs was seen as a way of increasing sales abroad. As a result, the balance of payments position of many more rapidly growing economies deteriorated, obliging them to follow suit. In this way the economies of the West were locked into a cumulative downward spiral movement. The consequences of the fall in aggregate demand were, however, not shared equally. In the competitive struggle to control markets, national economies with the lowest efficiency wages were successful but largely at the expense of weaker countries.

What also resulted, however, was an acceleration of the development of a new principle of work organisation: automation. Automation is associated with two major changes in the sphere of production. On the one hand, it allows production to be controlled as it occurs. On the other, the machine system itself acquires an increased flexibility: instead of specialised machines and specialised workers repetitively executing a single task, machines which can carry out a variety of different tasks and which can be switched from one to another quickly and under computer control are used. Production can therefore be made more dependent on design and marketing, and the value embodied in a machine can be realised through the sale of a variety of commodities.

Declining profitability and the stagnation and saturation of markets gave an added impetus to automation technologies as a means not simply of reducing production costs but also of increasing product heterogeneity, of adapting more quickly to the structural instability and volatility of demand, and more generally of increasing flexibility (see Boyer and Coriat, 1986, pages 19−23).

With the crisis and with automation went other changes in the factory and in the market for labour. On the one hand, the work of core workers in particular was reorganised in accordance with strategies of job enrichment, job rotation, job redesign, and the recomposition of tasks. On the other, subcontracting increased, as did irregular work. As a result, the dualism in the market for labour and in the wage relation was increased. The size of the core working population declined, whereas temporary and irregular jobs and 'moonlighting' or second jobs proliferated.

In the sphere of wages policy there was a move to a situation in which the wages, at least of workers not covered by collective agreements, showed zero or negative real growth, widening inequalities in earnings. With at best only irregular work, a growing marginalised population depended, in the intervening periods of unemployment or of no official employment, on incomes supplied by the welfare state. In this way a significant part of the costs of reproduction of a large section of the population were transferred to the state. Yet in the face of the growing fiscal strains the logic of social policy was also modified, changing from one of welfare and of "collective guarantees on behalf of the worse-off members of society" to one of insurance, in which benefits came to depend on an individual's ability to pay. Social benefits were increasingly targeted, and attempts were made to cut spending (see Coriat, 1984a, pages 44-45).

In the 1970s these developments were accompanied by important changes in the organisation of factory work and in the spatial distribution of industry. With the crisis the size of plants in metropolitan areas was reduced, and work was put out, subcontracted and decentralised to smaller and more geographically dispersed installations. What was emerging was in fact a new type of dispersed production in which the levels of technological sophistication and the conditions of employment could vary considerably.

In short, a paradox exists. On the one hand, the possibility exists of increasing productivity very radically and of reducing the amount of work necessary for society to meet its socially determined needs. On the other, the crisis of long-established industries and many of the transformations occurring in the sphere of work are contributing to the reinforcement of a dual and polarised society.

What I want to suggest is that the crisis is not simply one to be solved by changing industry and accepting new methods of work. Indeed, insofar as new methods of flexible specialisation are an adjustment to the instability and stagnation of markets, current technological trends do not in themselves offer the conditions on which the emergence of a new engine of growth depends (see Boyer and Coriat, 1986, page 51). The development of society is not a simple reflection of exogenous changes in technology but is mediated by social relations. The composition of output, the choice of technology, the organisation of work, the distribution of income are all a consequence of decisions whose content is essentially social and political. At the same time, important macroeconomic questions concerning aggregate resource use and the coordination of economic activity are involved. In a capitalist society, investment and growth depend in fact on the simultaneous fulfillment of two conditions. On the one hand, what is produced must be capable of being sold, and sales depend upon investment demand and the spending of incomes formed through employment. On the other, what is produced must be capable of being produced profitably. Under capitalism the squaring of that circle is particularly problematic.

14.7 Beyond the crisis?
In the 1970s and early 1980s what coexisted, in other words, were major innovations in the spheres of technology and production, together with job losses and unemployment, social and spatial polarisation, and international stagnation. As in the 1930s, moreover, the prevailing social and political

conditions were in turn acting as a constraint on the realisation of the potential of transformations in technology.

The problem that has to be dealt with is, in essence, the following. The old model of development has been placed in crisis as has the type of regulation characteristic of Fordism: the mechanisms of wage determination, the welfare state, and Keynesian techniques of economic management have all been brought into question, as have existing methods of spatial planning. With the rise of monetarism and a politics of austerity, however, automation itself has been used primarily to restore capitalist authority in the factory and office and to deepen the division of conception and execution. Increases in value added have been used to augment profits and the incomes of a minority of well-off and powerful individuals and of a relatively large group of people with stable jobs. The composition of output has been reoriented towards the needs of the well-off, whereas increases in productivity unmatched by increases in mass consumption have resulted in increasing unemployment. As a result, at the other pole of a segmented and dual society are left a significant minority dependent on irregular and ill-paid work, state transfers, and minimal services. In addition, at an international level what prevails is a kind of competitive stagnation.

Another model of development can, however, be identified. A reskilling of workers aimed at developing knowledge and control over new types of machinery could accompany the introduction of new technologies, and democratic control over work could be enlarged. Increases in productivity could be reapportioned to confer benefits on wider sections of the community, in particular via a reduction in the length of the working week.

The problem of employment can in fact be dealt with in two ways. One is through an increase in demand. But if demand is to increase, productivity must rise sufficiently to enable the incomes distributed to people in work to be increased. The problem with that path is twofold. On the one hand, it will reinforce the dualism between people in and out of work. On the other, current increases in productivity do not seem sufficient to sustain increased incomes. The reason is that the actual investments involved in introducing new technologies are quite expensive and frequently subject to rapid obsolescence. Although major gains in productivity are capable of attainment, the gains are frequently not sufficiently high to repay the capital investment involved and allow an expansion of incomes. The second way of coping with the problem and of squaring the circle identified in chapter 2 (sections 2.8 and 2.9) is to implement a major reduction in the length of the working week. In addition, with a reduced working week, access could be increased to new types of consumer goods whose use requires active involvement, involves the acquisition of new types of knowledge, and entails the use of time instead of economising on it (see also Lipietz, 1984b, pages 36-42).

The adoption of a model of that kind, which is a precondition for the full exploitation of the potential of new methods of production, is politically problematic. The reason why lies in the fact that the individual interests of powerful sections of society do not coincide with strategies that are more rational and just in a collective sense. In particular, if the length of the working week were to fall, abstracting from what happens to wages, the costs for an individual firm would increase. At a societal level, however, that increase in costs would be offset by a fall in the cost of the welfare state: incomes transferred to individuals making no contribution to measured output would fall. In addition, at the level of the firm, hourly productivity would in all probability increase—someone working for thirty-two hours a week would almost certainly work more efficiently than someone working for forty hours a week. In spite of the existence of these offsetting factors, the consequence of a major reduction in the length of the working week would nevertheless be an increase in real social wage costs. In that situation, no individual employer is going to introduce that change voluntarily. Collective rationality and individual rationality do not, in other words, coincide.

What has reemerged is a problem with historical parallels. The way out of the crisis of the 1930s involved a linking of wages with productivity, as well as new roles for the state in the economy. Yet from the point of view of individual enterprises the first of these steps was one that flew in the face of a search for competitiveness: if some firms had raised wages while others had introduced the same kind of technology and methods of work organisation but paid lower wages, the firms in the first group would have been undercut on the market by competitors in the second group. A precondition for the growth of the postwar years was therefore the generalisation of new methods and new institutional procedures of wage determination.

A second instance is provided by the struggle to reduce the length of the working day in mid-19th century Britain. At that point there were many economists who argued that a reduction in the length of the working day simply could not be introduced because it would undermine the competitiveness and profitability of the enterprises concerned. Indeed, no employer would want to reduce the length of the working day of the workers he or she employed to about ten hours if others were able to employ people for sixteen or eighteen hours. The trajectory of social and political struggle was such, however, that the working week was reduced. What followed was the great Victorian boom.

At present there is a fundamental contradiction between developments in the spheres of production and work and the institutional organisation of economic, social, and political life. Individual and collective interests, moreover, do not coincide. In that situation new national policies and a major shift in the way in which economic life is regulated are major priorities. New regional planning mechanisms are one component element of strategies aimed at ensuring a fuller and more equitable use of resources. Also involved, however, are new types of wage relation, other changes in state intervention, and new ways of life. What is more, insofar as the part of people's lives structured by the wage relation is reduced, a margin of manoeuvre within which new social relations can be explored could be created.

In the face of the consequent crisis a variety of positions have emerged. One useful set of distinctions has been presented by Lipietz (1985a, pages 21–22). What he identified were four elements out of which the competing economic and political projects evident in Europe are constructed:
(1) reactionary positions associated with a wish to return to a type of regulation that preceded the one in crisis;
(2) conservative positions involving a wish to return to the days that preceded the crisis;
(3) modernist views whose goal is to adapt society to contemporary transformations in technology and work while guaranteeing the reproduction of capitalist social relations; and
(4) radical positions pressed by social and political movements whose goal is to transform existing social relations and that include a variety of socialist, ecological, feminist, and peace movements.
These empirically useful distinctions cannot, however, act as a substitute for class analysis. Underlying these movements are different social classes and different social and political coalitions with identifiable material and social interests.

At present, to consider just one example, any project of modernisation faces the problem posed by the tendency of capital in an epoch of crisis to assume more fluid monetary forms and the tendency of indirect costs associated with land and other kinds of speculation to increase.

In the 1960s the share of banking capital increased, as did rentier incomes. In the 1970s the concepts of an aggressively assertive economic liberalism and of rentier perspectives that reflected the interests in particular of the holders of money capital regained hegemony. These concepts achieved ascendancy, however, not just on account of the increasing weight of their usual advocates, such as commercial capitalists and financiers, small shopkeepers, owners of small firms with a low organic composition of capital, and "entrepreneurs whose enrichment proceeds faster than their social ascendancy" (van der Pijl, 1984; pages 8–20). Owing to the difficulties of accumulation, the concepts of economic liberalism also gained ground in the ranks of industrial capitalists.

With the unfolding of the crisis, interests and strategies do of course change, opening up the possibility of new compromises. Achievement of the goals of radical economic and social movements ultimately depends, however, not on compromises with capitalist modernism, but on the transformation of the wage and commodity relations. As Marx wrote,

"No social order is ever destroyed before all the productive forces for which it is sufficient have been developed, and new superior relations of production never replace older ones before the material conditions for their existence have matured within the framework of the old society. [Humankind] thus always sets itself only such tasks as it is able to solve, since closer examination will always show that the task itself arises only when the material conditions for its solution are already present or at least in the course of formation" (Marx, 1975, page 426).

Just as in the face of earlier crises, the character and mode of operation of capitalism may be changed, adapting it to the causes of the current breakdown, extending its developmental potential and stability, and altering the conditions of maturation of its contradictions. In that evolution radical social and political movements can of course make various advances. Capitalism's objective contradictions nonetheless operate underneath all adjustments circumscribing the solutions to particular sets of difficulties. Not only is the cost of adjustment high. Capitalist solutions have also proved quite incapable of coming to grips with problems of inequality, and, as critiques of capitalist growth have shown, the ways in which development of the productive forces occurs are frequently wasteful and damaging. "As long, moreover, as transformations unfold on an antagonistically contested terrain no emancipatory step is safe from the dangers of retrogression" (Mészaros, 1986, page 4). Such emancipatory steps are, however, a precondition of a type of development of the productive forces that is capable of making real inroads into some of the problems discussed in this and earlier chapters.

Glossary of abbreviations and acronyms

(a) General

BP	British Petroleum
COMECON	Council for Mutual Economic Assistance
CPE	centrally planned economy
DME	developed market economy
ECSC	European Coal and Steel Community
ECU	European currency unit
EEC	European Economic Community
GATT	General Agreement on Tariffs and Trade
ICI	Imperial Chemical Industries
ILO	International Labour Office
IMF	International Monetary Fund
LDC	less developed country
LD converter	Linz – Donawitz converter
LPG	liquefied petroleum gas
LWS converter	Loire – Wendel – Sprunk converter
OECD	Organisation for Economic Cooperation and Development

(b) Italian

AGIP	Azienda Generale Italiana Petroli
ANAS	Azienda Nazionale Strade Statali
ANIC	Azienda Nazionale Idrogenazione Combustibili
ASI	Area di Sviluppo Industriale
CGIL	Confederazione Generale Italiana del Lavoro
CIPAA	Comitato Interministeriale per la Politica Agricola e Alimentare
CIPE	Comitato Interministeriale della Programmazione Economica
CIPI	Comitato dei Ministri per il Coordinamento della Politica Industriale
CIS	Credito Industriale per la Sardegna
CISL	Confederazione Italiana dei Sindacati Lavoratori
CNEN	Comitato Nazionale per l'Energia Nucleare
DC	Democrazia Cristiana
ENI	Ente Nazionale Idrocarburi
ESPI	Ente Siciliano Promozione Industriale
FIME	Società Finanziaria Meridionale
FINAM	Finanziaria Agricola per il Mezzogiorno
FNCD	Federazione Nazionale dei Cotivatori Diretti
FORMEZ	Centro di Formazione e Studi per il Mezzogiorno
IASM	Istituto per l'Assistenza allo Sviluppo del Mezzogiorno
IMI	Istituto Mobiliare Italiano
INEA	Istituto Nazionale di Economia Agraria
INSUD	Nuove Initiative per il Sud
IRFIS	Istituto Regionale per il Finanziamento delle Industrie Piccole e Medie in Sicilia

IRI	Istituto per la Ricostruzione Industriale
ISTAT	Istituto Centrale de Statistica
ISVEIMER	Istituto per lo Sviluppo Economico dell'Italia Meridionale
NI	Nucleo di Industrializzazione
PCI	Partito Comunista Italiano
PLI	Partito Liberale Italiano
PRI	Partito Repubblicano Italiano
PSDI	Partito Socialista Democratico Italiano
PSI	Partito Socialista Italiano
PSIUP	Partito Socialista di Unità Proletaria
SFIRS	Società Finanziaria Industriale Rinascità Sardegna
SIR	Società Italiana Resine
SIT Siemens	Società Italiana Telecomunicazione Siemens
SPI	Sviluppo e Promozione Industriale
SVIMEZ	Associazione per lo Sviluppo dell'Industria nel Mezzogiorno
UIL	Unione Italiana del Lavoro

(c) French

AL	Air Liquide
AMM	Aire Métropolitaine Marseillaise
ARBED	Aciéries Réunies de Burbach–Eich–Dudelange SA
CCIM	Chambre de Commerce et d'Industrie de Marseille
CDC	Caisse des Dépôts et des Consignations
CEPII	Centre d'Études Prospectives et d'Informations Internationales
CEPREMAP	Centre d'Études Prospectives d'Économie Mathématique Appliquées à la Planification
CFDT	Confédération Française Démocratique du Travail
CFEM	Compagnie Française d'Entreprises Métalliques
CFR	Compagnie Française de Raffinage
CGT	Confédération Générale du Travail
CIAT	Conseil Interministériel pour l'Aménagement du Territoire
CICC	Compagnie Industrielle Chiers-Châtillon
CLIF	Compagnie Lorraine Industrielle et Financière
CNAT	Commission Nationale de l'Aménagement du Territoire
CODER	Commission de Développement Économique Régional
CREI	Centre de Recherche en Économie Industrielle
CSSF	Chambre Syndicale de la Sidérurgie
DATAR	Délégation à l'Aménagement du Territoire et à l'Action Régionale
DNEL	Denain-Nord-Est-Longwy
DPF	Dépôts Pétroliers de Fos
EDF	Électricité de France
EPA	Établissement Public d'Aménagement

Glossary

EPAREB	Établissement Public d'Aménagement des Rives de l'Étang de Berre
Esso SAF	Esso Société Anonyme Française
FDES	Fonds de Développement Économique et Social
FEOGA	Fonds Européen d'Organisation et de Garantie Agricole
FIAT	Fonds d'Intervention pour l'Aménagement du Territoire
FSAI	Fonds Spécial d'Adaptation Industrielle
GCVN	Groupe Central des Villes Nouvelles
GDF	Gaz de France
GI-FOS	Groupement pour le Financement de la Région de Fos
GIS	Groupement de l'Industrie Sidérurgique
HLM	Habitation à Loyer Modéré
INSEE	Institut National de la Statistique et des Études Économiques
IRSID	Institut de Recherche de la Sidérurgie
MAEB	Mission d'Études et d'Aménagement des Rives de l'Étang de Berre
MIAFEB	Mission Interministérielle pour l'Aménagement de la Région de Fos – Étang de Berre
MIDAM	Mission Interministérielle de l'Aménagement des Bouches du Rhône
OREAM	Organismes d'Études d'Aménagement des Aires Métropolitaines
PAM	Port Autonome de Marseille
PCF	Parti Communiste Français
PCUK	Produits Chimiques Ugine Kuhlmann
PME	Petites et moyennes entreprises
POS	Plan d'Occupation du Sol
PS	Parti Socialiste
PUK	Péchiney – Ugine Kuhlmann
SACILOR	Société des Aciéries et Laminoirs de Lorraine
SAFE	Société des Aciers Fins de l'Est
SCA	Syndicat Communautaire d'Aménagement
SDAU	Schéma Directeur de l'Aménagement et de l'Urbanisme
SIDELOR	Union Sidérurgique Lorraine
SIVOM	Syndicat Intercommunal à Vocation Multiple
SNCF	Société Nationale des Chemins de Fer
SOLLAC	Société Lorraine de Laminage Continu
SOLMER	Société Lorraine et Méridionale de Laminage Continu
SPLSE	Société du Pipeline Sud-Européen
UCNM	USINOR – Châtillon – Neuves-Maisons
UCSIP	Union des Chambres Syndicales de l'Industrie du Pétrole
USINOR	Union Sidérurgique du Nord de la France
ZAC	Zone d'Aménagement Concerté
ZIP	Zone Industrialo-portuaire

References

• References of interest not cited in text.

Aglietta M, 1979 *A Theory of Capitalist Regulation* (New Left Books, London)

• Aglietta M, 1980, "La dévalorisation du capital: études des liens entre accumulation et inflation" *Économie Appliquée* **33**(2) 387–423

Aglietta M, 1982a, "Avantages comparatifs, valeur internationale et taux de change tendanciel", in *Économie et Finance Internationale* Ed. J L Reiffers (Dunod, Paris) pp 320–346

Aglietta M, 1982b, "World capitalism in the eighties" *New Left Review* number 136, 5–41

Aglietta M, Brender A, 1984 *Les Métamorphoses de la Société Salariale. La France en Projet* (Calmann-Lévy, Paris)

Aglietta M, Orléan A, Oudiz G, 1980, "L'industrie française face aux contraintes de change" *Économie et Statistique* number 119, 35–63

Aglietta M, Orléan A, Oudiz G, 1981, "Des adaptations différenciées aux contraintes internationales: les enseignements d'un modèle" *Revue Économique* **32**(4) 660–712

Allen K J, MacLennan M, 1970 *Regional Problems and Policies in Italy and France* (George Allen and Unwin, Hemel Hempstead, Herts)

Allen K J, Stephenson A A, 1974 *An Introduction to the Italian Economy* (Martin Robertson, Oxford)

Allum P, 1973a *Italy: Republic without Government?* (Weidenfeld and Nicolson, London)

Allum P, 1973b *Politics and Society in Post War Naples* (Cambridge University Press, Cambridge)

Allum P, 1981, "Thirty years of southern policy in Italy" *Political Quarterly* **52** 314–323

Amin A, 1982, "La ristrutturazione alla Fiat e il decentramento produttivo nel Mezzogiorno" *Archivio di Studi Urbani e Regionali* new series, numbers 13–14, 47–88

Amin A, 1983, "Industrial restructuring, state intervention, and regional growth: the example of Alfa Sud in Southern Italy" *Reading Geographical Papers* number 77, University of Reading, Whiteknights, Reading

• Amin A, 1985, "Restructuring in Fiat and the decentralisation of production into Southern Italy", in *Uneven Development in Southern Europe. Studies of Accumulation, Class, Migration and the State* Eds R Hudson, J Lewis (Methuen, Andover, Hants) pp 155–191

Arcangeli F, Vitiello A, 1982, "Le nuove condizioni per lo sviluppo del Mezzogiorno emerse negli anni '70", in *Italia: Centri e Periferie* Ed. S Goglio (Franco Angeli, Milan) pp 99–147

Arlacchi P, 1983 *Mafia, Peasants and Great Estates: Society in Traditional Calabria* (Cambridge University Press, Cambridge)

Armstrong G, 1983, "Woman to get pension at 33" *The Guardian* 14 January, page 5

Atkinson J, 1984, "Flexibility, uncertainty, and manpower management" Institute of Manpower Studies Report number 89, University of Sussex, Falmer, Brighton

Aymard M, 1982, "From feudalism to capitalism in Italy: the case that doesn't fit" *Review* **6**(2) 131–208

Bagnasco A, 1977 *Tre Italie. La Problematica Territoriale dello Sviluppo Italiano* (Il Mulino, Bologna)

• Bagnasco A, Messori M, Trigilia C, 1978 *Le Problematiche dello Sviluppo Italiano* (Feltrinelli, Milan)

Bairoch P, 1981, "The main trends in national economic disparities since the industrial revolution", in *Disparities in Economic Development since the Industrial Revolution* Eds P Bairoch, M Lévy-Leboyer (Macmillan, London) pp 3–17

Becchi Collidà A, 1979, "Città meridionale e sovraurbanizzazione", in *Gli Anni '70 nel Mezzogiorno* Eds A Accornero, S Andriani (De Donato, Bari) pp 168-221

Belhadj, Raked, Chapponière, Courlet, 1975, "La politique de développement mise en oeuvre dans le Mezzogiorno Italien et ses effets", Institut de Recherche Économique et de Planification, Université des Sciences Sociales de Grenoble, Grenoble

- Bethemont J, Pelletier J, 1983 *Italy. A Geographical Introduction* (Longman, Harlow, Essex)
- Biard R, 1973 *Groupe Sacilor (Wendel-SIDÉLOR)* (Économie et Politique, Paris)

Biarez S, 1982, "'Aménagement du territoire' in France: state interventionism or regulation?" *West European Politics* **5**(3) 270-286

Birnbaum P, 1980, "The state in contemporary France", in *The State in Western Europe* Ed. R Scase (Croom Helm, Beckenham, Kent) chapter 2

Bleitrach D, Chenu A, 1975, "L'aménagement: régulation ou approfondissement des contradictions sociales? Un exemple: Fos-sur-Mer et l'Aire Métropolitaine Marseillaise" *Environment and Planning A* **7** 367-391 [English translation: "Regional planning—regulation or deepening of social contradictions? The example of Fos-sur-Mer and the Marseilles metropolitan area", in *London Papers in Regional Science 11. Regional Planning in Europe* Eds R Hudson, J Lewis (Pion, London), 1979, pp 148-178]

Bleitrach D, Chenu A, 1977, "Discipline d'usine et modes de vie" *La Pensée* number 193, 3-30

Bleitrach D, Chenu A, 1979 *L'Usine et la Vie. Luttes Régionales: Marseille et Fos* (Maspero, Paris)

Blok A, 1969, "South Italian agro towns" *Comparative Studies in Society and History* **11**(2) 121-135

Blok A, 1974 *The Mafia of a Sicilian Village, 1860-1960. A Study of Violent Peasant Entrepreneurs* (Basil Blackwell, Oxford)

Bologna S, 1973a, "Questioni di metodo per l'analisi del Piano Chimico" *Quaderni Piacentini* numbers 48-49, 40-56

- Bologna S, 1973b, "Ancora sul Piano Chimico: materiali per una discussione" *Quaderni Piacentini* number 50, 61-94

Boudeville J R, 1966 *Problems of Regional Economic Planning* (Edinburgh University Press, Edinburgh)

Boyer R, 1978, "Les salaires en longue période" *Économie et Statistique* number 103, 27-57

Boyer R, 1979, "La crise actuelle: une mise au point en perspective historique. Quelques réflexions à partir d'une analyse du capitalisme français en longue période" *Critiques de l'Économie Politique* new series, numbers 7-8, 5-113

- Boyer R, 1980, "Rapport salarial et analyses en terme de régulation. Une mise en rapport avec les théories de la segmentation du marché du travail" *Économie Appliquée* **33**(2) 491-509

Boyer R, Coriat B, 1986, "Technical flexibility and macro stabilisation: preliminary insights" paper presented to the Conference on Innovation Diffusion, Venice, 17-21 March 1986

Boyer R, Mistral J, 1978 *Accumulation, Inflation, Crises* (Presses Universitaires de France, Paris)

- Boyer R, Mistral J, 1983a, "Le temps présent: la crise (1). D'une analyse historique à une vue prospective" *Annales* **38**(3) 483-506
- Boyer R, Mistral J, 1983b, "Le temps présent: la crise (2). Pesanteur et potentialité des années quatre-vingt" *Annales* **38**(4) 773-789
- Boyer R, Petit P, 1980, "Emploi et productivité dans la CEE" *Économie et Statistique* number 121, 35-59

Broda J, 1976, "Le travail temporaire dans la zone de Fos" *Sud Information Économique* number 5, 25 - 32

Broda J, Demailly S, La Bruyère C, 1978, "Crise de la sidérurgie et recomposition du procès de travail. La sous-traitance à la Solmer" *Sociologie du Travail* **8**(4) 423 - 447

Broda J, La Bruyère C, 1979, "Articulation de la sous-traitance et du travail temporaire dans la constitution des systèmes industriels modernes. L'example de la sidérurgie à Fos-sur-Mer" *Sud Information Économique* number 39, 24 - 45

Bruno S, 1979, "The industrial reserve army, segmentation and the Italian labour market" *Cambridge Journal of Economics* **3**(2) 131 - 151

Burris V, 1980, "Class formation and transformation in advanced capitalist societies: a comparative analysis" *Social Praxis* **7**(3 - 4) 147 - 179

Cafiero S, 1979, "La questione urbana oggi nel Mezzogiorno" *Informazioni Svimez* **32**(23 - 24) 859 - 865

Cafiero S, Busca A, 1970 *Lo Sviluppo Metropolitano in Italia* (Giuffré Editore, Rome)

Caizzi B (Ed.), 1973 *Nuova Antologia della Questione Meridionale. I Maestri del Meridionalismo Classico* third edition (Edizioni di Comunità, Milan) (originally published in 1948 by Edizione Agricole, Bologna)

• Cames A, Fontaine F, 1979, "La sidérurgie dans le Nord - Pas-de-Calais" *Profils de l'Économie Nord - Pas-de-Calais* number 2, 1 - 5

Cammet J M, 1967 *Antonio Gramsci and the Origins of Italian Communism* (Stanford University Press, Stanford)

Capuggi L, 1981, "The financing of industrial investment" *Review of Economic Conditions in Italy* number 1, 41 - 83

Cassa per il Mezzogiorno, annually *Bilancio e Relazione* Cassa per Opere Straordinarie di Pubblico Interesse nell'Italia Meridionale, Rome

Castells M, 1975 *Sociologie de l'Espace Industriel* (Anthropos, Paris)

Castells M, 1976, "Crise de l'état, consommation collective et contradictions urbaines", in *La Crise de l'État* Ed. N Poulantzas (Presses Universitaires de France, Paris) pp 179 - 208

Castells M, 1978 *City, Class and Power* (Macmillan, London)

Castells M, Godard F, 1974 *Monopolville. Analyse des Rapports entre l'Entreprise, l'État et l'Urbain* (Mouton, The Hague and Paris)

Castronovo V, 1980 *L'Industria Italiana dall'Ottocento a Oggi* (Mondadori, Milan)

Centre d'Information des Industries Lorraines, 1974a, "Un milliard de tonnes de fer" *Actualités Industrielles Lorraines* numbers 148 - 149, 10 - 18

Centre d'Information des Industries Lorraines, 1974b, "Les mines de fer Lorraines en 1973" *Actualités Industrielles Lorraines* numbers 148 - 149, 19 - 25

Centre d'Information des Industries Lorraines, 1974c, "Les sociétés sidérurgiques Lorraines" *Actualités Industrielles Lorraines* numbers 148 - 149, 38 - 71

CEPII, 1983 *Économie Mondiale: la Montée des Tensions* Centre d'Études Prospectives et d'Informations Internationales (Economica, Paris)

Chapman G, 1983 *The Theory and Politics of Underdevelopment in Southern Italy* DPhil thesis, University of Sussex, Brighton

Clough S B, 1965 *Storia dell'Economia Italiana* (Cappelli, Bologna)

• Coing H, 1982 *La Ville, Marché de l'Emploi* (Presses Universitaires de Grenoble, Grenoble)

Colletti L, 1975, "Introduction", in *Early Writings* K Marx (Penguin Books, Harmondsworth, Middx) pp 7 - 56

Coriat B, 1983 *L'Atelier et le Chronomètre. Essai sur le Taylorisme, le Fordisme et la Production de Masse* second edition (Christian Bourgois, Paris)

Coriat B, 1984a, "Labour and capital in the crisis: France, 1966-82", in *The French Workers' Movement: Economic Crisis and Political Change* Eds M Kesselman with G Groux (George Allen and Unwin, Hemel Hempstead, Herts) pp 39-47

Coriat B, 1984b, "Crise et électronisation de la production: robotisation d'atelier et modèle fordien d'accumulation du capital" *Critiques de l'Économie Politique* new series, numbers 26-27, 71-94

Corner P, 1979, "Fascist agrarian policy and the Italian economy in the Inter-war Years", in *Gramsci and Italy's Passive Revolution* Ed. J A Davis (Croom Helm, Beckenham, Kent) pp 239-274

Cosentino V, Fanfani R, Gorgoni M, 1979, "Alcuni aspetti dello sviluppo dell'agricoltura meridionale dal secondo dopoguerra ad oggi", in *Investimenti e Disoccupazione nel Mezzogiorno* Eds A Graziani, E Pugliese (Il Mulino, Bologna) chapter 4

• CREI, 1983 *L'Industrie en France* Centre de Recherche en Économie Industrielle (Flammarion, Paris)

Crouch C, Pizzorno A, 1978, "Appendix I: selected economic and other statistical data", in *The Resurgence of Class Conflict in Western Europe since 1968, volume 1: National Studies* Eds C Crouch, A Pizzorno (Macmillan, London) pp 307-319

CSSF(a), annually *Bulletin Statistique de la Chambre Syndicale de la Sidérurgie Française* Chambre Syndicale de la Sidérurgie, Paris

CSSF(b), annually *La Sidérurgie Française* Chambre Syndicale de la Sidérurgie, Paris

Cultiaux D, 1975 *L'Aménagement de la Région Fos-Étang de Berre* Notes et Études Documentaires, numbers 4164-4166 (La Documentation Française, Paris)

Curry D, 1978, "French steel rescue: control without nationalisation" *The Financial Times* 22 September, page 18

Dahmani A, 1983, "La sidérurgie. Le poids de l'assistance permanente", in *L'Industrie en France* Centre de Recherche en Économie Industrielle (Flammarion, Paris) pp 121-156

DATAR, 1965 *Aides du Développement Régional* Délégation à l'Aménagement du Territoire et à l'Action Régionale, Paris

Davis J A, 1979, "The South, the Risorgimento and the origins of the Southern Problem", in *Gramsci and Italy's Passive Revolution* Ed. J A Davis (Croom Helm, Beckenham, Kent) pp 67-103

Davis M, 1984, "The political economy of late-imperial America" *New Left Review* number 143, 6-38

Davis J A, 1985, "Reaganomics' magical mystery tour" *New Left Review* number 149, 45-65

Del Monte A, 1984, "The effects of regional policy on the industrial development of the South of Italy" *Mezzogiorno d'Europa* **4** 563-583

Del Monte A, 1986, "The impact of Italian industrial policy, 1960-1980", in *European Industrial Policy* Ed. G Hall (Croom Helm, Beckenham, Kent) pp 128-164

Del Monte A, Giannola A, 1978 *Il Mezzogiorno nell'Economia Italiana* (Il Mulino, Bologna)

Delorme R, André Ch, 1983 *L'État et l'Économie* (Éditions du Seuil, Paris)

• Demailly S, 1977, "La région Provence-Alpes-Côte d'Azur entre la crise et la Méditerranée" *Revue Française d'Études Politiques Méditerranéennes* number 25, 9-36

De Vroey M, 1984, "Inflation: a non-monetarist monetary interpretation" *Cambridge Journal of Economics* **8**(4) 381-399

Di Lampedusa G T, 1959 *Il Gattopardo* (Feltrinelli, Milan)

References

- Donolo C, 1981, "Uneven development and social disaggregation: notes for an analysis of classes in the South", in *Contemporary Italian Sociology. A Reader* Ed. D Pinto (Cambridge University Press, Cambridge; Éditions de la Maison des Sciences de l'Homme, Paris) pp 124-158
Dulong R, 1976, "La crise du rapport état/société locale vue au travers de la politique régionale", in *La Crise de l'État* Ed. N Poulantzas (Presses Universitaires de France, Paris) pp 209-232
Dulong R, 1978 *Les Régions, l'État et la Société Locale* (Presses Universitaires de France, Paris)
Duménil G, 1983, "Beyond the transformation riddle: a labour theory of value" *Science and Society* **47**(4) 427-450
- Duménil G, 1984, "The so-called 'transformation problem' revisited: a brief comment" *Journal of Economic Theory* **33** 340-348
Dunford M, Perrons D, 1983 *The Arena of Capital* (Macmillan, London)
Edwards C, 1985 *The Fragmented World. Competing Perspectives on Trade, Money and Crisis* (Methuen, Andover, Hants)
EEC Commission, 1982 *Pig Iron and Steel. Basic Prices and Iron and Steel Undertakings* 1981 edition (EEC Commission, Brussels)
EEC Commission: Eurostat, 1979 *Regional Statistics* 1978 edition (Office des Publications Officielles des Communautés Européennes, Luxembourg)
EEC Commission: Eurostat, 1983 *Iron and Steel 1952-1982* (Office des Publications Officielles des Communautés Européennes, Luxembourg)
EEC Commission: Eurostat(a) *Iron and Steel Yearbook* (Office des Publications Officielles des Communautés Européennes, Luxembourg)
EEC Commission: Eurostat(b) *Quarterly Iron and Steel Bulletin* (Office des Publications Officielles des Communautés Européennes, Luxembourg)
ENI, 1976 *Sommario Statistica* Ente Nazionale Idrocarburi, Rome
- Essig F, 1979 *Datar: des Régions et des Hommes* (Stanké, Paris)
Fabre M, 1976, "Fos: le gâchis", in *Les Régions dans la Crise* Eds M Fabre, N Pluet (Notes et Études d'Économie et Politique, Paris) pp 2-13
Fine B, Harris L, 1976a, "State expenditure in advanced capitalism" *New Left Review* number 98, 97-112
Fine B, Harris L, 1976b, "Controversial issues in Marxist economic theory", in *The Socialist Register 1976* Eds R Miliband, J Saville (Merlin Press, London) pp 141-178
- Fissore G, Meinardi G (Eds), 1976 *La Questione Meridionale* (Loescher, Turin)
Foerster R F, 1924 *The Italian Emigration of Our Times* reprinted in 1969 (Arno Press, New York)
Foley D K, 1982, "The value of money, the value of labour power and the Marxian transformation problem" *Review of Radical Political Economics* **14**(2) 37-47
Forte F, 1979 *Stato e Regioni nella Politica Regionale per l'Italia Meridionale* (Guida, Naples)
Franklin S H, 1961, "Social structure and land reform in Southern Italy" *The Sociological Review* new series **9**(3) 323-349
- Frémont A, 1978, "L'aménagement régional en France. La pratique et les idées" *L'Espace Géographique* **7**(2) 73-84
Freyssenet M, 1979a *La Sidérurgie Française 1945-1979* (Savelli, Paris)
Freyssenet M, 1979b *Division du Travail et Mobilisation Quotidienne de la Main-d'Oeuvre* (Centre de Sociologie Urbaine, Paris)
Freyssenet M, 1983, "Crise de la sidérurgie Lorraine et échec de la diversification industrielle" *Archivio di Studi Urbani e Regionali* new series **14** number 16, 67-81

Freyssenet M, Imbert F, 1975a *Capital Sidérurgique et Classe Ouvrière en Lorraine* (Centre de Sociologie Urbaine, Paris)
Freyssenet M, Imbert F, 1975b *La Centralisation du Capital dans la Sidérurgie 1945-1975* (Centre de Sociologie Urbaine, Paris)
Friedman A, 1977 *Industry and Labour. Class Struggle at Work and Monopoly Capitalism* (Macmillan, London)
Fröbel F, Heinrichs J, Kreye O, 1980 *The New International Division of Labour: Structural Unemployment in Industrial Countries and Industrialisation in Developing Countries* (Cambridge University Press, Cambridge)
Garofoli G, 1976a, "Produttività del lavoro e salari: un'analisi dei differenziali intersettoriali e interregionali", in *Mezzogiorno e Crisi* Ed. F Indovina (Franco Angeli, Milan) pp 97-139
Garofoli G, 1976b, "Un'analisi critica della politica di riequilibrio regionale in Italia: il caso del Mezzogiorno", in *Mezzogiorno e Crisi* Ed. F Indovina (Franco Angeli, Milan) pp 165-183
Garofoli G, 1978, "Decentramento produttivo, mercato del lavoro e localizzazione industriale" *Archivio di Studi Urbani e Regionali* number 4, 21-64
Garofoli G, 1981, "Lo sviluppo delle 'aree periferiche' nell'economia Italiana degli anni settanta" *L'Industria Rivista di Economia e Politica Industriale* **11** number 3, 391-404
Garofoli G, 1985, "Uneven regional development and industrial restructuring: the Italian pattern in the 1970s" *City and Region* number 9, 47-77
Giannola A, 1982, "The industrialisation, dualism and economic dependence of the Mezzogiorno in the 1970s" *Review of Economic Conditions in Italy* number 1, 67-117
Ginsborg P, 1984, "The Communist Party and the agrarian question in Southern Italy, 1943-1948" *History Workshop Journal* number 17, 81-101
• Gourc G, Gourc J, 1981, "La restructuration de la sidérurgie dans les usines performantes: la Solmer à Fos-sur-Mer" *Critiques de l'Économie Politique* new series, numbers 15-16, 135-184
Gouverneur J, 1983 *Contemporary Capitalism and Marxist Economics* (Martin Robertson, Oxford)
Gramsci A, 1971a, "Notes on Italian history", in *Selections from the Prison Notebooks of Antonio Gramsci* Eds Q Hoare, G Nowell Smith (Lawrence and Wishart, London) pp 52-126
Gramsci A, 1971b, "Americanism and Fordism", in *Selections from the Prison Notebooks of Antonio Gramsci* Eds Q Hoare, G Nowell Smith (Lawrence and Wishart, London) pp 279-318
Gramsci A, 1978 *Selections from Political Writings 1921-6* (Lawrence and Wishart, London)
• Grassini F A, 1980, "The Italian enterprises: the political constraints", in *State Owned Enterprise in the Western Economies* Eds R Vernon, Y Aharoni (Croom Helm, Beckenham, Kent) chapter 5
Graziani A (Ed.), 1972 *L'Economia Italiana: 1945-1970* (Il Mulino, Bologna)
Graziani A, 1976, "Mercato interno e relazioni internazionali", in *L'Italia Contemporanea, 1945-75* Ed. V Castronovo (Einaudi, Turin) pp 307-336
Graziani A, 1977, "Introduzione", in *Tecnologia e Decentramento Produttivo. L'Esperienza Italiana dal Dopoguerra a Oggi* Eds A Del Monte, M Raffa (Rosenberg and Sellier, Turin) pp 7-23
Graziani A, 1978, "The Mezzogiorno in the Italian economy" *Cambridge Journal of Economics* **2**(4) 355-372

Graziani A, 1979, "Il Mezzogiorno nell'quadro dell'economia Italiana", in *Investimenti e Disoccupazione nel Mezzogiorno* Eds A Graziani, E Pugliese (Il Mulino, Bologna) pp 7-65
• Graziani A, 1981, "Regional inequalities in Italy", in *Disparities in Economic Development since the Industrial Revolution* Eds P Bairoch, M Lévy-Leboyer (Macmillan, London) pp 319-330
• Graziani A, Pugliese E (Eds), 1979 *Investimenti e Disoccupazione nel Mezzogiorno* (Il Mulino, Bologna)
Green D, 1979a *The Dunkirk Maritime Industrial Zone: An Assessment* (HMSO, London)
Green D, 1979b *The Fos Maritime Industrial Zone: An Assessment* (HMSO, London)
Green D, 1979c *The Fos Maritime Industrial Zone: A Progress Report* (Department of Industry, London)
Guglielmetti P, Padovani R, 1981a, "I grandi impianti nel Mezzogiorno" *Informazioni Svimez* new series **34** numbers 9-10, 315-327
Guglielmetti P, Padovani R, 1981b, "Grandi e piccoli impianti nell'industria meridionale" *Informazioni Svimez* new series **34** numbers 9-10, 369-383
• Hirsch J, 1976, "Remarques théoriques sur l'état bourgeois et sa crise", in *La Crise de l'État* Ed. N Poulantzas (Presses Universitaires de France, Paris) pp 103-129
Hirsch J, 1977, "What is the fiscal crisis of the state?" paper presented at the Annual Conference of the Conference of Socialist Economists, University of Bradford, 2-4 July 1977
Hirsch J, 1978, "The state apparatus and social reproduction: elements of a theory of the bourgeois state", in *State and Capital. A Marxist Debate* Eds J Holloway, S Picciotto (Edward Arnold, London) chapter 5
• Hirsch J, 1985a, "Auf dem Wege zum Postfordismus? Die aktuelle Neuformierung des Kapitalismus und ihre politischen Folgen" *Das Argument* number 151, 325-342
• Hirsch J, 1985b, "Fordismus und Postfordismus. Die gegenwärtige gesellschaftliche Krise und ihre Folgen" *Politische Vierteljahresschrift* **26**(2) 160-182
Hirschman A O, 1958 *The Strategy of Economic Development* (Yale University Press, New Haven, CT)
Holland S, 1971, "Regional underdevelopment in a developed economy: the Italian case" *Regional Studies* **5**(2) 71-90
Holland S, 1972, "Introduction", in *The State as Entrepreneur. New Dimensions for Public Enterprise: The IRI State Shareholding Formula* Ed. S Holland (Weidenfeld and Nicolson, London) pp 1-4
Holland S, 1976 *Capital versus the Regions* (Macmillan, London)
Holloway J, Picciotto S, 1977, "Capital, crisis and the state" *Capital and Class* number 2, 76-101
Hytten E, Marchioni M, 1970 *Industrializzazione senza Sviluppo: Gela, una Storia Meridionale* (Franco Angeli, Milan)
IASM, 1979 *Documentazione sugli Agglomerati delle Aree e dei Nuclei Industriali del Mezzogiorno* Istituto per l'Assistenza allo Sviluppo del Mezzogiorno, Rome
ILO, annually *Yearbook of Labour Statistics* International Labour Office, Geneva
INEA, 1947 *Distribuzione della Proprietà Fondiaria in Italia* Istituto Nazionale di Economia Agraria, Rome
• INSEE, 1985 *Données Sociales, Édition 1984* Institut National de la Statistique et des Études Économiques, Paris
IRI, annually *Esercizio* Istituto per la Ricostruzione Industriale, Rome
ISTAT, annually *Annuario di Contabilità Nazionale* 2 volumes, Istituto Centrale di Statistica, Rome

ISTAT, 1973 *Occupati Presenti in Italia 1951-1972* Istituto Centrale di Statistica, Rome

ISTAT, 1982 *Occupati per Attività Economica e Regione 1970-81* Istituto Centrale di Statistica, Rome

Jessop B, 1982 *The Capitalist State. Marxist Theories and Methods* (Martin Robertson, Oxford)

Jessop B, 1983a, "Accumulation strategies, state forms, and hegemonic projects" *Kapitalistate* **10** 89-111

Jessop B, 1983b, "The capitalist state and the rule of capital: problems in the analysis of business associations" *West European Politics* **6**(2) 139-162

Judet P, 1982 *L'Évolution des Débouchés de la Sidérurgie Française et ses Perspectives à Moyen Terme. Un Rapport* Ministère de l'Industrie (La Documentation Française, Paris)

Kaldor N, 1970, "The case for regional policies" *Scottish Journal of Political Economy* **17** 337-348

Kaldor N, 1972, "The irrelevance of equilibrium economics" *The Economic Journal* **82** number 328, 1237-1255

Kaplinsky R, 1984 *Automation. The Technology and Society* (Longman, Harlow, Essex)

King R, 1973 *Land Reform: The Italian Experience* (Butterworth, Sevenoaks, Kent)

King R, 1977, "Recent industrialisation in Sardinia: rebirth or neocolonialism?" *Erdkunde* **31** 87-102

King R, 1985 *The Industrial Geography of Italy* (Croom Helm, Beckenham, Kent)

• King R, Strachan A, 1978, "Sicilian agro towns" *Erdkunde* **32** 110-123

Kinsey J, 1978, "The application of growth pole theory in the Aire Métropolitaine Marseillaise" *Geoforum* **9** 245-267

Laborie J-P, Langumier J-F, de Roo P, 1985 *La Politique Française d'Aménagement du Territoire de 1950 à 1985* (Documentation Française, Paris)

• Lajugie J, Delfaud P, Lacour C, 1979 *Espace Régional et Aménagement du Territoire* (Dalloz, Paris)

Lancaster K, 1974 *Introduction to Modern Microeconomics* second edition (Rand McNally, Chicago, IL)

Lange P, Vannicelli M, 1982, "Strategy under stress: the Italian union movement and the Italian crisis in developmental perspective", in *Unions, Change and Crisis: French and Italian Union Strategy and the Political Economy, 1945-1980* Eds P Lange, G Ross, M Vannicelli (George Allen and Unwin, Hemel Hempstead, Herts) part 2

Läpple D, 1985, "Internationalisation of capital and the regional problem", in *Capital and Labour in the Urbanised World* Ed. J Walton (Sage, London) pp 43-75

Läpple D, van Hoogstraten P, 1980, "Remarks on the spatial structure of capitalist development: the case of the Netherlands", in *Regions in Crisis. New Perspectives in European Regional Theory* Eds J Carney, R Hudson, J Lewis (Croom Helm, Beckenham, Kent) pp 117-166

Le Boucher E, 1984a, "La restructuration de la sidérurgie. Faut-il construire le 'train universel' de Gandrange?" *Le Monde* 28 March, page 30

Le Boucher E, 1984b, "Sidérurgie: un choix financièrement et technologiquement fondé" *Le Monde* 31 March, page 22

Levi C, 1982 *Christ Stopped at Eboli* (Penguin Books, Harmondsworth, Middx)

Lill R, 1984, "Historical reasons for the delay in the development of Southern Italy" *Mezzogiorno d'Europa* **4** 489-502

Lipietz A, 1974 *Le Tribut Foncier Urbain. Circulation du Capital et Propriété Foncière dans la Production du Cadre Bâti* (Maspero, Paris)

Lipietz A, 1977 *Le Capital et son Espace* (Maspero, Paris)
Lipietz A, 1979 *Crise et Inflation, Pourquoi? L'Accumulation Intensive* (Maspero, Paris)
Lipietz A, 1980, "Conflits de répartition et changements techniques dans la théorie marxiste" *Économie Appliquée* **33**(2) 511 – 537
Lipietz A, 1982a, "The so-called 'transformation problem' revisited" *Journal of Economic Theory* **26**(1) 59 – 88
Lipietz A, 1982b, "Derrière la crise: la tendance à la baisse du taux de profit. L'apport de quelques travaux français récents" *Revue Économique* **33**(2) 197 – 233
Lipietz A, 1982c, "Towards global Fordism?" and "Marx or Rostow?" *New Left Review* number 132, 33 – 58
• Lipietz A, 1982d, "Quelle base sociale pour le 'changement'?" *Les Temps Modernes* number 430, 1898 – 1930
Lipietz A, 1984a *L'Audace ou l'Enlisement. Sur les Politiques Économiques de la Gauche* (Maspero, Paris)
Lipietz A, 1984b *Accumulation, Crises et Sorties de Crise: Quelques Réflexions Méthodologiques autour de la Notion de 'Régulation'* (CEPREMAP, Paris)
Lipietz A, 1985a, "Le national et le régional: quelle autonomie face à la crise capitaliste mondiale?" paper presented at the seminar on Spatial Structure and Social Process held on Lesvos on 26 – 30 August 1985 (copy from the author, CEPREMAP, 142 rue du Chevaleret, 75013 Paris)
Lipietz A, 1985b *Mirages et Miracles: Problèmes de l'Industrialisation dans le Tiers Monde* (Éditions La Découverte, Paris)
Lojkine J, 1976, "Contribution to a Marxist theory of capitalist urbanisation", in *Urban Sociology: Critical Essays* Ed. C G Pickvance (Methuen, Andover, Hants) pp 119 – 146
Lojkine J, 1977 *Le Marxisme, l'État et la Question Urbaine* (Presses Universitaires de France, Paris)
Low-Beer J R, 1978 *Protest and Participation. The New Working Class in Italy* (Cambridge University Press, Cambridge)
Lyttelton A, 1979, "Landlords, peasants and the limits of liberalism", in *Gramsci and Italy's Passive Revolution* Ed. J A Davis (Croom Helm, Beckenham, Kent) pp 104 – 135
Malézieux J, 1980, "Crise et restructuration de la sidérurgie française. Le groupe USINOR" *L'Espace Géographique* number 3, 183 – 196
Marger P-L, 1979, "Situation et avenir de la sidérurgie française" *Problèmes Économiques* number 1639, 19 September, pp 8 – 16
• Margirier G, 1978 *Division Internationale du Travail et Emploi: Italie* Institut de Recherche Économique et de Planification, Université des Sciences Sociales de Grenoble, Grenoble
Martinelli A, 1980, "Organised business and Italian politics: Confindustria and the Christian Democrats in the postwar period", in *Italy in Transition. Conflict and Consensus* Eds P Lange, S Tarrow (Frank Cass, London) pp 67 – 87
Martinelli A, 1981, "The Italian experience: a historical perspective", in *State Owned Enterprise in the Western Economies* Eds R Vernon, Y Aharoni (Croom Helm, Beckenham, Kent) pp 85 – 98
Martinelli F, 1985, "Public policy and industrial development in Southern Italy: anatomy of a dependent industry" *International Journal of Urban and Regional Research* **9**(1) 47 – 81
Marx K, 1969 *Theories of Surplus-Value* part 1 (Lawrence and Wishart, London)
Marx K, 1973 *Grundrisse: Foundations of the Critique of Political Economy* (Penguin Books, Harmondsworth, Middx)

Marx K, 1975 *Early Writings* (Penguin Books, Harmondsworth, Middx)
Marx K, 1976 *Capital. A Critique of Political Economy, Volume 1* (Penguin Books, Harmondsworth, Middx)
Marx K, 1981 *Capital. A Critique of Political Economy, Volume 3* (Penguin Books, Harmondsworth, Middx)
Marx K, Engels F, 1976, "The German Ideology", in *Collected Works. Volume 5 (1845-1847)* (Lawrence and Wishart, London) pp 19-539
Mesplier A, 1983 *L'Agriculture des Dix et la Politique Agricole Commune* CEREC, 2 rue Mérimée, 75782 Paris, Cedex 16
• Messerlin F, Saunders C, 1983, "Steel: too much investment too late", in *Europe's Industries. Public and Private Strategies for Change* Eds G Shepherd, F Duchêne, C Saunders (Frances Pinter, London) chapter 3
Mészáros I, 1986, "The cunning of history in reverse gear" *Radical Philosophy* number 42, 2-10
Miliband R, 1977 *Marxism and Politics* (Oxford University Press, Oxford)
Ministero per il Mezzogiorno, 1974 *SpA Finsider: V Centro Siderurgico* Ministero per il Mezzogiorno, Rome
Mistral J, 1979, "Une politique de l'offre. Recentrer la politique industrielle" *Les Cahiers Français* number 192, 14-18
Mistral J, 1982, "La diffusion internationale de l'accumulation intensive et sa crise" in *Économie et Finance Internationale* Ed. J L Reiffers (Dunod, Paris) pp 205-237
Mottura G, 1980, "Notes for a study of work organisation in Italian agriculture" *International Journal of Urban and Regional Research* 4(3) 389-404
Mottura G, Pugliese E, 1972, "Observations on some characteristics of Italian emigration in the last fifteen years" *International Review of Community Development* numbers 27-28, 3-20
Mottura G, Pugliese E, 1980, "Capitalism in Agriculture and capitalistic agriculture: the Italian case", in *The Rural Sociology of Advanced Societies: Critical Perspectives* Eds F H Buttel, H Newby (Croom Helm, Beckenham, Kent) pp 171-199
Murray R, 1971, "The internationalisation of capital and the nation state" *New Left Review* number 67, 84-109
• Mutti A, Poli I, 1975 *Sottosviluppo e Meridione* (Mazzota, Milan)
Myrdal G, 1957 *Economic Theory and Underdeveloped Regions* (Gerald Duckworth, London)
Napoleoni C, 1975 *Smith, Ricardo, Marx. Observations on the History of Economic Thought* (Basil Blackwell, Oxford)
• Needleman L (Ed.), 1968 *Regional Analysis: Selected Readings* (Penguin Books, Harmondsworth, Middx)
Noirel G, 1981, "L'histoire sociale du Pays-Haut Lorrain" *Le Mouvement Social* number 115, 77-87
Noirel G, with Azzaoui B, 1980 *Vivre et Lutter à Longwy* (Maspero, Paris)
Nuova Italsider, 1985 *Siderurgico in Cifre: Lo Stabilimento di Taranto* Nuova Italsider, Taranto
OECD, annually *OECD Economic Surveys: Italy* Organisation for Economic Cooperation and Development, Paris
OECD, 1973 *Latest Results and New Features of Official Action in the Mezzogiorno (Italy)* Organisation for Economic Cooperation and Development, Paris
• Paci M (Ed.), 1978 *Capitalismo e Classi Sociali in Italia* (Il Mulino, Bologna)
• Paci M, 1981, "Class structure in Italian society", in *Contemporary Italian Sociology. A Reader* Ed. D Pinto (Cambridge University Press, Cambridge) pp 206-221
• Paci M, 1982 *La Struttura Sociale Italiana. Costanti Storiche e Trasformazioni Recenti* (Il Mulino, Bologna)

Padioleau J G, 1981 *Quand la France s'Enferre. La Politique Sidérurgique de la France depuis 1945* (Presses Universitaires de France, Paris)

Paillard B, with Fischler C, 1981 *La Damnation de Fos* (Éditions du Seuil, Paris)

Palloix C, 1975 *L'Internationalisation du Capital: Éléments Critiques* (Maspero, Paris)

Palloix C, 1976, "The labour process: from Fordism to Neo-Fordism", in *The Labour Process and Class Strategies* Conference of Socialist Economists (Stage 1, London) pp 46-67

• Palloix C, 1982, "Crise et nouvelles formes de l'impérialisme. Économie de crédit international et extension internationale du salariat", in *Économie et Finance Internationale* Ed. J L Reiffers (Dunod, Paris) pp 131-157

PAM, 1980 *Activités 1979* Port Autonome de Marseille, Marseilles

PAM, 1983, "Structure des emplois industriels permanents sur la zone de Fos de 1975 à fin 1981", internal document, Port Autonome de Marseille, Marseilles

Pennacchi L, 1977, "Struttura e prospettive del settore chimico" *Politica ed Economia* new series **8**(4) 31-41

Pinnarò G, Pugliese E, 1979, "Changes in the social structure of Southern Italy" *International Journal of Urban and Regional Research* **3**(4) 492-515

Piore M J, Sabel C F, 1984 *The Second Industrial Divide. Possibilities for Prosperity* (Basic Books, New York)

Pizzorno A, 1981, "Middle strata in the mechanisms of consensus", in *Contemporary Italian Sociology. A Reader* Ed. D Pinto (Cambridge University Press, Cambridge) pp 101-123

Planque B, 1983, "Fos, dix ans après" *Sud Information Économique* number 56, 2-6

• Podbielski G, 1974 *Italy: Development and Crisis in the Post-war Economy* (Oxford University Press, London)

Podbielski G, 1978 *Twenty-five Years of Special Action for the Development of Southern Italy* (Giuffré Editore, Milan)

Posner M V, Woolf S J, 1967 *Italian Public Enterprise* (Gerald Duckworth, London)

Poulantzas N, 1973 *Political Power and Social Classes* (New Left Books, London)

Poznanski K Z, 1983, "International diffusion of steel technologies: time lag and the speed of diffusion" *Technological Forecasting and Social Change* **23** 305-323

Poznanski K Z, 1985, "The extinguishing process: a case study of steel technologies in the world industry" unpublished report, Virginia Polytechnic Institute and State University, Blacksburg, VA

Preteceille E, 1976, "The contradictions of capitalist urbanisation" *Antipode* **8**(1) 69-76

Preteceille E, 1985, "Collective consumption, urban segregation, social classes" paper presented at the Fifth Urban Change and Conflict Conference, on *Industrial Restructuring, Social Change and the Locality* University of Sussex, 16-19 April 1985

Preteceille E, Terrail J-P, 1985 *Capitalism, Consumption and Needs* (Basil Blackwell, Oxford)

Procacci G, 1973 *History of the Italian People* (Penguin Books, Harmondsworth, Middx)

Prud'homme R, 1974, "Regional economic policy in France, 1962-72", in *Public Policy and Regional Economic Development* Ed. N M Hansen (Ballinger, Cambridge, MA) pp 48-51

Pugliese E, 1979, "Evoluzione della struttura di classe nel Mezzogiorno", in *Investimenti e Disoccupazione nel Mezzogiorno* Eds A Graziani, E Pugliese (Il Mulino, Bologna) Chapter 2

Pugliese E, 1980, "The Mansholt Plan and the Mezzogiorno", in *Contemporary Italian Sociology. A Reader* Ed. D Pinto (Cambridge University Press, Cambridge) pp 47-65

Pugliese E, 1985, "Farm workers in Italy: agricultural working class, landless peasants, or clients of the welfare state?", in *Uneven Development in Southern Europe. Studies of Accumulation, Class, Migration and the State* Eds R Hudson, J Lewis (Methuen, Andover, Hants) pp 123-139

Regalia I, Regini M, Reyneri E, 1978, "Labour conflict and industrial relations in Italy", in *The Resurgence of Class Conflict in Western Europe since 1968* Eds C Crouch, A Pizzorno (Macmillan, London) chapter 4

Regini M, 1980, "Labour unions, industrial action and politics", in *Italy in Transition. Conflict and Consensus* Eds P Lange, S Tarrow (Frank Cass, London) pp 49-66

Rhodes M, 1985, "Organised interests and industrial crisis management: restructuring the steel industry in West Germany, Italy, and France", in *Organised Interests and the State. Studies in Meso-Corporatism* Ed. A Cawson (Sage, London) pp 192-220

Ricardo D, 1951 *The Works and Correspondence of David Ricardo, Volume 1. On the Principles of Political Economy and Taxation* (Cambridge University Press, Cambridge)

Ricossa S, 1976, "Italy, 1920-1970", in *The Fontana Economic History of Contemporary Europe: Contemporary Economies, Part 1* Ed. C Cipolla (Fontana Books, London) pp 266-232

Robert G, 1974, "L'opération Fos. Un test de l'aménagement capitaliste du territoire" *Urbanisme* number 145, 63-76

Romeo R, 1959 *Risorgimento e Capitalismo* (Laterza, Bari)

Ross G, 1982, "French labour and economic change", in *France in a Troubled World Economy* Eds S S Cohen, P A Gourevitch (Butterworth, Sevenoaks, Kent) chapter 8

Ross G, 1984, "The CGT, economic crisis, and political change", in *The French Workers' Movement: Economic Crisis and Political Change* Ed. M Kesselman, with G Groux (Allen and Unwin, Winchester, MA) pp 49-74

Ross G, Jenson J, 1981, "Strategy and contradiction in the victory of French Socialism", in *The Socialist Register 1976* Eds R Miliband, J Saville (Merlin Press, London) pp 72-103

• Ross S, Cohen S, 1975, "The politics of French regional planning", in *Regional Policy: Readings in Theory and Applications* revised edition, Eds J Friedmann, W Alonso (MIT Press, Cambridge, MA) pp 727-750

Rossi-Doria M, 1948 *Riforma Agraria e Azione Meridionalista* (Edizioni Agricole, Bologna)

Rossi-Doria M, 1950, "Il lavoro" *Annuario dell'Agricoltura Italiana* **4** 369-404

• Rossi-Doria M, 1958a, "The land tenure system and class in Southern Italy" *The American Historical Review* **64**(1) 46-53

• Rossi-Doria M, 1958b *Dieci Anni di Politica Agraria nel Mezzogiorno* (Laterza, Bari)

Rossi-Doria M, 1972a, "La situazione delle campagne Italiane", in *L'Economia Italiana: 1945-70* Ed. A Graziani (Il Mulino, Bologna) pp 209-212

Rossi-Doria M, 1972b, "Un po' di storia", in *L'Economia Italiana: 1945-70* Ed. A Graziani (Il Mulino, Bologna) pp 242-249

Rossi-Doria M, 1973, "Cos'è il Mezzogiorno agrario?", in *Nuova Antologia della Questione Meridionale. I Maestri del Meridionalismo Classico* third edition, Ed. B Caizzi (Edizioni di Comunità, Milan) pp 165-192 (originally published in 1948 in *Riforma Agraria e Azione Meridionalista* by Edizione Agricole, Bologna)

• Rossi-Doria M, 1982 *Scritti sul Mezzogiorno* (Einaudi, Turin)

Sabel C F, 1982 *Work and Politics: The Division of Labour in Industry* (Cambridge University Press, Cambridge)
Sallois J, Cretin J, 1976, "Le rôle social des hauts fonctionnaires et la crise de l'état", in *La Crise de l'État* Ed. N Poulantzas (Presses Universitaires de France, Paris) pp 233–259
Salvati M, 1972, "The impasse of Italian capitalism" *New Left Review* number 76, 3–33
Salvati M, 1975 *Il Sistema Economico Italiano: Analisi di una Crisi* (Il Mulino, Bologna)
Salvati M, 1979, "Economia e politica in Italia dal 1969 al 1979. Una cronaca" *Quaderni Piacentini* **18** numbers 70–71, 51–67
Salvemini G, 1973a, "La piccola borghesia intellettuale nel Mezzogiorno d'Italia", in *Nuova Antologia della Questione Meridionale. I Maestri del Meridionalismo Classico* third edition, Ed. B Caizzi (Edizioni di Comunità, Milan) pp 377–392 (revised version published in *Scritti sulla Questione Meridionale 1896–1955* by Einaudi, Turin, in 1955 of an article originally published in *La Voce* 16 May 1911)
Salvemini G, 1973b, "La deviazione oligarchica del movimento socialista", in *Nuova Antologia della Questione Meridionale. I Maestri del Meridionalismo Classico* third edition, Ed. B Caizzi (Edizioni di Comunità, Milan) pp 367–375 (originally published in 1922 in *Tendenze Vecchie e Necessità Nuove del Movimento Operaio Italiano* by Capelli, Bologna)
Saraceno P, 1980, "Cattedrali nel deserto? Gli impianti di maggior dimensione nell'industrializzazione meridionale" *Informazioni Svimez* new series **33**(1) 20–30
Scott A J, 1980 *The Urban Land Nexus and the State* (Pion, London)
Secchi B, 1974 *Squilibri Regionali e Sviluppo Economico* (Marsilio, Venice)
Shaikh A, 1979, "Foreign trade and the law of value: part 1" *Science and Society* **43**(4) 281–302
Shaikh A, 1980a, "Foreign trade and the law of value: part 2" *Science and Society* **44**(1) 27–57
Shaikh A, 1980b, "The laws of international exchange", in *Growth, Profits and Property: Essays in the Revival of Political Economy* Ed. E Nell (Cambridge University Press, Cambridge) pp 204–235
Smith N, 1984 *Uneven Development. Nature, Capital and the Production of Space* (Basil Blackwell, Oxford)
Souyri P, 1983, "La crise de 1974 et la riposte du capital" *Annales* **38**(4) 790–820
Stoffaes C, 1984 *Politique Industrielle* Institut d'Études Politiques de Paris (Les Cours de Droit, Paris)
• Tarantelli E, Willke G (Eds), 1981 *The management of Industrial Conflict in the Recession of the 1970s: Britain, Germany and Italy* (Bruylant, Brussels; Klett-Cotta, Stuttgart; Le Monnier, Florence; Sijthoff and Noordhoff, Alphen aan den Rijn)
Tarrow S G, 1967 *Peasant Communism in Southern Italy* (Yale University Press, New Haven, CT)
• Tarrow S, Katzenstein P J, Graziano L (Eds), 1978 *Territorial Politics in Industrial Nations* (Praeger, New York)
Thévenot L, 1977, "Les catégories sociales en 1975: l'extension du salariat" *Économie et Statistique* number 91, 3–31
Thévenot L, 1985, "Des cadres moyens aux professions intermédiaires", in *Données Sociales 1984* Institut National de la Statistique et des Études Économiques, Paris, pp 551–557
Thirlwall A P, 1974, "Regional economic disparities and regional policy in the Common Market" *Urban Studies* **11** 1–12

Trevisan P, 1979, "Montedison e Piano Chimico. Lotte operaie e ristrutturazione a Maghera" *Materiali Veneti* number 12, 15-16

Turri E (Ed.), 1974 *L'Italia. Una Nuova Geografia* (Istituto Geografico de Agostini, Novara)

UCSIP, 1980 *L'Industrie Française du Pétrole 1979* Union des Chambres Syndicales de l'Industrie du Pétrole, Paris

United Nations Economic Commission for Europe *Quarterly Bulletin of Steel Statistics for Europe* (United Nations, New York)

van der Pijl, 1984 *The Making of an Atlantic Ruling Class* (Verso, London)

Vieille P, 1977, "Une séquence de Kriegspiel Méditerranéen: la bataille des rives de l'Étang de Berre (1972)", in *Aménagement du Territoire et Développement Régional: Les Faits, les Idées, les Institutions. Volume 7* Université de Grenoble, Institut d'Études Politiques, Grenoble, pp 376-406

Viola S, 1985, "Un salto nell'Italsider: cosi Taranto si è uccisa. L'industrializzazione sbagliata della più sporca città italiana" *La Repubblica* 29 September, page 7

Walsh V C, 1970 *Introduction to Contemporary Microeconomics* (McGraw-Hill, New York)

Walsh V, Gram H, 1980 *Classical and Neoclassical Theories of General Equilibrium. Historical Origins and Mathematical Structure* (Oxford University Press, New York)

Weaver C, 1984 *Regional Development and the Local Community: Planning, Politics and Social Context* (John Wiley, Chichester, Sussex)

Williams R, 1981, "For Britain see Wales" *The Times Higher Educational Supplement* 15 May, page 14

Williamson J G, 1965, "Regional inequality and the process of national development: a description of the patterns" *Economic Development and Cultural Change* **13** 3-45

Wormald A, 1972, "Growth promotion: the creation of a modern steel industry" in *The State as Entrepreneur. New Dimensions for Public Enterprise: The IRI State Shareholding Formula* Ed. S Holland (Weidenfeld and Nicolson, London) chapter 4

Index

Absentee landlords 66
Abstract labour 13
Accumulation
 of capital 28-29, 52-53, 231, 238, 347
 regimes 359, 363
 strategies 52-53, 117-119, 125, 137, 139-144, 232
Activity rates, trends in Italian 123-124, 214-215
Aglietta 11, 18, 20-23, 25-27, 34, 38, 41, 43, 44, 47, 204, 229, 357
Agricultural development 81
 social and spatial differentiation of 98-105
Agricultural policies 101-103
Agricultural structures 84-91
 intensive farming districts 89
 mixed farming zones 89-91
 capitalist 66
Agro-towns 86-89
Alfa Romeo (including Alfa Sud) 179, 182, 184, 200-202, 206, 351
Allen 108, 122, 147-150, 153, 247
Alliance of northern workers and southern peasants 76
Allum 114, 115, 154
Amin 200, 202, 203, 206, 207
Arcangeli 172
Areas of industrial development, see Growth areas
Arlacchi 85, 87, 90, 91
Armstrong 222
Assembly line, semiautomatic 23-24, 129, 202-207
Atkinson 27
Austerity measures 333, 358
Automation 22, 24-26, 143, 202, 206, 207, 229, 310, 313, 344, 358, 360
Autonomy, responsible 207
Autumno caldo 169
Azienda Generale Italiana Petroli (AGIP) 78, 187
Azienda Nazionale Idrogenazione Combustibili (ANIC) 78, 186, 187, 189, 190, 193-195, 198

Bagnasco 111, 121
Bagnoli 72, 78, 173, 179, 181, 184
Bairoch 1
Banking capital 58-59, 357, 362

Banks, Italian deposit and investment 72
Becchi-Collidà 113
Belhadj 155, 172, 176, 193
Birnbaum 243
Black economy 138, 215, 227-228
Bleitrach 252, 283, 296
Blocco storico, see Hegemonic bloc
Blok 86, 88, 95
Bologna 190, 191, 193
Boscher Law 287-288, 291
Bouches-du-Rhône département 269, 274, 283, 287, 294
Boudeville 245, 249, 349
Braccianti 86, 88, 94, 103-104
Brescia 311, 334
Broda 270-273
Bruno 215
Burris 120

Cafiero 224
Cammet 69
Capacity utilisation 195, 272-273
Capital
 centralisation of 26, 28-29, 128, 204, 238-239, 242, 262, 301, 344
 constant 16, 18, 262, 301, 344
 devalorisation of 22-23, 37, 199, 239, 268, 352-353
 financial 58-59, 301
 forms of 14-17, 58-59
 industrial, circuit of 14-17
 interest-bearing 58-59
 internationalisation of 9, 128, 203, 239, 357
 merchant 58-59, 229
 money 58-59, 362
 organic composition of 31-32, 357
 productive 58-59, 362
Capital formation, the role of regional aid 167-169
Capital-intensive industrialisation 198-200, 232
Capitalism 9-12
Capitalist sector, articulation with other sectors 12, 100-101, 354
Capuggi 167, 195
Cassa Integrazione Guadagni 134, 352
Cassa per il Mezzogiorno 93, 97-101, 114-115, 145-167, 178, 179, 184, 219, 352
 nonadditionality of spending 150, 162

Castells 238, 244, 254
Castronovo 113
Cathedrals in the desert 198–202, 281
Centralisation of capital 26, 28–29, 128, 204, 238–239, 242, 262, 301, 344
Centrally planned economies 337, 339–340
Centre d'Études Prospectives et d'Informations Internationales (CEPII) 143
Centre d'Information des Industries Lorraines 298, 304, 312, 313
Centre-left government 125–129, 135, 151
Chambre Syndicale de la Sidérurgie Française (CSSF) 301–302, 305, 313, 314, 323, 330, 337–340
Chapman 177, 186, 195
Chemical industry 72, 121, 152–153, 164, 167, 171, 172, 185–198, 200, 203, 212, 227, 232, 235, 238, 239, 252, 260, 261, 351–353
Chemical Plan 190–193, 195
Chemical war 189
Circular and cumulative causation 2–3, 38, 44–47, 357, 358
Circulation, sphere of 12, 15, 16, 58–59
City states, development of 61
Civil Society 49–50
Class conflicts and struggles 18, 24, 26, 28, 36–37, 76–79, 94–95, 117–118, 124–126, 129–137, 184, 201–204, 206, 207, 225, 226, 228, 282, 311–312, 317, 322, 328, 335, 354–355, 357
Class relations, class interests, and class domination 5, 6, 9–12, 14–16, 18–21, 49–53, 56–57, 62–69, 73, 76, 105, 168, 176, 242–244, 290, 345–346, 350–351, 362
Class structure, of Italian South 67, 103–105, 111–116, 118–120
Clientelism 66, 67, 93, 100, 115, 119, 126, 141, 146, 223
Clough 96
Coal industry, in Nord 236
Collective bargaining 37
Collective goods and services 12, 56–57, 118, 123, 133, 136, 294–295
Collective worker 7–8

Colletti 49, 50
Comitato Interministeriale della Programmazione Economica (CIPE) 150–154, 156–158, 179–181, 190, 201
Commercial capital 58–59, 125, 362
Commercial role, of the port of Marseilles 274
Commissariat du Plan 245, 302
Commodity production 8–9, 11–14
Common use rights 64
Comparative advantage 38–44, 343, 354
Competition 29–32
Concentration of capital 28–29, 128, 204, 238, 239, 242, 301, 344
Confindustria 139, 141
Congés de conversion 335
Constant capital 16, 18
Construction industry 108–109, 113–114, 277–278
Continuous casting 300, 310
Continuous rolling 299–302
Contrattazione programmata 151, 154, 155
Convention Générale État–Sidérurgie 309–315
Cooperation 7–8, 57
Coriat 23
Corner 77
Cosentino 84, 86, 97, 99–101
Credit money (see also Industrial incentives) 37
Crisis, fiscal 137–138, 222, 223, 359
Crisis of Fordism 23–24, 126, 227, 357–359
Crisis of steel industry 281–282, 319–347
crisis cartel 331
Crisis, oil 137–139
Critique 352
Crouch 131
Cultiaux 253, 255–257, 259, 260, 266, 275, 277, 279, 280, 286, 294
Curry 320

Dahmani 311, 340, 344
Davignon Plan 320, 331
Davis 35
Decentralisation of production (see Productive decentralisation)
Delegati 129, 134

Délégation à l'Aménagement du Territoire et à l'Action Régionale (DATAR) 245, 246, 248, 250, 253, 284
Del Monte 93, 99, 110, 156, 160, 161, 170
Delorme 48
Demand forecasts, and industrial plans 175–177, 191–192, 316, 320–321, 345–346
Departments of production 32–33, 222, 356
Dependent development 223, 231
Deposit and investment banks, Italian 72
Devalorisation of capital 22–23, 37, 199, 239, 268, 352–353
Development
 agricultural 81, 98–105
 dependent 223, 331
 differentiation of 2–3
 equalisation of 2–3
 of the spheres of consumption and social reproduction 283, 294–295
 uneven 1–6, 44, 98–103, 139, 165, 223, 349, 350
Development areas, maritime industrial 231–238, 240–241, 252, 254, 257, 268, 271, 273, 274, 276, 277, 279, 280, 282, 283, 285, 286, 291, 294
De Vroey 352
De Wendel 265, 301, 305, 308, 309, 314–318
Di Lampedusa 65, 115
Direct reduction 181, 310
Disproportionality 57
Division of labour
 coordination of 7, 8
 international 38–44, 143–144, 228, 318–320, 337–343, 357
 social 5–12, 299
 territorial 5, 7–10, 38–44
Division of the working class 228
Domestic sector 12
Dualism 27–28, 98–105, 123–125, 139, 358–360
Dulong 243
Duménil 13, 14, 17, 18
Dunford 6, 8, 9
Dunkirk 233–235, 237, 238, 249, 262, 281, 296, 299, 307–309, 314, 315, 325, 328, 332, 339, 341, 345

Economic integration 61–62, 122, 145, 151, 208, 241, 343, 346
Economic liberalism 58–59, 92, 93, 241, 341, 362
Economic miracle 91, 92, 117–122, 123–125
Economic structure and growth
 French 241–242
 Italian 80–83, 91–94, 117–144
Efficiency wage 45, 358
Elections 321, 322, 346
Electric arc methods 334
Electronics sector 26–27, 333, 335
Emigrants' remittances 110–111, 220
Emigration 74–75, 104, 108–111, 220, 329
Employment
 cross border 318
 in French iron and steel industry
  job losses 269–270, 314, 317, 324–325, 328–330, 332, 333, 340
  job transfers 269–270, 278–279, 317
 in Italian agriculture 103–105
 in Italian chemical industry 192
 in Italian iron and steel industry 180, 182
 in Italian vehicle manufacturing industry 201–205
 in the Mezzogiorno 80–83, 106–108, 208–220
Employment agencies, temporary 269–272
Employment problems in Aire Métropolitaine Marseillaise 274–282
Employment relation 27–28, 269–272
Energy and raw materials, imported supplies of 176, 238, 239, 262, 307, 311
Energy sector 3, 8, 15, 22, 23, 25, 35, 72, 162, 169, 172, 188–190, 194, 200, 201, 208, 220, 231, 232, 234, 236–239, 252, 254, 257, 261, 269, 276, 281, 282, 294, 319, 334, 340, 347, 356
Ente Nazionale Idrocarburi (ENI) 122, 139, 188, 189, 195
Equilibrium growth 32–34
Établissement Public d'Aménagement (EPA) 287–288, 293

European Coal and Steel Community (ECSC) 302
European Commission 4, 174, 307, 310, 332, 338, 342, 343
European Economic Community 122, 145, 206, 241, 247, 320, 331, 335, 341, 343
Exchange, law of 13-14
Exchange rate 39-44, 137, 138, 149
Export-led growth 45, 47, 91, 93-94, 117-123, 125-127, 136, 151, 356-357
Exposed sector 38, 47
External constraint 39-44, 343
External economies 277
Externalities 5, 56, 124, 147

Fabre 270
Factionalism in Italian politics 67
Falling rate of profit 29-32
  in Italian chemical industry 193
Fascism 76-78
Feudalism 9-10, 61, 64-65
FIAT 72, 78, 117-118, 128-130, 141, 174, 175, 177, 201, 203-207, 306, 351
Filière acier 344, 345
Financial capital 58-59, 301
Financial restructuring 262-266, 301-305, 314-316, 318, 321-325, 331, 344
Fine 57
Finsider 173, 176-178, 181, 182, 184
Fiscal crisis 137-138, 222, 223, 359
Fiscal incentives 148-149, 153, 158
Flexible specialisation 24-27, 227-229, 358, 359
Foerster 75
Foley 13, 14, 16, 17
Fonds de Développement Économique et Social (FDES) 264, 265, 314
Fonds d'Intervention pour l'Aménagement du Territoire (FIAT) 292
Fonds Spécial d'Adaptation Industrielle (FSAI) 330
Forces of production, contradictions with social relations of production 9-10, 360, 361
Fordism
  adaptations to inflexibility 226-227
  as an industrial paradigm 22-24, 128, 133, 204, 226-227

Fordism (continued)
  as a regime of accumulation 34-38, 121, 355-360
  crisis of 23-24, 126, 227, 357-359
Forte 148, 156, 159, 161
Fos-sur-Mer 233, 237, 238, 249, 252-296, 315-317, 339, 341, 345, 351
Franklin 98
Free trade, its impact on southern development 69-70
French Socialist Party 334
Freyssenet 203-205, 266, 269, 296, 299, 301-306, 308, 309, 311, 314, 315, 317, 318, 320, 322-325, 328-330, 340, 344
Friedman 207
Fröbel 357

Garofoli 128, 200, 229
General conditions of production 54-55, 252-256
Geographical inequalities 1-5, 56, 61-62, 68-69, 208
Giannola 93, 99, 110, 156, 171
Ginsborg 95
Gioia Tauro 90-91, 180-182
  as a site for the fifth integrated steel centre 180-182
Gouverneur 32
Government, see State
Gramsci 6, 68, 76
Graziani 94, 111, 122, 123, 140, 145, 146, 168, 199, 208, 212, 215, 218, 220, 226, 228
Great depression 72
Green 234, 235, 237, 260, 261
Groupement de l'Industrie Sidérurgique (GIS) 265, 301, 325
Growth centres and areas 147, 148, 151, 152, 165-167, 231-238, 240-241, 249-250, 252-295, 350
Growth, export led 45, 47, 91, 93-94, 117-123, 125-127, 136, 151, 356-357
Growth poles 147, 349
Guglielmetti 209-211

Habitations à Loyer Modéré (HLMs) 294
Hegemonic bloc 52-53, 64, 66, 71-73, 78, 111-115, 146, 242, 355, 356

Hegemonic project 35, 52–53,
    117–118, 125–126, 232, 244
Hirsch 51
Hirschman 349
Historical materialism 6–7
Holland 108, 109, 139, 151
Hot autumn 129–131, 146, 187, 351
Hytten 187

Ideal causality 6, 351
Immigrant and temporary workers
    132, 270, 278, 308, 329
Import substitution 175
Income determination 11, 14, 30, 46
Increasing returns 41, 45
Indebtedness 70, 143–144, 189, 223,
    267–268, 320, 324
Indicative planning 37–38, 57–59,
    125–126, 129, 150–151,
    153–156, 240, 247–249, 251, 252,
    255–256, 262, 293, 300–301, 305,
    308, 313, 315–316, 320–321
Industrial capital, circuit of 14–17
Industrial complexes 191–193,
    196–198, 203, 231–238, 249,
    257–264, 307, 313, 344–345
Industrial conflicts (see also Class
    conflicts) 207
Industrial decentralisation, see
    Productive decentralisation
Industrial development
    collapse of local industries 69–70,
        108, 212–213, 218–219, 280
    Italian 62–63, 69–73, 76–78,
        81–82, 106–108, 121–122,
        169–213
Industrial discipline 35, 300
Industrial diversification
    of areas 236, 314, 322, 328, 332,
        335
    of companies 200–202, 318, 351
Industrial incentives 59, 139–140,
    148–156, 158–169, 176–178,
    181–182, 189–190, 194, 198, 199,
    204–205, 248–249, 264–266,
    315–316, 332
    misappropriation of 198
    strength of Italian 161
Industrialisation, capital-intensive 137,
    165, 167, 172, 177, 189, 198–200,
    232
Industrial linkages 273

Industrial location 7–8, 10, 176–177,
    189–190, 200, 204–206,
    231–235, 257–274, 296–299,
    307, 341
Industrial reserve army mechanism 28,
    108–111, 118, 215
Industrial structures 226–230,
    233–236, 257–261, 270–272,
    325–328
Industrial training schemes 280
Industrial triangle 72
Inequalities
    geographical 1–4, 61–62, 68–69,
        83, 123, 128, 145, 150, 208,
        223–226, 235–237, 244–251,
        274–276, 345
    measurement of 2
Inflation 121, 123–126, 135, 280,
    352
Infrastructural investments 54–55,
    96–98, 108–109, 145, 151, 152,
    154–156, 158, 181, 237, 240–241,
    247, 249, 252–256, 266, 268, 350
    and growth strategies 55, 247
Input–output methods 17, 46–47,
    349
Integrated shore-based iron and steel
    plant 173, 239–240, 252,
    261–262, 307, 350
Integration (and interfirm specialisation)
    188, 189, 191, 194, 206, 229, 318,
    322, 331, 344
Integration, spatial 7–8, 349
Intensification of work 128, 129, 214
Intercapitalist competition and conflict
    39–44, 177–178, 188–189,
    194–198, 200–201, 305–306, 351
    within state 232, 320
Interest-bearing capital 58–59
Interindustry relations, see Input–
    output methods
International division of labour
    38–44, 143–144, 228, 318–320,
    337–343, 357
Internationalisation of capital 9, 128,
    203, 239, 357
International Labour Office (ILO) 120
International values 38–44
Interregional relations 353
Iron and steel industry 34, 71, 72,
    76–78, 121, 139, 143, 169,
    172–182, 184, 185, 198, 203, 212,

Iron and steel industry (continued)
213, 227, 231, 233–239, 252, 257, 261, 262, 264–273, 281, 282, 292, 296, 297, 299–302, 305–325, 328–333, 335–347, 350–352, 354, 356
   French social agreements 314, 329, 335–359
   miniplants 175, 311, 333, 334, 347
   oxygen steelmaking 307
   products and processes 179, 267, 299–301, 309–311, 347
   role in growth promotion 175
   role of capital costs 267–268
   shore-based complexes 173, 175–176, 179, 180, 231, 238–239, 241, 252, 261, 262, 351
   state-industry plans 175–176, 179–180, 262–264, 300–305, 308–309, 314–317, 320–336, 344–345
Iron foundry industry 311
Iron mines 311–313
Istituto Centrale di Statistica (ISTAT) 80–83, 104, 106–107, 169–171, 216–217, 221
Istituto di Economia Agraria (INEA) 90
Istituto Mobiliare Italiano (IMI) 77
Istituto per l'Assistenza allo Sviluppo del Mezzogiorno (IASM) 196–197
Istituto per la Ricostruzione Industriale (IRI) 77, 78, 122, 173, 175, 176, 178, 179, 181–184, 201
   financial difficulties in the 1970s 182
Italian Christian Democrat Party (DC) 35, 53, 92, 95, 114, 115, 125, 126, 138–141, 143
Italian Communist Party (PCI) 91–93, 117, 138, 139, 156
Italian fascism 76–78
Italian Socialist Party (PSI) 75, 92, 117, 125, 126, 129, 135
   and the southern question 75–76
Italsider 179, 180, 331

Jessop 52
Job enrichment 25, 133, 202, 206–207, 229, 358
Job loss, see Employment
Judet Report 332

Kaldor 44
Kaplinsky 26
Keynesianism 37–38, 360
King 96, 97, 185–187, 195, 198
Kinsey 277

Labour, abstract 13
Labour commanded 19, 39
Labour force
   mobilisation of 128, 195, 201–203, 205–206, 277–280
   occupational and skill composition of 299–300
Labour market
   segmentation of 27–28, 141–142, 215, 227–228, 269–272, 277–280
   structure and development of 108–109, 123–124, 176, 237, 274, 277–280
Labour power
   reproduction of 15–16, 35, 56–57, 278, 280, 294–295, 356
   value of 18–22, 29, 55, 57, 110, 117–118, 124, 126–127, 129, 132–134, 355, 358–359
Labour process 15–16, 20–27, 173, 175–176, 179, 203, 204, 206–207, 238–239, 299–300, 309–311, 333–334, 347, 351, 355
Land and property development and speculation 95, 113–114, 123, 284, 362
Land ownership 12, 58, 64–66, 70, 85–91, 94–97, 112
Land policies 54, 252, 253, 268, 295, 308
Land reform 94–105, 111, 113, 114
Land tenure, in Italian South 64–66, 85–91
Lange 92, 117, 126, 129, 134, 137
Läpple 5–8
Latifondo
   capitalist 85–87, 94–95
   peasant 87–89, 95, 101
Le Boucher 332, 335
Levi 67
Liberal economics 119–122, 126, 138
Lipietz 2, 5, 7, 17–19, 29–32, 34, 121, 242, 330, 346, 353–355, 357, 360, 362
Lojkine 8

Lorraine 261, 262, 265, 269, 270, 278, 296, 301, 302, 305, 308, 311, 312, 314, 316–318, 321, 322, 328–330, 332, 335, 339
Low-Beer 130
Lyttleton 66

Malézieux 323, 326, 327, 329
Marger 325
Maritime industrial development areas 231–238, 240–241, 252, 254, 257, 268, 271, 273, 274, 276, 277, 279, 280, 282, 283, 285, 286, 291, 294
Maritime transport 139, 238–240, 252, 257, 262
Market mechanisms, inadequacies of 54–60, 112, 194, 267–268, 341, 345–347, 353, 361
Marseilles 252, 253, 255–257, 283–293
Martinelli A 128, 140, 141
Martinelli F 172, 213
Marx 3, 7–9, 11, 13, 15, 17, 19, 20, 28–32, 43, 48–50, 54, 55, 58, 352, 362, 363
Mass consumption 34–38, 121
Mass production 34, 301
Material causality 6, 352
Mechanisation 22, 299, 344
Merchant capital 58–59, 229
Mergers 188–189, 301, 302–305, 314–315, 317, 322, 323, 325, 336
Merit goods 56
Mesplier 103
Mészáros 363
Métropoles d'équilibre 237, 249, 283–285
Mezzadria or contractual sharecropping system 66
Mezzogiorno 61, 64, 66, 67, 73, 78, 80–84, 122, 128, 145–162, 164, 165, 167–170, 172, 176, 177, 180, 182, 185, 189, 190, 198–200, 203, 204, 208, 212–214, 218–220, 223–226, 231, 232, 349, 351–354
Middle strata, role in consensus building 118–119, 125, 139
Ministero del Bilancio e della Programmazione Economica 195
Ministero dell'Industria 186
Ministero per il Mezzogiorno 182
Mistral 47
Mode of consumption 230, 355

Modes of production 8–10, 362
Monetarism 331, 343, 360
Monetary constraint 11–12, 38–44
Money
  quantity theory of 43
  value of 13
Money capital 58–59, 362
Mono-industrial areas 308, 337, 344
Monopolies, natural 55
Monopolistic regulation 34–38, 352
Montedison 137, 140, 187, 189, 190, 192–195, 198
Mottura 99, 101, 103, 109
Multiplier effects 107–108, 201, 213, 277, 280, 281, 350
Murray 53
Myrdal 44

Napoleoni 19
Nation states 9, 354
  hegemonic role of 2–3, 356
  hierarchies of 2–3, 38, 356
Nationalisation 59, 125, 139, 188, 322, 331, 347
Natural monopolies 55
Natural resources, ownership of 12
Neoclassical economics 38, 43
New Deal 37, 356
New international division of labour, see International division of labour
Newly industrialising countries 1–3, 337
New towns 237, 255, 287, 292, 293
Nord 73, 233–235, 270, 296, 299, 302, 311, 314, 328–330, 332, 339
Nuclei of industrialisatoin, see Growth areas
Nuova Italsider 180

Occupational structures 36, 103–105, 119, 120
Oil crisis 137–139
Oil industry 130, 139, 143, 185
Oligopolistic markets 37, 189
Organic composition of capital 31–32, 357
Organisation for Economic Cooperation and Development (OECD) 38, 138, 142, 144, 155
Organismes d'Études d'Aménagement des Aires Métropolitaines (OREAM) 246, 283, 287, 292
Overdevelopment 2–3

Padioleau 301, 302
Paillard 252, 262–263, 265, 269, 278, 291, 296
Palloix 20, 22
Passive revolution 64
Pennacchi 194
Petrochemical industry 172, 186–188, 190, 233, 234, 237, 238, 258, 260, 261
Petty commodity production 12
Pinnarò 95, 113, 115
Pizzorno 117, 119, 126, 131
Plan Acier 273, 319–322
Plan de Conversion de Wendel-SIDELOR (Plan Dherse) 315–318
Plan de Sauvetage de la Sidérurgie 323–330
Plan Professionnel (see also Convention Générale État-Sidérurgie) 314–315
Planque 281
Podbielski 83, 98, 102, 109, 156, 158, 159, 162, 163, 167, 169, 172, 199, 213, 214
Political economy 11–60, 351
Pollution 268–269, 292
Port Autonome de Marseille (PAM) 253, 254, 257, 258, 268, 279
Posner 140, 144, 189
Poulantzas 49
Poznanski 307, 310
Premier Plan de Modernisation et d'Équipement 302
Preteceille 8, 56
Price controls 306, 313, 320
Procacci 76
Production quotas 320
Productive capital 58–59, 362
Productive decentralisation 26, 138–139, 142–143, 203–207, 227–230, 284–285
Proposition force trade unionism 345–346
Protectionism 71, 218, 320
Prud'homme 251
Pugliese 95, 99, 101, 103, 105, 109, 112–116

Quantity theory of money 43

Raddoppiamento of the Taranto steel works 179–180

Rate of profit
  determination of 31–32, 110, 124, 129, 135–136
  falling 31–32, 264–265, 306, 313, 320, 323, 331–333, 357
Regalia 130–134, 136, 137
Regimes of accumulation 32–38, 229
Regini 130–134
Region, concepts of 9
Regional planning and policies 92–93, 122, 129, 133, 136, 145–162, 231, 241, 242, 244–251, 274–277, 282–283, 286, 317–318, 330, 332, 345, 350
  as instrument of national economic planning 111, 247–248
  Italian Law 646 (1950) 97–98
  Italian Law 634 (1957) 147–150
  Italian Law 717 (1965) 150–153
  Italian Law 853 (1971) 153–156
  Italian Law 183 (1956) 156–159
Regional planning theory 349
Regional problems 3–10
  definition of 4–5
  in Lorraine 308, 311, 317–318, 328, 330, 335
  in Nord 235–237
  in Provence 238, 274–276
Regulation, modes of 354–356, 362
Rentier incomes 58–59, 124, 141, 357, 362
Reproduction schemata 32–34
Responsible autonomy 207
Rhodes 272, 302
Ricardo 39, 43
Ricossa 118
Risorgimento 61–64, 66
Robert 259, 264, 280
Rollier 207
Romeo 69
Ross 330, 345
Rossi-Doria 84, 85, 87, 94, 112

Sabel 117–118, 124, 129, 130, 132
Sallois 242, 247
Salvati 91, 115, 124, 126–128, 135–139
Salvemini 73, 76
Saraceno 175–177, 209–211
Scala mobile 135
Schéma d'aménagement 284–285

Schéma Directeur de l'Aménagement et de l'Urbanisme (SDAU) 284–285, 293
Scientific management 22–23, 226
Scott 53
Seaports 181, 182, 192, 232–235, 237, 238, 240, 241, 252–257, 268, 269, 273, 274, 276, 278, 280–286, 288, 292–296, 351
Secchi 68
Selective state intervention, see State intervention
Self-centred form of economic development 345
Semi-autonomous work groups 202, 207
Service sector, development of 35–36, 113, 118–119, 130, 140, 284
Shaikh 43
Sharecroppers 86, 88, 94
Sharetenants 86, 88
Sheltered sector 38, 47, 124
Simmonet Plan 320
Skills and attitudes 22–25, 27–28, 35, 133, 240, 299–300, 310, 356
Smith 2
Social accounts 45–47
Socialisation of costs 134, 352–353
Social relations
  of patriarchy and ethnicity 355
  of production 5–6, 8–12, 14, 359, 362
Social reproduction 6–8, 11–12
  definition of 6–8
  differentiation of 6–10
Social security charges, reductions in 158
Società Italiana Resine (SIR) 187, 189, 190, 193–198
Société des Aciéries et Laminoirs de Lorraine (SACILOR) 262, 269, 315–317, 320, 323, 324, 331–333, 335, 336
Société Lorraine de Laminage Continu (SOLLAC) 261, 262, 264, 265, 269, 302, 308, 316, 317, 320, 323, 324, 332, 335, 351
Société Lorraine et Méridionale de Laminage Continu (SOLMER) 257, 261, 262, 264–266, 268–273, 277–279, 281, 316, 317, 321
Southern question, origins of 61–79

Southernist writers
  classical 73–74
  new 92–93
Space 5–11, 282, 353
Spatial differentiation, Italian 225–230
Special credit institutes 145, 149, 157, 167, 190
Special programme for Fos and the Étang-de-Berre included in the Sixth Plan 255, 256, 286
Special projects 154, 158, 181
Spread effects 45, 47
State, and economy 52–60, 145–161
State bourgeoisie 79, 113–116
State, concepts of 48–53
State economic plans, see Indicative planning
State entrepreneurship (see also State holding companies) 59–60, 77–78
State expenditure (including transfers) 48, 73, 83, 105, 114, 141, 220, 222, 250, 254–256
State holding companies 115, 122, 128, 139–140, 143–147, 149, 152, 154, 167, 169, 171, 184, 200, 208, 322, 324, 341
State induced jobs in old industrial areas 318, 322, 328, 330, 335
State–industry relations 139–141, 143, 184, 314, 321
State intervention 12, 48–60, 118–122, 125–126, 168, 202, 231, 240, 268, 302, 323, 341, 347
  selectivity of 101–103, 105, 150, 152–153, 241, 245
State, organisation and reorganisation of 60, 150, 153–154, 157, 158, 242, 243, 246, 283–284, 287–293
  central–local government relations 60, 246–247, 287–293
  relations with dominant groups 60, 168
  relations with political parties 60
Statuto dei Lavoratori 133, 134, 202
Stoffaes 321, 323, 330–333, 347
Strikes 130–137
Structure plans, see Schéma Directeur de l'Aménagement et d'Urbanisme
Subcontracting 142, 206, 269, 270, 359
Subproletariat 225

Surplus-value 14-22, 25, 28-34, 54-55, 58-59, 247, 357
Synthetic textile industry 187, 188, 190, 194-198
Systemofacture 22, 25, 358

Taranto 146, 167, 172, 176-182, 199, 224, 281
Tarrow 85
Taylorism 22-24, 34, 121, 128, 133, 204, 299, 355
Technical change 20-22, 29-32, 299-301, 307, 309-311, 340
Temporary employment agencies 269, 270-272
Textile industry 63, 71-72, 121, 139, 143, 235
Theoretical analysis, indeterminacy of 61, 352, 353
Thévenot 36
Three Italies 80, 121, 226
Time and motion studies 22-23
Trade balance 38-44, 47, 208, 220
Trade unions 45, 53, 92, 105, 117, 125, 126, 129-131, 138, 141, 215, 228, 236, 269, 272, 314, 322, 345, 346
Transnational restructuring 323, 336
Transport investments 285
Trasformismo 68
Trevisan 194
Turri 75

Ugine-Aciers 234, 273
Underdevelopment 2-3, 66-69, 73-75
Unemployment 76, 77, 118, 127, 138, 177, 201, 214, 215, 223, 225, 231, 236, 237, 274, 278, 280, 340, 346, 357-360
Unequal exchange 14, 39
Uneven development 1-6, 44, 98-103, 139, 165, 223, 349, 350
Unification of Italy 61-64, 66-69
Union Franc 260
Union Sidérurgique du Nord de la France (USINOR) 234, 265, 297, 302, 305, 307, 309, 314, 316, 318, 320, 321, 323-325, 328, 331-333, 335, 336
United Nations 337
Universal rolling mill at Gandrange 335

Urban congestion 201, 203, 204, 226, 229
Urbanisation 108-110, 113-114, 123, 133, 224, 255, 284, 286-288, 291, 293-295
Urban renewal 284
Usi civici 64

Valorisation of capital 14-17
Value 13-19, 307, 309
  international 39
  law of 13-14, 29
  transfers from South to North 73
  transformation of values into prices of production 17-19
Van der Pijl 58, 59, 357, 362
Vannicelli 92, 117, 126, 129, 134, 137
Vehicle manufacturing industry 23, 72, 121, 177, 200-207, 236, 306, 322, 328, 351
  in Nord 236
  Italian 200-207
Verdoorn's Law 45
Vieille 291
Viola 180
Virtuous circles, see Circular and cumulative causation
Vicious circles, see Circular and cumulative causation

Wage determination, see Labour power, value of
Wage relation 11-12, 14, 22
Walsh 5
Ways of life 35, 56-57, 272
Weaver 349
Welfare economics 5, 53, 56
Welfare state 35, 37-38, 105, 140, 141, 356-358, 360, 361
Wendel-SIDELOR 262, 264, 265, 269, 302, 309, 314-317
Williams 6
Williamson 68
Working class, division of 228
Working day
  intensity of 20-22, 133
  length of 20-22, 360, 361
Work organisation 21, 25, 206
Wormald 173, 175, 178

Zone d'Aménagement Concerté (ZAC) 294